THE LITERATURE
OF SLANG

By W. J. BURKE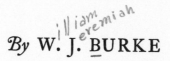

With an Introductory Note by
ERIC PARTRIDGE

NEW YORK
THE NEW YORK PUBLIC LIBRARY
1939

Republished, 1965 – Gale Research Company – Book Tower – Detroit, Michigan 48226

Paper used in this edition is
a fine acid-free, permanent/durable paper
of the type commonly referred to as
"300-year" paper

REPRINTED FROM THE

BULLETIN OF THE NEW YORK PUBLIC LIBRARY

1936-1938

PRINTED AT THE NEW YORK PUBLIC LIBRARY

form p400 [1i1-20-39 5c]

CONTENTS

INTRODUCTORY NOTE

◆

WHEN I received an invitation to write a brief note introducing Mr. Burke's vast bibliography of slang (and cant and dialect), I felt both pleased and embarrassed.

I still feel quite pleased — and horribly embarrassed. It is easy, far too easy, to write about the bad, the mediocre, and the merely good; but it is appallingly difficult to write pertinently about the excellent. If I had more courage, I'd say, "This is an extremely fine and irrefutably useful piece of work," and leave it at that: and such laconic brevity might have been kindest to all parties (especially myself): but because I have, for my sins, become, in the eyes of a few, an authority on slang and other kinds of unconventional English, I cannot take that short cut.

As a lexicographer and student of British and American slang and cant and other pleasant things, I know the tremendous odds with which Mr. W. J. Burke has had to contend. I know, therefore, the excellence of his method and the incredible richness of his results.

There have been other lists and bibliographies of slang and its congeners. But how meagre they are beside Mr. Burke's! (Moreover, Mr. Burke uses the word *bibliography* in its correct sense.)

His knowledge of the repositories and dormitories of British slang (including that of the outlying Empire) is astounding: I could pick no holes in his bibliography of slang proper, and precious few — tiny ones, at that! — in his researches into cant (the language of the underworld); these latter, only because I am engaged on intensive work in this field, work that will not be completed for some time yet; work in which I have been greatly assisted by this bibliography.

But what of American? Well, Mr. Burke has reduced me to prostration. Almost, indeed, to silence. I thought that I knew something of the sources of American slang . . . Well, I suppose I did, though I'm not quite so sure now as I used to be. He has had the happy idea of including dialect and Americanisms: that neither of them, pedantically considered, is strictly relevant, does not matter. What matters a great deal is that he has done invaluable work in both these branches of American.

Nor has Mr. Burke been content — as he well might have been content — to record his findings. He has added comments defining the scope and determining the degree of usefulness of the books and articles he has listed; nor are his comments, as too often comments are in bibliographies and *catalogues raisonnés,* jejune or woolly. They are sane and pointed and helpfully informative.

Here, then, is a storehouse of knowledge. Here is an apparatus for countless research workers. Here, too, is a reference book of inestimable value to all those persons who wish, or certainly will wish, to obtain information on this, that, or the other aspect of the English and American language — or, as Mr. H. L. Mencken would prefer me to say, the English and American languages.

Finally. Lexicographers have been called the hod-carriers of scholarship; bibliographers, the hangers-on of literature. Mr. Burke has proved, once for all, the gross libellousness of that epigram — insofar, at least, as it affects bibliographers. He richly adorns that select band of unpublicized martyrs.

To Mr. W. J. Burke, I "dips me lid."

ERIC PARTRIDGE

PREFACE

◈

SLANG was invented as an antidote to grammar. The rigid formalism of the schools was tempered by the gay and sometimes ribald democracy of street slang, that unconventional and undisciplined language of irreverent youth. Some of these picaresque expressions found their way into the chaste pages of the dictionaries, but not until they had been fumigated. In eugenics it is commonly asserted that the marriage of the blue-blooded aristocracy with red-blooded peasant stock keeps a nation sturdy, and in like manner slang brings new blood to a language eternally threatened with over-refinement. Slang keeps a language fresh and flexible. The bibliography which follows was compiled in the belief that slang is worthy of serious study; that slang has an important function to perform; and that philologists cannot afford to neglect a field of investigation so rich in material and so close at hand. The psychological factors involved in the creation and use of slang locutions are highly important, for after all slang is fundamentally a state of mind, a manifestation of man's inherent sense of humor and satire, that ever-present corrective for prudery, snobbishness and hypocrisy.

I have been assisted in this study by numerous persons in this country and abroad, and I wish to express my thanks to them all, and would gladly mention their names if space permitted. I would indeed be ungrateful if I did not make public acknowledgment of my indebtedness to the entire staff of The New York Public Library. I am particularly grateful for the editorial assistance of Mr. Daniel C. Haskell, whose perspicacious attention to bibliographical detail made this work presentable. Such errors as remain in the body of the work are entirely mine, and all bibliographical improvements of the original copy are his. I wish to express my thanks for the kind approbation placed on my humble efforts by Mr. Eric Partridge and Mr. H. L. Mencken, whose extensive contributions to the study of slang in England and America are too well known for comment.

Bibliography, I fear, is dull enough at best. I have tried as far as possible to make my numerous notes interesting. It would be presumptuous to feign a scholarship I do not possess. I undoubtedly have included in my informal notes much material which the trained philologist would eschew, but by so doing I may have inadvertently suggested a new method of approach to the investigation of our speech habits. I feel that many more students would choose this field if they could penetrate the Chinese Wall of technical jargon which bars their approach. Once beyond the wall the fields are fresh and green.

WILLIAM JEREMIAH BURKE

THE LITERATURE OF SLANG

ORDER OF ARRANGEMENT

BIBLIOGRAPHIES

AMERICAN speech. v. 1 – date. Baltimore, 1925–32; New York: Columbia University Press, 1933 – date. 4°.   RNA
Issued monthly from Oct., 1925, to Sept., 1927; bi-monthly, from Oct., 1927, to August, 1932; quarterly, from 1933 to date.
Founded and edited by Louise Pound, Kemp Malone, and Arthur Garfield Kennedy. From 1933 the editor-in-chief has been William Cabell Greet.
This periodical has had a salutary effect on the study of American speech habits. It combines popular and scholarly articles on all phases of American speech, including many articles on slang and trade jargons, as well as individual word studies. The bibliographical department, under the direction of Professor A. G. Kennedy, of Leland Stanford University, is a strong feature, and serves as a continuation, in a sense, of his standard work, *A Bibliography of writings on the English language from the beginning of printing to the end of 1922, 8–RN* (q.v.).

BURKE, WILLIAM JEREMIAH.
American slang — where to find it. (The Wilson bulletin. New York, Dec., 1933. 8°. v. 8, p. 220–221, 254.)   *HA
A classified list of 100 slang glossaries culled from American periodicals to aid librarians in running down requests for modern slang.

KENNEDY, ARTHUR GARFIELD.
A bibliography of writings on the English language from the beginning of printing to the end of 1922... Cambridge & New Haven: Harvard University Press, Yale University Press, 1927. xvii, 517 p. 4°.   *RG – RN
A standard bibliography indispensable to the student of the English language. Contains 13,402 items gleaned from the library collections of Harvard, Yale, the Library of Congress, The Boston Public Library, The New York Public Library, the British Museum, the Bodleian Library, and many others. The volume is carefully indexed. Books and periodical articles have been analyzed. The sections most useful to the student of slang are: Modern English, p. 196–203; American English, p. 404–416; Unconventional English, cant, slang and colloquialisms, p. 419–424; Current slang, p. 433–435.
Professor Kennedy, of Leland Stanford University, was one of the founders and editors of *American speech.*
Some additions and corrections were made by Arvid Gabrielson in an article entitled "Professor Kennedy's Bibliography of writings on the English language. A review with a list of additions and corrections" in *Studia neophilologica*, 1929, v. 2, p. 117–168, *RAA.*
Reviewed in *Journal of English and Germanic philology*, Bloomington, July, 1928, v. 27, p. 437–440, *RKA* (Geo. F. Flom); *American speech*, Baltimore, Feb., 1928, v. 3, p. 239–240, *RNA* (Louise Pound); *Modern philology*, May, 1928, v. 25, p. 495–497, *NAA* (James F. Royster); *Anglia, Beiblatt*, June, 1928, Jahrg. 39, p. 166–174 (Hermann M. Flasdieck), *RNA; Review of English studies*, London, Jan., 1929, v. 5, p. 120–121 (R. B. McKerrow), *RNA.*

KÖRTING, GUSTAV CARL OTTO.
Encyklopaedie und Methodologie der englischen Philologie. Heilbronn: Verlag von Gebr. Henninger, 1888. xx, 464 p. 8°.   RNB
"Die Dialecte des Englischen," p. 106–127.
This chapter contains bibliographical material on old and new English dialects, colloquialisms, Americanisms, slang, cant, and vulgarisms. Körting defines slang as the special speech of occupations, such as military, sea, student, etc., which today would generally be defined as jargon, or if a secret language, as cant. He associates cant with the underworld and says it is the lowest species of slang, much of it springing from obscenity. Philology has made many forward steps since Körting's celebrated handbook appeared, but it is still an indispensable guide to the student of English speech.

MENCKEN, HENRY LOUIS.
The American language. A preliminary inquiry into the development of English in the United States. New York: Alfred A. Knopf, 1919. 374 p. 8°.   8–RNB
Bibliography, p. 323–339.
Not all of these references have to do with slang, but a great many of them fall under that classification. The bibliography in the 1921 edition occupies p. 427–457. For a complete description, reviews, etc., of later editions see the entry in the general classification.

MODERN HUMANITIES RESEARCH ASSOCIATION.
...Bibliography of English language and literature... v. 1 – date. Cambridge: Bowes and Bowes, 1921 – date. 8°.   *RG – RN
Annual publication covering the period 1920 to date. There is a section devoted to cant and slang in each issue, containing items collected from the leading European and American journals, and carefully edited under the direction of philological scholars. There are also sections devoted to word studies, dictionaries, semantics, dialects, etc. Book reviews are noted. Memorial studies and anniversary papers are analyzed. It is the most comprehensive study of the English language now available.

A NEW English dictionary on historical principles...edited by James A. H. Murray, Henry Bradley, William A. Craigie, C. T. Onions. Introduction, supplement, and bibliography, by W. A. Craigie, C. T. Onions... Oxford: Clarendon Press, 1933. 2 v. f°.   M.R.R. Desk
A list of books quoted in the Oxford English dictionary, p. 1–91, at end of volume. Three columns to the page. This stupendous list of works which served as the basis for the dictionary is an excellent check list for all books relating to English and American slang, cant, jargon, and related forms of speech. It is a straight alphabetical list, compiled by F. J. Sweatman and H. J. Bayliss, of the editorial staff.
Reviewed in *English studies*, Amsterdam, June, 1934, v. 16, p. 101–105, *RNA;* New York *Times*, Oct. 3, 1933, p. 22, col. 4, *A.*
Ernest Weekley devotes a chapter to this N. E. D. Supplement in his *Something about words*, New York: E. P. Dutton & Co. [1936], p. 51–68, *RNF.*

Bibliographies, continued

NORTHUP, CLARK SUTHERLAND.
A bibliography of the English and French languages in America from 1894 to 1900. (Dialect notes. New Haven, 1901. 8°. v. 2, p. 151–178.) RNZ
Continuation of the bibliographical lists published in *Dialect notes*, v. 1, p. 13–16, 53–56, 80–83, 254–258, 344–347. Includes slang and Americanisms as well as dialect.

OLIVER, THOMAS EDWARD.
The modern language teacher's handbook...

New York [etc.]: D. C. Heath and Company, 1935. 706 p. 8°. RAV
"Slang and popular language," p. 595–598.
Mostly French slang dictionaries, but some German, Spanish, Italian, and English slang sources are included.

WRIGHT, JOSEPH.
The English dialect dictionary... v. 6. London [etc.]: Henry Frowde; New York: G. P. Putnam's Sons, 1905. 4°. * R – † RNX
Vol. 6 contains a bibliography.
"Cant, colloquial, and slang," v. 6, p. 41–42.

DICTIONARIES

NOTE: Listed here are those general dictionaries which include all types of slang. Dictionaries which confine themselves to one subject are listed under the subject.

BARENTZ, M. E.
Woordenboek der Engelsche spreektaal. Anglicismen en americanismen. Slang, cant, colloquialisms and idiomatic phrases... Amsterdam: S. L. van Looy [1895]. xvi, 333 p. 8°. RNM
The imprint is covered with a label reading "Milwaukee, Wisconsin, C. N. Caspar Co., Book Emporium."
This book is based largely on Hotten's *Slang dictionary*. The definitions are popular rather than scholarly.

BARRÈRE, ALBERT.
Argot and slang. A new French and English dictionary of the cant words, quaint expressions, slang terms and flash phrases... New and revised edition. London: Whittaker and Co., White Hart Street, Paternoster Square, 1889. 483 p. 8°. RFN
Although the French words come first, the definitions, which are in English, contain thousands of English slang synonyms. Barrère was an authority on English slang. The introductory matter contains many canting songs in English and French. There is a bibliography, p. ix–xii. Horsley's "Autobiography of a thief" is reprinted from *Macmillan's magazine*, London, Oct., 1879, v. 40, p. 500–506, * DA.

BARRÈRE, ALBERT, AND CHARLES G. LELAND.
A dictionary of slang, jargon & cant, embracing English, American, and Anglo-Indian slang, pidgin English, tinkers' jargon, and other irregular phraseology. Compiled and edited by Albert Barrère...and Charles G. Leland... [Edinburgh:] Printed for subscribers only at the Ballantyne Press, 1889–90. 2 v. 8°.
v. 1. A–K; v. 2. L–Z. M.R.R. Desk
675 copies only printed, of which this is no. 174.
"We are getting ahead with the Slang dictionary. I wrote Dr. Holmes, offering him £20 to write something in 'the Yankee dialect' and hope to get a lot of contributions... In the *main*, it will be a dictionary like Bartlett's, — but there will be a wider range, more anecdotes and poems — and a great deal more etymology — Anglo-Saxon, Norse, and Dutch. It will be deeper and a broader book." — Letter from Leland to E. R. Pennell, Brighton, May 12, 1888.
See Elizabeth Robbins Pennell, *Charles Godfrey Leland*, Boston: Houghton, Mifflin & Co., 1906. 2 v. 12°. AN. For a bibliography of Leland, see Joseph Jackson, *A Bibliography of the works of Charles God-*frey Leland. Reprinted from the Pennsylvania magazine of history and biography [Philadelphia, 1926]. 129 p. 4°. NBC.
In v. 1 of the Dictionary Leland contributes: "A brief history of English slang," p. xiii–xxiii. The preface, p. v–vi, is by Barrère, author of *Argot and slang*. The dictionary includes many Americanisms, and many gypsy words, thanks to Leland, who was a native of America, born in Philadelphia, Aug. 15, 1824, and who was an authority on gypsies. He died in Florence, March 20, 1903. He wrote the Hans Breitmann ballads.
The second edition was issued by George Bell & Sons, London, 1897. This popular edition was somewhat curtailed in text. Kennedy 12012.
Reviewed in *The Spectator*, London, Sept. 27, 1890, v. 65, p. 408–409, * DA; *Blackwood's magazine*, London, May, 1888, v. 143, p. 690–704, * DA (Charles Mackay); *The Scots observer*, Sept. 28, 1889, v. 2, p. 508–509, * DA (W. E. Henley?); *The Nation*, New York, Oct. 1, 1891, v. 53, p. 261–263, * DA; *Athenæum*, London, Feb. 14, 1891, v. 97, p. 211–213, * DA. (Review of the edition published by Whittaker & Co. in *Notes and queries*, London, 1889, series 7, v. 8, p. 341–342, * R–* DA.)

BARTLETT, JOHN RUSSELL.
Dictionary of Americanisms. A glossary of words and phrases, usually regarded as peculiar to the United States. By John Russell Bartlett, corresponding secretary of the American Ethnological Society, and foreign corresponding secretary of the New York Historical Society. New York: Bartlett and Welford, No. 7, Astor House, 1848. 412 p. 8°. RNZ
This was the first attempt to make a comprehensive dictionary of American speech, and it still holds front rank as a popular reference tool in libraries. There were numerous editions. It was translated into Dutch in 1854. Its appearance gave rise to numerous magazine articles on Americanisms, both here and in Europe, and much of our most valuable information concerning slang and Americanisms may be culled from these reviews, which were rather lengthy for the most part.
John Russell Bartlett (1805–1886) was a Rhode Island antiquarian and bibliographer. He came to New York in 1836 and formed a partnership with Charles Welford, a bookseller. He helped form the American Ethnological Society. He published many valuable works on Rhode Island history, and from 1865 to 1882 he published the *John Carter Brown catalogue*, a real contribution to the bibliography of Americana. See the *Dictionary of American biography* for details of his life and works. See also *Life and services of the Hon. John Russell Bartlett. A paper read before the Rhode Island Historical Society, November 2, 1886, by William Gammell, president of*

Dictionaries, continued

the society, Providence: Printed by the Providence Press Company, 1886. 20 p. *A p.v.54.*
This first edition was reissued in 1849. It was the same except for the date. The New York Public Library has a copy, *Stuart 10989.* This reissue also appeared in London in 1849, with the added imprint "London: John Russell Smith, 4, Old Compton Street, Soho Square."

Dictionary of Americanisms... 2d ed. greatly improved and enlarged. Boston: Little, Brown, and Company [etc.], 1859. xxxii, 524 p. 8°. Ref. Cat. 1192
"The second edition of this Dictionary was published in Boston in 1859, and a third the following year. The former was greatly enlarged from the first edition, the latter was a reprint of the second edition without alterations." — *Preface to 4th edition.*

Dictionary of Americanisms... 3rd ed. enlarged. Boston: Little, Brown, and Company; London: Trübner and Company, 1860. 524 p. 8°. RNI
The author says in the preface to the 2nd ed. that he had worked on the new edition for years, three of which were spent on the Mexican border as commissioner on the Mexican boundary, during which time he learned of many terms peculiar to the Southwest, mostly of Spanish origin. He is of the opinion that the new edition contains twice as many words as the 1848 edition. He said he consulted the manuscript of Dr. A. L. Elywn, of Philadelphia, who had collected a great many Americanisms. He mentions the Dutch edition of his work: *Woordenboek van Americanismen, etc. Bewerkt door M. Keijzer,* Gorinchem, 1854, but found it of little use in settling the etymology of some old Dutch words still used in New York.

Dictionary of Americanisms... 4th ed. greatly improved and enlarged. Boston: Little, Brown, and Company [etc.], 1877. 813 p. 8°. * R – RNZ
The fourth edition contains the names of states and principal cities with their nicknames, and a list of similes, in addition to the regular sections of the dictionary.
Among the many reviews of Bartlett may be cited: *National quarterly review,* London, March, 1861, v. 2, p. 230–240, * *DA; Atlantic monthly,* Boston, April, 1878, v. 41, p. 495–502, May, 1878, v. 41, p. 656–664, July, 1878, v. 42, p. 97–106, Sept., 1878, v. 42, p. 342–348, Nov., 1878, v. 42, p. 619–631, Jan., 1879, v. 43, p. 88–98, March, 1879, v. 43, p. 379–392, May, 1879, v. 43, p. 656–666, Nov., 1879, v. 44, p. 654–665, May, 1880, v. 45, p. 669–678, May, 1881, v. 47, p. 697–707 (Richard Grant White), * *DA; All the year round,* London, Feb. 18, 1871, v. 25, p. 270–275, * *DA; North American review,* Boston, July, 1849, v. 9, p. 94–110, * *DA* (Henderson ascribes this article to S. G. Brown); *Athenæum,* London, Oct. 20, 1849, v. 22, p. 1062, July 30, 1859, v. 34, p. 137–139, * *DA; The Galaxy,* New York, Sept., 1877, v. 24, p. 376–383, Nov., 1877, v. 24, p. 681–688, Jan., 1878, v. 25, p. 94–101, * *DA* (Richard Grant White); *Blackwood's magazine,* London, April, 1861, v. 89, p. 421–439, * *DA: The Nation,* New York, March 7, 1878, v. 26, p. 171–172, * *DA; Saturday review,* London, Oct. 15, 1859, v. 8, p. 457–459. * *DA; North American review,* Boston, Jan., 1883, v. 136, p. 64–67, * *DA* (Gilbert M. Tucker); *Atlantic monthly,* Boston, Nov., 1859, v. 4, p. 638–644, * *DA; Living age,* New York, Jan. 13, 1849, v. 20, p. 79–80, * *DA; Southern literary messenger,* Richmond, Oct., 1848, v. 14, p. 623–629, * *DA; The Southern review,* Baltimore, July, 1871, v. 9, p. 290–319. * *DA; The Literary world,* New York, Aug. 19, 1848, v. 3, p. 561–562, *NAA; Christian examiner,* Boston, Jan., 1849, v. 46, p. 146–147 (Edward Everett Hale), * *DA.*
Some additional words which correspondents sent to Bartlett are reprinted in *Dialect notes,* New Haven, July, 1935, v. 6, p. 452–454, *RNZ.*

Keijzer, M.

Woordenboek van Americanismen, een lijst van woorden en zinnen gewoonlijk als eigenaardig aan de Vereenigde Staten beschouwd. Bewerkt door M. Keijzer. Gorinchen, 1854. 96 p. 12°.
Copy in British Museum.
This is an abridgment of Bartlett's *Dictionary.*

Koehler, Friedrich.

Wörterbuch der Americanismen. Eigenheiten der englischen Sprache in Nordamerika. Leipzig, 1866. 183 p. 8°.
Copy in British Museum.
This is from the third edition of Bartlett's *Dictionary.*

THE BRITISH EMPIRE universities modern English dictionary... London: The Syndicate Publishing Company, Ltd., 1927. [rev. ed.] 1154 p. 12°. RNI
Glossary of automobile terms, p. 803–811; Glossary of aeronautical terms, p. 812–815; Glossary of cricket terms, p. 816–818; Glossary of football terms, p. 818–824 (Rugby); Glossary of football terms, p. 825–826 (Association); Glossary of golf terms, p. 827–829; Glossary of lawn tennis terms, p. 830–836.
These glossaries contain a few expressions which may properly be designated as jargon.

BURGESS, GELETT.

Burgess unabridged. A new dictionary of words you have always needed... New York: Frederick A. Stokes Company [cop. 1914]. xxii, 120 p. 12°. NBX
These hilarious neologisms were proposed in fun, and defined at length in prose and verse, but one at least was taken seriously and has been accepted in the dictionaries. That word was "blurb," used so much on book jackets and other advertising media.

CLAPIN, SYLVA.

A new dictionary of Americanisms. Being a glossary of words supposed to be peculiar to the United States and the dominion of Canada... New York: Louis Weiss & Co. [1902.] 581 p. 8°. 9-RNZ
Contains 5,258 entries. The dictionary proper occupies p. 1–424.
Appendix 1. Contains a list of words which have been taken over into American speech, p. 425–435. Appendix 2. A subject classification of Americanisms, but without definitions, p. 437–505. Appendix 3. Contains reprints of articles on Americanisms. Dr. Aubrey's "Americanisms" from *Leisure hour* (q.v.); Edward Eggleston's "Wild flowers of English speech in America," from the *Century magazine* (q.v.); E. B. Tylor's "The philology of slang" from *Macmillan's magazine* (q.v.); and Brander Matthews's "The function of slang" from *Harper's monthly* (q.v.).
Reviewed in *The Critic,* New York, May, 1903, v. 42, p. 474–475, * *DA* (C. J. Wood); *Modern language notes,* Baltimore, Jan., 1903, v. 18, p. 30–31, *RAA* (Clark S. Northup).

DARLING, CHARLES H.

The jargon book... Aurora, Illinois: The Aurora Company [1919]. 57 p. 8°. RNB p.v.25
"Contains over two thousand odd, unique and novel expressions, words and phrases, and verbal shortcuts used by high class people, and slang words and phrases, nicknames... jargon, words, phrases and parlance adopted and used by the police and those classed as the underworld."

Dictionaries, continued

DAVIES, THOMAS LEWIS OWEN.
A supplementary English glossary... London: G. Bell and Sons, 1881. 736 p. 8°.
* R – RNM
A supplement to Halliwell-Phillipps.
"Several slang expressions will be found in the glossary... A great deal of slang is ephemeral, neither preserved nor worth preserving, but when an eminent writer employs it, he bestows on it a species of immortality." — *Preface.*

DAWSON, ARTHUR H.
A dictionary of English slang and colloquialisms. New York: E. P. Dutton & Co. [1913.] viii, 213 p. 32°. (Miniature reference library. [no. 64.])
RNM
Also published in London by G. Routledge & Sons, 1913.

DE VERE, MAXIMILIAN SCHELE.
Americanisms; the English of the new world ... New York: Charles Scribner & Co., 1872. 685 p. 8°.
RNZ
Contents: 1. The Indian; 2. Immigrants from abroad: the Dutchman, the Frenchman, the Spaniard, the German, the negro, John Chinaman; 3. The Great West; 4. The church; 5. Politics; 6. Trade of all kinds; 7. Afloat; 8. On the rail; 9. Natural history; 10. Old friends with new faces; 11. Cant and slang; 12. New words and nicknames.
This is the first notable attempt to classify American speech by occupation, race, and section. It has a word index which aids the user. Many sources are cited in the text, but there is no separate bibliography. The chapter on slang and cant is arranged alphabetically. De Vere has suffered at the hands of his more severe critics, but his book is still a repository of many Americanisms which otherwise might never have been preserved.
Reviewed in *The Canadian monthly,* Toronto, Jan., 1872, v. 1, p. 87–90, * *DA; The Nation,* New York, Jan. 11, 1872, v. 14, p. 28–29, * *DA* (Gilbert M. Tucker characterized this as "a savage review"); *Scribner's monthly,* New York, Jan., 1872, v. 3, p. 379–383, * *DA; London quarterly review,* London, Jan., 1882, v. 57, p. 392–411, * *DA; Old and new,* Boston, Jan., 1872, v. 5, p. 104–105, * *DA.* See also G. A. Barringer, *Étude sur l'Anglais parlé aus États Unis,* 1874.
Maximilian Schele De Vere was the son of a Swedish father and a French mother. He was born at Wexio, Sweden, Nov. 1, 1820, and died at Washington, D. C., May 10, 1898. He was educated at Berlin and Greifswald. He came to America in 1843, was at Boston a year, and through the poet Longfellow was appointed to the chair of modern languages at the University of Virginia, a position he held from 1844 to 1895. Among his students were W. P. Trent who later became professor of English at Columbia University, Alcée Fortier, professor of Romance languages at Tulane University, Thomas R. Price, professor of English at Columbia University, and many others who made names for themselves in the field of language studies.

A DICTIONARY of American English on historical principles, edited by Sir William Craigie [and others]. Chicago: The University of Chicago Press [1936] – date. f°. M.R.R.Desk
Parts 1–3. A-Butterfly.
This great dictionary of American English will be the most exhaustive repository of our American English when completed. It is modelled on Murray's *New English dictionary.* The story of this monumental work may be found in the following articles.

Craigie, Sir William Alexander.
Collecting for the historical dictionary of American English. (American speech. New York, Feb., 1931. 4°. v. 6, p. 173–179.) RNA
Outlines the problems facing the small staff of

experts who are laboring to bring forth the first truly American dictionary, and pleads for outside help. Gives the fields still inadequately investigated and offers suggestions for recruits. See also the article on the same subject by Florence Elberta Barns in *The English journal,* Chicago, 1927, v. 16, p. 624–632, *RNA.* Sir William gives further information in regard to collecting for this dictionary in *American speech,* New York, June, 1931, v. 6, p. 338–340, *RNA.* Specimen slips are given to aid the collector in supplying information on standardized forms.

The historical dictionary of American English. (The English journal. Chicago, Jan., 1926. 8°. v. 15, p. 13–23.) RNA
A clear outline of the simple procedure to be followed by the voluntary workers on the new dictionary project. Rules and samples are given, and a plea is made to the American people to finance the stupendous work. "The University of Chicago will do its share, but it cannot bear the whole burden of what experience shows will be a costly enterprise, and I am much mistaken if a great nation will hesitate to bear the cost of learning for the first time the full history of its own tongue." See also *English journal,* Jan., 1929, v. 18, p. 34–50.

The historical dictionary of American English. (The University record. Chicago: University of Chicago Press, July, 1927, new series, v. 13, p. 209–214.) STG
More or less of a digest of the previous article.

The historical dictionary of American English. (English studies. Amsterdam, Oct., 1934. 8°. v. 16, p. 161–165.) RNA
A brief description of the aims and progress of the dictionary, with a specimen page to show the style and format.

The progress of the historical dictionary of American English. (American speech. Baltimore, April, 1930. 4°. v. 5, p. 259–263.) RNA
It would take fifty years to collect and digest anything like a complete dictionary of the type Sir William proposes. He is of the opinion that a usable one, done in a few years, is needed, and he outlines some of the work under his direction at the University of Chicago, and gives a few samples from the words beginning with the letter A.

The study of American English. (Society for Pure English. Tract no. 27. Oxford: At the Clarendon Press, 1927. 8°. p. 199–216.) RND
An historical essay on the English language in America, and an outline of the work to be done in the compilation of an *Historical dictionary of American English.* This dictionary, to be complete, must be supplemented by a slang dictionary and a dialect dictionary. Some of the words to be included in the new dictionary are given in their regular dictionary arrangement to give a clear idea of what is being done.

Brock, Henry Irving.
A dictionary of the American language. Now its long suspected existence is to be officially recognized. (World today. London, Dec., 1928. 8°. v. 53, p. 36–42.) * DA
A glowing tribute to Sir William A. Craigie, with a few biographical facts concerning him, and a description of the type of work he has undertaken in editing *The Historical dictionary of American English.*

Dollard, John.
Dictionary of English in America. Chicago, 1928. 11 p. 8°. (University of Chicago. Humanities research series. Booklet no. 8.)
STG (Chicago)
Outlines the work being done by Sir William Craigie on the *Historical dictionary of American English.*

Dictionaries, continued

Gates, Floy Perkinson.
The Historical dictionary of American English in the making. (American speech. Baltimore, Oct., 1930. 4°. v. 6, p. 36–44.)   RNA
Describes the painstaking work of the group compiling the dictionary. Gives samples from the letter B.

Read, Allen Walker.
The scope of the American dictionary. (American speech. New York, Oct., 1933. 4°. v. 8, p. 10–20.)   RNA
Outlines aims of the dictionary which Prof. W. A. Craigie is directing. "The American dialect dictionary has its field which the Historical dictionary will not usurp."
Words coined later than the year 1900 will not be included. Words before that will be treated historically down to the year 1925. Gives samples of the methods employed. Urges voluntary workers and lists some of the fields which need to be covered.

'Whoopee' traced to British origin. (New York Times. Oct. 9, 1935, p. 25.)   * A
An interview with Sir William A. Craigie reveals that many so-called American slang words are in reality old English words of respectable antiquity. Whoopee, lift, blizzard, booze, O. K., and beaver are mentioned in connection with the *Historical dictionary of American English,* which Sir William is editing.

Wolfort, Ira.
Ten years' study put in new dictionary. (New York Times. June 9, 1935.)   * A
Long article on Sir William A. Craigie's *Dictionary of American English.*

DIXON, JAMES MAIN.
English idioms. London: Thomas Nelson and Sons [1927]. 288 p. 16°.   RNL
"Instead of attempting to divide the work into chapters treating of 'colloquial phrases,' 'cant phrases,' 'slang phrases,' and so forth, I have thrown the whole into alphabetical form, and have marked by letters the category to which, in my opinion, the phrases ought to belong... This volume does not pretend to exhaust the list of slang phrases, but only to give those which have crept into ordinary use, and are understood, although they may not be used, by all educated people." — *Preface.*

EDWARDS, ELIEZER.
Words, facts, and phrases. A dictionary of curious, quaint, & out-of-the-way matters... Philadelphia: J. B. Lippincott and Co. [1881.] 631 p. 12°.   * AY
One of the older dictionaries, but compiled on historical principles. Contains many slang terms, old English dialectal phrases, and numerous Americanisms. A list of authorities is given, p. vii–viii. There are other editions of this work, and it was always advertised as a companion volume to Brewer's *Reader's handbook* (q.v.).

ELWYN, ALFRED LANGDON.
Glossary of supposed Americanisms. Collected by Alfred L. Elwyn, M.D. Philadelphia: J. B. Lippincott & Co., 1859. 122 p. 12°.   RNZ
This work does not take rank with Pickering, Bartlett, Thornton, and other dictionaries of Americanisms. The quotations are undated.

FALLOWS, SAMUEL.
A complete dictionary of synonyms and antonyms... New York: Fleming H. Revell, 1898. 512 p. 12°.   RNL
"A dictionary of Briticisms, Americanisms, colloquial phrases, etc., in current use," p. 295–342.
Numerous slang synonyms are given for each word. The Americanisms are not differentiated from the Briticisms.

FARMER, JOHN STEPHEN.
Americanisms, old & new. A dictionary of words, phrases and colloquialisms peculiar to the United States, British America, the West Indies, &c. &c. Their derivation, meaning and application, together with numerous anecdotal, historical, explanatory, and folk-lore notes. ... London: Privately printed by Thomas Poulter & Sons, 1889. 564 p. 8°.   8–RNZ
Autographed copy. No. 237.
Authorities and references to periodical literature, p. xvi–xx. Most of the references are to American newspapers and periodicals, the greater portion of them bearing the date 1888. The definitions are full, and often followed by apt quotations. Some of the definitions betray Farmer's insularity.
Reviewed in *Athenæum,* London, July 13, 1889, v. 94, p. 62, * *DA; Nation,* New York, July 4, 1889, v. 49, p. 15–16 (F. Hall), Oct. 9, 1890, v. 51, p. 288–290, Oct. 1, 1891, v. 53, p. 261–263, * *DA.*

FARMER, JOHN STEPHEN, AND W. E. HENLEY.
Slang and its analogues past and present. A dictionary, historical and comparative, of the heterodox speech of all classes of society for more than three hundred years. With synonyms in English, French, German, Italian, etc. Compiled and edited by John S. Farmer... Printed for subscribers only. 1890–1904. 7 v. 8°.
6–RNK
Limited to 750 copies. This is no. 283, and is signed by John S. Farmer.
Vol. I. A to Byz. 1890. Printed by Thos. Poulter & Sons, Limited, 6, Arthur Street West, London Bridge, E. C. (Poulter refused to print the second volume on account of alleged indecencies. Farmer sued for breach of contract, but was sued himself on a counter claim, and Poulter won a judgment of £114.) v. II. C to Fizzle. 1891. Printed by Harrison and Sons, St. Martin's Lane, London. On some printings of v. II, Henley's name appears on the title-page. v, III. Fla. to Hyps, 1893. v. IV. I to Myz. 1896. v. v. N. to Razzle-dazzle, 1902. v. VI. Rea to Stozzle, 1903. v. VII. Stra to Z. 1904. v. VII was printed by Neill and Co., Ltd., Edinburgh. Some copies of this work were printed by H. C. A. Thieme.
The Library also has v. I of a revised edition, Parts 1–3. 1903–09. Part 1. A to Bang; part 2–3, Bang to Byte. Part one contains an editorial note by Farmer in which he pays tribute to Henley and tells about Henley's work on the revised edition just before his death, July 11, 1903.
This has been the standard dictionary of slang ever since its publication. A set brings an enormous price when put on the market. It contains upwards of 100,000 illustrative quotations.
Reviewed in the *Scots observer* (known also as *National observer*), London, Feb. 15, 1890, v. 3, p. 341–342,* *DA; The Nation,* New York. Oct. 9, 1890, v. 51, p. 288–290, Oct. 1, 1891, v. 53, p. 261–263, * *DA* (T. R. Lounsbury, according to Kennedy); *Spectator,* London, May 3, 1903, v. 64, p. 630–631, * *DA; Athenæum,* London, March 14, 1903, v. 121, p. 332–333, Sept. 10, 1904, v. 124, p. 341–343, * *DA; Notes and queries,* London, Dec. 2, 1893, series 8, v. 4, p. 460; March 14, 1903, series 9, v. 11, p. 218–219; April 11, 1903, series 9, v. 11, p. 300; Aug. 15, 1903, series 9, v. 12, p. 138–139; Dec. 26, 1903, series 9, v. 12, p. 519–520, * *R–* DA.*
The abridged edition published by E. P. Dutton & Co. was reviewed by Llewelyn Powys in *The Freeman,* New York, Sept. 20, 1922, v. 6, p. 43–44, * *DA.*

Dictionaries, continued

HALLIWELL-PHILLIPPS, JAMES ORCHARD.

A dictionary of archaic and provincial words, obsolete phrases, proverbs, and ancient customs, from the fourteenth century... 2d ed. London: J. R. Smith, 1850. 2 v. 8°.   RNM
Much on the same order as Nares's glossary (q.v.). Includes old cant words and slang.

—— Third edition. London: T. and W. Boone, 1855. 2 v. 8°.   RNM

—— 7th edition. New York: E. P. Dutton & Co., 1924. 960 p. 8°.   RNM

HARGRAVE, BASIL.

Origin and meanings of popular phrases & names. London: T. Werner Laurie, n. d. 350 p. 12°.   RNF
Many of these popular phrases fall into the classification of slang. The definitions are full, dated in some cases, and illustrated with quotations to a great extent.

HOLT, ALFRED HUBBARD.

Phrase origins. A study of familiar expressions. New York: Thomas Y. Crowell Co. [1936.] 328 p. 12°.   RNM
Bibliography, p. 327–328.
A dictionary of popular phrases based on a careful combing of *Notes and queries* and thirty-four standard works as listed in the bibliography. The work was compiled at the Williams College Library, with the assistance of the staff. It contains a large percentage of slang and Americanisms, and the style shows the influence of Fowler's *Modern English usage.*

HORWILL, HERBERT WILLIAM.

Dictionary of modern American usage. Oxford: At the Clarendon Press, 1935. 360 p. 12°.   M.R.R. Desk
Not a companion volume to Fowler's *Modern English usage.* Chiefly a dictionary of Americanisms, collected on the compiler's many trips to America over a period of thirty-five years. The quotations which form the bulwark of the definitions are dated as far as possible, lending a historical value to this delightfully informal repository of our changing speech.
Reviewed in *Saturday review of literature,* New York, Aug. 3, 1935, v. 12, p. 13 (Christopher Morley), *NAA; New York Times,* Aug. 11, 1935, p. 3 (C. G. P.), * A; *Times literary supplement,* London, July 18, 1935, p. 461; *New York Herald Tribune,* July 31, 1935 (Lewis Gannett), * A; *New statesman and nation,* July 27, 1935, v. 10, p. 131 (S. K. Ratcliffe), * DA; *Revue anglo-américaine,* Dec., 1935, p. 147–148 (F. Mossé), * DM; *Review of English studies,* London, July, 1936, v. 12, p. 368–372, RNA; *American speech,* New York, Dec., 1935, v. 10, p. 307, Dec., 1936, v. 11, p. 302–306, RNA; *Oxford magazine,* Oct. 17, 1935, v. 54, p. 10, 12–14, † STK; *The Spectator,* London, Sept. 6, 1935, p. 361, Sept. 20, p. 431, * DA (Alistair Cooke).

HOTTEN, JOHN CAMDEN.

A dictionary of modern slang, cant, and vulgar words, used at the present day in the streets of London; the universities of Oxford and Cambridge; the houses of parliament; the dens of St. Giles; and the palaces of St. James. Preceded by a history of cant and vulgar language from the time of Henry VIII; shewing its connection with the gipsey tongue; with glossaries of two secret languages, spoken by the wandering tribes of London, the costermongers, and the patterers. By a London antiquary [John Camden Hotten]... London: John Camden Hotten, antiquarian bookseller, Piccadilly, 1859. 160 p. 12°.   RNM
Not in The New York Public Library.
This was the first edition of Hotten's celebrated dictionary. The preface by Hotten was dated Piccadilly, June 30, 1859. It has a cadger's map showing a begging district, as frontispiece.
Contents: The history of cant, or the secret language of vagabonds, p. i-xlvii; The history of slang, or the vulgar language of fast life, p. xlix–lxxxvi; A dictionary of modern slang, cant, & vulgar words; many with their etymologies traced, p. 1–118; Some account of the back slang, the secret language of costermongers, p. 119–124; Glossary of back slang, p. 125–131; Some account of rhyming slang, the secret language of chaunters and patterers, p. 133–139; Glossary of rhyming slang, p. 141–146; The bibliography of slang, cant, and vulgar language; or, A list of the books which have been consulted in compiling this work, comprising nearly every known treatise upon the subject, p. 147–160.
For many years the bibliography in Hotten was the most comprehensive of all the works on slang. A few changes were made in it in later editions.
John Camden Hotten (1832–1873) went to work for John Petheran, a London bookseller, at the age of fourteen. He lived in America from 1848 to 1856. Returning to England, he began a voluminous publishing business. After his death the business was purchased by Chatto & Windus, who continued to publish editions of the "Slang dictionary." Hotten published cheap reprints of *Dr. Syntax,* written by William Combe and illustrated by Thomas Rowlandson, and *Life in London,* by Pierce Egan, and many other books of a sporting or humorous character. How much of the slang dictionary was actually compiled by Hotten is not definitely known, but there is reason to suspect he contributed very little. "Somewhat more than a generation ago John Camden Hotten, of London, a publisher of 'rare and curious books,' put out a slang dictionary. If my memory serves, its compiler-in-chief was that accomplished scholar, George Augustus Sala. It was afterwards revised by Henry Sampson." — Ambrose Bierce, in *Cosmopolitan magazine,* New York, July, 1907, v. 43, p. 335, * DA.

A dictionary of modern slang, cant, and vulgar words, used at the present day in the streets of London; the universities of Oxford and Cambridge; the houses of parliament; the dens of St. Giles; and the palaces of St. James. Preceded by a history of cant and vulgar language; with glossaries of two secret languages, spoken by the wandering tribes of London, the costermongers, and the patterers. By a London antiquary... Second edition, revised, with two thousand additional words. London: John Camden Hotten, Piccadilly, 1860. 300 p. 12°.   RNM
"The first edition of this work had a rapid sale, and within a few weeks after it was published the entire issue passed from the publisher's shelves into the hands of the public... The first had been found incomplete and faulty in many respects, and the author determined to thoroughly revise and recast before again going to press." — *Preface.*
The bibliography is slightly increased.

The slang dictionary; or, The vulgar words, street phrases, and "fast" expressions of high and low society. Many with their etymology, and a few with their history traced.... [Drawing of the "Wedge" and the "Wooden spoon."] London: John Camden Hotten, Piccadilly, 1865. 305 p. 12°.   RNM
Nearly 10,000 words appear in this edition. With the exception of one item, the bibliography is the same.

Dictionaries, continued

HOTTEN, JOHN CAMDEN, *continued*

The slang dictionary, etymological, historical and anecdotal. A new edition, revised and corrected, with many additions. [Drawing of the "Wedge" and the "Wooden spoon."] London: Chatto and Windus, publishers <successors to John Camden Hotten>, 1874. 382 p. 12°. RNM
The bibliography is the same, except that one additional item is included.

The slang dictionary. Etymological, historical and anecdotal. [Wedge and spoon emblem.] A new impression. London: Chatto & Windus, 1910. 382 p. 12°. RNM
Except for the title-page this is an exact reprint of the 1874 edition.
Some of the reviews of various editions of Hotten may be found in *The Academy*, London, Nov., 1874, v. 6, p. 582, * *DA; The New statesman*, London, May 4, 1929, v. 33, p. 116–117 (G. W. Stonier), * *DA; Revue des deux mondes*, Paris, 1864, tome 53, p. 462–481, * *DM; Chambers's journal*, Edinburgh, Sept. 10, 1859, v. 32, p. 172–174, * *DA; Harper's magazine*, New York, April, 1865, v. 30, p. 601–607 (Charles Nordhoff), * *DA; The Dartmouth*, Hanover, N. H., Feb., 1869, v. 3, p. 54–59, *STG; The Reader*, London, Oct. 22, 1864, v. 4, p. 505, * *DA*.
See Robert Pierpont and others, " 'The Slang dictionary' published by John Camden Hotten: its author" in *Notes and queries*, London, Dec. 19, 1914, series 11, v. 10, p. 488; Jan. 9, 1915, series 11, v. 11, p. 30–31; Jan. 23, 1915, series 11, v. 11, p. 77; Feb. 6, 1915, series 11, v. 11, p. 111–112; Feb. 27, 1915, series 11, v. 11, p. 178, * *R-* DA*.
This raises the question as to whether Hotten was the actual compiler of the slang dictionary. It is proved in subsequent correspondence that he was. A later edition was enlarged by Henry Sampson, who wrote sports articles for *The Weekly dispatch* and *The Referee*, both of which he edited at one time. He wrote under the pseudonym of "Pendragon."
A bibliography of Hotten's publications may be found in *Notes and queries*, London, May 8, 1915, series 11, v. 11, p. 357–358, by F. J. Hytch.

HYAMSON, ALBERT MONTEFIORE.

A dictionary of English phrases, phraseological allusions, catchwords, stereotyped modes of speech and metaphors, nicknames, sobriquets, derivations from personal names, etc. With explanations and thousands of exact references to their sources or early usage... London: G. Routledge & Sons, 1922. 365 p. 8°. * R – RNM
The title is self-explanatory. There are many slang and cant words included.
Reviewed in *The Independent*, New York, April 22, 1922, v. 108, p. 395 (E. L. Pearson), * *DA; The Nation*, New York, June 7, 1922, v. 94, p. 698, * *DA; Outlook*, New York, May 31, 1922, v. 131, p. 216, * *DA; Times literary supplement*, London, March 2, 1922, † *NAA; New statesman*, London, Feb. 11, 1922, v. 18, p. 538, * *DA; Spectator*, London, March 11, 1922, v. 128, p. 307, * *DA; Nation-Athenæum*, London, March 11, 1922, v. 30, p. 867, * *DA; Saturday review*, London, Jan. 21, 1922, v. 133, p. 67, * *DA*.

JOHNSON, TRENCH H.

Phrases and names: their origins and meanings... London: T. Werner Laurie [1906]. vi, 384 p. 12°. * R-* AY
"A great many Americanisms have been included, but as the number is daily increasing it would require a monthly publication of such home-made phrases to keep fully abreast with the times... It has been thought advisable to incorporate in the text a number of slang terms."
Contains the usual *Olla podrida*. cf. Edwards, Brewer, Reddall, etc.

JOHNSON's dictionary, improved by Todd, abridged for the use of schools...and an appendix of Americanisms. Boston: Jenks & Palmer, 1839.
Not in The New York Public Library.
Kennedy 11378.
Appendix of Americanisms, p. 384–395.

KASTNER, LÉON ÉMILE, AND JOSEPH MARKS.

A glossary of colloquial and popular French; for the use of English readers and travellers... London: J. M. Dent & Sons, Ltd. [1929.] vii, 376 p. 8°. M.R.R. Desk
The English definitions of French slang and colloquialisms are couched in colloquial English, and a good deal of English slang may be winnowed from this work in this roundabout way. "Linguistic and historical notes have been added in all cases where such additional information seemed helpful."
Reviewed in *John o' London's weekly*, London, Dec. 7, 1929, v. 22, p. 378–379, * *DA; The French quarterly*, London, June, 1930, v. 12, p. 87–94 (Félix Boillot), * *DA*.

KRON, RICHARD.

Amerikanismen. (In his: Verdeutschungs-Wörterbuch der englischen Umgangssprache ... Karlsruhe (Baden): J. Bielefelds Verlag, 1903. 16°. p. 197–202.) RLK
A short dictionary of Americanisms with their German and English equivalents.

KWONG KI CHIU.

A dictionary of English phrases with illustrative sentences... New York [etc.]: A. S. Barnes & Co. [etc.], 1881. 914 p. 8°. RNK
"Slang and cant phrases," p. 371–428, 745–754.
"Terms and phrases of the stock exchange," p. 755–762.
The larger sections on colloquial phrases, and idiomatic phrases are also of value to the student of Americanisms.
"That a Chinese scholar should have produced, in the heart of New England, a book in English and about English which gives proof of so much knowledge, discrimination, and industry, is a fact which thoughtful people will like to ponder." — *Charles W. Eliot, president of Harvard University.*

LEGRAS, CHARLES.

Dictionnaire de slang et d'expressions familières anglaises. Nouvelle édition entièrement refondue. Paris: Garnier frères, 1922. 182 p. 12°. RNM
A straight dictionary, with no introductory treatise or bibliography. There are numerous citations to English books, however, scattered through the text.
Legras is a laureate of the French Academy.
Cf. J. Manchon, *Le slang*, 1923, *RNM.*
The early edition of this work was published in Paris in 1898, by Garnier. There is a note respecting this edition in *Literature*, London, Dec. 24, 1898, v. 3, p. 611, * *DA*.

LOARING, HENRY JAMES.

A selection of common sayings, words, and customs: their origin and history. London, 1870. 8°.
Copy in the British Museum.

Dictionaries, continued

LYELL, THOMAS REGINALD GUIRE.

Slang, phrase and idiom in colloquial English and their use... Kanda, Tokyo, Japan: The Hokuseido Press, 1931. xxx, 764, 5, 54 p. 16°.
RNM

The author, a lecturer in English at Waseda University and the Tokyo Foreign Language School, has compiled a dictionary for Far Eastern needs. The introduction and preface acquaint the student of the English language with the history and nature of slang and the forces which add to the colloquial accretions of the language.
Reviewed in *American speech*, New York, Feb., 1935, v. 10, p. 61–65, *RNA* (Harold W. Bentley).

MACKAY, CHARLES.

The Gaelic etymology of the languages of western Europe and more especially of the English and Lowland Scotch, and of their slang, cant, and colloquial dialects... London: N. Trübner and Co., 1877. 604 p. 8°.   RPC

Arranged in dictionary form. Contains many slang words. The definitions are full and there are many quotations. Some of the Gaelic etymologies for slang expressions advanced by Dr. Mackay seem far-fetched, according to a reviewer in *Blackwood's magazine, American edition*, New York, July, 1878, v. 124, p. 59–71, * *DA*. The word "cant" seems to be of Gaelic origin, but an attempt to show that the word "slang" itself is a Gaelic word seems to miss the mark. Ernest Weekley has said the last word about this dictionary in his *Something about words*, New York: E. P. Dutton & Co. [1936], p. 170–174, *RNF*.

MACRAGH, ESTEBAN.

Diccionario Amaltea, inglés y español, de modismos, localismos, jergas, argot, frases y palabras que no están incluidas en los diccionarios inglés-españoles. Barcelona: Librería Sintes, 1933. vi, 261(1), viii, 222 p., 1 l. 12°.   RGK

The English-Spanish part occupies p. 1–262.
This dictionary of slang, cant, jargon, etc., lists several thousand English expressions, with their Spanish equivalents. Each word or phrase is classified according to subject. There is no attempt to trace the origin of the expression or date in any way.

MAITLAND, JAMES.

The American slang dictionary. Embodying all American and English slang phrases in current use, with their derivation and philology. Chicago, 1891. 308 p. 8°.   RNM

Limited to 250 copies.
On verso of title-page: Chicago, Ill.: Printed and published for the author by R. J. Kittredge & Co., 52 to 58 West Jackson Street, 1891.
Reviewed in *The Critic*, New York, March 26, 1892, v. 20, p. 180–181, * *DA*. "It is a supplement to Schele de Vere, Bartlett, Hotten, Grose, Egan, and others, far from complete indeed, not immaculate in its accuracy, but racy, full and pointed, well printed and modest in its request to editors for help." Also reviewed in *The Nation*, New York, June 23, 1892, v. 54, p. 469–470, * *DA*. "If the precise truth must be told, seldom has labor been spent to less purpose than in the compilation of this volume. Seldom has the accomplishment of a task of peculiar difficulty fallen into hands so ill-equipped for accomplishing it properly." Mencken and Partridge echoed these sentiments later on.

MANCHON, J.

Le slang, lexique de l'anglais familier et vulgaire. Précédé d'une étude sur la prononciation et la grammaire populaires... Paris: Payot, 1923. 343 p. 12°.   RNM

This work, according to the preface, is compiled for the aid of those who know the classic English literature, but who are unfamiliar with the popular speech. It is in three parts, the first being pronunciation, the second grammar, and the third a dictionary of terms. The French equivalents are given, but many English slang words can scarcely be translated into understandable French. The works cited in the text are listed. Cf. Charles Legras, *Dictionnaire de slang*, 1922. Manchon was professor at the French Institute in London at the time the book was published.
Reviewed in *John o' London's weekly*, London, Sept. 22, 1923, v. 9, p. 792, * *DA* (Sidney Dark); *National review*, London, Nov., 1923, v. 82, p. 438–440, * *DA* (Edgar Preston); *Saturday review*, London, Sept., 1923, v. 136, p. 308, * *DA; Times literary supplement*, London, July 12, 1923, † *NAA*.

MEYSENBUG, HERMANN ULRICH.

Amerikanisches Englisch. Leitfaden der amerikanischen Umgangs- und Handelssprache... Ettlingen (Baden) u. Leipzig: J. Bielefelds Verlag, 1929. 104 p. 8°.   RNZ

The introduction gives a short history of American speech and its peculiarities. This is followed by a dictionary of Americanisms, p. 40–104. A great deal of slang and commercial jargon is included. This book is designed chiefly for German writers and travellers who wish to know more about the every-day speech of Americans. It goes well with *The Little Yankee. A handbook of idiomatic English treating of the daily life, customs and institutions of the United States*, by Alfred D. Schoch and R. Kron. This is also a Bielefeld publication.

MORWITZ... Wörterbuch der englischen und deutschen Sprache mit besonderer Berücksichtigung der Amerikanismen. Leipzig, 1885. 8°.

Mentioned in *Dialect notes*, 1890, v. 1, p. 81, *RNZ*. Not in The New York Public Library.

MUTSCHMANN, HEINRICH.

A glossary of Americanisms. Tartu-Dorpat, 1931. 70 p. 8°. (Tartu. — Ülikool. Acta et commentationes Universitatis Tartuensis, Dorpatensis. B. Humaniora. [v.] 23, [no.] 4.)
STZ (Tartu)

On verso of title-page: Printed by K. Mattiesen, Inc., Tartu, 1931.
"The following list of Americanisms is intended for the use of those who wish to read contemporary American novels, journals, and similar literature." The works of Professors Weseen and Krapp, and *American speech* were used to a great extent in compiling the glossary. The historical method is not employed.

NARES, ROBERT.

A glossary; or, Collection of words, phrases, names, and allusions to customs, proverbs, &c., which have been thought to require illustration, in the works of English authors, particularly Shakespeare, and his contemporaries... London: Printed for Robert Triphook, Old Bond Street; Messrs. Rivington and Co., Waterloo Place and St. Paul's Churchyard; W. and C. Tait, Prince's Street, Edinburgh; and George Mullen, Nassau Street, Dublin, 1822. 538 p. 4°.
†* NCW

Contains many canting words. Full quotations are given. Added to later by the editors, J. O. Halliwell Phillipps and Thomas Wright.

—— London: J. R. Smith, 1859. 2 v. 8°. RNM

—— v. 1. London: J. R. Smith, 1867. 8°. RNM

—— London: J. R. Smith, 1872. 8°.   RNM

—— London: G. Routledge & Sons, Ltd., 1905. ix, 981 p. 8°.   RNM

See H. J. Massingham. "Nares' glossary" in his *Letters to X.*, London: Constable, 1919, p. 186–191, *NCZ*.

Dictionaries, continued

A New English dictionary on historical principles...edited by James A. H. Murray, Henry Bradley, William A. Craigie, and C. T. Onions. Introduction, supplement, and bibliography, by W. A. Craigie, C. T. Onions... Oxford: Clarendon Press, 1933. f°. M.R.R. Desk
While the main body of this great dictionary contains a rich store of slang and Americanisms, the supplementary volume is particularly rich in modern American slang. Although earlier quotations for some of the words should have been found, the attempt to date the words represents the most successful effort in that direction yet made.
A preliminary list of these words, inviting readers to send in the earliest quotations which could be found, appeared in *The Periodical*, Oxford University Press, from Oct., 1928 to Dec., 1932, * *GAA*.
Reviewed in Manchester Literary Club, *Papers*, 1934, v. 60, p. 222–227, *NAA* (C. L. Barnes).

NUTTALL'S popular dictionary of the English language... Extended and improved by James Wood, with supplement of new words. London and New York: Frederick Warne & Co., Ltd., 1932. 816 p. 8°. RNI
"Supplement," p. 1–16.
Contains new words, many of which are slang creations of the twentieth century.

ODELL, TALBOT.
Dictionary of slang and idioms. Distributed by The Washington Bureau, 1322 New York Avenue, Washington, D. C., n. d. 4 double-column pages, 7 x 8½ in.
Contains American slang.

PARTRIDGE, ERIC HONEYWOOD.
A dictionary of slang and unconventional English... London: George Routledge & Sons, Limited, 1937. 999 p. 4°. M.R.R. Desk
Published in America by Macmillan & Co.
This is the most ambitious dictionary of slang ever created by one man, and it places the compiler among the front rank of modern lexicographers. It includes all slang locutions of any real importance from the earliest English records to the present day. Governed by historical principles rather than prudery, this comprehensive dictionary contains many expressions not ordinarily found in dictionaries. It mirrors the speech of men in every walk of life, and is a virile record of the English language. Almost every entry is dated, and the bibliographical references are extensive. Partridge approaches slang with delightful informality, and is thereby able to instruct without being dry. He admits that the groundwork of his dictionary was the old standby, "Farmer and Henley," but he has the advantage of the extensive slang literature which was published in the years following the appearance of *Slang and its analogues* (q.v.).
Reviewed in *The Fortnightly review*, London, April, 1937, new series, v. 147, p. 460–466, * *DA* (G. W. Stonier); Army quarterly, July, 1937, v. 34, p. 355–360, *VWA; The Listener*, London, March 10, 1937, v. 17, supplement, p. vii, * *DA* (Raymond Mortimer); *The Observer*, London, Feb. 21, 1937, * *A* (Ernest Weekley); *The Times literary supplement*, London, March 20, 1937, p. 206, † *NAA; The Times*, London, Feb. 15, 1937, * *A; The Morning Post*, London, Feb. 15, 1937; *The New statesman and nation*, London, Feb. 20, 1937, new series, v. 13, p. 288, * *DA* (David Garnett); *Manchester Guardian*, Feb. 19, 1937; *The Nation*, New York, April 24, 1937, v. 144, p. 478, * *DA* (George Genzmer); *Saturday review of literature*, New York, April 10, 1937, * *DA* (H. L. Mencken); *Time*, New York, April 12, 1937, * *DA; Springfield Republican*, March 14, 1937.

—— Second edition. New York: Macmillan and Company, 1938. 1051 p. 4°.

Slang to-day and yesterday. With a short historical sketch and vocabularies of English, American, and Australian slang... London: George Routledge & Sons, 1933. 476 p. 8°. M.R.R. Desk
Contents: I. General considerations. 1. Slang: definition, etymology, synonyms, range. 2. Origin, uses, reasons for use, attitudes toward slang. 3. Characteristics of slang: in relation to language in general. 4. The essence of slang. II. A sketch of the history of slang. 1. Introductory. 2. The sixteenth century. 3. The seventeenth century. 4. The eighteenth century. 5. The nineteenth century. 6. The twentieth century. 7. Some tendencies of the present. III. Particular aspects. 1. The affiliations of slang. 2. The standard and norm of slang. 3. Kinds of slang other than the standard. a. Cockney, b. public house, c. workmen, d. tradesmen, e. commerce, f. publicity, g. journalism, h. literary criticism, i. publishing and printing, j. the law, k. medicine, l. the church, m. parliament and politics, n. public schools and universities, o. society, p. art, q. the theatre, r. sports and games, s. the turf, Epsom's attic salt, t. circus life, u. sailors, v. soldiers, w. Yiddish, x. cant, y. miscellaneous. 4. Oddities. Rhyming, back, centre slang; Gibberish and Ziph; spoonerisms; blends. 5. A glance at colonial slang. India, South Africa, New Zealand, Australia, Canada. IV. American slang. 1. Introductory, 2. affiliations, 3. characteristics, 4. theorists, 5. practitioners. V. Vocabularies. 1. English, 2. Australian, 3. American. Index of theorists, exponents, and themes.
Partridge has written many articles on slang. He is the most active of the British slang collectors, and has been a close student of American idiom.
Reviewed in *Notes & queries*, London, Dec. 30, 1933, v. 165, p. 468, * *R–* *DA; Week-end review*, London, Oct. 14, 1933, v. 8, p. 380–381, * *DA* (Rose Macauley); *Times literary supplement*, London, Nov. 16, 1933, p. 781, † *NAA; New statesman and nation*, London, Oct. 14, 1933, supplement, p. xvi, * *DA; New York Herald Tribune Books*, April 1, 1934, p. 14, † *NAA; John o' London's weekly*, London, Sept. 30, 1933, v. 29, p. 919, * *DA* (John o' London), same continued on Oct. 7, 1933, v. 30, p. 33; *American speech*, New York, Feb., 1935, v. 10, p. 61–65, *RNA* (Harold W. Bentley); *Word study*, Springfield, Mass., March, 1934, v. 9, p. 2, *RNA; Observer*, London, Oct. 15, 1933, * *A* (Ernest Weekley).
Partridge also edited an edition of Grose's *Classical dictionary of the vulgar tongue* (q.v.), and has written much on soldier slang, in collaboration with John Brophy (q.v.).

—— Second edition, carefully revised; somewhat augmented. London: George Routledge & Sons, Ltd., 1935. 476 p. 8°. M.R.R. Desk

PICKERING, JOHN.
A vocabulary, or collection of words and phrases which have been supposed to be peculiar to the United States of America. To which is prefixed An essay on the present state of the English language in the United States. Originally published in the Memoirs of the American Academy of Arts and Sciences; and now republished with corrections and additions. By John Pickering. [Latin quotation.] Boston: Published by Cummings and Hilliard, No. 1, Cornhill; Cambridge: Hilliard and Metcalf, 1816. 206 p. 8°. RNZ
This was the first dictionary of Americanisms and created quite a stir on both sides of the Atlantic. Pickering (1777–1846) was born at Salem, Mass., attended Harvard, and afterwards studied law at Philadelphia, but he was always an ardent Anglomaniac in matters of speech. He began to make his list of so-called Americanisms in 1799–1801, while secretary to Rufus King, in London. The dictionary gives full quotations and dates in an attempt to give a true history of the words, and he pays his respects to John Witherspoon (q.v.) and Benjamin Franklin,

Dictionaries, continued

PICKERING, JOHN, *continued*

pioneers in the study of the English language in America.

Thomas Jefferson and Noah Webster believed in creating a new language in America, free from the cramping influence of England, but Pickering was a staunch champion of the opposite tendency. Pickering, in a letter to his father, dated Feb. 17, 1817, says: "At the time I read my Memoir to the Academy, Judge Dawes (who, you will recollect, is Mr. Webster's brother-in-law) said to me in a very emphatic manner, as soon as I had finished: 'There! that is what I have been trying to bring my brother Webster to agree to; but he won't do it.' And this is the fact; W. wants to make an American language, and will of course feel hostile to those who take the opposite ground."

Webster did feel hostile and soon wrote *A Letter to the Honorable John Pickering, on the subject of his vocabulary* . . ., Boston, 1817 (q.v.).

The *Dictionary of American biography* has a good account of Pickering, with a bibliography.

Among the reviews of Pickering's book are Thomas R. Lounsbury, "The first dictionary of Americanisms," *Harper's monthly*, New York, June, 1914, v. 129, p. 103–110, *DA;* S. Willard, "A vocabulary, &c.," *North American review*, Boston, Sept. 18, 1816, v. 3, p. 355–361, *DA; Eclectic review*, London, April, 1820, new series, v. 13, p. 356–363, * *DA; National quarterly review*, London, March, 1861, v. 2, p. 230–240, * *DA; The Portico*, Baltimore, July–Aug., 1817, v. 4, p. 1–11, * *DA.*

See obituary in *Southern literary messenger*, Richmond, Aug., 1847, v. 13, p. 496–500, * *DA.*

REDDALL, HENRY FREDERIC.

Fact, fancy, and fable . . . comprising personal sobriquets, familiar phrases, popular appellations, geographical nicknames, literary pseudonyms, mythological characters, red-letter days, political slang, contractions and abbreviations, technical terms, foreign words and phrases, Americanisms, etc . . . Chicago: A. C. McClurg & Co., 1892. 536 p. 8°.   * R – * AY

Two columns to a page.

The title is self-explanatory.

RICE, EMMA LEE.

Handbook of better speech . . . Kingsport, Tennessee, 1932. 165 p. 8°.   RND

Bibliography, p. 165.

Designed to correct errors of speech. Colloquialisms, slang, vulgarisms, etc., make up a large part of the work. The book is arranged in dictionary form.

ROSE, HOWARD N.

A thesaurus of slang. New York: The Macmillan Company, 1934. x, 120 p. 12°.   RNM

Compiled for the use of short story writers. Divided into the following groups: aviation, college, detective, hobo, lumber-jack, New England, newspaper, oilfield, railroad, sea-fishing, sports, theatre, western, war.

Reviewed in *Times literary supplement*, London, Dec. 6, 1934, v. 33, p. 878, † *NAA; Commonweal*, New York, Sept. 21, 1934, v. 20, p. 494, * *DA; New York Times*, Sept. 2, 1934, p. 9, * *A; New republic*, New York, Nov. 21, 1934, v. 81, p. 55, * *DA; American speech*, New York, April, 1935, v. 10, p. 142–144, *RNA* (J. Louis Kuethe); *National review*, Nov. 21, 1934, v. 81, p. 55, * *DA; Nation*, New York, Sept. 19, 1934, v. 149, p. 331–332 (H. L. Mencken), * *DA.* Other reviews are listed in the *Book review digest*, New York, 1934, p. 808.

RUSSELL, T. BARON.

Current Americanisms: a dictionary of words and phrases in common use . . . London: Saxon & Co. [1897.] 158 p. 24°.   RNZ

The introduction traces the history of the study of Americanisms. The dictionary proper seems to be a digest of Bartlett and other American compilers, to which is added a considerable number of words taken directly from American newspapers.

Americanismen. Alphabetisch gerangschikte verzameling van de meest gebrinkelijke, special amerikaansche woorden en zegswijsen met verklarende ophelderingen door J. H. van der Voort. Gouda, 1894. 150 p.

Not in The New York Public Library.
Kennedy 11515.

SCHOCH, ALFRED D., AND RICHARD KRON.

The little Yankee: a handbook of idiomatic American English, treating of the daily life, customs and institutions of the United States, etc. Freiburg: Bielefeld, 1912. 192 p.

Not in The New York Public Library.
Kennedy 11587.

See also Kron's *The little Londoner,* 1911.

TENNER, ARMIN, EDITOR.

Amerika . . . Berlin: Stuhr'sche Buchhandlung; New York: Westermann & Co., 1886. xii p., 1 l., 484 p., 2 l., 116 p. 2. ed. 8°.

ILD (Amerika)

At the end of this volume is *Tenner's Deutsch-amerikanisches Vademecum; oder, Kurzgefasste Erläuterungen amerikanischer Eigenthümlichkeiten im Sprache und Leben,* 116 p. This dictionary contains geographical and personal names, along with Americanisms and slang. Based on Bartlett.

THORNTON, RICHARD HOPWOOD.

An American glossary. Being an attempt to illustrate certain Americanisms upon historical principles. Philadelphia: J. B. Lippincott Company, 1912. 2 v. 8°.   M.R.R. Desk

A work of high merit, and the only one of its kind prior to the more ambitious *Historical dictionary of the American language,* now being published under the direction of Sir William Craigie. Thornton has included: 1. Forms of speech now obsolete or provincial in England, which survive in the U. S. 2. Words and phrases of distinctly American origin. 3. Nouns which indicate quadrupeds, birds, trees, articles of food, etc. 4. Names of persons and classes of persons, and of places. 5. Words which have assumed a new meaning. 6. Words and phrases of which "I have found earlier examples in American than in English writers."

The definitions are clarified by numerous dated quotations.

Some of these words were discussed in a correspondence initiated by Thornton in *Notes and queries.* See June 12, 1909, series 10, v. 11, p. 469; July 3, 1909, series 10, v. 12, p. 10–11; July 17, 1909, series 10, v. 12, p. 50–51; Aug. 7, 1909, series 10, v. 12, p. 107–108; Oct. 2, 1909, series 10, v. 12, p. 270–271; Dec. 18, 1909, series 10, v. 12, p. 492–493, * *R–* *DA.*

Reviewed in *Athenæum*, London, May 25, 1912, v. 1, p. 593, June 29, 1912, v. 1, p. 728–729, * *DA; Spectator*, London, June 15, 1912, v. 108, p. 958, * *DA; Nation*, New York, July 4, 1912, v. 95, p. 11–12, * *DA; Literary digest*, New York, June 21, 1913, v. 46, p. 1386, 1388, * *DA; Revue germanique*, Paris, 1913, v. 9, p. 91–94, * *DM* (F. C. Danchin); Englische Studien, Leipzig, 1912, Bd. 46, p. 133–136 (Johannes Hoops), *RNA.*

Some editions have the imprint: Philadelphia: J. B. Lippincott Company; London: Francis & Co., 13, Bream's Buildings, Chancery Lane, E. C., 1912. These were printed in England.

An American glossary: a specimen passage. (Dialect notes. New Haven, 1919. 8°. v. 5, p. 43–53.)   RNZ

Outlines his third volume of Americanisms, which he could not publish on account of lack of funds. His appeal to a number of wealthy men was in vain, although ten thousand dollars would have paid for the publication. He gives a sample of what the new volume would contain, when published.

An American glossary. (Dialect notes. New Haven, 1931–date. 8°. Dec., 1931, v. 6, part 3, p. 100–104, Foreword and Introductory note, p. 105–216, A–Dip; July, 1932, v. 6, part 4, p. 238–280, Dipping-Frog pond; Dec., 1932,

Dictionaries, continued

v. 6, part 5, p. 286–312, Front office–Half horse and half alligator; July, 1933, v. 6, part 6, p. 336–352, Halfway covenant-Horse sense; Dec., 1933, v. 6, part 7, p. 368–384, Horse sense-Johnnycake; July, 1934, v. 6, part 8, p. 392–416, Johnny-jump-up-Longs and shorts; Dec., 1934, v. 6, part 9, p. 424–448, Long sauce and short sauce-Nigger; July, 1935, v. 6, part 10, p. 456–480, Nigger in the woodpile-Perique; Dec., 1935, v. 6, part 11, p. 488–512, Persimmon-Puts and calls; July/Dec., 1936, parts 12/13, p. 528–576, Put through-Slang; July, 1937, v. 6, part 14, p. 600–616, Slang-whanger-Spoils system; Dec., 1937, v. 6, part 15, p. 624–648, Spook-Under ditch.

The third volume of *An American glossary* appeared in *Dialect notes* after Thornton's death. He had made a plea for financial help for the furtherance of his project, but this met with failure, and it was through the graces of the Dialect Society of America that Thornton's notes, the work of many years of assiduous study, were finally brought to press. Had he lived many pages of new material would have been added.

TOONE, WILLIAM.
A glossary and etymological dictionary of obsolete and uncommon words, antiquated phrases, proverbial expressions, obscure allusions, and of words which have changed their signification... London: William Pickering, 1832. 467 p. 16°.   RNM
Contains a great many cant words. A valuable illustrative quotation from some old play or poem helps to date the expression.

TORRENS, R. K., AND HERBERT PARKER.
English idiomatic and slang expressions done into German. Strassburg: Karl J. Trübner, 1914. 119 p. 16°.   RNM
An amusing and instructive dictionary of slang. "In the compilation, it has been my aim always to select such expressions as are generally omitted from ordinary dictionaries and phrase-books. . . These expressions constitute conversational small change."

VIZETELLY, FRANCIS HORACE.
A desk book of errors in English, including notes on colloquialisms and slang to be avoided in conversation. New York: Funk & Wagnalls, 1907. 232 p. 12°.
Dr. Vizetelly has always had an interest in slang words and has looked at them with the eye of the lexicographer, ready to acclaim those which were vital, and ready to kill those which were ephemeral. This is an early compilation, and Dr. Vizetelly's English ears were alert to catch American barbarisms.

VIZETELLY, FRANCIS HORACE, AND LEANDER DE BEKKER.
...A desk-book of idioms and idiomatic phrases in English speech and literature... New York: Funk & Wagnalls Co., 1923. 498 p. 8°.   M.R.R. Desk
This handy reference volume by the editor of *The New standard dictionary* and his associate includes much of our modern slang. Origins are given when known, and quotations are numerous.

VOORT, J. H. VAN DER.
Hedendaagsche Amerikanismen; alphabetisch gerangschikte verzameling van de meest gebruikelijke, speciaal Amerikaansche woorden en zegswijzen. Gouda: G. B. van Goor Zonen [1894]. vi, 150 p. obl. 16°.   RNM

WARE, JAMES REDDING.
Passing English of the Victorian era. A dictionary of heterodox English, slang, and phrase... London: George Routledge & Sons [1909]. 271 p. 8°.   RNM
A companion volume to Farmer and Henley's *Dictionary of slang and colloquial English*. This is a popular dictionary, and not arranged according to the strict historical lines laid down by the *O. E. D.*
Reviewed by W. J. Ghent, *Harper's weekly*, New York, Aug. 1, 1914, v. 59, p. 105, * *DA*; by Edmund Lester Pearson, *Nation*, New York, Aug. 13, 1914, v. 99, p. 189–190, * *DA*; *The Independent*, New York, Aug. 26, 1909, v. 67, p. 477–478, * *DA*.

WESEEN, MAURICE HARLEY.
Crowell's dictionary of English grammar and handbook of American usage. New York: Thomas Y. Crowell Company [cop. 1928]. 703 p. 8°.   RND
Filled with American slang and colloquialisms. Has a special glossary of college slang, p. 123–128. See also coined words, p. 118–121.

A dictionary of American slang... New York: Thomas Y. Crowell Company [1934]. 543 p. 8°.   M.R.R. Desk
Contents: 1. Crooks' and criminals' slang, p. 1–45; 2. Hoboes' and tramps' slang, p. 46–67; 3. Railroaders' slang, p. 68–76; 4. Loggers' and miners' slang, p. 77–87; 5. Oil drillers' slang, p. 88–91; 6. Cowboys' and Westerners' slang, p. 92–111; 7. Soldiers' slang, p. 112–124; 8. Sailors' slang, p. 125–131; 9. Aviators' slang, p. 132–134; 10. Theatre slang, p. 135–156; 11. Circus and carnival slang, p. 157–164; 12. Radio slang, p. 165–172; 13. College slang, p. 173–202; 14. Baseball slang, p. 203–225; 15. Football slang, p. 226–228; 16. Boxing and prizefighting slang, p. 229–245; 17. Sports slang — miscellaneous, p. 246–271; 18. Drinking slang, p. 272–287; 19. Eating slang, p. 288–293; 20. Money slang, p. 294–300; 21. General slang, p. 301–422; Index, p. 423–543.
Modern slang for the most part. Does not give dates, or definitions in the historical manner. Weseen is connected with the University of Nebraska as associate professor of English. He is the compiler of *Words confused and misused*, New York, Crowell, 1932.
This dictionary contains about 15,000 expressions. Does not contain a bibliography.
Reviewed in *Saturday review of literature*, New York, Feb. 2, 1935, v. 11, p. 462 (John S. Kenyon), *NAA*; *New York Times*, Nov. 11, 1934, p. 18, * *A*; *Nation*, New York, Nov. 28, 1934, v. 139, p. 628, * *DA*; *American speech*, Feb., 1935, v. 10, p. 61–65, *RNA* (Harold W. Bentley); *Review of reviews*, New York, Dec., 1934, v. 90, p. 6, * *DA*; *Revue anglo-américaine*, Paris, Dec., 1935, p. 146–147 (F. Mossé), * *DM*; *Oxford magazine*, Oct. 17, 1935, v. 54, p. 10, 12–14, † *STK* (D. W. B.); *American speech*, New York, Dec., 1936, v. 11, p. 293–297, *RNA* (J. Louis Kuethe); *Everyman*, London, Nov. 8, 1935. See also *Book review digest*, New York, 1934, p. 1001.

WILLIAMS, HENRY LLEWELLYN.
The American standard dictionary... New York: Hurst & Co. [cop. 1881.] 928 p. 12°.   RNK
Objectionable words and terms, p. 398–419 (includes slang); Americanisms, p. 419–421; Popular names of states, p. 348–350; Vocabulary of business, p. 353–360; Nautical vocabulary, p. 360–371; Supplement of additional words and definitions, p. 661–681 (made up largely of slang).

WOOD, CLEMENT, AND GLORIA GODDARD.
A dictionary of American slang. Girard, Kansas: Haldeman-Julius, 1926. 64 p.   NAC
A handy list of American slang, strong in sports slang. The definitions are brief.

GENERAL WORKS

AYRES, HARRY MORGAN.
The English language in America. (Cambridge history of American literature. Cambridge: The University Press, 1921. 4°. v. 4, p. 554–571.)   * R–NBB
Does not treat of slang *per se*, but shows the historical background of American speech and its fundamental differences from so-called standard English.

CAIRNS, WILLIAM B.
British criticism of American writings, 1783–1815. Madison, 1918. 97 p. 8°. (University of Wisconsin studies in language and literature. no. 1.)   NAA (Wisconsin)

British criticisms of American writings, 1815–1833. Madison, 1922. 319 p. 8°. (University of Wisconsin studies in language and literature. to. 14.)   NAA (Wisconsin)
Scattered references to Americanisms may be found in these studies, along with useful bibliographical notes.

FISCHER, WALTHER PAUL.
Amerikanisches Englisch. (In: Handbuch der Amerikanakunde... Frankfurt a. M.: Verlag Moritz Diesterweg, 1931. 8°. p. 153–178.)   IDS
Contents: 1. Allgemeines — Die geschichtliche Entwicklung. 2. Bibliographisches. 3. Die drei amerikanischen Aussprachegruppen. 4. Wortschatz — Wortschöpfung — Slang. 5. Bemerkungen zur Formenlehre und Syntax.
The German critic of our speech has read all the important works on American English and approaches the study in the strictly historical manner. This is one of the better foreign surveys of American English. Reviewed in *American speech*, Oct., 1931, v. 7, p. 63–64, *RNA*.

Neuere und neue Arbeiten über amerikanische Englisch. (Die Neueren Sprachen. Marburg in Hessen, Sept., 1927. 8°. Bd. 35, p. 449–456.)   RAV
Historical survey of American English, with emphasis on Pickering, Thornton, Mencken, Krapp, and others who have dealt with the thorny subject of Americanisms.

HIGH-CLASS slang. (Temple Bar. London, Feb., 1871. 8°. v. 31, p. 309–321.)   * DA
Some possible derivations for the word slang are discussed. The Greeks and Romans used much slang, as did the early church. English slang is of great antiquity. A number of Elizabethan slang words are mentioned, along with some nicknames, Scotch slang, and other varieties.

MESICK, JANE LOUISE.
The English traveller in America. New York: Columbia University Press, 1922. 370 p. 8°.   IID
The books of about seventy-five English travellers are studied. English opinions on the language spoken in America may be traced by following up the citations listed by Miss Mesick on p. 240–245.

NIEBERG, GEORGE FREDERIC.
The American slanguage. (Forum. New York, Dec., 1930. f°. v. 84, p. 371–376.) * DA
Historical sketch of slang; its vagaries and varieties. Shows that many American slang words of the present day are really old English cant. A few slang words indigenous to the United States are gone into.

AN OLD mine re-opened. (All the year round. London, Oct. 17, 1874. 8°. v. 33, p. 6–10.)
                                                       * DA
A study of the words *cant* and *canting*. The author holds that "the true root of the word cant is the Gallic and ancient British *cainnt*, which simply signifies language; the language, in fact, of the British people before the irruption of the Anglo-Saxons and Danes." An alphabetical list of slang words is given with an attempt to trace them to this ancient language.

READ, ALLEN WALKER.
British recognition of American speech in the eighteenth century. (Dialect notes. New Haven, July, 1933. 8°. v. 6, part 6, p. 313–334.)
                                                       RNZ
Many quotations from English lexicographers, travellers, and magazine critics, exhibiting their opinion of the speech of Americans. They range from faint praise to vicious denunciation. A great many Americanisms crop up in the study and much light is thrown on the early development of our national speech habits.
Some additional comments are to be found in *Dialect notes*, July, 1935, v. 6, part 10, p. 454–456.

TANDY, JENNETTE REID.
Crackerbox philosophers in American humor and satire. New York: Columbia University Press, 1925. 181 p. 8°.   NBW
A survey of American humor from Royall Tyler's comedy, *The Contrast* (1787) to the twentieth century. Has much to say about "Jack Downing" and "Sam Slick" and their creators, also about the *Biglow papers*, and the story-tellers of the South. Bibliography of early Yankee poems, p. 20–23; bibliography of southern humor and satire, p. 97–102; bibliography of Montague Glass and Frank McKinney Hubbard, p. 173–175.

SEVENTEENTH CENTURY

BATEN, ANDERSON MONROE.
Slang from Shakespeare, together with literary expressions... Compiled by Anderson M. Baten. [Hammond, Ind.: Printed by W. B. Conkey, cop. 1931.] vii p., 1 1., 153 p. 12°. * NCR
Author's autograph on flyleaf, written at Dallas, Texas, Nov. 2, 1931.
Alphabetical list of slang words and phrases in Shakespeare, but the plays from which they are taken are not mentioned.

CLARKE, CHARLES COWDEN, AND MARY COWDEN CLARKE.
The Shakespeare key... London: Sampson, Low, Marston, Searle & Rivington, 1879. xi, 810, xvi p. 8°.   * NCW
"Cant terms," p. 38–42.
Glossary of the cant terms found in Shakespeare's plays.

General Works, continued

Seventeenth Century, continued

COMBS, JOSIAH HENRY.

Early English slang survivals in the mountains of Kentucky. (Dialect notes. New Haven, 1921. 8°. v. 5, p. 115–117.) RNZ

"Much of the slang of the Elizabethan period is still used in the southern mountains." Gives a list.

EGGLESTON, EDWARD.

Mother English; folk-speech, folk-lore, and literature. (In his: Transit of civilization from England to America in the seventeenth century. New York: D. Appleton & Co., 1901. 8°. p. 96–140.) IF

The first part of this chapter gives a few early Americanisms and shows how new conditions of life called for a new terminology.

ERNST, C. W.

Words coined in Boston. (New England magazine. Boston, 1896. 8°. new series, v. 15, p. 337–344.) *DA

The Pilgrim fathers, although grounded in Elizabethan English, coined new expressions to fit local conditions, and Bostonians have clung persistently to these old expressions. Some notable additions have been made in subsequent generations, among which are "paper money," "trust," "caucus," "gerrymander," "warden."

GERARD, WILLIAM RUGGLES.

Virginia's Indian contributions to English. (American anthropologist. Lancaster, Pa., 1907. 8°. v. 9, p. 87–112.) HBA

A number of common Americanisms which were taken over from the native Indian languages are mentioned.

Cf. Alexander F. Chamberlain's article "Algonkian words in American English," *Journal of American folk-lore*, Boston, 1902, v. 15, p. 240–267; 1903, v. 16, p. 128–129; 1908, v. 21, p. 82, *HBA*.

LODGE, HENRY CABOT.

The origin of certain Americanisms. (Scribner's magazine. New York, June, 1907. 8°. v. 41, p. 653–660.) *DA

Many so-called Americanisms are shown to be good old English words. "To possess English as a birthright opens to every man so born, without effort and without price, the greatest literature except that of Greece... The importance of uniformity in usage, not only to the quality, but to the growth and spread of the language, can hardly be overestimated."

Reprinted in his volume of essays, *The Democracy of the constitution*, New York: Charles Scribner's Sons, 1915, p. 246–273, *NBQ*.

Shakespeare's Americanisms. (In his: Certain accepted heroes, and other essays in literature and politics... New York: Harper & Brothers, 1897. 12°. p. 96–114.) NBQ

French and Spanish have become more fixed than the English language, due to less colonization. Even so, the changes in the English language are more apparent than real, particularly in the case of so-called Americanisms. Shakespeare's plays are combed for expressions now obsolete in England but still a part of the living speech in America. With true reverence for the sacred bond of language which makes us forever a part of England, the author closes with the hope that both countries will continue to defend the common language against barbarous impurities.

MARQUARDT, FREDERIC S.

Shakspere and American slang. (American speech. Baltimore, Dec., 1928. 4°. v. 4, p. 118–122.) RNA

Many of Shakespeare's slang words have survived in American speech, but the meanings now attached to them are not always those intended by the poet.

See also J. Weiss, *Wit, humor and Shakespeare*, Boston, 1876, p. 121–150, * *NCV*; *Harper's magazine*, New York, 1895, v. 90, p. 252–256; A. M. Baten, *Slang from Shakespeare*, 1931, 153 p., * *NCR*; C. W. Stearns, "'Americanisms' in Shakespeare's plays," in his *The Shakespeare treasury*, New York: Putnam, 1869, p. 386–393, * *NCR*; Margaret Galway, "Flyting in Shakespear's comedies," in *The Shakespeare Association bulletin*, New York, Oct., 1935, v. 10, p. 183–191; Burton Stevenson, *The homebook of Shakespeare quotations*, New York: Charles Scribner's Sons, 1937.

MUNDUS FOPPENSIS, or the Fop displayed; being the Ladies vindication: in answer to 'Mundus Muliebris, etc.; in Burlesque. With a Supplement to the 'Fop Dictionary,' for the use of the Town Beaus. Printed for J. Harris at the Harrow in the Poultrey. 1690. 4°.

Title from Arber, *The Term catalogues*, v. 2, p. 337.

We have not examined the contents of the "Fop Dictionary" but we strongly suspect it is in the slang of the period.

MUNDUS MULIEBRIS, or The Ladies' dressing Room unlock'd, and her Toilette spread; in Burlesque. Together with the Fop Dictionary, compiled for the fair Sex: with a rare receipt to make Pig-or Puppy dog-water. Printed for R. Bentley in Russel street in Covent Garden. 1690. 22 p. 4°.

Title from Arber, *The Term catalogues*, v. 2, p. 336.

OLD Americanisms. (T. P.'s weekly. London, 1907. f°. July 26, 1907, v. 10, p. 108; Aug. 16, 1907, v. 10, p. 224.) *DA

Traces many so-called Americanisms to older English authors. The article by Henry Cabot Lodge in *Scribner's magazine* is discussed.

RICHARDS, WALTER.

Some colloquialisms in Shakespeare. (Temple Bar. London, July, 1902. 8°. v. 126, p. 175–180.) *DA

Many of the common "up-to-date expressions of to-day have, if not their origin, at least their imprimatur in Shakespeare." Cites many examples.

SHAKESPEARE'S slang. (National repository. Cincinnati, Dec., 1878. 8°. v. 4, p. 565.) *DA

Brief conjecture as to the origin of the word *Bezonian*, found in the speech of ancient Pistol.

STEARNS, CHARLES WOODWARD.

The Shakspeare treasury of wisdom and knowledge... New York: G. P. Putnam & Son, 1869. viii, 436 p. 12°. *NCR

"Americanisms in Shakspeare's plays," p. 386–393.

Many Shakespearian words are still used in the Southern Highlands of the United States.

General Works, continued

Eighteenth Century

ANSONIUS, PSEUD.
Whimsical peculiarities of expression. (Spirit of the public journals for 1798. London, 1805. new ed. 12°. p. 382–387.)   * DA

Reprinted from *The Monthly magazine*. This essay dated Wells, July 20, 1798, concerns itself with popular phrases of the day, including some university slang.

BOUCHER, JONATHAN.
Boucher's glossary of archaic and provincial words, edited by the Rev. Joseph Hunter... with large additions...by Joseph Stevenson, Esq., forming a supplement to the dictionaries of the English language, particularly those of Dr. Johnson and Dr. Webster. London: Black, Young, and Young, 1833. 4°.   † RNM

Part II according to title on paper wrapper cover. This volume goes only from A to Blade. There is an introduction by Boucher, written, according to the editors, in 1800. Boucher came to America in 1759 and became a tutor in Virginia. He was a student of language and he soon noticed the peculiarities of American speech. In this introductory essay, he lists a number of Americanisms, although he does not use the term "Americanism." The list is on p. xlix. He also reprints a poem entitled "Absence, a Pastoral: drawn from the life, from the manners, customs and phraseology of planters (or, to speak pastorally, of the rural swains) inhabiting the banks of the Potomac, in Maryland." The poem was written before 1775, and is therefore earlier than Witherspoon's "The Druid," which was long considered the first serious treatment of Americanisms. The importance of the poem is fully explained by Allen Walker Read in *Dialect notes*, Dec., 1933, v. 6, part 7, p. 353–360, with additional comment by M. M. Mathews, p. 360–363. Boucher puts the dialect words in italics, and carefully explains them in his notes, which were probably written circa 1800. In many respects this is one of the most important studies of the American language ever made, considering the time it was written. See *D.N.B.* and *D.A.B.*

MATHEWS, MITFORD McLEOD.
The beginnings of American English. Essays and comments. Edited by M. M. Mathews. Chicago: The University of Chicago Press [1931]. 181 p. 8°.   RNZ

Contents: Some preliminary observations. 2. Rev. John Witherspoon (1722–94). 3. Four additional commentators. 4. Noah Webster (1758–1843). 5. David Humphreys (1752–1818). 6. John Pickering (1777–1846). 7. Theodore Romeyn Beck (1791–1855). 8. Mrs. Anne Royall (1769–1854). 9. Americanisms in the *Virginia literary museum*. 10. Western and southern vernacular. 11. James Fenimore Cooper (1789–1851). 12. English travelers. 13. John Russell Bartlett (1805–86). 14. Southwestern vernacular. Index.
Gives a survey of American speech by printing excerpts from the recognized pioneers in this field, accompanied by biographical and critical material. Witherspoon's series of articles on language entitled "The Druid" are reproduced. Letters of Webster to Thomas Dawes and Benjamin Franklin are reprinted. David Humphrey's glossary of Americanisms which appeared in the back of his play *The Yankey in England*, 1815, is given. Pickering's introductory essay to his *A Vocabulary or collection of words and phrases which have been supposed to be peculiar to the United States of America*, 1816, is reproduced. Beck's notes on Pickering's *Vocabulary*, read before the Albany Institute, March 18, 1829, is given. Excerpts from Anne Royall's various writings are commented upon. Dunglison's list of Americanisms which appeared in the *Virginia literary museum*, 1829, and Sherwood's provincialisms which appeared in his *Gazetteer of the state of Georgia*, 1827, are reprinted. Selections are made from Marryat, Cooper, and Bartlett, and the chapter on southwestern slang is a reprint of Socrates Hyacinth's article in the *Overland monthly*, San Francisco, Aug., 1869, v. 3, p. 125–131, * DA.

MATTHEWS, ALBERT.
Colonial and early pioneer words. (Dialect notes. New Haven, 1917. 8°. v. 4, p. 375–385.)   RNZ

Items from the collectanea of Albert Matthews, prepared by the editor of *Dialect notes*. The words are dated and handled much in the manner of those in Thornton's *American glossary*.

Remarks on early discussions of Americanisms. (Colonial Society of Massachusetts. Publications. Boston, 1913. 8°. v. 14, p. 257–264.)   IAA

The remarks by Matthews were made at the March, 1912, meeting of the society. The works of Witherspoon and Pickering are mentioned and the attempt, on the part of John Adams and others to form an "American Academy for refining, improving, and ascertaining the English language" is outlined.

MITCHELL, HUGH.
Scotticisms, vulgar Anglicisms, and grammatical improprieties corrected, with reasons for the corrections. Glasgow, 1799. 12°.

Copy in the British Museum.

OBSERVATOR, PSEUD.
On new words. (Annual register. London, 1773. 8°. 1772, p. 190–191.)   * R-BAA

Speaks of the "kind of amphibious animals, between fools and wits, fops and slovens, rakes and enthusiasts," who attempt to make new words the fashion. Observator especially disliked the words "immense," "humbugg'd," "shaver," "flabbergasted," and "bored," as they were currently used.

[On fashionable and cant phrases.] (The World. London, Dec. 12, 1754. no. 102.) * DA

Reprinted in *British essayists*, by Alexander Chalmers, London, 1802, v. 27, p. 266–270, *NCY*; and also in *London magazine*, London, 1754, v. 23, appendix, p. 597–599, * DA.
The essay was signed: C. D.
It is in polite disagreement with those who would add neologisms to a dictionary before they proved their right to be there. Blames women for new words. "Novelty is their pleasure; singularity and the love of being beforehand is greatly flattering to the female mind... From hence only can we account for that jargon which the French call the *bon ton*, which they are obliged to change continually, as soon as they find it prophaned by any other company but one step lower than themselves in their degrees of politeness."

PLATT, JOAN.
The development of English colloquial idiom during the eighteenth century. (Review of English studies. London, 1926. 4°. v. 2, p. 70–81, 189–196.)   RNA

This article was based on research undertaken in the course of preparing a thesis for the degree of Ph.D. in the University of London. Most of the well-known eighteenth-century writers were gleaned for odd and striking colloquialisms. The words are studied in connection with their social and psychological backgrounds.

SWIFT, JONATHAN.
[On the corruptions of the English language.] (The Tatler. London, Sept. 28, 1710. f°. no. 230.)   †* KSD

Swift attributed the vulgarity which was creeping into the English language to ignorance and lack of taste. He gives examples of corrupt English, such as "mobb," "bamboozle," "banter," "kidney," etc. These remarks have been often quoted by the writers dealing with the English tongue.
The New York Public Library has numerous reprints of *The Tatler*.

General Works, continued

Eighteenth Century, continued

WITHERSPOON, JOHN.

"The Druid." No. V–VII. (Pennsylvania journal and the weekly advertiser. Philadelphia, May 9, 16, 23, 30, 1781.)   Reserve

"The Druid" series was contributed by the distinguished president of Princeton College. Nos. 5, 6, and 7 of the series were devoted to language, and the peculiarities of American speech. It was in this series that Witherspoon coined the word *Americanism*. In "The Druid" No. 5, he says: "The first class I call Americanisms, by which I understand an use of phrases or terms, or a construction of sentences, even among persons of rank and education, different from the use of the same terms or phrases, or the construction of similar sentences in Great Britain... The word Americanism, which I have coined for the purpose, is exactly similar in its formation and signification to the word Scotticism."

"The Druid" series was reprinted in Witherspoon's collected works, and in M. M. Mathews, *The Beginnings of American English. Essays and comments...*, Chicago: The University of Chicago Press [1931], p. 14–30, *RNZ*. Mathews also reprinted some of the comments *in re* "The Druid" which appeared in the *Pennsylvania Journal*, June 20, 1781, and June 30, 1781.

Witherspoon was one of the first writers to make a serious study of the language differences between the inhabitants of Great Britain and America. He was born in Scotland in 1722, and entered the University of Edinburgh at the age of 14. In 1766 he was elected president of the College of New Jersey, later known as Princeton University, but he did not arrive in America until 1768. He was one of the signers of the Declaration of Independence. A statue to his memory was unveiled in Washington, D. C., May 20, 1909.

The best account of his life and works is Varnum Lansing Collins's *President Witherspoon. A biography*, Princeton: Princeton University Press, 1925, 2 v. 8°. A bibliography of Witherspoon's writings may be found in the second volume of this work, p. 235–266. The

descriptions of the following editions of Witherspoon are taken from Collins:

The works of the Rev. John Witherspoon, D.D., L.L.D. Late president of the college, at Princeton New-Jersey. To which is prefixed An Account of the author's life, in a sermon occasioned by his death, by the Rev. Dr. John Rodgers, of New York. In three volumes. Philadelphia: Printed and published by William W. Woodward. No 17 Chesnut [*sic*] near Front street, 1800. 4 v. 8°.

The 4th volume was dated 1801.

—— Second edition, revised and corrected. Philadelphia: Printed and published by William W. Woodward, No. 52 South Second Street, 1802. 4 v. 8°.

—— The works of John Witherspoon, D.D. Sometime minister of the gospel at Paisley and late president of Princeton College, in New Jersey. Containing essays, sermons, &c., on important subjects; intended to illustrate and establish the doctrine of salvation by grace, and to point out its influence on holiness of life. Together with his lectures on moral philosophy, eloquence and divinity; his speeches in the American Congress; and many other valuable pieces never before published in this country. Edinburgh: Printed for Ogle & Aikman; J. Pillans & Sons; J. Ritchie; and J. Turnbull, 1804–05. 9 v. 8°.

"The Druid" appears in v. 9 of this edition, p. 224–291. Nos. 5, 6, and 7, on language, occupy p. 267–291.

—— Edinburgh: Printed for J. Ogle, Parliament Square; M. Ogle, Glasgow; Ogles, Duncan & Cochran, London; and T. Johnston, Dublin, 1815. 9 v. 8°.

WOOD, EDWARD J.

Words and phrases of the eighteenth century. (Gentleman's magazine. London, Sept., 1867. 8°. v. 223, p. 357–358.)   * DA

"While reading the *Tatler* (1709–1710), I met with certain curious, and now almost obsolete words and phrases... Perhaps some of your readers can elucidate and explain this verbal coinage of the time of 'Isaac Bickerstaff.'"

The writer, in this letter to Mr. Urban, gives a list of words taken from *The Tatler*.

NINETEENTH CENTURY

1801–1820

BARKER, JAMES NELSON.

Tears and smiles. A comedy. In five acts. Performed at the theatre Philadelphia. By J. N. Barker. First acted Wednesday, 4th March, 1807. Philadelphia: Printed by T. & G. Palmer, for G. E. Blake, No. 1 South Third-street, 1808. iv, 85 p. 16°.   * KL

In the preface to this play the author speaks of *Columbianisms*, which English theatre-goers objected to as crude. *Columbianisms* meant not only speech, but manners. The Yankee in this play helped to create the type which appeared in literature and caricature. See Paul H. Musser, *James Nelson Barker, 1784–1858*, Philadelphia: University of Pennsylvania Press, 1929. 230 p. 8°. *NBC. Tears and smiles* is reprinted in Musser. There is also a bibliography, p. 211–223.

The Library has a second copy in *NAFH p.v.9, no.5.*

BARROW, SIR JOHN?

Inchiquen's favourable view of the United States. (Quarterly review. London, Jan., 1814. 8°. v. 10, p. 494–539.)   * DA

In reviewing Inchiquen's book all the ill feeling created in the War of 1812 comes to the fore. On p. 528 the language used by Americans comes in for a scathing attack. Other Americanisms are italicized throughout the text of the review. The custom of *bundling* is mentioned.

Timothy Dwight is the supposed author of a reply

to this review. It was called *Remarks on the review of Inchiquin's Letters, published in the Quarterly review; addressed to the Right Honorable George Canning, Esquire. By an Inhabitant of New-England.* Boston: Published by Samuel F. Armstrong, No. 50, Cornhill, 1815. 176 p., *IID.*

Dwight takes up the matter of American and English speech, p. 139–144. He says: "The Review of Inchiquin's Letters, as I have been lately informed, has in this country been attributed to Mr. Southey."

Walter Graham in his *Tory criticism in the Quarterly review, 1809–1853*, New York: Columbia University Press, 1921, p. 10, attributes the review to James Barrow, of the Admiralty. It seems more likely that Sir John Barrow of the Admiralty was meant, for he contributed 195 articles to the *Quarterly review*. See *D. N. B.*

Barrow has a good account of the *Quarterly review* in his *Autobiography*, London: John Murray, 1847, p. 492–515, *AN.*

BIRCH, BARTLEMY.

Instances of English pseudography reprobated. (Gentleman's magazine. London, May, 1818. 8°. v. 86, p. 418–420.)   * DA

"When I find one extreme of the Illiterati express themselves thus: *A fearful fine day*, and a *devilish pratty* [sic] *woman;* and the other extremity of this sapient order, who are equally guilty of breaking poor Priscian's head, talk of *all the go, all the rage*, and to *quiz* the fellow for his *truisms*, which are all *twaddle*, I turn aside: *O profanum vulgus!* alike from the low and the high vulgar: being as unwilling to be a disciple of the stable, the kennel, and the sty, as of the other precious slang, the dialect of Newgate."

General Works, continued

Nineteenth Century — 1801–1820, continued

ENGLISH, JAMES.

A new vocabulary of fashionable phrases. (European magazine. London, August, 1813. 8°. v. 64, p. 111–112.) * DA
A country visitor to London had to learn the fashionable phrases of the day. About fifty homely words and phrases are listed in one column and their fashionable equivalents in the opposite column. Some of the phrases are French importations, and some reveal a sense of verbal modesty.

THE ENGLISHMAN. No. III. (The Satirist. London, June, 1811. 8°. v. 8, p. 465–473.) * DA
On p. 471 there is an interesting paragraph on slang. "Your readers will be well aware that the dialect I allude to is now dignified by the name of the slang. A dictionary of this dialect has been recently published, replete with the grossest obscenity selected from the expressions of coachmen, fishwomen, gamblers, and highwaymen. This dictionary is now the constant companion of every man who aspires to the dignity of a buck of the first head."
The Satirist is filled with slang and dialect, and is a rich field for the lexicographer. The New York Public Library has v. 1–9, 1808–1811, * DA.

ESSAY on American language and literature. (North American review. Boston, Sept., 1815. 8°. v. 1, p. 307–314.) * DA
A plea for an American language and an American literature, free of the enslaving effects of England's language and literature. This was written close enough to the War of 1812 to contain a strong touch of American independence.

FESSENDEN, THOMAS GREEN.

The ladies monitor; a poem. Bellows Falls, Vt.: printed by Bill Blake & Co., 1818. xii, (1)14–180 p. 12°. NBHD
The works of this poet are filled with Americanisms. A number of "Yankeyisms" are listed on p. 171–173. This list is reprinted by P. G. Perrin in *Dialect notes*, New Haven, 1926, v. 5, p. 383–384, RNZ.

JEFFERSON, THOMAS.

The writings of Thomas Jefferson. Edited by H. A. Washington. New York: Riker, Thorne & Co., 1853–54. 9 v. 8°. IAW
Letter to John Waldo, Aug. 16, 1813, v. 4, p. 184–189:
"I am no friend, therefore, to what is called *Purism,* but a zealous one to the *Neology* which has introduced these two words without the authority of any dictionary. I consider the one as destroying the nerve and beauty of language, while the other improves both, and adds to its copiousness... The new circumstances under which we are placed, call for new words, new phrases, and for the transfer of old words to new objects. An American dialect will therefore be formed."

Letter to Joseph Milligan, April 6, 1816, v. 6, p. 568–575:
"Where brevity, perspicuity, and even euphony can be promoted by the introduction of a new word, it is an improvement to the language... In giving a loose to neologism, indeed, uncouth words will sometimes be offered; but the public will judge them, and receive or reject, as sense or sound shall suggest."

Letter to John Adams, Aug. 15, 1820, v. 7, p. 172–177:
"I am a friend to *neology.* It is the only way to give a language copiousness and euphony. Without it should still be held to the vocabulary of Alfred or of Ulphilas... Dictionaries are but the depositories of words already legitimated by usage. Society is the workshop in which new ones are elaborated. When an individual uses a new word, if ill formed, it is rejected in society; if well formed, adopted, and after due time, laid up in the depository of dictionaries.

And if, in this process of sound neologisation, our trans-Atlantic brethren shall not choose to accompany us, we may furnish, after the Ionians, a second example of a colonial dialect improving on its primitive."

LENGTHY, LEMUEL, PSEUD.

Americanisms. (Analectic magazine. Philadelphia, May, 1814. 8°. v. 3, p. 404–409.) * DA
"Old nations, like old belles, are naturally inclined to be jealous of young ones... I maintain that we have a right to make what alterations and additions we please in the language. It is ours by right of conquest, for when we wrested these States from England, we subdued the language with them... We shall never be truly independent, I am afraid, till we make our own books and coin our own words."

LETTICE, JOHN.

On the analysis of English idioms. (European magazine. London, 1813. 8°. May, v. 63, p. 385–387; June, v. 63, p. 499–501; July, v. 64, p. 18–20; Aug., v. 64, p. 109–111; Sept., v. 64, p. 226–228; Nov., v. 64, p. 395–397.) * DA
About a dozen common English phrases are carefully dissected in each article. The fifth essay contains some remarks about boxing slang, the idiom of the "milling fancy." An article signed "A Word Catcher," contains further remarks on boxing, in the Nov., 1813, issue, p. 398.

LOUNSBURY, THOMAS RAYNESFORD.

The first dictionary of Americanisms. (Harper's monthly magazine. New York, June, 1914. 8°. v. 129, p. 103–110.) * DA
A study of Pickering's vocabulary of Americanisms. Pickering was a pioneer in American philology, and stands as a type, represents a state of mind. Although a recognized scholar, Pickering's knowledge in the technique of philology was very poor. He was blind to the value of new words and their ways. He relied too much on English friends and English periodicals for information concerning proper usage. "His faith in the dicta of English reviewers generally was of the kind that removes mountains. Their assumption of a knowledge which they did not possess, their attitude of patronage, whether kindly or hostile, he received with unquestioning humility." Pickering did not like Scotticisms and being an ardent Federalist did not like anything from France, hence his contempt for Gallicisms.

MALONE, KEMP.

John Davis on American speech. (American speech. Baltimore, Aug., 1929. 4°. v. 4, p. 473–476.) RNA
In 1803 John Davis published his *Travels of four years and a half in the United States of America.* His linguistic observations are extracted from the body of the work to form the basis of the above article.

MATHEWS, MITFORD McLEOD.

Humphreys' glossary. (Dialect notes. New Haven, 1926. 8°. v. 5, p. 375–382.) RNZ
David Humphreys (1752–1818), one of the "Hartford wits," published a glossary of Americanisms in the back of his play *The Yankey in England,* in 1815. This was one year before Pickering published his *Vocabulary.* The complete glossary is reprinted. Humphreys has the distinction of publishing the first American sonnet.

ON Americanisms, with a fragment of a trans-Atlantic pastoral. (The New monthly magazine. London, Dec., 1820. 8°. v. 14, p. 629–632.) * DA
Sees the development of new words in America as inevitable, due to the distance between England and the United States. Several lines of a poem entitled "A Backwoodsman and a squatter" are quoted, with a glossary.

General Works, continued

Nineteenth Century — 1801–1820, continued

PALMER, JOHN.

Journal of travels in the United States of North America and in Lower Canada, performed in the year 1817... London: Printed for Sherwood, Neely and Jones, Paternoster-Row, 1818. vii, 456 p., 1 map. 8°.　　IID
On p. 129–132 the author gives a specimen of Kentucky tavern talk, with a note or two on *gouging*.

SILLIMAN, BENJAMIN.

A journal of travels in England, Holland and Scotland, and of two passages over the Atlantic, in the years 1805 and 1806. New-York: Printed by D. & G. Bruce, for Ezra Sargeant, 1810. 2 v. 8°.　　CBD
In v. 1, p. 234 there is a comment by Major Rennel to the effect that "The Americans had improved the English language, by the introduction of some new words and phrases very energetic and concise, instead of diffuse circumlocution," etc. In v. 2, p. 236–239, the author advances the view that the rank and file of Americans speak a purer English than the rank and file in England. These comments contain no slang or Americanisms, but they are important historically, coming at such an early date.
A review of this work may be found in *The Quarterly review*, London, 1816, v. 15, p. 555–562, *DA.*

WEBSTER, NOAH.

A letter to the Honorable John Pickering, on the subject of his vocabulary; or, collection of words and phrases, supposed to be peculiar to the United States of America. Boston: published by West and Richardson, no. 75, Cornhill. T. W. White, printer, 1817. 60 p. 8°.　　RNB p.v.19, no.7
With autograph of author and a few of his mss. notes. "It is not my intention to animadvert upon every word in your collection. This would require a book larger than yours," Webster says at the beginning of his letter. He takes up a number of the so-called Americanisms and tears them to pieces. His closing paragraph has much of the spirit of Samuel Johnson's letter to Lord Chesterfield.
The Library has a second copy in *KF.*

1821–1830

BECK, THEODORIC ROMEYN.

Notes on Mr. Pickering's "Vocabulary of words and phrases, which have been supposed to be peculiar to the United States," with preliminary observations. (Albany Institute. Transactions. Albany: Webster and Skinners, 1830. 8°. v. 1, p. 25–31.)　　*EA
Read before the Institute, March 18, 1829. Consists chiefly of notes made on seventeen of the words and phrases mentioned by Pickering. The history of the words is traced.
Reprinted in M. M. Mathews, *The Beginnings of American English*, Chicago, 1931, *RNZ.*

BIRSS, JOHN HOWARD.

Some Americanisms of a hundred years ago. (American speech. Baltimore, Dec., 1931. 4°. v. 7, p. 96–98.)　　RNA
Reprints a list from the *Virginia literary museum*, Dec., 1829. Based largely on Pickering.

CANDLER, ISAAC.

A summary view of America... By an Englishman [Isaac Candler]. London: Printed for T. Cadell, in the Strand; and W. Blackwood, Edinburgh, 1824. 503 p. 8°.　　IID
p. 326–334 deal with the English language in America. Sectional differences in speech are discussed and a few stock Americanisms such as "fall," "guess," "dry goods," "stores," etc., are mentioned.
Reviewed in *Blackwood's magazine*, Edinburgh, Dec., 1824, v. 16, p. 620–652, * DA.

FARRAND, MAX.

A word-list of 1823. (Dialect notes. New Haven, 1913. 8°. v. 4, p. 46–48.)　　RNZ
A list for the use of emigrants published in the *Mississippi Intelligencer*, May 1, 1823. Western and Yankee dialect.

FLINT, JAMES.

Letters from America... Edinburgh: Printed for W. & C. Tait...1822. viii, 330 p. 8°.　　IID
See p. 262–264. American manners in speech are pointed out. A list of Americanisms may be found on p. 264.

HALL, BASIL.

Americanisms. (Polar star. London, 1829. 8°. v. 1, p. 134.)　　* DA
Excerpts from his *Travels in North America in the years 1827 and 1828*, London, 1829. Reports an interview with Noah Webster on the subject of Americanisms.

MACTAGGART, JOHN.

Three years in Canada... London: Henry Colburn, 1829. 2 v. 12°.　　HWY
Speaks of the sharpers and vagabonds and convicts who bring to America the low jargon of the European underworld, v. 2, p. 324–327. A few Americanisms are scattered throughout the text.

MATHEWS, CHARLES.

...The London Mathews; containing an account of this celebrated comedian's trip to America... Baltimore: Printed and published by J. Robinson...1824. 35 p. 16°.　　NCO p.v.299, no.1
Contains many Americanisms; also several comic songs, including "Opossum up a gum tree," and "Illinois inventory."
At head of title: [Robinson's fourth edition.]

MATHEWS, MITFORD McLEOD.

Sherwood's provincialisms. (Dialect notes. New Haven, 1927. 8°. v. 5, p. 415–421.)　　RNZ
Adiel Sherwood (1791–1879) published his *Gazetteer of the state of Georgia* in 1827, including a short list of provincialisms. This was omitted in the 1829 edition. The 3rd edition, 1837, had a longer list. The two lists are herein reprinted. There was an 1860 revised edition, which Mathews does not mention.

NEILSON, PETER.

Recollections of a six years residence in the United States of America... Glasgow: David Robertson, 1830. 358 p. 8°.　　IID
On p. 186–188 a conversation between a judge and a young man accused of shooting a pig belonging to someone else is recorded in order to bring out peculiar speech habits. A short list of Americanisms appears on p. 188.

General Works, continued

Nineteenth Century — 1821–1830, continued

PAULDING, JAMES KIRKE.
John Bull in America; or, The new Munch-ausen. New York: Charles Wiley, no. 3, Wall street, 1825. 226 p. 12°.   NBY
A parody on the English travel books. The British travellers in America had stressed only the barbarous side of American life and literature. The barbarity of American speech was always pointed out to re-spectable English readers as a defilement of the mother tongue.
Paulding's *The New mirror for travellers; and guide to the Springs,* New York: G. & C. Carvill, 1828, 12°, 292 p. *NBY.* was written in the same light mood, and contains many Americanisms.
A typical British animadversion on American speech and customs may be found in Thomas Hamilton's *Men and manners in America,* Edinburgh: William Blackwood, 1833, 2 v., 8°, *IID.* Hamilton was a member of the so-called "Blackwood group." The book was reviewed at great length by Andrew : Norton, in *The North American review,* Boston, Jan., 1834, v. 38, p. 210–270, * *DA,* who stoutly defended Ameri-can manners, expressing the hope that at some not too distant date an English traveller would visit America and see the real America in much the same manner that Madame de Staël saw the Germany of her time. This review was printed separately by John Miller, London, 1834, 62 p., 8°, *IAG p.v.89.*

READ, ALLEN WALKER.
Dunglison's glossary (1829–1830). (Dialect notes. New Haven, 1927. 8°. v. 5, p. 422–432.)
                                                      RNZ
Robley Dunglison (1798–1869) was appointed to the chair of medicine at the University of Virginia in 1824, by Thomas Jefferson. In the *Virginia literary museum and journal of belles lettres, arts, &c.,* Dec. 16, 1829, p. 417–420; Dec. 30, 1829, p. 457–460; and Jan. 6, 1830, p. 479–480, appeared a glossary of Americanisms. Professor Read, of the University of Missouri, reprints the glossary in the above article.

SCREVELIUS RADIX, PSEUD.
Vulgarity of slang. (Literary museum. 1822. v. 1, p. 138–139.)
Kennedy 11929.

WALN, ROBERT, JR.
The hermit in Philadelphia. Second series ... By Peter Atall, Esq. [Robert Waln, Jr.]... Philadelphia: Published for the author by J. Maxwell and Moses Thomas, and by Haley and Thomas, New York, 1821. 228 p. 12°.   ISD
"Dandy-slang," p. 20–31.
Burlesque on the popular book of the day, *The Hermit in London.* The whole book is written in slang. Waln was one of the editors of the *Biography of the Signers of the Declaration of Independence,* published by R. W. Pomeroy, Philadelphia. He also wrote second-rate poetry, contributed to many magazines, and wrote a history of China, after shipping there as a super cargo. This is one of the earliest lists of slang published in America.

1831–1840

ALEXANDER, SIR JAMES EDWARD.
Transatlantic sketches, comprising visits to the most interesting scenes in North and South America and the West Indies. London: Rich-ard Bentley, 1833. 2 v. 8°.   HAY
Capt. Alexander was a keen observer of customs and manners and had an ear for speech peculiarities. Both volumes of his entertaining work are sprinkled with Americanisms.

——— Philadelphia: Kay and Biddle, 1833. 378 p. 8°.   HAY

ALEXANDER, JAMES WADDELL.
English language in America. (Southern literary messenger. Richmond, Jan., 1836. 8°. v. 2, p. 110–111.)   * DA
Signed: Borealis.
"It is not enough to avoid Americanisms; nor is it expedient to manufacture a pye-bald dialect, of vul-garisms and provincialisms for the mere satisfaction of calling it our own." Urged a standard of classic taste to save the "noble tongue of freemen from becoming an unwieldly cacophonious, inconsistent mess of crudities."

C., A. B.
On the phraseology of the Americans. (New England magazine. Boston, Dec., 1832. 8°. v. 3, p. 485–487.)   * DA
The changes in the English language apparent to the visitor to the United States are caused by (1) the peculiar circumstances attending the settlement of the country; (2) the want of a common and acknowl-edged standard.

DAVIS, ELVICK B.
John Mason Peck and the American language. (American speech. Baltimore, Oct., 1926. 4°. v. 2, p. 20–33.)   RNA
Peck (1789–1858) in his *Gazetteer of Illinois* used Americanisms unknown to the editors of the *N. E. D.* It is a veritable treasure trove for the lexicographer. At least 124 words from Peck's book were overlooked by the *N. E. D.*

THE ENGLISH language as spoken in the United States. (The Penny magazine. London, July 21, 1838. f°. v. 7, p. 278–279.)   * DA
Claims that Americans had no chance to hear pure English, on account of the ignorance of the average English emigrant in this respect. Decries the Ameri-can penchant for coining new words and making new dictionaries.

H.
Americanisms. (Southern literary messenger. Richmond, March, 1836. 8°. v. 2, p. 257.) * DA
A patriotic assertion that Americans have a right to coin their own words without first asking England's permission.
The author was probably James E. Heath.

MARRYAT, FREDERICK.
A diary in America, with remarks on its institutions... London: Longman, Orme, Brown, Green & Longmans, 1839. 12°.   IID
Marryat's chapter on language, v. 2, p. 217–247, is amusing, and highly uncomplimentary. Thinks American lower classes speak a better English than the English lower classes, but that the educated Ameri-cans speak a language inferior to that used by the upper classes in England. Gives examples of our speech, our place-names, our verbal modesty, etc.
The Library also has the following editions: Phila-delphia: Carey and Hart, 1829; New York: W. H. Colyer, 1839; and Paris, 1839.

SAVAGE, W. H.
The vulgarisms and improprieties of the Eng-lish language... London: T. S. Porter, 1833. 139 p. 12°.
Kennedy 11939.
Copy in the British Museum.

SCATTERED observations about words. (Cham-bers's journal. London, Dec. 12, 1835. 4°. v. 4, p. 365–366.)   * DA
Points out that Englishmen who laugh at American speech make errors of the same kind.

General Works, continued

Nineteenth Century — 1831-1840, continued

SLANGOLOGY. (The Comic almanack for 1836. London: Chatto & Windus, n. d. 12°. p. 43–44.)
                                                    NDE
A poem written in the London slang of 1836. These almanacs, written largely by Thackeray and the brothers Mayhew, and illustrated by George Cruikshank, had a vogue from 1835 to 1853. They contain some slang expressions.

UNCLE SAM'S peculiarities. (Bentley's miscellany. American edition. New York, 1838-40. 8°. v. 2, p. 40–48, 134–140, 294–300, 581–590; v. 4, p. 262–271; v. 5, p. 619–626.)   * DA
These articles are replete with the Americanisms met with by visiting Englishmen. Many of the words are explained in footnotes. It is chiefly the language heard around New York streets, the Hudson River steamboats, Long Island, and that picked up en route from New York to Philadelphia.

VIGNE, GODFREY THOMAS.
Six months in America... London: Whittaker, Treacher & Co., 1832. 2 v. 12°.   IID
Americanisms and slang are briefly described in v. 2, p. 73–77, of the 1832 ed.
The Library also has an edition published by T. T. Ash in Philadelphia, 1833.

WESTON, RICHARD.
The United States and Canada in 1833; with the view of settling in America... Edinburgh: Richard Weston and Sons, 1836. 312 p. 12°.
                                                    IID
Filled with American expressions. See particularly p. 59–60. His description, p. 196–204, of an "apple-bee" with the songs and dances is a contribution to American folk ways.

YANKEEISMS. (The New England magazine. Boston, Nov., 1832. 8°. v. 3, p. 377–381.) * DA
"Even some of our own writers do not seem to know when they have got to the proper limits of burlesque; but, as if there could not be too much of a good thing, cram into the mouth of one man, all the queer, cant phrases they ever heard, either at first or second hand, from all the uncouth fellows, idiots included, that they ever met with in the course of their lives, doubling the stock to boot out of their own invention, and then send the crambo out to the world, as caricature of Yankeeisms; witness, for instance, Joe Strickland and Enoch Timbertoes... The technicalities of crafts and classes, or the cant and slang of the felon and his consorts, is by no means to be considered as making a part of the legitimate language of a nation; that is, in speaking of it generally, or entitled to a place among its peculiarities. The nautical phraseology of a sailor, is only to be regarded as a part of the language in its application to maritime purposes and subjects; his transfer of it to objects and occurrences on shore, is the peculiarity of the class to which he belongs, and does not entitle it to be considered among the idioms at large of the country. Such is the case also with the slang of the boatmen on our great western rivers, and their intimates; it is but the peculiarity of the race, and not deserving of the appellation of an Americanism. It is on the same footing with the slang of the smugglers, the gipsies, or the coal-heavers of England, appropriate only when put into the mouths of those to whom it belongs. The only kind of phraseology that can be properly spoken of, or used as designating a real national peculiarity, is that which is used by the people at large, independent of their peculiar pursuits. Making this ground of distinction, — and it seems the only legitimate one, — the peculiarities of the Yankee dialect will be wonderfully narrowed down."

1841-1850

AMERICANISMS. (Encyclopedia Americana. A new edition. Philadelphia: Lea & Blanchard, 1847. 8°. p. 210–211.)   * AK
Lists a few Americanisms, and early writers on the subject of American speech.

AMERICANISMS. (The Literary world. New York, March 17, 1849. 4°. v. 4, p. 247–248.)
                                                    NAA
Reprinted from *American review*, March, 1849.
"There are two great and distinct classes in the United States, the Yankee and the Virginian... The farther south you travel, the more rude, wild and energetic, the language you will hear." Attributes many odd phrases to the semi-annual meetings of the southern gentlemen of the bar.

AMERICANISMS. (Southern literary messenger. Richmond, Oct., 1848. 8°. v. 14, p. 623–629.)
                                                    * DA
A review of Bartlett's *Dictionary of Americanisms* (1848 ed.). A number of Bartlett's definitions are given and the reviewer adds observations of his own. He thinks Americans speak a better English than the English themselves. Says the lingo of the Bowery is not as bad as that of St. Giles, that the slang of Yale is about the same as that of Oxford, and the good speech of Belgrave Square is matched by educated people in Baltimore, Richmond, or Boston.

CHANGES in the English language in America. (Princeton magazine. Princeton, 1850. 8°. v. 1, p. 6–9.)   * DA
Prophecies in regard to the changes in American speech which are to come about as the result of immigration. The German influence will have the strongest effect. A few samples of foreign speech infiltrations are given.

COOK, ELIZA.
A word on slang. (Eliza Cook's journal. London, June 30, 1849. 8°. v. 1, p. 138–139.)
                                                    * DA
"It is a mistake to suppose that slang is allied to 'vulgarity' only." Lists some ballroom, technical, legal, medical, and political slang. Slang "has its embossed and gilt-edged encyclopedia, as well as its coarsely printed hornbook."

CROLL, HERMANN.
Leben in London. W. Moncrieff's Life in London. Durch englische und deutsche Noten und ein Wörterbuch der Vulgar Tongue... erläutert von H. Croll. Stuttgart [1842]. 230 p. 8°.
Kennedy 11943.
Copy in the British Museum.
English text, with annotations in German and a copious and very curious slang dictionary.

FLÜGEL, FELIX.
Die englische Sprache in Nordamerika. (Archiv für das Studium der neueren Sprachen und Literaturen. Elberfeld und Iserlohn, 1848. 12°. Bd. 4, p. 130–156.)   RAA
A survey of American speech, based largely on Pickering, but with additional material gleaned from books and periodicals. This was one of the first studies of Americanisms by a German writer.

HARRISON, MATTHEW.
The rise, progress, and present structure of the English language... London: Longman, Brown, Green, and Longmans, 1848. 12°. RNB
"Sources of corruption," p. 94–109.
This section embraces foreign words, phrases, and idioms, unauthorized terms, inflated terms, incongruity of terms, talkee-talkee, extraneous words, and the effects of colonization. Under the last named a few Americanisms are mentioned.

General Works, continued

Nineteenth Century — 1841–1850, continued

HURD, SETH T.
A grammatical corrector; or, Vocabulary of the common errors of speech... Philadelphia: E. H. Butler & Co., 1848. 124 p. 16°.   RND
Contains nearly two thousand barbarisms, cant phrases, etc. There is a special list of Americanisms, p. 122–124. Numerous quotations explain the popular usage of the words.

KOHL, JOHANN GEORG.
Land und Leute der Britischen Inseln. Beiträge zur Charakteristik Englands und der Engländer... Dresden und Leipzig: Arnoldische Buchhandlung, 1844. 3 v. 8°.   CN
English slang and dialect occur throughout the three volumes, but the last chapter of the third volume, p. 449–542, is devoted exclusively to English speech, and numerous slang expressions are defined.

LACY's acting edition of plays... London: S. French, 1850–1913. v. 1–163. 16°. NCO (Lacy)
Title varies: v. 101–163, French's acting edition of plays.
Many of these plays, chiefly of the eighteenth and nineteenth centuries, abound in slang, cant, and jargon. A close examination of the set will amply repay the student of slang.

μ.
Contributions to a fashionable vocabulary. (The New monthly magazine. London, 1842. 8°. v. 66, p. 213–221.)   * DA
Discloses some of the verbal artificialities of London society, which are termed the *"pontes asinorum* of *bon-ton* deportment." *Faux pas,* in 1842, was pronounced *fore-paw* and meant a "lapse from female virtue" which it still means in France, but Americans have broadened it to include a social blunder of any sort.

MACKAY, CHARLES.
Popular follies in great cities. (In his: Memoirs of extraordinary popular delusions... London: Richard Bentley, 1841. 8°. v. 1, p. 323–341.)   YNH
This edition, the first and the best, is in three volumes. The only illustration is a frontispiece. The chapter on popular follies is concerned with London slang, "Quoz," "What a shocking bad hat!" "There he goes with his eye out!" and other expressions are discussed. "These are the whimsies of the mass — the harmless follies by which they unconsciously endeavour to lighten the load of care which presses upon their existence."
See *American speech,* Baltimore, Nov., 1926, v. 2, p. 89–92, *RNA.*
Mackay was a journalist and poet, with several volumes of poetry to his credit. He came to America as British war correspondent during the Civil war. On this phase of his life see *South Atlantic quarterly,* Jan., 1927, v. 26, p. 50–62, * DA.

—— Philadelphia: Lindsay and Blakiston, 1850. 2 v. in 1. illus. 8°.   YNH

—— London: Office of the National Illustrated Library, 1852. 2 v. 12°.   YNH

—— London: Routledge, 1892. illus. 2 v. in 1. 8°.   YNH

Extraordinary popular delusions and the madness of crowds...a verbatim reprint, with reproductions of original illustrations, of the edition of 1852, with a foreword by Bernard M. Baruch. Boston: L. C. Page & Company, 1932. xxiv p., 1 l., 724 p. 8°.   YNH

P., P.
Idioms and provincialisms of the English language. (The American review. New York, March, 1849. 8°. v. 9, p. 251–265.)   * DA
A long review of Bartlett's *Dictionary of Americanisms,* Halliwell's *Dictionary of archaic and provincial words,* etc. There are two great classes in the United States — the Yankee and the Virginian. "Should he *guess,* write him down a Yankee; does he *reckon,* you may swear him a Southron...the Yankee *calculates...*the Southron *allows."*

THE YANKEE tongue — and its corruptions. (Brother Jonathan. New York, Aug. 26, 1843. 4°. v. 5, p. 494–495.)   * DA
A commentary on Judge Haliburton's *Sam Slick in England.* The words are not pure Yankee, but only about five per cent Yankee. The reviewer insists that the series of letters being sent to *Brother Jonathan* at that time by Jonathan Slick is genuine Yankee. The Jonathan Slick letters were written by Ann Sophia Winterbotham Stephens.

1851–1860

AMERICANISMS. (The New American cyclopædia. Edited by George Ripley and Charles A. Dana. New York: Appleton & Co., 1858–63. 4°. v. 1, p. 470–473.)   * AK
The article on Americanisms appears in all subsequent editions of this encyclopaedia. About 150 words are listed to show the difference between American English and British English.
This article was reviewed in *Archiv für das Studium der neueren Sprachen,* Braunschweig, 1861, Bd. 29, p. 63–66, *RAA.*

BREEN, HENRY HEGART.
Modern English literature: its blemishes and defects. London: Longman, Brown, Green, & Longmans, 1857. 307 p. 8°.   NCB
"Slang terms and foreign words," p. 69–73.
Prevalence of slang is due "to that quintessence of Rebellion and Radicalism; that amalgamation of Socialism and Slavery; that galaxy of Stars and Stripes; our encroaching, annexing, intermeddling, repudiating friend; our outlandish, off-handish, wholehoggish, go-a-headish brother, Jonathan Yankee."

BRISTED, CHARLES ASTOR.
The English language in America. (In: Cambridge essays, contributed by members of the university. 1855. London: John W. Parker and Son [1855?]. 8°. p. 57–78.)   NCY
A study of the better-known Americanisms of the period with a few predictions as to the future of American speech. Argot and slang are not included. Bristed entered Yale at the age of fifteen, and later took high honors at the University of Cambridge. He wrote much for sporting journals under the name of Carl Benson. He was a member of the American Philological Association, and a trustee of the Astor Library in New York, from its founding until his death.
Reviewed in *Chambers' journal,* London, April 19, 1856, v. 25, p. 249–251, * DA.

BURGESS, WALTON.
...Five hundred mistakes of daily occurrence in speaking, pronouncing, and writing the English language, corrected... New York: Daniel Burgess & Co., 1856. 73 p. 12°.   RND
Some common vulgarisms of America, including a few slang expressions. Many of the colloquialisms are still heard in provincial America.

General Works, continued

Nineteenth Century — 1851–1860, continued

CLEMENT, K. I.
Americanische Provincialismen. (Archiv für das Studium der neueren Sprachen und Literaturen. Braunschweig, 1853. 8°. Bd. 12, p. 236–239.) RAA
Brief note on Bartlett; on Johnson's *Notes on North America;* and the Rev. J. Blackmar's *A Practical grammar of the English language: designed to amuse the curious, and to benefit all,* Providence, R. I., 1847. This latter book is filled with samples of provincial speech.

CRIES from the past. (Household words. London, July 28, 1855. 4°. v. 11, p. 606–609.) *DA
Old street cries and familiar sayings are discussed. "Flare up" and "What a shocking bad hat" are treated at length.

DAVIES, MAURICE.
Slang. (The Train. London, 1856. 8°. v. 2, p. 216–219.) *DA
A representative collection of London slang locutions of the John Camden Hotten period.

THE ENGLISH language in America. (North American review. Boston, Oct., 1860. 8°. v. 91, p. 507–528.) *DA
A long review of George P. Marsh's *Lectures on the English language,* New York, 1860.
Scoffs at the theory that American speech is a serious divergence from the mother tongue. English literature rises above Americanisms and Briticisms. The reviewer thinks the King James version of the Bible gave the American colonists their literary background. He shows that this beautifully written book served as a standard for both countries.
The so-called Americanisms are analyzed closely, and some are shown to be rooted in older English provincial dialects. Others are not Americanisms, but *Websterisms* as the reviewer calls them.

GRATTAN, THOMAS COLLEY.
Civilized America... London: Bradbury and Evans, 1859. 2 v. 8°. IID
In v. 1, p. 62–63, the author comments on barbaric Americanisms heard during his travels in America. Slang expressions appear in various parts of the book. There is no glossary.

GRIFFIN, R. M., AND A. FARNSWORTH.
Everybody's table. (The New York monthly. New York, 1854. 8°. v. 1, p. 89–106, 201–220, 313–332, 427–444.) *DA
The editorial department of this magazine was written in the current New York slang.

HERRIG, LUDWIG.
Die englische Sprache und Literatur in Nord-America. (Archiv für das Studium der neueren Sprachen und Literaturen. Braunschweig, 1853. 8°. Bd. 12, p. 241–265; Bd. 13, p. 76–115, 241–268; Bd. 14, p. 1–35.) RAA
The first article takes up the subject of American speech, based largely on a study of Bartlett. The remaining articles deal more with the literature of the United States. Herrig utilizes this material in his *Handbuch der nordamerikanischen Literatur,* Braunschweig: G. Westermann, 1854, p. 1–8.

LESLIE, ELIZA.
The behaviour book. A manual for ladies... Philadelphia: Willis P. Hazard, 1853. 336 p. 3. ed. 12°. SBD
"Incorrect words," p. 216–224. Taboo expressions are listed.

Miss Leslie's behaviour book. A guide and manual for ladies. Philadelphia: T. B. Peterson and Brothers [1859]. 336 p. 12°. SBD

MADDOX, JOHN MEDEX.
A fast train! High pressure!! Express!!! A short trip. London: Thomas Hailes Lacy, n. d. 20 p. 12°. (Lacy's acting edition of plays. v. 10.) NCO (Lacy)
First performed at the Royal Lyceum Theatre, London, April 25, 1853.
Filled with Yankeeisms, spoken by a Yankee in London.

NEW Americanisms. (American notes and queries. Philadelphia, Feb., 1857. 8°. v. 1, p. 75–76.) *DA
Invites readers to send in slang expressions and promises to publish them. A few samples are given.

REVIEWS and literary notices. (Atlantic monthly. Boston, Nov., 1859. 8°. v. 4, p. 638–644.) *DA
A group review of Bartlett, Ducange Anglicus, Hotten, Craik, Trench, and Swinton. "The first allusion we know of to an Americanism is that of Gill, in 1621, — '*sed et ab Americanis nonnulla mutuamur, ut MAIZ et KANOA.*'" Says the speech of Americans, despite the mingling of races is more uniform than that of any European nation, thanks to our common schools, and the universal reading of newspapers. "We have but one fault to find with Mr. Bartlett's dictionary...no accents are given."

SALA, GEORGE AUGUSTUS.
Slang. (Household words. London, Sept. 24, 1853. 4°. v. 8, p. 73–78.) *DA
This article appeared anonymously, but it is known that Sala wrote it. It was reprinted in *Living age,* New York, Nov. 12, 1853, *DA. It was also reprinted in Sala's *Looking at life,* London, 1860, p. 31–43, *NCZ.*
Slang of the Victorian era. Advocated a new dictionary which would include slang terms, and listed a few words which would properly be included in such a dictionary, such as slang terms for money, drinks, thieves' slang, fashionable slang, etc.
For an account of Sala and his contributions to *Household words* see Percy Fitzgerald's *Memories of Charles Dickens, with an account of "Household words" and "All the year round" and of the contributors thereto,* Bristol, 1913, *AN.*
Sala, according to Ambrose Bierce, was the compiler-in-chief of Hotten's *Dictionary of slang* (q.v.).

SLANG literature. (The Titan. London, 1859. 8°. v. 29, p. 352–360.) *DA
Review of Hotten's *Dictionary of modern slang, cant and vulgar words,* 1859. Other slang books are mentioned.

TAYLOR, E. S.
Slang expressions. (Notes and queries. London, June 25, 1853. 8°. v. 7, p. 617–618.) *R–*DA
An enquiry into slang used by educated men as opposed to the more vulgar argot such as St. Giles' Greek. One of the expressions "just the cheese" is explained in *Notes and queries,* July 23, 1853, v. 8, p. 89.

THOMSON, MORTIMER.
Doesticks' letters: and what he says...by Q. K. Philander Doesticks, P. B. (Mortimer Thomson)... Philadelphia: T. B. Peterson and Bros. [cop. 1855.] 330 p. 12°. NBX
Pre-Civil war stories abounding in slang and Americanisms. A great part of the jargon is peculiar to New York; and the Bowery, the theatre, and Barnum's Museum are described along with other New York landmarks.
The book was copyrighted by Edward Livermore, New York, and first published by him in 1855.
Thomson was also author of a parody on Longfellow's Hiawatha, entitled *Plu-ri-bus-tah,* New York: Livermore & Rudd, 1856, 12°, *NBX,* and many other humorous works.

General Works, continued

Nineteenth Century — 1851–1860, continued

THE Two tongues. (Atlantic monthly. Boston, Dec., 1860. 8°. v. 6, p. 667–674.)   * DA
A defence of slang and American idiom. Of the latter the author says: "Sharp, energetic, incisive, they do the hard labor of speech, — that of carrying heavy loads of thought and shaping new ideas... We cannot do without them... We declare for the prolétaires. We vote the working-words ticket." Lists many political Americanisms, nicknames, colloquialisms, and slang words used by boys.

UNEDA, AND OTHERS.
Americanisms (so called). (Notes and queries. London, Oct. 30, 1852. series 1, v. 6, p. 411.)   * R–* DA
Uneda discusses expressions "I guess," "I reckon," etc. He added a further note in the same issue, p. 423. B. B. Woodward adds a note, Dec. 4, 1852, series 1, v. 6, p. 543, and Uneda continues the discussion in the Dec. 11, 1852, issue, series 1, v. 6, p. 554. J. S. S. comments on the words in the Jan. 8, 1853, issue, series 1, v. 7, p. 51, and E. D. adds a note, in the Jan. 22, 1853, issue, series 1, v. 7, p. 97.

UNITED STATES. Collection of songs and ballads. 1850–73. 4 v. f°.   * MP (U. S.)
This is a scrapbook collection of songs and ballads. Many of them contain slang. Among them are: "There goes another guy" by T. K. Symns, published by D. H. De Marsan, 54 Chatham street, New York; "Since Terry first joined the gang," words by W. Scanlon, and music by William Cronin, published by Bell & Co., San Francisco, from music first published by E. H. Harding, 229 Bowery, New York; "Kole Oil Tommy," as sung by E. C. Melville, published by T. C. Boyd, San Francisco. The collection abounds in Civil War songs.

YANKEE phrases traced home. (Emerson's United States magazine. New York, July, 1857. 8°. v. 5, p. 88–90.)   * DA
Quotes from Dean Swift's introduction to "Polite conversation" to show the vulgar speech of Queen Anne's time, and from Thackeray to illustrate the then current tendency towards "cant phraseology." American writers, the author is happy in pointing out, never resort to such "coarseness and vulgarity."

1861–1870

AMENT, WILLIAM S.
Some Americanisms in Moby Dick. (American speech. Baltimore, June, 1932. 4°. v. 7, p. 365–367.)   RNA
Compares the bowdlerized English edition with the original American edition. Some of the Americanisms have been altered in the English edition.

AMERICANISMS. (National quarterly review. London, March, 1861. 8°. v. 2, p. 230–240.)   * DA
Review of Pickering's *A Vocabulary of words and phrases supposed to be peculiar to America*, and Bartlett's *Dictionary of Americanisms*. "If we do not think deeply and calmly as a people, we think rapidly and strongly. What requires labor and toil, among other people, in reaching ultimate conclusions, we gain at a single bound... We are prehensile if not comprehensive. The Patent Office affords a striking example of this peculiar quickness of thought and power of combination."

AMERICANISMUS. (Deutsch-amerikanisches Conversations-Lexicon... New York: Friedr. Gerhard, 1869. 8°. v. 1, p. 421–424.)   * AM
Two or three hundred Americanisms explained for the benefit of German readers.

BACHE, RICHARD MEADE.
Slang. (In his: Vulgarisms and other errors of speech. Philadelphia: Claxton, Remsen, and Haffelfinger, 1869. 2. ed. 16°. p. 18–21.) RND
"Familiarity is insulting, and slang is familiar. Let it never be considered as having a foothold in our language."

BROOKS, BRADFORD.
Epidemic language. (Brooklyn monthly. Brooklyn, June and July, 1869. 8°. v. 1, p. 305–307.)   * DA
"English slang is intensely local, and is either the production of dandyism, cockneyism, or tally-ho-ism. Ours is the production of various American localities, Yankeeism, and general *cuteness*." A few phrases like "face the music" and "he can't keep a hotel" are mentioned.

BYGONE cant. (All the year round. London, March 5, 1870. 8°. v. 23, p. 320–324.)   * DA
A casual essay filled with illustrations from the accepted cant and flash dictionaries of the eighteenth and nineteenth centuries.

CALDWELL, J. P.
The rationale of slang. (Overland monthly. San Francisco, Feb., 1870. 8°. v. 4, p. 187–190.)   * DA
Slang abounds most in the language of Teutonic stock. Compares slang with the grotesque in architecture. The power of slang is characterized: "This material slang is brutalizing in its effect on the genius of people, and destructive of the poetic principle which slang should tend to foster." Gives American examples.

COLERIDGE, HERBERT.
On the exclusion of certain words from a dictionary. (Philological Society. Transactions. London, 1860–61. 8°. p. 37–44.) RAA
Coleridge placed before the society the question of exclusion, i.e., what words should a dictionary omit? Mentions such words as "devilship" and similar words which he defines as "vocabular parodies," devilship being a parody of lordship, etc. Such coinages as "foolometer" and "Correggiosity" were discussed, and words on the borderland of slang were included.

COZZENS, FREDERICK SWARTWOUT.
Does Queen Victoria speak English? (In his: The sayings of Dr. Bushwhacker and other learned men... New York: A. Simpson & Co., 1867. 12°. p. 81–101.)   NBX
"Let us with one hand soothe the American lexicographical eagle, while with the other we smooth the bristling mane of the British polyglot." Mentions cockneyisms, slang, chinook jargon, etc.
Reprinted from the *New York Ledger*.
Autographed presentation copy to Evert A. Duyckinck.

CRANE, W. W.
The American language. (Putnam's magazine. New York, Nov., 1870. 8°. v. 6, p. 519–526.)   * DA
One of the manifestations of the philological activity occasioned by the appearance of Bartlett's *Dictionary of Americanisms*.

DEPRAVATIONS of English. (All the year round. London, Oct. 17, 1863. 4°. v. 10, p. 179–181.)   * DA
"The national love of slang has a good deal to do with the growing depravation of our classical tongue. Slang, no doubt, has existed at all times, but never with such grave and respectable countenance as now." States that most slang expressions originate in America, but are adopted eagerly in England.

General Works, continued

Nineteenth Century — 1861–1870, continued

DODGE, N. S.
Guesses and queries. (Lippincott's magazine. Philadelphia, May, 1870. 8°. v. 5, p. 545–552.)
* DA
Study of Americanisms and the evolution of language, with a few English slang words added to make the article comparative. Carelessness in speech, the mental laziness which creates slang, is a fool's paradise.

THE ENGLISH of the newspapers. (The Nation. New York, Dec. 28, 1864. 4°. v. 1, p. 814–815.)
* DA
Newspaper jargon corrupts the English language. Does not like the new-fangled word "pessimistic." "But if we say 'pessimistic' why may we not say 'optimistic'?" Also dislikes "aldermanic" and "telling." This use of the word "pessimistic" is earlier than the first recorded date in the O. E. D.

FERGUSON, J.
Genesis of slang and street-swearing. [By J. Ferguson.] (The American quarterly church review, and ecclesiastical register. New York, Jan., 1866. 8°. v. 17, p. 535–552.)
ZRA (Church)
Chiefly a review of Hotten's Dictionary of slang (1863); the Life and writings of Major Jack Downing (1834); and the Clockmaker (1840). The use of slang is deprecated, and books on the subject should be avoided.

FITZGERALD, PERCY HETHERINGTON.
Pickwickian manners and customs. Westminster: The Roxburgh Press [1898]. xv, 128 p. 12°.
NCC (Dickens)
Contains many of the slang terms used by Dickens, with explanations of some of them.

FORGUES, ÉMILE DAURAND.
La langue du monde excentrique en Angleterre. (Revue des deux mondes. Paris, 1864. 8°. période 2, v. 53, p. 462–481.)
* DM
Reviews of Hotten. One of the earliest and ablest of the attempts to make the copious slang of the English-speaking world intelligible to Frenchmen.

FRISWELL, JAMES HAIN.
The question of "slang" in writing and conversation. (In his: The gentle life... 9. ed. London: Sampson Low, Son, & Marston, 1868. 12°. p. 153–163.)
YFE
Lists many slang and cant expressions to show their lowly origin and advises against their use in polite circles. "Slang lames thought and clogs it with unmeaning repetition."

—— Third edition. New York: Walter Low, 1894. 12°.
YFE
See p. 153–163.

GARDNER, CHARLES.
Down East and out West. (Western monthly. Chicago, Nov., 1869. 8°. v. 2, p. 339–343.)
* DA (Lakeside)
Short essay on the speech differences of the two sections of the United States. The Westerner's broader physical outlook begets "a correspondingly broader mental horizon...there comes to be less twang in his speech as well as his theology. He 'calculates' less and 'speculates' more."

GRAHAM, GEORGE FREDERICK.
Slang and Americanisms. (In his: A book about words... London: Longmans, Green and Co., 1869. 16°. p. 169–184.)
RNF
"It may be laid down as a rule that words, as they grow older, degenerate in meaning and contract in form." Thus we get bus from omnibus, fancy from fantasy, etc. Gives samples of contemporary London slang. Americanisms come in for considerable attention.

HERMENTRUDE, PSEUD., AND OTHERS.
Americanisms. (Notes and queries. London, 1866. 8°. Feb. 10, 1866, series 3, v. 9, p. 118; March 10, 1866, series 3, v. 9, p. 205.) * R–* DA
A few notes on Americanisms by Hermentrude, D. M. Stevens, and others. "Tenement-house," "johnny-cake," "rye mush," and "squirrel cups" are mentioned.

INROADS upon English. (Blackwood's Edinburgh magazine. Edinburgh, Oct., 1867. 8°. v. 102, p. 399–417.)
* DA
English-speaking people use Bible or old Saxon English when they go to church, vernacular or colloquial English (slang) when they talk to one another in the ordinary intercourse of life, and literary English when they write or make speeches. Americanisms fall for the most part in the second class. Several hundred Americanisms are explained — mostly borrowings from Bartlett.

LUCAS, SAMUEL CUSHING.
English cant and slang. (In his: Mornings of the recess. 1861–64. A series of biographical and literary papers. Reprinted, by permission, from the "Times," and revised by the author [Samuel Lucas]. London: Tinsley Brothers, 1864. 8°. v. 1, p. 334–347.)
NCZ
A rather lengthy review of an informal kind on the first edition of Hotten's The slang dictionary, 1859. Holds that the word "slang" is of gipsy origin. Dwells on the influence of Lingua Franca, or bastard Italian spoken in Mediterranean seaport towns.

McALPINE, R. W.
A word about slang. (United States service magazine. New York, June, 1865. 8°. v. 3, p. 535–540.)
* DA
"Slang is to a language what any gross perversion of a usage of society is to the etiquette of refinement... More than one philosopher has observed that the degeneration of a people's language marks the degeneration of the people." Complains of the use of slang among army men in the Civil war. Speaks of the gaucheries of the Faubourg Bowery. A few samples of slang common to the American army camp are given. "Language, like water, is a common necessity. Impure, it causes disease."

MACRAE, DAVID.
Americanisms. (In his: The Americans at home. Edinburgh: Edmonston and Douglas, 1870. 12°. v. 2, p. 329–338.)
ILD
Gives a list of town names. Enumerates over a hundred Americanisms common to daily speech immediately following the Civil war. The odd uses of the word "fix" are given at some length. Defines "chicken fixings."

MATHEWS, WILLIAM.
The use and abuse of words. (The Western monthly. Chicago, 1869–71. 8°. Nov., 1869, v. 2, p. 343–350; Dec., 1869, v. 2, p. 407–414; June, 1869, v. 3, p. 431–438; June, 1871, v. 5, p. 445–451.)
* DA (Lakeside)
Slang and Americanisms are not stressed, but the whole background of word-making is gone into so thoroughly, and so many sources are quoted as to make the study worthy of close attention.

General Works, continued

Nineteenth Century — 1861–1870, continued

NICHOLS, THOMAS LOW.
American peculiarities and eccentricities. (In his: Forty years of American life. London: John Maxwell and Company, 1864. 2 v. 8°. v. 2, p. 384–392.) IID
"Yankee speech" is listed among the peculiarities. "A Yankee does not swear... The western man has no trouble about swearing, and has a remarkable breadth of expression... I am inclined to think the western vocabulary more copious than that of the Yankee proper. The language, like the country, has a certain breadth and magnitude about it."

—— London: Longmans, Green, & Co., 1874. 509 p. 2. ed. 12°. IID

OUR cousins' conversation. (All the year round. London, April 16, 1864. 4°. v. 11, p. 224–227.)
* DA
The impressions of a British traveller in America. The speech peculiarities are recorded with accuracy and they throw light on the American character during the Civil war. Most of the speech specimens were collected at Boston.

THE QUEEN's English and Brother Jonathan's. (Hours at home. London, Aug., 1867. 8°. v. 5, p. 360–367.) * DA
A reply to Dean Alford's strictures on the American language. A few Americanisms are discussed.

QUINTILLIAN, NEWCOME, PSEUD.
Curiosities of slang. (Beecher's magazine. Trenton, N. J., Jan., 1870. 8°. v. 1, p. 52–55.)
* DA
Mostly slang words used in England, but a few American expressions are included. Examples from thieves' slang, prize-ring slang, nautical slang, and a poem from *Punch.*

REEVES, HENRY.
Our provincialisms. (Lippincott's magazine. Philadelphia, March, 1869. 8°. v. 3, p. 310–321.) * DA
Distinguishes between an *Americanism,* which is national, and a *provincialism,* which is limited to one section of the country. Provincialisms are listed with etymological notes in the following order: New England, New York, New Jersey, Pennsylvania, Southern States, Western States. This is one of the earliest studies of our sectional speech and anticipated the type of work done later by the Dialect Society.

SLANG. (Public opinion. London, Oct. 15, 1870. f°. v. 18, p. 490.) * DA
"The growth of slang means the decay of language... Slang is of very modern date." Says Gay required no glossary for his opera, and that Swift did not use slang. Many samples of slang are given. "Ignorance uses slang, because ignorance copies Idleness, which is the parent of synonym."
Reprinted from an article in *Court circular.*

SLANG phrases. (Our boys and girls. Boston, June 27, 1868. 8°. v. 4, p. 416.) NASA
In all the early magazines for boys and girls it was customary to point out the evils of slang, and this article is not unlike the rest.

SOME thoughts on language. (Western monthly. Chicago, Feb., 1870. 8°. v. 3, p. 154–155.)
* DA (Lakeside)
"Americanisms are not necessarily vulgarisms. Language, like everything else, is progressive... The health of a tree is shown by the vigor with which it sends off new shoots and increases its spread of foliage." America should develop its own language and not ape Europe.

VILES, EDWARD, AND OTHERS.
Illustrations of slang and cant. (The Reader. London, 1864. f°. v. 4, Oct. 22, p. 505; Oct. 29, p. 545; Nov. 12, p. 609–610; Nov. 19, p. 641–642; Nov. 26, p. 673–674; Dec. 3, p. 707.) * DA
A list of words, with illustrative definitions, proposed as corrections and additions to Hotten's *The Slang dictionary.*

WAKEMAN, GEORGE.
Babel in our midst. (Putnam's magazine. New York, March, 1870. 8°. v. 15, p. 294–303.)
* DA
Study of class dialects and technical jargons. Includes medical jargon, stock exchange jargon, and the special words of the sea, the turf, the prize-ring, law, architecture, chemistry, etc.

Live metaphors. (The Galaxy. New York, Oct., 1866. 8°. v. 2, p. 272–280.) * DA
"Slang is live metaphor. It is the result of the strong, rude, unconscious mind of the crowd, creative, actually performing the process of using things to tell thoughts... Slang is ready-coined wit... Slang tickles the fancy, and indulges the universal love of the fantastic." Several hundred examples are given. Most of the words were current in America in the 1860's.

Verbal anomalies. (The Galaxy. New York, Sept., 1866. 8°. v. 2, p. 29–39.) * DA
Very little attention given to slang, but this is the first of a series of articles published by Wakeman in the *Galaxy,* and should be read in connection with them. A few drinking terms, p. 35.

WHITE, RICHARD GRANT.
British English and "American" English. (In his: Words and their uses... New York: Sheldon and Company, 1870. 12°. p. 44–62.)
RND
A defence of the use of the English language in America in reply to the critics who would deny Americans the propensity to handle the mother tongue with the ease and grace of the true Briton.
The Library also has several later editions.

1871–1880

AN AMERICAN.
English Americanisms. (Spectator. London, Aug. 9, 1873. f°. v. 46, p. 1012.) * DA
A letter remonstrating against the Englishman's habit of attributing vulgarity of speech to all Americans.

AMERICAN English. (Chambers's journal. London, Sept. 25, 1875. 8°. v. 52, p. 609–612.) * DA
A garland of slang phrases taken from daily American life, from politics, religion, railroads, nicknames, and the writings of the American humorists.

AMERICAN nicknames. (Chambers's journal. London, Nov. 13, 1875. 8°. v. 52, p. 171–173.)
* DA
State names, political phrases, religious sects.

AMERICANISMS. (Leisure hour. London, 1877. 8°. v. 26, p. 110–112.) * DA
"The locomotive habits of Americans, and their universal habit of reading the newspaper, have saved them from provincialisms."
The Englishman arriving in the United States immediately hears words and reads signs which puzzle him. A number of instances are noted. There is less swearing in America, due to the Puritan influence. Reprinted in part in *Living age,* New York, March 31, 1877, v. 132, p. 821–822, * *DA;* and in part in *Public opinion,* London, March 3, 1877, v. 31, p. 270, * *DA.*

General Works, continued

Nineteenth Century — 1871–1880, continued

AMERICANISMS: a study of words and manners. (Southern review. Baltimore, 1871. 8°. April, v. 9, p. 290–317; July, v. 9, p. 529–560.) * DA

An omnibus review of Bartlett's *Dictionary of Americanisms*, 1859; Webster's *An American dictionary*, 1855; B. H. Hall's *A collection of college words and customs*, 1856; William C. Fowler's *The English language in its elements and forms*, 1855; William Dwight Whitney's *Language and the study of language*, 1867; Rufus W. Griswold's *Curiosities of American literature*, 1856; Captain Marryatt's *A Diary in America*, 1839; Lowell's *The Bigelow papers*, 1858; Charles G. Leland's *Breitmann's ballads*, 1869; Whitman's *Leaves of grass*, 1856; and Duyckinck's *A Cyclopedia of American literature*, 1856.

This hodge-podge is a helpful survey of American speech trends, with quotations from many sources. The author predicts that Whitman's poetry will become the American speech of the future. Makes a plea for the development of American culture, and has no patience with the vulgar display of American humorists and provincial reformers.

THE ARGOT of polite society. (Belgravia. London, April, 1877. 8°. v. 32, p. 235–241.) * DA

A judicious selection of London slang words of the 1870's, of value to those who wish to create period speech.

B., E.

Americanisms in England. (Lippincott's magazine. Philadelphia, April, 1877. 8°. v. 19, p. 513–514.) * DA

E. B. observes that England does not scruple to borrow a few good Americanisms, and mentions "skedaddle," "annex," "smart," etc.

BABEL in our midst. (The Broadway. A London magazine of society and politics. London, May, 1871. 8°. series 3, v. 2, p. 424–429.) * DA

A study of class dialect and jargon, including classical terminology, medical lingo, nautical lingo, law terms, sports, and heraldry.

This is a reprint, apparently without mentioning the source, of George Wakeman's article by the same name in *Putnam's magazine*, New York, March, 1870, v. 15, p. 294–303, * DA. The latter part of Wakeman's article is omitted in the *Broadway* reprint, and a few sentences changed.

BARRINGER, GEORGE A.

Étude sur l'anglais parlé aux États-Unis. (Société philologique. Actes. Paris, 1874. 8°. tome 3, p. 295–310.)   RAA

A discussion of many Americanisms, excerpted without acknowledgement from De Vere.

Reviewed in *The Nation*, New York, June 11, 1874, v. 18, p. 380–381, * DA.

BENET, W. C.

Americanisms: English as spoken and written in the United States. An essay, read before the Abbeville Literary Club by W. C. Benet. Abbeville, S. C.: Wilson & Wardlaw, printers, 1880. 18 p. 8°.   * C p.v.358

Appeared originally in the *Abbeville Press and Banner*. Words borrowed from Europe are not Americanisms, Indian words are not Americanisms, negroisms are not, misspellings and mispronunciations are not Americanisms, slang words are not, nor are vulgarisms, archaisms or obsolete words. Dialects are not Americanisms. Benet, with these classes of words disposed of, lists what he terms genuine Americanisms.

They fall into these classes: new words which are malformations; new words which owe their origin to un-English circumstances; new meanings and new uses of good words, which may be divided into literary Americanisms, and colloquial Americanisms; substitutes, or words substituted by Americans for English equivalents and in this class belong words substituted through verbal modesty.

This copy is inscribed: "With the author's compliments to his old Professor, John Stuart Blackie."

CERTAIN Americanisms. (Atlantic monthly. Boston, Aug., 1877. 8°. v. 40, p. 233–235.) * DA

Discussion of the word "skedaddle." See same magazine, Dec., 1877, v. 40, p. 748.

CHAMPLIN, JOHN DENISON, JR.

Slang. (The American cyclopedia. Edited by George Ripley and Charles A. Dana. New York, 1876. 4°. v. 15, p. 85–87.)   * AK

"A burlesque or colloquial form of expression, the language of low humor, or the jargon of thieves and vagrants." Speaks also of argot, germania, Rotwelsch, calão of Portugal, the Czech hantyrka, the Dutch bargoens or dieventaal, the Scandinavian fantasprog, the Asiatic balaibalan, and the Hindu ramaseena.

DENIKE, C. W.

"Pull down your vest." (Record of the year. New York, June, 1876. 8°. v. 1, p. 627.) * DA

An item for the collector of slang poems. The slang expression "pull down your vest" had a vogue in 1876, and still survives.

DRAWING room slang. (The Victoria magazine. London, Sept., 1872. 8°. v. 19, p. 462–464.) * DA

Reprinted from the *Saturday review*. Deplores use of slang by women. "Amongst the many strong cards in woman's hand is her acknowledged subtlety and refined strength in the use of language; but she throws it away when she rivals men in 'talking shop,' and in professional slang and the jabber of the season."

ELLIS, CHARLES T.

Since Mary Ann learned the slang. (In: Murphy & Morton songster. New York: Dick & Sullivan [cop. 1879]. 24°. p. 9.) NBH p.v.16

Song contains a few slang words. It was sung to the tune of "The hat my father wore." The music hall songs of this period borrowed many expressions from London music halls.

FASHIONS and tricks of speech. (Blackwood's magazine. Edinburgh, April, 1875. 8°. v. 117, p. 437–450.)   * DA

GAELIC lore and modern slang. (Blackwood's magazine. American ed. New York, July, 1878. 8°. v. 124, p. 59–71.)   * DA

A review of Charles Mackay's *The Gaelic etymology of the languages of western Europe, and more especially of the English and Lowland Scotch, and of their slang, cant, and colloquial dialects*, London: Trübner, 1877. The reviewer challenges the etymology of some of the slang words offered by Dr. Mackay.

GILES, RICHARD.

Slang and vulgar phrases and forms as used in the different states of the Union. Explained, corrected and arranged for easy reference. New York: Hurst & Co., 1873. 1 p.l., 30 p. 12°.

Copy in the Library of Congress.

Kennedy 11970.

General Works, continued

Nineteenth Century — 1871–1880, continued

HALL, FITZEDWARD.
English rational and irrational. (Nineteenth century. London, Sept., 1880. 8°. v. 8, p. 424–444.)   * DA
An essay on good and bad English in general, and on the mistakes of William Cullen Bryant, in particular. Copious footnotes. Reprinted in *Eclectic magazine*.
See *New York Evening Post*, Oct. 15, 1880. Hall wrote to the editor of *The Nation* (New York) relative to certain slanders of the *New York Evening Post*. See Kennedy 5586. Hall's letter was published as a separate, London, 1881, 27 p.

Modern English... New York: Scribner, Armstrong & Co., 1873. 394 p. 12°.   RNB
An attack on the purists who seek to conform to antiquity. Hall's spirit and style have been captured by H. L. Mencken in his *The American language*. For an account of Hall see the *Dictionary of American biography*, v. 8, p. 124–126. See also his attack on Richard Grant White's *Words and their uses* (q.v.) in *Recent exemplifications of false philology*, New York: Scribner, Armstrong & Co., 1872, 124 p., 8°, *RND*.

JACOX, FRANCIS.
Idiomatic iterations or the humour of Corporal Nym. (Belgravia. London, Aug., 1874. 8°. v. 24, p. 157–164.)   * DA
A study of pet words, stereotyped phrases, etc. "The frequent use of interjections, expletives, and vague or unmeaning phrases of all kinds, is held to be inadmissible in a really elegant and graceful conversational style."

KINGTON-OLIPHANT, THOMAS LAURENCE.
Good and bad English in 1873. (In his: The sources of standard English. London: Macmillan and Co., 1873. 12°. p. 322–348.)   RN
Reviews the speech of America and England with amused tolerance and draws examples from a wide range of sources, culling them at random from a well-stocked mind.

L., D. C. (Oxon.)
Modern corruptions of the English language. (The St. James magazine. London, May, 1872. 8°. v. 30, p. 201–205.)   * DA
"Most of the present corruptions of our language may be traced to America." A number of Americanisms and slang words are given.

LANDON, MELVILLE DE LANCEY.
Eli Perkins on cant words and phrases. (The Galaxy. New York, Feb., 1872. 8°. v. 13, p. 281–282.)   * DA
Some slang words prevalent on Fifth Avenue, New York, in the 1870's.

LOUNSBURY, THOMAS RAYNESFORD.
The English language in America. (The International review. New York, 1880. 8°. May, 1880, v. 4, p. 472–482; June, p. 596–608.) * DA
The first article was incorrectly signed J. F. Lounsbury.
This is a sound article on American and English speech, written by an authority. Lounsbury holds that there are few indigenous words in America. Mentions the good and bad features of Bartlett's *Dictionary*. Thinks the colloquial speech of educated America is rather more archaic than that of Englishmen, and gives the reasons for this.
In the second article the archaic character of the American speech is dwelt upon in detail. The differences in dialect and popular usage between Englishmen and Americans are pointed out. Warns against the pedants. "The preservation of the purity of language, fortunately, has never been and never can be

in the hands of *dilettanti* students of speech or of professed scholars... It is the men, whoever they be and whatever their station, who strive to realize for themselves the highest intellectual and moral development of which their natures are capable, who are the real guardians of any tongue." Prof. Lounsbury's opinions on the archaic nature of much that passes for American speech are discussed from the opposite point of view by George Philip Krapp, in an article entitled, "Is American speech archaic?," in the *Southwest review*, Dallas, Summer 1927, v. 12, p. 292–303, * DA (q.v.).

MARTIN, ALMA (BORTH).
A vocabulary study of "The gilded age." With an introduction by Robert L. Ramsay, professor of English, University of Missouri, and a foreword by Hamlin Garland. [Webster Groves, Mo.:] Published by Mark Twain Society, 1930. 55 p. 8°.   RAE p.v.54, no.2
A detailed study of Mark Twain's book which was first published in 1873. A list of Americanisms appearing in the work is noted (283 words) and nineteenth-century words are grouped. Most of the words are earlier than the dates recorded in the *O. E. D.* Bibliography, p. 52–54.

THE ORIGIN of some slang phrases. (Chambers's journal. London, Feb. 9, 1878. 8°. v. 55, p. 85–87.)   * DA
Says slang came from the Norman *slengg-or* (meaning insulting words). The slang words defined are taken, admittedly, from Brewer's *Dictionary of phrase and fable*.

PERKINS, ELI, PSEUD. *See* LANDON, MELVILLE DE LANCEY.

PHOEBUS, PSEUD.
Concerning slang. (Brooklyn monthly. Brooklyn, Nov., 1878. 4°. v. 2, p. 341–342.)   * DA
Lists a number of slang words of the 1870's. "Whoa, Emma," "pull down your vest," "off color," "fresh," "wrecker," "deadbeat," "bucket-shop," and others are listed.

POPULAR American phrases. (All the year round. London, Feb. 18, 1871. 4°. new series, v. 5, p. 270–275.)   * DA
An attempt to make American slang intelligible to the English reading public. Bartlett's dictionary is reviewed.

RICHARDS, J.
"Words, words, words." (The Californian. A western monthly magazine. San Francisco, Sept., 1880. 4°. v. 2, p. 266–270.)   * DA
The author's purpose is "not to discuss nomenclature so much as the misuse and misapplication of terms, induced by circumstances that are peculiar to this country, and stronger on the Pacific coast than elsewhere." Discusses the word "lumber" at length.

SLANG. (The Arcadian. New York, 1873. f°. v. 1, no. 12, July 3, 1873, p. 4.)   * DA
Americans use more slang than Englishmen. Slang denotes bad breeding.

SLANG phrases. (Notes and queries. London, 1878. 8°. April 6, series 5, v. 9, p. 263–264; May 18, series 5, v. 9, p. 398; Aug. 17, series 5, v. 9, p. 138; Aug. 24, series 5, v. 9, p. 158; Sept. 14, series 5, v. 9, p. 214; Oct. 5, series 5, v. 9, p. 276.)   * R–* DA
"The *Reader* (an extinct literary periodical) published in 1864 some notes on slang words, forwarded by various contributors. Dictionary makers will probably not think of looking there for them... I therefore send you my cuttings reduced to alphabetical order." This list is amended in subsequent correspondence.

General Works, continued

Nineteenth Century — 1871–1880, continued

SLANG in the pulpit. (Public opinion. London, March 18, 1871. f°. v. 19, p. 332–333.) *DA
Reprinted from the New York *Herald.* Condemns the use of slang by preachers.

SLANG and vulgar phrases and forms as used in the different states of the Union... New York: Hurst & Co. [1873.] 30 p. 16°. RND
A dictionary of vulgarisms and Americanisms. Title is misleading. Book is not a guide to sectional slang.

SOLLY, EDWARD.
Slang and proverbs. (Notes and queries. London, 1877. 8°. June 16, series 5, v. 7, p. 466.) *R–*DA
Mentions an article in *The Times* on slang and says that the author did not know what slang really was. Holds that proverbs are not to be confused with slang. "Slang words are words misapplied, so as to have no real meaning or an incorrect one."

THOMAS, FRANK RHYS.
The age of slang. (Victoria magazine. London, Nov., 1877. 8°. v. 30, p. 23–28.) *DA
Slang is sham. Slang is lazy thinking. The main source of slang is the language of sport. Women alone can purge the language of slang. Slang is an index to national character.
Reprinted in *Public opinion,* London, Dec. 1, 1877, v. 32, p. 684, *DA.

TYLOR, SIR EDWARD BURNETT.
The philology of slang. (Macmillan's magazine. London, April, 1874. 8°. v. 29, p. 502–513.) *DA
A well-informed article on the etymology of slang terms, based on a close study of Grose, Michel, Hotten, Bartlett, Halliwell, Hoppe, Schele de Vere, etc. "My present task — is to choose a few typical examples out of the multitude of slang words in the published vocabularies, and to treat them etymologically in groups, so as to display in each group a philosophical principle, or the operation of a common cause."
Reprinted in *Living age,* New York, May 9, 1874, v. 121, p. 367–377, *DA; also in *Eclectic magazine,* New York, June, 1874, new series, v. 19, p. 722–732, *DA; and also in Sylva Clapin, *A new dictionary of Americanisms,* 1902, appendix III. Reprinted in part in *Public opinion,* London, May 2, 1874, v. 25, p. 555, *DA.

UNITED STATES English. (Chambers's journal. London, Dec. 20, 1873. 4°. v. 50, p. 801–803.) *DA
A glance at American neologisms and corruptions of the mother tongue, with emphasis on the outstanding differences between the daily speech of America and England. Reprinted in *Living age,* New York, Jan. 24, 1874, v. 120, p. 240–243, *DA.

VULGARISMS. (The Family herald. London, Feb. 5, 1876. 4°. v. 36, p. 221–222.) *DA
Lists a number of current vulgarisms. "When a person uses a word or phrase out of place — as a catch-word or a catch-phrase — then such a word or phrase degenerates into a vulgarism, or a piece of slang."

WHITE, RICHARD GRANT.
Americanisms. (Atlantic monthly. Boston, 1878–81. 8°. April, 1878, v. 41, p. 495–502; May, 1878, v. 41, p. 656–664; July, 1878, v. 42, p. 97–106; Sept., 1878, v. 42, p. 342–348; Nov., 1878, v. 42, p. 619–631, [643]; Jan., 1879, v. 43, p. 88–98, [109]; March, 1879, v. 43, p. 379–392; May, 1879, v. 43, p. 656–666; Nov., 1879, v. 44, p. 654–665; March, 1880, v. 45, p. [428]; May, 1880, v. 45, p. 669–678 [British Americanisms]; May,

1881, v. 47, p. 697–707 [correspondence with a British critic].) *DA
The page numbers in brackets indicate comments on White's articles by other Atlantic monthly contributors.
These articles were a continuation of those published in *The Galaxy,* occasioned by the 1877 edition of Bartlett's *Dictionary of Americanisms.* Anything in language which is distinctly American is bad. "There is a craze for 'the American thing.' There is a cry for the novel of American society, for the American poem, the American what-not... Let the American thing be bad, only let it be something new." The words supposed to be peculiarly American are dissected. Taken as a whole these essays form an authoritative study of our speech, and have been frequently quoted by English and American writers. They are strictly on the conservative side.

Americanisms. (The Galaxy. New York, 1877–78. 8°. Sept., 1877, v. 24, p. 376–383; Jan., 1878, v. 25, p. 94–101.) *DA
A review of Bartlett's *Dictionary of Americanisms.* White is critical of Bartlett and says the dictionary "seemed to me a very misleading and untrustworthy book — a book injurious in its effect both at home and abroad." It simply showed how the English language had been "corrupted, perverted, and overlaid with slang." The question of what constitutes a real American is discussed and the loose use of the term "Americanism" pointed out.

Cant, trading and other. (In his: Everyday English. Boston: Houghton, Mifflin & Co., 1880. 12°. p. 484–493.) RNB
In slang, humor or satire is an element to be considered, but such is not the case with cant, or special language. "Cant is not so respectable; and yet it is, on the whole, more enduring." Gives some examples of business cant.

—— Boston: Houghton, Mifflin & Co., 1882. 8°. RNB

—— Boston: Houghton, Mifflin & Co., 1908. 8°. RNN

"The Federal language." (Galaxy. New York, Nov., 1877. 8°. v. 24, p. 681–688.) *DA
A continuation of the Bartlett review. Traces the history of Noah Webster's attempt to create a "Federal language."

WORDSWORTH, CHRISTOPHER.
Social life at the English universities in the eighteenth century... Cambridge: Deighton, Bell, and Co. [etc.], 1874. 727 p. 12°. STH
A few slang terms may be traced by using the index to this volume. The history of the words is gone into carefully and scrupulously documented.

1881–1890

ALLEN, EDWARD A.
The origin in literature of vulgarisms. (The Chautauquan, Meadville, Pa., Nov., 1890. 8°. v. 12, p. 192–198.) *DA
A professor at the University of Missouri cites numerous vulgarisms from Chaucer to the *Biglow papers* of Lowell.

AMERICANISMS. (The American universal cyclopedia... A reprint of the last Edinburgh and London edition of Chambers's encyclopædia. New York, 1882. 4°. v. 1, p. 372–376.) *AL
Several hundred expressions with English equivalents if any are known. In two parts. The first part is the original article which appeared for years in Chambers's encyclopedia. The second and larger one was added by the American editors.

General Works, continued

Nineteenth Century — 1881-1890, continued

AMERICANISMS. (Chambers's journal. London,
Jan. 9, 1886. 8°. v. 63, p. 31–32.)   * DA
Short article on American slang words which have
so little meaning for the Englishman. A few gambling
and railroad terms are listed. Reprinted in *Taalstudie*,
1886, v. 7, p. 233–234.

AMERICANISMS. (London quarterly review.
London, Jan., 1882. 8°. v. 57, p. 392–411.) * DA
Review of M. Schele De Vere's *Americanisms:
the English of the New World* (q.v.).
Points out some inaccuracies in the work, but thinks
it an important contribution. Thinks the author lacked
a ready knowledge of colloquial English, and criticizes
the arrangement of the book, but hastens to add:
"He is the first who has entered this important field
with the energy of an explorer."

AUBREY, DR.
Americanisms. (Leisure hour. London, 1887.
8°. v. 36, p. 827–829.)   * DA
"It must also be cheerfully admitted that average
people in the United States speak with much greater
ease and appropriateness than persons of corresponding position and education in England. This is to be
accounted for partly by the system of recitations pursued in the schools, and partly by the social freedom
which permits ready talk on almost every subject."
A great many Americanisms are explained. One or two
samples of verbal modesty are given. The newspapers
of the lower type are credited with propagating American slang.

BOOTT, FRANCIS.
On certain neologisms. (Andover review.
Boston, Feb., 1885. 8°. v. 3, p. 135–149.) * DA
Discursive study of vulgarisms, Americanisms —
an extension of ideas set forth by Richard Grant White,
the Rev. M. Harrison, and Fitzedward Hall.

CARTER, ALICE P.
American English. (The Critic. New York,
Sept. 1, 1888. f°. v. 13, p. 97–98, 104, 115, 154.)
          * DA
A plea for purer English in America. The dif-
ferences between American and English pronunciation
are outlined. A letter approving this article, signed
Argus, appeared Sept. 8, 1888, p. 115. Mary D.
Leonard added further comment, Sept. 29, p. 154.

COCKAIGNE, PSEUD.
"English as she is spoke" on different sides
of the ocean. (Public opinion. Washington,
D. C., Oct. 30, 1886. f°. v. 2, p. 53–54.) * DA
Excerpts from an article from the San Francisco
Argonaut, written under the nom-de-plume of Cock-
aigne. Americanisms versus Briticisms.

COTTON, JAMES SUTHERLAND.
Americanisms. (Academy. London, May 2,
1889. f°. v. 35, p. 151.)   * DA
Short note on a few Americanisms observed in the
New York *Nation*.

COXE, ARTHUR CLEVELAND.
Americanisms in England. (The Forum. New
York, Oct., 1886. 8°. v. 2, p. 117–129.) * DA
Marshals a few quotations to prove that some reputed Americanisms are old English words. Makes
an eloquent plea for the preservation of the beautiful
language common to educated Englishmen and Americans. Coins the word *angliloquent* to express this idea.

CROFTON, FRANCIS BLAKE.
Society slang. (The Week. Toronto, May
13, 1886. f°. v. 3, p. 382.)   * DA
Comment on London society slang of the period.

ERRINGTON, DUDLEY.
Fashionable English. (Gentleman's magazine. London, June, 1883. 8°. v. 254, p. 576–
594.)   * DA
"For a good or apt word, and a happy phrase, all
readers ought to be grateful, but writers ought to
beware of repeating them too often, or introducing
them on all occasions relevant or irrelevant, especially
if they be inferior writers — mere parrots and mock-
ing-birds — who catch a word by the ear and use
it without intelligence or necessity. Such words and
phrases soon degenerate into slang."
Mentions many stock phrases of the daily press.
"But language always deteriorates when the morals
of a people become depraved, when the growth of
political corruption hardens the heart and dulls the
conscience of a nation; when men, and worse still
when women, lose the feeling and the habit of reverence, and when the cynical sneer or the senseless
ridicule of the high and low vulgar are fashionable."

FONBLANQUE, ALBANY DE GRENIER.
The English of America. (Tinsley's magazine. London, October, 1881. 8°. v. 29, p. 330–
334.)   * DA
"Our American cousin prides himself upon his contempt of forms, his fertility of invention, and claims
entire freedom from 'old world' ways, customs, and
methods of thought."
Cites a few differences between English and American speech.

FREEMAN, EDWARD AUGUSTUS.
Some impressions of the United States...
New York: Henry Holt and Company, 1883.
12°.   ILD
This enlightened traveller's observations, p. 49–91, on
our speech is above the usual casual criticism made by
visitors from England. Cites differences between
Americanisms and Scotticisms, comments on the pseudo-
classical names of our cities, our speech habits, etc.
Appeared originally in *Fortnightly review*, London,
Aug., 1882, v. 38, p. 133–155; Sept., 1882, v. 38, p. 323–
346, * DA.
Reviewed in *The American*, Philadelphia, Jan. 20,
1883, v. 5, p. 233–234, * DA.

Some points in American speech and customs.
(Longmans' magazine. London, 1882–83. 8°.
Nov., 1882, v. 1, p. 80–98; Jan., 1883, v. 1, p. 314–
334.)   * DA
A long essay written after a visit to the United
States, on American English, with specific references
to the divergence of this speech from that of England.
The difference is of degree, not of kind.
The second article deals chiefly with the differences
between American town and country life and the effects
of environment on speech habits.

FRENCH-ENGLISH. (The Cornhill magazine.
London, March, 1890. 8°. v. 61, p. 279–286.)
          * DA
Reprinted in *Living age*, New York, April 19, 1890,
v. 185, p. 157–161, * DA.
A most amusing collection of English words as
they are spelled and pronounced by Frenchmen. Slang
expressions often grow out of this linguistic aberration,
due to an erroneous apprehension of the sound of
words on foreign tongues.

GEORGE.
Words, idioms, etc., of the vulgar. (Wal-
ford's antiquarian magazine and bibliographical review. London, 1887. 8°. April, 1887,
v. 11, p. 250–254; August, 1887, v. 12, p. 91–
95.)   CA
A study of "gutter English," or the speech of the
street Arab. Includes such words as buster, cadey, chock,
half snags, heady-whop, napper, splawger, benge, etc. In
the second article about fifty additional words are added.
Thomas J. Jeakes selects the word "cadey" from the
above list and goes into its etymology at some length
in a later number of the same magazine, Sept., 1887,
v. 12, p. 139–142. It has come to mean hat, but the
usual spelling is "cady."

General Works, continued

Nineteenth Century — 1881–1890, continued

THE GREAT American language. (Cornhill magazine. London, Oct., 1888. 8°. v. 58, p. 363–377.)   *DA
Dislikes our westernisms. Says American English is still in the jelly-fish stage, quoting the authority Sayce. The American language "palpitates with actuality." Cites many regional words. All that saves American slang is its humor. This lengthy article goes into many phases of our speech peculiarities.
Reprinted in *Living age*, New York, Nov. 3, 1888, v. 64, p. 298–305, * *DA*. Excerpts appeared in *The Critic*, New York, Nov. 24, 1888, v. 13, p. 263, * *DA*.

HESSE-WARTEGG, ERNST VON.
Mississippi-Fahrten. Reisebilder aus dem amerikanischen Süden (1879–1880)... Leipzig: Verlag von Carl Reissner, 1881. 354 p. illus. 8°.   ILD
Does not contain a glossary or index, but the text abounds in Americanisms, which are italicized and easy to find in skimming the page. Several hundred words may be gleaned from this work.

HILL, ADAMS SHERMAN.
Our English... New York: Harper & Brothers, 1889. 245 p. 16°.   RNC
Contents: 1. English in schools. 2. English in colleges. 3. English in newspapers and novels. 4. English in the pulpit. 5. Colloquial English.
Adams Sherman Hill was the Boylston professor of rhetoric and oratory at Harvard University. He says in a preliminary note: "The five papers which make up this volume have already been published, substantially in their present form; I. and V. in Harper's monthly magazine; II. and III. in Scribner's magazine; and IV. in The Christian register."
There is a page or two on verbal taboos in "English in schools," a good deal of slang is mentioned in "English in newspapers and novels."

—— New York: Harper & Brothers, 1897. 245 p. 16°.   RNC

HOWELLS, WILLIAM DEAN.
[Americanisms.] (Harper's magazine. New York, Jan., 1886. 8°. v. 72, p. 324–325.) *DA
"No language is ever old on the lips of those who speak it, no matter how decrepit it drops from the pen."

KELLNER, LEON.
Zur englischen Umgangs- und Vulgarsprache. (Zeitschrift für Realschulwesen. [1890.] Bd. 15, p. 65–74, 132–139.)
Kennedy 11995.

LIENEMANN, OSKAR.
Eigenthümlichkeiten des Englischen der Vereinigten Staaten, nebst wenig bekannten Amerikanismen. Osterprogramm des kgl. Real-Gymnasiums in Zittau. Leipzig, 1886. 52 p. 4°.
Reviewed in *Englische Studien*, Bd. 10, p. 498–500, *RNA*, by A. E. Schönbach.
Based largely on writings of O. W. Holmes, J. R. Lowell, Bret Harte, Harriet Beecher Stowe, and Joel Chandler Harris, etc.
Not in The New York Public Library.

MACKAY, CHARLES.
English slang and French argot: fashionable and unfashionable. (Blackwood's magazine. Edinburgh, May, 1888. 8°. v. 143, p. 690–704.)   *DA
Advances thesis that slang permeates the language of peoples living under a democracy "where liberty has more or less degenerated into license, both in speech and action." Despite this tendency to be Victorian and insular, and to moralize in the spirit of the times, the article gives many useful facts about word origins; and reviews the book on argot by Barrère.

MATHEWS, WILLIAM.
Americanisms. (In his: Literary style, and other essays... Chicago: S. C. Griggs, 1881. 12°. p. 320–336.)   NBQ
Advances the theory that our separation from England brought about an immediate divergence of speech. Neologisms have always met with opposition. Caesar said: "Avoid a new word as you would a rock." Robert Mannyng and Richard Rolle in the fourteenth century protested against "strange Ynglyss." So did Ascham in the sixteenth century. A number of Americanisms are explained and justified.

PROCTOR, RICHARD A.
English and American English. (The Gentleman's magazine. London, Aug., 1881. 8°. new series, v. 27, p. 315–325.)   *DA
Reprinted in *Appleton's journal*, New York, Oct., 1881, new series, v. 11, p. 315–325, * *DA*.
Chiefly concerned with pronunciation. A few of the more familiar Americanisms are mentioned.

RANSONE, L. J.
"Good form" in England. By an American resident in the United Kingdom [L. J. Ransone]. New York: D. Appleton and Co., 1888. 315 p. 12°.   SBD
The chapter on language, p. 172–193, gives the differences between the American and English usage, with a special section on slang. Americanisms and their English equivalents are arranged in a special list, p. 180–185. A list of words "strictly American slang" appears on p. 186–187.

REPPLIER, AGNES.
Some curious idioms. (The American. Philadelphia, Nov. 17, 1888. 4°. v. 17, p. 72.) *DA
The word "colored" for a negro, and the various names for a servant woman from "girl" to "lady" seem to be used thoughtlessly, and with harm to clear thinking.

RUNKLE, LUCIA GILBERT.
Slang. (St. Nicholas. New York, Oct., 1884. 8°. v. 11, p. 907–909.)   *DA
An imaginary conversation between two children and their uncle in which the latter points out the danger of using slang.

S., I. G.
Slipshod English. (National review. London, Dec., 1887. 8°. v. 10, p. 521–528.)   *DA
"Just as debased coinage speaks ill for commercial integrity, so, when the mintage of speech is tampered with, when the coins of social intercourse are clipped and defaced without scruple, there is danger to other things more important even than literary excellence." Defines slang as "the application of an illustration ludicrously incommensurate with the thing, to which it is applied, and, accidentally, the familiar use of technical expression in a sense, for which it was not intended originally. Slang is, in short, giving nicknames to things." Over a hundred words and phrases are used for illustration.

SALA, GEORGE AUGUSTUS.
America revisited... 2. ed. London: Vizetelly & Co., 1882. 2 v. illus. 8°.   ILD
Has no glossary, but almost every page contains an Americanism or bit of slang, some calling for a special footnote. Sala was always a close observer of manners and customs, and was particularly interested in popular speech.

Living London... London: Remington & Co., 1883. 568 p. 8°.   COB (London)
This work is a scrap-basket of literary odds and ends collected by Sala in his many years of journalism and world travel. A good part of it is of an etymological nature, Sala having a penchant for new and bizarre words. Sala had a remarkable collection of Americanisms at his command, and many of them appear in this book.

General Works, continued

Nineteenth Century — 1881–1890, continued

SLANG. (The Family herald. London, Sept. 22, 1888. 4°. v. 61, p. 333–334.)   * DA
The nature of slang and its dangerous influence on society is shown. The history of slang is briefly outlined, and a great many well-chosen slang words of the Victorian era are given. The compiler designates the eighteenth century as "the century of the gallows" and it gave us much of our criminal slang.
Reprinted in part in *Public opinion*, London, Oct. 5, 1888, v. 54, p. 426–427, * DA.

SLANG. (The Literary era. Philadelphia, Nov., 1884. 4°. v. 2, p. 313–314.)   * DA
Reprinted from the Oct., 1884, issue of *St. Nicholas*. A few of the better-known slang words which prove the theory of the survival of the fittest in the life struggle of words are given.

SMITH, CHARLES FORSTER.
Some more of Bartlett's "Americanisms." (The Current. Chicago, June 28, 1884. f°. v. 1, p. 439–440.)   * DA
Points out a number of instances in which Bartlett's so-called Americanisms turn out to be old English expressions.

SOME Americanisms. (Chambers's journal. London, Jan. 30, 1886. 8°. v. 63, p. 70–71.) * DA
Says dialect of Americans which is represented on the English stage is incorrect and unfair. Thinks the speech of educated Americans differs but slightly from the speech of educated Englishmen. A few English words have simply taken on a new shade of meaning in the United States.

SOME etymological curios. (All the year round. London, Aug. 20, 1887. 4°. v. 61, p. 125–131.)   * DA
Study of words "queer," "news," "gin," "jerked beef," "bobby," "upper crust," "halloo," "jockey," "cravats," "blue-stocking," "white elephant," etc.

SOME slang phrases. (All the year round. London, June 9, 1888. 4°. v. 62, p. 541–543.) * DA
Divides bulk of common words into two classes, the colloquial and the literary. "Attached to the colloquial section of the language are two important but ill-defined tributary classes of words, the larger is known as slang, while the smaller consists of dialectal forms and modes of speech."
Some of the many uses of "Dutch" and "blue" are given, such as "Dutch uncle," "blue funk," etc.

STORM, JOHAN FREDERIK BREDA.
Englische Philologie. Anleitung zum wissenschaftlichen Studium der englischen Sprache ... Heilbronn: Verlag Gebr. Henninger, 1881. 468 p. 8°.   RNB
Slang und Cant, p. 152–163.
Die Umgangssprache (colloquial English), p. 206–258.
Die Vulgarsprache, p. 259–298.
Amerikanische Literatur, p. 299–300.
Amerikanismen, p. 301–340.
The number of slang expressions listed in Storm is very large. Most of them are taken, with due credit, from Dickens, Hotten, and Schele de Vere. Haliburton's *Clockmaker* is also drawn on for illustrations of American dialect.
This work first appeared in Norwegian, and was published at Christiania in 1878. Storm was a professor at the University of Christiania.

TINSON, HENRY.
On some cockneyisms. (Time. London, April, 1881. 8°. v. 5, p. 79–84.)   * DA
Discusses the nature of cockneyisms, and the speech habits of Londoners of the Victorian era.

TOWNSEND, MALCOLM.
U. S. An index to the United States of America... Boston: D. Lothrop Company [1890]. 482 p. 8°.   IAG
Gives the derivation of state names; state nicknames; nicknames applied to the peoples of the states; geographical terms; political parties, including their slang names; soubriquets of the presidents; college cheers (originated at Harvard-Yale boat race in 1860); money slang; origin of "Yankee Doodle," etc.

TROLLOPE, THOMAS ADOLPHUS.
What I remember... London: Richard Bentley and Son, 1887. 2 v. 2. ed. 8°.   AN
In v. 1, p. 50–52, the author speaks of the slang of his youth, and differentiates between slang which is vulgar and that which is not.

—— New York: Harper & Bros., 1888. vi, 546 p. 8°.   AN

TUCKER, GILBERT MILLIGAN.
American English. (The Albany Institute. Transactions. Albany, N. Y., 1883. 8°. v. 10, p. 334–360.)   * EA
A paper read before the Institute, June 6, 1882. Bibliography, p. 358–360.
Appeared in abridged form in the *North American review*, Boston, Jan., 1883, v. 136, p. 55–67, * DA. Defends American speech against uninformed British criticism. Our lower classes speak less cant than the London cadgers. Changes in spelling in the United States are always in the direction of simplicity. Selects a few blunders in standard English authors. Reviews the work of Pickering, De Vere, and Bartlett, in some detail.
The bibliography was continued in *Dialect notes*, Boston, 1890, v. 1, p. 13–16, 80–83, *RNZ*.
George Augustus Sala had a few remarks to make about this paper in the *Illustrated London news*, Jan. 27, 1883, v. 82, p. 87; April 12, 1884, v. 84, p. 339, * DA.

American English. New York: Alfred A. Knopf, 1921. 375 p. 8°.   * R-RNZ
"The following pages are the development of a chapter on the same subject in the author's earlier book, 'Our common speech,' published in 1895 and long out of print, that chapter being itself the development of a paper read before the Albany Institute in 1882, printed in the tenth volume of the Transactions of that body, and also printed, in somewhat different form, in the *North American review* for January, 1883." — *Foreword.*
Contents: 1. Is our English degenerating? 2. Ten important treatises. 3. Exotic Americanisms. 4. Some real Americanisms. 5. Misunderstood and imaginary Americanisms. 6. The bibliography of the subject. 7. Index of words and phrases.
Reviewed in *Scribner's magazine*, New York, Dec., 1921, v. 70, p. 730–736, * DA (Thomas G. Tucker); *North American review*, Boston, Nov., 1921, v. 214, p. 628–635, * DA (Archibald Marshall); *Bookman*, New York, June, 1921, v. 53, p. 353–355, * DA (H. L. Mencken); *Archiv für das Studium der neueren Sprachen und Literaturen*, Braunschweig, 1921, Bd. 143, p. 297–299, RAA (Georg Kartzke); *New republic*, New York, Nov. 16, 1921, v. 28, p. 357, * DA (Stark Young); *New York Times book review*, April 10, 1921, p. 4 (Brander Matthews), † *NAA; Boston Transcript*, May 7, 1921, p. 6; *Book review digest*, 1921, v. 17, p. 433; *Dialect notes*, New Haven, 1921, v. 5, p. 190–194, *RNZ* (A. G. Kennedy); *Modern language review*, Cambridge, Oct., 1922, v. 17, p. 429–430, *NAA* (J. H. G. Grattan); *The Pacific review*, Seattle, Dec., 1921, v. 2, p. 510–512, * DA (R. M. G.); *Zeitschrift für französischen und englischen Unterricht*, Berlin, 1923, v. 22, p. 144–145, *NAA* (H. Jantzen); *Philological quarterly*, Iowa City, Oct., 1924, v. 3, p. 318, *NAA* (T. A. Knott); *Weekly review*, New York, April 13, 1921, v. 4, p. 340, * DA (Edmund Lester Pearson).

General Works, continued

Nineteenth Century — 1881–1890, continued

WASTE basket of words. (Journal of American folk-lore. Boston, 1888–94. 8°. v. 1, p. 78–79, 161; v. 2, p. 64, 155, 229; v. 3, p. 64, 311; v. 4, p. 70–71, 159–160; v. 5, p. 61, 145–146; v. 6, p. 143; v. 7, p. 150.)   HBA

A collection of Americanisms, slang, and dialect words contributed by readers of the journal from various parts of the United States.

WHITMAN, WALT.
An American primer of Walt Whitman, with facsimiles of the original manuscript. Edited by Horace Traubel. Boston: Small, Maynard & Co., 1904. 35 p. 8°.   RNB

Limited to 500 copies.
An eloquent plea for the American language. Predicts that Americans will become the most fluent and melodious voiced people in the world, and the most perfect users of words. Words follow character, nativity, independence, individuality. A mine of quotable sentences.
Also printed in the *Atlantic monthly*, Boston, 1904, v. 93, p. 460–470, * DA.

Slang in America. (The North American review. Boston, Nov., 1885. 8°. v. 141, p. 431–435.)   * DA

Whitman's *Leaves of grass* did more to freshen the English language than any other single work issued in the latter half of the nineteenth century. The freedom it advocated has since been carried to excess. On account of the wide influence he had on later writers anything he has to say about slang is important historically. "Slang," he says, "profoundly considered is the lawless germinal element, below all words and sentences, and behind all poetry, and proves a certain freedom and perennial rankness and protestantism in speech... Such is slang, or indirection, an attempt of common humanity to escape from bald literalism, and express itself illimitably." Gives many examples. He designates the western states as "the special areas of slang."
See Leon Howard, "Walt Whitman and the American language," *American speech*, Baltimore, Aug., 1930, v. 5, p. 441–451, *RNA*.

WILLIAMS, RALPH OLMSTED.
Some peculiarities, real and supposed, in American English. (In his: Our dictionaries and other English language topics. New York: H. Holt and Company, 1890. 8°. p. 71–160.)
Not in The New York Public Library.

WILLIAMS, S. FLETCHER.
English: literary and vernacular. (Literary and Philosophical Society of Liverpool. Proceedings. London [and] Liverpool, 1889. 8°. v. 43, p. 211–245.)   * EC

1891–1900

ADAMS, JOHN COLEMAN.
Democracy and the mother tongue. (Cosmopolitan. New York, Feb., 1893. 8°. p. 459–464.)   * DA

"The pressure of much that passes for slang is the voice of the people at the gates of speech... The interests of linguistic purity do not demand that we make our language prim, particular or prudish. Nor ought we to turn our backs on the new-comers among words... 'There is death in the dictionary' observed Lowell... 'Sharp sabre-cuts of Saxon speech' was what Bret Harte termed the slang of the camps of our Civil war."

THE "AMERICAN dialect." (America. Chicago, June 11, 1891. 4°. v. 6, p. 290–291.)   * DA

Comments on an article in praise of Americanisms by E. A. Freeman (q.v.). Admits that Americans do create words of their own, but thinks a philological conference to unify the English speech would be a boon. Criticized the United States government for making a wholesale change of geographical names, changing Behring to Bering and Chili to Chile, etc.

AN AMERICAN language. (The Arena. Boston, Oct., 1898. 8°. v. 20, p. 537–539.)   * DA

Comment on article by Professor Mark H. Liddell in the *Atlantic monthly*, Oct., 1898, who made a plea for an English which would enable us to read Shakespeare without having to translate him, a new, every-day, practical English. Notes the emergence in America of a new tongue.

AMERICANISMS. (The Columbian cyclopedia. Buffalo, 1897. 12°. v. 1, p. 3.)   * AK

"Words and phrases current in the United States, not current in England."
Lists a few words. "The tendency to the use of slang is excessive in America."

AMERICANISMS. (The International cyclopedia. New York, 1892. 4°. v. 1, p. 368–372.)   * AK

One of the better of the encyclopedia articles on the subject. Follows the plan of De Vere's *Americanisms* (q.v.). Cites many examples.

ANDREWS, ELIZA FRANCES.
Linguistic parvenus. (Chautauquan. Meadville, Pa., May, 1896. 8°. v. 23, p. 216–220.)   * DA

"A new word struggling for admittance into the vocabulary of good English is like a parvenu seeking recognition in good society."
"Language is like a coral reef, always dying at the bottom and growing at the top... When a language ceases to grow it is a sure sign that the people who used it have ceased to progress."
Over a hundred new expressions are mentioned — mostly American.

Slang and metaphor. (Chautauquan. Meadville, Pa., July, 1896. 8°. v. 23, p. 462–466.)   * DA

Slang proper (or improper) including catchwords and popular phrases, is defined as "linguistic vermin." "Like toadstools they spring up in a night, but having no root in the solid subsoil of our speech they wither in a day."
Several slang terms of the 1890's are listed to prove Miss Andrews' point. Some older expressions are mentioned, some for "the degraded argot of vagrancy and crime...not properly to be classed as slang."

Some vagabond words. (St. Nicholas. New York, Sept., 1898. 8°. v. 25, p. 913–914.)   * DA

Shows how vulgar expressions were once words of beauty and good standing. "Laws a mussy!" was once "Lord have mercy!" "Grog" was once the French gros-grain.

ARCHER, WILLIAM.
America and the English language. (Pall Mall magazine. London, Oct., 1898. 8°. v. 16, p. 231–235.)   * DA

So-called Americanisms are to be regarded as increasing the power and stability of the language rather than destroying its purity.

American jottings. (The New York Times. March 23, March 30, April 6, April 14, April 20, April 27, May 4, May 11, May 18, May 26, 1899.)   * A

Written by the dramatic critic of the *London World*, during his first visit to America. They appeared simultaneously in the *Pall Mall Gazette*. They contain observations on American speech.

General Works, continued

Nineteenth Century — 1891–1900, continued

A BLUE book of slang. (The Leisure hour. London, 1894. 4°. v. 43, p. 468–469.)   * DA
"The glossary of technical terms used in the evidence given before the Labour Commission, which the indefatigable Mr. Drage has now published, is really a dictionary of trade slang." Selections are made from this publication.

BURTON, RICHARD.
American English. (In his: Literary likings. Boston: Copeland & Day, 1898. 12°. p. 341–361.)
Not in The New York Public Library.
Comments on the English attitude towards certain so-called Americanisms. Mentions a few slang terms. Defends independence of America in her speech ways.

The use of English. (East and West. New York, Sept., 1900. 8°. v. 1, p. 345–351.)   * DA
The latter part of this essay is devoted to slang. Not all slang is bad. Some of it is delightful. Foreign elements in speech are for ornamentation. The vernacular is the backbone of speech.

CARLETON, E.
Slang in literature. (The Critic. New York, 1897. f°. v. 30, p. 47.)   * DA
Short note on some slang found in the writings of Lawrence Hutton, and the *Bookman.*

CLARK, KATE (UPSON).
The slaves and sources of slang. (Independent. New York, Oct. 25, 1900. 8°. v. 52, p. 2572–2573.)   * DA
Title is somewhat misleading. Sources of slang words are not traced. A few current expressions are noted.

COLLIER, PRICE.
American English. (In his: America and the Americans, from a French point of view. 6. ed. New York: C. Scribner's Sons, 1897. 12°. p. 156–168.)   ILD
Boston English is contrasted with British English. A number of Americanisms are given. Newspaper English is condemned. The American's love of exaggeration shows in his speech. "Language is, after all, but the passing cloud picture of the mind." The expression "God's own country" was already in vogue. The book was a great success in the "gay nineties." Published in February, 1897, it went into a fourth edition before the end of April, one English publisher purchasing a thousand copies in one order.

COURTNEY, WILLIAM PRIDEAUX, AND OTHERS.
[Slang.] (Notes and queries. London, 1900–03. 8°. Jan. 13, 1900, series 9, v. 5, p. 28; March 17, 1900, series 9, v. 5, p. 212; Feb. 28, 1903, series 9, v. 11, p. 166–167.)   * R–* DA
A few early appearances of the word "slang" are discussed.

DE BLAQUIER, DORA.
American slang. (Girl's own paper. London, 1894. 4°. v. 15, p. 555.)
The compiler has not seen this.

DESMOND, SHAW.
London nights in the gay nineties… New York: Robert M. McBride & Company, 1928. 252 p. 8°.   COB (London)
Filled with slang of the street, the restaurant, and the music hall.

DUTCHER, EDWARD WILLIAM.
Slang. (Education. Boston, Jan., 1899. 8°. v. 19, p. 309.)   SSA
A poem in praise of good English.

ELLIS, EDWARD SYLVESTER.
Slang. (In his: Common errors in writing and speaking… New York: Woolfall Pub. Co., 1894. 16°. p. 24–26.)   RND
"We shall always be a slang speaking and a slang loving people. But we can refrain from an over-indulgence in it."

"ENGLISH as she is spoke." (Atlantic monthly. Boston, Nov., 1895. 8°. v. 76, p. 717–719.) * DA
Speaks of English as the "maddest yet the greatest language in the world." It has the "wild lawlessness of Nature herself."
With all its lawless vagaries English promises to be the world-language.

ENGLISH slang. (St. Louis Globe Democrat. Feb. 5, 1893.)
The ease with which a cant expression finds entrance into the mother tongue is illustrated. Length of article about 3,000 words.

FOR hasty writers. (The Academy. London, June 18, 1898. 4°. v. 53, p. 661–662.)   * DA
An Index expurgatorius of incorrect words and phrases with the correct equivalents given. Reprinted from A. G. Compton, *Some common errors of speech.*

THE FUNCTION of slang. (Current literature. New York, Aug., 1893. 8°. v. 13, p. 540–542.)   * DA
Comment on Brander Matthews' article of the same title, with some additional observations. See Matthews.

HALL, FITZEDWARD.
"Scientist," with a preamble. By F. H. [Fitzedward Hall.] (The Academy. London, Feb. 23, 1895. f°. v. 47, p. 169–171.)   * DA
The subject of Americanisms comes up in the discussion of the word "scientist." Andrew Lang wrote a reply to this in the March 2nd number of *Academy.* Hall replied to Lang in the March 30th number, p. 278–279, taking Mr. Lang to task. In the April 13th number of *Academy,* George Newcomen makes a plea for " — isms" in language, p. 317.
Many of Hall's numerous writings are listed in *Dialect notes,* New Haven, v. 1, p. 345; v. 2, p. 163, *RNZ.*

"Slang." (The Nation. New York, Aug. 31, 1893. f°. v. 57, p. 155.)   * DA
Traces the word to its earliest uses. It appears for instance in Foote's *The Orators* (1762), act 1. Other references are cited. See Arthur C. Hayward, O. Ritter, and H. F. Reves, for other articles on the early history of the word slang.

Sundry "Americanisms" [by] F. H. [Fitzedward Hall.] (The Nation. New York, Dec. 28, 1893. f°. v. 57, p. 484–485.)   * DA
Explanation of a few Americanisms occasioned by reading T. W. Higginson's *Hints on writing and speech-making,* principally "I reckon" and "I guess." See also *The Nation,* New York, July 20, 1893, v. 57, p. 45, * DA.

HARTT, IRENE WIDDEMER.
Americanisms. (Education. Boston, Feb., 1893. 8°. v. 13, p. 367–374.)   SSA
A number of representative Americanisms traced to their source. Some examples of otosis are given, such as Bob Ruly for *Bois bule.*

HAYWARD, ARTHUR C.
[Slang.] (The Academy. London, March 17, 1894. f°. v. 45, p. 232–233.)   * DA
A report of a paper read by Hayward before the Elizabethan Society, Feb. 21, 1894. He said that Grose was the first to recognize the word "slang," in 1785. Maria Edgeworth used the word in 1796.

General Works, continued

Nineteenth Century — 1891–1900, continued

HERMANN.
Ueber Wortverstümmelung im englischen Slang und in der englischen Umgangssprache. (Archiv für das Studium der neueren Sprachen und Litteraturen. Braunschweig, 1899. Bd. 102, p. 382–383.)   RAA
"Merely a report of a paper read before the Berliner Gesellschaft." — Kennedy 12019.

HIGGINSON, THOMAS WENTWORTH.
English and American phrases. (Independent. New York, Feb. 15, 1900. 8°. v. 52, p. 410–411.)
* DA
A number of words are selected from the older English literature to demonstrate that American English so-called is but a survival.

English and American speech. (Harper's bazar. New York, Nov. 20, 1897. f°. v. 30, p. 958.)   * DA
Thinks speaking of bad English is frowned upon in America as well as in England, and that the desire for speech improvement is pretty general. America stresses a finical, pedantic mode of speech rather than paying strict regard to usage, as in England.

On the transplantation of slang. (Harper's bazar. New York, July 29, 1893. f°. v. 26, p. 607.)   * DA
Reprinted in *Public opinion,* New York, Aug. 5, 1893, v. 15, p. 419, * DA.
Discourse on the numerous slang words occurring in a book entitled *Across France in a caravan.* Thinks English slang is coarser than American slang. "Slang represents original force, and cultivation represents acquired force." Higginson conducted a column entitled "Men and women" in *Harper's bazar,* and many of his articles are devoted to slang, dialect, and speech problems.

HILDRETH, CHARLES LOTIN.
American slang. (Belford's monthly. Chicago, Dec., 1891. 8°. v. 7, p. 451–458.)   * DA
"A clever gamin might invent slang; a scholar never would. And it is the gamin who is the true language builder."
"Half a century ago slang appears to have been drawn from the thieves' dictionary... Modern slang, if less pregnant, is also less ominous. Generally speaking, it is the vehicle of coarse humor or blunt and uncompromising satire."

I speak United States. (Saturday review. London, Sept. 22, 1894. 4°. v. 78, p. 321.)   * DA
" 'I am free, white, twenty-one, and I speak United States' is the modern Declaration of Independence of every native adult American citizen."
Compares English colloquial expressions with American.

LANG, ANDREW.
Americanisms. (The Academy. London, Nov. 2, 1895. 4°. v. 47, p. 193.)   * DA
A letter written for the benefit of an American correspondent (F. H.) who objected to the term "Americanisms." Lang says: "Yet there exist such things as we style 'Americanisms,' and if F. H. will only give us a soothing term for them, he will find us grateful. A Scot does not draw dirk when he hears of a 'Scotticism.' " Thinks these "— isms" began to appear in America after 1816 — our earlier colonial writers made no use of them.
The F. H. was Fitzedward Hall (q.v.).

A little tiff. (The Illustrated London news. London, Jan. 21, 1893. f°. v. 102, p. 90.)   * DA
This is a spirited review of Brander Matthews, *Ameri-*

canisms and *Briticisms,* New York: Harper & Bros., 1892 (q.v.).
"Still, as Mr. Matthews honours me by not infrequent mention, perhaps he expects a countercheck (not quarrelsome), and it would be a pity to disappoint him."

M.
A new dictionary and some omissions. (The Academy. London, June 18, 1898. 4°. v. 53, p. 665–666.)   * DA
A comparative study of English dictionaries as regards their inclusion or omission of slang.

MATTHEWS, BRANDER.
Americanisms and Briticisms, with other essays on other isms. New York: Harper & Brothers, 1892. 16°.   NBQ
Comments on Australianisms and Americanisms and predicts a wider divergence between the speech of the colonies and that of the mother country. Castigates British critics for their remarks on the American language. "No American writer worth his salt would think of withdrawing a word or of apologizing for a phrase because it was not current within the sound of Bow Bells."
Augustine Birrell took exception to these essays in his own essay, *Americanisms and Briticisms* (q.v.).
Matthews was rebuked for his "patriotic pugnacity" in *The Critic,* New York, Nov. 19, 1892, v. 21, p. 271, * DA.
Reviewed by Andrew Lang in *The Illustrated London news,* London, Jan. 21, 1893, v. 102, p. 90, * DA, in an article entitled "A little tiff." Lang was mildly rebuked for some of these statements by Henry Cabot Lodge in *The Critic,* New York, Feb. 18, 1893, v. 22, p. 97–98, * DA.

The function of slang. (Harper's monthly magazine. New York, July, 1893. 8°. v. 87, p. 304–312.)   * DA
Outlines the history of slang and cant, and makes sharp distinctions between the two classes of words. Both bear the "bend sinister of illegitimacy." Slang of a metropolis is always stupid, be it New York or London or Paris, but of the metropolitan slang the most virile is that of outlaws. Balzac detected this virility in the argot of Vidocq. Our raciest Americanisms spring from the open spaces of the West. "A man should choose his words at least as carefully as he chooses his clothes."
Reprinted in his *Parts of speech,* New York: Charles Scribner's Sons, 1901, p. 185–213, RNB.
A divergent and gently chiding opinion concerning this article appeared in *The Speaker,* London, July 15, 1893, v. 7, p. 42–43, * DA.
See letter by Pitts Duffield, in *The Dial,* Chicago, Aug. 16, 1893, v. 15, p. 86, and Matthews's reply in the Sept. 1, 1893, issue, p. 108, * DA.

The future literary centre of the English language. (The Bookman. New York, Nov., 1900. 8°. v. 12, p. 238–242.)   * DA
The growing population of the United States will mean a gradual shift of the literary center from London to America, with the corresponding ascendancy of American speech with its vigor and flexibility.

A note on recent Briticisms. (Modern language notes. Baltimore, Dec., 1894. 4°. v. 9, columns 449–454.)   RAA
A supplement to his article "Briticisms and Americanisms" in *Harper's monthly magazine,* New York, July, 1891, v. 83, p. 215–222, * DA.
Reprinted in *The Critic,* New York, March 20, 1895, v. 26, p. 245, * DA.

Another note on recent Briticisms. (Modern language notes. Baltimore, Dec., 1895. 4°. v. 10, columns 449–454.)   RAA
A continuation of the previous title. Thinks there should be a dictionary of Briticisms and lists a number of words he considers fit candidates for such a dictionary.

A final note on recent Briticisms. (Modern language notes. Baltimore, Feb., 1897. 4°. v. 12, columns 65–69.)   RAA

General Works, continued

Nineteenth Century — 1891–1900, continued

MR. HOWELLS's "Americanisms." (The Critic.
New York, Sept. 22, 1894. 4°. v. 25, p. 193.)
                                              * DA
Reprinted from the Springfield *Republican*. Comments on a review of Howells' *Traveler from Altruria*
in the London *Athenæum*, in which the reviewer lamented the use of so many Americanisms.

NISBET, J. F.
A plea for purer English. (The Academy.
London, March 19, 1898. f°. v. 53, p. 329–330.)
                                              * DA
Deplores the slipshod practices of newspaper reporters, especially in grammatical construction. Suggests
greater use of provincialisms as opposed to pedantic and
stilted literary form.

PAUL, CHARLES KEGAN.
The American language. (The Month. London, July, 1899. 8°. v. 94, p. 63–68.)   * DA
"It would appear, however, that our age, which has
seen such a wonderful development of philological
science, is assisting at the birth of a new language,
the *Sprachscheide*, from which are to flow two great
fertilizing streams, and that in years to come, just
as we now speak of German and Dutch, so will men
speak of English and American."

PECK, HARRY THURSTON.
What is good English? and other essays.
New York: Dodd, Mead, and Co., 1899. 318 p.
12°.   NBQ
"What is good English?" appeared originally in *The
Bookman*, New York, 1898, v. 7, p. 125–130. "It is a
national superstition with us that 'the dictionary' came
down direct from heaven, and that it contains all that
is necessary to our linguistic salvation, when supplemented by the cut-and-dried pronouncements of a
grave grammarian." Thinks English should be taught
orally, and not out of text books. Despite the school-
men our language has been renewed by the "rich stream
of spoken English."
The second essay in the book is entitled "The little
touches." It was first printed in *The Bookman*, New
York, Feb., 1889, v. 8, p. 549–555, * DA. "In private
life, the unenlightened person is very apt to dread
colloquialisms. He will wish to speak book-language...
The truly enlightened person uses language with carelessness, but it is a masterly carelessness that always
keeps within the limits of good taste. It is usually
colloquial, but not vulgarly colloquial. It draws freely
upon slang, yet always upon the slang which a gentleman can use... It is, indeed, in the use of slang
that the little touches become very subtle." Gives
samples of slang, Americanisms, and Briticisms.

THE PHILOSOPHY of slang. (Saturday review.
London, Aug. 19, 1899. f°. v. 88, p. 226–227.)
                                              * DA
A defence of slang.
"The essence of slang is that it embodies the instinct
of familiarity precisely in the same way as does a
nickname when applied to a person...it is by no means
confined to the rude and humbler classes. It is mur-
mured in Mayfair as well as shouted in Whitechapel."
Reprinted in *Living age*, New York, Nov., 1899,
v. 223, p. 324–326, * DA.

PHIPSON, EVACUSTES A.
British vs. American English. (Dialect notes.
Norwood, Mass., 1896. 8°. v. 1, p. 428–437.)
                                              RNZ
An Englishman's view of American speech, with
numerous comparisons, and emphasis on usage.

RALEIGH, SIR WALTER ALEXANDER.
Style. London: Edward Arnold, 1897. 129 p.
12°.   NAD
The good slang, p. 27–29. The bad slang, p. 29–32.
Distinguishes between the technical slang, "the nat-
ural efflorescence of highly cultivated agilities of brain,

and hand, and eye" and that which is "the offspring
of mental sloth, and current chiefly among the idle,
jocular classes to whom all art is a bugbear and a
puzzle."
This copy belonged to James Huneker. He wrote on
the flyleaf: "After Stevenson's essay on the technical
elements of style this is the most satisfactory study
on the elusive and dangerous subject."

RALPH, JULIAN.
The language of the tenement folk. (Harper's
weekly. New York, Jan. 23, 1897. f°. v. 41,
p. 90.)   * DA
Street slang of New York City in the gay nineties.
A number of slang expressions are explained. The
author contends that New York slang is more refined
than London or Paris slang.

REUSCH, J.
Die alten syntaktischen Reste in modernen
Slang. Münster diss., 1894. 40 p. Fock's
Bibliogr. Monatsbericht.
Kennedy 12002.
Not in The New York Public Library.

RUSSELL, T. BARON.
The American language. (Gentleman's magazine. London, Nov., 1893. 8°. v. 275, p. 529–
533.)   * DA
Lists a number of Americanisms, real and spurious,
with a stout defence of some of them.

SCHRÖDER, GEORG.
Ueber den Einfluss der Volksetymologie auf
den Londoner Slang-Dialekt. Rostock dissertation. 1893. 50 p.
Kennedy 8844.

SHERMAN, ELLEN BURNS.
A study in current slanguage. (The Critic.
New York, Sept. 18, 1897. 4°. v. 31, p. 153.)
                                              * DA
Argument against the slang-*geist*. It lacks dignity,
it is too emotional. It soon becomes mildewed. "A
careful study of the qualities of men and women who
habitually interlard their remarks with slang will
furnish anybody with a world of convincing conclusions
in favor of pure English."

SILLARD, R. M.
Transatlantic whimsicalities. (The New century review. London, 1899. 8°. July, v. 6, p. 62–
68; Aug., v. 6, p. 110–113.)   * DA
Reviews a list of Americanisms, including names
for drinks, nicknames of States, slang of imprecation,
verbal modesty, etc. "There are few London waiters
who could tell you that a Yankee meant pigs' feet if
he called for 'Cincinnati oysters.'" [We suspect Mr.
Sillard was also ignorant of the meaning if Cincinnati
oysters by any chance are synonymous with what the
Middle-Westerners call "mountain oysters." W. J. B.]

SLANG. (All the year round. London, Nov. 25,
1893. 4°. v. 73, p. 510–515.)   * DA
Gives slang words peculiar to the politician, the
writer, the artist, the sportsman, the criminal, the
man of the streets, and others. It is a reply to an
article in an American magazine by Brander Matthews.
"Slang is almost universal... It is very much a
question of temperament."

SLANG. (Atlantic monthly. Boston, March,
1893. 8°. v. 71, p. 424–426.)   * DA
"The distinctive test of good slang from bad is
that it has a real meaning. Bad slang has no meaning
... Good slang is idiomatically expressive, and has
a narrow escape sometimes from being poetical."

General Works, continued

Nineteenth Century — 1891–1900, continued

SLANG. (Harper's bazar. New York, 1897. f°.
Feb. 6, v. 30, p. 112.)   * DA
Girls should use slang sparingly. Slang should be
"utilized in speech as red pepper is employed in cooking
— very lightly, and with great discretion."

SLANG. (Literature. London, May 13, 1899.
f°. v. 3, p. 485.)   * DA
Comments on the "Anti-slang league" formed at New
Albany, Indiana.

SMITH, CHARLES FORSTER.
Americanisms. (The Quarterly review of the
M. E. Church, South. Louisville, Jan., 1891.
8°. new series, v. 9, p. 248–266.)   ZTA
Caption-title of the periodical: Methodist quarterly
review.
Points out the difficulty of determining what an
Americanism really is, and cites the mistakes of Bartlett and Schele de Vere. The compiler of a dictionary of Americanisms must have an exhaustive
knowledge of English idiom, past and present. The
works of W. C. Benet, Richard Grant White and
James Russell Lowell are studied and many words
are taken up in alphabetical order and freely discussed.
Smith was a professor at Vanderbilt University.

SOME so-called Americanisms. (All the year
round. London, Jan. 12, 1895. 4°. v. 76, p. 38–
42.)   * DA
Some of the expressions treated in this article are
from T. B. Russell's *Current Americanisms.* Others
are gathered from Bartlett and other familiar sources.
Reprinted in *Living age,* New York, 1895, v. 204,
p. 438, * *DA.*

SYKES, FREDERICK HENRY.
American speech and standard English. (Our
language. New York, 1892. 8°. Aug., v. 2,
p. 33–35; Sept., v. 2, p. 45–47; Oct., v. 2, p. 52;
Nov., v. 2, p. 55–56.)   RNEH
A paper read before the Modern Language Association of Ontario, at Toronto, April 19, 1892, and reprinted from the *Educational journal,* Toronto.
A study of sectional speech in the United States.
Includes a number of political phrases, and words
selected from Lowell, Bret Harte, Miss Murfree, Maitland, and Norton.

THOMPSON, MAURICE.
The triumph of jargon. (Methodist review.
New York, May, 1898. 8°. v. 80, p. 426–433.)
                                            * DA
American dialects create a language problem when
the words are written down. It is hard to give literary
form to "gombo," "Hoosier," "cracker," and other
dialects. The author of this article looks with fear
upon the rising tide of dialect in fiction. Cautions the
young writers to return to classic language.

TOWNSEND, EDWARD WATERMAN.
"Chimmie Fadden," Major Max and other
stories... New York: Lovell, Coryell & Company [1895]. 346 p. 12°.   NBO
On verso of title-page: "Copyright, 1895, by United
States Book Company."
Also published by Dodd, Mead and Co. [1895.] The
preliminary note states that "Chimmie Fadden" was
first published in the New York *Sun.* This book is
considered to be the best account of the slang of the
New York Bowery for the period of the so-called
"gay nineties." The high and low life of New York
is seen through the eyes of a Bowery newsboy. Town-

send wrote other "Chimmie Fadden" stories besides
those contained in the above volume.
The success of *Chimmie Fadden* led to the publication
of George Vere Hobart's *John Henry.* Hobart wrote
under the pseudonym of Hugh McHugh. Compare
also with Ernest Jarrold's *Tales of the Bowery,* New
York: J. S. Ogilvie, *NBO.* Jarrold was the creator
of the character Mickey Finn. This was definitely an
era of slang and character-sketching. It was the age
of O. Henry, George Ade, Peter Finley Dunne, George
Vere Hobart, and many others of like stamp.

TURNER, GODFREY.
The vulgar tongue. (Macmillan's magazine.
London, March, 1893. 4°. v. 47, p. 390–397.)
                                            * DA
"Ten thousand terms, made to accommodate technical
necessity, or physical investigation and experiment,
could not add a doit to the wealth of a language."
Numerous vulgarisms are mentioned, mostly mal-
apropisms, to show the carelessness of speech. Reprinted in *Living age,* New York, March 31, 1883,
v. 156, p. 814–820, * *DA.*

TWAIN, MARK, PSEUD. OF S. L. CLEMENS.
Concerning the American language. (In his:
The stolen white elephant. New York: Charles
L. Webster & Co., 1894. 8°. p. 265–269.) NBO
Mark Twain reproduces a conversation he had on a
train with an Englishman concerning the difference
between the speech of England and America. Deals
chiefly with pronunciation.
This may be found in various editions of Mark
Twain's collected works. *The Stolen white elephant*
was published originally in 1882 by James R. Osgood
& Co., Boston, 1882.

WAGNER, LEOPOLD.
The significance of names. New York:
Thomas Whittaker, 1893. 287 p. 12°. (Whittaker's library. no. 50.)   RNF
Includes nicknames of American states; things theatrical; titles of honor; the Senate; firearms and
projectiles; matrimony; schools of philosophy; articles
of attire; counties and their subdivisions; insects;
education; the sea; music; cordials and beverages;
printing types; fishes; lawyers and courts of law;
quadrupeds; trees, plants, herbs, and barks; poets
and poetry; weapons of steel; the church; pet names
of American cities; fruits and vegetables; the army.

WALLACE, A.
Popular sayings dissected. New York: Frederick A. Stokes Company [cop. 1895]. 168 p.
16°.   RNM
Several hundred expressions, many of them of slang
origin, are traced. Has a complete word index, p. 157–
168.

WHEELER, BENJAMIN IDE.
Americanisms. (The Universal cyclopedia.
New York, 1900. 4°. v. 1, p. 157–158.)   * AK
Numerous samples of native and borrowed Ameri-
canisms, with a bibliography.

WILLIAMS, RALPH OLMSTED.
Some questions of good English, examined
in controversy with Dr. Fitzedward Hall...
New York: Henry Holt & Co., 1897. viii, 233 p.
12°.   RND
Includes the article "The American dialect" by
Hall, which appeared in *The Academy,* London, March
25, 1893, v. 43, p. 265–267, * *DA,* with Williams's
reply. "Not so very American," by Williams, appeared in *Modern language notes,* Baltimore, Dec.,
1893, v. 4, p. 239–242, *RAA.* Hall's "A rejoinder"
appeared in *Modern language notes,* Nov., 1894, v. 9,
p. 221–224, and Williams's "Dr. Hall's rejoinder" came
out in *Modern language notes,* Jan., 1895, v. 10, p. 29–
31. These battles were fought over a handful of
Americanisms, real and spurious.

General Works, continued

TWENTIETH CENTURY

1901–1910

ADE, GEORGE.
Fables in slang. Illustrated by Clyde J. Newman. New York & Chicago: Herbert S. Stone and Co., 1902. 200 p. 16°.   NBX
Published also in 1899 by Herbert S. Stone & Co. The fables appeared originally in the Chicago *Record*. Ade was one of the first of modern American writers to popularize the slang essay. He has had many imitators.

AMERICAN English. (Outlook. New York, May, 1908. 8°. v. 89, p. 236.)   * DA
Praise for Prof. Walter H. Skeat, who declared that Americans speak as good English as the English themselves. There is slang in England as well as in America.

THE AMERICAN language. (T. P.'s weekly. London, 1905. f°. Feb. 24, v. 5, p. 246; April 7, v. 5, p. 444; April 21, v. 5, p. 508; May 12, v. 5, p. 588.)   * DA
The first and longest article gives a number of American slang words, including the Harvard "fusser." "To 'fuss' a woman is to show a Platonic attachment to her." The other articles are discussions of particular words, sent in by correspondents.

THE AMERICAN language. (T. P.'s weekly. London, Jan. 10, 1908. f°. v. 11, p. 35.) * DA
Comment on Charles Whibley's article in *Blackwood's* (q.v.).
In the April 24, 1908, issue of *T. P.'s weekly*, v. 11, p. 533, comment on Boynton's reply to Whibley, which appeared in *The Bookman*, New York, is made.

THE AMERICAN language again. (The Nation. New York, Jan. 10, 1907. 4°. v. 84, p. 28–29.)
* DA
Scouts the idea of American speech growing away from English. The differences are more apparent than real. Refers to an article by Enid Campbell Dauncey in the *Monthly review* (q.v.).
Reprinted in *Living age*, New York, July 13, 1907, v. 254, p. 123–125, * DA.

AMERICANISMS. (The Anglo-American encyclopedia and dictionary. New York, 1902. 4°. v. 1, p. 87–88.)   * AK
Lists about one hundred words and definitions.

AMERICANISMS. (T. P.'s weekly. London, April 1, 1910. f°. v. 15, p. 416.)   * DA
Study of a few so-called Americanisms, with earlier quotations from English works. The word "bug" is cited. Poe's *The Gold bug* was read in England under the title *The Golden beetle*.

ARGOT: peculiar class phraseology. (American review of reviews. New York, July, 1910. 8°. v. 42, p. 116–117.)   * DA
Short essay on trade and class argot, inspired by an article in *La Revue* (Paris).

BAEDEKER, KARL.
The United States... Handbook for travellers... 4th ed., rev. Leipzig: K. Baedeker, 1909. cii, 724 p. maps, plans. 12°. M.R.R. Desk
On p. xxvi–xxvii is a glossary of Americanisms, a "short list of words in frequent use in the United States in a sense not commonly known in England."

BELL, FLORENCE EVELEEN ELEANORE (OLLIFFE), LADY.
Our present vocabulary. (The Albany review. London, Oct., 1907. 8°. new series, v. 2, p. 40–45.)   * DA
Our vocabulary equipment should be kept in the best condition possible. Words such as "rotter," "gnogger," "umbies," "deaser" and "proggers" are roundly scored as intruders.
Reprinted in *Living age*, New York, 1907, v. 255, p. 416–419, * DA. Also reprinted in her *Landmarks*, London [cop. 1929], p. 39–47, *NCZ*.

BELL, RALCY HUSTED.
Slang. (In his: The worth of words. New York: The Grafton Press [cop. 1902]. 12°. p. 193–220.)   RND
"Language serves man according to his needs." This essay is followed by a glossary of slang words with full definitions.
Third edition published in 1903.

BICKNELL, FRANK MARTIN.
The Yankee in British fiction. (The Outlook. New York, Nov. 19, 1910. 8°. v. 96, p. 632–639.)   * DA
Andrew Lang, Grant Allen, J. A. Stewart, F. C. Philips, E. W. Hornung, and numerous other English writers fail miserably as soon as they attempt to reproduce American characters and American speech, and samples of their mistakes are given.

BIERCE, AMBROSE.
Some sober words on slang. (Cosmopolitan magazine. New York, July, 1907. 8°. v. 43, p. 335.)   * DA
Bierce remonstrates against slang, and takes a fling at George Ade's and Wallace Irwin's works. "Slang has as many hateful qualities as a dog bad habits, but its essential vice is its hideous lack of originality, for until a word or phrase is common property it is not slang."

BIRRELL, AUGUSTINE.
Americanisms and Briticisms. (In his: Collected essays. New York, 1902. 2. ed. 12°. v. 2, p. 325–330.)   NCZ
A spirited attack on the nationalism in letters advocated by Brander Matthews, in his *Americanisms and Briticisms, with other essays on other isms* (q.v.).

BOWEN, EDWIN WINFIELD.
Questions at issue in our English speech... New York: Broadway Publishing Co. [1909.] 154 p. 12°.   RNE
Contents: 1. On English spelling of yesterday. Why antiquated, p. 1–24; 2. A question of preference in English spelling, p. 25–37; 3. Authority in English pronunciation, p. 38–59; 4. Vulgarisms with a pedigree, p. 60–81; 5. Briticisms versus Americanisms, p. 82–107; 6. What is slang? p. 108–129; 7. Standard English. How it arose and how it is maintained, p. 130–154.
"Briticisms versus Americanisms" appeared in *Popular science monthly*, New York, 1906, v. 69, p. 324–337, * DA. This is a defence of Americanisms. Gives difference between climate, conditions of life, orthoepy, dialects, provincialisms, etc. Takes up a few Elizabethan survivals, and gives a number of Americanisms with their British equivalents.
"What is slang?" appeared in *Popular science monthly*, New York, Feb., 1906, v. 68, p. 127–138, * DA. This is considered to be one of the best articles written by an American on the subject of slang. Nice distinctions are made between slang, cant, and jargon. The history of slang is traced. Slang repairs the

General Works, continued

Twentieth Century — 1901–1910, continued

waste in the spoken language, feeds the language. Swift's article on language which appeared in *The Tatler* is discussed at some length. "The laws governing speech development are very imperfectly known ... Language is an involuntary product and does not result from any determined concert of action... It is the heighth of folly for any one, no matter how highly esteemed as an author, to attempt the rôle of reformer of the speech."

"Vulgarisms with a pedigree" is based on two articles which appeared in the *Atlantic monthly* and the *North American review*.

BOYNTON, HENRY WALCOTT.
"The American language." (The Bookman. New York, March, 1908. 8°. v. 27, p. 63–71.)
* D A
A reply to Charles Whibley's article on "American language" in the Jan., 1908, issue of *The Bookman*. See Whibley.
Whibley's article is reprinted below the line, in small type, to enable the reader to make a comparison of the two articles. Boynton claims that Whibley did not know what he was talking about, his impressions being hasty and prejudiced. He claims further that Whibley picked unrepresentative specimens of the American tongue. The reader can judge for himself.

BURGESS, GELETT.
A defence of slang. (In his: The romance of the commonplace... San Francisco: Paul Elder and Morgan Shepard [cop. 1902]. 12°. p. 72–76.) NBQ
"Could Shakespeare come to Chicago and listen curiously to 'the man in the street,' he would find himself more at home than in London... Slang has been called 'poetry of the rough,' and it is not at all coarse or vulgar."
Compares slang in America with slang in England.

CAMERON, AGNES DEANS.
English as she is Americanized. (Pacific monthly. Portland, Ore., 1908. 8°. Jan., 1908, v. 19, p. 96a–96h; March, 1908, v. 19, p. 324–329; July, 1908, v. 20, p. 90–94.) * D A
This is a series of articles on western slang, anticipating the type of article published years later in *American speech*. Such studies as this help date some of the twentieth century expressions.

CHESTERTON, GILBERT KEITH.
A defence of slang. (In his: The defendant. New York: Dodd, Mead & Co., 1902. 12°. p. 105–111.) NCZ
"The one stream of poetry which is continually flowing is slang. Every day a nameless poet weaves some fairy tracery of popular language... Nothing is more startling than the contrast between the heavy, formal, lifeless slang of the man-about-town and the light, living, and flexible slang of the coster... All slang is metaphor, and all metaphor is poetry."
Reprinted in his *A Defence of nonsense, and other essays*, New York: Dodd, Mead & Co., 1911, p. 55–63. *NCZ.*
This article first appeared in *The Speaker*, London, April 27, 1901, new series, v. 4, p. 101–102, * D A. It was reprinted in part in *Public opinion*, London, May 3, 1901, v. 79, p. 559–560, * D A.
Reviewed in *T. P.'s weekly*, London, Dec. 26, 1902, v. 1, p. 201–202, * D A.

COLEY, LOUIS B.
Rubaiyat of the East Side. (The Commentator. New York, Jan., 1902. 12°. v. 1, p. 103–105.) * D A
A poem written in the slang of the New York Bowery.

CROSLAND, THOMAS WILLIAM HODGSON.
The abounding American... London: A. F. Thompson, 1907. 116 p. 12°. ILH
A comic satire on American life, with numerous samples of American slang of the "Teddy" Roosevelt era.

DAUNCEY, ENID CAMPBELL.
The American language. (The Monthly review. London, Oct., 1906. 8°. v. 25, p. 24–32.)
* D A
Holds to the opinion that a new language is developing in America, and attributes most of the changes to the influx of foreigners speaking diverse tongues.
Reprinted in *The Living age*, New York, Dec. 15, 1906, v. 251, p. 654–658, * D A.

GALES, RICHARD LAWSON.
The rightness of popular speech. (In his: Studies in Arcady. 2d series. London: Herbert & Daniell [1910–12]. 12°. p. 228–237.) NCZ
"The people have always loved to call a spade a spade." Defends the common speech and points out that the speech of "superior persons" is lifeless in comparison. Other kindred essays appear in this volume and in other works by the same author.

GOULEY, JOHN WILLIAM SEVERIN.
Dining and its amenities... New York: Rebman Company [cop. 1907]. 470 p. 8°. VTB
"Slang speech," p. 302–326.
Traces the history of slang.

GREENOUGH, JAMES BRADSTREET, AND G. L. KITTREDGE.
Words and their ways in English speech... New York: The Macmillan Company, 1901. 431 p. 8°. RNF
p. 55–79, "Slang and legitimate speech." This is one of the really noteworthy studies of slang. "A peculiar kind of vagabond language, always hanging on the outskirts of legitimate speech, but continually straying or forcing its way into the most respectable company, is what we call *slang*." Slang is often made by the use of "harsh, violent, or ludicrous metaphors, obscure analogies, meaningless words, and expressions derived from the less known or less esteemed vocations or customs... Provincialisms or dialect words are often adopted into slang... Slang delights in fantastic coinages and in grotesque combinations or distortions of existing words... It appears then, that there is no real difference between the processes of slang and those of legitimate speech. Slang is only the rude luxuriance of the uncared-for soil, knowing not the hand of the gardener." Says that slang shocks the sensitive. It is evanescent. "Finally, the unchecked and habitual use of slang even polite slang is deleterious to the mind...slang tends to level all those nice distinctions of meaning, all those differentiations between word and word, which the consensus of the language has been at so much pains to build up."

HOBART, GEORGE VERE.
Down the line with John Henry. By Hugh McHugh [pseud. of George Vere Hobart]... New York: G. W. Dillingham Co. [cop. 1901.] 114 p. 16°. NBX
The works of this American humorist abound in slang. He was a forerunner of the Ring Lardner school of humorists. He was born in Nova Scotia, and went as a young man to Cumberland, Maryland, where he entered the newspaper profession. He worked later on papers in Baltimore and New York. He created a character in Dinkelspiel, a German-American who spoke the idiom of Hans Breitmann. This was about the time of Peter Finley Dunne's *Mr. Dooley*. Hobart was the first newspaper man to report baseball games in verse. Every line he wrote was filled with slang. In New York he created the character John Henry, a man about town, sportsman, *bon vivant*, who talked only in the slang of the day. By 1904 Hobart had sold over 445,000 copies of his

General Works, continued

Twentieth Century — 1901–1910, continued

HOBART, GEORGE VERE, *continued*

John Henry series. In format and content, these stories are very much like the "Chimmie Fadden" stories by E. W. Townsend, which appeared in the 1890's, except that Townsend's chief character was a Bowery boy. Other Hobart books are: *Its up to you,* 1902, *NBO; John Henry,* 1901, *NBO; You can search me,* 1905, *NBX; I need the money,* 1903, *NBO; Out for the coin,* 1903, *NBO;* and many others, all published in the same format by G. W. Dillingham Co.
See Arthur K. Taylor, "Poets and humorists of the American press," *Inland printer,* Chicago, Sept., 1904, v. 33, p. 839–840, †* *IPA.*

IMPROVISED words. (Atlantic monthly. Boston, Nov., 1908. 8°. v. 102, p. 714–716.)   * DA
"There is hardly a family but has some expressive improvised word." "Streely," "uppy," "neb," "obsniptious," etc., are mentioned.

J., W. C.
Current slang. (Notes and queries. London, Sept. 29, 1906. 8°. series 10, v. 6, p. 247.)
* R–* DA
Comment on new expressions current among the educated classes.
Alfred F. Robbins adds a note in the Nov. 17, 1906, issue of *Notes and queries,* p. 393.
R. L. Moreton adds a final word in the Dec. 29 issue, p. 517, on the exclamation "What?"

JAMES, HENRY.
The question of our speech. (Appleton's booklovers magazine. New York, Aug., 1905. 8°. v. 6, p. 199–210.)   * DA
Address delivered before the graduating class at Bryn Mawr College, June 8, 1905. Vulgarism in speech has seldom been attacked with more dignified fury than in the case of James vs. barbarism. It has become a little classic of speech criticism. It was published in book form by Houghton, Mifflin & Co., Boston, 1905, 115 p., 12°, * *KP (Rogers).*
The book was designed by Bruce Rogers.

KIRK, JOHN FOSTER.
"Words, words, words." (Lippincott's monthly magazine. Philadelphia, July, 1906. 8°. v. 78, p. 62–68.)   * DA
An informal essay on Americanisms, with special emphasis on the terms which came in with the development of the railroads.

KLEBERG, ALFRED LEON.
Slang fables from afar. Baltimore: Phoenix Pub. Co. [1903.] 94 p. 16°.   NAC p.v.329
Slang fables in the manner of George Ade.

KNORTZ, KARL.
Amerikanische Redensarten und Volksgebräuche... Leipzig: Teutonia Verlag, 1907. 82 p. 8°.   ZBD
Not an important contribution. A few American slang words are examined for the benefit of the German reader who knows nothing whatsoever about the subject.

KRAPP, GEORGE PHILIP.
Slang. (In his: Modern English. New York: Charles Scribner's Sons [1909]. 12°. p. 199–211.)   RNB
Slang is a necessary element in the freshening of language, but "it is almost always more expressive than the situation demands. It is indeed a kind of hyperesthesia in the use of language. It differs thus from idiom, which is normally expressive."

KRUEGER, GUSTAV.
Was ist *slang,* bezüglich *argot?* (In: Festschrift Adolf Tobler zum siebzigsten Geburtstage. Braunschweig: Georg Westermann, 1905. 8°. p. 229–240.)   RAE
Proves the need of a clear cut definition of slang. A number of representative dictionary definitions are compared and many differences of opinion noted. Webster's definition: "Low, vulgar, unauthorized language," to quote but a part of it, seems to prevail. Another school holds that slang words are potentially respectable. As Victorien Sardou said: "L'argot c'est le français de l'avenir."
See also Reves, Ritter, Hayward.

LITTMANN, ENNO.
"23" and other numerical expressions. (Open court. Chicago, Feb., 1908. 8°. v. 22, p. 119–124.)   * DA
"23" and "skiddoo" were the slang coinages of 1906. A number of possible origins for the expression "23" are brought to light, and the essay becomes involved in the symbolism of numbers.
Littmann makes no mention of it, but the term "skiddoo" was coined in 1906 by the musical comedy star, Billy B. Van. See *Indianapolis Morning Star,* March 31, 1906.

MATTHEWS, BRANDER.
The American language. (Munsey's magazine. New York, Dec., 1908. 8°. v. 40, p. 345–349.)   * DA
America lacks a specific national name, its race is a mixture of European stock, and it lacks a national language. American English is unlike the English spoken in Great Britain. The literature of America is not much different from English literature. The twentieth century will see the triumph of American literature and idiom.

Americanisms once more. (The Cosmopolitan. New York, Jan., 1901. 8°. v. 30, p. 274–280.)   * DA
American and English bickering over the English language is a retarding factor. English writers show a great lack of appreciation of American speech, and condemn as Americanisms many old words rooted in Elizabethan English. The American Middle West will add new life to the English language with its freedom and its swift directness. "The function of slang as a true feeder of language is certain to get itself more widely recognized as time goes on; and there is no better nursery for these seedlings of speech than the territory west of the Mississippi and east of the Rockies."
Reprinted in his *Parts of speech,* New York: Charles Scribner's Sons, 1901, p. 95–123, *RNB.*

Briticisms of all sorts. (Harper's monthly magazine. New York, April, 1903. 8°. v. 106, p. 709–712.)   * DA
Defines Americanisms and Briticisms. Neither should be used as a term of reproach. A standard of English speech is somewhat of a scholar's utopia. In the matter of "sporadic innovation" England lags behind America.

The speech of the people. (In his: The American of the future, and other essays. New York: Charles Scribner's Sons, 1909. 12°. p. 177–194.)   NBQ
Professor Matthews does not fear the encroachments of slang. "Most of us have failed to lay firm hold of this principle — that the spoken word is primary and that the written word is secondary only." Thinks the French Academy is hide-bound. Writers like Rudyard Kipling and Mark Twain try to put in their pages as much as possible of the "elemental energy of the spoken word."

MAYALL, ARTHUR.
American slang. (Notes and queries. London, Aug. 3, 1901. 8°. series 9, v. 8, p. 111–112.)
* R–* DA
Discussion of the word "bunt" and its origin.

General Works, continued

Twentieth Century — 1901–1910, continued

MEAD, LEON.

Among the word-makers. (The Booklovers magazine. Philadelphia, June, 1905. 8°. v. 5, p. 844–848.) *DA

A continuation of the study of neologisms which appeared in his *Word-coinage*, New York, 1902, RNF.

Word-coinage, being an enquiry into recent neologisms. Also a brief study of literary style, slang, and provincialisms. New York: T. Y. Crowell & Co. [cop. 1902.] 281 p. 16°. RNF

Slang, p. 161–191.

"Slang is a necessity — to Wall St., to fashionable clubs, to the college youth, to pugilists, to thieves, to the police, to the factory, to the politicians, to sportsmen, to the stage, to sailors, to soldiers, to shop-keepers, and what not."

Gives several pages of slang expressions, some of them by class.

Provincialisms and Americanisms, p. 192–210. Study of regional speech in America.

Other chapters in the book are on related subjects. Mead wrote to most of the prominent writers of the period and asked them to submit a list of words they had coined. One collection of these letters appeared under the title: "Word-coinage by living American authors" in *The Chautauquan*, Meadville, Pa., Nov., 1899, v. 30, p. 131–135. Further letters appeared in the same volume for Feb., 1900, p. 485–88, *DA.

The book has a good word index.

MORSE, JAMES HERBERT.

The new vocabulary. (Independent. New York, Sept. 24, 1908. 8°. v. 65, p. 765–767.) *DA

Praises the fresh creations of American slang. Calls it Sophoclean. Back of these expressions is the eternal spirit of youth. College slang is always in the vanguard of new words.

OUR unhappy language. (Macmillan's magazine. London, June, 1902. 8°. v. 86, p. 122–132.) *DA

The latter part of this long essay is devoted to the peculiarities of American speech, as observed by an Englishman.

OVERLOOKED conversational asset. (Scribner's magazine. New York, Aug., 1909. 8°. v. 46, p. 250–251.) *DA

Remarks occasioned by the passage of a bill by the New York Legislature to prevent "joy riding." Other slang words of the period are mentioned such as "glad hand."

PLAIN United States. (The Academy. London, Aug. 10, 1901. 4°. v. 61, p. 117–118.) *DA

An analysis of the American novel, *John Henry*, by Hobart, with emphasis on slang.

RALPH, JULIAN.

The English of the English. (Harper's magazine. New York, Aug., 1901. 8°. v. 103, p. 446–448.) *DA

The American visitor to London finds he must acquaint himself with the English names for common objects. Pronunciation is also discussed and there is a sample or two of cockney pronunciation.

RANKIN, GEORGE VALLER.

America guilty of languicide. (Harper's weekly. New York, Aug. 13, 1910. v. 54, p. 6.) *DA

An Englishman residing in Seattle complains of the

bad manners of American journalists in referring to educated Londoners as though they were all coster-mongers — judging from the speech attributed to them.

RITTER, OTTO.

Zur Herkunft von ne. slang. Mit einem Anhang über das 'bewegliche *s*' im Englischen. (Archiv für das Studium der neueren Sprachen und Literaturen. Braunschweig, 1906. 8°. Bd. 116, p. 41–49.) RAA

Thinks *slang* is a slang word itself, that it comes from a shortening of the word *language*, plus the liaison (Verbindungen) with final (s). Thus beggar's lang, thieves' lang, sailors' lang. Gradually *lang* became *slang*, through this liaison. Gives other examples of this word evolution. For the origin of the word *slang* see also Hayward, Reves, and Krueger.

RUSSELL, GEORGE WILLIAM ERSKINE.

Slang. (In his: Sketches and snapshots. London: Smith, Elder & Co., 1910. 8°. p. 444–449.) NCZ

In a reminiscent mood the author recalls the slang of his boyhood at Harrow, some Dickensian slang, and some of the more picturesque expressions of his contemporaries. He mentions a book called *Happy thoughts*, which contained much slang of the 'sixties.

SLANG. (The Academy. London, March 18, 1905. f°. v. 68, p. 279–280.) *DA

"In dictionary-making the right thing is to choose from the number of slang words such as have distinctive significations well marked, and such as have proved their usefulness in long years of service... As for the rest, half of them should be discarded altogether for what they are — fresh from the ditch and smelling of it, or, at the best, without a shade of meaning that isn't nasty even when it is new."

Reprinted in *Living age*, New York, April 22, 1905, v. 245, p. 252–253, *DA.

SMITH, CHARLES FORSTER.

Darwin's Americanisms. (The Independent. New York, Nov. 14, 1901. 8°. v. 53, p. 2706–2708.) *DA

Wonders if Bartlett read very many English books in compiling his dictionary of Americanisms. Smith found 24 of Bartlett's Americanisms in *Tom Brown at Rugby*, and a great many others in the works of Charles Darwin.

SOME Americanisms and Irishisms. (T. P.'s weekly. London, Jan. 30, 1903. f°. v. 1, p. 377.) *DA

Inspired by a perusal of Florence Howe Hall's *The Correct thing in good society*. Also comments on the word-duel between the London *Daily Chronicle* and the New York *Sun* anent the word "fall" for autumn. The *Sun* called the opinion voiced in the *Chronicle* as a "hunk of flubdub," which elicited queries from England as to the meaning of "flubdub."

THE SPECTATOR. (Outlook. New York, Jan. 2, 1909. 8°. v. 91, p. 17–19.) *DA

Notes the speech changes one observes in crossing the American continent, with a few specific terms used by miners, cowboys, the Japanese in California, etc.

SPENCER, HERBERT.

A few Americanisms. (In his: Facts and comments. New York: D. Appleton & Co., 1902. 12°. p. 16–18.) NCZ

"If purists had ruled from the beginning language would never have progressed." Criticizes a few Americanisms. "It should be a matter of conscience not to misuse words; it should also be a matter of conscience to resist misuse of them."

General Works, continued

Twentieth Century — 1901–1910, continued

SPENCER, HERMAN.
Language in the making. A defense of slang.
(Booklovers magazine. Philadelphia, Dec.,
1903. 8°. v. 2, p. 658–665.)   * DA
    In Europe the use of slang seems to be "reprobated
by the educated classes." In America slang is used
by all classes. Slang is a character index. We not
only talk slang, we live slang. Gives many samples
of slang words and lingers on the word "rubber-neck."
"In slang we most vigorously and most freely express
our hatred of all indirection and of all sham and
hypocrisy. It is the antipodes of bathos... It is blunt,
it is crude, it is brutal sometimes, but it is always
honest and it is always sane."

SWYNNERTON, C.
Fashionable slang of the past. (Notes and
queries. London, May 10, 1902. 8°. series 9,
v. 9, p. 368–369.)   * R–* DA
    "Will not some expert contributor also tell us the
life story of a selected number of fashionable slang
words which from time to time have had their little
day among the *jeunesse dorée* of both sexes and then
died out?"
    Herbert B. Clayton replies June 21, 1902, series 9,
v. 9, p. 495. Other notes are added by Chas. Welsh and
Henry Gerald Hope, Aug. 2, 1902, series 9, v. 10,
p. 98.

VIZETELLY, FRANCIS HORACE.
The talk of the town. illus. (The Bookman.
Deposit, New York, May, 1908. 8°. v. 14, p. 634–
644.)   NBA
    A defence of slang by the managing editor of *The
Standard dictionary.* Many of the better-known American slang words are traced. The word "rubber-neck"
was then in vogue. Says "dude" originated in London
in the 1880's. "Yeggman" came from a thief named
John Yegg. Explains yellow journalism, which followed in the wake of the much publicized "yellow
kid" whose sensational adventures gave way to sensational news columns.

WHIBLEY, CHARLES.
American language. (Bookman. New York,
Jan., 1908. 8°. v. 26, p. 533–539.)   * DA
    The visiting Englishman seems to have found the
American language rather barbaric, and cites examples
to prove his case. It is based more on books the
author has read than on speech he has heard, and
smells of the candle, and H. W. Boynton was quick
to refute Whibley's claims, in the March issue of the
Bookman (q.v.). Whibley's article also appeared in
Blackwood's magazine, London, Jan., 1908, v. 183,
p. 118–126, * DA.

Slang and its uses. (Living age. New York,
April 20, 1901. 8°. v. 229, p. 196–199.)   * DA
    Reprinted from *Literature.*
    Discourses on British slang, old 'thieves' Latin,' etc.
"The further we get from civilization and the re-
straints imposed by it, the more eloquent and quick-
witted grows the lingo of street and hedgerow... What
Rabelais did for France...our Elizabethans did for
England. They sought new words as they sought new
continents."
    Also in *Eclectic magazine,* June, 1901, v. 136, p. 739–
742.

WILSTACH, FRANK JENNERS.
"He couldn't come back." Five typewritten
pages of ms. presented to The New York Public Library by Mr. Wilstach. Several American
phrases are traced and a wide variety of subjects
treated.
    Printed, with revisions, in the New York *Review,*
July 23, 1910, p. 2, under the title: "America wrongly
accused of picturesque slang," * A.

WORD-COINING and slang. (The Spectator. London, May 18, 1907. f°. v. 98, p. 790–792.) * DA
    "Pedantry in language is folly... Slang is commonly,
indeed, the expression of concentrated vitality... Vil-
lon's slang was a language in itself. So is the *argot*
of the Parisian *apache* of today." Gives examples of
lively slang words which should be put into the dictionary. Reprinted in *Living age,* New York, July 13,
1907, v. 254, p. 115–118, * DA.

1911–1920

ALLEN, EDWARD A.
A word about slang. (The Forum. New
York, June, 1914. 8°. v. 51, p. 916–918.)   * DA
    "Much of the better sort of slang is an unconscious
endeavor to turn into vigorous Saxon English, readily
understood, the highly Latinized English of the learned
... Slang is the spare-ribs of speech, cut to the bone."

AT last! An American language. (The Literary
digest. New York, Sept. 30, 1916. f°. v. 53,
p. 848–849.)   * DA
    Amusing illustrations of the strange forms which
the spoken English in America often assumes.

ATROCITIES in English. (The Literary digest.
New York, Aug. 12, 1916. f°. v. 53, p. 355.)
                                            * DA
    Excerpts from an article in the *Saturday review.*
British officials were credited with speaking atrocious
English during the war, due to the influence exerted
by American slang.

BECHTEL, JOHN HENDRICKS.
Slang. (In his: Slips of speech. Philadelphia:
Penn Publishing Company, 1913. 16°. p. 22–23.)
                                            RND
    "Slang is somewhat like chicken-pox or measles,
very catching, and just as inevitable in its run; and
very few of us escape it." Lists a few words from
society, commercial, and common slang.

BOSSON, OLOF.
Slang and cant in Jerome K. Jerome's works.
Cambridge: W. Heffer & Sons, Ltd., 1911. 71 p.
8°.
    Copy in Columbia University Library.
    "By slang, I mean *the easy, natural, semi-technical
language of special classes of society...* By cant or
vulgarism (low slang) I mean *the easy, natural
language of the uneducated people.*"
    Reviewed in *Beiblatt zu Anglia,* Jahrg. 26, p. 149–
150, *RNA.*

BRITISH-AMERICAN war over language. (The
Literary digest. New York, July 17, 1920. f°.
v. 66, p. 35.)   * DA
    Comment on E. B. Osborn's article in the London
Morning Post concerning Rupert Hughes's plea for the
independence of American literature. The British can
get along without understanding the Americans but the
reverse is not true.

BRITISH struggles with our speech. (The Literary digest. New York, June 19, 1915. f°. v. 50,
p. 1468–1469.)   * DA
    Views of Cecil Chesterton in the *New witness,*
London, after a trip to the United States. Americans
are more foreign than Frenchmen. The American speech
is more difficult to read than French, for the dictionary
offers no aid in interpreting American newspaper headlines. Also local differences. A city "block" in New
York is a "square" in Philadelphia.

General Works, continued

Twentieth Century — 1911–1920, continued

BROWN, IVOR JOHN CARNEGIE.
The decay of English. (The Athenæum. London, July, 1919. f°. v. 151, p. 614–615.) * DA
"So we can pass over the lifeless metaphor in the morning's news without noticing it, but shudder to see it in a book of quality." Does not condemn slang, but abhors the cheap arm-waving of the publicist and his employment of a "cumbrously evasive phraseology."
Reprinted in the *Living age*, New York, Aug. 30, 1919, v. 302, p. 524–526, * DA, under the title "One's morning paper and the English language."

BURTON, RICHARD.
English as she is spoke. (The Bookman. New York, July, 1920. 4°. v. 51, p. 513–517.) * DA
"No wonder Brander Matthews speaks of English as a 'grammarless tongue.' America has done and is doing her full share to make it so." American sectionalism makes the job of the linguist a hard one. These sectionalisms in speech refresh the language. We have nothing to fear from their inroads. "Chaucer wrote in a dialect; but he became the first great English poet."

Vulgarizing speech. (In his: Little essays in literature and life... New York: The Century Co., 1914. 12°. p. 319–323.)   NBQ
A plea for purity of speech and the preservation of the noble English tongue.

CATEL, JEAN.
Sur la poésie américaine d'aujourd'hui. (Les Marges. Paris, Jan., 1920. 12°. v. 18, p. 41–49.) * DM
Observations on the new American idiom which is creeping into contemporary poetry. Cites Carl Sandburg as a striking example.

COLTON, ARTHUR WILLIS.
Gains and losses in language. (Harper's monthly magazine. New York, April, 1920. 8°. v. 140, p. 707–709.) * DA
Disagrees with Herbert Spencer's ideas on Americanisms. Thinks that no Englishman should write on American usages.

DAUNCEY, ENID CAMPBELL.
The snobbery of synonyms. (The Eye-witness. London, Aug. 29, 1912. 4°. v. 3, p. 339–341.) * DA
Weeps the passage of old words like "rooms," "petticoat," etc., and the advent of "lodgings," "joop," and other modern synonyms. A few slang words are included. In the Sept. 5 issue, p. 372, R. H. Pott makes a few comments on the above essay.

DILNOT, FRANK.
The written and spoken word. (In his: The new America. New York: The Macmillan Company, 1919. 12°. p. 22–28.)   ILH
Favorable comment by a visiting Englishman on the slang of America. "Show me the alert Englishman who will not find a stimulation in those nuggety word-groupings which are the commonplaces in good American conversation... They come from all kinds of people, who are brilliantly innocent of enriching the language."

DOOLITTLE, MAUD M.
Rhymes in prose on my verbal throes. (The Outlook. New York, Nov. 13, 1918. 4°. v. 120, p. 433.) * DA
Some of the modern slang expressions are woven into a rhymed complaint to the editor.

FAULKNER, W. G.
Yankee slang increasing. (London Daily Mail. Overseas edition. London, June 21, 1913.)
Not in The New York Public Library.
This article attempts to show the corrupting influence upon English speech of the American "movies." The charge was challenged by the *Detroit Journal*, Aug. 9, 1913. The writer claims that the English used in the *Daily Mail* was a dead language. Cites Kipling's language as a live language.

FITZGERALD, JOSEPH.
Americanisms. (The Americana. A universal reference library. New York, 1912. 4°. v. 1.) * AK
About five columns long. Includes bibliography. Puts Americanisms in three main divisions: (1) Those originating in America; (2) Those which have emigrated from Britain; (3) Those which have undergone here an essential change of meaning.

FRANK, GLENN.
Slang and jargon. (The Century magazine. New York, Nov., 1920. 8°. v. 101, p. 137–139.) * DA
A conjecture as to the survival of certain slang words created by the British soldier in the World war. "Jargon is the fog of language; slang the lightning of language... Jargon is abstract; slang is concrete... Jargon is circumlocution become a habit." The definitions of slang, cant, and jargon are reexamined and considerably clarified.
Appearing anonymously in *The Century*, it was reprinted in Glenn Frank's *An American looks at his wo·ld*, Newark, Delaware; University of Delaware Press, 1923, p. 100–110, SB.

GRAHAM, STEPHEN.
The American language. (In his: With poor immigrants to America... New York: The Macmillan Co., 1914. xviii, 306 p. 8°.)   SEV
"Britain lives in a tradition; America in a passion." Graham shows the differences between American and English speech tendencies, and the influence of immigrant speech on the American language.

A GUIDE to the English language... London: T. C. & E. C. Jack, 1915. viii, 455 p. 8°.   RNB
A cooperative work, under the general editorship of H. C. O'Neill. "Enlargement of vocabulary through slang," p. 137–138. "Slang," p. 227–230.

HALL, FLORENCE MARION (HOWE).
A. B. C. of correct speech. New York: Harper & Bros. [1916.] 118 p. 16°.   RND
Slang and over-precision of speech, p. 24–30. Condemned words and phrases, p. 55–62. Briticisms and Americanisms, p. 63–69.

HAMPSON, J. M. C.
How to speak American. (To-day. London, March, 1919. 12°. v. 5, p. 19–24.) * DA
A veritable repository of current American slang as culled from our picturesque speech by an observing Englishman. Includes about 100 expressions.

HAWTHORN, W. J.
Slanguage. (The Saturday review. London, July 31, 1920. f°. v. 130, p. 93–94.) * DA
To strengthen the claim made in a previous article in the *Saturday review*, entitled "The degradation of English," July 24, p. 69–70, the writer adds several examples of barbarous American slang, the result of the war and of the movies.

General Works, continued

Twentieth Century — 1911–1920, continued

HILLYARD, ANNA BRANSON.
"American written here." (The Athenæum.
London, Dec. 19, 1919. f°. v. 151, p. 1362–1363.)
                                                    * DA
An essay written in lighter mood, in which the
author proposes to furnish, for a small stipend, correct
Americanisms for H. G. Wells, Stephen McKenna,
Sir James Barrie, and others. She thinks most English-
men are ignorant concerning the proper handling of
American argot in narrative writing. Reprinted in
Living age, New York, Jan. 24, 1920, v. 304, p. 235–
237, * DA.

HOLLIDAY, ROBERT CORTES.
Caun't speak the language. (In his: Walking-
stick papers. New York: George H. Doran
Company [1918]. 12°. p. 201–213.)   NBQ
The trials and errors of an American in England,
with remarks on the difference in speech between the
two countries, including slang.

HUGHES, RUPERT.
Our statish language. (Harper's magazine.
New York, May, 1920. 8°. v. 140, p. 846–849.)
                                                    * DA
"But let us sign a Declaration of Literary Inde-
pendence and formally begin to write, not British, but
United Statesish." This article was roundly criticized
in England.

"I'M from Missouri." Pet slang phrase of St.
Louis star in Passing Show. (St. Louis star.
March 19, 1915.)
Marilyn Miller discourses on slang. A number of
regional phrases are recounted. This press notice was
written by Frank J. Wilstach. The original typewritten ms. was found in the Wilstach papers presented
to The New York Public Library.

KEARNS, JOHN.
The vogue of slang. (The Writer. Boston,
Nov., 1917. 8°. v. 29, p. 161–162.)   * DA
A few contemporary slang expressions. Deplores
the use of slang by American writers.

KELLY, R. J., AND OTHERS.
Some Americanisms. (Notes and queries.
London, 1915. 8°. Sept. 18, 1915, series 11,
v. 12, p. 218–219; Oct. 16, 1915, series 11,
v. 12, p. 307–308.)   * R–* DA
A list of Americanisms compiled by Judge Ruppenthal, of Kansas, in the course of his experience. In
the subsequent article a number of additions and corrections are made by other contributors.

KRON, RICHARD.
The little Londoner. A concise account of
the life and ways of the English with special
reference to London... 12th ed. Freiburg
(Baden): J. Bielefelds Verlag, 1911. 203 p.
16°.   RNPH
On p. 175–193 of this popular and entertaining
book we have a good selection of London colloquialisms,
slang, and cockney dialect — just the things the ubiq-
uitous German traveller would be proud to acquire.
This is a companion piece to the *Petit Parisien,* by the
same author.

LANE, JOHN, AND OTHERS.
Americanisms? (Notes and queries. London,
1916–17. 8°. Oct. 17, 1916, series 12, v. 2, p. 287–
288; Oct. 21, p. 334; Nov. 18, p. 414; Dec. 16,
p. 496–497; Jan. 13, 1917, series 12, v. 3, p. 35–
36; Feb. 10, p. 115–116; May, p. 313; July,
p. 364–365.)   * R–* DA
John Lane notes that some of the so-called Americanisms were familiar to him as words heard in Devon

in his youth. W. B. H., St. Swithin, E. Rimbault
Dibdin, R. E., John T. Page, Thomas Bayne, Richard
H. Thornton, John Murray, Penry Lewis, Avern Pardoe, N. W. Hill, and William Francis Crafts toss
the discussion back and forth, and a good many Americanisms crop up in this transatlantic correspondence.

LEE, FRANCIS HERBERT.
Not so modern as we think. (The Ladies'
home journal. Philadelphia, Aug., 1913. f°.
v. 30, p. 20.)   * DA
A hundred or more slang expressions are shown
to be quite ancient, and quotations from English
literature bolster the claim.

LINTOT, BERNARD.
[New York slang.] (T. P.'s weekly. London,
Sept. 6, 1912. f°. v. 20, p. 297.)   * DA
In Lintot's page entitled "At Number 1 Grub
street." Comments on the slang of George Ade, Robert
W. Sneddon, and Barry Pain, with a long quotation
from a story by Sneddon purporting to give a typical
specimen of East Side New Yorkese.

[Slang.] (T. P's weekly. London, March
29, 1912. f°. v. 19, p. 393.)   * DA
Supplements the remarks of William Archer on the
slang expressions used by Arnold Bennett in his play
"Milestones." Bennett replied that he obtained his
slang by poring through all the numbers of *Punch*
for the year 1860, which was the period background
of the play.

LOUNSBURY, THOMAS RAYNESFORD.
Americanisms, real or reputed. (Harper's
monthly magazine. New York, Sept., 1913.
8°. v. 127, p. 586–592.)   * DA
"Nationality is a hard, almost an impossible thing
to disguise." The Englishman and the American do
use different words to convey the same meanings.
The English novelists seldom put American speech
into the mouths of their American characters. Haliburton's character, Sam Slick, of Onion county, Connecticut, gave the English a great store of pseudo-
Americanisms, and they have drawn from it freely.
The work of John Witherspoon is recounted at some
length.

Differences in English and American usage.
(Harper's magazine. New York, July, 1913.
8°. v. 127, p. 274–280.)   * DA
"To set off the speech of the illiterate American
against the speech of the cultivated Englishman is as
unscientific as it would be to set off the speech of the
London cockney against that of the cultivated American." Lexicographers in this country have thrown
almost every word they could find into their dictionaries
and labelled them Americanisms without much study,
and Englishmen assume that our daily speech is made
up of such words. Prof. Lounsbury believes that a
dictionary of legitimate Americanisms would make a
very thin volume indeed.

Linguistic causes of Americanisms. (Harper's
monthly magazine. New York, June, 1913. 8°.
v. 127, p. 133–139.)   * DA
The tendency for words to pass from one part of
speech to another creates much of our slang, and the
expressions known as Americanisms. The use of "ad-
vocate" and "progress" as verbs created quite a controversy as far back as the time of Webster and
Franklin. The same is true of "degenerate," "test,"
and "deed" when used as verbs.

Scotticisms and Americanisms. (Harper's
magazine. New York, Feb., 1913. 8°. v. 126,
p. 417–424.)   * DA
The emeritus professor of English, at Yale University, makes a few remarks on the hostility of
lexicographers towards neologisms. Hume tried to rid
his speech of Scotticisms, and made a list of words
to be avoided. Some of them were not Scotticisms
at all. Scotticisms have been freely adopted in America.
The *N. E. D.* is praised for its attempt to clarify
word origins.

General Works, continued

Twentieth Century — 1911–1920, continued

LOUNSBURY, THOMAS RAYNESFORD, *continued*

What Americanisms are not. (Harper's magazine. New York, March, 1913. 8°. v. 126, p. 618–624.)   *DA

The idea that the American Revolution was the precursor of a linguistic separation from England was soon exploded. Technical and scientific words have been labelled as Americanisms simply because they happened to be invented by Americans. The words of science are international. Considerable space is given to the word "female," and a few errors of lexicographers pointed out.

LOW, SIR SIDNEY JAMES MARK.
[Americanisms.] (Westminster Gazette. London, 1913.)

See H. L. Mencken, *The American language*, New York: A. A. Knopf, 1936, p. 36–37, *M. R. R. Desk.*

LUCAS, EDWARD VERRALL.
Of slang — English and American. (In his: Cloud and silver. New York: George H. Doran Co., 1916. 12°. p. 94–100.)   NCZ

English slang is seldom descriptive. American slang applies and illustrates. "American slang very often is poetry." Criticizes English rhyming slang, and gives some horrid examples.

McKNIGHT, GEORGE HARLEY.
Slang and the King's English. (The Nation. New York, Sept. 14, 1918. 4°. v. 107, p. 296.)   *DA

Letter to the editor praising the use of slang by President Wilson, Lloyd George, Lord Northcliffe, and others.

MATTHEWS, BRANDER.
American English and British English. (Harper's magazine. New York, Nov., 1920. 8°. v. 68, p. 621–626.)   *DA

Our standards of speech are "first of all personal; secondly, local and sectional; and thirdly, national." The list of Americanisms in Baedeker's *Guide to the United States* is hardly adequate. Thinks that much of the so-called antagonism between Americans and British anent the language divergencies is "poppycock."

Reprinted in his *Essays on English*, New York: Charles Scribner's Sons, 1921, p. 61–77, *RNB.*

The art of making new words. (The Unpopular review. New York, Jan. – March, 1918. 8°. v. 9, p. 58–69.)   *DA

Reflections on the lexicographer's task in selecting words from the welter of technical terminology. The bugbear of usage is mentioned. Vaugelas says: "There is only one master of language, who is the king and tyrant; that is usage." Origins of some slang and technical words are given. The author confesses that he coined the words "osteocephalic" and "short-story."

The latest novelties in language. (Harper's monthly magazine. New York, June, 1920. 8°. v. 141, p. 82–87.)   *DA

"Where do all the new words come from?... Huxley manufactured 'agnostic'... But where did 'jazz' come from? Who was responsible for this fit name for misfit music?" Other words are traced. Mentions the linguistic device known as "back-formation," verbs back-formed from nouns, such as "to burgle" from burglar, "to buttle" from butler.

MEARNS, HUGHES.
Our own, our native speech. (McClure's. New York, Oct., 1916. 4°. v. 47, p. 87.)   *DA

Contrasts American speech with English and French, and shows amazement and enthusiasm in "attaboy" and other liaison words.

Reprinted in part in *Literary digest*, New York, Sept. 30, 1916, v. 53, p. 848, 850, *DA.*

MENCKEN, HENRY LOUIS.
The American: his language. (Smart set. New York, August, 1913. 8°. v. 40, p. 89–96.)   8–NBA

Scores the "clumsy English of the pundits" and appeals to the schools to teach an American grammar which would permit the usage of yourn, ourn, stang, knowed, throwed, etc. Cites numerous Americanisms to prove their advantage over similar terms in British speech. Gives fifty slang expressions for whiskers. The tendency to reduce grammar to common sense is hampered on all sides by the conservative attitude of school teachers.

The American language. A preliminary inquiry into the development of English in the United States. New York: Alfred A. Knopf, 1919. 374 p. 8°.   8–RNB

First edition. This copy is no. 277 of a limited edition of 1,500.

This widely discussed work, despite the author's insistence that it is but a preliminary inquiry, stands as the most comprehensive work on the subject of American speech emanating from a single pen. Mencken has eschewed the pedantic terminology so often associated with works of this kind and has produced a readable volume. He traces the development of American speech from colonial days to the present, and holds to the theory throughout that American speech has an indigenous quality and that it is developing independently of the so-called standard English, and that our environment, our mental habits, etc., have produced an American language destined to diverge from English more and more. He gives a list of American expressions side by side with English ones, p. 97–101; there is a chapter on slang, p. 304–312; an imposing bibliography, p. 323–339; and a list of words and phrases, p. 340–367. H. L. Mencken, in addition to this work, has written a number of newspaper and magazine articles on the "American Vulgate" over a period of many years. As editor of *The American mercury* he added not a little to the picturesque vocabulary of post-war America, drawing to his banner writers noted for their ability to handle the "Americanese."

Reviewed in *Atlantic monthly*, Boston, July, 1919, Bookshelf (T. L. H.), * *DA; The Bookman*, New York, Dec., 1921, v. 54, p. 361–363 (William McFee), * *DA; Current opinion*, New York, June, 1919, v. 66, p. 390–392, * *DA; Boston Transcript*, April 2, 1919, p. 2, * *A; The Nation*, New York, May 3, 1919, v. 108, p. 698, * *DA; New republic*, New York, May 31, 1919, v. 19, p. 155–156 (F. H.), * *DA; New York Times*, March 30, 1919, section viii, p. 157, col. 2 (Brander Matthews), * *A; North American review*, Boston, May, 1919, v. 209, p. 697–703 (Lawrence Gilman), * *DA; Book review digest*, New York, 1919, v. 15, p. 345, *Pub. Cat.; English journal*, Chicago, May, 1919, v. 8, p. 337–339 (Clarence Stratton), *RNA; Modern language notes*, Baltimore, June, 1919, v. 34, p. 379–383 (J. W. B.), *RAA; Journal of English and Germanic philology*, Urbana, Ill., 1919, v. 18, p. 480–483 (George O. Curme), *RKA; Modern philology*, Chicago, Sept., 1919, v. 17, p. 118–119 (James Root Hulbert), *NAA; Archiv für das Studium der neueren Sprachen und Literaturen*, Braunschweig, 1921, Bd. 141, p. 181–198, Bd. 145, p. 298–299 (Georg Kartzke), *RAA; Literary digest international book review*, New York, April, 1924, v. 2, p. 341–343 (Enrique Blanco), *NAA; Saturday review*, London, March 25, 1922, v. 133, p. 313–314, * *DA; Queen's quarterly*, Kingston, Ontario, April/June, 1923, v. 30, p. 353–362 (Henry Alexander), * *DA; Yale review*, New Haven, July, 1923, new series, v. 12, p. 889–892 (G. Van Santvoord), * *DA; Zeitschrift für französischen und englischen Unterricht*, Berlin, 1923, Bd. 22, p. 154–155, *NAA; The Nation*, London, May 6, 1922, v. 31, p. 193–194, *DA; The Nation*, New York, April 12, 1922, v. 114, p. 430–431 (John Macy), * *DA; Englische Studien*, Leipzig, 1924, Bd. 58, p. 115–119 (Arthur G. Kennedy), *RNA; Times literary supplement*, London, 1922, p. 217–218, *NAA; New English weekly*, London, Oct. 19, 1933, v. 4, p. 9–10 (William Carlos Williams), * *DA; Litteris*, Lund, March, 1925, v. 2, p. 1–7 (O. Jespersen), *RAA.* See also entries for the 1921, 1923, and 1936 editions.

General Works, continued

Twentieth Century — 1911–1920, continued

O'BRIEN, ROBERT J.
Why we should have an American language.
Columbus, Ohio: Heer Printing Co., 1919. 37 p.
"A most patriotic effort." — Kennedy 11628.
Not in The New York Public Library.

PEARSON, EDMUND LESTER.
The cruel and abusive treatment of slang.
(The Nation. New York, Aug. 13, 1914. 4°.
v. 99, p. 189–190.)   *DA
"Does American slang suffer a sea-change in crossing the Atlantic?" Comments on W. J. Ghent's review of J. Redding Ware's *Passing English of the
Victorian era* (q.v.). "To be a maker of a slang
dictionary one must chloroform one's sense of humor
... A slang dictionary and a collection of beautifully mounted dead butterflies are, to me, very much
the same. Slang words and phrases are, in their
own way, as beautiful as moths and butterflies. Their
gay life is on the lips of the people. They are held
captive in literature — and this is not only excusable,
but necessary. But in a dictionary they are smothered,
impaled, dried, and mounted."
The death of Mr. Pearson in 1937 was a great
loss to the compiler. He always had a keen interest
in slang and helped the compiler with scholarly hints.
At the time of his death he was busy finding out
about the life and works of John S. Farmer. Farmer
was a prolific lexicographer and editor, but there is
very little biographical information available. The compiler would appreciate any correspondence which would
throw light on this man who contributed so much
to the history of slang.

READ, RICHARD P.
The American language. (New York Sun,
March 7, 1918.)   *A

The American tongue. (New York Sun, Feb.
26, 1918.)   *A

RIVERS, JOHN.
What is slang? (The Academy. London,
April 12, 1913. 4°. v. 84, p. 465–466.) *DA
"The essential difference between dialect and slang
is that the former is a property of words, the latter
of ideas; one is on the lips, the other is in the mind.
A slang phrase is a metaphor of limited significance.
This limitation may be in time, in place, or in both.
If in time, we may call it topical or ephemeral, and
if in place, local or professional slang."

SCOTT, FRED NEWTON.
The standard of American speech. (The English journal. Chicago, Jan., 1917. 8°. v. 6,
p. 1–11.)   RNA
The prevailing opinion has been that American
speech is a degraded form of English. Henry James
and Rudyard Kipling have fostered this idea. "The
idea that somewhere, in some linguistic British Utopia,
there exists a standard English which all cultured
Englishmen use alike and cannot help but use, and to
which distracted Americans may resort for chastening
and absolution, is a pleasing hallucination, which a
single glance into Mr. Henry Sweet's *Primer of spoken
English* should have dissipated forever."
Reprinted in his *The Standard of American speech,
and other essays*, Boston: Allyn and Bacon, 1926.
Reviewed in *American speech*, Baltimore, 1926, v. 1,
p. 618–619 (A. G. Kennedy), *RNA; Quarterly journal
of speech education*, Chicago, Nov., 1926, v. 12, p. 384–
385 (Everett L. Hunt), *NANA; American mercury*,
New York, Oct., 1926, v. 9, p. 255 (H. L. Mencken),
DA; Modern language notes, Baltimore, Dec., 1926,
v. 41, p. 557–558 (Kemp Malone), *RAA; Times
literary supplement*, London, June 10, 1926, p. 390,
NAA.

SECHRIST, FRANK KLEINFELTER.
The psychology of unconventional language.
(The Pedagogical seminary. Worcester, Mass.,
Dec., 1913. 8°. v. 20, p. 413–459.)   SSA
The most satisfying study of the psychology of
slang in English. Traces the history of slang, defines
it, classifies it, gives examples. The speech of children receives special attention. A bibliography is given.
"Conventional language is the language of confederated
groups. Slang rises in limited groups whose contact
with the world is necessarily immediate, and intimate...
It is the language of social intercourse rather than
that of written communication and books. The sources
of unconventional language lie deep and its power
is irresistible as a force of nature. It is the individual
speaking from the racial substratum, while conventional
language is the language of expediency, of social deference, and reverence of the past... The rise of the
unconventional is due to the play impulse; to the desire for secrecy, for economy of effort, for accuracy,
and for reality."

SLANG as a democratic agent. (Literary digest.
New York, July 21, 1917. f°. v. 55, p. 29.) *DA
Digest of the comment in *Reedy's Mirror* on a slang
article in *The London Morning Post*, on the amazement of the English over the war slogans of America.
Excerpts are also made from an article in the Atlanta *Constitution* which shows how war popularizes
slang.

"SOME" American slang. (The New York dramatic mirror. New York, April 29, 1914. f°.
v. 71, p. 4.)   *T–*DA
Cyril Maude's impressions of American slang.
"Four-flusher" and "stunt" intrigued him.

SPEAKING American in England. (Literary digest. New York, June 21, 1919. f°. v. 61, p. 31.)
                                         *DA
Digest of an article which appeared originally in
the London *Daily Mail*. American slang is praised
for its picturesque imagination and pointedness. "English never was rigid, and there are some who think
it is receiving added vitality from American slang
through the medium of the films."

SQUIRE, SIR JOHN COLLINGS.
A parody in slang. (In his: Books in general.
By Solomon Eagle [J. C. Squire]. New York:
A. A. Knopf, 1919. 12°. p. 150–151.)   NCZ
A clipping cut from "some American newspaper
before the war" gives Heine's *Lorelei* in slang. The
spelling "booze-parlour," which appears in the poem,
seems to indicate an English rather than an American
paper.

TITTERTON, W. R.
Locke on the understanding. Should American slang be barred? (Bookman's journal &
print collector. London, Oct. 22, 1920. 4°.
v. 2, p. 419.)   *IAA
A shocked comment on W. J. Locke's proposal that
there be a marriage between the English and American
tongues. "The Americans are a great people. They invented wooden nutmegs, nigger ragtime, and the
League of Nations... Every country has the language
it deserves. This is a hard saying, but America has
brought it on herself... We shall not bar the door to
American slang unless we bar the door to American
drama."

To teach the American tongue in Britain. (Literary digest. New York, Aug. 9, 1913. f°. v. 47,
p. 212–213.)   *DA
Sir Sidney Low, writing in the *Westminster Gazette*,
laments the fact that the American language is not
taught in the English schools along with French and
German and Hindustani. He searched the bookstalls
in vain to find "How to learn American in three
weeks" or some similar compendium. He points out
some samples of American speech and shows how they
fall on deaf ears of Englishmen unless a glossary is
attached.

General Works, continued

Twentieth Century — 1911–1920, continued

WEBER, CARL JEFFERSON.
Do we speak English? (North American review. Boston, Jan., 1918. 8°. v. 107, p. 91–101.)
* DA
Reflects the opinion that it takes a trip to the mother country really to convince Americans that they do not speak English. Americans are too prone to consult so-called authorities. They are slaves to the dictionary habit, and believe in the finality of any definition they find in print. The writer claims that the dictionaries are conservative, and that they follow rather than lead usage. The dictionary fiend is quite likely to use archaic, obsolete, and conservative words. "At some future date, the American schoolboy may have as great difficulty in reading Kipling and Bernard Shaw as the college student of today experiences in reading Beowulf." Numerous Americanisms are given.

1921–1930

ABBATT, WILLIAM.
Popular phrases and quotations not found in "Bartlett" or "Norton." (In his: The colloquial who's who. Tarrytown: W. Abbatt, 1924. 8°. v. 1, p. 87–95.)   Ref. Cat. 187
Not exclusively American sayings. Some are very striking, such as "Missouri nightingale" for mule, and "Taunton turkey" for herring, and "Hudson county warblers" for mosquitoes.

AMERICAN ACADEMY OF ARTS AND LETTERS. —
EVANGELINE WILBOUR BLASHFIELD FOUNDATION.
Academy papers. Addresses on language problems of members of the American Academy of Arts and Letters... New York: Charles Scribner's Sons, 1925. 282 p. 8°.
RNA (American)
Contents: English and Englistic, by Paul Elmore More; The American Academy and the English language, by William Milligan Sloane; The Academy and the language, by William Crary Brownell; The English language and the American Academy, by Brander Matthews; The Academy and the language, by Bliss Perry; The American language, by Paul Shorey; The fringe of words, by Henry Van Dyke; Style, by William Crary Brownell; "The glory of words," by Robert Underwood Johnson.
Slang and Americanisms figure prominently in these addresses. The address by Paul Shorey is the longest, and devotes itself exclusively to the Anglo-British quarrel over language, and the effects of American slang on the British.
Reviewed in *The Independent,* New York, Dec. 5, 1925, v. 115, p. 647 (Ernest Boyd), * DA; *New York Times,* Jan. 3, 1926, p. 9; *New York Tribune,* Nov. 29, 1925, p. 9; *Saturday review of literature,* New York, Dec. 12, 1925, v. 2, p. 413, † *NAA.*

"AMERICAN" as she is spoke. (The Literary digest. New York, May 17, 1924. f°. v. 81, p. 30.)   * DA
Remarks on Robert Bridges' opinion on H. L. Mencken's statement that America is drawing away from England linguistically. An article from the Portland *Oregonian* on Bridges and Mencken is digested, and reference is made to a series of articles on the standardization of the English language, written by Robert Donald, former editor of the London *Daily Chronicle.*

AMERICAN made easy. An amusing book on transatlantic slang. (John o' London's weekly. London, May 9, 1925. f°. v. 13, p. 182.)   * DA
Review of *Spoken in jest* by "Chadets," published by Hutchinson, 1925. A glossary is given. American and British slang is given in parallel columns.

AMERICAN slang as Paris sees it. (The New York Times. Nov. 3, 1929, section 9, p. 20, col. 1.)   * A
The Times said that the article first appeared in *Transition,* an American magazine published in Paris, and was then reprinted in *The Manchester Guardian.* Over a hundred words are given.
A writer in the *New York Mirror,* Nov. 5, 1929, says: "Its history follows: In the *N. Y. Sunday World* of May 5, first: 'Transition,' the intellectual magazine of Paris lifted it, sans credit. A few months later the *Manchester (Eng.) Guardian* burgled it without saying where it got it, and then *The Times* took it and called it 'American slang as Paris sees it.'... In fewer words it is not American slang 'as Paris sees it' at all, but slang as a New York newspaperman named Theodore D. Irwin sees it."

ARE we colonials in our speech? (The Literary digest. New York, Jan. 8, 1927. f°. v. 92, p. 27.)   * DA
Comment on Sidney Howard's article in the New York *Sun* on the subject of the English language, occasioned by charges in London that our plays were colonial and filled with atrocious barbarisms. He disagrees with H. L. Mencken that America is developing a speech of her own. "London, naturally and inevitably looks on us as mischievous linguistic children. We had better get over the teachings of our amateur patriot philologists and remember that London is our true linguistic mother."

BELL, RALCY HUSTED.
Slang. (In his: The mystery of words. New York, Philadelphia [etc.]: Hinds, Hayden, & Eldredge [1924]. 12°. p. 109–124.)   RAB
An elegant apostrophe to the spirit of slang.

"BETTER in himself." (The Spectator. London, Oct. 22, 1921. f°. v. 127, p. 520–521.)   * DA
Americans do not understand this expression. On the other hand Englishmen understand very few American slang words. "American slang seems to be in a constant state of flux... We have fewer of these national evanescent verbal delights."

BONNER, G. H.
Slang: its use and misuse. (The Nineteenth century and after. London, Dec., 1924. 8°. v. 96, p. 833–842.)   * DA
Slang is creative. Men are the greatest inventors of guage." Slang grows from the "hatred of repetition." It springs from "the impulse to make an impression." Slang is creative. Men are the greatest inventors of slang — being more creative. Slang falls into six main classes: (1) Words which become slang by metonymy; (2) Metaphorical slang; (3) The onomatopœic, or alliterative; (4) Abbreviations; (5) Words of foreign origin; (6) Words which are used more or less arbitrarily, such as rhyming slang.
Over a hundred words are given. "Slang terms are not applied to that which is truly beautiful, but only to that which is pretentious and pompous. Man in his present condition cannot live always on the heights, and so in ordinary life...slang has its place. But to introduce it where it does not belong is an error in artistry."

BRADLEY, HENRY.
The collected papers of Henry Bradley. With a memoir by Robert Bridges. Oxford: At the Clarendon Press, 1928. x, 296 p. 8°.   NDH
Slang, p. 145–156. This is reprinted from Bradley's contribution to the *Encyclopedia britannica,* 11th ed., v. 25, p. 207–210. Bradley was one of the editors of the *O. E. D.*
Reviewed in the *Times literary supplement,* London, May 31, 1928, p. 408, *NAA; Modern language review,* Cambridge, Oct., 1928, v. 23, p. 477–481 (H. C. Wyld), *NAA; Oxford magazine,* Oxford, Nov. 29, 1928, p. 251 (H. T. McM. Buckhurst), *STK; Review of English studies,* July, 1929, v. 5, p. 371–374 (A. W. Reed), *RNA; Commonweal,* London, April, 1929, v. 9, p. 661–662, *TIQA; Antiquity,* Gloucester, Dec., 1929, v. 3, p. 499–500, *MTA.*

General Works, continued

Twentieth Century — 1921–1930, continued

BRADLEY, HENRY, AND G. P. KRAPP.
Slang. (In: Encyclopedia britannica. 14th edition. London: Encyclopedia Britannica, 1929. 4°. v. 20, p. 765–770.) * R–*AL
The short historical sketch is based on Bradley's earlier article, but Professor Krapp has added to the bibliography, and has included four selected glossaries of slang, namely: British slang, British war slang, American slang, and Australian slang.

A BRITON concedes our language. (The Literary digest. New York, May 6, 1922. f°. v. 73, p. 36–37.) * DA
Digests an article by E. B. Osborn in the London *Morning Post.* "The Americans have always coined new words and similitudes much faster and with more audacity than we do, and the result is that we really need a guide to their speech and grammar, such as Mr. H. L. Mencken, who has just published a revised edition of his famous treatise — a much more entertaining work than any lexicon that was ever compiled, not excepting Dr. Johnson's."

BROCKELHURST, J. H.
Slang, and pamphlet no. XXIV of the Society for Pure English on American slang. (Manchester Literary Club. Papers. Manchester, 1928. 8°. v. 53, p. 247–267.) NAA
Using Prof. Fred Newton Scott's pamphlet as a beginning, the author enlarges upon the question of American slang, showing a firmer grasp upon the subject than is usually shown by British critics. Most of the words are of post-war coinage, and English equivalents are given when they exist.

BROWN, BARBARA.
The great American language. (Outlook and independent. New York, Nov. 12, 1930. 8°. v. 156, p. 417, 435.) * DA
Amusing memories of an American in Paris; a few samples of the foreigner's bewilderment when he comes in contact with American slang for the first time.

BBOWN, STEPHEN JAMES MEREDITH.
Metaphor in common speech. (In his: The world of imagery. London, 1927. 8°. p. 257–279.) NADD
Most of the homely metaphor of common speech is slang. Numerous examples are given, chiefly from modern slang. A lengthy extract from Krapp's *The English language in America,* dealing with slang, is appended as Note A, p. 275–278.

Metaphor in every-day speech. (Thought. New York, Dec., 1926. 8°. v. 1, p. 445–457.) * DA
Slang as metaphor is discussed on p. 451–453. Quotes from G. K. Chesterton and Joseph Vendryes who have written on the metaphorical nature of slang.

BUCKHURST, HELEN THÉRÈSE MCMILLAN.
Some recent Americanisms in standard English. (American speech. Baltimore, Dec., 1925. 4°. v. 1, p. 159–160.) RNA
England slowly absorbs the more conservative Americanisms, particularly those which have no satisfactory English counterpart. For example: "jazz," "cocktail," "sundae."

BURKE, THOMAS.
The outer circle; rambles in remote London. London: George Allen and Unwin, Ltd. [1921.] 221 p. 12°. COB (London)
Modern rhyming slang is criticized. Dekker's cant is commented upon, p. 209–213.

BURTON, RICHARD.
Why do you talk like that? Indianapolis: Bobbs-Merrill Company [cop. 1929]. 294 p. 12°. RND
Contains much information about slang and its use. Important chapters include: British or American English? p. 70–88; English as she is spoke, p. 101–111; Calling a spade a spade, p. 89–100 (verbal taboos); High-sounding words: an American tendency, p. 124–136 (mostly slang); Clipped words, p. 213–223.

CARNOY, ALBERT JOSEPH.
The semasiology of American and other slangs. (Leuvensche Bijdragen. 1921. v. 13, p. 49–68, 181–212.)
Kennedy 12385.
A technical analysis filled with philological jargon, but highly important as a scientific approach.
Copy in Columbia University Library.

CATLIN, GEORGE EDWARD GORDON.
The American language. (New republic. New York, May 8, 1929. f°. v. 58, p. 335.) * DA
A letter criticizing a statement by Virginia Woolf that the English and American languages are different tongues.
Herbert G. Purchase adds further comment in a letter to the same magazine, May 22, 1929, v. 59, p. 26.

CHAMPION DE CRESPIGNY, SIR CLAUDE, 4TH BART.
American and English. (American speech. Baltimore, June, 1926. 4°. v. 1, p. 490–494.) RNA
Disagrees with H. L. Mencken's statement that the American language is different from the English language. The academic and technical literature is the same, but an American "will find it just as hard to understand W. W. Jacobs as an Englishman to understand George Ade or Ring Lardner."

THE COMMON speech of America. (The Catholic world. New York, March, 1925. 8°. v. 120, p. 825–826.) * DA
An observation on the so-called standard-speech of America, by way of reviewing the writings of H. L. Mencken, Ring Lardner, and others.

COWDEN, R. W.
Slanging English words. (The English journal. Chicago, Nov., 1925. 8°. v. 14, p. 697–706.) RNA
"Slang should also be distinguished from dialect. The natural speech of a people is the dialect. The American's use of 'elevator' where the Englishman uses 'lift' is essentially a dialect use... The strangest source of confusion, however, lies in linking slang and profanity... Profanity has a scalding quality unknown to slang... Slang does not as a usual thing bring new words into the language but rather contents itself with the full form or the modification of old symbols... The old word is not slang but it may be 'slanged.' 'Dumb' and 'bell' in the meaning of 'dumbbell' have been slanged." The author seeks answers to the three questions: "First, What is done when a word is slanged? Second, Why are words slanged? and third, What effect does slanging have upon a word?"

CURTISS, PHILIP EVERETT.
The psychology of tripe. (Harper's magazine. New York, Aug., 1929. 8°. v. 159, p. 385–388.) * DA
Reflections on such terms as "tripe," "bologny," "raspberry," "good egg," "bad egg," etc., and their psychological implications.

General Works, continued

Twentieth Century — 1921–1930, continued

EINENKEL, EUGEN.
London slang. (Anglia. Halle, 1928. 8°. Bd.
52, p. 192.) RNA
A note on George Bernard Shaw's *Captain Brass-
bound's conversion*. Shaw, in his notes to this play,
had a few words to say on London dialect.

ENGLAND deluged by American slang. (The
Literary digest. New York, March 16, 1929.
f°. v. 100, p. 23.) *DA
The *Manchester Guardian* held a slang contest to
decide which were the six most expressive slang
phrases. It was found that American slang predominated. Some samples are given.

THE ENGLISH Big Six. (The New York Times.
Feb. 10, 1929, section 3, p. 4, col. 4.) *A
Editorial comments on the *Manchester Guardian's*
contest to find the six most expressive slang phrases.

ENGLISH has pitfalls for the tourist. (Writer's
monthly. Springfield, Mass., Oct., 1927. 8°.
v. 30, p. 335–337.) *IH
Points out the difference between common English and American words for everyday things which
confuse the American tourist. Reprinted from the
New York *Times Magazine*.

FASHIONS in slang. (The World's work. New
York, Nov., 1929. 4°. v. 58, p. 40.) *DA
Expresses the hope that the meeting in New
Haven of representatives from fifty American uni-
versities, for the purpose of laying a plan for the
scientific study of American dialects, will include
American slang.

FOSTER, HELEN HERBERT.
Lazy man's language. (World review.
Chicago, March 11, 1929. f°. v. 8, p. 91.) *DA
Quotes Robert Underwood Johnson, of the Ameri-
can Academy of Arts and Letters, and Dr. Johnson
(Boswell's) to the effect that slang is to be avoided by
cultivated people. Only the lazy intellects employ slang
words.

"The sideshow of speech." (The World review. Chicago, March 4, 1929. f°. v. 8, p. 78–
79.) *DA
Defence of slang. Quotes a good deal from Frank
H. Vizetelly.

FOWLER, HENRY WATSON.
A dictionary of modern English usage...
Oxford: Clarendon Press, 1926. viii, 742 p.
12°. M. R. R. Desk
See the instructive paragraph under the heading
"jargon," p. 307–308. A few slang words may be
found here and there in the dictionary which is a
lexicographical delight.
For the best account of Fowler see "H. W. Fowler," by G. G. Coulton, in Society for Pure English,
Tract no. 43, Oxford, 1934, p. 97–158, *RNA*. This
article contains several good photographic likenesses
of Fowler.

FRANZ, WILHELM.
Amerikanisches und britisches Englisch.
(In: Festschrift Friedrich Kluge zum 70. Ge-
burtstage. Tübingen, 1926. 8°. p. 29–39.) RK
Points out the difference between American and
British speech, with emphasis on the deliberate bad
grammar of writers like Ring Lardner and other
American humorists. "Sam Slick" is drawn upon,
and Galsworthy's *Strife* and Herbert Jenkins's *Bindle*
are also used as examples.

GALSWORTHY, JOHN.
On expression. [Oxford: The Oxford Uni-
versity Press,] 1924. 18 p. 8°. (The English
Association. Pamphlet no. 59.)
NADB p.v.13,no.10
Introduces a few paragraphs on slang, Ameri-
canisms, and the cockney dialect, p. 7–9.

GAY, ROBERT MALCOLM, EDITOR.
Fact, fancy and opinion; examples of present
day writing. Boston: Atlantic Monthly Press
[1923]. xix, 393 p. 12°. NCY
Includes an article from the New York *Sun* entitled "Curiosities of American speech," p. 155–158.
This is based on a volume of *Dialect notes*.

GLICKSMAN, HARRY.
Gesture-language. (The English journal.
Chicago, Oct., 1924. 8°. v. 12, p. 564–566.)
RNA
"Anyone who has taken the pains must have
observed, within the past few years, let us say since
1910, the increasing dependence, among all classes of
people, upon the bare theatrical mechanics of speech —
the gestures and jazz, in other words, of vocal expression."

GODWIN, MURRAY.
The American slanguage. (Irish statesman.
Dublin, Oct. 9, 1926. f°. v. 7, p. 106–107.)
*DA
A letter written to the editor, attacking the British
attitude towards the American language with violent
humor.

GRANDGENT, CHARLES HALL.
Here either. (In his: Prunes and prism...
Cambridge: Harvard University Press, 1928.
8°. p. 39–48.) NBQ
A general essay on slang, how it starts, and how it
falls by the wayside or reaches dictionary respect-
ability. The slang psychology of the British and the
Americans is compared.

GREIG, JOHN YOUNG THOMSON.
Breaking Priscian's head; or, English as
she will be spoke and wrote... New York: E.
P. Dutton & Co. [cop. 1929.] 96 p. 16°. RN
On p. 68–96 there is an account of the richness of
the English language through its borrowings and
word-coining. "The attitude now fashionable in the
educated classes of England towards all Americanisms
in speech is smug and ill-informed." Lists a number
of racy Americanisms. "Good slang, that is virile and
expressive slang, is irresistible... And since the slang
coined from year to year in England is, most of it
...feeble stuff when compared with the output
of America, it is to America that we must chiefly
look in future for this replenishment and freshening
of our language."

HARMON, LUCY.
A study of the vocabulary of Carl Sandburg.
1926.
Master's thesis in the English Department of the
University of Chicago. Contains much slang.
Typewritten.

HEARN, EDMOND.
A blurb for slang. (American speech. Baltimore, Dec., 1928. 4°. v. 4, p. 95–97.) RNA
Uses slang in a defence of slang. "A bloke who
described himself as a sugar daddy once puzzled me
by complaining that he had been given the raspberry
by a dizzy blonde."

General Works, continued

Twentieth Century — 1921–1930, continued

HELM, CARL.
An Englishman censors American speech. (The World today. London, March, 1929. 8°. v. 53, p. 367–372.) * DA
A sketch of the life and work of Dr. Frank H. Vizetelly, editor of the *Standard dictionary*. He "bears an Italian name and was born in England, and educated in France... Dr. Vizetelly traces his ancestry back to Venetian glassmakers." The Vizetellys became master printers in England. The lexicographer came to New York in 1891. He soon got a job with Benjamin Funk. In 1912 he succeeded Isaac Funk as editor of the *Standard dictionary*. A few terms picked from the dictionary are discussed.

HILLS, ELIJAH CLARENCE.
New words in California. (Modern language notes. Baltimore, March, 1923. 4°. v. 38, p. 187–188.) RAA
Explanation of the "irradiation" of Bréal, who held that some word endings have come accidentally to denote certain ideas. In California "teria," "ery" and "atorium" have become the rage. Hence "marketeria," "doughnutery," "healthatorium," etc.

JACKDAW, PSEUD.
The way they talk over there. (John o' London's weekly. London, Dec. 10, 1927. f°. v. 18, p. 360.) * DA
Essay on American slang based on an article by Frank H. Vizetelly, written by Donald Parker. Other articles by Jackdaw on the subject of slang may be found here and there in *John o' London's weekly*.

KARPF, FRITZ.
Neuere Werke über das amerikanische Englisch. (Die Neueren Sprachen. Marburg in Hessen, 1928. 8°. Bd. 36, p. 514–518.) RAV
Criticism of recent works by Sir William Craigie, Fred Newton Scott, Johann Alfred Heil, Otto Jespersen, G. P. Krapp, and others.

KARTZKE, GEORG.
Die Amerikanische Sprache. (Archiv für das Studium der neueren Sprachen und Literaturen. Braunschweig und Berlin, 1921. 8°. Bd. 141, p. 181–198.) RAA
A survey of American speech from colonial times to the present. Chiefly a review of H. L. Mencken's *The American language*. Gives several hundred Americanisms.

KAY, LLOYD.
Slang as it was and is. (Writer's monthly. Springfield, Mass., Aug., 1921. 8°. v. 18, p. 122–125.) * IH
A slang writer defends his craft, and finds solace in the fact that Shakespeare made free use of slang.

KENNEDY, ARTHUR GARFIELD.
Hothouse words versus slang. (American speech. Baltimore, July, 1927. 4°. v. 2, p. 417–424.) RNA
A study of Thomas Blount's *Glossographia*. Takes the words which begin with the letter D, all jawbreaking words, and gives simple meanings. Slang has grown up around these words, like weeds, and smothered them, a circumstance no one regrets. Who would weep at the fall of a word like decacuminate?

KRAPP, GEORGE PHILIP.
The English language in America. New York: The Century Co., 1925. 2 v. 8°. * R–RNZ
Filled with Americanisms, and has a few pertinent remarks on slang. Generally conceded to be an indispensable work for the student of American speech. Professor Krapp of the English Department of Columbia University, devoted many years to the study of our speech habits, and wrote a great deal on the subject. See Elliott V. K. Dobbie, "Bibliography of the writings of George Philip Krapp," *American speech*, New York, 1934, v. 9, p. 252–254, RNA. In the second volume of *The English language in America* there is a bibliography, p. 273–284, and an excellent word list, p. 299–355.
Reviewed in *The Literary digest international book review*, New York, Dec., 1925, v. 4, p. 27–28 (Brander Matthews), * DA; *The Nation*, New York, Nov., 1925, v. 121, p. 599, * DA; *Review of English studies*, London, 1927, v. 3, p. 223–227 (J. H. G. Grattan), RNA; *New York Tribune*, Jan. 10, 1926, p. 5; Boston *Transcript*, Dec. 5, 1925, p. 4; *Catholic world*, New York, 1926, v. 123, p. 106–107, * DA; *Theatre arts monthly*, New York, Feb., 1926, p. 135–137 (C. H. Grandgent), *NBLA; Anglia, Beiblatt*, Halle, Aug., 1926, p. 225–230 (O. Jespersen), RNA; *Saturday review of literature*, New York, June 12, 1926, v. 2, p. 856 (F. P. Magoun), † NAA; *New republic*, New York, Jan. 20, 1926, v. 45, p. 248–250 (John M. Manly), * DA; London *Times Literary supplement*, Jan. 21, 1926, p. 40, NAA; *New York Times*, Feb. 7, 1926, section 3, p. 2, col. 1, * A; *American speech*, Baltimore, March, 1926, v. 1, p. 340–346 (A. G. Kennedy), RNA; *Studia neophilologica*, 1930, v. 2, p. 216–218 (R. E. Zachrisson).

Is American English archaic? (Southwest review. Dallas, summer 1927. 8°. v. 12, p. 292–303.) * DA
"The distinctive thing about an archaism is not that it is old, but that it has survived in certain special aspects of the language, dialectal, poetical, liturgical, technical, after it has passed out of general practice. The slang of yesterday becomes archaic today." Airs the opinion that American English is an Elizabethan survival, and refutes it. This has been a favorite subject among philologists on both sides of the Atlantic. "The great historic changes in the English language have always coincided with periods of folk-wandering and of social disturbance... One cannot prove that English in America is more archaic than English in England by contrasting rustic and provincial American English with cultivated British English... Slang does not in fact manifest itself vigorously in America until the early nineteenth century. It is the child of the new nationalism, the new spirit of joyous adventure that entered American life after the close of the war of 1812."

KUCK, CLARA E.
The American variety. (Theatre and school. Berkeley, Cal., March, 1928. 8°. v. 6, p. 15–17.) MWA
European disdain of the American variety of English arouses the ire of this writer. "The speech of an individual is the immediate index of his refinement and worth." Americans should take pride in correct speech.

LINDSAY, NICHOLAS VACHEL.
The real American language. (American mercury. New York, March, 1928. 8°. v. 13, p. 257–265.) * DA
An interesting account of the American language of the hills and crossroads as encountered by a tramp philologist in his search for beauty and bread. "Wherever there is a touch of Virginia left, there is the United States language."

LITTELL, ROBERT.
Enlarge your vocabulary. (The New republic. New York, Jan. 26, 1927. 4°. v. 49, p. 277–278.) * DA
An odd assortment of slang terms current in America, mostly trade lingo. "Runk," "peglams," "snollops," "plints," "peckstindle," are a few samples.

General Works, continued

Twentieth Century — 1921–1930, continued

LYND, ROBERT.
The King's English and the Prince's American. (New statesman. London, Feb. 4, 1928. f°. v. 30, p. 524–525.)   *DA
Comment on the use of slang in two speeches delivered by the Prince of Wales. "I should like to see England building a high tariff wall against the slang of America, and America building a high tariff wall against the slang of England." Movie films corrupt a language.

McKINSTRY, H. E.
The American language in Mexico. (The American mercury. New York, March, 1930. 8°. v. 19, p. 336–338.)   *DA
Brief discussion of the jargon of the border land between the United States and Mexico, and the gradual infiltration of American words into daily Mexican speech.

McKNIGHT, GEORGE HARLEY.
Conservatism in American speech. (American speech. Baltimore, Oct., 1925. 4°. v. 1, p. 1–17.)   RNA
Noah Webster was one of the first to fight for speech independence in America. The tendency was to ape the English. The writers, schoolmasters, and Tories sought to uphold the conventional. W. D. Howells and Henry James preserved this tradition in later years.

English words and their background. New York: D. Appleton & Co., 1923. x p., 1 l., 449 p. 12°.   *R–RNF
American English, p. 23–36. Slang, p. 37–69. These chapters furnish an historical introduction to the subject of unconventional language.

Modern ' English in the making... New York: D. Appleton and Company, 1928. 590 p. 12°.   *R–RN
Contains several cogent remarks on slang and its part in the development of language. See particularly p. 122, 252, 301, 372, 408ff, 507–508, 551–552. Reviewed in *Modern philology*, Chicago, Nov., 1929, v. 27, p. 243, *NAA; American speech*, Baltimore, April, 1929, v. 4, p. 316–318, *RNA; Quarterly journal of the University of North Dakota*, April, 1929, v. 19, p. 327–329, *STG; Times Literary supplement*, London, Feb. 21, 1929, p. 130, *NAA; Saturday review of literature*, New York, Nov. 17, 1928 (George Philip Krapp), *NAA.*

McLOON, WALTER H.
The use of slang in fiction. (Writer's monthly. Springfield, Mass., Jan., 1921. 8°. v. 17, p. 17–19.)   *IH
"The free use of slang in fiction, by either experienced or inexperienced writers, is a thing to be avoided... Nothing changes more quickly than slang. It is essentially a thing of the moment."

MALONE, KEMP.
The International Council for English. (American speech. Baltimore, April, 1928. 4°. v. 3, p. 261–275.)   RNA
An account of the first meeting of the council in London, June, 1927. Comments, mostly unfavorable to America, quoted from the London *Times* of June 20, 1927, the *Nation and Athenæum*, June 25, *The Spectator* of July 2, and the *New statesman* of June 25, draw from the author a defence. The statements are challenging and not to be treated lightly.

MANY books on slang found in New York Public Library. (The New York Times, July 14, 1929, section 10, p. 8, col. 1.)   *A
"The New York Public Library offers wide opportunity for the study of slang and colloquialisms."

MARSHALL, ARCHIBALD.
American speech and English language. (North American review. Boston, Nov., 1921. 8°. v. 214, p. 628–635.)   *DA
"One of the most amusing minor sports to be followed by an Englishman — like myself — travelling in America is to note and discuss the differences of speech and language that have come about between us... It seems to me that it (American educated speech) is distinctly nearer to ours than when I last visited the United States over twenty years ago."
A spirited criticism of the "Exotic Americanisms" listed by Gilbert Tucker in his *American English* is the raison d'être of this article.

MASSEY, W. A.
The divergence of American from English. (American speech. Baltimore, Oct., 1930. 4°. v. 6, p. 1–9.)   RNA
Thinks the new historical dictionary for America will duplicate the *O. E. D.* There is not enough divergence between written words by American and English authors to justify a mammoth new dictionary. What is needed is a dialect dictionary.

MASSON, ROSALINE ORME.
Use and abuse of English... With a preface by the late Professor David Masson. Fourth edition. Revised. Edinburgh: James Thin, 1924. 108 p. 12°.   NAC p.v.150, no.6
Preface to fourth edition, p. xi–xiv, by Rosaline Masson, is confined almost exclusively to the subject of slang. There is a short section on slang, p. 55–56.

MASSON, THOMAS LANSING.
Speech, common and preferred. Word-manufacture in the United States. (Century magazine. New York, Nov., 1926. 8°. v. 113, p. 80–89.)   *DA
Calls attention to our over-refinement in the teaching of English. Thinks our language can be kept alive by the masses and by the creative writers, but not by the academicians. Edna Ferber, H. L. Mencken, Gertrude Stein, Quiller-Couch, and others are quoted. Points out a few clichés and shows the folly of trying to avoid them.
Reprinted in *Essays of today (1926–1927). Selected by Odell Shepard and Robert Hillyer*, New York: Century Co. [1928], p. 19–36, *NBP.*

MATTHEWS, BRANDER.
Essays on English... New York: Charles Scribner's Sons, 1921. 248 p. 12°.   RNB
Contents: 1. Is the English language degenerating? 2. What is pure English? 3. American English and British English. 4. The vicissitudes of the vocabulary. 5. The latest novelties in language. 6. Newspaper English. 7. The permanent utility of dialect. 8. A confusion of tongues. 9. Learning a language. 10. The advertiser's artful aid. 11. A standard of spoken English. 12. Style from several angles. 13. Mark Twain and the art of writing. 14. One world-language or two?
Most of these essays were originally magazine articles.
Reviewed in *The Independent*, New York, Oct. 15, 1921, v. 108, p. 64 (E. L. Pearson), *DA; New York Times*, Oct. 2, 1921, p. 2; *The Dial*, New York, March, 1922, v. 72, p. 328, *DA; Literary review*, New York *Evening Post*, Dec. 3, 1921, p. 224 (Henry Bradley); *Saturday review*, London, March 15, 1922, p. 314–315, *DA; The Spectator*, London, May 6, 1922, v. 128, p. 560–561, *DA.*

General Works, continued

Twentieth Century — 1921–1930, continued

MEIKLEJOHN, M. J. C.
American English. (The Spectator. London,
Aug. 6, 1927. f°. v. 139, p. 212–213.)   *DA
An attempt to prove that many American expressions are old English terms, pure and undefiled.

MENCKEN, HENRY LOUIS.
The American language. An inquiry into the
development of English in the United States.
Second edition. Revised and enlarged. New
York: Alfred A. Knopf, 1921. 492 p. 8°.   RNB
This edition is characterized chiefly by the addition
of samples of the "American Vulgate," and the influence of non-English dialects upon American speech.

The *American* language. (The Freeman. New
York, May 16, 1923. f°. v. 7, p. 222–224.)
*DA
A spirited disagreement with H. L. Mencken's contention that there exists a distinct American language. "The most that can be said for our American
variants is that they show a greater energy and gusto
in speech than the British Islanders...but as yet
there is no promise of equivalent returns in literature."

MENCKEN, HENRY LOUIS.
Americanisms. (Encyclopedia Britannica.
New York: Encyclopedia Britannica Co., 1929.
4°. v. 1, p. 773–775.)   *R–*AL
Gives a short historical survey and a short bibliography. The main part of the article is devoted to
parallel columns of Americanisms with their British
counterparts. Mencken holds that Americans are more
creative in picturesque language, more resourceful.
"Cow-catcher" is better than the English "plough"
and "movie" more direct than "cinema."

Die amerikanische Sprache (das Englisch der
Vereinigten Staaten). Deutsche Bearbeitung
von Heinrich Spies. Leipzig und Berlin: B. G.
Teubner, 1927. viii, 176 p. 8°.   RNB
Reviewed in *Archiv für das Studium der neueren
Sprachen und Literaturen*, Dec., 1928, Bd. 154, p. 299–
303 (K. Brunner), *RAA; Zeitschrift für französischen
und englischen Unterricht*, Bd. 27, p. 555–556 (Oczipka), *NAA; Anglia, Beiblatt*, Feb., 1929, Bd. 40, p. 33–
38 (Fritz Karpf), *RNA; Deutsche Literaturzeitung*,
Berlin, 1930, Folge 3, Jahrg. 1, col. 400–403 (H.
Lüdeke), *NAA*.

"Shooting-the-chutes" with English. (The
World review. Mt. Morris, Ill., Dec. 6, 1926.
f°. v. 3, p. 175.)   *DA
Americans have a penchant for abbreviations: this is
verbal economy, independence, efficiency. Contrasts
signs in English and American institutions. In the
British Museum washroom is the placard: "These
basins are for casual ablutions only." The American
"Stop! Look! Listen!" is a sample of direct English.
Between the two cultures lies a great abyss, two
habits of mind, two rapidly diverging tongues.

MONTAGUE, CHARLES EDWARD.
A living language. (In his: A writer's notes
on his trade. London: Chatto & Windus, 1930.
12°. p. 15–24.)   NAD
"And everybody who loves the language enough to
want to keep it always young and racy ought to turn
out too and keep the pedants from running amuck...
A list of American slang words and phrases should
gladden everyone who delights in the way Elizabethan
English was made... Perfect slang has a cunning
brevity that braces you. It should taste sweet and keen,
like a nut. If it does, it will make its way into that
holy of holies where 'literary' English lives in state.

For this queenly figure has the sagacity of every
successful ruling caste. She does not build the wall
round her fastness too high; and she makes good the
natural losses of her establishment by opening a postern
gate now and then and letting in the pick of the lusty
upstarts of the period."

MOORE, H. E.
American language crucible. (English review. London, Feb., 1925. 8°. v. 40, p. 226–232.)
*DA
Reprinted under the title "The American language"
in *Living age*, New York, Nov., 1925, v. 327, p. 416–
420. *DA*.
"No large nation has as many foreigners as America
... The linguist finds there a modern Babel." Cites
examples of hybrid speech, and discusses American
intellectual background. "One American free-lance
scholar predicts standard English for pedants and
American for the world."

MORGAN, BAYARD QUINCY.
Simile and metaphor in American speech.
(American speech. Baltimore, Feb., 1926. 4°.
v. 1, p. 271–274.)   RNA
"When we examine the figurative expressions in
current use, we are soon struck by the fact that the
great majority of them exhibit one or all of three
tendencies: they strive to be vivid and emphatic, they
try to make a humorous appeal, they are almost universally disparaging." Slang fills the bill.

MUSSER, BENJAMIN FRANCIS.
The fetish of catch phrases. (Catholic world.
New York, June, 1924. 8°. v. 119, p. 301–304.)
*DA
An enquiry into the American habit of phrasemaking. Why do Americans invent such things as:
"keep off the grass," "watch your step," "over the
top," "the three R's," "full dinner pail," "the four
hundred," "sweet sixteen," etc., etc. Conversation
is full of such verbal tags.

A study in American slang. (Catholic world.
New York, July, 1923. 8°. v. 117, p. 471–476.)
*DA
Approves of slang when used intelligently. Gives
numerous examples of good and bad slang, and cites
standard American references on the subject. "All
one should strive for is the ability to discriminate
between cheap vulgarity and respectability."

NATHAN, GEORGE JEAN.
England and the American language. (American mercury. New York, Oct., 1926. 4°. v. 9,
p. 242.)   *DA
England is using more and more Americanisms in
daily speech thanks to the movies, Sinclair Lewis,
Anita Loos, and other writers of best sellers.
A few years ago George Ade's *The College widow*
was unintelligible to the English audience, even with
a glossary.

THE NEW American language. (Forum. New
York, 1927. 8°. Feb., v. 77, p. 265–268; May, v.
77, p. 752–756; Aug., v. 78, p. 271–272; Nov., v.
78, p. 756–757.)   *DA
An open forum for word-coiners. Prizes were
offered for the best creations. Many contributions
were sent in answer to this editorial request for
"needed words" in the American vulgate.

NEW saws for old. (The Nation. New York,
Sept. 4, 1929. 4°. v. 129, p. 240.)   *DA
"The pressure upon modern writers is intense...
The old-time novelist was allowed six pages in which
to describe the weather on the day when his story
opened."
The editorial cry for speed and pep has led to a
wider use of slang and "wise-crackery."

General Works, continued

Twentieth Century — 1921–1930, continued

NICOLSON, MARJORIE HOPE.
"Ici on parle — " (American speech. Baltimore, Feb., 1926. 4°. v. 1, p. 257–263.) RNA
Reviews the commercial words America has borrowed from France, with a few of the errors made in spelling and pronouncing them. Many have been adopted in our English dictionaries.

NOCK, S. A., AND HEINRICH MUTSCHMANN.
Spoken American. Conversations in American on American subjects... Leiden: N. V. Leidsche, 1930. 70 p. 12°. RAE p.v.135, no.4
Contains much slang. The conversations, covering almost every phase of American daily life, were written by S. A. Nock, of Houston, Texas, and the notes were largely the work of H. Mutschmann, professor of English at the University of Dorpat.

OSBORN, EDWARD BOLLAND.
Life, literature, and slang. (John o' London's weekly. London, April 28, 1928. f°. v. 19, p. 79–80.) *DA
Believes that slang keeps a language alive. Speaks of American slang, and goes into the derivations of many slang phrases, old and new, British and American.

OUR wisecracks live fleetingly. (The New York Times. Oct. 13, 1929, section 10, p. 13, col. 6.) *A
An article dealing with the transitory life of "banana oil," "skidoo," "23," etc., with a few current wisecracks.

PAGET, ED. O.
Neue Amerikanismen. (Die Neueren Sprachen. Marburg in Hessen, 1927. 8°. Bd. 35, p. 350–355.) RAV
New American slang words are culled from newspaper headlines, the films, the Volstead Act, etc. An attempt is made to translate them into modern German. Additions to this article were made by H. Mutschmann in *Die Neueren Sprachen*, April, 1928, Bd. 36, p. 203–205.

POLLOCK, F. WALTER.
The current expansion of slang. (American speech. Baltimore, Dec., 1926. 4°. v. 2, p. 145–147.) RNA
Gives examples of the slang in vogue in 1926, choosing many words that seek to disparage, and a few that seek to praise. Slang often invented by the educated mind, although it smacks of the slums.

POUND, LOUISE.
Research in American English. (American speech. Baltimore, June, 1930. 4°. v. 5, p. 359–365.) RNA
An historical account of American speech investigations, beginning with John Witherspoon (1722–94). Opportunities for present-day students to do good work in the field of philology are outlined.

REVES, HAVILAND FERGUSON.
What is slang? A survey of opinion. (American speech. Baltimore, Jan., 1926. 4°. v. 1, p. 216–220.) RNA
Traces the definition of slang from the time it appeared in Webster's Dictionary in 1828, to the present day.
Additions to this article were contributed by Fr. Klaeber in the April, 1926, issue of *American speech*, v. 1, p. 368.
See also entries under Hayward, Arthur C.; Ritter, O.; and Krueger, G.

RHODES, EUGENE MANLOVE.
Say now Shibboleth. (In: Present-day essays. Edited by Edwin Van B. Knickerbocker ... New York: Henry Holt & Company [1923]. 12°. p. 236–261.) NBP
A genial and philosophical revery on speech habits, with a gentle prod at the "purists" who would rob America of its Lincolnesque quality of speech by too much attention to the letter and too little to the spirit of those imaginary laws which regulate our written and spoken intercourse.

ROOF, KATHARINE METCALF.
American slang. (Times literary supplement. London, July 14, 1921, p. 450; July 21, p. 468; July 28, p. 484; Aug. 4, p. 500; Aug. 11, p. 517; Sept. 1, p. 565.) †NAA

SCHAUFFLER, ROBERT HAVEN.
Peter Pantheism. New York: Macmillan Company, 1925. 215 p. 12°. NBQ
"Unborn words," p. 34–61. "There are not nearly enough words to allow us to say what we mean." Americans borrow freely from other languages to make up for this deficiency. Some become slanged. Lists many portmanteau words and neologisms.
"Timesquarese," p. 140–153. Lingo of Times Square newsboys. The language of the newsboy must reach the ear in competition with the many street noises of New York City. Noise has a great influence on the American vulgate. This essay appeared originally in the *Saturday review of literature*, New York, June 13, 1925, v. 1, p. 817–818, †NAA, and was reprinted in *Essays of 1925*, selected by Odell Shepard, and published at Hartford, Conn., by Edwin Valentine Mitchell, 1926, p. 120–127, *NBP*.
Reviewed in Boston *Transcript*, Dec. 12, 1925; *Saturday review of literature*, New York, Dec. 26, 1926, v. 2, p. 451, †NAA; *The Independent*, New York, Dec., 1926, v. 115, p. 743, *DA*.

SCHOCH, ALFRED D., AND R. KRON.
The little Yankee; a handbook of idiomatic American English, treating of the daily life, customs and institutions of the United States; with the vocabulary of the spoken language incorporated in the text. Freiburg, Baden: J. Bielefeld, 1927. 192 p. 16°.
An adaptation of Kron's *Little Londoner*.
Reviewed in *American speech*, Baltimore, Feb., 1928, v. 3, p. 237–239 (Lowry Charles Wimberly), *RNA*.

SCOTT, FRED NEWTON.
American slang. (Society for Pure English. Tract no. XXIV. Oxford: Clarendon Press, 1926. 8°. p. 118–127.) RND
A list of slang words for "British readers who are struggling with the works of Sinclair Lewis and similar contributions to American literature." Some slight corrections by R. W. H. are published in *Tract no. 27*, p. 217–219.
Reprinted in *Emerson quarterly*, Boston, Nov., 1927, v. 8, p. 17–18, 22, 24, 26, †NANA.

English and American vernacular. (McNaught's monthly. London, May, 1925. 4°. v. 3, p. 144–145.) *DA
Speaking of the divergence of the English and American tongues, the hypothesis is advanced that the "degree of divergence between the two vernaculars varies inversely as the degree of importance of the subject matter. That is, when the ideas to be expressed are trivial or facetious, the two vernaculars differ so widely that they may almost be said to be foreign languages one to the other. When, on the other hand, the subject matter is purely practical or commonplace the divergence, though noticeable, is of secondary importance. And, finally, when the subject matter is of the highest quality, being concerned with ideal values and fundamental concepts, the divergence is so slight as to be almost negligible."
See Society for Pure English, *Tract no. 22*, 1925, p. 58–62.

General Works, continued

Twentieth Century — 1921–1930, continued

SCOTT, SAMUEL M.
The American language. (Harvard graduates magazine. Boston, June, 1923. 8°. v. 31, p. 487–494.)   STG (Harvard)
Deplores the defilement of the founts of pure English by the uncultured; and the spread of jargon by the industrial classes, sports writers, and yellow journalists. Expresses fear of the wholesale spread of corrupt English by immigrants.

SCULLY, FRANK.
Slanguaged language. (Variety. New York, Jan. 8, 1930. f°. v. 97, p. 77.)   NAFA
A few slang words are, explained, and a tribute is paid to Jack Conway, "king of American slang writers." What Conway didn't coin himself he borrowed from carnivals and tent shows.

SHOREY, PAUL.
The American language. (In: American Academy of Arts and Letters. — Evangeline Wilbour Blashfield Foundation, Academy papers. Addresses on language problems by members of the American Academy of Arts and Letters... New York: Charles Scribner's Sons, 1925. 8°. p. 127–189.)   RNA
Discusses the "American scholar's game" of discovering Americanisms and American slang in the older English literature. Points out some amusing mystifications of Englishmen over American slang. Other interesting essays appear in this volume. See main entry.
Reviewed by Ernest Boyd in *The Independent,* New York, Dec. 5, 1925, v. 115, p. 647, * DA.

SLANG in evolution. (Literary digest. New York, Feb. 14, 1925. f°. v. 84, p. 28–29.)   * DA
Résumé of an article by Ada Lewis, the character actress. Ada Lewis was an adept at Bowery lingo.

SMITH, MR.
The King's English — and the President's. (The Literary digest international book review. New York, April, 1925. 4°. v. 3, p. 317.)
* DA
Speaks of the "progressive infiltration of Americanisms into British speech." Mentions "highbrow," "joyride," "skyscraper," "bootlegger," etc.

Manhandled Americanisms. (The Literary digest international book review. New York, May, 1926. 4°. v. 4, p. 368.)   * DA
Criticism of John Galsworthy's *Silver spoon.* "Mr. John Galsworthy can write good English, but he writes bad American."

SMITH, LOGAN PEARSALL.
Words and idioms. Studies in the English language... London: Constable & Co., 1925. 299 p. 12°.   RNF
Contents: 1. English sea terms, p. 1–27; 2. The English element in foreign languages, p. 28–65; 3. Four romantic words, p. 66–134; 4. Popular speech and standard English, p. 135–166; 5. English idioms, p. 167–278; Appendix: Somatic idioms, p. 279–292. Index.
The essay on sea terms appeared originally in *The English review,* London, 1912. "English idioms" and "Four romantic words" appeared in the *Tracts of the S. P. E.* in 1922 and 1924, respectively.
"If I may be accused of encouraging or inventing a new vice — the mania, or 'idiomania,' I may perhaps call it — of collecting what Pater called the 'gypsy phrases' of our language, I have at least been punished

by becoming one of its most cureless and incorrigible victims."
Reviewed by Robert Littell in the *New republic,* New York, Oct. 21, 1925, v. 44, p. 235–236, * DA; *New statesman,* London, June 20, 1925, v. 25, p. 286, 288, * DA; *Times literary supplement,* London, July 16, 1925, p. 469–470, NAA; *New York Tribune. Books,* Oct. 4, 1925, p. 9 (G. P. Krapp), † NAA; *Saturday review,* London, May 30, 1925, v. 139, p. 589, * DA; *Saturday review of literature,* New York, Dec. 19, 1925, v. 2, p. 432 (Lowry Charles Wimberly), NAA; *Spectator,* London, May 30, 1925, v. 134, p. 892, Oct. 24, 1925, v. 135, p. 720, * DA; *New York Times Book review,* Sept. 13, 1925, p. 2 (Henry B. Fuller), † NAA; *The Dial,* New York, Jan., 1926, v. 80, p. 59–60 (Kenneth Burke), * DA; *Nation and Athenæum,* London, July 4, 1925, v. 37, p. 431 (Bonamy Dobrée), * DA; *Literary digest. International book review,* New York, March, 1926, v. 4, p. 254–255 (Brander Matthews), * DA; *American mercury,* Baltimore, Sept., 1925, v. 6, p. 126–127 (H. L. Mencken), * DA; *Sewanee review,* Sewanee, Tenn., Jan. – March, 1926, v. 34, p. 128, * DA; *American speech,* Baltimore, May, 1926, v. 1, p. 450–452, RNA; *London mercury,* Oct., 1925, v. 12, p. 661–662, * DA; *Bookman,* London, Oct., 1925, v. 69, p. 28, * DA; *Englische Studien,* 1926, v. 40, p. 322–327 (E. Rosenbach), RNA; *Revue anglo-américaine,* Paris, Oct. – Dec., 1926, v. 4, p. 180 (A. Koszul), * DM.

SPIES, HEINRICH.
Kultur und Sprache im neuen England... Leipzig und Berlin: Verlag von B. G. Teubner, 1925. 216 p. 8°.   RNB
This interesting book on English speech (with emphasis on British rather than on American English) gives a survey of the English studies and language developments of the period 1880–1920. It is well buttressed with bibliographical footnotes. The detailed table of contents and name and subject index facilitate the use of the volume. Parts of interest to the student of slang are: U. S. Englisch und britisches Englisch, p. 50–54; the study of the words "camouflage," "snaffer" and "napoo," p. 68–72; Soldatensprache — War slang, p. 83–91; Der Slang im neuen England, p. 140–143; and the study of the word "swank," p. 172–177.
Reviewed in *Archiv für das Studium der neueren Sprachen und Literaturen,* 1926, Bd. 151, p. 120–125 (K. Brunner), RAA; *Die Neueren Sprachen,* Marburg, 1926, Bd. 34, p. 113–125 (G. Kirchner), RAV; *Literatur,* Berlin, 1926, Bd. 28, p. 556 (A. Ludwig), NAA; *Zeitschrift für französischen und englischen Unterricht,* Berlin, 1926, Bd. 25, p. 377 (W. Preusler), NAA.

STABILIZING Anglo-American speech. (Literary digest. New York, Jan. 28, 1922. f°. v. 72, p. 27–28.)   * DA
Digest of an article by Dean Inge in the *London Evening Standard* concerning the formation of a joint commission to standardize English speech. American variants are pointed out.

STRACHEY, JOHN ST. LOE.
The myth of an American language. (The Independent. New York, May 15, 1926. f°. v. 116, p. 579, 587–588.)   * DA
Strachey's confessed love for American slang does not lead him into the popular belief that America is developing a separate language. He finds much of our language, particularly our legal phraseology, and our theological and philosophical writings, extremely conservative in the accepted British sense.

THOMA, WILHELMINA M.
Slang. (In her: Language in the making. New York: Harcourt, Brace & Co., 1922. 12°. p. 112–117.)   RNF
"There are two kinds of slang, that which is too ephemeral or coarse to survive and that which is a source of vigor to the language." The chapter on "British and American speech," p. 118, 122, lists some of the differences of colloquial expression.

General Works, continued

Twentieth Century — 1921–1930, continued

TOWNE, CHARLES HANSON.
Our passion for haste. (Harper's monthly magazine. New York, Nov., 1924. 8°. v. 149, p. 798–800.) *DA
"The fundamental decencies and niceties of our language are utterly ignored by a new riff-raff who have taken complete possession of the publicity field."
"The truth is that any bit of art is seldom achieved in haste."

TUCKER, THOMAS GEORGE.
British English and American English. (Scribner's magazine. New York, Dec., 1921. 8°. v. 70, p. 730–736.) *DA
"No supreme authority has ever legislated, or ever could effectively legislate, for an immutable English." Only in "smart" fiction and jaunty journalism does the American write a language unintelligible to the British reader. American writers who specialize in slang use it much more freely in their books than they do in ordinary speech, and it is unfair to judge American speech on the exaggerated product of these professional slangsters. This article, a review of Gilbert M. Tucker's *American English*, was written by an emeritus professor of the University of Melbourne.

UNWELCOME Americanisms. (The Literary digest. New York, June 25, 1921. f°. v. 69, p. 25.) *DA
Excerpts from the New York *Evening Post* in praise of William Archer's plea for tolerance on the part of Englishmen towards American slang.

UP from slangery. (Word study. Springfield, Mass., Dec., 1930. 4°. v. 6, p. 4.) RNA
Twelve words of slang origin which have been accepted by the lexicographers as good English. Reprinted from *The Golden book.*

UTTER, ROBERT PALFREY.
The idiom of democracy. (In his: Pearls and pepper... New Haven: Yale University Press, 1924. 8°. p. 61–81.) NQB
"Slang is the boiling surface on the melting-pot of language; we burn our fingers if we try to deal with it without sense of humor and an intimate knowledge of its ways. That is the trouble with international comments on slang — British discussions of American slang, for example. By the time our slang gets to England, the specimens are about as valuable as stuffed birds in a museum. Dissection of a dead form of words does not reveal the vital breath of humor."
Printed originally in *Harper's monthly magazine,* New York, June, 1917, v. 135, p. 66–72, * DA, under the title "Our upstart speech."

VAN DOREN, CARL CLINTON.
Beyond grammar. Ring W. Lardner: philologist among the low-brows. (The Century. New York, July, 1923. 8°. v. 106, p. 471–475.) *DA
A study of American humor as represented in the writings of Ring Lardner, with comment on his utilization of slang.

VIZETELLY, FRANCIS HORACE.
A ramble in the garden of words. The ectoplasm of the Puritans and the incubus of the cavaliers. (American speech. Baltimore, Oct., 1925. 4°. v. 1, p. 32–35.) RNA
An essay on dictionary making and the aims, mistakes, moral background, and short-sightedness of lexicographers.
For a biographical sketch of Dr. Vizetelly see Carl Helm's article, "An Englishman censors American speech," in *The World today,* London, March, 1929, v. 53, p. 367–372, * DA.

VOORHEES, T. V.
Slang. (Educational review. Boston, June, 1926. 8°. v. 72, p. 44–45.) SSA
"We are a nation of phrase-snatching, word-peddling, idea-copying addicts, and slang at its best shows us at our worst."

W. W.
The Anglo-American language. (The New statesman. London, June 25, 1927. 4°. v. 29, p. 341–342.) *DA
An unfriendly account of the International Conference on English, held in London, June 27, 1927. "The only way to preserve the purity of the English language is to present a steadily hostile resistance to every American innovation." J. Y. T. Greig, commenting on this article in his *Breaking Priscian's head,* New York, 1929, p. 71, says: "And, as if to prove that the English have lost none of their notorious smugness in recent years, one 'W. W.' published in the New Statesman, on 25th June, 1927, one of the most arrogantly stupid articles I ever read."

WADE, MARK SWEETEN.
The American language. (Canadian magazine. Toronto, Jan., 1923. 8°. v. 60, p. 218–220.) *DA
Criticizes H. L. Mencken's review, in *The Bookman,* of Gilbert M. Tucker's *American English.* Says there can never be an American language.

WATTS, HARVEY MAITLAND.
The king's English vs. American English. (Philadelphia Forum. July, 1927.)
The compiler has not seen this item.

WEBB, WILLIAM TREGO.
English of to-day. London: G. Routledge & Sons, Ltd., 1925. viii, 198 p. 12°. RND
Colloquialisms, p. 156–160. A few slang expressions are listed.

WEEKLEY, ERNEST.
Americanisms. (In his: Adjectives — and other words. New York: E. P. Dutton and Co., Inc., 1930. 12°. p. 162–183.) RNB
Reprinted from an article in the *Quarterly review,* London, July, 1926, v. 247, p. 140–154, * DA.
This is a review of Mencken's *The American language,* Sinclair Lewis's *Martin Arrowsmith, Americana,* ed. by H. L. Mencken, C. H. Bretherton's *Midas, or the United States and the future,* and George Philip Krapp's *The English language in America.*
Here we have the perfect reviewer, one versed in the subject of the English language and endowed with critical tolerance towards the aberrations of the mother tongue on the more vulgar side of the Atlantic. The spoken English in America is something quite different from the written English. Bret Harte, Mark Twain, and their robust fellow humorists really sowed the seeds of slang in England, and the crop has flourished ever since. Englishmen enjoy American slang, even when criticizing it.

WITWER, HARRY CHARLES.
The classics in slang. New York: G. P. Putnam's Sons, 1927. 331 p. 12°. 8-NBX
A reprint of stories which appeared originally in *Popular magazine* and *Collier's weekly.* The adventures of One-Punch McTague, a prize fighter, are carried through parodied versions of The Taming of the shrew, Hamlet, Uncle Tom's cabin, Macbeth, Romeo and Juliet, The Merchant of Venice, The Count of Monte Cristo, The Last of the Mohicans, Gulliver's travels, Ali Baba and the forty thieves, Sinbad the sailor, Faust, Carmen, Robinson Crusoe, The Hunchback of Notre

General Works, continued

Twentieth Century — 1921–1930, continued

WITWER, HARRY CHARLES, *continued*

Dame, Oliver Twist, The Three musketeers, Les Miserables, Gil Blas, Ivanhoe, Mysteries of Paris, and Nicholas Nickleby. The slang or jargon of the prize ring predominates. Witwer's other stories in various numbers of *Collier's weekly* are rich in slang. Witwer published a number of slang stories between 1918 and 1929, the year of his death. Among his books with a prize fighter as hero are: *The Leather pushers,* 1921, *Fighting back,* 1924, *Fighting blood,* 1923, and *Kid Scanlan,* 1925. He also wrote books in baseball slang.

WOOLF, VIRGINIA (STEPHEN).
American fiction. (Saturday review of literature. New York, Aug. 1, 1925. f°. v. 2, p. 1–3.). † NAA
The American writer ignores the army of English words and seeks new ones. "The English tradition is formed upon a little country...crowded with people who know each other intimately...ruled...by the spirit of the past... In America there is baseball instead of society...tin cans...prairies...cornfields."
The English writer points out, however, that England borrows from American slang when she wishes to freshen her speech.

WORK, JAMES A.
The American slanguage. (Educational review. New York, April, 1927. 8°. v. 73, p. 222–224.) SSA
The adding of "ie" to words is a special irritant to this member of the speech department of Brown University. He mentions "all rightie," "dearie," "sweetie," "hotsie totsie," etc.

'Y. O.'
The American slanguage. (Living age. New York, Nov. 15, 1926. 8°. v. 331, p. 336–339.) * DA
Reprinted from the *Irish statesman,* Aug. 21, 1926. Shows the need for a dictionary of the American language. "The slang of to-day may be classical speech to-morrow. I am told that the French language has become so perfect that it is pallid or near death." Lists a few American slang words, and shows great admiration for them.

YEAMAN, M. V. P.
Speech degeneracy. (American speech. Baltimore, Nov., 1925. 4°. v. 1, p. 92–95.) RNA
The average American overworks certain words, repeats words too often, uses silly and meaningless words, overworks slang expressions, mispronounces, gives wrong meanings to words, and is careless about points of grammar. Some glaring examples are given.

YOUNG, STARK.
Mad money. (In his: Encaustics. New York: New Republic, 1926. 12°. p. 1–10.) NBQ
The distress of an educated man in a barbaric world of slang. The readers of popular magazines find slang congenial and perfectly adequate. The reader of Santayana is perplexed by it.

1931–

ADKINS, NELSON FREDERICK.
Americanisms. (American speech. Baltimore, Feb., 1933. 4°. v. 8, p. 75–76.) RNA
A list of old words reprinted from the *New York Mirror* of Sept. 7, 1833, v. 11, p. 80.

AGAR, HERBERT.
Anglo-American tension. (New statesman and nation. London, Aug. 8, 1931. f°. new series, v. 2, p. 162–163.) * DA
America profanes herself through her "loathsome pictures" which pour steadily from Hollywood, but on the other hand "the English should try to cope with their philological ignorance" and make an honest effort to understand the American speech and literature, and not assume such an absurd attitude of intellectual snobbery.

AGATE, JAMES.
I loathe this American slang. (London Daily Express. June 4, 1936.)

ALEXANDER, ROSE.
Slang and popular phrases used by Shakespeare... Los Angeles, California: Rose Alexander, 743 North Lafayette Park Place.
A pamphlet which the compiler has not seen.

ALMANAC for New Yorkers 1937. Compiled by workers of the Federal Writers Project... New York: Simon and Schuster, 1937. 128 p. 8°.
Slang, p. 122.

ANDERSON, CUTTER.
Words with a wanderlust. (Education. Boston, Sept., 1933. 8°. v. 54, p. 38–40.) SSA
"Some words are like gypsies; they wander all over the world. Beefsteak, cowboy, chopsuey, naiveté, automobile, sombrero, igloo, golf, skoal, and polka, are words like that, and each betrays by its accent the country of its origin." Some pidgin English is included. "Wandering words... serve as messengers of good will and mutual understanding."

ARONSTEIN, PHILIPP.
Zur Biologie des amerikanischen Englisch. (Leuvensche bijdragen. 's Gravenhage, 1934. jaarg. 26, p. 12–35, 81–111.)
Based on a study of Krapp, Mencken, Spies, Sinclair Lewis, and Dreiser.
Copy in Columbia University Library.

AYRES, HARRY MORGAN.
England's English — and America's. (Current history. New York, Sept., 1932. 8°. v. 36, p. 702–706.) BAA
The divergence from the speech of England as noted in the United States by countless critics is more imaginary than real. Certain factors do have an influence in speech differences, however, such as spelling, intonation, emotional reactions to words, traditions, etc. Americans are "school conscious." The English rely on family or neighborhood tradition in spelling and pronunciation.

BEATH, PAUL ROBERT.
Winchellese. (American speech. Baltimore, Oct., 1931. 4°. v. 7, p. 44–46.) RNA
A study of the wise-cracking language of the *New York Daily Mirror's* columnist, including the words "whoopee" and "blessed event."

BIRTH pangs of slang. (The Literary digest. New York, Aug. 5, 1933. f°. v. 116, p. 20.) * DA
Résumé of statements anent slang made by Gelett Burgess, who is credited with coining "blurb," "bromide," etc. Will Irwin is credited with creating "highbrow."

General Works, continued

Twentieth Century — 1931-   , continued

BODENHEIM, MAXWELL.
Naked on roller skates. New York: Live-right, 1931. 279 p. 12°.
Filled with the slang of low life in New York. "The author never explains what it is that causes him to deal so extensively with filthy places and filthy people — such slang as Mr. Bodenheim uses is more than a kind of language; it is an attitude of mind." — Gerald Sykes in *Herald Tribune Books*, Jan. 25, 1931, p. 16.
Reviewed also in *The Nation*, New York, Feb. 18, 1931, v. 132, p. 195, * DA, and in the *Saturday review of literature*, New York, April 25, 1931, v. 7, p. 783, † NAA.

BROPHY, JOHN.
Idiom and slang. (In his: English prose. London: A. & C. Black, 1932. 12°. p. 59–65.)
NAD
"Good slang is that which gives fresh life to old or abstract ideas... Bad slang lacks both the precision of statement and the defined function of good slang. It arises from mental sloth instead of from mental acuteness. It desires to be witty but lacks the ability, and it puts the imagination to sleep instead of awakening it. It is usually cumbersome, where good slang is compact." Criticizes American movies but makes the generous statement that 99 per cent of American books can be read by Englishmen without their being doubtful of the meaning.

BUTLER, KATE.
Slang. American and English. (London Daily Telegraph, March 6, 1935.)

BYINGTON, STEVEN TRACY.
Slang and Bible translation. (American speech. New York, Feb., 1932. 4°. v. 7, p. 188–191.)
RNA
In a new translation of the Bible certain passages will gain by a judicious use of slang.

CHARMLEY, BEULAH.
The great god slang. (Modern thinker. New York, April, 1935. v. 6, p. 22–26.)   * DA

CHESTERTON, GILBERT KEITH.
The worst slang. (G. K.'s weekly. London, May 9, 1931. f°. v. 13, p. 135.)
"I have the greatest respect for American slang so long as it is really slang... American juvenility has a good deal to do with the real powers and dangers of American slang... It is not a primitive thing... It is sophisticated." The American's use of the "silly slang of popular science" is deprecated, as is his misuse of psychological terms. The terms of quackery are prevalent.

COOKE, ALISTAIR.
'That dreadful American.' (The Listener. London, Jan. 30, 1935. 4°. v. 13, p. 207.)   * DA
Finds *American* a foreign language, and thinks it should be studied as such. The American films should not be criticized by Englishmen on the point of corrupt English. The film "The Thin man" is taken as a case in point.

CRAIGIE, SIR WILLIAM ALEXANDER.
An American language. (The Saturday review of literature. New York, Feb. 21, 1931. f°. v. 7, p. 614–615.)   † NAA
Prof. Craigie views the so-called differences between American and English speech with an intelligence and sanity too often lacking in a discussion of this controversial subject. He shows that Americans began to speak of their language as American as early as 1837, and this spirit finds modern champions in such authorities as Mencken, Krapp and Tucker. Many differences are being reconciled by closer communication, and with the growth of Canada and the United States the English language center is shifting westward. Fears that the movies will do great damage to English speech. "The results may at first dismay the purists, but unless the English of the future is to be unworthy of its past, it may be trusted to select what is worth preserving and to allow the rest to fall into the rubbish-shoot of obsolete slang, which is as dead as anything in language can be."

Americanisms. (The Nation. New York, Nov. 26, 1930. f°. v. 131, p. 572.)   * DA
Comment on an article on Americanisms by Sir William A. Craigie in a recent issue of the London *Times*. A few samples of Americanisms are given.

ELLBY, DAVID, PSEUD.
Shooting the bull. London: Grayson, 1933. 259 p. 8°.
Contains much modern English and American slang. David Ellby is a pseudonymn.

FISCHER, WALTHER PAUL.
Amer. Slang guy 'Fellow, chap, person.' (Anglia. Halle, 1931. 8°. Bd. 55, p. 443–448.)
RNA
Traces the changes in meaning of "guy." This word has one meaning in England and another in America.
See also Robert Withington's article in *American speech*, Baltimore, April, 1930, v. 5, p. 280–281, *RNA*, entitled, " 'Guy' — a case of rehabilitation."

GARY, LORENA M.
Anglo-American altercation. (Overland monthly. Los Angeles, March, 1935. 4°. v. 93, p. 5, 6, 20.)   * DA
Americanisms — Briticisms, with a patriotic flourish at the end.

GRATTAN, JOHN HENRY GRAFTON.
On slang, cant and jargon. (Yorkshire Dialect Society. Transactions. York, Nov., 1935. v. 5, p. 9–22.)   RNY
One of the best articles on the subject of slang, cant, and jargon; with lucid differentiations.

GRIFFIN, FRANK LOXLEY.
Learn English before you go. (Atlantic monthly. Boston, June, 1932. 8°. v. 149, p. 775–776.)   * DA
A few tips for the American about to sail for England. English terms for everyday things are not at all like their American equivalents, and English slang is particularly difficult.

GROOM, BERNARD.
A short history of English words. London: Macmillan and Co., Ltd., 1934. vi, 221 p. 12°.
"Popular word making," p. 46–68.   RNF
"Many cant words in English can be traced back to Tudor times, when the underworld of rogues was beginning to be explored as a fruitful subject for literary men."

HALE, EDWARD EVERETT, JR.
Geographical terms in the Far West. (Dialect notes. New Haven, July, 1932. 8°. v. 6, part 4, p. 217–234.)   RNZ
Contains many words which may properly be called Americanisms. The list of books from which these terms have been gleaned is given. Bluff, prairie, chute, slash, swag, dome, crawl, butte, bad-lands, etc., have interesting origins.

HALFELD, ADOLF.
Der slang. (In his: England, Verfall oder Aufstieg? Jena: Eugen Diederichs Verlag [1933]. 8°. p. 38–41.)   CBA
Comments on the prevalence of jargon in America, and its popularity in the talking films.

General Works, continued

Twentieth Century — 1931–   , continued

HARDY, THOMAS JOHN.
Some eccentricities of common speech. (In his: Books on the shelf. London: Philip Allan, 1934. 12°. p. 236–247.) NCZ
A defence of slang, but warns against clipped words. "The unfinished word insults the flag!" A few expressions, including World War slang, are traced.

HAYDON, BROWNLEE.
Technique of the U. S. slang. (London Morning Post. July 3, 1936.)

HERBERT, ALAN PATRICK.
What a word... London: Methuen [1935]. 286 p. 12°. RND
Slang receives no particular emphasis in this work, but the popular linguistic processes which create unnecessary and uncouth verbal novelties are exposed by one who would cleanse the English language of its impurities by holding them up to merited ridicule. Most of the material appeared originally in *Punch.*

JAMES, RIAN.
All about New York...with a foreword by Ogden Nash, and decorations by Jay. New York: The John Day Company [cop. 1931]. 316 p. 8°. IRGV
"A New York glossary," p. 306–309.
Includes Broadway slang, drinking terms, argot, journalese, and other New York words.

JOHNSON, GAYLORD.
Old words get new meanings in queer trade lingoes. (Popular science monthly. New York, Feb., 1933. 8°. v. 122, p. 28–29, 98.) *DA
Selection of slang words from railway, telegraph, radio, circus, oil fields, mining, theatre, and movie speech. A popular article with no historical data.

JONES, P. J.
American jargon. (London Daily Telegraph. March 4, 1935.)

KEATON, ANNA LUCILE.
Americanisms in early American newspapers. Chicago, 1936. 1 p.l., 27, 61–73, 75–85, 144–150 p. 8°.
Part of thesis (Ph.D.), University of Chicago. Photolithographed.

KENNEDY, ARTHUR GARFIELD.
The future of the English language. (American speech. Baltimore, Dec., 1933. 4°. v. 8, p. 3–12.) RNA
Not an article on slang, but in part devoted to colloquial English. The student is advised not to take such speech too seriously "because so much of it is transitory and ephemeral and superficial." Admits the rejuvenating effect slang has on the language.

Standard English and its variants. (In his: Current English... Boston: Ginn and Company [1935]. 8°. p. 22–69.) RNB
In this well-grounded chapter, the well-known compiler of the *Bibliography of writings on the English language,* 1927 (q.v.), examines with care the subjects of pure English, colloquial speech, slang, grotesque English, archaic English versus neologisms, newspaper English, children's English, dialects of English, and jargons. Professor Kennedy shows the marked differences between colloquial speech, slang, and jargon, and warns against the misuse and loose application of those terms. Slang is not condemned en masse as "bad English," for many slang terms soon reach dictionary sanctity, but the intellectual laziness and linguistic poverty which slang betrays is

lamented. Writers on the subject of American English would do well to familiarize themselves with this enlightening chapter. A bibliography of the subjects covered in this chapter is given, p. 621–626.

KIRCHNER, GUSTAV.
Englische Sprachecke. (Zeitschrift für neusprachlichen Unterricht. Berlin, 1936. 8°. Bd. 35, p. 120–122, 172–174, 257–261.) NAA
Study of British and American slang locutions of today, with bibliographical footnotes.

MACAULAY, ROSE.
Slang. (Week-end review. London, Oct. 14, 1933. 8°. v. 8, p. 380–381.) *DA
A review of Eric Partridge's *Slang to-day and yesterday* and *Words, words, words.* "I am disposed to believe that (a) there is no slang, (b) everything said or written is slang. If I am wrong, what is slang, and where the shadowy frontiers that divide it from idiom, from mere vulgarism, or even from standard language?" Some of Partridge's slang expressions are questioned. "Why, for instance, 'museum headache' (a malaise contracted while waiting in the B. M. reading-room for one's books) should be called slang, I do not know. You might as well call seasickness, or Indian cholera, slang." On the whole the review is favorable — and amusing. "Mr. Partridge knows his slang of to-day through and through, and you can tell him little about it."

MacCARTHY, DESMOND.
Handy words. (In his: Experience. London: Putnam [1935]. 8°. p. 270–271.) NCZ
Short essay on the words "bilk," "bird," "snag," "mim," "moonflaw," "yonderly," "squelch," "swank," "to gowl," "scritch," and a few others.

McKNIGHT, GEORGE HARLEY.
Words and human comedy. (Words. Los Angeles, Oct., 1934. 8°. v. 1, p. 9–12.) RNA
The nature and function of slang is mentioned in this article.

MARK, HEINZ.
Die Verwendung der Mundart und des Slang in den Werken von John Galsworthy. Breslau: Priebatsch, 1936. 3 p.l., v–x, 137 p. 8°. (Sprache und Kultur der germanischen und romanischen Völker. A. Anglistische Reihe. Bd. 23.) RNA

MASON, WILLIAM LESLEY.
Slanguage. (In his: How to say it — correctly; a useful "elbow" volume... New York: A. L. Burt, 1932. 12°. p. 165–169.) RND
Defines slang and gives "a few of the more objectionable slang words and phrases."

MATHEWS, M. A.
Some fashions in English slang. (Sprachkunde. March, 1937. Bd. 1, p. 4–5.)

MATTHEWS, WILLIAM.
Cockney past and present. A short history of the dialect of London. London: George Routledge & Sons, Ltd. [1938.] xv, 245 p. 8°. RNY
Excellent survey. "Cockney mannerisms and slang," p. 105–155.

MENCKEN, HENRY LOUIS.
...The American language. An enquiry into the development of English in the United States ... Fourth edition, corrected, enlarged and rewritten. New York: Alfred A. Knopf, 1936. xi, 769, xxix p. 8°. M. R. R. Desk
This edition is a thorough revision, containing hundreds of passages based on newspaper and magazine articles on American speech which had appeared subsequent to the third edition, 1923. The disarming preface explains the nature of the revisions. There is

General Works, continued

Twentieth Century — 1931-   , continued

no separate bibliography, but hundreds of references are given in footnotes, which are copious and specific.

The chapter on slang is up-to-the-minute, and hundreds of words are mentioned to illustrate the text, p. 555–589. The appendix, p. 616–697, contains material showing the influence of foreign dialects upon the American vulgate. The foreign elements are reviewed in the following order: German, Dutch, Swedish, Dano-Norwegian, Icelandic, Yiddish, French, Italian, Spanish, Portuguese, Rumanian, Czech, Slovak, Russian, Ukranian, Serbo-Croat, Lithuanian, Polish, Finnish, Hungarian, Gaelic, Arabic, Modern Greek, Chinese, Japanese, Armenian, Hawaiian, Gipsy.

There is a list of words and phrases, p. 699–769, which gives the work a dictionary aspect, and doubles its handy reference value.

See *Times literary supplement,* London, Oct. 10, 1936, p. 797–798, † *NAA; Readers' digest,* Pleasantville, N. Y., Oct., 1936, p. 67–70, * *DA; American speech,* New York, Oct., 1937, v. 12, p. 185–189 (Stuart Robertson), *RNA.*

Dying words. (Words. Los Angeles. Jan., 1935. 8°. v. 1, p. 7.)   RNA
Shows how our political terms of one generation die out in the next. This applies to all classes of slang. Reprinted from New York *American.*

MITCHELL, RONALD ELWY.
The American language. (In his: America. A practical handbook. [London:] Hamish Hamilton, 1935. 12°. p. 75–109.)   KNF
A handbook for the British traveller in the United States. Speech differences are noted, and parallel lists of Americanisms and their British counterparts are given, p. 89–93. Slang is defended. "It is better for British people to avoid slang... Moreover the British are known all over America for the slowness of their humour and for their well-meaning use of out-of-date American slang."

NOT yet in the dictionary. (The Kablegram. Mount Morris, Ill., 1935. 8°. Jan. – May.)
This volume not in The New York Public Library. A number of neologisms, mostly slang, appeared in this trade publication of Kable Brothers. They were arranged alphabetically.

PARTRIDGE, ERIC HONEYWOOD.
Colloquial speech and colloquialisms. (Everyman. London, Feb. 19, 1931. f°. v. 5, p. 116.)
* DA
Colloquial speech is divided into three main classes: dialect, technical words, and slang. Examples are given.

Words, words, words!... London: Methuen & Co., Ltd. [1933.] 230 p. 12°.   RNB
Contents: I. An etymological medley. 1. "Offensive nationality," published in *John o' London,* 1932; 2. "Footpads and highwaymen," published in *Everyman,* March, 1931; 3. "The devil and his nicknames," published in *John o' London,* July, 1931; 4. "Familiar terms of address," published in *Action,* October, 1931; 5. "Rhyming slang, back slang, and other oddities," published in *Everyman,* February, 1931; 6. The art of lightening death; 7. "The philology of Christmas," published in *The Week-end review,* Dec., 1931; 8. "All fools' day," published in *The New statesman,* March, 1931; 9. "Representative names," published in *John o' London,* March, 1933; 10. "American cant," published in *The New statesman,* Jan., 1931; 11. The word bloody; 12. Euphemism and euphemisms; II. Semi-biographical. "One of John Wesley's sidelines," published in *London quarterly review,* Oct., 1932; "Johnson's dictionary," published in *Everyman,* April, 1932; "A Falstaff among antiquaries," published in *Everyman,* Jan., 1931. III. Aspects of soldiers' slang: 1914–1918. 1. "British soldiers' slang with a past," published in *The Quarterly review,* April, 1931; 2. "German army slang," published in *The New statesman,* April, 1932; 3. "The slang of the poilu," published in *The Quarterly review,* April, 1932; 4.

Soldiers' slang of three nations. Appendices. 1. "Boxing day," published in *Everyman,* Dec., 1931; 2. "Some groups of 'Tommy' words," published in *A Martial medley,* May, 1931; 3. "The poilu on himself and others," published in *John o' London,* Feb., 1932. Index.

PFEILER, WILHELM KARL.
...Uncle Sam and his English. 1. Auflage. Berlin-Schöneberg: Langenscheidtsche Verlagsbuchhandlung [1932]. 152 p. 12°. (Langenscheidts fremdsprachliche Lektüre. Bd. 32.)
RAE p.v.138
Dr. Pfeiler was assisted in this work by Miss Elizabeth Wittmann, of the University of Nebraska. A number of articles from American newspapers and periodicals were selected for their free use of Americanisms and current slang, and definitions of the terms unfamiliar to German readers are given (in German) in the margins.

READ, ALLEN WALKER.
Amphi-Atlantic English. (English studies. Amsterdam, Oct., 1935. 8°. v. 17, p. 161–178.)
RNA
A documented survey of the attitude of Englishmen towards Americanisms from the seventeenth century to the present, with bibliographical footnotes, excerpts from books of travel, and apt quotations from numerous literary periodicals. It is a study of an attitude of superiority, a transatlantic duel of the neologists on the one side and the philological "diehards" on the other.

RHOTEN, EDWARD T.
Wizardry in words. (The Editor. Highland Falls, New York, Aug., 1934. 4°. v. 102, p. 86–87.)
NARA
A list of Americanisms, with a few British slang words thrown in. Some of the words are from *Alice's adventures in wonderland.* The author continues the subject in the April, 1935, issue, v. 102, p. 272–273, under the title "Some apt phrases."

ROBERTSON, STUART.
The development of modern English. New York: Prentice-Hall, 1934. 559 p. 8°.   RN
Modern English: British and American, p. 65–97; The making of words, p. 358–421; Changing meanings and values of words, p. 457–472; American English, p. 473–490. These and other parts of the book touch upon the subject of slang and other unconventional forms of speech. The slang of today the author thinks is a "desire for a tongue that shall be sophisticated and intelligible only to the initiated."

SALMON, LUCY MAYNARD.
The record of language. (In her: Historical material. New York: Oxford University Press, 1933. 8°. p. 77–90.)   BAL
A treatment of words as basic historical material. The evolution of man is to be found in the words he uses. A few samples are given from religion, politics, inventions, foods, geography, amusements, clothing, conveyances, military life, etc. The words are given in footnotes.

SARFATTI, MARGHERITA (GRASSINI).
L'Americano come lo si parla. (Nuova antologia. Roma, Dec., 1934. 8°. serie 7, v. 298, p. 416–434.)   NNA
A detailed and illuminating study of Latin influence on American speech, along with other peculiarities of the American idiom. One extremely interesting observation is made; namely, that from the time of Caesar the pure Latin was vulgarized by the barbarians of Gaul, that this vulgarization passed to England with William the Conqueror, became slang in some instances, was carried to America in Elizabeth's time, became pidgeon English in modern times and spread from the west coast of America to the South Seas and Asia and then around the world, becoming a lingua franca. In recent years Italian immigrants to America, uncultured and illiterate, tried

General Works, continued

Twentieth Century — 1931–   , continued

SARFATTI, MARGHERITA (GRASSINI), *continued*
to adapt this slang of America into Italian colloquial speech. Gradually they broke the word down into its original elements and the original Latin word and Latin meaning was recaptured, quite by accident. This linguistic atavism is worthy of further study.

SAY it in American. (London Morning Post. Sept. 11, 1936.)

SHIGEMI, HOKUICHI.
On Americanisms. (Studies in English literature. Tokyo: Imperial University, 1934. 8°. v. 14, p. 267–277.)
Text in Japanese. The New York Public Library lacks this number.

SIMPSON, J. H.
Oddities of American speech. (Canadian Bankers Association. Journal. Toronto, Oct., 1934. 8°. v. 42, p. 56–59.)   THA
A comparison of the speech habits of Americans with those of their Canadian neighbors, with a paragraph or two on the subject of American slang.

SMITH, A. M.
This slanguage of ours. (Chambers's journal. London, Oct., 1934. 4°. series 8, v. 3, p. 769–771.)   * DA
"Slang is the Cinderella of language. It is never in favour, yet never out of use... To find the true language of a nation it is always safe to go to its songs and popular poems, and the ballads of the seventeenth century in particular do not disappoint us." Lists a few slang words taken from ancient sources. Other words of more recent vintage are examined.

STONE, RUTH MATILDA.
Studien über den deutschen Einfluss auf das amerikanische Englisch. Bochum-Langendreer: H. Poppinghaus, 1934. vii, 90 p. 8°.   * CX p.v.45
Dissertation, University of Marburg.

TATE, ALLEN.
The American language. (The New English weekly. London, Dec. 1, 1932. f°. v. 2, p. 157–158.)   * DA
"The American language, since the appearance of Dickens' 'American notes' nearly a century ago, has fascinated the Englishman as no other feature of American life has ever succeeded in doing." A commentary on the literary views held by William Carlos Williams.

THOMPSON, BLANCHE JENNING.
The lure of illiteracy. (Catholic review. New York, July, 1936. 8°. v. 143, p. 463–467.)   * DA
Samples of vulgar American speech. "If America has come of age, some evidences of maturity should begin to appear. If not, let *Homo sapiens* be written correctly in the jargon of the day — simply and justly *Homo Sap.*"

TOWNSEND, CHARLES WENDELL.
Concerning Briticisms. (American speech. Baltimore, Feb., 1932. 4°. v. 7, p. 219–222.)   RNA
By giving examples from old English dictionaries a good case is made for the assertion of George Arliss that many words considered by his countrymen to be Americanisms are really old English words.

TYSELL, HELENE TRACE.
The English of the comic cartoons. (American speech. New York, Feb., 1935. 4°. v. 10, p. 43–55.)   RNA
Much of the dialogue in comic strips is pure slang.

There is an effort to keep the language down to the level of the masses. Hundreds of examples of names, epithets, wise-cracks, etc., are taken from American newspapers.

VIZETELLY, FRANCIS HORACE.
American English. (Lecture recorder. London, July, 1936. 4°. v. 5, p. 365–367.)   * DA

WASMUTH, HANS WERNER.
Slang bei Sinclair Lewis... Hamburg: H. Schimkus, 1935. 84, iii p. 8°.   NBF p.v.
Takes up all the works of Lewis and classifies the slang they contain.
There is a glossary in the London edition (1922) of *Babbitt*.

WEBSTER, HAROLD TUCKER.
They don't speak our language. (Forum. New York, Dec., 1933. 4°. v. 90, p. 367–372.)
                    * DA
Webster ran a number of cartoons in the *New York Herald Tribune* and other papers, entitled "They don't speak our language," in which he gave short glossaries of the various trades and professions. This article is written in slang and gives the results of the original studies which lead to the appearance of the cartoons.

WEEKLEY, ERNEST.
English as she will be spoke. (Atlantic monthly. Boston, May, 1932. 8°. v. 149, p. 551–560.)   * DA
Takes up the problem of spelling reform, pronunciation, disputes concerning usage (Mr. Fowler always figures in such a study), divergences in grammatical practice in England and America, and the entry of new words into language. This latter process is of interest to the student of slang. "The idea that language can be 'improved' is fantastic... standardization must gradually kill idiom and degrade language to the level of the Morse code."

Something about words... New York: E. P. Dutton and Company [1936]. 233 p. 12°.   RNF
A potpourri of word studies. "This is a very mixed bag," the author says. It includes references to slang words, Briticisms and Americanisms, dialect locutions, etc.; with a chapter on "Etymological monomaniacs"; "The Oxford Dictionary Supplement"; "Proverbs"; "Proper names and common nouns"; "The future of English"; etc. Contains a word index, p. 221–233.
Reviewed in *Revue anglo-américaine*, Paris, Dec., 1935, p. 145 (Marie Betbeder-Motibet), * DM.

WHITMAN, D. B.
American slang in England. (Manchester Guardian weekly. Manchester, England, May 7, 1937. p. 374.)

WINCHELL, WALTER.
Lending a hand to Mr. Mencken. (New York Daily Mirror. June 20, 1936.)
Slang additions to the 4th edition of H. L. Mencken's *The American language*, drawn from the theatre, sports, and movies.

WITHINGTON, ROBERT.
Some neologisms from recent magazines. (American speech. Baltimore, April, 1931. 4°. v. 6, p. 277–289.)   RNA
Magazines, like *Time*, coin new words freely. Some get into the dictionaries. The long list of coinages are defined and dated.

ZIPF, GEORGE KINGSLEY.
[Slang.] (In his: The psycho-biology of language. Boston: Houghton Mifflin Company, 1935. 12°. p. 36, 201–202.)   RAD
Just a few succinct lines about slang, but interesting in the light of the new psychological approach to language problems.

UNDERWORLD CANT AND ITS SUBSIDIARIES

THE temptation to write a lengthy history of cant must be resisted by the compiler, but a word or two may be said concerning the nature of this form of locution. *Shelta,* or the secret language of Gaelic bards and tinkers, goes back over a thousand years, but it is still understood in part by certain tribes of gipsies, although it is not to be confused with pure *Romany* or *Hindustani.* Canting, or secret begging language, is as old as organized beggary, and has been handed down from generation to generation. The first attempt to make a study of this language was in the sixteenth century, and that is the beginning of our bibliography. Slang lexicography began in Germany and made its way through the Low Countries to England. English canting words are mixed with Gipsy cant; Latin corruptions brought in by pardoners and begging friars; Dutch words brought over by smugglers, fishermen, adventurers, returning soldiers, and banished gipsies, rogues and vagabonds; common English words applied in a figurative sense, thus taking on a new meaning to the initiated; onomatopoeic or echoic words which imitate the sounds of things; words born of that linguistic process known as otosis, which is the alteration of words caused by an erroneous apprehension of the sound, for instance, the corruption of *bacchanales* into *bag of nails;* and the mixture of secret words handed down by various guilds, brotherhoods, religious sects, and secret societies. Cant is always secret, it is usually anti-social, and is low and vulgar. When it loses its secrecy and passes into common speech it becomes colloquial. Appropriated by fashionable circles it becomes slang. Continued usage may legitimize it, and then it passes into standard English.

HISTORICAL STUDIES

AYDELOTTE, FRANK.
...Elizabethan rogues and vagabonds. Oxford: At the Clarendon Press, 1913. 187 p. 8°. (Oxford historical and literary studies...)
CBA (Oxford)
Traces the history of Elizabethan rogue literature. Includes excerpts from Harman, Greene, Dekker, and others who utilized canting language in their works. Illuminating footnotes clarify the authentic text, and many bibliographical references are cited. The contents are: Introduction; Origins; The art of begging; Laws against vagabonds; The art of conny-catching; Laws against conny-catching; The rogue pamphlets; Documents; Plagiarism in Elizabethan pamphlets. *Cf.* F. W. Chandler's *The literature of roguery,* q. v.
See also M. St. Clare Byrne, "The queen's highway" in her *Elizabethan life in town and country,* London: Methuen, 1934. 12°, p. 79–91, *CN,* which describes roguery and some of the books on the subject.

BRADLEY, HENRY.
Shakespeare's English. (In: Shakespeare's England... Oxford: Clarendon Press [1932]. 8°. v. 2, p. 539–574.) * NCLD
Bibliography, p. 574.
This scholarly account of Elizabethan English, by one of the editors of the O. E. D. contains many thoughtful remarks on the colloquialisms and slang of Shakespeare's plays, and the influence of dialects on the dramatist. "Under the head of slang may, without serious inaccuracy, be reckoned the enormously extensive vocabulary of profane oaths and euphemistic or burlesque substitutes for them. Many hundreds of expressions of this kind are to be found in the Elizabethan writers." In 1606 an Act of Parliament forbade the profane use of the names of God, Christ, the Holy Ghost, and the Trinity, in any stage show or play, which acted as a check on blasphemous slang. This period was marked by reduplicating formations, such words as hurly-burly, hugger-mugger, helter-skelter, etc.

CHANDLER, FRANK WADLEIGH.
The literature of roguery... Boston and New York: Houghton, Mifflin & Co., 1907. 2 v. 16°. (The types of English literature. Ed. by William Allan Neilson.) NCBX
"In the broadest sense, this history follows the fortunes of the anti-hero in literature. More narrowly, it is a study of realism, for it investigates the role enacted in literary art by the observation of low-life." To the student of canting literature the bibliographies at the end of each chapter are rich in useful suggestions. Of particular interest is chapter three of the first volume. It deals with: 1. beggar books; 2. conny-catching pamphlets; 3. prison tracts and repentances; 4. canting lexicons and scoundrel verse; 5. sociological studies of roguery.
This is one of the most notable contributions to the history of rogue literature ever written, and Professor Chandler deserves the thanks of all students who have been aided by his researches.

FULLER, RONALD.
The beggars' brotherhood. London: George Allen & Unwin [1936]. 253 p. 8°. SGS
"The villains of the Middle Ages have become romantic to the twentieth century, however monstrous they may have appeared to the fourteenth. The sordid is transformed to the picturesque... The golden age of the tramp was from 1530 till 1630."
A well-written history of English beggars, with ample attention given to the literature of the subject, particularly of the Elizabethan period. At this time rogues and beggars figured very prominently in poetry and drama.

HARRISON, WILLIAM.
Harrison's Description of England in Shakspere's youth. Being the second and third books of his Description of Britaine and England. Edited from the first two editions of Holinshed's chronicle, A. D. 1577, 1587, by Frederick J. Furnivall... Part I. The second book... London: Publisht for The New Shakspere Society, by N. Trübner & Co...1877. 368 p. 8°. (New Shakspere Society. Series VI.) * NCK (New)
Part I. Second book, p. 212–232.
This is one of the earlier descriptions of the rogues of England and the condition of the poor. Describes the language and tricks of rogues and vagabonds. The vocabulary is based largely on Harman's *Caveat* (q.v.).

Underworld Cant and Its Subsidiaries, cont'd

Historical Studies, continued

JUDGES, ARTHUR VALENTINE.

The Elizabethan underworld. A collection of Tudor and early Stuart tracts and ballads telling of the lives and misdoings of vagabonds, thieves, rogues and cozeners, and giving some account of the operation of the criminal law. The text prepared with notes and an introduction by A. V. Judges... London: George Routledge & Sons, Ltd., 1930. lxiv, 543 p. illus. 4°.   SLG

Contents: (An asterisk denotes that portions of the original have been omitted.) Preface, p. xi; Introduction, p. xiii–lxiv; The Highway to the Spital-house (1535–6), Robert Copland, p. 1; A Manifest Detection of Dice-play (1552), Gilbert Walker (?), p. 26; The Fraternity of Vagabonds* (1561), John Awdeley, p. 51; A Caveat for Common Cursitors (1566), Thomas Harman, p. 61; A Notable Discovery of Cozenage (1591), Robert Greene, p. 119; The Second Part of Cony-catching (1591), Robert Greene, p. 149; The Third Part of Cony-catching (1592), Robert Greene, p. 179; A Disputation between a He-cony-catcher and a She-cony-catcher (1592), Robert Greene, p. 206; The Black Book's Messenger (1592), Robert Greene, p. 248; The Black Dog of Newgate (c. 1596), Luke Hutton, p. 265; Luke Hutton's Lamentation (1596), p. 292; The Testament of Laurence Lucifer (being a part of the Black Book,* 1604), Thomas Middleton (?), p. 296; The Bellman of London* (1608), Thomas Dekker, p. 303; Lantern and Candlelight* (1608), Thomas Dekker, p. 312; O per se O (1612), Thomas Dekker (?), p. 366; Martin Markall, Beadle of Bridewell (1610), Samuel Rid (?), p. 383; The Counter's Commonwealth (1617), William Fennor, p. 423; The Song of a Constable (1626), James Gyffon, p. 488; Notes to the text, p. 491; Glossary, p. 522; Index, p. 533.

In a lengthy introduction the editor traces the history of rogue literature, and gives the sociological background for Elizabethan rogues, and many old laws and customs are surveyed. A number of facsimile title-pages are reproduced along with quaint old woodcuts, etc. The glossary of canting words, p. 522–532, is almost a dictionary, running two columns to a page and containing several hundred words and definitions. The editor has not retained the old spelling of the original texts but has made it into modern English for the most part and suitable for popular reading. Biographical and bibliographical material is supplied in the section devoted to notes, p. 491–521.

KNIGHT, CHARLES, EDITOR.

Old London rogueries. (In his: London. London: Charles Knight & Co., 1843. 8°. chapter 85, p. 145–160.)   CO (London)

A detailed study of the early canting works of Harman, Dekker, Greene, Rowlands, etc., to trace the development of pickpockets in London, and the rise of the canting language.

LELAND, CHARLES GODFREY.

A brief history of English slang. (In: A. M. V. Barrère and C. G. Leland, A dictionary of slang, jargon & cant. Edinburgh: Ballantyne Press, 1889. 8°. v. 1, p. xiii–xxiii.)
M.R.R. Desk

Leland was an authority on gipsies, and knew the early history of canting, which he outlines in the introduction to the above work. This dictionary will be described elsewhere.

MASSINGHAM, HAROLD JOHN.

On cant. (In his: Letters to X. London: Constable & Co., Ltd., 1919. 12°. p. 226–235.) NCZ

Traces the history of the word cant, and shows changes of meaning.

MICHEL, FRANCISQUE, AND ÉDOUARD FOURNIER.

Histoire des hotelleries, cabarets, hotels garnis, restaurants et cafés... Paris: Librairie

historique, archéologique et scientifique de Seré, 1851. 2 v. in 1. 348, 410 p. 4°.   VTB

A curious collection of songs, anecdotes, and excerpts illustrating the jolly life of road and tavern in all countries of the world through the ages. Contains much argot, and considerable English cant and jargon, collected by Michel, who was an authority on the language of low life. The English section covers p. 219–260 of v. 2. Contains excerpts from an article by M. Ph. Chasles, in the *Revue de Paris*, March 24, 1844. Mentions *L'Histoire de Colly le Rossignol*, *Grandes annales des voleurs de mer et de rivière*, and *Gémissements de John Ketch* among other works. Points out that Jonathan Wild was the original of *Peachum* in Gay's *The beggar's opera*. Contains much information on gipsies, with illustrations from Callot.

PARTRIDGE, ERIC HONEYWOOD.

Slang to-day and yesterday; with a short historical sketch and vocabularies of English, American, and Australian slang. Second edition, carefully revised; somewhat augmented. London: George Routledge & Sons, Ltd., 1935. 476 p. 4°.   M.R.R. Desk

One of the best historical approaches to the study of slang and congeneric types of speech which are treated in full. A complete analysis of this work will be given in another section of this bibliography. The first edition appeared in 1933. Partridge has made the most notable contributions to slang lexicography since Farmer and Henley.

RIBTON-TURNER, CHARLES JAMES.

A history of vagrants and vagrancy and beggars and begging... London: Chapman and Hall, 1887. 720 p. 8°.   SGS

The whole book is of value to the slang collector, but chapter xx, "The secret jargon of the vagrant and the mendicant," p. 466–479, which is an historical study of cant; and chapters xxix, p. 576–600, xxx, p. 601–624, and xxxi, p. 625–665, which contain excerpts from canting literature and the slang of vagrancy from 1383 to 1886, are of value to the student of slang. The numerous references are a great aid to the bibliographer of unconventional language. The book takes in all of Europe, but the greater emphasis is put on vagrancy in the British Isles. Has a good chapter on gipsies.

SIMPSON, VIOLET A.

Beggars and begging songs. (Virginia quarterly review. University of Virginia, The Lawn, Jan., 1928. 8°. v. 4, p. 40–51.)   *DA

A study of beggars and their songs from the time of the *Liber Vagatorum*, circa 1509, to the end of the eighteenth century. The chief emphasis is on the vocabularies of Awdelay and the *Liber Vagatorum*.

A short history of beggars in England may be found in John Thomas Smith, *Vagabondia; or, Anecdotes of mendicant wanderers through the streets of London. A new edition.* London: Chatto and Windus, 1874, p. 1–36, † *MMK*.

TSCHOPP, ALBERT.

Terms, phrases and proverbs connected with beggars. (In his: The beggars of England in prose and poetry. <Part 1.> From the earliest times to the end of the 17th century... Bern, 1902. 8°. p. 77–88.)   NCBX

This inaugural dissertation, an historical study of beggary in all its forms, gleans its information chiefly from old English ballads and plays. A list of books used is given. Copious footnotes furnish further bibliographical information.

WHIBLEY, CHARLES.

Rogues and vagabonds. (In: Shakespeare's England. Oxford: Clarendon Press [1932]. 8°. v. 2, p. 484–510.)   *NCLD

An excellent survey of the rogue literature of Shakespeare's time, beginning with Awdelay and Harman. Bibliography on p. 510. Illustrated.

Underworld Cant and Its Subsidiaries, cont'd

Historical Studies, continued

WILDE, WILLIAM CUMMING.
Some words on thief talk. (Journal of American folk-lore. Boston, 1889. 8°. v. 2, p. 301–306.)   HBA
A concise historical account of cant. The theory that cant derives from the gipsies is herein refuted. There is but one gipsy word in Harman's *Caveat*, none in the first American canting glossary, compiled by Henry Tufts (q.v.) and so it is with the first dictionaries of argot, Rotwelsch, zerga, etc. It is pointed out that one canting dictionary copied the errors of an earlier one and this goes on for centuries. Harman's "morts" should read "mots," and Tufts' "kin" should read "ken," etc. Wilde was the son of the Southern scholar and statesman, Richard Henry Wilde, who was a Dante authority, and who discovered Giotto's head of Dante in the Bargello Chapel, in Florence, July, 1840.
Wilde thought that the expression "O. K." was originally a coinage of the American underworld.

BIBLIOGRAPHY

Included in this section are those bibliographies which have been of most use in tracing the development of the canting language. Other bibliographies, more general in character, appear in other sections. It may be added, however, that the *British Museum Catalogue* has been of great help in verifying authors, titles, and editions of the various canting books. The Library of Congress card catalogue has also been helpful in this respect. The list of philological journals which have supplied pertinent information is too long for inclusion.

HAMILTON, WALTER.
Slang, cant, and flash. (In his: Parodies of the works of English and American authors. London: Reeves and Turner, 1889. 4°. v. 6, p. 282–287.)
Copy in Columbia University Library.
This bibliography is based on Hotten's list, with a few additions, including a few American references and the better known French sources.

HOTTEN, JOHN CAMDEN.
The slang dictionary... London: John Camden Hotten, 1865. xxi, 305 p. 12°.   RNM
There was also an 1874 edition, and later editions by Hotten's publishing successors, Chatto & Windus. Each contains a lengthy bibliography of slang, being particularly strong in early canting dictionaries. It contains a few minor mistakes, but was the first serious attempt at bibliography of the subject.
A full description of Hotten's work will be found under the section devoted to general dictionaries.

KENNEDY, ARTHUR GARFIELD.
A bibliography of writings on the English language from the beginning of printing to the end of 1922... Cambridge & New Haven: Harvard University Press, Yale University Press, 1927. xvii, 517 p. 4°.   * RG–RN
"Unconventional English, cant slang and colloquialisms," p. 419–424.
This is the standard authority on the English language, and the compiler makes acknowledgement for the help it has afforded him. For a full description of this work, see the later section devoted to general bibliographies.

MICHEL, FRANCISQUE.
Études de philologie comparée sur l'argot et sur les idiomes analogues parlés en Europe et en Asie, par Francisque Michel... Développement d'un mémoire couronné par l'Institut de France. Paris: Librairie de Firmin Didot Frères, Fils et Cie., imprimeurs de l'Institut... 1856. 516 p. 8°.   RFN
One of the first scholarly studies of slang, and the basis of many later studies. The section on English slang, "Argot anglais," p. 455–474, is made up of words taken from the older canting dictionaries, and full bibliographical descriptions of the more important English slang dictionaries.

SKEAT, WALTER WILLIAM, AND J. H. NODAL.
English Dialect Society. A bibliographical list of the works that have been published, or are known to exist in Ms., illustrative of the various dialects of English. Compiled by members of the English Dialect Society, and edited by the Rev. Walter W. Skeat...and J. H. Nodal. London: Published for the English Dialect Society, by Trübner and Co., Ludgate Hill, 1877. 163 p. 8°.   RNX
Slang and cant, p. 157–165. This section was compiled by Nodal. "In preparing this list I have been much assisted by the catalogue of cant and slang works in Bohn's edition of Lowndes, and the Bibliography appended to Mr. J. Camden Hotten's *Slang dictionary*. I have, however, arranged the several publications in chronological order, revised and verified the titles, and made considerable additions." Covers the period 1565–1877.
English gipsy dialect, p. 171.

VATER, JOHANN SEVERIN.
Litteratur der Grammatiken, Lexika und Wörtersammlungen aller Sprachen der Erde ... Zweite, völlig umgearbeitete Ausgabe von B. Jülg. Berlin: In der Nicolaischen Buchhandlung, 1847. xii, 592 p., 2 l. 8°.   R
A bibliography of canting books on p. 112, 481. Only a few works noted, and all may be found in Kennedy, Nodal, or Hotten.

WAGNER, JOS. MARIA.
Die Litteratur der Gauner- und Beheim-Sprachen seit 1700. (Neuer Anzeiger für Bibliographie und Bibliothekwissenschaft. Herausgegeben von Dr. J. Petzholdt. Berlin, 1861–63. 8°. März, 1861, p. 81–87; April, 1861, p. 114–124; Mai, 1861, p. 147–153; Juni, 1861, p. 177–181; Mai, 1862, p. 151–153; März, 1863, p. 69–75.)   * GAA
Under "England," May, 1861, p. 147–150, a number of works are listed. *Gaunersprache* is enlarged to include cant, thieves' Latin, pedlar's French, St. Giles's Greek, slang, gibberish, flash, flash-lingo, and Romany. Additions appear in the March, 1863, number, p. 71–74. Items of American slang and cant are listed, p. 74–75. Most of the entries seem to be based on Hotten's bibliography.

Underworld Cant and Its Subsidiaries, cont'd

Sixteenth Century

AWDELAY, JOHN.

The Fraternitye of Vacabondes. As wel of ruflyng Vacabondes, as of beggerly, of women as of men, of Gyrles as of Boyes, with their proper names and qualities. With a description of the crafty company of Cousoners and Shifters. Whereunto also is adioyned the xxv Orders of Knaues, otherwyse called a Quartern of Knaues. Confirmed for ever by Cocke Lorell... Imprinted at London by Iohn Awdeley, dwellyng in little Britayne streete without Aldersgate. 1575.

This edition is reprinted in Early English Text Society, *Extra series 9. Edited by Edward Viles & F. J. Furnivall*. London: N. Trübner, 1869. 8°. p. 1–16, NCE. It is in the same volume with Harman's *Caveat* (q.v.) and other canting pieces. The first appearance of this work was in 1560–61, according to Payne Collier. The writer was known variously as John Awdeley, John Sampson, and Sampson Awdelay. The various knaves and rogues are listed with descriptions. The Viles and Furnivall edition of Awdelay was reprinted in New Shakspere Society, *Series 6, no. 7.* London: N. Trübner, 1880. 8°. p. 1–16, * NCK. The 1575 edition is in the Bodleian Library, Oxford.

Awdelay's *The fraternity of Vagabonds* is reprinted in part in A. V. Judges, *The Elizabethan underworld,* London: George Routledge & Sons, 1930, p. 51–60, SLG. There is another reprint bearing the imprint: "Westminster. Reprinted for Machell Stace, No. 12, Little Queen street, and R. Triphook, St. James Street, 1813." 12°. Copy in Columbia University Library.

According to W. Oxberry in his *The actor's budget,* London, 1820, 12°, p. 246, strolling players who shorten a piece during its actual performance are said to be "John Audleying" it. Whether this has anything to do with the above John Awdelay we do not know. Is the circus expression "John Orderly," meaning about the same thing, a corruption of John Awdelay?

COPLAND, ROBERT.

The Hye Way to the Spyttell Hous. [Woodcut.] Copland and the Porter. [Four lines of verse.] n. d. [circa 1535.]

This work belongs to the first half of the sixteenth century. Copland was an assistant to the printer, Wynkyn de Worde. This edition was reprinted in *Select pieces of early popular poetry...[by E. V. Utterson]...* London: Longman, Hurst, Rees, Orme, and Brown, 1817, v. 2, p. 1–50, NCI. The glossary to these select pieces, v. 2, p. 223–236, contains many cant words. The porter in *The hye way to the spyttell hous* talks in the language of rogues, and there are passages entirely in cant.

Also reprinted in A. V. Judges, *The Elizabethan underworld,* London: Routledge, 1930, p. 1–25, SLG. A facsimile of the title-page is reproduced. Judges fixes the date as 1535–36, and shows how it was influenced by *Cock Lorel's Boat* (circa 1500) and Alexander Barclay's *Ship of Fools* (1509).

Copland's *Jyl of Breyntford's Testament,* which was privately printed in 1871, and edited by F. J. Furnivall, abounds in the coarse speech of low life.

See H. R. Plomer. "Robert Copland," in *Transactions of the Bibliographical Society,* London: The Society, 1895, v. 3, p. 211–225, * GAA.

W. G. Moore, writing of "Robert Copland and his Hye Way" in the *Review of English studies,* London, Oct., 1931, v. 7, p. 406–418, RNA, says that the *Hye Way* is not an original work, but Copland's adaptation of a French work, *Le chemin de l'ospital,* by Robert de Balzac, an offspring of Brant's *Narrenschiff,* which was translated by Alexander Barclay in 1508 as *The shyp of foles of the world.*

James A. S. McPeek's article "Shakespere and the fraternity of unthrifts," in *Harvard studies and notes in philology and literature,* Cambridge, 1932, v. 14,

p. 35–50, RAA, traces the provenance of the *Hye Way* and shows how Thomas Nash utilized Copland in his *Summer's last will and testament;* he also shows that Harman and Awdelay knew Copland's work. Its influence on Shakespeare is given.

GREENE, ROBERT.

A Notable Difcouery of Coofnage *Now daily practifed by fundry lewd perfons,* called Connie-catchers, and Croffe-biters... London. Printed by Iohn Wolfe for T. N. and are to be fold ouer againft the great fouth doore of Paules. 1591.

Copy in British Museum.

Facsimile of title-page may be found in *The Life and complete works in prose and verse of Robert Greene... Edited by Alexander B. Grosart...* [London and Aylesbury:] Printed for private circulation only, 1881–86, v. 10, p. 3, NCF. The text occupies p. 15–61. This edition is a part of the Huth library.

There was a second edition in 1592, of which there is a copy in the Bodleian Library.

A part of this work, that dealing with the coosenage of colliers, was reprinted in *Reprints of rare tracts... chiefly illustrative of the history of the Northern counties; and printed at the press of M. A. Richardson. Miscellaneous,* Newcastle, 1849, 19 p., 12°, C.

The Second part of Conny-catching. *Contayning the difcouery of certaine wondrous Coofenages,* either fuperficiallie paft ouer, or vtterlie vntoucht in the firft... London, Printed by Iohn Wolfe for William Wright, and are to be fold at his fhop in Pauls Church yard, neare to the French fchoole. 1591.

Reprinted in Grosart's edition, v. 10, p. 67 (reproduction of title-page). Text, p. 69–133.

The Thirde and laft Part of Conny-catching. With the new devised knauifh Art of Fooletaking... Imprinted at London by *Thomas Scarlet,* for Cutberd Burbie, and are to be folde at his fhoppe in the Poultrie, by S. Mildreds Church. 1592.

Copy in British Museum.

In Grosart's edition, v. 10, p. 139–192, text. Title-page on p. 137.

A Difpvtation Betweene a Hee Connycatcher, and a Shee Conny-catcher, whether a Theefe or a Whoore, is moft hurtfull in Coufonage, to the Common-wealth. Discovering the Secret Villanies *of alluring Strumpets...* Imprinted at London, by A. I. for T. G. and are to be folde at the Weft ende of Paules. 1592.

See Grosart's edition, v. 10, p. 195, for facsimile of title-page. Text, p. 197–278.

The Blacke Bookes Messenger. Laying open the Life and Death of *Ned Browne* one of the moft notable Cutpurfes, *Crofbiters, and Connycatchers, that euer liued in England...* Printed at London by Iohn Danter, or *Thomas Nelfon* dwelling in Siluer ftreete, neere to the figne of the Red-Croffe. 1592.

See Grosart's edition, v. 11, p. 3, for full title. Text, p. 5–37. Reprinted in *Bodley Head quartos,* London: John Lane, 1924, 12°, no. 10, p. 1–32, NCE *(Bodley).* The original of this text is in the British Museum.

Underworld Cant and Its Subsidiaries, cont'd

Sixteenth Century, continued

GREENE, ROBERT, *continued*

The Defence of Conny catching. or a Confvtation of those two iniurious Pamphlets publiſhed by R. G. againſt the practitioners of many Nimble-witted and myſticall Sciences. By Cuthbert Cunny-catcher, Licentiate in Whittington Colledge. Printed at London by A. I. for *Thomas Gubbins* and are to be ſold by *Iohn Buſbie.* 1592.

Copy in British Museum.

See Grosart's edition, v. 11, p. 41, for facsimile of title-page. Text, p. 43–104. Reprinted in the *Bodley Head quartos,* London: John Lane, 1924, 12°, no. 10, edited by G. B. Harrison, *NCE (Bodley).*

In v. 15 of Grosart's edition of Greene's works, p. 229–238, is a glossary entitled "Thieves' vocabulary."

Samuel Rowlands's *Greenes ghost haunting coniecatchers...* London: R. Jackson and I. North, 1602, should be read along with Greene's works. Copy in British Museum.

HARMAN, THOMAS.

A Caveat or Warening, for commen cursetors vvgarely called Vagabones, set forth by Thomas Harman, Esquiere, for the utilite and proffyt of his naturall contrey. Augmented and inlarged by the fyrst authir here of. Anno Domini M.D.LXVII... Imprinted at London, in Fletestrete, at the signe of the falcon, by William Gryffith, and are to be sold at his shoppe in Saynt Dunstones Churche yarde, in the West. Anno Domini. 1567.

Reprinted in Early English Text Society, *Extra series 9,* London: N. Trübner, 1869, p. 17–91, *NCE.* This reprint was edited by Edward Viles and F. J. Furnivall, from the 3rd edition of 1567, belonging to Henry Huth, collated with the 2nd edition of 1567 in the Bodleian Library, Oxford, and with the reprint of the 4th edition of 1573.

Harman's book was considered by many bibliographers to be earlier than John Awdelay's *The fraternitye of vacabondes,* 1560, but Viles and Furnivall have proved in the preface to the above reprint that Awdelay's book was prior to Harman's. Copland's *The hye waye to the spyttel house,* published sometime between 1517 and 1537, was even earlier. All three were no doubt influenced by the *Liber vagatorum,* published in Germany circa 1514. Martin Luther wrote a preface to the 1528 edition of the *Liber vagatorum.* Viles and Furnivall have gone into the various editions of Harman and have shown how Dekker, Head, and others made free and unblushing use of Harman's material. The editors also give all the biographical facts at their disposal. This edition of Viles and Furnivall was reprinted under the title "The rogues and vagabonds of Shakespeare's youth," by the New Shakspere Society, *Series 6, no. 7,* London: N. Trübner, 1880, p. 17–91, * *NCK.* Included in Early English Text Society volume and the New Shakspere Society reprint, besides Harman's book, are John Awdelay's *The fraternitye of vacabondes, A sermon in praise of thieves and thievery,* by Parson Haben or Hyberdyne, and *The groundworke of conny-catching,* 1582 edition (only such parts as differ from Harman's *Caveat).* The bibliographical notes of Viles and Furnivall constitute a scholarly bibliography of early English canting dictionaries.

Harman lists the various classes of rogues and cheats, with full descriptions, and also gives the names of some of the vagabonds. He gives a glossary of words used by them. "Here I set before the good Reader the leud, lousey language of these lewtering Luskes and lasy Lorrels, where with they bye and sell the common people as they pas through the countrey. Whych language they terme Peddelars Frenche..."

The *Caveat,* in modernized English spelling, may be found in A. V. Judges, *The Elizabethan underworld,* London, 1930, p. 61–118, *SLG (q.v.).*

HIGGINS, JOHN, AND ABRAHAM FLEMING.

The nomenclator, or Remembrancer of A. J... Written in Latine, Greeke, French and other forrein tongues and now in English by J. Higins. With a dictional index. London, 1585. 8°.

Copy in the British Museum.

C. H. Cooper and T. Cooper in their *Athenae Cantabrigienses,* Cambridge, 1861, v. 2, p. 462, attribute this translation to Higgins and Fleming. In commenting upon the word "applesquire" as used by Joseph Hall in his *Satires,* 1824 edition, the editor, Thomas Warton, says the word was also in "that curious little manual, Junius's Nomenclator, by Abraham Fleming, 1585, *in voce* Aquariolus."

See "A note on sixteenth century vernacular English," by Don Cameron Allen, in *Language,* Baltimore, March, 1935, v. 11, p. 17–19, *RAA,* and "The English of the 'Nomenclator'" by Sir William A. Craigie, *Language,* Sept., 1935, v. 11, p. 242–243.

Hadrian Junius published the *Nomenclator* in 1567. He went to England in 1542 as personal physician to the Duke of Norfolk. He compiled his dictionary by associating with workmen and by visiting taverns. John Higgins translated the work, which was originally in Greek, Latin, German, Dutch, French, Italian, Spanish, and English, into English in 1585.

HINDLEY, CHARLES.

The old book collector's miscellany; or, A collection of readable reprints of literary rarities, illustrative of the history, literature, manners, and biography of the English nation during the sixteenth and seventeenth centuries. London: Reeves and Turner, 1871–73. 3 v. 8°. NCE

The first volume contains a reprint of Harman's *Caveat* among others. Volume 2 contains Dekker's *The Gull's hornbook,* and several works by John Taylor, the water poet. Hindley has added several interesting bibliographical comments on canting dictionaries.

NASH, THOMAS.

The complete works of Thomas Nashe. In six volumes. For the first time collected and edited...by the Rev. Alexander B. Grosart... [London and Aylesbury:] Printed for private circulation only, 1883–85. 12°. (The Huth library.) NCF

Limited to 50 copies.

v. 6 contains a "glossarial-index," p. 173–256. In this list are found scores of cant and slang words of the sixteenth century. Nash was unexcelled at picaresque idiom.

The works of Thomas Nashe edited from the original texts by Ronald B. McKerrow. London: Sidgwick & Jackson [1910]. 5 v. 8°. NCF

In the index in v. 5 cant and slang words used by Nash are included with other material. By comparing this index with Grosart's edition of Nash one may gather considerable etymological information of the sixteenth century.

Underworld Cant and Its Subsidiaries, cont'd

SEVENTEENTH CENTURY

BEAUMONT, FRANCIS, AND JOHN FLETCHER.
Beggars' Bush. (In: The works of Francis
Beaumont and John Fletcher. Variorum edition... London: George Bell and Sons & A. H.
Bullen, 1905. 8°. v. 2, p. 339–453.)   NCP
     The work first appeared in folio, in *Comedies, etc.,*
printed for Humphrey Robinson, at the three Pidgeons,
and for Humphrey Mosely at the Princes Armes in
St. Paul's church-yard, 1647. "Beggars Bush" is the
seventh play in this volume.
     It was published singly, in quarto, in 1661.
     This play borrows many canting words from Dekker.
The numerous canting terms are explained by the
editor, P. A. Daniel.
     The Library also has numerous other editions of
Beaumont and Fletcher's works.

BROME, RICHARD.
A joviall crew: or, The merry beggars. Presented in a comedie, at the cock-pit in Drury
Lane, in the yeer 1641... London: printed by
J. Y. for E. D. and N. E., and are to be sold
at the gun in Ivy-Lane. 1652.
     Reprinted in *The dramatic works of Richard Brome
containing fifteen comedies now first collected in three
volumes.* London: John Pearson, 1873, v. 3, p. 341–
452, *NCP.*
     This play is filled with canting slang. "The central
figure is Oldrents, a sort of fictional Harmon, who
welcomes to his estate all tatterdemalions. His daughters
share his tastes, and even run away with their lovers
to become 'stark, errant, downright beggars.'" —
Chandler, Literature of roguery, v. 1, p. 255.

—— London: J. Watts, 1731. 68 p. 12°.
                                                  NCO p.v.31

—— London: J. & R. Tonson, 1767. 46 p.
12°.   NCOF

—— London: T. Lowndes, 1774. 46 p. 8°.
                                                  NCO p.v.190

—— (In: R. Dodsley, A select collection of
old plays. London, 1780. 16°. v. 10, p. 319–443.)
                                                  NCO (Dodsley)

—— (In: Ancient British drama. London,
1810. 8°. v. 3, p. 179–216.)   NCO (Ancient)

—— London: J. Barker, 1813. 55 p. 8°.
                                                  NCP

THE CATTERPILLERS of this Nation anatomized,
in a brief yet notable Discovery of House-breakers, Pick-pockets, &c... London: Printed for
M. H. at the Princes Armes, in Chancery-
lane, 1659.
     See Early English Text Society, *Extra series 9,*
p. xxi, *NCE.*

COLES, ELISHA.
An English dictionary... London: Printed
by S. Collins, for R. Bonwick, T. Goodwin
[etc., etc.], 1717. 12°.   RNM
     Pages unnumbered.
     Contains many canting words, designated by the
letter (c). Has hundreds of English dialect words.
Has some trade jargon.
     The first edition noted by Kennedy is London:
S. Crouch, 1676. This dictionary was also published
in 1677, 1685, 1692, 1696, 1701, 1708, 1713, 1717,
1724, 1732. See Kennedy 6183, 6189, 6196, 6202, 6207,
6217, 6223.
     See Gerald Mander, "The identity of Elisha Coles,"
in *The Library,* London, 1919, v. 10, p. 34–44, * *HA.*
Mander mentions a 1676 edition printed for Peter
Parker, also a 1670 edition entitled, *The English*

*dictionary, or an expositor of hard English words,
newly refin'd...,* printed for W. Miller, 12°, but the
ascription of this book to Coles in the *Term catalogues*
of Arber is probably incorrect.

COTTON, CHARLES.
Burlesque upon burlesque: or, The scoffer
scoft; being some of Lucians Dialogues newly
put into English fustian, for the consolation of
those who had rather laugh and be merry, then
be merry and wise. [By Charles Cotton.] London: H. Brome, 1675. 200 p. 12°.   * KC 1675
     First edition.
     Filled with ribald slang. Cotton is best known
as the author of the dialogue between "Piscator" and
"Viator" written in 1676, which is the second part
of the fifth edition of Izaak Walton's *Compleat Angler,*
and for his translation of Montaigne's *Essays,* 1685.

Scarronides: or, Virgile travestie. A mock
poem. Being the first book of Virgil's Aeneis
in English... [By Charles Cotton.] London: H. Brome, 1664. 112 p. 16°.   Reserve
     Replete with the popular slang of the period.

DEKKER, THOMAS.
The Belman of London: Bringing to Light
the most notorious villanies that are now Practiced in the Kingdome. Profitable for Gentlemen, Lawyers, Merchants, Citizens, Farmers,
Masters of housholds, and all sorts of seruants,
to marke, and delightfull for all men to reade.
Lege, Perlege, Relege. [Woodcut of the Belman.] Printed at London for Nathaniel Butter,
1608.
     Copy in British Museum.
     Reprinted in *The non-dramatic works of Thomas
Dekker... For the first time collected and edited...
by the Rev. Alexander Grosart...* [London and Aylesbury:] Printed for private circulation only, 1884–86,
v. 3, p. 61–169, *NCF.*
     The edition by Grosart is limited to 50 copies.
The title-page is reproduced in facsimile.
     F. J. Furnivall states that Thomas Dekker in his
Belman of London pilfered from Harman's *Caveat.*
Dekker's work was pilfered by Richard Head in his
English rogue. See Early English Text Society, *Extra
series 9, NCE,* which contains a reprint of Harman's
Caveat (q.v.).
     The *Belman of London* was reprinted in part in
A. V. Judges, *The Elizabethan underworld,* London:
Routledge, 1930, p. 303–311, *SLG.*
     The "glossarial index" to Grosart's edition, v. 5,
p. 243–280, is a repertory of canting words.

The Guls Horne-booke: *Stultorum plena sunt
omnia.* Al Sauio meza parola Basta. By T.
Deckar. *Labore et Constantia.* Imprinted at
London for R. S. 1609.
     Copy in British Museum.
     Reprinted in Grosart's edition, v. 2, p. 193–266.
Title-page is reproduced.
     There was an 1812 edition edited by Dr. Nott.
     This witty book concerns itself with rules for a
young gallant in the city, and every page contains the
racy slang and idiom of an age not given over-much
to prudery.

The gull's hornbook. Edited by R. B. Mc-
Kerrow. London: De La More Press, 1904.
107 p. 4°. (The king's library. De La More
Press quartos. [no.] 2.)   * KP (De La More)

Underworld Cant and Its Subsidiaries, cont'd

Seventeenth Century, continued

DEKKER, THOMAS, *continued*

The guls hornbook, and The Belman of London. London: J. M. Dent and Co., 1904. 291 p. 24°. (Temple classics.)   COB (London)
A part of the *Guls Horne-booke* was reprinted in Leland Stanford Junior University. — English Club, *The true historie of the knyght of the burning pestle, full of mirthe & delight, by Francis Beaumont and John Fletcher, gent...and a notable account of How a young gallant should behave himselfe in a play-house, reprinted from the Gulls horne-book by T. Deckar.* San Francisco: P. Elder and M. Shepard, 1903. 58 p. illus. 16°, NCOM.

Lanthorne and Candle-light. Or, The Bell-Mans second Nights-walke. In which He brings to light, a Brood of more strange Villanies than euer were till this yeare difcouered. *Decet nouisse malum, fecisse, nefandum. The second edition, newly corrected and amended.* London *Printed for* Iohn Busby, *and are to be solde at his shop in Fleete-streete,* in Saint Dunstans Church-yard. 1609.
Copy in British Museum.
Reprinted in the Grosart edition, v. 3, p. 171–303. Dekker continues his canting speech in this work, and opens with a discourse on canting. "The first Inventor of it, was hang'd; yet left he apt schollers behind him, who have reduced that into *Methode,* which he on his death-bed <which was a paire of gallowes> could not so absolutely perfect as he desired." He goes on to explain thieves' language and gives a short dictionary of their terms, with a canting song or two thrown in.
Excerpts from Dekker's works were printed in William Beloe's *Anecdotes of literature and scarce books,* London: F. C. and J. Rivington, 1807, v. 2, p. 137–158, * GBH. Includes the list of canting terms in *Lanthorn and candle light.*
Reprinted in part in A. V. Judges, *The Elizabethan underworld,* London: Routledge, 1930, p. 312–365, SLG.

O per se O. London: Printed for John Busbie, and are to be sould at his shop in Fleetestreet in S. Dunstans Church-yard. 1612.
Copy in British Museum.
Reprinted in A. V. Judges, *The Elizabethan underworld,* London: Routledge, 1930, p. 366–382, SLG. "This book was published anonymously in 1612, and consists of two parts. The first is merely a reprint of Dekker's *Lantern and Candlelight;* the second is a not altogether successful attempt at continuation. We leave the city rogue, and return to the abram-man, the clapperdudgeon, and their colleagues of the country highway... Offers fresh and interesting information on beggar life. There are for instance two useful receipts for the production of artificial sores." — *Judges, p. 514.*
Judges hazards the guess that the work was by one of Dekker's hack-writing contemporaries. See also Frank Wadleigh Chandler, *The literature of roguery,* Boston: Houghton, Mifflin & Co., 1907, v. 1, NCBX.

THE DUTCH Whore, or the Miss of Amsterdam; being a new discovery of the Humours and Intrigues of Bullies, Pimps, Bauds, Cracks, and their Cullies; with a pleasant account of the Siege of the Black Castle, the place of the Rendezvous. 1690. 12°.
Title from Arber, *The term catalogues,* v. 2, p. 339. We have not seen this item, but the cant words in the title suggest contents couched in similar language.

E., B., GENT.
A new dictionary of the terms ancient and modern of the canting crew, in its several tribes of gypsies, beggars, thieves, cheats, &c., with an addition of some proverbs, phrases, figurative speeches, &c... By B. E., gent. London: Printed for W. Hawes at the Rose in Ludgatestreet, P. Gilbourne at the corner of Chancerylane in Fleet-street, and W. Davis at the Black Bull in Cornhill. [1698.]   8–RNM
Pages unnumbered. 92 leaves.
Various dates of publication have been given for this celebrated little dictionary, ranging from 1690 to 1720. Hawes was at the Rose in Ludgate street in 1698, and Gilbourne was at Chancery-Lane in Fleet street in the years 1697–1698. The only year common to both printers, therefore, is 1698.
Nothing is known of B. E., gent. From his dictionary one gathers that he was an antiquary. Some of his words and definitions bear no relation to slang and cant, but merely gratify his whim for curiosa. He may have known Rochester, D'Urfey, and the Earl of Dorset, and a close study of their literary remains may give a clue to his identity. See Victoria Sackville-West Nicolson's *Knole and the Sackvilles,* London, 1923, for a canting glossary similar to B. E.'s. This dictionary is perhaps the most important dictionary of slang ever printed, since it had such an influence on later compilations. *The New canting dictionary, Bacchus and Venus, The scoundrel's dictionary;* the canting dictionary appended to Nathan Bailey's *Dictionary,* Grose's *Classical dictionary of the vulgar tongue* — all are based on B. E., gent.

—— Facsimile reprint. [n. d.]   RNM
According to the British Museum Catalogue there was an American edition, Philadelphia, 1813, abridged from the London edition. There is also a reprint in John S. Farmer's *Choice reprints of scarce books and unique MSS., no. 3,* London: Smith, Kay & Company, 1899.
The compiler's copy is from the library of Richard Brinsley Sheridan, but bears no marginalia.

FACETIAE. The counter-scuffle. Whereunto is added the counter rat. Written by R. S. Quaint ... London: Printed by J. C. for Andrew Crook, 1670. 8°.
"Broad farcical ballads of London."
"The Counter-Rat is rich in the patter of the prison and the underworld." — *Argosy Book Stores, Catalogue no. 85.*

HEAD, RICHARD.
The canting academy, or the devil's cabinet opened. Wherein is shewn the mysterious and villanous practices of the wicked crew; commonly known by the names of hectors, trapanners, gilts, etc. London, sold by most booksellers, 1673. 12°.

The canting academy; or, Villanies discovered. Wherein is shewn the mysterious and villanous practices of that wicked crew, commonly known by the names of hectors, trapanners, gilts, &c. With several new catches and songs. Also a compleat canting dictionary. Both of old words, and such as now are most in use... The second edition. London: printed for F. Leach, for Mat. Drew... 1674. 12°.

The English rogue: described in the life of a complete history of the most eminent cheats Meriton Latroon, a witty extravagant. Being of both sexes. London, printed for Henry Marsh, at the Princes Arms in Chancery Lane, 1665.
Copy in the British Museum.
Reprinted by Chatto & Windus, London, 1874.
See W. Kollman, "Nash's 'Unfortunate traveller' and Head's 'English Rogue' " in *Anglia,* Halle, 1899, Bd. 22 [N. F. Bd. 10], p. 81–140, RNA.
"The opening chapters...are based on Head's own career... When the manuscript of 'The English rogue'

Underworld Cant and Its Subsidiaries, cont'd

Seventeenth Century, continued

HEAD, RICHARD, *continued*

was first presented to the censors of the press, licence was refused on the ground of its indecency... The original work was published by Henry Marsh in 1665, and in the following year was reissued by Francis Kirkman, bookseller. In spite of its popularity Kirkman applied in vain to Head to write a second part... Kirkman himself thereupon wrote a second part, which was licenced for the press, February 22, 1668, but no earlier edition than that of 1671 has been met with. In 1671, third and fourth parts were issued, with a promise of a fifth part. The four parts were republished uniformly in 1680. An abridgement of the first part, prepared by Head, appeared in 1679, and was reissued in 1688. A 'fifth' part is appended to an abridgement of the whole, issued in 1689." — H. N. Cary, *The slang of venery*, 1916, p. 9.

The English rogue described in the life of Meriton Latroon a witty extravagant. Being a complete history of the most eminent cheats of both sexes... London: George Routledge & Sons, 1928. 660 p. 4°.   8–CN

"The present edition contains Head's original volume and two of Kirkman's added volumes. The text has been left untouched except for certain necessary typographical corrections."
Based on the 1665 and 1671 volumes.
Chapter 5, p. 24–34 is devoted to the gipsy crew and their language, with a canting song and a glossary.
Chapter 14, p. 337–339, describes a company of canting beggars.
Chapter 15, p. 340–345, gives the orders and degrees of canting beggars. Contains a canting song.
The above sections of the book are based on Dekker's *The Belman of London*, which in turn was pilfered from Harman's *Caveat*.

—— New York: Dodd, Mead and Co., 1928. viii, 660 p. 4°.   8–CN

The life and death of the English rogue, or his last legacy to the world; containing most of his notorious robberies, cheats, and debauch'd practices. With a full discovery of a high-way rogue: the manner of his being apprehended. To which is added, an alphabetical canting dictionary. London: Printed for C. Passenger at the seven stars on London Bridge, 1679. 4°.

Copy in British Museum.
According to Arber, *Term catalogues*, v. 1, p. 358, this is an abridgement of the larger work by Head and Kirkman.

Proteus Redivivus, or The art of wheedling or insinuation, obtained by general conversation; and extracted from the several humours, inclinations, and passions, of both sex, respecting their several ages, and suiting each profession or occupation. Collected and methodised by the author of the first part of the 'English Rogue.' London: Sold by Peter Parker at the Leg and Star in Cornhill, 1675. 8°.

See Arber, v. 1, p. 197.
Richard Head "was the author of 'Hic et ubique, or the Humours of Dublin,' a comedy, printed in 1663, by which he acquired much reputation, and of several other pieces; particularly 'Nugae Venales,' which would have served for a general title to his works. Roguery, fornication, and cuckoldom, were the standing topics of this author, who was persuaded that his books would sell in proportion to the prevalency of those vices." — William King, in his *Works*, London, 1776, v. 2, p. 182, *NCF*.
King's own works contain much slang. King says of Kirkman, Head's publisher, "He was famous for publishing plays, farces, and drolls; and dealt as largely in drollery of various kinds as Curl did in

bawdry and biography. Kirkman, indeed, had no objection to trading in the former commodity, if he thought it would turn the penny. He has given us Memoirs of his own Life, and probably led the way to John Dunton." — *v. 1, p. 180.*
See the account of Richard Head in William Winstanley's *Lives of the English poets,* London: H. Clark, 1687, p. 207–210, *NADB.*

JONSON, BEN.

Bartholomew fair. (In his: Works...with notes critical and explanatory, and a biographical memoir, by W. Gifford... London: Printed for G. and W. Nicol [and others], 1816. 8°. v. 4, p. 357–542.)   NCP

This comedy was produced at the Hope Theatre, London, Oct. 31, 1614. It was printed in folio, 1631–1641. It contains many words in the canting language. The cant words are explained in the footnotes by Gifford.

MIDDLETON, THOMAS, AND THOMAS DEKKER.

The Roaring girle, or Moll Cut-Purse. (In: The works of Thomas Middleton, now first collected...by the Reverend Alexander Dyce ... London: Edward Lumley, 1840. 12°. v. 2, p. 423–562.)   NCP

This play is profusely studded with the cant of Shakespeare's day, and was first produced in 1611. Dyce explains the cant in footnotes. Middleton's other plays abound with slang. Thomas Dekker, quite a slangster in his own right, collaborated with Middleton on this particular play.

—— (In: Robert Dodsley, A select collection of old plays. London, 1780. 2. ed. 16°. v. 6, p. 1–132.)   NCO

—— (In: Ancient British drama. London, 1810. 8°. v. 2, p. 325–362.)   NCO (Ancient)

—— (In: Robert Dodsley. A select collection of old plays. London, 1825–27. 12°. v. 6, p. 1–111.)   NCO

NICOLSON, VICTORIA MARY (SACKVILLE-WEST).

Knole and the Sackvilles, by V. Sackville-West. London: William Heinemann, 1923. 230 p. 8°.   CO (Knole)

Thieves slang, p. 135–137.
"I find also, dated 1690, this curious vocabulary of thieves' slang, scribbled on the back of some particulars relating to the appointment of a new incumbent for Sevenoaks. Unfortunately half the alphabet is missing." This list was no doubt the work of Charles, Earl of Dorset and Middlesex, the then incumbent of Knole. The list of words and their definitions goes to the letter (M) and all but a few of them may be found in *A new dictionary of the terms ancient and modern of the Canting Crew*, by B. E., gent. He led a "devil-may-care" life in those gay times of Charles II, and he must have been familiar with the sporting and canting phrases of the day. Slang has always flourished in the time of gay monarchs, particularly in the reigns of Henry VIII, Charles II, and George IV. In those periods we had Copland, B. E., Gent., and Pierce Egan, and their companions.
A note on cant is given in the Appendix, p. 221–222.

—— Another copy.   CO (Knole)
See note under D'Urfey, Thomas, in the section devoted to the eighteenth century.

OVERBURY, SIR THOMAS.

A canting rogue. (In his: Miscellaneous works... 10th ed. London: W. Owen, 1756. 12°. p. 202–203.)   NCF

This little essay on the canting rogue was written circa 1613. Contains a remark or two about the manners and language of the Elizabethan rogue.

Underworld Cant and Its Subsidiaries, cont'd

Seventeenth Century, continued

ROWLANDS, SAMUEL.

The complete works of Samuel Rowlands, 1598–1628, now first collected... [Glasgow:] Printed for the Hunterian Club [by R. Anderson], 1880. 3 v. 8°. NCF

On cover: Hunterian Club. [Reprints] no. 1–4, 7–10, 14–15, 19–24, 29–30, 33–34, 37–39, 45, 51, 61. Issued in 26 parts, with special title-pages, dated 1872–1886.

"Notes to the works of Samuel Rowlands," p. 1–83, at end of volume three. Contains explanations of cant words.

"Glossary," p. 3–35 of terminal material in volume three. The notes and glossary were compiled by Sidney J. H. Herrtage.

Greenes ghost haunting conie-catchers, 1602, appears in volume two, 26 p. It is filled with cant.

Martin Mark-all, beadle of Bridewell; His defence and answere to the Belman of London, 1610, appears in volume one, 60 p. It contains a glossary of cant and canting songs.

The bibliographical index, by Sir Walter Scott, volume one, 46 p., goes into the history of the first editions of Rowlands's works, and locates copies. There is also a memoir of Rowlands by Edmund W. Gosse, in v. 1, p. 1–24. The title-pages are reproduced in facsimile.

See Edward D. McDonald, "An example of plagiarism among Elizabethan pamphleteers: Samuel Rowlands' 'Greenes ghost haunting conie-catchers'" in *Indiana University studies,* [v. 1], no. 11, p. 145–170, *STG.*

The Library has other editions of Rowlands's works, but this edition was chosen for its glossarial feature.

SHADWELL, THOMAS.

The squire of Alsatia. (In his: Dramatic works. London: James Knapton and Jacob Tonson, 1720. 12°. v. 4.) NCP

The play was first produced in 1688. At the beginning of this volume is a page of cant words used in the play.

—— London: J. Knapton, 1715. 76 p. 16°. NCO p.v.19

—— London: W. Feales, 1736. 102 p. 16°. NCP

—— (In: D. Macmillan, and H. M. Jones, editors, Plays of the Restoration and eighteenth century. New York [1931]. 8°. p. 257–306.) NCO

SHIRLEY, JOHN.

The triumph of wit, or ingenuity display'd in its perfection; being the newest and most useful academy, in three parts... Illustrated with poems, songs, etc., in the canting language ... Printed for N. Bodington at the Golden Ball in Duck lane. 1688. 12°.

See Arber, *Term catalogues,* v. 2, p. 218. British Museum has 5th ed., 1707; 6th, 1712; and 8th, 1724.

TAYLOR, JOHN.

The works of John Taylor, the water poet. Edited by Charles Hindley... London: Reeves and Turner, 1872. 4°. † NCF

John Taylor, 1580–1653, was a voluminous writer of prose and verse and his works abound in cant phrases. Hindley has explained the greater part of these in his footnotes. The New York Public Library has the rare first edition, *All the works of John Taylor, the water poet.* London: J. Boler, 1630. f°. *Stuart 13993.* The Library also has numerous single works by this author. Taylor's works have also been reprinted in the *Publications* of the Spenser Society, v. 2–4, 7, 14, 19, 21, 25, *NCE.*

W., J.

Youth's safety, or Advice to the Younger sort of each Sex, more valuable than Gold; laying open the wicked Practices of the Town shifts, Sharks, Beaus, Sweetners, Rakes, intraguing Town Jilts, to cheat, ruin, and disgrace, Gentlemen, Shopkeepers, Apprentices, Gentlewomen, Servant-Maids, etc... Printed for T. Ballard at the Ring in *Little Britain.* 1698. 4°.

See Arber, *Term catalogues,* v. 3, p. 97. Another edition is listed in v. 3, p. 97 for the year 1698; a 1699 edition, v. 3, p. 159; a 1700 edition, v. 3, p. 178; and a 1703 edition, v. 3, p. 376.

A WARNING for housekeepers; or, A discovery of all sorts of thieves and robeers which go under these titles, viz. — the Gilter, the Mill, the Glasier, Budg and Snudg, File-lifter, Tongue-padder, the private Theif[*sic*]... Written by one who was a prisoner in Newgate. Printed for T. Newton, 1676.

Described in Early English Text Society, *Extra series 9,* p. xxi, *NCE (Early).*

WINSTANLEY, WILLIAM.

A new help to discourse; or, Wit, mirth, and jollity, intermixt with more serious matters. By W. W., Gent. [William Winstanley.] London: printed by T. J. and sold by Peter Parker in Pope's Head Alley, in Cornhill, 1672.

Some of the editions of this work contain a canting dictionary. In the 4th edition, 1696, the dictionary occupies p. 93–97, so it cannot be a very large one.

In Capt. Charles Johnson's *A general history of the lives and adventures of the most famous highwaymen,* London: Olive Payne, 1736, p. 127, there is an account of Jack Bird, the highwayman, holding up Winstanley on the highway and robbing him of fifteen shillings and his new hat, despite Poor Robin's protestations that he was a friend and literary champion of many a notorious thief, having canonized many of them in his celebrated almanack.

Poor Robin. An almanack after a new fashion. London: Printed for the company of stationers [etc.], 1665–1828. 16°. CAC

The New York Public Library has the years 1665, 1669, 1671, 1673, 1678, 1680, 1685, 1689–1691, 1693, 1695, 1700, 1706, 1708–1709, 1711–1777, 1779–1780, 1782–1783, 1785, 1786, 1788, 1790, 1792–1805, 1811–1812, 1816, 1818, 1828.

The almanac was started in 1662. Winstanley's name does not appear on the title-page, but in the 1671 issue the compiler discloses his name in the following manner:

1 2 3 5 4
Thy will I am sure doth stan d to win true fame.

6
Ly then secure, thy works merrit the same.

These almanacs were burlesques of the standard almanacs of the time. They are filled with ribald slang and cant, enough to fill a small dictionary. The almanacs were continued long after Winstanley's death. The title was changed to *Old Poor Robin* in 1777. There are other slight variations of title from time to time. Sir Samuel Egerton Brydges called Winstanley the "barber biographer," in his *Censura literaria,* London, 1807, p. 129. Other men of the day feared Poor Robin's lampoons. Edward Ravenscroft, in his play, *The London Cuckolds,* London, 1682, says: "I shall be talk'd of in every Coffee-house, and Poor Robin wil make me a jest o'r all the nation." Articles on the obscenity of almanacs of the *Poor Robin* type appear in *Athenaeum,* London, 1828, v. 1, p. 5–6, 43–45, * *DA.* The word *obscenometer* is coined as a needed device to measure the degrees of indecency in printed matter.

Underworld Cant and Its Subsidiaries, cont'd

EIGHTEENTH CENTURY

ACADEMY of wit, with the mystery and art of canting, illustrated with poems, songs in the canting language. London, 1735. 12°.

AMOROUS Gallant's tongue tipp'd with golden expressions; or, The art of courtship refined, being the best and newest academy; containing select sentences, forms of courtship; choice letters; interpretations of dreams: to which is added bills, bonds, releases, letters of attorney, &c.; together with a canting academy, or the pedlar's French dictionary, 16th edition. London, for C. Hitch and L. Hawes, n. d. [1740.] 12°.

Mentioned by Hotten.

ASH, JOHN.
The new and complete dictionary of the English language... To which is prefixed, a comprehensive grammar... London: Printed for E. and C. Dilly [etc.], 1775. 2 v. 8°. * KF

Presentation copy from George Coningsby, 5th earl of Essex, to Thomas Moore; with two holograph letters from Essex to Moore inserted at end of v. 1. Bookplates of Thomas Moore. See *Bulletin*, The New York Public Library, Dec., 1933, v. 37, p. 1030.
Contains many cant words.

—— A second copy.   RNI

—— A third copy.   RNI

—— 2d ed. London, 1795. 2 v. 8°.   RNI

BACCHUS and Venus: or, A select collection of 200 near of the most witty and diverting songs and batches in love and gallantry, many whereof never appeared in print before. To which is added, a collection of songs in the canting dialect, with a dictionary explaining all the burlesque and canting terms used by the several tribes of gipsies, beggars, and other class of cheats and villains... With a preface giving an account of the original progress, etc., of the canting crew... London: Printed for R. Montague at the book-warehouse and general post-office, that end of Great Queens-street next Drury Lane, 1737. 12°.

Full title may be found in Michel.
Wood-engraving of boozing-ken for frontispiece.
One hundred and eighteen pages of songs, followed by "A collection of xix songs in the canting dialect being wholly new. By B. E. Gent. London" 26 p., signatures A–N. This is followed by "A new canting dictionary," unpaged, signatures B–L. — *Michel.*
Reprinted, with slight modifications in title, in 1738. See Kennedy 11890.
See Scoundrel's dictionary.
See Sir John Stainer, *Catalogue of English song books*, London, 1891, p. 9, * MC.
Bacchus and Venus is a page for page theft from *A new canting dictionary*, 1725 (q.v.).

BAILEY, NATHAN.
An universal etymological English dictionary ... The sixth edition, with considerable improvements. London: Printed for J. J. and P. Knapton... [and others], 1733. 472 l. 12°. RNI

This dictionary contains numerous canting words. They are indicated by the abbreviation "cant."

A collection of the canting words and terms, both ancient and modern, used by beggars, gyp-

sies, cheats, house-breakers, shop-lifters, footpads, highway-men, etc. 16 l. 8°.   RNI

Appended to his: The new universal etymological English dictionary. 4. ed. London: T. Waller, 1756. v. 2.
This canting dictionary also appears in the 3. ed., London: Thos. Cox, 1737, v. 2.
The dictionary occupies 31 unnumbered pages, two columns to a page. In other editions cant words are scattered through the text of the dictionary.
This dictionary formed the groundwork for Capt. Grose (q.v.) in his *Classical dictionary of the vulgar tongue*. Grose copied some of the definitions verbatim, but added so many new words of a later period that his dictionary stands on its own merit.
This is in reality the *A new canting dictionary*, London, 1725, which in turn is largely based on the celebrated dictionary of B. E., Gent. (q.v.).
"Nat Bailey should not be forgotten: he is even older than Grose, and twice as nasty." — Jon Bee, in preface to his *Sportsman's slang*, 1825, p. iii.

BAKER, THOMAS.
An act at Oxford. A comedy. By the author of the Yeoman O' Kent [Thomas Baker]... London: Printed for Bernard Lintot at the Middle-Temple-Gate in Fleetstreet. 1704. 60 p. 8°.   NCO p.v.309, no.7

Contains some of the London and Oxford cant and slang of the period, with emphasis on the slang of ribaldry.

BRIDGES, THOMAS.
Homer travestie: being a new translation of the four first books of the Iliad. By Cotton, Junior [Thomas Bridges?]. To which is prefix'd some small account of the author. London: R. Marriner, 1762. 231 p. 12°.

Copy in British Museum.
Filled with the slang and cant of the eighteenth century. It has been attributed to Francis Grose as well as to Thomas Bridges. *Cf.* Charles Cotton's works.

A burlesque translation of Homer <i. e. of Books i–xii of the Iliad. By T. Bridges>... Third edition, greatly enlarged and improved. London: S. Hooper, 1770. 2 v. 12°.

Copy in British Museum.

A burlesque translation of Homer. In two volumes. The fourth edition improved. London: Printed for G. G. and J. Robinson, 1797. 2 v. 8°.   NRLW

—— New-York: Published at the sentimental epicure's ordinary, 1809. 2 v. 16°.   NRLW

—— A second copy. 2 v. in 1.   NRLW

BROWN, THOMAS.
The works of Mr. Thomas Brown, serious and comical in prose and verse...with the life and character of Mr. Brown, and his writings, by James Drake... The seventh edition carefully corrected... London: Printed by and for Edward Midwinter, 1730. 4 v. 8°.   NCF

Contains much slang in the manner of Ned Ward, Tom D'Urfey, Poor Robin, and Charles Cotton, Brown's contemporaries. Brown was credited with the authorship of many books he did not write, including Ward's *The London spy*. Brown spent much of his time in brothels and coffee houses and was a keen observer of London night life.
Much of this material was reprinted in *A collection of all the dialogues written by Mr. Thomas Brown* ..., London: John Nutt, 1704, *NDF*; and *Amusements serious and comical and other works. By Tom Brown*. Edited with notes by Arthur L. Hayward, New York: Dodd, Mead & Co., 1927, 476 p., *NCF.*

Underworld Cant and Its Subsidiaries, cont'd

Eighteenth Century, continued

BURNS, ROBERT.
The jolly beggars. (In his: Poetry of Robert Burns. Edited by William Ernest Henley and Thomas F. Henderson... Edinburgh: T. C. and E. C. Jack, 1896. 8°. v. 2, p. 1–19.) NCL
  The extensive notes on this poem, p. 291–313, trace the canting elements in the poem, and review the literature of roguery.

CAREW, BAMPFYLDE MOORE.
The Life *and* Adventures of Bampfylde-Moore Carew, the noted Devonshire Stroler and Dog-Stealer; As related by Himself, during his Passage to the Plantations in *America.* Containing, A great Variety of remarkable Transactions in a vagrant Course of Life, which he followed for the Space of Thirty Years and upwards. EXON: Printed by the Farleys, for Joseph Drew, Bookseller, opposite *Castle-Lane,* 1745. *<Price two shillings.>* 8°.
  Copy in British Museum.
  "The specimen of the language of the community of gipsies, reprinted in one form or another in almost every subsequent edition <after the second> is an unacknowledged selection of the words given in *A new canting dictionary."* — *C. H. Wilkinson.*

The King of the beggars Bampfylde-Moore Carew. Edited by C. H. Wilkinson... Oxford: At the Clarendon Press, 1931. 307 p. port., facsims. 8°. AN
  A reprint of the 1745 and the 1749 editions. The introduction gives an accurate account of the Carew legend and the various editions of the books describing his adventures. The original title-pages of the 1745 and the 1749 editions are reproduced in facsimile.

The Accomplished Vagabond, or, The compleat Mumper: Exemplify'd in the Bold & artful Enterprises, & merry Pranks, of Bampfylde Carew, The notorious Dog-stealer... Exon: Printed by A. and S. Brice; by whom sold; and may also be had of Mess. Score, Thorn, and Tozer, Booksellers, in the same city. 1745. Price Sixpence.
  Lowndes wrongly attributed this to Oxon instead of Exon. No Oxford copy was ever found.
  There is a copy of this unique edition in the Dickson collection at Yale University. It is described by Ralph L. Collins in *Modern language notes,* Baltimore, April, 1933, v. 48, p. 249–251, RAA. "Published in the same year and at the same place as the first account of Carew, this volume was evidently designed to profit by the popularity of the earlier work. The poor grade of paper, its lack of ornaments and of a preface, the small type — which allows fifty-one lines to a page — the cheaper price, all point towards a piracy... Many new cant terms are made use of..." — *Ralph L. Collins.*

An APOLOGY for the LIFE of Bampfylde-Moore Carew, (son of the Rev. Mr. *Carew,* of *Bickley.*) Commonly known throughout the West of *England,* by the Title of KING of the BEGGARS; and DOG-MERCHANT-GENERAL. Containing, An Account of his leaving *Tiverton* School, at the Age of Fifteen, and entering into a Society of Gypsies; His many and comical Adventures, more particularly, a full and faithful Relation of his Travels twice through great Part of *America,* his Manner of living with the wild *Indians,* his bold Attempt in swimming the River *Delaware,* and many other extraordinary Incidents; His return Home, and Travels since in *England, Wales, Scotland,* and *Ireland.* The Whole taken from his own Mouth. *Totus Mundus agit Histrionem.* Printed by R. Goadby, and Sold by W. Owen, Bookseller, at *Temple-Bar, London.* [1749.] 8°.
  Frank Wadleigh Chandler, in the first volume of his *Literature of roguery* (q.v.) speaks of this 1749 edition, and says that the publishers, Goadby and Owen, issued under similar title, the third and most important biography. "This combines both the others, is twice as long as either, and has served as the basis of all future accounts. It is divided into chapters and includes laws of the gypsies, with a 'Gypsy' dictionary drawn in part out of Harman and Dekker." Chandler speaks of the thirty editions of Carew's biography and states that from 1871 forward the editions contain additional matter concerning vagabonds and their speech, derived from Simson's *History of the Gypsies,* 1865.
  The British Museum has an edition [1750?]; a second edition, London: W. Owen [1750?], 343 p., 8°; the sixth edition, London: R. Goadby [1765?], 350 p., 12°; the eighth edition, London: R. Goadby, 1768, 347 p., 12°; and the ninth edition, London: R. Goadby, 1775, 342 p., 12°.

The life and adventures of Mr. Bampfylae-Moore Carew, commonly called the king of the beggars. Being an impartial account of his life, from his leaving Tiverton School, at the age of fifteen, and entering into a society of gipsies ...with his travels twice through great part of America. Giving a particular account of the origin, government, laws, and customs of the gipsies...and a dictionary of the cant language, used by the mendicants. London: Sold by T. Forster, R. Armstrong, J. Digby, and W. Locke, 1779. 246 p., front. (port.) 12°. * KF 1779
  See Sabin 27615.
  Canting dictionary, p. 235–246

The life and adventures of Mr. Bampfylde-Moore Carew, commonly called the king of the beggars: Being an impartial account of his life, from his leaving Tiverton School, at the age of fifteen, and entering into a society of Gypsies, to the present time; wherein the motives of his conduct will be explained, and the great number of characters and shapes he has appeared in through Great Britain, Ireland, and several other places of Europe, be related; with his travels twice through great·part of America. A particular account of the origin, government, language, laws, and customs of the gypsies; their method of electing their king, &c. *Totus Mundus agit Histrionem.* A new edition. London: Printed for, and sold by the booksellers in Town and Country [n. d.]. 202 p. 16°.
  From compiler's copy.
  Portrait frontispiece.
  The dictionary of the gipsy language is on p. 197–202, but contains no Romany. It is simply an abridgement of the *New canting dictionary.*
  The "Advertisement to the reader" says in part: "The proprietors of this Edition beg leave to premise to the Public, that they have taken the liberty of omitting the parallel which has been carried on in the former Editions of this work, between Mr. Carew and Tom Jones...[etc.]."

—— London: R. Whiston, 1782. 240 p. 16°.
  Copy in Library of Congress.
  Contains the dictionary.

Underworld Cant and Its Subsidiaries, cont'd

Eighteenth Century, continued

CAREW, BAMPFYLDE MOORE, *continued*

The life and adventures of Mr. Bampfylde-Moore Carew, commonly called the king of the beggars. Being an impartial account of his life, from his leaving Tiverton School, at the age of fifteen, and entering into a society of gipsies ...with his travels twice through great part of America. Giving a particular account of the origin, government, laws, and customs of the gipsies...and a dictionary of the cant language, used by the mendicants. London: Printed for J. Wren and W. Hodges, 1785. 244 p. 12°.

Same dictionary as the 1779 edition.   * KF 1785

The life and adventures of Bampfylde-Moore Carew, commonly called the king of the beggars: being an impartial account of his life, from his leaving Tiverton School at the age of fifteen, and entering into a society of gipsies... with his travels twice through great part of America: giving a particular account of the origin, government, laws, and customs of the gipsies, with the method of electing their king: and a dictionary of the cant language used by the mendicants. London: Printed for W. Cavill, 1791. 222 p., 3 l. 12°.   * KF 1791

The dictionary occupies the last six unnumbered pages, two columns to a page. The words are the same as those in the 1779 edition.

—— London: J. Buckland, 1793. 235 p. 12°.
Copy in the British Museum.

—— London: R. Bassam, 1798. 182 p. 12°.
Copy in the British Museum.

A brief relation of the adventures of Bamfylde Moore Carew, who was for more than forty years king of the beggars. Glasgow [180–?]. 24 p. 16°.   NDP p.v.3, no.88

—— London: T. Hughes, 1804. 104 p. 12°.
Copy in the British Museum.

The life, voyages and adventures of Bampfylde-Moore Carew; commonly called, king of the beggars. Being an impartial account of his life, from his leaving Tiverton School, at the age of fifteen, and entering into a society of gypsies, to his death...with a history of his travels twice through great part of America. Collected and amended from his own writings, by Thomas Price... To which is added, a dictionary of the cant language, used by the mendicants. London: Printed for J. Barker; Mr. Brown, Bristol; and Mr. Fish, Exeter [1785?]. 2 p.l., 212 p., front. (port.) 12°.   * KF 1785

—— London: J. Barker [1810?]. 212 p. 12°.
Copy in the British Museum.
Canting dictionary, p. 205–212, same as 1779 edition. The text is changed from earlier editions.

The life and adventures of Bampfylde-Moore Carew, commonly called the king of the beggars. Being an impartial account of his life, from his leaving Tiverton School at the age of fifteen, and entering into a society of gipsies... with his travels twice through great part of America: containing a particular account of the origin, government, laws, and customs, of the gipsies, with the method of electing their king, and a dictionary of the cant language used by the mendicants. Derby: H. Mozley [1811?]. 159 p., 5 l., front. 12°.   AN

—— Gainsborough: H. Mozley, 1811. 165 p. 12°.
Copy in the British Museum.
The text, and the dictionary of the cant language, is the same as the 1779 ed. Preface omitted.

The surprising adventures of Bampfylde Moore Carew, king of the beggars, containing his life, a dictionary of the cant language, and many entertaining particulars of that extraordinary man. A new edition corrected & much improved. Tiverton: Printed for W. Salter, 1812. 288 p., front. (port.), plates. 12°.

Engraved title-page.   * KF 1812
A dictionary of the cant language, p. 273–288. The vocabulary has been enlarged from the 1779 edition. The main text is the same, but the preface is different.

...The king of the beggars; or, The history of Bampfylde Moore Carew who was the son of a gentleman near Plymouth, and ran away from his father and joined a gang of gypsies, detailing the numerous tricks and impositions practised by him in various disguises, with an account of his coronation as king of the gypsies. London: O. Hodgson [1840?]. 23 p., col'd front. 8°.   * KVD

At head of title: Hodgson's edition.

The history and curious adventures of Bampfylde-Moore Carew, king of the mendicants. London: R. Davies [1882?]. 160 p. 12°.   AN
"A dictionary of the cant language generally used by the mendicants," p. 151–160.
The authorship has been ascribed variously to Thomas Price, Robert Goadby, Mrs. Goadby and Carew himself. Text same as 1812 edition. The dictionary is based on the 1812 edition, with a few additions.

—— London: W. Tegg, 1871. 414 p. 16°.
Copy in the British Museum.

The life of Bamfylde Moore Carew, some time king of the beggars, containing an accurate history of his travels, voyages, and adventures. New York: Published by D. Felt & Co.; Pittsburgh: Cook and Schoyer, 1834. 29 p., front. 12°.   * KF 1834

See Sabin 27615.
A chapbook in original paper covers.

—— Edinburgh [1800?]. 24 p. 12°.
Copy in the British Museum.

—— London [1800?]. 24 p. 12°.
Copy in the British Museum.

—— Glasgow: J. & M. Robertson, 1802. 24 p. 12°.
Copy in the British Museum.

—— Glasgow, 1808. 24 p. 12°.
Copy in the British Museum.

—— Penrith: A. Soulby [1810?]. 20 p. 12°.
Copy in the British Museum.

—— Newcastle: G. Adams [1820?]. 36 p. 12°.
Copy in the British Museum.

—— London: J. Bailey [1820?]. 36 p. 12°.
Copy in the British Museum.

—— Devonport: E. Keys [1820?]. 12 p. 12°.
Copy in the British Museum.

—— London: Dean and Munday [1820?]. 36 p. 8°.
Copy in the British Museum.

Underworld Cant and Its Subsidiaries, cont'd

Eighteenth Century, continued

CAREW, BAMPFYLDE MOORE, *continued*

Jensen, Gerard Edward.
Concerning the use of slang. (American speech. Baltimore, Oct., 1927. 4°. v. 3, p. 12–13.)   RNA
Calls attention to the terseness of the expressions in the cant dictionary appended to the *Apology* of Bampfylde Moore Carew, circa 1750.
See also Edward Abbott Parry, *Vagabonds all...* New York: Charles Scribner's Sons, 1926, p. 229–260, *SLG.*

CAREY, HENRY.
Chrononhotonthologos... London: W. Lowndes, 1806. 16 p. 8°.   NCP
Also printed in his *Dramatick works,* London, 1743, p. 151–182, *NCP.*
This play was first published in 1734.
It is a burlesque, filled with jargon, an attempt to ridicule the use of big words on the stage. Compare this with Archibald Campbell's *Lexiphanes,* a satire on Dr. Johnson. Other burlesques on Dr. Johnson were *Anecdotes of the learned pig,* London: Hockham, 1786, and *The etymologist,* London: Printed for J. Jarvis, 1785.
Another play containing jargon is *Lingua: or, The combat of the tongue and the five senses for superiority,* London: G. Eld, for Simon Waterson, 1607, attributed to Anthony Brewer. In *The muse's looking-glass,* Oxford: Leonard Lichfield, for Francis Bowman, 1638, vanities of high-flown speech are criticized as "the idle timpanies of a windy brain." In John O'Keeffe's drama, *The agreeable surprise,* there is a character by the name of Lingo. *Cf.* the character Jeremiah Lingo in George Daniel's *Sworn at Highgate,* a musical farce.
Carey, in his *Chrononhotonthologos* satirizes the poetaster "who with his big bellowing Bombast rend our Ears."
In his *The honest Yorkshireman,* first acted in 1735, there is a character called "Slango." If this is a play on the word "slang" it is one of the earliest recorded. Could the original word have been *slango* (Gipsy?) later to be shortened to *slang?* Lingo and slango are closely related in sound and meaning.
The New York Public Library has many editions of *Chrononhotonthologos.* It may also be found in standard collections such as Lacy, Cumberland, Dodsley, etc.
Carey will be remembered for his celebrated song, "Sally in our alley."

CAULFIELD, JAMES.
Blackguardiana or, Dictionary of rogues, bawds, &c...with portraits. [By James Caulfield.] 1795.
"This work, with a long and very vulgar title, is nothing but a reprint of Grose, with a few anecdotes of pirates, odd persons, &c., and some curious portraits inserted. It was concocted by Caulfield as a speculation, and published at one guinea per copy; and, owing to the remarkable title, and the notification at the bottom, that 'only a few copies were printed,' soon became scarce. For philological purposes it is not worth so much as any edition of Grose." — *Hotten.*
James Caulfield (1764–1826) was the compiler of *Portraits, memoirs, and characters of remarkable persons,* 1790–95. *The Dictionary of national biography* says of this work: "Caulfield's 'Remarkable characters' are persons famous for their eccentricity, immorality, dishonesty, and so forth." For his complete works see DNB.

CHARACTERISM, or, the Modern Age display'd; being an attempt to expose the pretended virtues of both sexes. (Part one, Ladies; part two, Gentlemen.) London: E. Owen [1750?]. 8°.
"An anonymous work, from which some curious matter may be obtained." — *Hotten.*
Copy in the British Museum.

THE CHOIR of Anacreon; Or, Captain Morris's Lyric Repository. London: Printed for C. Curl ...1790.
This anthology contains some cant. Copy owned by Mr. Walter N. H. Harding, of Chicago.

A COLLECTION of Favourite Songs sung at the Beaf Steak Club, and the Anacreontic Society. By Messrs. Edwin, Dodd, Dignum... London. Printed and Sold by J. Fentum the Corner of Salisbury Street in the Strand, n.d.
Probably published in the 1780's. Contains 106 songs, many of a canting nature. Copy owned by Mr. Walter N. H. Harding, of Chicago.

CONSTANT READER, PSEUD.
The cant language of thieves. (Monthly magazine. London, Jan., 1799. 8°. v. 7, p. 22–23.)   *DA
Short list of current terms used by the English thieves.

DEFOE, DANIEL.
Street robberies considered. The reason of their being so frequent, with probable means to prevent 'em. To which is added, three short treatises: — 1. A warning for travellers: with rules to know a highwayman, and instructions how to behave upon the occasion. 2. Observations on housebreakers. How to prevent a tenement from being broke open. With a word of advice concerning servants. 3. A caveat for shopkeepers: with a description of shoplifts, how to know 'em, and how to prevent 'em; also a caution of delivering goods: with a relation of several cheats, practiced lately upon the publick. Written by a converted thief [Daniel Defoe]. To which is prefix'd some memoirs of his life. *Set a thief to catch a thief.* London: Printed for J. Roberts, in Warwick Lane, 1728. 72 p. 8°.
Most bibliographies attribute this work to Defoe. Contains a long list of slang words. Some of them are listed in Early English Text Society, *Extra series 9,* London, 1869, p. xxii–xxiii, *NCE* (*Early*). This authority lists the work as being anonymous.
Defoe is also credited with writing a life of the famous prison breaker, Jack Sheppard. See Horace Bleackley, *Jack Sheppard,* Edinburgh, 1933, *SLN,* for the latest bibliographical information *in re* Defoe.

DODSLEY, ROBERT.
A select collection of old English plays... 4th edition. Now first chronologically arranged, revised and enlarged with the notes of all the commentators, and new notes. By W. Carew Hazlitt... London: Reeves and Turner, 1876. 15 v. 8°.   NCO
"Glossarial index," by Richard Morriss, v. 15, p. 459–509, contains many slang and cant words and phrases. See index to notes, v. 15, p. 435–455.

D'URFEY, THOMAS.
The bath, or, The western lass. A comedy, as it was acted at the Theatre Royal in Drury-lane, by his majesty's servants. London: Printed for Peter Buck, at the sign of the Temple, at the Middle Temple Gate in Fleetstreet, 1701. 56 p. 8°.   NCO p.v.46
Filled with the slang of the period.

Underworld Cant ana Its Subsidiaries, cont'd

Eighteenth Century, continued

D'URFEY, THOMAS, *continued*

Wit and mirth: or Pills to purge melancholy; being a collection of the best merry ballads and songs, old and new... 4th ed... London: Printed by W. Pearson, for J. Tonson, 1719–20. 6 v. 16°.   6–NDE

Collected by Tom D'Urfey, song-writer and playwright of the gay period of Charles II, who was a special patron of this prolific writer, these not overly chaste songs abound in the ribald slang of the times. It was at this time that B. E., Gent brought out his dictionary of canting phrases. D'Urfey was a scurrilous writer, but enjoyed the friendship of the principal wits and noblemen, and even the crowned heads of the period, who delighted in his wit and humor. He was often at the home of the Duke of Dorset, at Knole. A good account of D'Urfey may be found in the introduction, p. 3–44, of *The songs of Thomas D'Urfey*, by Cyrus Lawrence Day, Cambridge, Mass.: Harvard University Press, 1933. 8°. (Harvard studies in English. v. 9), * *MP* (*English*). Day also gives the earlier editions of D'Urfey's songs, p. 41–44. See also *DNB* and *The original works of William King*, London, 1776, 12°, v. 2, p. 119, *NCF*. There is a portrait of D'Urfey in Day's excellent work, painted by van der Gucht, while D'Urfey was staying with the Duke of Dorset, and now in the possession of Baron Sackville, a direct descendant of the Dorsets of Knole. Dorset was a gay blade and delighted in the company of tavern wits. He even compiled notes for a canting dictionary.

FIELDING, SIR JOHN.

A brief description of the cities of London and Westminster, the public buildings, palaces ... To which are added some proper cautions to the merchants, tradesmen, and shopkeepers, journeymen, apprentices, porters, errand-boys, bookkeepers, and innkeepers; also very necessary for any person going to London, either on business or pleasure. London, 1776. 12°.

Copy in the British Museum.
Contains some cant.

Thieving detected: being a true and particular account of the various methods and artifices used by thieves and sharpers to take in and deceive the public; with proper cautions to guard against such destructive measures... London, 1777. 8°.

Copy in the British Museum.
Reprinted in Gilbert Armitage, *The history of the Bow Street runners, 1729–1829*, London: Wishart & Co. [1932], p. 268–293, *SLE*.
Describes "The Kidd," "House-breaking, or, in the flash language, to Mill a Kin," "The drag lay," "The knuckle," "The jump," "The sneak," "The drop," "Starring the glaze," "The pinch or truck," "Flying the basket," "The thrust," and "The lift or hoist."

GROSE, FRANCIS.

A classical dictionary of the vulgar tongue. London: Printed for S. Hooper, no. 212, High Holborn, 1785. Entered at Stationers Hall. 1785. 182 p. 12°.   RNM

A reprint of the first edition.
"Grose's Classical Dictionary of the Vulgar Tongue appeared in 1785, the slightly enlarged second edition in 1788, and the third — the last to incorporate its editor's additions and corrections — in 1796.. (The additions of 1811, known as the Lexicon Balatronicum, and 1823, Pierce Egan's, need not concern us further than this bare mention.) The first edition contained about 3,000, the third nearly 4,000 entries, and except in the few instances in which he reproduces, with only verbal changes, the definitions — this applies almost solely to cant — of B. E. or of the editor of the 1725 Canting Dictionary, every entry bears the unmistakable imprint of the vivid accuracy and the jolly, jovial earthiness of 'the greatest antiquary, joker, and porter-drinker of his day' and one of the happiest wits of 1760–1790." — Eric Partridge, in his *Slang of to-day and yesterday*, London, 1933, p. 75–76.

A classical dictionary of the vulgar tongue. The second edition, corrected and enlarged. London: Printed for S. Hooper, No. 212, High Holborn, facing Bloomsbury Square. 1788. xv, 248 p. 8°.   RNM

Pages unnumbered.
"The second edition is much the better of the three." — *Nodal*.

A classical dictionary of the vulgar tongue. 3rd ed., corrected and enlarged. London, Hooper & Widstead, 1796.

A classical dictionary of the vulgar tongue, by Captain Francis Grose: edited with a biographical and critical sketch and an extensive commentary by Eric Partridge... London: Issued for private subscribers by the Scholartis Press, 1931. 396 p. 4°.   RNM

The text is that of the 3rd edition, 1796.
Reviewed in *London Times literary supplement*, Dec. 31, 1931, p. 1052, *NAA*; *Saturday review*, London, Aug. 29, 1931, p. 152, 269, * *DA*; *Notes & queries*, Oct. 3, 1931, v. 161, p. 234, * *R–* DA*.

Grose's classical dictionary of the vulgar tongue, revised and corrected, with the addition of numerous slang phrases, collected from tried authorities. By Pierce Egan... London: Printed for Sherwood, Neely, and Jones, Paternoster-Row, 1823. 123 l., 1 port. 8°.   RNM

Contains the prefaces to the first and second editions, and a preface written by Pierce Egan. There is a biographical sketch of Grose, p. xxix–xl. The frontispiece is a supposed likeness of the famous antiquary.
The New York Public Library has an interleaved edition of this 1823 enlargement of Grose, differing only in the imprint, which reads, London: Printed for the editor, no. 71, Chancery-Lane, and sold by all booksellers, 1823. *RNM*.

Lexicon balatronicum. A dictionary of buckish slang, university wit, and pickpocket eloquence. Compiled originally by Captain Grose. And now considerably altered and enlarged, with the modern changes and improvements, by a member of the Whip Club. Assisted by Hell-Fire Dick, and James Gordon, Esqrs. of Cambridge; and William Soames, Esq. of the Hon. Society of Newman's Hotel. London: Printed for C. Chappel, Pall Mall; Sold by J. Johnston, Cheapside; Goddard, Pall-Mall, and all other booksellers. 1811. 8°.   RNM

Col'd frontispiece by G. Cruikshank is missing from this copy.
Pages unnumbered. 14 sheets of 16 p. each, B–P².
The compiler of this dictionary, according to Jon Bee, was H. Clarke. Kennedy gives Hewson Clarke. See no. 11919. Bee, in his *Sportsman's slang*, 1825, p. ix, says: "Hell-fire Dick's name, with some others bore a prominent feature on the first leaf; Dick Owen, or Vowen, or Vaughan, had, however, nought whatever to do with 'the writing part,' not being in the habit of penmanship; and he was, moreover, previously dead and buried. The other names on the title were fictitious, or not allowable — it was, in fact, a printer's job." In another place Bee says that Hell-fire Dick Owen was a Cambridge coachman. He says moreover that this was the best edition of Grose. Bee's statements are often inaccurate and are not to be trusted. See *Bang-up dictionary*.
For a biographical account of Grose see the *Dictionary of national biography*. There is a portrait and short memoir in the *European magazine*, London, July,

Underworld Cant and Its Subsidiaries, cont'd

Eighteenth Century, continued

1797, v. 32, p. 3–4, * DA. There is a brief memoir of Grose in *Anthologia Hibernica*, Dublin, Nov., 1794, v. 4, p. 321–322, * DA. The latter is accompanied by a "striking likeness of him from an original etching by Bartolozzi." The memoir states that a movement was under foot to erect a monument to Grose in Christ Church, Dublin, and a model had been made by the "celebrated architect, Mr. Gandon."

HALL, JOHN.
Memoirs of the right villainous J. H. [John Hall] the late famous robber... Also a... representation of Newgate, and its inhabitants ...to which is added the cant...us'd by those sort of people, etc. London, 1708. 8°.
Copy in the British Museum.

—— 4th edition. London: H. Hills, 1708. 8°.
Copy in the British Museum.

—— 4th edition. London, 1714. 8°.
Copy in the British Museum.
Hall's "An interpretation of the several qualities of rogues," a part of the *Memoirs*, is reprinted in Raymond Postgate's *Murder, piracy, and treason*, London: Jonathan Cape [1925], p. 239–242, *SLN*. Postgate, however, does not reprint the glossary of flash words.

THE HISTORY of the lives of Jonathan Wild, thief taker, Joseph Blake, alias Blueskin, footpad, and John Sheppard, housebreaker, giving a full and exact account of Jonathan's being crown'd king of the gypsies...as also a true relation of the pranks Jack Sheppard played and of his being retaken. Taken from several papers found since Jonathan's death with letters and private confessions to friends never yet published. The third edition. London. Printed for Edw. Midwinter at the three crowns and looking glass in St. Paul's churchyard [1725].
Described in the bibliography in Horace Bleackley's *Jack Sheppard*, Edinburgh, 1933, p. 128, *SLN*. S. M. Ellis, who compiled the bibliography, says that there is a quaint portrait of each of the three criminals, and at the end a canting dictionary by Jonathan Wild.

HITCHIN, CHARLES.
The regulator; or a discovery of the thieves, thief-takers, and locks, alias receivers of stolen goods in and about London; also an account of all the flash words now in vogue amongst the thieves... [London,] 1718. 8°.
Copy in the British Museum. Contains a woodcut. "Published anonymously. The author was Charles Hitching [*sic!*], sometimes City Marshal, but wrote his book when a prisoner in Newgate. It contains a violent attack upon Jonathan Wild." — *Nodal*.
Hitchin's glossary is reprinted in Raymond Postgate's *Murder, piracy, and treason; a selection of notable English trials*, London: Jonathan Cape [1925], p. 233–238, *SLN*.

THE / HONEST FELLOW, / or / Buck's necessary Companion. / Wherein / Mars and Venus, assisted by Bacchus, are in conjunction to exhibit the Humours of the World, / In a Collection of such / Jocular Songs, / As will provoke the Laugh in spite of Grief, Care, Distress, the Hyp or Vapours. / To which is added, / A Collection of Comic Sentiments, and other Matters to make an accomplished Toper. / Published at no. 8, Mary Street, Dublin. /
The only copy the compiler knows about is the one owned by Mr. Walter N. H. Harding, of Chicago. Mr. Harding writes: "This is the way the first title-page reads and each of the six reads differently. That to no. IV has the imprint... Published at no. 36, Denmark-street, Dublin, 1794, thus fixing the date. The volume was issued in six parts of 28 pages each so that it has 166 pages plus the first title-page. It is 6¾ by 8½ inches but is without signatures. It is probably an oblong octavo with only 6 leaves in the second gathering of each part. There is music to every song. This song book contains the most erotic collection of English songs I have ever seen containing all those popular in England during the period 1780 to 1795; the age of Hewerdine, Morris and the other bon vivants ... I suspect the volume is unique."

JOHNSON, CHARLES.
A general history of the lives and adventures of the most famous highwaymen, murderers, street-robbers, &c... To which is added, a genuine account of the voyages and plunder of the most notorious pirates... London: Printed and sold by Olive Payne...1736. 484 p. f°.   * KC
Contains much cant. The stories of Moll Cut-purse, Jack Sheppard, Jonathan Wild, Blueskin, etc., are of interest. There is much cant in the section devoted to William Nevison. The section on Tom Sharp contains a number of words probably taken from Harman via Dekker.

LOGAN, WILLIAM HUGH.
A pedlar's pack of ballads and songs... Edinburgh: William Paterson, 1869. 479 p. 12°.   NCK
Contains eleven canting songs from *Bacchus and Venus*, London, 1737. The greater part of the preface to *Bacchus and Venus* is reprinted. The songs are: The canter's holiday: The thief-catcher's prophecy; The life and death of the Darkman's budge; Clear out — look sharp; The strowling mort's praise of her clapper-dogeon; The beggar's curse; The canter's serenade; Retoure, my dear Dell; All men are beggars; Jack Sheppard (with bibliographical notes); Blueskin (with bibliographical notes). The latter two were taken from John Thurmond's *Harlequin Jack Sheppard*, 1724.
Also includes "Ye scamp, ye pads, ye divers" from Messink's *The choice of Harlequin, or the Indian chief*, acted in 1781.
In the appendix is an "Explanation of the terms used in the canting songs," p. 452–457.

MILLER, WILLIAM DAVIS.
Thomas Mount and the flash language. (Rhode Island Historical Society. Collections. Providence, July, 1929. 8°. v. 22, p. 65–69.) IAA
Speaks of the *Voluntary Confession of Thomas Mount*, by the Rev. William Smith, of Newport, Rhode Island, written between 1790 and 1797. This is the first account of an organization of thieves called the Flash Company, organized in London, with members in the American colonies. A note on the history of the flash languages, and a flash song, are also included.

A NEW canting dictionary: comprehending all the terms, antient and modern, used in the several tribes of gypsies, beggars, shoplifters, high-waymen, foot-pads, and all other classes of cheats and villains... Being a complete collection of all that has been publish'd of that kind, with very large additions of words never before made publick... To which is added a complete collection of songs in the canting dialect. London: printed; and sold by the booksellers of London and Westminster, 1725. 12°.
Copy in the British Museum.
156 unnumbered pages.
Lowndes says that this volume contains a frontis-

Underworld Cant and Its Subsidiaries, cont'd

Eighteenth Century, continued

A NEW canting dictionary, *continued*

piece. There is none in the British Museum copy. My own copy does not have one.

This is based largely on B. E., Gent [q.v.]. The first part of the preface is almost identical with B. E., Gent's preface. Some remarks on the canting dialect are new, and an attempt to trace the gipsies is made. The episodes of Jack Sheppard are mentioned.

The last 26 pages contain canting songs, some of them from "Harlequin Shepherd."

A NEW collection of poems relating to state affairs, from Oliver Cromwell to this present time. By the greatest wits of the age. Wherein, not only those that are contain'd in the three volumes already published are incerted [*sic*], but also large additions of chiefest note, never before published. The whole from their respective originals, without castration. London: printed in the year 1705. 591 p. 8°.   NCI

Contains much slang and cant, chiefly from the time of the Restoration to the beginning of Queen Anne's reign.

The Library also has v. 2 and 3 of the earlier edition, dated 1703 and 1704 respectively, 8°, *NCI*. These earlier volumes contain more slang words of a ribald nature.

THE NIGHT before Larry was stretched. (Walker's Hibernian magazine. Dublin, 1787. 8°.)   Music Div.

This Irish slang song was never bound in The New York Public Library's copy of *Walker's Hibernian magazine*, 1787, or was removed by a vandal. It is likewise missing from the Newberry Library's copy, and the one in the Trinity College Library, Dublin, but thanks to Mr. J. Hanna, of the latter institution, a photostat copy was obtained from the National Library of Ireland, and is now available in the Music Division. Mr. Hanna was of the opinion that the song was never included in a great many copies.

John S. Farmer included this song in his anthology *Musa Pedestris*, and was of the opinion that it was written circa 1816. He says: "Neither the authorship nor the date of these inimitable verses are definitely known. According to the best authorities, Will Maher, a shoemaker of Waterford, wrote the song. Dr. Robert Burrowes, Dean of St. Finbar's, Cork, to whom it has so often been attributed, certainly did not." Stimulated by Farmer's uncertainty the compiler tried to trace the origin and authorship, but got no farther than the 1787 anonymous song which was set to music in *Walker's Hibernian magazine*. It contains six stanzas. It has for sub-title: "An Irish Slang Song; to be pronounced as spelled."

There are several versions of the poem. Francis Sylvester Mahony, better known as Father Prout, translated the song into French for *Fraser's magazine*, Dec., 1834, v. 10, p. 671–672, * *DA*, under the title "La Mort de Socrate," with a parallel English version in seven stanzas, the fourth stanza beginning "Then the cards being called for, they played," which is an interpolation, since it did not occur in the 1787 version. Mahony definitely assigned the authorship to the Rev. Robert Burrowes, Dean of St. Finbar's Cathedral, Cork.

In *Blackwood's magazine*, Dec., 1821, v. 10, p. 615–616, * *DA*, appears a song entitled "Saint Patrick," set to the music of "The night before Larry was stretched." In a note written by Christopher North, we learn that "the tune to which Mr. Mulligan has put these words is a great favourite in Ireland. It is said the original words ("The night before Lary [*sic*] was stretched") were written by a very learned gentleman, who is now a dignitary of the established church in Ireland. It is a first-rate slang song."

Also attributed to Kane O'Hara, the Irish playwright, to Henry Grattan Curran, to Edward Lysaght, and others.

Mr. Walter N. H. Harding, of Chicago, who owns the finest collection of songs of this nature in America, including the famous Stainer collection which he pur-

chased in 1932, informed the compiler that "Larry" appeared in *The Festival of Anacreon II*, 1788, in *Paddy Whack's Bottle Companion*, 1791, and in *The Honest Fellow*, Dublin, 1794, "an extremely rare and curious book of songs." The Harding collection is a rich, untapped field for the student of canting songs.

Versions of the song may be found in *The Universal songster*, London, 1834; H. Halliday Sparling, *Irish minstrelsy*, London: Walter Scott, 1888, *NDM;* Alfred Percival Graves, *The reciter's treasury of Irish verse and prose*, London: Routledge [1915], *NDM;* Broadstreet ballads, *being a collection of Irish popular songs with an introduction by Padraic Colum*, Dublin: Maunsel & Co. [n. d.], *NCK;* and M. J. Barry, *The songs of Ireland*, Dublin: James Duffy, 1854, *NDM*. The Graves and Sparling versions are the same, containing nine stanzas. Most versions have seven stanzas.

S. J. Adair Fitz-Gerald, in his *Stories of famous songs*, London: John C. Nimmo, 1898, p. 368–369, assigns the song to Will Maher, who kept a cloth shop in Waterford. Fitz-Gerald gleaned this information from *Ireland ninety years ago*, published in 1876. That would throw the song close to the year 1787. The subject of the song was one Lambert.

The *Hibernian magazine* contained other flash songs. In the Jan., 1785, issue was a song entitled "Your rhino rattle"; in the Nov., 1773, issue, "The new fol de rol tit," which was reprinted under the title "The flash man of St. Giles" in Farmer's *Musa pedestris;* and other issues contain poems which are sprinkled with slang words.

O'HARA, KANE.

The golden pippin. An English burletta, in two acts... By the author of Midas [Kane O'Hara]. A new edition. London: Printed for T. Becket... 1777. 34 p. 8°.   NCO p.v.356

This burletta was first acted at Covent Garden, Feb. 6, 1773. The Library also has a copy of the first edition, London: T. Becket, 1773, *NCO p.v.159*.

Written in rollicking cant and slang. The family of actors and musicians by the name of D'Amici had introduced the Italian burletta in Ireland, and O'Hara wrote a travesty of it in his burletta *Midas* in 1759, which was published in 1764. There are many editions of *Midas* in the Library. O'Hara, according to the account given in the DNB, is one of the alleged authors of the Dublin slang ballad *The night before Larry was stretched*. A popular Dublin slang song was entitled *Kane O'Hara's cruel tall*, a parody of an Italian glee, *Che no' hanno crudeltà*. John O'Keeffe's *Olympus in an uproar* is an alteration of O'Hara's *The golden pippin*. Both playwrights were artists of note, and both were blind in their later years.

O'KEEFFE, JOHN.

The farmer... London: Printed by A. Strahan...for T. N. Longman and O. Rees...1800. 48 p. 8°.   NCO p.v.169

, Performed at the Theatre Royal, Covent Garden, in 1787.

Jemmy Jump, a farmer's boy, returns to the farm from London a full-fledged dandy. He talks in the slang of London to impress the country bumpkins. All of O'Keeffe's plays, like Kane O'Hara's, abound in colloquialisms and slang, and might be made the subject of an interesting study.

PARKER, GEORGE.

Life's painter of variegated characters in public and private life, by George Parker, librarian to the college of wit, mirth, and humour, and author of the View of society of manners, &c. To which is added, a dictionary of modern flash, or cant language, so much in use with the swells of the town... London, Printed by R. Bassam, no. 53, St. John's street, West Smithfield... [1789?] 176 p. port., front. 32°. * KF (1789)

Glossary, p. 123–163.

This edition was published circa 1789. In that year J. Ridgway published the book in octavo.

"The publisher has omitted the dedication to subscribers, preface, and compliment to his friends of

Underworld Cant and Its Subsidiaries, cont'd

Eighteenth Century, continued

Ireland. Also the poems of Carravaggio, and a long list of 2,210 subscribers, where a number of respectable names appear, being of no consequence to the beauties of the work, and only served to swell the book to a handsome octavo volume, that his friends might see how well he was respected — that book was sold at 4s. and this is offered for 1s. notwithstanding the exorbitant price of paper, and labour, to what it was when the first edition was printed." — *From verso of title-page.*

Parker's work was filled with numerous slang and flash songs in addition to the excellent glossary. He defines *slang boys* as "Boys of the slang; fellows who speak the slang language, which is the same as flash and cant, but the word slang is applied differently; when one asks the other to shake hands, that is, slang us your mauly. To exhibit anything in a fair or market, such as a tall man, or a cow with two heads, that's called slanging, and the exhibiter is called the slang cull." Many of the slang songs in Parker are reprinted in Farmer's *Musa pedestris* (q.v.). For an account of Parker, an itinerant actor, see the DNB.

A view of society in high and low life, being the adventures in England, Ireland, &c., of Mr. G. Parker. A stage itinerant. Printed for the author, 1781. 12°.

"Contains many cant words, with 100 orders of rogues and swindlers." — *Nodal.*

POSTGATE, RAYMOND WILLIAM.
Murder, piracy, and treason. A selection of notable English trials. London: Jonathan Cape [1925]. 254 p. 12°.   SLN

In the appendix, p. 233–242, Postgate reprints the flash glossary from Charles Hitchin's *The regulator*, London, 1718 (q.v.); and "An interpretation of the several qualities of rogues" from John Hall's *Memoirs*, London, 1708 (q.v.).

Contains chapters on Jack Sheppard and Jonathan Wild.

POTTER, HUMPHRY TRISTRAM.
A new dictionary of all the cant and flash languages, both ancient and modern; used by gipsies, beggars, etc. Carefully arranged and selected from the most approved authors, and from the MSS. of Jonathan Wild, Baxter, and others. Rev. and corrected. London: W. Mackintosh [1790]. 62 p. 8°.

Kennedy 11905.
Also published in 1797, and [1800?], Kennedy 11908, 11914.
Nodal gives the name as H. Tristram Potter of Clay, Worcestershire.
Lowndes describes the 1790 edition.

POULTER, JOHN.
The discoveries of John Poulter, alias Baxter ...written wholly by himself... 12th ed. Printed for R. Goadby in Sherborne; and sold by W. Owen, bookseller, at Temple Bar, London, 1761. 48 p. 12°.   SLN p.v.5, no.8

The author, who was caught for robbing Dr. Hancock of Salisbury, wrote this book to make amends for his villainies. He tells of the manners and language of crooks so that innocent visitors to London may be on their guard. A quaint and useful volume.

RANN, JOHN.
An account of John Rann, commonly called Sixteen String Jack; being a narrative of his principal transactions and his amours, etc. London [1774?]. 8°.

Copy in the British Museum.

The life & trial of John Rann, alias Sixteen-string Jack, for robbery; to which is added A narrative of the life & trial of William Cox, for robbery. [London:] Printed for and sold by J. Ker [1810?]. 38 p. 16°.   * KVD

A chapbook. Contains a colored portrait.

The life of John Rann, otherwise Sixteen Strings Jack, who was sentenced to death for robbing Dr. W. Bel... Together with the anecdotes of Miss Roche, and several other persons connected with Rann. London: F. Wheeler, 1884. 32 p. 8°.

Copy in the British Museum.

Rede, Leman.
Sixteen-string Jack: a romantic drama in three acts... London: G. H. Davidson, n. d. 57 p. 24°.   NCO p.v.682

Has an introduction by G. D. [George Daniel.] The play is filled with cant. Contains two songs in slang, "Kit Clayton" and "Adelgitha and Kit."

—— New York: Samuel French, n. d. 57 p. 12°.   NCOF

Wilks, Thomas Egerton.
Sixteen string Jack; or, The knaves of knaves' acre. A romantic original drama in two acts... London [and] New York: Samuel French, n. d. 40 p. 16°. (Lacy's acting edition of plays. v. 105.)   NCO

THE SCOUNDREL'S dictionary; or, an explanation of the cant words used by thieves, housebreakers, street-robbers, and pickpockets about town. To which are prefixed some curious dissertations on the art of wheedling, and a collection of their flash songs, with a proper glossary. The whole printed on a copy taken on one of their gang, in the late scuffle between the watchmen and a party of them on Clerkenwell Green; which copy is now in the custody of one of the constables of that parish. London: printed for J. Brownell, in Pater-noster row, 1754. 32 p. 8°.

Described in Michel, p. 462.
Kennedy 11895.
Copy in the British Museum.
The editor of *Notes and queries*, says in the Jan. 24, 1852, issue, series 1, v. 5, p. 79–80, "The most complete *Lexicon Balatronicum et Macaronicum* was published in 1754, enriched with many 'a word not in Johnson', and which leaves at a respectful distance the glossarial labours of Spelman, Ducange, Junius, and even the renowned Francis Grose and his *Classical dictionary of the vulgar tongue.*"
Reprints the section devoted to canting and canting songs from the *Triumph of Wit*, 1688.

SHEPPARD, JACK.
Harlequin Jack Shepherd, with a night scene in grotesque characters. 1736. 8°.

"Contains songs in the canting dialect." — *Nodal.*
Mr. Walter N. H. Harding questions this edition. He says, "I cannot find any trace of the 1736 Harlequin Jack Shepherd that you quote from Nodal. There was a 1724 Harlequin Shepherd, which I have, songs from which appear in *The New Canting Dictionary*, 1725, but this 1736 item seems unlisted by any of the dramatic authorities."

Underworld Cant and Its Subsidiaries, cont'd

Eighteenth Century, continued

SHEPPARD, JACK, *continued*

Ainsworth, William Harrison.

Jack Sheppard. (Bentley's miscellany. London, Jan., 1839 – Feb., 1840. 8°. v. 5, p. 1–29, 113–133, 221–253, 329–371, 447–463, 563–582; v. 6, p. 1–23, 109–139, 221–252, 325–340, 429–449, 543–560; v. 7, p. 92–105, 137–152.) * DA

Ainsworth was one of the first to capitalize on the Newgate school of literature which sought to bring into popular form the escapades of rogues and prison breakers. Of all the historic prison breakers Jack Sheppard was the most romantic, and Ainsworth's novel, which ran serially in *Bentley's*, and was illustrated by George Cruikshank, caught the public eye. It was filled with the cant of prisons and low life. The novel appeared in book form in 1839, being published by Richard Bentley, in three volumes, 8°. It contained twenty-seven illustrations by George Cruikshank. For bibliographical details see Horace Bleackley, *Jack Sheppard*, London [1933], p. 131, *SLN*. *Jack Sheppard* is also in Ainsworth's *Complete works*, London: G. Routledge, 1897–1900, v. 6, *NCG*.

Rookwood. A romance... By W. Harrison Ainsworth. From the second London edition. In two volumes. Philadelphia: Carey, Lea & Blanchard, 1834. 12°.   NCW

This is the earliest edition the Library owns. The original edition was published by Richard Bentley, London, 1834, 8°, in three volumes. It did not bear the author's name. The second and third editions carried Ainsworth's name. The fourth edition, 1836, is the most sought after on account of 12 plates by George Cruikshank. See Harold Locke, *A bibliographical catalogue of the published novels and ballads of William Harrison Ainsworth*, London: Elkin Mathews, 1925, *NCC*.
Rookwood was Ainsworth's first novel. It glorified gipsies and highwaymen and contained the cant of the lower classes in the early days of Queen Victoria's reign. "Jerry Juniper's chant," and the even more famous "Nix my dolly, pals, — fake away" were set to music later and became the rage. Ainsworth has much to say of the latter ballad in the preface to *Rookwood*. The glorification of the English rogue became so widespread that Dickens wrote *Oliver Twist* to counteract the tendency by vivid realism.

Rookwood. A romance...with illustrations by George Cruikshank. London: Chapman & Hall, 1851. xl, 344 p., 11 pl., 1 port. 8°.
                                 MEM C955 ain
Also in *Complete works*, London: G. Routledge and Sons [1887–1900], v. 12, *NCG*.
According to Horace Bleackley *Rookwood* was plagiarized by the opportunist, Henry Downer [*sic*] Miles in his novel *Dick Turpin* (q.v.). On the other hand Dr. Shelton Mackenzie, in his memoir of William Maginn says that Ainsworth used flash poems which Maginn wrote and gave to Ainsworth, and used them without giving credit.

Buckstone, John Baldwin.

Jack Sheppard... New York: Samuel French, n. d. 92 p. 12°. (The minor drama. Edited by F. C. Wemyss. no. 53.) NCO p.v.512
Based on the Ainsworth novel of that name. Contains slang.

Greenwood, Thomas.

Jack Sheppard; or, The House-breaker of the last century. A romantic drama. In five acts. Dramatized from Harrison Ainsworth's novel... London: John Cumberland. 68 p. 24°.

Embellished with an engraving by R. Cruikshank.
G. D. [George Daniel] contributes some remarks on Jack Sheppard, p. 5–9.

The *Life* and death of Jack Sheppard. A drama, in four acts. Adapted from Harrison Ainsworth's popular romance. London: Thomas Hailes Lacy, n. d. 63 p. 12°. (Lacy's acting edition of plays. v. 23.)   NCO

Phillips, Jonas B.

Jack Sheppard; or, The life of a rotter. Melodrama in three acts, founded on Ainsworth's novel. [New York, 1839.] f°.
Manuscript in the theatre collection of Harvard College Library. First performed at the Bowery Theatre, New York, Dec. 30, 1839.

Planché, James Robinson.

An old offender. A comic drama in two acts ... London: Samuel French, n. d. 40 p. 12°.
                                 NCO p.v.507, no.4
Based on the exploits of the famous housebreaker, Jack Sheppard. Filled with flash cant.
Edmund Yates, in the *Illustrated Times*, London, Jan. 8, 1859, dedicated some stanzas to Planché, in which he lamented the use of slang by contemporary dramatists.

The *Prison* breakers; or, The adventures of Jack Sheppard. A farce as intended to be acted at the Theatre Royal in Lincoln's-Inn-Fields... London: Printed for A. Moore near St. Paul's, 1725.
This work was reproduced, with additions and new songs written or arranged by John Watts, as The *Quaker's opera, as it is perform'd at Lee's and Harper's great theatrical booth in Bartholomew Fair. With the musick prefix'd to each song*, London: printed for J. W., and sold by J. Roberts in Warwick Lane; A. Dodd, at the Peacock without Temple Bar; and E. Nutt and E. Smith at the Royal Exchange, 1728.
The above information was obtained from Horace Bleackley's *Jack Sheppard*, London: William Hodge, 1933, p. 128–129, *SLN* (q.v.).
This play influenced Gay's *The Beggar's opera*. See William Harrison Ainsworth's *Jack Sheppard;* and W. Roberts, "Jack Sheppard in literature, in *National review*, London, May, 1924, v. 83, p. 432–440, * DA.
See Alban M. Phillip, *The prison-breakers*, New York: Henry Holt [1928], p. 26–61, *SLT*.

Stephens, Henry, and W. Yaroley.

Little Jack Sheppard. A three act burlesque-operatic-melodrama. London: W. S. Johnson, 1885. 56 p. 12°.
From compiler's copy.
Written in the manner of Gilbert and Sullivan comic-operas. Contains the London slang of the period.

Bleackley, Horace William.

Jack Sheppard, by Horace Bleackley... With an epilogue on Jack Sheppard in literature and drama, a bibliography, a note on Jonathan Wild, and a Memoir of Horace Bleackley by S. M. Ellis... Edinburgh and London: W. Hodge and Co., Ltd. [1933.] 260 p. 8°. (Notable British trials.)   SLN
Bleackley died before the work came to press, and Ellis brought it out. The bibliography of Jack Sheppard, p. 127–136 is a mine of information.
Sheppard, the notorious prison-breaker, was the subject of many a drama and romance. W. Harrison Ainsworth was one of the most successful writers on the subject.
Numerous flash songs from the various plays and romances and biographies are reprinted in this work, and old prints are reproduced.
See also William McAdoo, *The procession to Tyburn*, New York: Boni & Liveright, 1927, *SLG*. He speaks of Sheppard on p. 272–288, and of Jonathan Wild, p. 70–107.

Underworld Cant and Its Subsidiaries, cont'd

Eighteenth Century, continued

SMITH, CAPT. ALEXANDER.

Compleat history of the lives and robberies of the most notorious highwaymen, foot-pads, etc. v. 1. Thieves' new canting dictionary, etc. 5th ed. London: S. Briscoe, 1719. 12°.
Copy in the British Museum.

A complete history of the lives and robberies of the most notorious highwaymen, footpads, shoflifts, & cheats of both sexes... Ed. by Arthur L. Hayward. New York: Brentano's [1926]. 3 v. in 1. 4°.　　　　　　　SLG
Reprint of the 5th ed., 1719.
Contains "The thieves' new canting dictionary," p. 201–210; "The thieves' key found out," p. 590–593; and the "Thieves' exercise," p. 594–596, all of which give numerous canting words of the period. Much of the material in Capt. Smith's book was reprinted in *The complete Newgate calendar*, ed. by J. L. Rayner and G. T. Crook, London: Privately printed for the Navarre Society, Limited, 1926. 6 v. 8°. 6–SLG.

STEVENS, GEORGE ALEXANDER.

Distress upon distress: or, Tragedy in true taste. A heroic-comi-parodi-tragedi-farci-cal burlesque... London: Reprinted from the Dublin edition, for R. Griffiths in St. Paul's church-yard, 1752. 99 p. 12°.　　　　NCO p.v.307, no.8
Contains a good deal of slang and jargon.
See the biographical sketch of Stevens in *DNB*. As a youth he joined a company of strolling players. He wrote many ballads, but his chief work was *A lecture on heads*, a pioneer monologue entertainment which netted its author over ten thousand pounds. He visited America around 1765. In 1752 he founded a jovial club in Dublin called "Nassau Court," where he and Lord Chief Joker Sparks held mock trials and other buffooneries. He and Sparks probably knew what we do not know — the authorship of *The night before Larry was stretched* (q.v.).

...TRICKS of the town. Being reprints of three eighteenth century tracts, with an introduction by Ralph Straus... London: Chapman and Hall, 1927. 256 p. 8°.　　CO (London)
Introduction, p. ix–xxiv; Tricks of the town laid open (1747), p. 1–110; A trip through the town (1735), p. 111–182; A trip from St. James's to the Exchange (1744), p. 183–256.
These tracts contain some slang, but not as much as the titles would imply. *Tricks of the town laid open* is in reality a reprint of *The Country gentleman's vade-mecum; or His companion for the town*, 1699. This work is well known as a source of much information on the game of tennis.

THE TRIUMPH of wit, or ingenuity displayed in its perfection, being the newest and most useful academy, songs, art of love, and the mystery and art of canting, with poems and songs in the canting language. London: J. Clarke, 1735. 16°.
"A shilling chap book. The same appeared in Dublin about 1760, in 12mo, 32 pages." — *Nodal*.
Also 1702 and 1707 editions, reprinted from the edition of 1688.

A TRUE discovery of the conduct of receivers and thief-takers, in and about the city of London, &c. &c. London, 1718.
Described in Early English Text Society, *Extra series*, v. 9, p. xxiii, *NCE*.

TUFTS, HENRY.

A narrative of the life, adventures, travels and sufferings of Henry Tufts, now residing at Lemington, in the district of Maine. In substance, as compiled from his own mouth... Dover, N. H.: Printed by Samuel Bragg, jun., 1807. 366 p. 12°.　　　　　　　　*KF
On p. 316–317 is a glossary of the flash language. "A number of my fellow prisoners were flashmen as they termed themselves an appellation appropriate to such rogues and sharpers, as make exclusive use of the flash lingo. This is partly English and party [*sic*] an arbitrary gibberish, which, when spoken, presents to such hearers, as are not initiated into its mysteries, a mere unintelligible jargon, but in the flash fraternity is, peculiarly significant... It was imported in gross from Europe, and no part of it, to my knowledge, has been hitherto communicated to the public."
It is generally believed that Tufts did not actually write this book, but its importance lies in the fact that it is probably the first published glossary of flash lingo in America.
This book was reprinted and edited by Edmund Pearson, and published in 1930 by Duffield and Company, New York, 12°, *AN*. Pearson's introduction throws much light on Tufts and his book.
See Thomas Wentworth Higginson's *Travellers and outlaws*, Boston: Lee and Shepard, 1889, p. 88–115, *IAG*.

VILLAINY unmask'd: containing an ample discovery of the many surprizing tricks, subtilities, and frauds, now practiced by rogues of all denominations, &c... By a lover of his country ... London: Printed for W. Owen, at Homer's head, near Temple-Bar, 1752. 96 p. 8°.
　　　　　　　　　　　　　　　* C p.v.759
Interesting for its descriptions of the many types of rackets practiced in London, with a few cant words.

WARD, EDWARD.

A compleat and humorous account of all the remarkable clubs and societies in the cities of London and Westminster... Compil'd from the original papers of a Gent. who frequented those places upwards of twenty years. London: Printed for the author and sold by Joseph Collier at Shakespear's Head in Ludgate-street, 1745. 327 p. 12°.　　　　　　　NDF
Written in the slang of the period.
Contents: Of clubs in general; the Vertuoso's club; of the Knights of the Order of the Golden Fleece; of the No-Nose club; of the Farting club; of the Man-Killing club; of the Surly club; the Atheistical club; club of Ugly faces; the Split-Farthing club; the club of broken Shopkeepers; the Man-Hunter's club; the Yorkshire club; the Wrangling club; the Quack's club; the Weekly Dancing club; the Bird-Fanciers' club; the Lying club; the Beggar's club; the Chatter-wit club; the Florist's club; the Bob Weden's club; the Mollies club; the Bawd's Initiating club; Sam Scot's smoking club; the Market Women's club; the Thieves' club; the Small-Coal Man's music club; the Kit-Kat club; the Beef-stake club.
Ned Ward (1667–1731) was a "tavern keeper and writer of Hudibrastic doggerel verse and coarse humorous prose." His best known book of London life was *The London spy* (1698–1709).
W. Matthews has made a study of the slang and cant in Ward's works and prints the result of his labors in *Notes and queries*, London, June 15, 1935, v. 168, p. 416–418; June 22, 1935, v. 168, p. 439–441; June 29, 1935, v. 168, p. 454–456, * R–* DA. Matthews compares the words in Ward with Grose's *Classical dictionary of the vulgar tongue*, 1785. He claims that Ward used a great deal of general slang, but scarcely any cant words.
There is an American reprint of *The London spy*, New York: Doran [1927]. 309 p. 8°. *COB (London)*.

Underworld Cant and Its Subsidiaries, cont'd

Eighteenth Century, continued

THE WHOLE art of thieving and defrauding discovered, etc., to which is added an explanation of most of the cant terms in the thieving language. 1786. 46 p. 8°.
Kennedy 11902.

WILD, JONATHAN.

D., H.
The life of Jonathan Wild, from his birth to his death... By H. D. late clerk to Justice R——. London: Printed for T. Warner, at the

Black Boy in Paternoster Row, 1725. 71 p. 12°. 　　　　　　　　　* C p.v.177, no.2

Lyons, Frederick J.
Jonathan Wild, prince of robbers. [London:] Michael Joseph, Ltd. [1936.] 320 p. illus. 8°. AN
Glossary, p. 303–309.

P., N.
Weighley, alias Wild. A poem in imitation of Hudibras...by N. P. many years his intimate acquaintance... London: Printed for J. Roberts, near the Oxford-Arms, in Warwick Lane, 1725. 48 p. 12°. 　　　　NCI p.v.79, no.12

NINETEENTH CENTURY

THE A. B. C. of a new dictionary of flash, cant, slang, and vulgar words, proverbs and provincialisms, their explication and illustration: compiled and methodically arranged, as well for the instruction of the curious, as the information of the ignorant: and for the benefit of students and journeymen from the country who are desirous of thoroughly understanding the cant words and flash sayings of London life. On the basis of Bailey and Captain Grose. London: Printed for the booksellers, n. d. 16°.
From compiler's copy.
Nodal mentions a similar title: Jervis, Captain. The A. B. C. of a new dictionary of flash cant, slang, and vulgar words, proverbs and provincialisms, compiled for the special use of old shipmates and friends. Foolscap 8°, for private circulation only. Jersey, 1870. Nodal adds: "Not published, and very few copies printed. The three letters A. B. and C. are all that were done." We have not seen the text of the dictionary mentioned by Nodal, but it would appear that the two texts are the same.

AINSWORTH, WILLIAM HARRISON.
Ballads, romantic, fantastical and humorous ... London, New York: George Routledge and Sons [1872]. xxiii, 326 p. 12°. 　　NCK
Includes: "A romany chant"; "The double cross," a prize fighting slang poem; "The modern Greek," in gamblers' slang; "The game of high Toby." All have glossarial footnotes.

AMONG thieves. (The Broadway. A London magazine of society and politics. London, Nov., 1871. 8°. series 3, v. 3, p. 404–412.) 　　* DA
An account of the habitual criminals of London in 1871 — the "prigs," the "rampsman," the "Charley Pitcher," the "Drummer," the "Mobsman," "sneaksman," "racket-men," etc., with many of their common slang phrases.

ANDREWES, GEORGE.
A dictionary of the slang and cant languages; ancient and modern. As used by Adam Tylers, badgers, bullies, etc., etc. London: George Smeeton, James street, Covent Garden [1809]. 12°.
Copy in the British Museum.
Contains a folding colored plate by George Cruikshank, entitled "The Beggar's carnival."

BADCOCK, JOHN.
A living picture of London, for 1828, and stranger's guide; shewing the frauds...and wiles of all descriptions of rogues...with sketches of cockney manners, etc. To which

is appended "Hints for the improvement of the police," by Jon Bee [pseud. of John Badcock]. etc. London [1828]. 12°.
Copy in the British Museum.
Contains some of the street slang of London. H. N. Cary, in his *Slang of venery* says that the above is the same as his *Sportsman's slang*, 1825, except for the difference in title.

Slang. A dictionary of the turf, the ring, the chase, the pit, of bon-ton, and the varieties of life, forming the completest and most authentic Lexicon Balatronicum hitherto offered to the notice of the sporting world, for elucidating words and phrases that are necessarily, or purposely, cramp, mutative, and unintelligible, outside their respective spheres. Interspersed with anecdotes and whimsies, with tart quotations, and rum-ones; with examples, proofs, and monitory precepts, useful and proper for novices, flats, and yokels. By Jon Bee [pseud. of John Badcock] Esq. Editor of the Fancy, Fancy gazette, Living picture of London, and the like of that. London: Printed for T. Hughes, 35, Ludgate-street, 1823. 216 p. 12°. 　　8–RNM
Published in the hey-dey of British sporting slang, this volume offers a complete picture of the language of the Regency. It was reprinted in 1825. See note under next entry.

Sportsman's slang; a new dictionary of terms used in the affairs of the turf, the ring, the chase, and the cock-pit; with those of bon-ton and the varieties of life; forming an original and authentic lexikon balatronicum et macaronicum; particularly adapted to the use of the sporting world, for elucidating words and phrases that are necessarily, or purposely, rendered cramp, mutative and unintelligible, outside their respective spheres. Interspersed with anecdotes and whimsies, with tart quotations and rum-ones; with examples, proofs and monitory precepts, useful and proper for novices, flats, and yokels. Editio altera. By Jon Bee, Esq. [pseud. of John Badcock] Editor of the original Fancy, Fancy gazette, Fancy-ana, Living picture of London, and the like of that... London: Printed by W. Lewis, 21, Finch-lane, Cornhill; for the author, 1825. 222 p. 12°.
Copy in the Racket & Tennis Club, New York City.
This is an interesting dictionary similar to Pierce Egan's enlargement of Grose. Jon Bee and Pierce Egan were rivals, and each claimed that the other plagiarized. Very little is known of Badcock, except

Underworld Cant and Its Subsidiaries, cont'd

Nineteenth Century, continued

that he was eccentric. Many of his statements have been found to be inaccurate. In a review of the above book in *Blackwood's*, Aug., 1825, v. 18, p. 177–183, * DA, Bee is described as "an active frequenter of all sorts of public houses, chaffing cribs, fives-courts, eccentrics, &c., as well as a most ardent and indefatigable street-walker at all hours and seasons — a man also well acquainted with the fair, and not unacquainted with those whose ways of life are generally foul. In his own words he has seen every variety of life, 'except being presented at court, and feeling the delights of a prison.'"

A BANG UP dictionary; or, The lounger and sportsman's vademecum; containing a copious and correct glossary of the whips, etc. London: M. Jones, no. 5 Newgate street, 1812. 8°.
224 unnumbered pages. Contains a folding colored plate by George Cruikshank entitled, "Bang up Dinner." The Library owns a copy of this illustration, but not the book.
This is the same as *Lexicon balatronicum*, which was based on Grose (q.v.).

BARHAM, RICHARD HARRIS.
The wondrous tale of Ikey Solomons! (In: R. H. D. Barham, The life and letters of the Rev. Richard Harris Barham... By his son. London: Richard Bentley, 1870. 8°. v. 2, p. 324–336.) AN
A squib on Disraeli's early novel *Alroy*. Ikey Solomons was a notorious receiver of stolen goods, a "fence." He escaped from Newgate in 1826 and was transported in 1830. This fragment contains some flash lingo.
See HEBRON, MOSES.

BEE, JON, PSEUD. See BADCOCK, JOHN.

BINNY, JOHN, JOINT AUTHOR. See MAYHEW, HENRY, AND JOHN BINNY.

BRAINARD'S half-dime hand-books. Tricks and traps of New York City... Boston: C. H. Brainard [1857]. 64 p. 32°. *KF
Has a few underworld terms of the period, but they are not in the form of a glossary.

BRANDON, H.
Poverty, mendicity and crime; or, The facts, examinations, &c. upon which the report was founded, presented to the House of Lords by W. A. Miles, Esq. to which is added a dictionary of the flash or cant language, known to every thief and beggar. Edited by H. Brandon, Esq. London: Shaw & Sons...1839. 168 p. 8°. SLG
On p. 161–168 appears the cant dictionary. Includes two specimens of flash, with translations. This is authentic speech for the period covered. It was widely copied.

BULWER-LYTTON, EDWARD GEORGE EARLE LYTTON, 1ST BARON LYTTON.
Paul Clifford. By the author of "Pelham," "The disowned," and "Devereux"... New-York: Printed by J. and J. Harper, 82 Cliff-street...1830. 2 v. 12°. NCW
This is the earliest edition owned by the Library. The Library has the 1842 Tauchnitz edition, 16°, *NCW;* London: G. Routledge, 1877, 8°, *NCW;* Philadelphia, 1868, 16°, *NCW;* Philadelphia: Lippincott, 1883, 12°, *NCW;* New York: Harper, 1842, 8°, *NCW;* New York: Harper, 1835, 12°, *NCW.* Also in *Complete works,* New York: P. F. Collier, 1850, 4°, v. 8, *NCG;* Leipzig: Tauchnitz, 1842, 16°, *NCG;* Philadelphia:

Lippincott, 1866, 12°, v. 30–31, *NCG;* London: Routledge [187–?], 8°, v. 15, *NCG.*
Paul Clifford contains much more slang than *Pelham.* It is a story of prison life and was designed with the object of improving English penal discipline. It is one of the first philanthropic novels. It had a great influence on Ainsworth and Dickens.

Webster, Benjamin.
Paul Clifford; the highwayman of 1770. A drama in three acts. Adapted from the novel of Edward Lytton Bulwer, Esq... London: John Cumberland, n. d. 76 p. 24°. (Cumberland's minor theatre. v. 6.) NCO
Introduction by George Daniel. This introduction gives a brief history of highwaymen in drama, and includes a flash song from *Harlequin Shepherd.* The play itself is filled with flash and cant. The opening line is: "Now then, my covies, down with the brads for the lush, and let's out on the tramp to fork a fogle or a ticker."

BULWER-LYTTON, EDWARD GEORGE EARLE LYTTON, 1ST BARON LYTTON.
Pelham; or, The adventures of a gentleman ... Second edition. In three volumes. v. I. London: Henry Colburn, New Burlington street, 1828. viii, 326 p. 12°. NCW
The Library has v. 1 only. The original edition also appeared in 1828. Neither the first nor second edition bore the author's name. The Library has other copies of *Pelham,* viz.: New York: Harper, 1867, 8°, *NCW;* Philadelphia: 1867, 16°, *NCW;* London: G. Routledge, 1877, 12°, *NCW;* London: G. Routledge, 1877, 8°, *NCW;* Philadelphia: Lippincott, 1883, 12°, *NCW;* New York: Harper, 1842, 8°, *NCW;* Philadelphia: L. A. Godey, 1836, 8°, *NCT p.v.46;* Boston: Colonial Press [18—?], 12°, *NCW.* Also in *Complete works,* New York: P. F. Collier, 1850, 4°, v. 8, *NCG;* London: G. Routledge [187–?], 8°, v. 16, *NCG;* Philadelphia: Lippincott, 1865, 12°, v. 26–27, *NCG;* Leipzig: Tauchnitz, 1842, 16°, *NCG.*
Pelham contains some of the slang of fashion in the days of the dandy. The Regency period, which saw the advent of the dandy in the persons of Beau Brummell and Count D'Orsay, gave rise to a number of novels of high life. The character of Thornton in *Pelham* was drawn from the notorious murderer, Thurtell. Thackeray has written amusingly of *Pelham* in his *Diary of Jeames de la Pluche. Pelham* set the fashion for black evening wear for men, a fashion which has remained unchanged ever since.

BURNHAM, GEORGE PICKERING.
American counterfeits. Boston: A. W. Lovering, 1879. 416 p. 8°. SLG
Glossary of terms used in familiar converse among counterfeiters, p. 417–421.

Memoirs of the United States Secret Service ... Boston: Lee and Shepard, 1872. 436 p. 8°. SLX
Glossary, p. iv–viii. The "vernacular of criminals, used in familiar converse among counterfeiters, middle men, thieves, receivers of stolen goods, and their confederates." Short sketches of some of the notorious American underworld characters.

BURROWES, J.
Life in St. George's Fields; or, The rambles and adventures of disconsolate William, Esq., and his Surrey friend, Flash Dick, with songs and a flash dictionary. London, 1821. 8°.
Copy in the British Museum.
Kennedy 11926 lists this as anonymous.

BYEGONE cant. (All the year round. London, March 5, 1870. 8°. v. 23, p. 320–324.) *DA
Several hundred canting terms of old England's rogues and thieves are revived in a jocular article — and defended against the cries of purists.

Underworld Cant and Its Subsidiaries, cont'd

Nineteenth Century, continued

BYRON, GEORGE GORDON NOËL BYRON, 6TH
    BARON.
    Don Juan. Cantos IX. — X. — and XI...
London: Printed for J. Hunt, 1823. 8°.   * KL
    First edition.
    Canto XI, stanzas xvi–xix. This section of the poem
contains a number of cant and flash words. *Don Juan*
first appeared in 1819 and came out in parts until
1824. Byron was well known in the sporting circles
of London, and was a friend of pugilists, as was his
close friend, Tom Moore, who wrote *Tom Crib's memorial to Congress,* 1819 (q.v.). See also Bohun
Lynch's *The prize ring,* London, 1925, for sporting
anecdotes concerning Byron and his crowd, and for
illustrations from the famous "Byron screen."
    There are many editions of *Don Juan.* In the 1833
edition of Byron's collected works, edited by Thomas
Moore, v. 17, p. 9–10, are some interesting notes on
the flash words used.
    See Farmer, *Musa pedestris,* p. 247–249.

CANTING: a poem, interspersed with tales
and additional scraps. London, 1814. 8°.
    "A few street words may be gleaned from this
rather dull poem." — *Nodal.*

CANTING; an eccentric poem. Interspersed
with tales, pathetic and ludicrous. To which
are added a few scraps. London [1815]. 8°.
    Copy in the British Museum.

CANTING: a poem. With tales of Judith and
Reuben; Dash; and Gruff the miller. 2. ed.
London, 1816. 8°.
    Copy in the British Museum.

CAREY, DAVID.
    Life in Paris, comprising the rambles, sprees,
and amours of Dick Wildfire of Corinthian
celebrity, and his bang-up companions, Squire
Jenkens and Captain O'Shuffleton, with the
whimsical adventures of the Halibut family...
London: Printed for John Fairburn, Broadway, Ludgate Hill [etc.], 1822. 489 p. 8°.
                                    MEM C955c
    Contains colored aquatints, drawn by G. Cruikshank.
This is patterned after Pierce Egan's *Life in London.* It has many flash expressions, but not as many
as may be found in Egan.
    The Library also has another edition, bearing the
imprint: London: John Cumberland, 19, Ludgate Hill,
1828. 489 p. 8°, *MEM C955c.* The illustrations are
not as good as those in the first edition.

CLOUSTON, WILLIAM ALEXANDER.
    English canting songs. (Notes and queries.
London, Feb. 9, 1889. 8°. series 7, v. 7, p. 104.)
                                    * R–* DA
    Notes on W. Harrison Ainsworth's *Rookwood.* Also
gives bibliographical notes on Richard Head.
    Geo. L. Apperson, H. C. Hart, R. H. Busk, and
Br. Nicholson make additions to this note in the March
23 issue, p. 229–230.

CROFTON, A. F. B.
    The language of crime. (Popular science
monthly. New York, April, 1897. 8°. v. 50,
p. 831–835.)   * DA
    Disagrees with those who hold that the *argot* of
thieves is a primitive language. Crofton thinks of
argot "only as a dialect, in which debased terms
replace the words of the parent tongue." "Thieves
reduce abstract words to concrete words, shorten long
words." "The criminal has no more conception of
abstract emotion than a blind man has of color."
"*Argot* is a poor language."

DANIEL, GEORGE.
    "Sworn at Highgate." A musical farce, in
two acts... London: John Cumberland, n. d.
41 p. 24°. (Cumberland's minor theatre. v. 6.)
                                    NCO
    Written in slang. Includes a number of songs,
written in the language of the Dickens era. Contains
some jargon spoken by one of the characters, Dr.
Jeremiah Jargon.

DAVITT, MICHAEL.
    Leaves from a prison diary; or, Lectures
to a "solitary" audience... New York: Ford's
National Library, 1886. 311 p. 12°.   SLG
    The author was sent to Portland prison in 1881.

THE DENS of London exposed... Third edition. London: Published by the author, 1835.
106 p., col'd front. 16°.
    Also bears the title: "A peep into the Holy Land,
or, Sinks of London laid open! ... Cadging made
easy, doings of the modern Greeks, unfinished gentlemen at home. Snoozing kens depicted. Description
of the cribs... The thieves school. The brothel...
The cadging house gallant [etc., etc.]. London: John
Wilson.
    Despite the title, which was designed to catch the
eye of the curious, the book contains little more than
the ordinary "slumming" trip of a sociologist. A
few flash terms are scattered throughout the book.

DIARY of a celebrated police officer. (Ramb-
ler's magazine. New York, 1810. 24°. v. 2,
p. 65–68.)   * DA
    Contains a "glossary of fashionable or cant phrases,"
p. 68.

DOWNEY'S Peter Napoleon campana old sport
songster. New York: Dick & Sullivan [cop.
1879]. 64 p. 24°.   NBH p.v.16, no.2
    Contains much slang. One song entitled "Peni-
tentiary" by P. I. Downey, is filled with slang. "The
Isle de Blackwell" sung by Harrigan & Hart in
Edward Harrigan's burlesque *Celebrated hard case* is
also written in criminal slang.

DUCANGE, ANGLICUS, PSEUD.
    The vulgar tongue: comprising two glos-
saries of slang, cant, and flash words and
phrases, principally used in London at the
present day... London: Bernard Quaritch,
1857. 44 p. 12°.   RNM
    A glossary of slang, to which is added a dictionary
of cant, which appeared originally in 1839 in a volume
entitled *Poverty, mendicity, and crime,* by H. Brandon (q.v.).
    "The first book to give rhyming slang at all, so
far as I know, was the Vulgar Tongue, by Ducange
Anglicus, 1857, 1859." — *Partridge, Slang to-day and
yesterday,* London, 1933, p. 274.
    "The *Vulgar Tongue*...is, as a glossary, of no
account whatever; the only thing not pilfered from
Brandon's *Poverty, mendicity and crime* being this
song [The Leary man]. Where that came from de-
ponent knoweth not." — *John S. Farmer, Musa pedestris,* 1896, p. 242.

DUNCOMBE, JOHN?
    Duncombe's dictionary of the cant words,
queer sayings and crack terms now in use in
flash cribb society. [1820.] 32°.
    Has a colored print.
    John Duncombe was a publisher.

EGAN, PIERCE.
    Life in London; or, The day and night scenes
of Jerry Hawthorn, Esq. and Corinthian Tom,
accompanied by Bob Logic, the Oxonian, in
their rambles and sprees through the metropolis
... A new edition. Embellished with thirty-six
scenes from real life, designed and etched by

Underworld Cant and Its Subsidiaries, cont'd

Nineteenth Century, continued

I. R. & G. Cruikshank; and enriched also with numerous original designs on wood by the same artists. London: Printed by C. Baynes, 13, Duke-street, Lincoln's-inn-fields, for G. Virtue, 26, Ivy Lane, Paternoster Row [1821]. xvi, 376 p., 35 pl., 1 song with music. 8°.

MEM C955e11

Dedication and frontispiece dated July, 1821.

The plates were published by Sherwood, Neely, & Jones, some bearing the date 1820, and some 1821.

Most bibliographies agree in saying that the work was first issued in monthly numbers beginning July 15, 1821, but they seem to have overlooked the fact that there was a review of the book in the *European magazine*, Nov., 1820, * *DA,* and that it was announced as being in the press, in the Aug., 1820, issue of the same magazine, v. 78, p. 145. The review does not mention monthly numbers but speaks of "the book before us," p. 436. This may have been a pre-view of the manuscript. Books were often announced far in advance of actual publication date.

—— Published by Sherwood, Neely, and Jones, 1822. xvi, 376 p., 36 pl. 8°.

MEM C955eg1.

Life in London took London by storm. "So great was the demand for copies, increasing with the publication of each successive number, month by month, that the colourists could not keep pace with the printers... Imitations and pirated copies appeared, both of the text and pictures... At many of the playhouses dramatic versions increased the notoriety. First of these was Mr. W. Barrymore's play, produced at the Royal Amphitheatre on Monday 17 Sept. 1821... At the Olympic, an extravaganza called 'Life in London', by Charles I. M. Dibdin the younger was produced on 12 Nov. 1821... W. T. Moncrieff (supposed pseudonym of W. J. Thoms) [this is an error. It should be William Thomas Thomas] wrote the dramatic version for the Adelphi... This version was adopted throughout the country and in the United States, everywhere securing crowded houses." — *Dictionary of national biography.* The DNB has quite a full account of Egan.

See Egan's edition of Grose's *Classical dictionary of the vulgar tongue,* 1823.

A study entitled "Pierce Egan und Dickens" by Wilhelm Dibelius appeared in *Archiv für das Studium der neuerem Sprachen und Literaturen,* 1910, v. 124, p. 306–317, *RAA.*

Life in London: or, The day and night scenes of Jerry Hawthorn, Esq. and Corinthian Tom, accompanied by Bob Logic, the Oxonian, in their rambles and sprees through the metropolis... New Orleans: For sale by W. M'Kean, 1837. 2 v. 12°. COB (London)

Imperfect: v. 2 lacks title-page and p. 1–12.

Illustrated by George Cruikshank, but it is not listed in Albert M. Cohn, *George Cruikshank. A catalogue raisonné,* London: The Bookman's Journal, 1924, *MDG.*

Life in London: or, The day and night scenes of Jerry Hawthorn, Esq., and his elegant friend Corinthian Tom, accompanied by Bob Logic, the Oxonian, in their rambles and sprees through the metropolis. By Pierce Egan...embellished with thirty-six scenes from real life designed and etched by I. R. & G. Cruikshank, and enriched also with numerous original designs on wood by the same artists. new ed. New York: D. Appleton & Co., 1904. xiv, 297 p., 36 col'd plates. 16°. COB (London)

Founded on the edition printed for Sherwood, Neely & Jones in 1821; a reprint of the title-page of that edition is included.

Tom and Jerry. Life in London; or, The day and night scenes of Jerry Hawthorn, Esq. and his elegant friend Corinthian Tom in their rambles and sprees through the metropolis... With numerous coloured illustrations from real life designed by I. R. & G. Cruikshank. London: John Camden Hotten, Piccadilly [1869]. 406 p. 12°. NDF

A cheap reprint of Egan's famous work. The illustrations are the veriest chromos. It is in the introduction to this edition that Hotten states that *Real Life in London* was written by Jonathan Bee, and not by Egan. He also gives quite a lengthy biographical account of Pierce Egan. Hotten was the publisher of *A dictionary of modern slang,* 1859 (q.v.) and also reprinted the celebrated *Tour of Dr. Syntax,* written by William Combe, illustrated by Thomas Rowlandson, and published by Rudolph Ackermann. The "Tours" of this amusing old gentleman, Dr. Syntax, really set the stage and created the taste for Egan's *Life in London.* The *Tour of Dr. Syntax* first appeared in the *Poetical magazine,* London, 1809. The appearance of these gay, slangy, sporty books by Combe, Egan, Bee, and others coincided with the heyday of the colored aquatint.

Pierce Egan's finish to the adventures of Tom, Jerry, and Logic, in their pursuits through life in and out of London, illustrated by the pencil of Mr. Robert Cruikshank... London: W. Strange [1829]. v–xvi, 368 p., 35 plates. 8°. MEM C956 ep

In the introduction to this work Egan lists over sixty imitations of his *Life in London.* They were of all kinds, some rank piracies, others cheap productions designed for quick sale among less sophisticated readers. There were Tom and Jerry games, drawings of them on handkerchiefs, ballads, songs, plays, chap-books, broadsides and every conceivable kind of imitation. Thomas Greenwood's *Tears of Pierce Egan for the Death of Life in London: or, The Funeral of Tom and Jerry* which was published to sell for two shillings, was pirated by Catnach, the notorious publisher of cheap reprints, in less than 12 hours and offered for sale for twopence.

There is a reprint, London: John Camden Hotten, n. d., 8°; and the English *Book prices current* lists an 1830 edition by G. Virtue, with 36 colored plates by R. Cruikshank.

Hindley, Charles.

The true history of Tom and Jerry; or, The day and night scenes of life in London. From the start to the finish. With a key to the persons and places, together with a vocabulary and glossary of the flash and slang terms occurring in the course of the work... London: Charles Hindley [186–?]. 216 p. 12°. Co (London)

The introduction gives a history of Pierce Egan's popular book *Life in London.* The present volume is an epitome of that story, with numerous additions, including a reproduction of Moncrieff's dramatic adaptation, 1821; *The Corinthian diary,* by T. Greenwood; *The treadmill at Brixton;* some Catnach ballads, etc., etc. The glossary, p. 153–216, is of particular value.

Dibdin, Charles Isaac Mungo.

Life in London; or, The larks of Logic, Tom, and Jerry, an extravaganza in three acts... Second edition corrected. London: Printed for John Lowndes, 1822. 40 p. 8°. NCO p.v.184

Founded on Pierce Egan's work. Filled with flash patter and race track cant.

Fitzball, Edward.

The tread mill; or, Tom and Jerry at Brixton... London: Published by J. Lowndes, 36, Bow-street, Covent-Garden, n. d. 28 p. 8°. NCO p.v.94

Colored aquatint frontispiece.

Contains some slang, but it is a very poor imitation of the original *Life in London* by Moncrieff. Library also has another copy, *NCO p.v.184.*

Underworld Cant and Its Subsidiaries, cont'd

Nineteenth Century, continued

EGAN, PIERCE, *continued*

Greenwood, Thomas.
The death of Life in London; or, Tom &
Jerry's funeral... Printed for John Lowndes,
36, Bow Street, Covent Garden [1823]. 20 p.
8°.   NCO p.v.184
Has a colored frontispiece.
First performed at the Royal Coburg Theatre, June
2, 1823.
Written in slang. Contains flash songs.

—— Baltimore: J. Robinson, 1823. 24 p.
24°.   NCO p.v.296

Moncrieff, William Thomas.
Tom and Jerry; or, Life in London in 1820.
A drama in three acts. From Pierce Egan's
celebrated work... London: T. H. Lacy, n. d.
72 p. 12°. (Lacy's acting edition of plays. v. 88.)
       NCO
The slang of London is profusely illustrated in
this rollicking drama, one of the many stage adaptations
of Pierce Egan's epoch-making book. See Egan, Pierce.
This play ran for two years and made slang popular.

—— London: J. Cumberland [1835]. 72 p.
24°. (Cumberland's British theatre. v. 33.)
       NCO

—— Second edition. London: Thomas Richardson [1828]. 72 p. 24°.   NCO p.v.444

Tom & Jerry in France; or, Vive la baga-
telle. A musical entertainment in three acts...
London: Printed for J. Lowndes, 36, Bow-
street, Covent-Garden, 1842. 44 p. 8°.
       NCO p.v.184
Colored frontispiece by S. R. G.
Contains some slang, but not as much as the usual
"Tom & Jerry" type of farce.
Library also has another copy, *NCO p.v.196.*

EGAN, PIERCE.
Life and extraordinary adventures of S. D.
Hayward, denominated the modern Macheath
... London: Sherwood & Co., 1822. 12°.
Copy in the British Museum.
Contains many flash words.

Real life in Ireland; or, The day and night
scenes, rovings, rambles, and sprees, bulls,
blunders, bodderation and blarney, of Brian
Boru, Esq. and his elegant friend Sir Shawn
O'Dogherty. Exhibiting a real picture of char-
acters, manners, &c. in high and low life, in
Dublin and various parts of Ireland... By a
real Paddy. Fourth edition. London: William
Evans & Co., 22 Warwick Square, Paternoster
Row [1821]. 296 p., col'd illus. 8°.   NDF
This fourth edition was reprinted by Methuen, Lon-
don, 1904. 16°, *NDF.*
Also published in London: B. Bensley, 1821, 8°,
with col'd plates by Henry Alken, F. Heath, and others.
There is some confusion as to dates and editions. The
English *Book prices current,* 1921, mentions a 3rd
edition, 1822; and a 4th edition, London: Jones &
Co., 1829.

Real life in London: or, The rambles and
adventures of Bob Tallyho, Esq., and his
cousin, the Hon. Tom Dashall, through the
metropolis; exhibiting a living picture of fashionable characters, manners, and amusements

in high and low life. By an amateur. Em-
bellished and illustrated with a series of col-
oured prints, designed and engraved by Messrs.
Heath, Alken, Dighton, Rowlandson, &c...
London: For Jones & Co., 1822–31. 2 v. col'd
fronts., 30 col'd plates. 8°.   Stuart 7363–4
Added title-pages, illus. in colors, dated 1821.
Volume 1 published in 1831.
Volume 2 "designed and engraved by Messrs. Heath,
Alken, Dighton, Rowlandson, &c."
Ascribed to Pierce Egan, but according to the *Cambridge history of English literature* it "is a pleasanter
book than its prototype...the author had a purer style,
a cleaner mind and a wider knowledge of London
than Egan." — *v. 14, p. 225, * R–NCB.*
"Originally published in 14 parts in pink pictorial
wrappers, afterwards in pictorial boards... Some copies
on large paper." — *J. H. Slater, Illustrated sporting
books, 1889, p. 96, MED.*
J. C. Hotten claims this was written by John Badcock, who wrote under the pseudonym of Jonathan
Bee. "Immediately Messrs. Sherwood & Co. issued
the first shilling number of Mr. Egan's work [*Life
in London*], out came Jones & Co. with... [*Real life
in London*] in sixpenny numbers." Jones & Co.,
Hotten goes on to say, were successors to the famous
Lackington, Finsbury Square. See Hotten's introduc-
tion to *Life in London,* London: Hotten [1869], 12°,
NDF.
Library has another set, dated 1829–1830, *MED;*
and a reprint, Methuen, London, 1905, *NCW.*
For full collation of Egan's books see R. V.
Tooley, *Some English books with coloured plates.
Their points, collations and values,* London: Ingpen
& Grant, 1935, p. 104–113, *MDTO;* and Albert M.
Cohn, *George Cruikshank. A catalogue raisonné,*
London: The Bookman's Journal, 1924, p. 85–92,
† *MDG.*

ELLIS, HAVELOCK.
Thieves' slang. (In his: The criminal. 2. ed.
London: Walter Scott, 1897. 12°. p. 201–218.)
       SLG
Sociological study of criminals and their speech
habits. Based on Davitt, Horsley, and Lombroso for
the most part.

EVERY night book; or, Life after dark. By
the author of "The cigar"... London: Published by T. Richardson, 98, High Holburn
[etc.], 1827. 192 p. 12°.   CO (London)
A few slang expressions may be found in this
work, and the chapters on "Belcher's" and "Cribb's
Cribb" contain pugilistic slang, the "Eganisms" of the
"Eganites."

FARMER, JOHN STEPHEN.
Musa pedestris. Three centuries of canting
songs and slang rhymes <1536–1896>. Collected and annotated by John S. Farmer. Privately printed for subscribers only, 1896. 253
[correctly 251] p. 12°.   NCK
Farmer in preparing his celebrated dictionary of
slang ran across a number of canting songs, which
he thought would make a useful volume by themselves.
This collection ranges from the early songs found in
Middleton, Copland, Dekker, Fletcher, and other early
writers to the latest canting songs the compiler could
find. It includes such old favorites as Pierce Egan,
Bon Gaultier, Ainsworth, G. R. Sims, A. Chevalier,
and William Maginn. A large number of anonymous
songs are given. The notes, p. 199–245, are of extreme value to the bibliographer. This is the best
anthology of this type to be had — when a copy can
be found.

FASHIONABLE characters. (The spirit of the
public journals. London, 1801. 12°. v. 4, p. 254–
255.)   * DA
Under the title "A kiddy," a short sketch of a London
pickpocket is given in the flash language. The words
are defined in footnotes. This article was reprinted
from *The Oracle,* noted for its breezy, slangy articles.

Underworld Cant and Its Subsidiaries, cont'd

Nineteenth Century, continued

THE FLASH language. (Ladies' repository. Cincinnati, Oct., 1848. 8°. v. 8, p. 315–317.)
* DA
The author had just visited the Western Penitentiary of Pennsylvania, at Pittsburgh, and got one of the inmates to make him a manuscript copy of the flash terms known to the "well-educated" rogues. He explains that most of the words came from England, but that they were well known in America, and that a number of new words had been added. About 250 words are defined. This is one of the first lists of criminal argot published in America.

FLOWERS of felonry. (The man in the moon. London, 1848. 16°. v. 3, p. 158–159.) NDF
Contains two flash poems entitled "The burglar's bride" and "The pickpocket's love."
The man in the moon was edited by Albert Smith and Angus B. Reach. It was a rival to *Punch* for the three years, 1847–1849.

FOX, RICHARD KYLE.
Slang dictionary of New York, London and Paris. A collection of strange figures of speech, expressive terms and odd phrases used in the leading cities of the world. Their origin, meaning, and application. Collected and arranged by a well-known detective. Containing portraits of celebrated criminals, with sketches of their lives. [By Richard K. Fox.] Published at the National Police Gazette Office, 183 William St., New York [cop. 1880]. 54 p. 8°. 8–RNM
The copyright was taken out by Richard K. Fox, proprietor of the *National Police Gazette*.
This is almost a verbatim reprint of Matsell's *Vocabulum; or Rogues Lexicon* (q.v.), 1859, although it is presented to the public as a new and original work. Both dictionaries were issued under the auspices of the *National Police Gazette*.
Library also has another copy, *RNM*.

GREENWOOD, JAMES.
Low-life deeps: an account of the strange fish to be found there... London: Chatto and Windus, 1876. 319 p. 12°. CO (London)
A series of articles on low life in London and vicinity, abounding in the slang of the period.

The seven curses of London... Boston: Fields, Osgood, & Co., 1869. 336 p. 12°. SLE
"The language of 'weeds' ", p. 64–66.
A glossary of professional thieves' cant.

Unsentimental journeys: or, Byways of the modern Babylon... London: Ward, Lock, & Tyler, 1867. 232 p. 12°. COB (London)
Contains some slang. Most of the works of Greenwood contain London low life slang, and are worth perusal. For a full list of his works consult the catalogue of the British Museum.

The wilds of London... London: Chatto and Windus, 1874. 364 p. 12°. CO (London)
Stories of London low life. Includes much slang. The publishers had just taken over the business of John Camden Hotten, a great exponent of slangy literature, and Greenwood's works are very much in the Hotten manner.

HAGGART, DAVID.
The life of David Haggart, alias John Wilson, alias John Morison, alias Barney M'Coul, alias John M'Colgan, alias Daniel O'Brien, alias the Switcher... Second edition. Edinburgh: W.

and C. Tait [etc.]; London: Longman, Hurst, Rees, Orme, and Brown, 1821. 173 p. 12°.
Glossary, p. 171–173.
"Advertisement" signed by Geo. Robertson. Dated July 20, 1821.
Contains facsimile of David Haggart's signature and a note stating that "This is a true account of my life partly written by myself and partly taken down from my own lips while under sentence of death."

The life of David Haggart, alias John Wilson, alias John Morison, alias Barney M'Coul, alias John M'Colgan, alias Daniel O'Brien, alias the Switcher. Written by himself while under sentence of death. Second edition. Edinburgh: Printed by James Ballantyne and Co., for W. and C. Tait, 1821. Reprinted by A. & G. Brown, Edinburgh, 1882. 76 p. 24°. * C p.v.374
"Glossary," p. 73–76.
See William Roughead, "The adventures of David Haggart," in *Juridical review*, Edinburgh, 1917, v. 29, p. 203–226, *SEA*.
According to Roughead the *Life* was reviewed in the *Scotsman*, July 28, 1821, and in *The Scots magazine*, Aug., 1821. There is an article on Haggart in the *DNB*. His life may also be found in the *Newgate calendar* and Camden Pelham's *Chronicles of crime*.
In Haggart's glossary the word "slang" meant a show. The word "whidding" meant to talk slang.
See chapter on Haggart in Alban M. Phillip's *The prison-breakers*, New York: Henry Holt [1928], p. 62–114, *SLT*.

HAYWARD, ARTHUR LAWRENCE.
The days of Dickens... London: George Routledge & Sons [1926]. xiv, 280 p. 8°.
COB (London)
Slang, p. 15–18. Contains some back-slang, rhyming slang, and a tailor's advertisement in slang, in addition to some popular catch phrases of the period.
"The songs they sang," p. 202–218, also contains some slang. Hayward points out that the famous slang song, "The chickaleary bloke" was popularized by the greatest of all music hall stars, "The Great Vance," who was in real life Alfred Peck Stevens. The song took London by storm and occasioned "grave words of disapproval from 'Household Words,' regarding the evil taste of the day."

HEBRON, MOSES.
...The life and exploits of Ikey Solomons, swindler, forger, fencer, and brothel-keeper. With accounts of flash and dress houses, flash girls, and coves of the hatch, now on Town... London: printed and published by Edward Duncombe, Middle-Row, Holborn [circa 1830]. 24 p. 16°.
This scarce item must have gone through more than one edition, for it is called the "only correct edition." Hebron describes himself "formerly a Jewish Rabbi, but now a Christian."
See Barham, Richard Harris.

HÖFER, H.
Die Londoner Vulgärsprache insbesondere nach dem Punch. (Die neueren Sprachen. Marburg in Hessen, May – Dec., 1896. 8°. Bd. 4, p. 89–104, 150–168, 296–304, 363–368, 431–442, 486–498.) RAV
Scientific study of the London dialect of low life, drawn chiefly from the pages of *Punch*. The grammatical structure of Cockney speech is emphasized.
Cf. Stoffel, C. Annotated specimens of "Arryese." 1894.
George Rose, who wrote under the pseudonym Arthur Sketchley, created a Cockney character, Mrs. Brown, and *Mrs. Brown in America, Mrs. Brown at the play, Mrs. Brown on the turf*, etc., are good examples of Cockney speech and manners.

Underworld Cant and Its Subsidiaries, cont'd

Nineteenth Century, continued

HORSLEY, JOHN WILLIAM.
Autobiography of a thief in thieves' language.
(Macmillan's magazine. London, Oct., 1879.
8°. v. 40, p. 500–506.)   * DA
Written by the chaplain of Clerkenwell Prison, this
slang study with its sociological aspect is frequently
cited in bibliographies.
Reprinted in *The Newgate garland, or Flowers of
hemp*, London: Desmond Harmsworth, 1932, p. 111–
129, *NCI*.
Reprinted in Albert Barrère, *Argot and slang*,
London: Whittaker and Co., 1889, p. xli–lx, *RFN*. In
parallel columns is printed the same story, done into
French argot.

HOWE, J. BURDETT.
Scarlet Dick. The king's highway... London: Samuel French, n. d. 44 p. 12°. (Lacy's
acting edition of plays. v. 114.)   NCO (Lacy)
Contains much flash lingo.

THE INDIVIDUAL. Cambridge, England. 1836.
Copy in the British Museum.
This periodical contained many canting songs.

JONES, JOHN WILTON.
...Book of the words of the grand, comic,
spectacular Christmas pantomime entitled The
forty thieves or Harlequin Ali Baba and the
robbers of the magic cave... Bristol: C. J.
Jefferies & Sons [1884]. 99 p. 12°.
                              NCO p.v.685, no.7
A burlesque written in slang and poor verse. The
slang is that of London in the 1880's.

JUDSON, EDWARD ZANE CARROLL.
The mysteries and miseries of New York: a
story of real life, by Ned Buntline [pseud. of
E. Z. C. Judson]. New York: Dick & Fitzgerald, n. d. 534 p. 8°.   NBO
"A glossary of flash terms and slang language used
in this work," p. 526–527.
A story of low life in New York in the 1850's,
somewhat in the manner of George W. M. Reynolds'
Mysteries of London, which may have served as a
model.

KENT, E.
Modern flash dictionary, containing all the
cant words, slang terms, and flash phrases now
in vogue. London, 1825. "18mo and also 48mo
for the waistcoat pocket."
Kennedy 11935.

KING, RICHARD.
...The new cheats of London exposed; or,
The frauds and tricks of the town laid open
to both sexes. Being a warning piece against
the iniquitous practices of that metropolis. Containing a new and clear discovery of all the
various cheats, frauds, villanies, artifices, tricks,
seductions, stratagems, impositions, & decep-
tions, which are daily practiced in London, by
bawds, beggars, bullies, children strippers, duf-
fers, fortune tellers, footpads, gossips, gamblers,
hangers on, highwaymen, house breakers, jilts,
intelligencers, Jew defaulters, informers, kid-
nappers, mock auctioneers, money droppers,

pimps, pretended friends, pettifoggers, procur-
ers, procuresses, pickpockets, quacks, ring droppers, receivers of stolen goods, spungers, sharpers, swindlers, smugglers, shop-lifters, street
robbers, trappers, way-layers, waggon-hunters,
whores, &c. &c. &c... Written from experience
and observation by Richard King, Esq... London: Alex. Hogg, No. 16 Paternoster Row,
n. d. 72 p. 12°.   SLG
Has an engraved frontispiece.
The "new" in the title indicates it was based on an
older work of similar character. Written probably at
the beginning of the nineteenth century.

LABERN, JOHN.
...Comic songs... London: J. Duncombe
[183–?]. 74 p. 16°.   NCM
At head of title: Seventh collection.
The previous collections were filled with London
slang, and this edition is also written in popular speech.
One of the best songs in the lot is "Hush, 'tis the
Peeler!"

LAWRENCE, THOMAS.
Cant or slang language. (Notes and queries.
London, Aug. 14, 1852. 8°. v. 6, p. 142–143.)
                              * R–* DA
A query in regard to the origins of early English
cant words. A list of canting expressions is jotted
down.

...THE LONDON guide and stranger's safe-
guard against the cheats, swindlers, and pickpockets that abound within the bills of mor-
tality; forming a picture of London, as regards
active life. Collected from the verbal com-
munications of William Perry, and others. To
which is added, a glossary of cant terms. By
a gentleman, who has made the police of the
metropolis, an object of enquiry twenty-two
years. London: Printed for J. Bumpus, 6, Holborn Bars [etc.], 1819. 240 p.   SLG
"Vocabulary," p. x–xii.
Frontispiece, "Example of early depravity" shows
three boys snatching a purse from a frightened woman.
The text is filled with much slang which does not
appear in the vocabulary. Slang is defined: "Covert
language of thieves."
Hotten says that Perry was in prison a good portion
of the twenty-two years which the title-page claims
was devoted to a study of the police. Jon Bee has a
few remarks about Perry in the introductory part of
his *Slang dictionary*, 1823 (q.v.).
Almost every type of London villainy is described
and the cant phrases of each dark calling are exposed
by an authority.

LORD TOMNODDY's comic songster... [Lon-
don?] Orlando Hodgson, n. d. 8°.
Contains "Nix my dolly, pals" and other flash
songs.

MCCABE, JAMES DABNEY.
The secrets of the great city: a work descriptive of the virtues and the vices, the mysteries, miseries and crimes of New York City.
By Edward Winslow Martin [pseud. of James
Dabney McCabe]... Philadelphia: Jones,
Brothers & Co., 1868. 552 p. illus. 8°.   IRGV
"The thief language," p. 358–359. A glossary of
criminal argot taken from *The detective's manual*. The
specimens are from the letter B only. Other slang
words may be found in the text.

Underworld Cant and Its Subsidiaries, cont'd

Nineteenth Century, continued

MacDONALD, ARTHUR.
Criminology... With an introduction by
Dr. Cesare Lombroso... Second edition. New
York: Funk & Wagnalls... 1893. 416 p. 12°.
SLG
Presentation copy from the author to Andrew Car-
negie.
"Slang," p. 105–109.
"Hieroglyphics and signatures of criminals," p. 109–
113.
"Bibliography of crime," p. 275–408.

MALCOLM, JAMES PELLER.
Anecdotes of the manners and customs of
London from the Roman invasion to the year
1700... The second edition. v. I. London:
Longman, Hurst, Rees, Orme, and Brown, 1811.
8°.   CO (London)
On p. 311–335, are descriptions of some of the
contents of *Proteus Redivivus, The Art of wheedling*,
written in the reign of Charles II.; *The Canting
academy*, second edition of 1674; and the *Compleat
gamester*, of 1674. One gathers from these excerpts
that the various orders of rogues and beggars and cheats
mentioned in the *Canting academy* (undoubtedly Richard Head's) were taken from Harman's *Caveat*.

MARTIN, SIR THEODORE.
Flowers of hemp; or, The Newgate garland.
By Bon Gaultier [pseudonym of Sir Theodore
Martin and W. E. Aytoun]. (Tait's Edinburgh
magazine. Edinburgh, April, 1841. 8°. v. 8,
p. 215–223.)   *DA
Introduces the work of Jack Fireblood and quotes
from his works which were left in ms. form to John
Dalgleish, a hangman. The particulars may be pursued
in Hanchant's reprint of *The Newgate garland*, 1932.
See also Otto Schwarz, *Ein historischer und kritischer
Überblick der Galgenliteratur*, Göttingen, 1910, 2. ed.,
Appendix H. "Martin ist Fireblood. Eine Betrachtung
der Verfasning von Flowers of Hemp."
" 'Bon Gaultier' was the joint *nom-de-plume* of
W. E. Aytoun and Sir Theodore Martin. Between
1840 and 1844 they worked together in the production
of *The Bon Gaultier ballads.*" — John S. Farmer, *Musa
pedestris*, 1896, p. 240, NCK.
See also Horace W. Bleackley, *Jack Sheppard*, Edinburgh, 1933, p. 85–87, *SLN*.
There is an article on Martin, with a photograph,
in *Dublin University magazine*, Dec., 1877, v. 90,
p. 674–691, * DA.

MATSELL, GEORGE WASHINGTON.
Vocabulum; or, The rogues' lexicon. Compiled from the most authentic sources. By
George W. Matsell, special justice, chief of
police, etc., etc. New-York: Published by
George W. Matsell & Co., Proprietors of the
National Police Gazette [cop. 1859]. 130 p.
12°.   RNM
The main body of the dictionary occupies the first
97 pages. Scene in a London Flash-Panny, p. 98–104;
Appendix. The Gambler's flash, p. 107–118; technical
words and phrases, used by billiard players, p. 119–
122; brokers' technicalities in brief, p. 123; A hundred
stretches hence (flash poem), p. 124; technical words
and phrases in general use by pugilists, p. 125–128.
This dictionary formed the basis of Richard K. Fox's
Slang dictionary of New York, London and Paris, 1880
(q.v.).
It is quite likely that the slang song "A hundred
stretches hence" was a parody on *Hundred years
hence*, written and sung by Tony Pastor, at about
that period, and published by Johnson, song publisher,
7 N. 10th Street, Philadelphia.

MAYHEW, HENRY.
London characters... A new edition... Lon-
don: Chatto and Windus, 1881. 477 p. illus. 8°.
CO (London)
"Dying with cotton in one's ears," p. 345–350, is a
chapter on London thieves' slang.

London labour and the London poor... London: Griffin, Bohn, and Co., 1861. 3 v. 8°. SGF
"Language of costermongers," p. 23–24. In addition
to this special vocabulary there is a great deal of slang
interspersed through the text. This noteworthy study
of the poor of London takes up every phase of life
among the lower classes, and describes their occupations, honorable or dishonorable, open and secret, and
some of the stories are written down as they fell from
the lips of the subjects themselves, and these are filled
with the slang of the period. It remains to this day
one of the most detailed studies of street life in the
English language.
Griffin & Bohn issued a fourth volume in 1862,
which dealt with prostitutes, thieves, swindlers and
beggars. 504 p. 8°. This was called the second edition,
extra volume, *SGF*.

—— London: [G. Woodfall and Son,] 1851.
3 v. 8°.   Stuart 11967–69

—— New York: Harper & Brothers, 1851.
2 v. in 1. 8°.   SGF

MAYHEW, HENRY, AND JOHN BINNY.
The criminal prisons of London, and scenes
of prison life... London: Griffin, Bohn, and
company, 1862. 634 p. 8°.   SLT
On p. 5–6, 45–47 are specimens of London prison
slang. "The word 'patter', which is the slang for
speech, is borrowed merely from the *'pater-nosters'* that
the old-established mendicants delighted to mumble."
The classification of the criminal classes is given in
argot, on p. 45–47, and criminal slang may be found
scattered freely throughout the text.

THE METROPOLIS of England displayed; or,
A pilot thro' London: giving an accurate de-
scription of all the cheats and villainies daily
practised therein... London: G. Smeeton, 139,
St. Martin's Lane [1812]. 18 p.
Col'd frontispiece by G. Cruikshank.
The 3rd edition of this was printed under the title:
The Villainies of London; or, The frauds and cheats
of the metropolis displayed. London: G. Smeeton,
n. d. 8°.
Contains some thieves' cant.

MILES, HENRY DOWNES.
Dick Turpin... London: Thomas White,
59, Wych street, Strand, 1841. 323 p. 8°.
8–NCW
A novel in the manner of Ainsworth's *Rookwood*.
It is embellished with an engraved portrait of Turpin,
and contains several curious woodcuts. It is filled
with slang and the flash language, and the words
are defined in footnotes. There is a flash poem called
"The Dubsman's chaunt" on p. 303–304. Horace
Bleackley in his *Jack Sheppard*, Edinburgh, 1933,
p. 90, claims that Miles was noted for his plagiarism
of other men's works. He claims that Miles para-
phrased much of Ainsworth in *Dick Turpin*. "His
piracy seems to have been eminently successful, for
in the fourth edition, which appeared in 1845, the
preface states that 20,000 copies had been sold to
date." Miles is the author of *Pugilistica* (q.v.) and
was the translator of Eugene Sue's *The wandering
Jew* and *The mysteries of Paris*. He also compiled
a dictionary of Anglo-Indian terms.
See A. M. P., "Dick Turpin: fact or fiction" in
Police journal, London, Jan., 1931, v. 4, p. 128–
145; April, 1931, v. 4, p. 285–302, *SLA*.

Underworld Cant and Its Subsidiaries, cont'd

Nineteenth Century, continued

MONCRIEFF, WILLIAM THOMAS.

All at Coventry: or, Love and laugh; a farcical entertainment in two acts... London: Printed for John Phillips...1816. 57 p. 8°.

NCO p.v.392

Characterized by its generous use of London slang. It was this propensity which fitted Moncrieff for the dramatization of Egan's *Life in London* a few years later.

According to the British Museum Catalogue, William Thomas Moncrieff was a pseudonym for William Thomas.

Eugene Aram; or, Saint Robert's cave: a drama in three acts... London: John Cumberland, n. d. 68 p. 24°. (Cumberland's minor theatre. v. 10.) NCO

Preface by G. D. [George Daniel.] Filled with flash slang.

This play was based on Bulwer Lytton's *Eugene Aram*, the novel which created a new interest in Aram, just as Ainsworth's *Jack Sheppard* ushered in a flood of *Jack Sheppard* literature. Moncrieff's play was first performed Feb. 9, 1832, at the Surrey Theatre, according to a playbill reproduced in Eric R. Watson's *Eugene Aram. His life and trial*, Edinburgh and London: William Hodge & Company [1913], *SLN*. Watson has an excellent bibliography of Aram appended to the above work, p. 207–219.

Gipsy Jack; or, The Napoleon of humble life... London: John Cumberland [183–?]. 36 p. 24°. (Cumberland's minor theatre. v. 9.) NCO

Introduction by G. D. [George Daniel.] The play contains some flash words, but no authentic Romany.

The heart of London; or, The Sharper's progress: a drama in three acts... [London: H. Robertson, printer, Russell Court, Covent Garden, 1839?] 80 p. 8°.

From compiler's copy.

"This drama owes its birth to some incidents narrated in the well-known memoirs of the notorious Vidocq, the French thief-taker."

Moncrieff's name does not appear on the title-page of this edition. The preface is dated Oct., 1839.

Filled with prison slang. "The heart of London" is a slang name for Newgate Prison. It was also called "The stone jug" and "The Whit," by virtue of its being founded by the London mayor, Richard Whittington. There is a flash poem in the play.

—— London: John Dicks, n. d. 23 p. 12°. (Dicks' standard plays. no. 430.) NCO p.v.666

Modern collegians; or, Over the bridge. An half-hour's comic sketch before dinner... London: Printed for John Lowndes, 25, Bow street, Covent-Garden, opposite the theatre. 1820. 23 p. 8°. NCO p.v.83

Filled with flash songs and slang. The King's Bench Prison is the scene of the action. It was sometimes referred to as the college, hence the title of the above play.

THE NEWGATE garland; or, Flowers of hemp. Being a choice nosegay gathered in the pleasant fields of such canting and flash literature as was written from approximately the hanging of those accomplished Burkers, Messrs. Bishop and Williams, to the execution of that discreet practicioner, Thomas Neill, alias Cream, including all the verses known to be extant of that rare spirit, Jack Fireblood... The whole diligently assembled and set forth for the delight

of the family and the benefit of the public by W. L. Hanchant. London: Desmond Harmsworth, 1932. 150 p. 12°. NCI

A collection of nineteenth-century songs and stories of English criminal life. Includes selections from Jack Fireblood, William Harrison Ainsworth, Bulwer Lytton, Bon Gaultier, Pierce Egan, Ducange Anglicus, Leman Rede, John Labern, G. R. Sims (Dagonet), and many others, mostly those contained in Farmer's *Musa pedestris* (q.v.).

Jack Fireblood's poems, edited by Sir Theodore Martin (q.v.) who wrote under the pseudonym of Bon Gaultier, were published in 1841, under the title *Flowers of hemp; or, The Newgate garland.*

NORDHOFF, CHARLES.

Thieves' jargon. [By Charles Nordhoff.] (Harper's new monthly magazine. New York, April, 1865. 8°. v. 30, p. 601–607.) *DA

A review of Hotten's *The Slang dictionary*. Each part of the book is reviewed and hundreds of slang words discussed.

PHILOLOGUS, PSEUD.

A defence of slang. (In: William Hone, The every-day book... London [1827]. 8°. v. 3, p. 853–856.) *R-* AY

A defence of flash terms, particularly blowin, fib, fogle, gam, leary, pal, to prig, seedy, togs, spree, spoony. The letter is dated Dec., 1827.

POOLE, JOHN.

Hamlet travestie. In three acts... [By John Poole.] New-York: Published by David Longworth, 1811. 64 p. 16°. NCO p.v.287

Written in slang. The notes explain some of the terms and refer to the St. Giles and to the Billingsgate editions of the *Slang dictionary*, both imaginary no doubt.

An earlier edition appeared in 1810.

REYNOLDS, GEORGE WILLIAM MACARTHUR.

The mysteries of the court of London...with numerous illustrations. London: Published by John Dicks, No. 313, Strand [1849–56]. 2 v. 4°. NCW

Filled with the slang of low life. Many of the slang words are explained in footnotes. The more important sections of slang are as follows: The station house, v. 1, p. 35–37; the boozing ken, v. 1, p. 45–49; the old house in Smithfield again, v. 1, p. 58–60; the plague ship, v. 2, p. 86–90; the boozing ken once more, v. 2, p. 139–142; flash songs may be found in v. 1, p. 72; v. 2, p. 140, 175, 189–190.

Reynolds also wrote the *Mysteries of London*, 6 v., 1846–50.

—— Another set. [1852–64.] NCW

In these sets v. 1–4 are known as the new edition; v. 3–4 form the second series; v. 5–6, the third series; and v. 7–8, the fourth series.

Pickwick abroad; or, The tour in France... illustrated with forty-one steel engravings, by Alfred Crowquill and John Phillips, and with thirty-three wood cuts, by Bonner. London: Printed for Thomas Tegg...1839. 628 p. 8°. NCW

Contains a flash song, p. 223–224, entitled "The house-breaker's song." Has a glossary.

Reynolds was editor of *Reynolds's miscellany of romance, general literature, science and art*, another good source for slang.

THE ROGUES and rogueries of New York. New York: Haney & Co. [1865.] 126 p. 12°. SB p.v.175

Describes all the swindles and rackets of New York City, with a few slang words associated with each subject sprinkled through the text.

Underworld Cant and Its Subsidiaries, cont'd

Nineteenth Century, continued

RUSSELL, WILLIAM.
The recollections of a policeman. By Thomas Waters [pseud.]. New York: Cornish, Lamport & Co., 1852. 238 p. 12°.　　　NCW
Some of the stories appeared in American magazines, and some were reprinted from *Household words*. Contains criminal cant. The word "detective," just then gaining currency, is used often. Russell was one of the first successful writers of crime fiction, and his antiquarian bent was revealed in his stories.

SCHRÖDER, GEORG.
Ueber den Einfluss der Volksetymologie auf den Londoner Slang-Dialekt. Rostock, 1893.
The compiler has not seen this dissertation, but it undoubtedly bolsters the work of Baumann, Stoffel, and Höfer (q.v.).
Another work not encountered by the compiler is R. Lasch, *Londonsprachen*, 1907, 36 p.

SIMS, GEORGE ROBERT.
[Ballads in *The Referee*.]
G. R. Sims, better known under the pseudonym "Dagonet," joined the staff of *Fun* on the death of Tom Hood the younger, in 1874. After 1877 he was a constant contributor to *The Referee*, an English sporting publication. His flash songs are of particular interest. Farmer has reproduced some of them in his *Musa pedestris*, 1896.
Dagonet ballads, London: J. P. Fuller, 1881, *NCM*, does not contain the flash poems reprinted in Farmer.
See British Museum Catalogue for other works by Sims.
See Sims' *My life; sixty years' recollections of Bohemian London*, London: Eveleigh Nash, 1917, *AN*.

SINKS of London laid open: a pocket companion for the uninitiated, to which is added a modern flash dictionary containing all the cant words, slang terms, and flash phrases now in vogue, with a list of the sixty orders of prime coves... Embellished with humorous illustrations by George Cruikshank. London: Published by J. Duncombe, 1848. 131 p. 12°.
Col'd frontispiece.
"Flash dictionary," p. 95–130.

SLANG advertisement. (Town talk. London, Aug. 7, 1858. f°. v. 1, p. 167.)
Copy in the Library of Congress.
A tailor's ad, entirely in flash slang.

SLEEMAN, SIR WILLIAM HENRY.
Ramaseeana; or, A vocabulary of the peculiar language used by the Thugs... Calcutta: G. H. Huttmann, Military Orphan Press, 1836. 515 p. 12°.　　　* OLT
The vocabulary occupies p. 67–140. This is not a list of English words, but was at one time a slang vocabulary the Indian police had to be familiar with, and some of the words have crept into the English language, including the word "thug" itself.

A report on the system of Megpunnaism... [Serampore:] From the Serampore Press, 1839. iv, 121 p. 8°.　　　SLG
Technical terms in the language of the Indian Thugs, p. 67–70. The Thugs called this language Pharsee.

SMEETON, GEORGE.
Doings in London; or, Day and night scenes of the frauds, frolics, manners, and depravities of the metropolis. With thirty-three engravings

by Bonner, from designs by Mr. R. Cruikshank. Tenth edition. London: Orlando Hodgson, 111 Fleet Street, n. d. 422 p. 8°.
Preface signed: G. S.　　　CO (London)
This is one of the many imitations of Egan's *Life in London*, but is more of an exposé of frauds and the low life of London. It is filled with the cant of the crooks, gamblers, cheats, beggars, etc. Smeeton published an edition in Southwark, 1828. 8°. A good deal of London history is interspersed with the desultory wanderings of Peregrine Wilson and his guide, Mentor.

SMITH, T.
Highgate Tunnel; or, The secret arch... By Momus Medlar, Esq. [T. Smith]... London: Printed for John Miller, 1812. 37 p. 8°.
NCO p.v.177
Contains London slang and anticipates the school of slang popularized so successfully by Pierce Egan.

SNOWDEN, R. L.
The magistrates assistant and constable's guide. With a glossary of the flash language. 1852. (Klöpper's Reallexicon.)
Copy in the British Museum.
The British Museum also lists the following editions: the 3rd, edited by J. F. Archbold, London, 1857, 12°; the 4th, edited by Archbold, London, 1859, 12°; the 5th, edited by W. C. Glen, London: Shaw & Sons, 1862, 12°; the 6th, edited by Glen, London: Shaw & Sons, 1866, 12°; the 7th, edited by Glen, London: Shaw & Sons, 1875, 8°; the 8th, edited by T. H. Lees, London: Shaw & Sons, 1885, 8°; the 9th, edited by T. H. Lees, London: Shaw & Sons, 1892, 8°; the 10th, edited by T. O. H. Lees, London: Shaw & Sons, 1897, 8°. Some of them may not contain the glossary.

STAINER, SIR JOHN.
Catalogue of English song books forming a portion of the library of Sir John Stainer... London: Printed for private circulation by Novello, Ewer and Co., 1891. 107 p. 8°. * MC
Contains many song books that have canting songs in them. This is not always clear from the titles, but a close study of the song books listed would prove of great value to the slang collector. The books are listed alphabetically by title, and not chronologically. Many of the music hall hits of the eighteenth and early nineteenth century, the golden age of the "flash" language, are included in these popular collections.
This superb collection is now owned by Mr. Walter N. H. Harding, of Chicago.

STOFFEL, CORNELIS.
Annotated specimens of "Arryese"; a study in vulgar English. (Taalstudie. 1889–90. v. 10, p. 291–296; v. 11, p. 8–13, 21–29, 57–77.)
These articles were greatly enlarged in Stoffel's *Studies in English written and spoken for the use of continental students. First series*, Zutphen: W. J. Thieme, 1894, p. 170–320. Copy in Columbia University Library.
Although these studies were based on the 'Arry poems in *Punch* they serve as a compendium of English slang of the nineteenth century. The 'Arry poems appeared quite frequently in *Punch* after 1877, and were the essence of Cockney speech. The slang of low life predominated.
Cf. Baumann's "Londinismen"; and Höfer's "Die Londoner Vulgarsprache, insbesondere nach dem Punch" in *Die Neueren Sprachen*, 1896, *RAV*.
See also E. J. Milliken's *'Arry ballads*, 1892.
Besides *Punch*, there were many other London magazines of the Victorian era rich in slang, particularly *Ally Sloper's Half Holiday*, *Judy*, and *Curried Fowl*.

Underworld Cant and Its Subsidiaries, cont'd

Nineteenth Century, continued

SUE, EUGÈNE.
The mysteries of Paris. London: Chapman and Hall, 1845–46. 3 v. 4°.   NKV
Illustrated by Charles Heath.
Eugène Sue created a vogue for criminal argot in his *Les Mystères de Paris*, 1842–43. It was soon translated into English. As it was necessary to give English equivalents for the French argot these translations are filled with criminal cant. In France special dictionaries of argot were published to help readers understand Sue.
See R. Yve-Plessis, *Bibliographie raisonnée de l'argot et de langue verte en France du XVe au XXe siècle...*, Paris: H. Davagon, P. Sacquet, 1901, p. 99–101, *RFN*.
There are many editions of Sue translated into English. The above edition is valuable for its footnotes containing cant definitions. An edition published by Hooper, Clarke & Co., Chicago [189–?], 648 p., 12°, *NKV*, may be mentioned because it brings some of the slang expressions up-to-date. Most of the early editions copied one another in the choice of slang words.

TERMS used by rogues. (The detective's manual and officer's guide. Springfield, Mass., 1868. 8°. v. 1, p. 115–116, 171–173.)   SLA
The letters B and C only. We have not been able to locate earlier and later numbers. The list was "cribbed" from Matsell's *Vocabulum; or, The rogue's lexicon* (q.v.)

THIEVES and thieving. (Cornhill magazine. London, Sept., 1860. 8°. v. 2, p. 326–344.) *DA
A sociological study of thieves. Contains a selection of thieves' slang, based largely on Hotten. "Let any thoughtful man ask himself, what must be the moral condition of a people with such a vernacular?"

THE TOM & JERRY flash dictionary. London: printed for the publisher; John G. Scobie, printer, 1825. 69 p.
Kennedy 11933.
Eric Partridge wrote to the compiler, "I doubt the existence of 'The Tom and Jerry Flash Dictionary.' It is probably identical with E. Kent's 'Modern Flash Dictionary,' 1825."

THE UNIVERSAL songster; or, Museum of mirth...embellished with a humorous characteristic frontispiece, and twenty-nine woodcuts, designed by George and Robert Cruikshank, and engraved by J. R. Marshall... London: Published by Jones and Co., Temple of the Muses [formerly Lackington's], Finsbury Square [1834?]. 3 v. 8°.   NCK
v. 1 has an engraved frontispiece dated 1832, and an engraved title-page, without date. v. 2 lacks engraved frontispiece and t.-p. v. 3 has an engraved title-page, without date. Each volume contains 448 p.
Stainer mentions an earlier edition. He describes v. 1 as having an engraved frontispiece dated 1825, and an engraved t.-p.; also an additional t.-p. and frontispiece dated 1827; v. 2 has an engraved frontispiece and t.-p. and is dated 1826; v. 3, is the same. Each volume has 448 p. It would appear from this that The New York Public Library set is a straight reprint, as far as the text goes, of the earlier edition mentioned by Stainer.
The *universal songster* contains many songs of slang, cant, flash, etc. The song "The night before Larry was stretched" is in v. 3, p. 140, and is attributed to Curren. See the annotation under Farmer's *Musa pedestris in re* this poem. Farmer reprints a number of slang songs from *The Universal songster*.

—— London: Jones and Co., 1834. 8°.
                                        MEM C955u

—— London: G. Routledge and Sons [1878]. 3 v. 8°.   NCK

VAGABONDIA: or, Anecdotes of mendicant wanderers through the streets of London, with portraits of the most remarkable, drawn from life by J. T. Smith. 1817. 30 etchings. 4°.
"Contains accounts and anecdotes of beggars and some of their songs." — *Nodal*.

VAUX, JAMES HARDY.
Memoirs of James Hardy Vaux. Written by himself. London: Printed by W. Clowes, Northumberland-court, Strand, and sold by all respectable booksellers, 1819. 2 v. in 1. 12°.
                                        AN
"A new and comprehensive vocabulary of the flash language, compiled and written by James Hardy Vaux," p. 147–227.
Reviewed in *Edinburgh monthly review*.

Memoirs of James Hardy Vaux, a swindler and theif [sic], now transported to New South Wales for the second time, and for life. Written by himself. Second edition. London: Printed for Hunt and Clarke, York Street, Covent Garden, 1827. 288 p. 24°. A(Auto. v.13)
This reprint occupied v. 13 of a set entitled "Autobiography. A collection of the most instructive and amusing lives ever published, written by the parties themselves."

—— London: Whittaker, Treacher, and Arnot, Ave-Maria-Lane, 1830.   A(Auto. v.13)
The flash dictionary, which was appended to the original edition, London: W. Clowes, 1819, 2 v. 12°, does not appear in the above reprints. See the British Museum Catalogue, and Lowndes, for early editions of Vaux. The bibliography in the Oxford English dictionary, Supplement, 1933, mentions an early work by Vaux entitled: "A new and comprehensive vocabulary of the flash language," London, 1812. This was reprinted in v. 1 of the *Memoirs*, 1819. The 1819 edition of the *Memoirs* was reviewed in the *London magazine*, London, Jan., 1820, v. 1, p. 25–31, *DA*. The review contains flash words also, and gives a selection of words taken from the flash dictionary appended to the *Memoirs*.
"His *Memoirs* were suppressed by reason of the vice they inculcated, and with them Viscount [sic] Collard's Cant went likewise to the trunk-makers." — *Jon Bee, Sportsman's slang*, 1825, p. ix.
Vaux was used as a character in W. T. Moncrieff's operatic drama, *Van Diemen's Land*. See Cumberland's minor theatre, v. 10, *NCO*.

VIDOCQ, EUGÈNE FRANÇOIS.
Mémoires de Vidocq, chef de la police de sureté jusqu'en 1827... [v. 1, compiled from Vidocq's notes by E. Morice; v. 2–4, by L. F. L'Héritier.] Paris, 1828–29. 4 v. 8°.
Copy in the British Museum.
Reviewed in *Monthly review*, London, Dec., 1828, series 3, v. 9, p. 514–522; Oct., 1829, v. 12, p. 278–297, *DA*. Gives publisher as Tenon. Says last two volumes were invented by the editor and that Vidocq didn't write a line of them.

Memoirs of Vidocq, principal agent of the French police until 1827: and now proprietor of the paper manufactory at St. Mandé. Written by himself... London, 1828–29. 24°. (Autobiography. A collection of the most instructive and amusing lives. v. 25–28.)
                                        A (Autobiography)
Volumes 1 and 2 were published by Hunt and Clarke; v. 3 and 4 by Whittaker, Treacher, and Arnot.
The translator of the French signs himself H. T. R. This translation is filled with English criminal slang, the nearest counterpart to the argot of Vidocq. In v. 3, p. 56–58, 59, 169–170 appear flash ballads. The translator gives them in translation in the appendix to v. 4, p. 259–267. The first one is reprinted from a

Underworld Cant and Its Subsidiaries, cont'd

Nineteenth Century, continued

translation by William Maginn, which appeared in *Blackwood's magazine*, Edinburgh, July, 1829, v. 26, p. 131–133, * DA. This version was also reprinted along with the French original in Farmer's *Musa pedestris* (q.v.). From internal evidence it appears that William Maginn was the translator of parts of the memoirs of Vidocq, concealed behind the initials H. T. R. Maginn wrote under a great number of pseudonyms. He had a knowledge of English and French criminal argot second to none. In fact there is reason to believe that no other Englishman then alive could have made such a faithful translation. Jon Bee (John Badcock) and Pierce Egan knew the English flash language, but they did not know the French. Maginn was in Paris shortly before the appearance of Vidocq's memoirs. Dr. Shelton Mackenzie, in his memoir of Maginn in v. 5 of the *Miscellaneous writings of the late Dr. Maginn*, New York: Redfield, 1857, p. lv–lvii, *NCG*, although making no statement to the effect that Maginn was the translator of Vidocq, or even hinting as much, has the following pertinent remarks to make: "This last (a reference to Maginn's *Blackwood's* translation of Vidocq's flash poem) showed a remarkable acquaintance with, and command over, the slang used by criminals not only in London but in Paris also. Dr. Maginn certainly could not have written it *before* his residence in France. He always considered this Slang Song as one of his greatest feats. It certainly was superior to the flash lyrics <clever though they were> which he afterward allowed to be published by, and accredited to, Mr. Ainsworth, in the Newgate romances of that author. No study, however serious and deep, of the Slang vocabularies of Captain Grose <the 'fat friend' of the last century immortalized by Burns>, and the redoubtable and more recent Jon Bee could have given Maginn, or any other literary man, such an intimate acquaintance with *thieves' patter* as he had acquired by trusting himself into the haunts of 'pickers-up of unconsidered trifles' — places where the police themselves hesitated to venture, when armed with the full authority of the law... Fearlessly trusting himself into the haunts of criminals, in Paris as well as in London, Dr. Maginn never once was subjected to insult. He made himself acquainted, very thoroughly, with what are called the *back slums* of the Quartier St. Denis, the Rue du Temple, and other haunts of each *mauvaise subjet* of the Lusetian [*sic*] capital. Equally, even in Bermondsey and 'The Mint' of Southwark <the worst localities in London>, he was tolerated."

Halkett and Laing's dictionary gives Maginn as a possible translator of Vidocq. The *DNB* makes no mention of the possibility. Miriam Thrall's *Rebellious Fraser's*, New York: Columbia University Press, 1934, * D, in her bibliography of Maginn makes no mention of it.

—— Philadelphia: T. B. Peterson and Brothers [1859]. 580 p. 12°.   SLG

—— Another edition. An exact reprint of the above, but bearing the imprint of J. C. Morgan & Co., New Orleans [1859].   SLG

—— New York: George Routledge & Sons [18—?]. 448 p. 12°.   SLG
The three American editions above reprinted the London edition word for word, but ended their reprints at the end of v. 3, for some unknown reason. The preface to the American editions published by Peterson were signed F. L. and they were stolen from the sequel of the 4th volume of the English edition.

—— Edited and translated by Edwin Gile Rich. Cambridge: Houghton Mifflin Co., 1935. 433 p. 8°.   SLG
A free translation which omits much. None of the flash ballads appear in this edition. Any translator lacking the skill of William Maginn would hardly dare attempt an English rendering of this most difficult French criminal argot.
See Moncrieff, William Thomas, *The heart of London.*

Maginn, William.
The pickpockets chaunt. (Blackwood's magazine. Edinburgh, July, 1829. 8°. v. 26, p. 131–133.)   * DA
A translation of the famous canting song of Vidocq. Maginn translates the opening line "En roulant de vergne en vergne?" in this wise: "As from ken to ken I was going," etc. There are fourteen stanzas in all, and they appeared in *Noctes Ambrosianae*, under Maginn's pseudonym, Sir Morgan Odoherty. The poem has been reprinted many times. The French verses are given alongside the English. Maginn was a friend of "The Fancy" and the other sporting men of the time, and helped bring the works of Jon Bee, Pierce Egan, and others, before the reading public of the respectable magazines.

VELLACOTT, C. H.
Thieves' slang. (Gentleman's magazine. London, Oct., 1896. 8°. v. 281, p. 346–351.)   * DA
Gives the history of cant, rhyming slang, backslang. Gives etymology of words used by criminals. Quotes from the works of J. W. Horsley, The Newgate chaplain, and Michael Davitt.

WARNER; a tragedy of the attic, Aristophanic, classic, comic, didactic, domestic, localic, moralistic, operatic, terpsichoric, <and every other essential ic> extravaganza class; interspersed with parodies; dedicated not by permission to an illustrious and well-known character on the pave of the metropolis. By a regular swell cove... London: printed for E. Duncombe, Theatrical Repository, n. d. 16 p. 12°.   NCO p.v.233
Colored aquatint of a London boozing ken, for frontispiece.
An inscription to Billy Waters, president of the Club of Cadgers, written in flash, p. [iii] is dated Dec. 24, 1822.
Warner is a parody on Byron's *Werner* and on the Tom and Jerry school of drama inaugurated by Pierce Egan. It contains many flash songs, and is written in flash verse.

WIGHT, JOHN.
Mornings at Bow Street... 4th ed. London: Thomas Tegg & Son, 1838. 300 p. 16°.   MEM C955wi
Illustrations by George Cruikshank. Contains a scattering of London slang.
This was wrongly attributed to T. Wright in Nodal's bibliography of slang and cant.

More mornings at Bow Street... London: James Robins & Co., Ivy Lane, Paternoster Row, 1827. 12°.   MEM C955wi
Illustrated by George Cruikshank.

WILDE, WILLIAM CUMMING.
Notes on thief talk. (Journal of American folk-lore. Boston, 1890. 8°. v. 3, p. 303–310.)   HBA
A selection, with notes, of the words in Matsell's *Vocabulum; or, The Rogue's lexicon* (q.v.). Wilde, a New Orleans bibliophile, died before the proof sheets of this article reached him. A note on this article appeared in the same volume of the *Journal of American folk-lore*, p. 314–315, signed W. W. N.
Arthur MacDonald in his *Criminology*, New York: Funk & Wagnalls, 1893, p. 330, *SLG*, mentions Wilde's "Notes on thief-lore," 1890, which must be the same as the above.

Underworld Cant and Its Subsidiaries, cont'd

TWENTIETH CENTURY

A NO. 1, PSEUD. *See* LIVINGSTON, LEON RAY.

ACKLOM, MOREBY.
"Wise-cracking" crook novels. (The Bookman. New York, April, 1919. 8°. v. 49, p. 208–209.)   * DA
For the benefit of readers of crook stories, a number of crook terms are presented in the form of an examination paper — the readers to go to the works of Bronson Howard and Mrs. E. T. Rath and other writers of crime fiction for the answers.

ALLINGHAM, PHILIP.
Cheapjack, being the true history of a young man's adventures as a fortune-teller, grafter, knocker-worker, and mounted pitcher on the market-places and fair-grounds of a modern but still romantic England... London: William Heinemann [1934]. 322 p. 12°.   TMT
"Glossary of grafters' slang," p. 316–322. "Some are rhyming slang, some Yiddish and some Romany, but together they make up the principal vocabulary of most grafters."
Reviewed in *New York Times book review*, Sept. 9, 1934, p. 11, † *NAA; Saturday review of literature*, New York, Sept. 8, 1934, v. 11, p. 94 (Arthur Ruhl), † *NAA; London Times literary supplement*, May 31, 1934, v. 33, p. 394–395, † *NAA.*

THE AMERICAN "ganguage." (The Literary digest. New York, April 9, 1932. 4°. v. 113, p. 36.)   * DA
The busy brains of the underworld coin new phrases constantly for self protection. A few samples from the Chicago "bad lands" are given.

AMERICAN hobo possessor of curious lingo. (New York Herald Tribune, Jan. 6, 1935, section 1, p. 23.)   * A
Article copied from the Baltimore *Sun*, written by Charles A. Scarpello. Scarpello's early life, and his adventures as a tramp in a number of countries and the vocabulary acquired en route, are reviewed.

ANDERSON, NELS.
The hobo; the sociology of the homeless man. A study prepared for the Chicago Council of Social Agencies under the direction of the Committee on Homeless Men. Chicago: The University of Chicago Press [cop. 1923]. 302 p. 12°.   SGS
Contains no glossary, but the text is filled with the cant of the American hobo.
Reviewed in *New republic*, New York, Aug. 22, 1923, v. 35, p. 364–365 (Harry Kemp), * DA.

The milk and honey route. A handbook for hobos by Dean Stiff [Nels Anderson]. With a comprehensive and unexpurgated glossary. Illustrated by Ernie Bushmiller. New York: The Vanguard Press, 1931. 219 p. 12°.   SGS
Glossary of terms, p. 218–219.
A first-hand account of the life of the American hobo.

ASBURY, HERBERT.
The gangs of New York... New York: Alfred A. Knopf, 1928. xviii, 400 p. illus. 8°.   SLE
Slang of the early gangsters, p. 375–379. Excerpts from Matsell's *Vocabulum* (q.v.).

BARR, A. J.
Let tomorrow come. New York: W. W. Norton & Company, Inc. [cop. 1929.] 269 p. 8°.   SLT
"Glossary," p. 265–269. American criminal cant. About 70 words and phrases defined.

BAUMANN, HEINRICH.
Londinismen (slang und cant); Wörterbuch der Londoner Volkssprache sowie der üblichsten Gauner-, Matrosen-, Sport- und Zunftausdrücke. Mit Einleitung und Musterstücken. Ein Supplement zu allen englisch-deutschen Wörterbüchern von H. Baumann, Master of Arts of London University... Dritte Auflage... Berlin-Schöneberg: Langenscheidtsche Verlagsbuchhandlung... [1913.] 285 p. 8°.   RNM
In many respects this is one of the leading books on London slang. The title is misleading, for the author goes far beyond the environs of London and snares slang and cant from England proper. The Cockney dialect is studied very carefully. The history of slang and cant is reviewed in the bibliography, and many illustrative excerpts enliven the bibliographical entries. This book had considerable influence on Eric Partridge and other English writers on slang. Besides the bibliography there is a dictionary of London slang, done in the historical manner. The words and phrases are in English and the definitions are in German. Some Yiddish is included, and there is a section devoted to the speech of gipsies.
Kennedy lists a 1903 edition and a still earlier one, the 1887 edition. He also mentions a number of reviews of the dictionary. See Kennedy 10979 and 10982.

BEATH, PAUL ROBERT.
More crook words. (American speech. Baltimore, Dec., 1930. 4°. v. 6, p. 131–134.)   RNA
Based on an article in the *Saturday evening post* of April 13, 1929, by Col. Charles G. Givens. The crook words in the article are taken out and put in a glossary.

BIRSS, JOHN W., JR.
English underworld slang. (American speech. Baltimore, June, 1931. 4°. v. 6, p. 391–393.)   RNA
Reprinted from *Variety*, New York, April 8, 1931, † *NAFA.*

BISHOP, CECIL.
From information received. London: Hutchinson & Co. [1932.] 286 p. 8°.   AN
Written by a member of the criminal investigation department of New Scotland Yard. Contains a good deal of argot. Bishop claims that he took George R. Sims (Dagonet), who wrote so many slang ballads in *The referee*, through the roughest section of Seven Dials in order that Sims could see low life at close hand. Sims never made a request for a second trip.

BOOTH, ERNEST.
The language of the underworld. (The American mercury. New York, May, 1928. 4°. v. 14, p. 78–81.)   * DA
Discusses the etymology of some of the present-day criminal words. Notes the prevalence of Australian slang in the argot of thieves.
Reprinted in *Gray shadows*, compiled by Joseph Lewis French, New York: The Century Co. [1931], p. 159–166, *SLE.*

Underworld Cant and Its Subsidiaries, cont'd

Twentieth Century, continued

BROWN, W. F.
Thieves and their argot. (The Police journal. London, Oct., 1931. 8°. v. 4, p. 500–505.) SLA
A first-hand study of modern London underworld slang by a superintendent of the metropolitan police. Excerpts from this article appeared in the *New York Times*, Oct. 18, 1931.

BURGLARS vocabulary. (New Broadway brevities. New York, Oct. 5, 1931.)
About one hundred expressions.

BURKE, JAMES P.
The argot of the racketeers. (The American mercury. New York, Dec., 1930. 4°. v. 21, p. 454–458.) *DA
"In this list I omit much of the slang that is common to all American criminals, and confine myself mainly to words and phrases used only by the new race of racketeers." Arranged in dictionary form and the parts of speech are indicated.

CALDWELL, JOHN.
Patter of the prisons. (Writer's digest. Cincinnati, Feb., 1930. 8°. v. 10, p. 25–27.) *IH
American prison slang. The compiler was aided by prisoner no. 57419, of Ohio State Penitentiary.

CASEY, PATRICK.
Flash. (The Editor. Highland Falls, N. Y., Feb. 24, 1917. 8°. v. 45, p. 150–155.) NARA
This is the best glossary that has appeared in *The Editor*. Gives a short historical sketch of slang and cant, followed by a glossary of "up-to-date flash language of America, heard in the 'jungles' and 'on the road,' the most of which my brother and I have already made use of in our several tramp stories: The Gay-cat, which appeared in the *Saturday evening post*, and To crack a safe, According to his caste, and The Phoney man, which have appeared or soon will appear in *Adventure.*"

CASEY, PATRICK, AND TERENCE CASEY.
The gay-cat... New York: H. K. Fly Company [1921]. 305 p. 12°. NBO
"Appendix," p. 301–305, contains a "glossary of flash language, that peculiar argot or slang of the thief and hobo. It is as old as history and has been used as a means of safe communication in public for years. How many words this lingo contains it is impossible to tell absolutely, but it is believed that over three thousand separate and distinct expressions are in use in this country today."

CHADWICK, ROY, PSEUD.
Heist guy. (Liberty. New York, July 5, 1930. 4°. v. 7, p. 18–20, 23–25.) *DA
A crook's story of how he got his start.

My racket is autos. (Liberty. New York, July 19, 1930. 4°. v. 7, p. 22–29.) *DA
Car stealing and its lingo.

I crack some Petes. (Liberty. New York, Aug. 2, 1930. 4°. v. 7, p. 36–42.) *DA
Argot of the safe-cracker.

Cleaning the jugs. (Liberty. New York, Aug. 23, 1930. 4°. v. 7, p. 30–34.) *DA
Bank-robbing lingo.

In my parlor. (Liberty. New York, Nov. 20, 1930. 4°. v. 7, p. 74–78.) *DA
The speakeasy racket.

Thieves' honor. (Liberty. New York, Oct. 11, 1930. 4°. v. 7, p. 27–30, 32.) *DA
The gangsters' code.

Meet the moll. (Liberty. New York, Nov. 1, 1930. 4°. v. 7, p. 36–38, 43–44.) *DA
The gangster's woman.

I get some steers. (Liberty. New York, Nov. 15, 1930. 4°. v. 7, p. 74–78.) *DA
The argot of the tipster.

With thanks to the fences. (Liberty. New York, Nov. 29, 1930. 4°. v. 7, p. 70–74.) *DA
The stolen goods racket.
Roy Chadwick is the pseudonym of an Ohio racketeer. He related the above stories to Eugene Segal. Each story contains a short glossary of crook slang for the benefit of the reader.

CLARK, CHARLES L., AND E. E. EUBANK.
Lockstep and corridor; thirty-five years of prison life... Cincinnati: The University of Cincinnati Press [cop. 1927]. 177 p. illus. 8°. (University of Cincinnati. Department of Sociology. Publication no. 1.) SA (Cincinnati)
Charles L. Clark was an inmate of the Illinois State Penitentiary, and Earle Edward Eubank, head of the Department of Sociology at the University of Cincinnati, helped prepare Clark's personal narrative for publication.
"Appendix B. A glossary of criminal jargon": p. 173–175.

CONVICT 12627.
Underworld slang. [Jackson, Tenn., May 20, 1936.] 13 unnumbered pages, 2 col. 4 x 6 in.

CONVICT 65,368.
The passing of the argot of the underworld. (The Editor. Highland Falls, N. Y., Feb. 24, 1917. 8°. v. 45, p. 177–179.) NARA
Reprinted from *The Star of hope*, a Sing Sing prison publication. Chiefly the argot of the American pickpocket, called a "gun." About 100 expressions are defined, by an "expert."

COURTNEY, THOMAS J.
Hot shorts. (Saturday evening post. Philadelphia, Nov. 30, 1935. f°. v. 208, p. 12–13, 72–74.) *DA
A story of automobile thieves, which contains a special glossary of their slang.

CRUMP, IRVING, AND JOHN W. NEWTON.
Our police. New York: Dodd, Mead & Co., 1935. x, 263 p. illus. 8°. SLX
"The bi-lingual police," p. 257–263.
American underworld slang, "chosen at random from the crook's slang book."

DARLING, CHARLES H.
The jargon book... Aurora, Ill.: The Aurora Co., cop. 1919. 57 p. 8°. RNB p.v.25, no.1
Contains over two thousand words, mostly those familiar to the underworld. Short definitions with no attempt to trace origins.

DAVIES, WILLIAM HENRY.
Beggars' slang. (In his: Beggars. [London:] Duckworth & Co., 1909. 12°. p. 97–104.) SGS
Beggar cant heard along English roads. Other parts of the book contain a few American tramp words.

DEVERE, WILLIAM.
Tramp poems of the West... Tacoma, Washington: Cromwell Printing Company, 1891. 102 p. 8°. NBF p.v.24, no.3
These poems are filled with tramp lingo.

Underworld Cant and Its Subsidiaries, cont'd

Twentieth Century, continued

Do YOU speak "yegg"? (The Literary digest.
New York, Aug. 19, 1916. f°. v. 53, p. 424–
425.)   * DA
"A yegg is a professional safe-blower... A dictionary of his terms would rival that of any other
language in size." Excerpts over a hundred words
from *The Star of hope*, a Sing Sing publication.

ENGLAND, GEORGE ALLAN.
   Underworld lingo. (The Writer's monthly.
Springfield, Mass., Nov., 1927. 8°. v. 30, p. 387–
394.)   * IH
   One of the longer glossaries of crook argot. Contains several hundred modern American expressions
known to criminals and those who hunt them. "Several years association with a 'swell mouthpiece,' or
lawyer whose principal business it has been to defend
crooks, have given me some idea of the underworld
lingo."

ERSINE, NOEL.
   Underworld and prison slang. Upland, Indiana: Published by A. D. Freese & Son [cop.
1933]. 80 p. 8°.   RNM
   Slang obtained from prisoners. Essay on slang,
p. 7–12. The dictionary gives brief but reliable definitions. Mentions the extensive glossary of criminal
slang which appeared in Jack Lait's syndicated column,
"Highlights of Broadway." See also Jack Lait's
Gangster girl, New York: Grosset & Dunlap, 1930,
which contains a glossary, p. 213–230.

FERRIER, J. KENNETH.
   Crooks & crime... London: Seeley, Service
& Co., 1928. 314 p. 8°.   SLG
   "Crime in the United States of America," p. 210–
229.
   This chapter defines American slang for the benefit
of English readers.

FINERTY, JAMES J.
   "Criminalese." Slang talk of the criminal.
Los Angeles: The author, P. O. Box 867, 1934.
   A word list compiled by a former chief of police.

GILL, MERLE AVERY.
   Underworld slang. [Kansas City, Missouri:
South Side Printing Co.,] 1929. 15 l. 24°.
   The compiler has not seen a copy of this pamphlet.

GIVENS, CHARLES G.
   The clatter of guns. (Saturday evening post.
Philadelphia, April 13, 1929. f°. v. 201, p. 48,
50, 54.)   * DA
   "American crooks are the slangiest in the world."
Shows that most of the slang used by criminals traces
back to Europe. Hotten's *The slang dictionary* (1859)
contains many words in common use today. "I have
yet to find a criminal, big or little, no matter how
widely travelled, who knew enough slang to permit
him to talk in the unknown tongue." Lists a number
of slang terms now in vogue in America.

GLOSSARY of terms used in labor espionage.
(New York Times, Dec. 22, 1937.)   * A

GLOVER, J.
   Thieves slang. (The Garda review. Dublin,
May, 1935. 8°. v. 10, p. 646–647.)   SLA
   Reprinted from the *Ulster constabulary gazette.*
A glossary of modern criminal slang in Ireland. De-
scribes some of the linguistic tricks and devices of
thieves.

GOODWIN, JOHN CUTHBERT.
   Sidelights on criminal matters... London:
Hutchinson & Co., 1923. 336 p. 8°.   SLE
   p. 164–167 gives a sample of criminal argot, and
a translation.

GORDON, CHARLES GEORGE.
   Crooks of the underworld. With an introduction by George Dilnot. London: Geoffrey Bles
[1929]. 255 p. 12°.   AN
   It is unfortunate that this book does not contain
a glossary, for it is filled with crook argot from
cover to cover. It is a genuine crook autobiography
and is not padded with fiction.

GRAY, HUGH.
   Rhyming slang. (The Bookman. London,
Oct., 1934. f°. v. 87, p. 33–34.)   †* GDD
   One of the best articles on this neglected and important subject. Contrary to learned opinion this variety
of London slang still flourishes. "There is not a 'cabby,'
a bricklayer or a Covent Garden porter to-day who does
not still use some of these expressions. Our learned
friend the philologist has perhaps not, in his day,
been a great patron of the music hall." A great
many examples of rhyming slang are given, and the
compiler acknowledges his debt to the glossary compiled by A. H. Williams. "Brass tacks," which has
baffled the etymologists, is rhyming slang for "facts,"
Gray asserts.

HAPGOOD, HUTCHINS.
   Types from city streets. New York: Funk
and Wagnalls, 1910. 379 p. 12°.   SLG
   Does not have a glossary, but it is one of the best
guides to the speech of the Bowery, in New York
City. The men of the Bowery are depicted with sympathetic understanding.

HARGAN, JAMES.
   The psychology of prison language. (The
Journal of abnormal and social psychology.
Princeton, Oct./Dec., 1935. 8°. v. 30, p. 359–
365.)   WPA
   Written by a psychologist connected with the classification clinic at Sing Sing prison. A glossary of
terms used by the prisoners at Sing Sing is given.
Does not include words of gross sexual signification,
but the compiler stated that such a list would be sent
to students interested in this phase of slang, upon
written application.

HENCH, ATCHESON L.
   From the vocabulary of automobile thieves.
(American speech. Baltimore, Feb., 1930. 4°.
v. 5, p. 236–237.)   RNA
   A few samples of the jargon of a new class of criminals, taken from an article "I wonder who's driving
her now?" in the *Journal of American insurance*, Feb.,
1929, p. 5–8, written by William G. Shepherd.

HENDERSON, GEORGE COCHRAN.
   Keys to crookdom...with an introduction by
August Vollmer... New York: D. Appleton
& Co., 1924. xix, 429 p. 12°.   SLG
   Appendix B. Criminal slang, p. 396–422. This
is a good glossary for modern criminalese. The author
got his information from numerous prison wardens,
police chiefs, and detectives.
   Reviewed in *London Times literary supplement,*
Nov. 27, 1924, v. 23, p. 785, † *NAA.*

HOBO COLLEGE, CINCINNATI.
   Hobo songs, poems, ballads, recitations,
etc... Cincinnati: Published by the· Hobo-
College Press Committee· [19—?]. 16 p. 4°.
                                               NAC p.v.181
   Hobo lingo collected by Nicholas Klein appears on
p. 6–7. The songs are filled with hobo slang. See
also the *Hobo world, official organ of the International
Brotherhood Welfare Association*, Cincinnati, 1920–
24, *TDRA.*

Underworld Cant and Its Subsidiaries, cont'd

Twentieth Century, continued

HOLBROOK, STEWART H.
Wobbly talk. (The American mercury. New
York, Jan., 1926. 8°. v. 7, p. 62–63.)   * DA
A wobbly is a member of the I. W. W. (Industrial
Workers of the World). "He has developed, within his
group, a peculiar argot, and it is little known outside
the ranks." A number of these expressions are defined.

HOPKINS, ROBERT THURSTON.
Life and death at the Old Bailey. London:
Herbert Jenkins [1935]. 318 p. illus. 8°.   SLT
This competent work is filled with slang. See
especially p. 58–68, 94–95. Includes some back slang,
and a great many slang terms for money.

HYATT, ROBERT M.
Correct underworld "lingo." (The Editor.
Highland Falls, N. Y., Feb. 6, 1932. 4°. v. 96,
p. 110–114.)   NARA
Glossary of criminal cant, old and new, for the
writer of American crime fiction.

INGRAM, GEORGE, PSEUD.
Hell's Kitchen. The story of London's underworld as related by the notorious ex-burglar
George Ingram to De Witt Mackenzie. London: Herbert Jenkins, Ltd. [1930.] 312 p. 12°.
"The underworld language," p. 113–121.   SLG
An excellent glossary, including much rhyming
slang. Other parts of the book contain additional
slang words.

IRWIN, GODFREY.
American tramp and underworld slang...
with a number of tramp songs...edited with
essays on the slang and the songs by Godfrey
Irwin. With a terminal essay on American
slang in its relation to English thieves' slang
by Eric Partridge. London: Eric Partridge, at
the Scholartic Press, 1931. 263 p. 8°.   RNM
"Changing modes and manners in tramp life and
language will make themselves plain to anyone who
goes back to the books by Josiah Flynt," writes Irwin.
The glossary is well selected, and the latest expressions are intermingled with a few words that go
back as far as Grose and Vaux. The definitions incline
to fullness. Partridge is the most active of the
modern English compilers of slang. See his various
books and articles.
Reviewed in *American speech,* New York, Dec.,
1934, v. 9, p. 303–304 (J. Louis Kuethe), *RNA; Review of English studies,* London, 1934, v. 10, p. 114–
116 (C. Sisley), *RNA; New statesman and nation,*
London, April 18, 1931, new series, v. 1, p. 286 (Richard
Sunne), * DA; Saturday review, London, May 16, 1931,
v. 151, p. 726, * DA; Saturday review of literature,
New York, Nov. 21, 1931, v. 8, p. 319, *NAA; London
Times literary supplement,* June 18, 1931, p. 489,
NAA; Spectator, London, June 20, 1931, v. 146, p. 980,
* DA; John O'London's weekly, London, May 2, 1931,
v. 25, p. 127, * DA (Jackdaw); New statesman, London, Jan. 24, 1931, v. 36, p. 465–466, * DA (Eric
Partridge); Life and letters, London, July, 1931, v. 7,
p. 74–75, * DA; London mercury, Oct., 1931, v. 24,
p. 572 (E. Weekley), * DA; Everyman, London, May
21, 1931, v. 5, p. 520, 522 (Charles Ashleigh), * DA.

IRWIN, WALLACE ADMAH.
The love sonnets of a hoodlum...with an
introduction by Gelett Burgess. San Fran-
cisco: Elder and Shepard, 1902. 16 l. 12°.
NBI p.v.8
Twenty-three sonnets in the slang of the road.
Gelett Burgess defends slang in his introduction and
calls it "the illegitimate sister of poetry."

JACKSON, LOUIS E., AND C. R. HELLYER.
A vocabulary of criminal slang with some
examples of common usages... Portland, Oregon [? Modern Printing Co., 1914]. 103 p.
12°.   RNB p.v.32
This lengthy vocabulary was compiled with the aid
of C. R. Hellyer, a detective of Portland, Oregon,
and the definitions are full.

JACQUOT, L.
Interprétation du langage secret des tramps,
chemineaux américains. (Société dauphinoise
d'ethnologie et d'anthropologie. Bulletin. Gre-
noble, 1914. 8°. v. 20, p. 75–79.)   QOA
Not an article on tramp slang, but on their signs
or hieroglyphics, which, in reality, are forms of communication by symbolic equivalents of spoken argot.
Compare this with the cadger's map in Hotten's *Dictionary of slang.*

JORDAN, RANDOLPH.
Idioms of the road and pave. (The Writer's
monthly. Springfield, Mass., June, 1925. 8°.
v. 25, p. 485–487.)   * IH
Crook and hobo lingo for the writers of fiction.
"I have compiled here only those terms that have lived."
About 125 words are listed.

KANE, ELISHA K.
The jargon of the underworld. (Dialect
notes. New Haven, 1927. 8°. v. 5, p. 433–467.)
RNZ
"The jargon of the underworld embraces the slang
of three general classes, criminals, tramps, and prostitutes." The comprehensive glossary is made up of
current slang terms. An attempt to classify the deni-
zens of the underworld is made, and we get such
distinctions as "bindle-stiff," "hobo," "scenery-stiff,"
"Jesus-stiff," etc.

KANE, H. F.
A brief manual of beggary. (New republic.
New York, July 15, 1936. f°. v. 87, p. 288–289.)
Contains a few slang words.   * DA

KILDARE, OWEN.
The jargon of low literature. (The Independent. New York, July 19, 1906. 8°. v. 61,
p. 139–142.)   * DA
"From time immemorial the Bowery has been cited
as the birthplace of slang." The author points out
that the slang used by writers of Bowery stories is
unintelligible to the Bowery loafer.

KLEIN, NICHOLAS.
Hobo lingo. (American speech. Baltimore,
Sept., 1926. 4°. v. 1, p. 650–653.)   RNA
"The following list of hobo words, presented in
glossary form, was collected by me during twenty
years of experience with hobo cases in my profession
of attorney-at-law."
Additions to this list were contributed by Howard
F. Barker in *American speech,* Aug., 1927, v. 2, p. 506,
RNA.

KUETHE, J. LOUIS.
Prison parlance. (American speech. New
York, Feb., 1934. 4°. v. 9, p. 24–28.)   RNA
The writer was an instructor in a penal institution
when this glossary was compiled. It has a number
of words peculiar to the negro element in American
prisons. Materials for this study first appeared in the
Baltimore *Evening Sun,* Dec. 9, 1932.

Underworld Cant and Its Subsidiaries, cont'd

Twentieth Century, continued

LAMSON, DAVID.
Conversations with criminals. (In his: We who are about to die. New York: Charles Scribner's Sons, 1935. 8°. p. 184–206.)   SLP
This chapter is written exclusively in the argot of the American criminal.
Reviewed in *London Times literary supplement,* 1935, p. 675, *NAA.*

LAVEN, GOAT.
Rough stuff; the life story of a gangster. London: Falcon Books [1933]. xiii, 214 p. 8°.
"Glossary," p. vii–xii.   SLG
"The slang, and American words and expressions which he used either explain themselves, or an explanation is given. We have added a short glossary." — *The editor.*
The narrative of an American criminal as dictated to a ghost writer.

LEACH, CHARLES E.
On top of the underworld... London: Sampson Low, Marston & Co. [1933.] vii, 248 p. 8°.
   SLG
Crooks' argot, p. 137–152. Compiled by the author, who was connected with New Scotland Yard. Twentieth century London argot.

LEDOUX, URBAIN.
...Ho-Bo-Ho. Medley no. 1. [New York, 1931.] 4°.   TDH
Bound with "Mr. Zero?" Filled with tramp slang. Urbain Ledoux, known as Mr. Zero, fed thousands of unemployed in New York during the depression years, and is almost a legendary figure in trampdom.

LEE, HENRY JAMES.
...Eagle police manual... Edited by Henry J. Lee... Brooklyn: Eagle Library Publications [cop. 1933]. 159 p. 12°. (Brooklyn Eagle library. no. 316.)
"Definitions of underworld terms," p. 144–156.

LEWIS, ALFRED HENRY.
The Apaches of New York... Chicago: M. A. Donohue & Company [1912]. 272 p. 12°.
   SLG
Does not contain a glossary, but the cant of the New York underworld of the era just preceding the World War may be found on almost every page.

LIST of works in The New York Public Library relating to beggars, mendicants, tramps, vagrants, etc. (The New York Public Library. Bulletin. New York, May, 1906. 8°. v. 10, p. 279–289.)   M.R.R. Desk
In four parts: bibliography, history, general works, regional. A few of the items have brief annotations of a bibliographical nature only. There is no separate division devoted to the speech of tramps, but some of the books contain tramp slang and cant.

LIVINGSTON, LEON RAY.
Mother Delcassee of the hoboes, and other stories, by A no. 1, the famous tramp [Leon Ray Livingston]. Erie, Pa. A. No. 1 Publishing Co., 1918. 136 p. 12°. SHD p.v.46, no.4
A no. 1, America's most celebrated tramp, wrote many other tramp books, including *Hobo camp-fire tales, The adventures of a female tramp, The ways of a hobo, Life and adventures of A no. 1, The curse of tramp life, The snare of the road, The trail of the tramps,* etc. All contain numerous examples of tramp argot.

LONDON, GEO.
Deux mois avec les bandits de Chicago. Paris: Éditions des Portiques [1930]. 256 p., 2 l. 12°.
"Lexique franco-gangster," p. 257–258.   SLG
Other American slang words are defined in the text.

LUCAS, NETLEY EVELYN.
London and its criminals... London: Williams & Norgate, 1926. 281 p. 12°.   SLG
The cant of London criminals appears plentifully in these pages.

LUDWIG, ALBERT.
Die Kriminaldichtung und ihre Träger. (Germanisch-romanische Monatsschrift. Heidelberg, 1930. Bd. 18, p. 57–71, 123–135.)   RAA
Includes English words.

MCCAULAY, LEON.
Underworld and prison slang.
See *New York World-Telegram,* Sept. 21, 1936.

MCCLELLAN, HOWARD.
Its Greek to you — but the crooks "get" it. (Collier's. New York, Aug. 8, 1925. f°. p. 30.)
   *DA
American underworld lingo of the prohibition era.

MCCOOK, JOHN J.
Leaves from the diary of a tramp. (Independent. New York, 1901–02. 8°. Nov. 21 1901, v. 53, p. 2760–2767; Dec. 5, p. 2880–2888, Dec. 19, p. 3009–3013; Jan. 2, 1902, v. 54, p. 23–28, Jan. 16, p. 154–160, Feb. 6, p. 332–337, March 13, p. 620–624, April 10, p. 873–874.)   *DA
An intimate study of tramps and their ways, with many photographs. The author lived with tramps and learned their argot. Many of these words are used in the series of articles.

MACDONALD, ARTHUR.
Slang. (In his: Man and abnormal man... Washington, D. C.: Government Printing Office, 1905. 8°. p. 511–513.)   SLG
58. cong., 3. sess. Senate doc. 187.
"The recidivists, who are collected together in large cities, have a language of their own." Gives samples from several languages.

MACKENZIE, KENNETH.
Living rough. London: Jonathan Cape [1936]. 287 p. 12°.   AN
A Scotch hobo's experiences in the Pacific Northwest. Written in slang.

MARSHALL, MATT.
Tramp-royal on the Toby... Edinburgh and London: W. Blackwood & Sons, 1933. 369 p. 12°.   SGS
Words and phrases, p. 365–368. The tramp lingo in this volume is authentic and up-to-date. The material for the book appeared originally in the Glasgow *Evening Times* over the signature of "Tramp-Royal." It is a vagabond's impressions of London and rural Britain.

MAURER, DAVID W.
The argot of the underworld. (American speech. Baltimore, Dec., 1931. 4°. v. 7, p. 99–118.)   RNA
Writer had access to Ohio State Penitentiary for nine months in order to make this study. An excellent glossary.

Underworld Cant and Its Subsidiaries, cont'd

Twentieth Century, continued

MAURER, DAVID W., *continued*

The lingo of the good people. (American speech. New York, Feb., 1935. 4°. v. 10, p. 10–21.)   RNA
Criminal slang of the pre-gangster era. The modern gangster refers to the old-fashioned criminals as "good people." A lengthy glossary is appended and the words well defined.

The lingo of the jug-heavy. (Writer's digest. Cincinnati, Oct., 1931. 8°. v. 11, p. 27–29.)   * IH
A glossary of terms used by the "aristocrat of thieves." His specialty is "blowing banks."

MILBURN, GEORGE.
Convicts' jargon. (American speech. Baltimore, Aug., 1931. 4°. v. 6, p. 436–442.)   RNA
Compiled by Daniel Conway, an inmate of Auburn prison, New York State.

The hobo's horn book. A repertory for a gutter jongleur... New York: Ives Washburn, 1930. 295 p. 8°.   8–NBH
A collection of hobo poems and ballads, familiar to the American tramp. Has a glossary, p. 283–288. "Tramps and hoboes are the last of the ballad makers ... Hoboes are migratory workers, while tramps have sources of livelihood other than toil."

MINEHAN, THOMAS.
Boy and girl tramps of America. New York: Farrar and Rinehart [1934]. xvii, 267 p. 8°.
Glossary, p. 264–267.   SGS
The great number of boys and girls wandering homeless across the country during the depression years led the author to investigate their life. They created a new and colorful argot.
Reviewed in New York Herald Tribune, *Books*, July 8, 1934, v. 10, p. 1 (Robert Lynd), † *NAA; New republic*, New York, Aug. 1, 1934, v. 79, p. 323–324 (Otis Ferguson), * *DA*. In the latter review two other books containing the argot of the underworld and the road are reviewed, namely, Benjamin Appel's *Brain Guy* and Asa Bordages' *There shall be laughter*.

NEVILLE, HIPPO.
Sneak thief on the road... London: Jonathan Cape [1935]. 349 p. 8°.   AN
There is a glossary of English tramp words on p. 347–348.

NEW YORK TIMES.
[Articles on criminal slang.] See issues: June 4, 1922, section 6, p. 7, col. 3, slang of detectives; Aug. 3, 1924, section 8, p. 16, col. 1; Oct. 10, 1926, section 8, p. 20, col. 1; Dec. 26, 1926, section 8, p. 3, col. 1; June 16, 1927, p. 26, col. 4, tramp slang; Aug. 22, 1929, p. 25, col. 2, Chicago police; March 27, 1932, p. 28, col. 3, gangster slang.
The *New York Times index*, 1913-date, is a valuable source for new slang locutions of all kinds. In England the *Manchester Guardian* carries articles on American slang quite frequently. H. L. Mencken has perhaps the most complete file of clippings from English newspapers on the subject of American slang. He has utilized many of them in his *The American language*, 4th ed., 1936.

No. 90613–A.
Prison jargon. (Writer's digest. Cincinnati, Aug., 1932. 8°. v. 12, p. 46–48.)   * IH
American prison slang, by an authority.

NEWTON, HENRY CHANCE.
Crime and the drama; or, Dark deeds dramatized. By H. Chance Newton ("Carados" of the *Referee*)... With an introduction by Sir John Martin-Harvey. London: Stanley Paul & Co. [1927.] 284 p. 8°.   NAF
The escapades of Jack Sheppard, Dick Turpin, Paul Clifford, and other famous English criminals, real and imaginary, are recounted, and the author writes of them in the breezy slang so characteristic of writers on the *Referee*. An index to the "blood and thunder" plays mentioned in the book may be found on p. 275–278.

NUMBER 1500, PSEUD.
Life in Sing Sing. Indianapolis: Bobbs-Merrill Co. [cop. 1904.] 276 p. 12°.   SLT
Slang among convicts, p. 244–265. "The use of slang by convicts is very general and is usually for decorative effect rather than for the purpose of concealing." The glossary, and excerpts from letters written by crooks, are of value for terms current in crookdom at the beginning of the twentieth century.

O'CONNOR, JOHN JAMES.
Broadway racketeers. New York: Horace Liveright, 1928. 255 p. 12°.   SLG
"Glossary," p. 249–255.
New York criminalese of the 1920's.

OLIVER, ROBERT T.
Junglese. (American speech. Baltimore, June, 1932. 4°. v. 7, p. 339–341.)   RNA
An attempt to distinguish between types of bums. "First is the tramp, who best exemplifies the true professional spirit. He never works. The second grade consists of the hoboes who work now and then... Last and lowest, of the divisions, is the Stetson, who is usually found in mining regions. He works to earn a grub-stake, then hits the road for a sort of pseudo-bumming expedition until his money is gone, after which he returns to work."

ORWELL, GEORGE.
Down and out in Paris and London. New York: Harper & Brothers, 1933. 292 p. 12°.   SGS
London slang, p. 239–244. A picturesque glossary of the modern argot peculiar to the underworld of London.
Reviewed in *New statesman and nation*, London, Nov. 18, 1933, supplement, p. 338, 340 (W. H. Davies), * *DA; New York Times book review*, Aug. 6, 1933, p. 4 (Herbert Gorman), † *NAA; London Times literary supplement*, Jan. 12, 1933, p. 22, † *NAA.*

PASLEY, FRED D.
Al Capone; the biography of a self-made man ... [New York:] I. Washburn, 1930. 355 p. 8°.   8–AN
Does not have a glossary, but every page contains the vigorous criminal argot of the racketeering era, words which will always be associated with the prohibition period.

POLLOCK, ALBIN JAY.
The underworld speaks; an insight into vice — crime — corruption. San Francisco: Published by Prevent Crime Bureau [1935]. [288 p.] 12°.   RNM
The dictionary is quite comprehensive, including drug addicts, counterfeiters, rackets, prostitution, smuggling, prohibition, gambling, money, firearms, shoplifting, weapons, and almost every phase of criminal life in America. Besides the main dictionary, there are classified lists in the back. The definitions are brief, and the historical method is eschewed.

RACKET slang explains itself. (New York Sun. Feb. 19, 1935. p. 28, col. 1–2.)   * A
"Odd phrases that are ingeniously devised to trap the unwary customer."
"Living on the fringe of legitimate trade are merchants and salesmen who find profit in ignoring copybook ethics."
About fifty words from racketeering argot are defined.

Underworld Cant and Its Subsidiaries, cont'd

Twentieth Century, continued

REEVE, ARTHUR BENJAMIN.
The golden age of crime... New York: The Mohawk Press, 1931. 272 p. 12°.   SLG
The story of racketeering in America by the author and creator of *Craig Kennedy.*

RHOADES, HOWARD PHILIP.
Police slang. (The Editor. Highland Falls, N. Y., May 6, 1916. 8°. v. 43, p. 487.) NARA
Slang words picked up in six years "spent in contact with the police." A short list.

RIMINGTON, CRITCHELL.
English underworld slang. (In his: The bon voyage book, by "Old Salt" [Critchell Rimington]. New York: John Day Company [1931]. 12°. p. 87–89.)   KBB
This list of modern criminal argot was printed originally in *Variety*, New York, April 8, 1931, v. 102, p. 63, † *NAFA.*

ROSE, HOWARD N.
A thesaurus of slang. New York: The Macmillan Company, 1934. x, 120 p. 12°.   RNM
The sections on detective slang and hobo slang are designed for the use of writers of the pulp-magazine school.

S., H.
Curiosities of rhyming slang. (Bookman's journal & print collector. London, March 26, 1920. 4°. v. 1, p. 420.)   *IAA
A few specimens of modern English rhyming slang with a query as to its origin and its scope.

SAMOLAR, CHARLIE.
The argot of the vagabond. (American speech. Baltimore, June, 1927. 4°. v. 2, p. 385–392.)   RNA
Tramp slang of the road, most of the words being of such a general nature as to be understood by the "vags" from New York to "Frisco."

SAUL, VERNON W. (ALIAS K. C. SLIM).
The vocabulary of bums. (American speech. Baltimore, June, 1929. 4°. v. 4, p. 337–346.)   RNA
"The following word-list is not intended to be an exhaustive glossary of underworld colloquialisms or vagabond argot." Roughly, close to 500 representative words are defined.

SCOTT, WELLINGTON, PSEUD.
Seventeen years in the underworld. Introduction by Lynn Harold Hough. New York: The Abingdon Press [1916]. 119 p. 12°.   SLG
Contains American criminal cant.

SHARPE, MAY CHURCHILL.
Chicago May. Her story... New York: The Macaulay Company [1928]. 336 p. 8°.
"Criminal jargon," p. 281–288.   AN (Sharpe)
"As I have been a badger, pay-off, note-layer, creep, panel, and blackmailer, mostly, I shall explain them in more detail than some other words."
Includes a great deal of rhyming slang.

SIDNEY, F. H.
Hobo cant. (Dialect notes. New Haven, 1919. 8°. v. 5, p. 41–42.)   RNZ
A few terms of "hobos" infesting transcontinental railroad lines.

SIMONS, HI.
A prison dictionary (expurgated). (American speech. New York, Oct., 1933. 4°. v. 8, p. 22–33.)   RNA
Argot of the inmates of the Federal prison at Fort Leavenworth, Kansas. The definitions are full, and furnish the readers with more information than the usual glossary. The compiler writes from personal experience.

SING SING NO. 65368.
The argot of the underworld. (Star of hope. Sing Sing Prison, Ossining, N. Y., June, 1916. f°. v. 18, p. 3–6.)   †† SLA
This magazine is published by the inmates of the prison. Many of the slang terms found in this article are not met with in the dictionaries. The article is well written.

SMITH, MAURICE G.
Crook argot. (American speech. Baltimore, Feb., 1928. 4°. v. 3, p. 254–255.)   RNA
List culled from an article by Norma Fuller in the Denver *Rocky Mountain news*, Nov. 13, 1927. Definitions were supplied by Bert Clark, night captain of the Denver detective force.

SPENSER, JAMES, PSEUD.
Limey. An Englishman joins the gangs. Second impression. London: Longmans, Green and Co., 1933. 303 p. 8°.   SLG
The story of an English immigrant who jumped his ship at Philadelphia, and later became a gunman in a New York gang. His narrative is in the argot of the American underworld.

SPINDRIFT.
Dictionary of American slang. Privately printed. 1932.
This dictionary was compiled by a Briton, and is described in a letter to the New York *Sun*, Dec. 7, 1932. Includes a special section on criminal argot. The compiler has not seen a copy.

SULLIVAN, JOSEPH MATTHEW.
Criminal slang. (American law review. Boston, Dec., 1918. 8°. v. 52, p. 885–894.)   XAA
"Slang had its birth in criminality... The peculiar language used by the underworld is to my mind due to their preverted [*sic*], but acute, mentality." Gives a few examples of criminal slang.
Reprint, with additions, of an article by the same author in *New England magazine*, Boston, July, 1910, v. 42, p. 585–588, * *DA.*

Criminal slang... Boston: Wayland B. Russell, 1908. 27 p. 24°.   RNB p.v.7, no.2
On outside cover: The Worcester Press, Boston.
A small dictionary for popular use. Short definitions, with no etymological notes.

TAYLOR, F. C.
The language of lags. (Word-lore. London, Oct., 1928. 12°. v. 3, p. 121–122.)   ZBA
"Lags" is the English word for convicts. Gives a letter in underworld lingo, with a translation, and a specimen of back-chat.

TEALL, FRANCIS HORACE.
Slang. (The Inland printer. Chicago, Sept., 1916. 4°. v. 57, p. 760–762.)   †*IPA
An article on the word "hoodlum," based on a newspaper clipping from the Wichita, Kansas, *Eagle.*

THE THIEVES' Thesaurus. (The Literary digest. New York, Dec. 4, 1926. f°. v. 91, p. 64, 66.)   *DA
Digest of an article in *The New York Times* on gangster speech. Two or three hundred modern words familiar to the underworld are defined. Old words survive, but the process of creation is still active.

Underworld Cant and Its Subsidiaries, cont'd

Twentieth Century, continued

TILLOTSON, F. H.
How to be a detective. A complete text book of the methods and practices used by the best detectives in dealing with the criminal, together with a criminal vocabulary. Kansas City, Mo.: Hailman Printing Company, 1909. 187 p.
Copy owned by Mr. Peter Tamony, San Francisco.

VAN CISE, PHILIP SIDNEY.
Fighting the underworld. Boston: Houghton Mifflin Company, 1936. xii, 369 p. 8°.   SLE
"Glossary of terms used by the underworld," p. 355–357.
Short definitions of 65 words and phrases. The locale is Denver, Colorado.

WESEEN, MAURICE HARLEY.
A dictionary of American slang... New York: Thomas Y. Crowell Company [1934]. xiii, 543 p. 8°.   M.R.R. Desk
This dictionary will be described in full elsewhere. The sections which apply to this division of the bibliography are "Crooks' and criminals' slang," p. 1–45; "hoboes' and tramps' slang," p. 46–67.

WILLARD, JOSIAH FLYNT.
Tramping with tramps...by Josiah Flynt [Willard]... New York: Century Co., 1899. 398 p. 12°.   SGS
The tramp's jargon, p. 381–398.
A sociological study of tramp slang, the fruit of personal observation made by the author in tramping tours through Europe and America. This is one of the more reliable articles on the subject of tramp speech.

The world of graft. By Josiah Flynt [Willard]... New York: McClure, Phillips & Co., 1901. 221 p. 12°.   SLG
"Glossary," p. 219–221. Contains criminal cant.

WILSTACH, JOHN.
New words. (The Saturday review of literature. New York, July 18, 1931. f°. v. 7, p. 978.)
                                                 NAA
A letter to the editor; includes a short glossary of racketeer argot.

Under cover man. New York: William Morrow & Co., 1931. 287 p. 12°.
This novel contains the argot of the racketeer. A glossary of racketeer slang was issued by the company as a press release. It contained 66 words and phrases.

WITMAN, FRED.
Jewelry auction jargon. (American speech. Baltimore, June, 1928. 4°. v. 3, p. 375–376.)
                                                 RNA
"This branch of the jewelry business is never wholly 'on the square,' and, like most branches of legalized plundering, is developing a jargon of its own."

WORBY, JOHN.
The other half. The autobiography of a spiv ... London: J. M. Dent and Sons, Ltd. [1937.] vi p., 1 l., 279 p. 8°.   AN
Glossary, p. 277–279.

"YEGGMEN" in the criminal class. (Seen & heard by Megargee. Philadelphia, July 13, 1904. 16°. v. 4, p. 4241–4252.)   *DA
Claims that "yegg" is a gipsy word.

YENNE, HERBERT.
Prison lingo. (American speech. Baltimore, March, 1927. 4°. v. 2, p. 280–282.)   RNA
A general list of prison argot.

YOUNG, EDGAR.
Tramp jargon. (The Editor. Highland Falls, N. Y., May 6, 1916. 8°. v. 43, p. 487–488.)
                                               NARA
"I can vouch for the authenticity of the following tramp words and expressions for I sojourned among tramps for several years as a 'blowed-in-the-bottle-stiff' myself."

CANT OF DRUG ADDICTS

BERG, LOUIS.
Revelations of a prison doctor. New York: Minton, Balch & Co. [cop. 1934.] 255 p. 8°.
                                                 SLT
This is an inside story of New York prison life, written in the slang familiar to the underworld. It is filled particularly with the slang of drug addicts, and of sexual perverts.

DE LENOIR, CECIL.
The hundredth man. Confessions of a drug addict... London: Jarrolds, 1933. 288 p. 8°.
                                                 VTY
Filled with scores of words associated with the drug traffic. The narrative embraces the experiences of a drug addict in England, the United States, and Mexico.

MAURER, DAVID W.
The argot of the underworld narcotic addict. (American speech. New York, 1936–38. 4°. v. 11, p. 116–127; v. 13, p. 179–192.)   RNA
The glossary is lengthy and accurate, and secured, as the introductory remarks explain, by interviews with police and welfare officers and the addicts themselves. Addicts are reluctant to divulge their slang, hence the value of this laborious glossary.

"Junker lingo," by-product of underworld argot. (American speech. New York, April, 1933. 4°. v. 8, p. 27–28.)   RNA
Speech of the drug addict. Additions by Victor

Folke Nelson in *American speech*, Oct., 1933, v. 8, p. 33–34, *RNA*.

MURPHY, EMILY FERGUSON.
The black candle... Toronto: Thomas Allen [1922]. 405 p. 12°.   VTY
A sociological study of drug addicts in Canada.

PAYNTER, RICHARD HENRY.
The language of drug addicts. (American speech. Baltimore, Oct., 1928. 4°. v. 4, p. 19–21.)   RNA
Outlines a proposed study of the slang used by drug addicts. The author accumulated a long list of words as research psychologist of the Philadelphia Committee for the Clinical Study of Opium Addiction.

TUOHY, FERDINAND.
Inside dope. London: Hamish Hamilton [1934]. 255 p. 12°.   VTY
An expose of the opium racket. Contains some of the terminology familiar to drug addicts.

WELLS, WHITNEY HASTINGS.
Words used in the drug traffic. (Dialect notes. New Haven, 1922. 8°. v. 5, p. 181–182.)
                                                 *DA
A few words from the San Francisco underworld.
See A. J. Pollock, *The Underworld speaks* (1935).

OCCUPATIONAL JARGON

THE jargon of various occupations is not slang. This distinction must be made at the outset. However, any student of our speech will admit that the highly specialized and technical jargon of the groups of people who follow a common trade has a direct bearing on the general subject of slang, since so many of the locutions pass sooner or later into common speech and thereby take on the nature of slang. These diversified groups speak a language of expediency. Speed is the conditioning factor. If a short, coined word can convey the meaning of a longer word or of a whole sentence it rapidly gains favor with the speaker and pushes the more formal words into the background. Quite often these words spring from humorous interpretations of little crises which arise in the course of the day's work, and this ridiculous quality of the words hastens their adoption by ever-widening groups of individuals; if they possess the true nature of slang they pass into the newspapers and trade magazines, first in quotation marks or italics, and finally as standard words known and accepted everywhere. The list which follows is but a weak selection at best, considering the fact that there are so many hundreds of occupations which have a language of their own, but it is a beginning.

In countless trade publications are useful articles on trade jargon which the compiler is almost certain to have overlooked. No attempt has been made to list all the technical dictionaries, despite the relevant material they contain. Their value is obvious, but their necessary exclusion from the bibliography is equally obvious. The reader should consult the section devoted to regional dialects for other occupational locutions.

ORDER OF ARRANGEMENT

ADVERTISING	GLASSBLOWING	OYSTER FISHERY	SODA FOUNTAIN
AQUARIUM	HOP FIELD	POLITICS	STEEL INDUSTRY
BOOK TRADE	HOSPITAL	POST OFFICE	STOCK YARDS
BUSINESS	LAW	QUICK LUNCH	SUGAR INDUSTRY
COOKERY	LIBRARY	SEA:	TELEGRAPHY
COWBOY	LUMBER INDUSTRY	U. S. NAVAL ACAD.	TELEPHONY
FARMING	MEN'S WEAR	SEALING	TRANSPORTATION:
FIRE INSURANCE	MINING	WHALING	AIRPLANE
FISHING	MOTOR BOAT	SHEEP HERDING	AUTOMOBILE
FRUIT FARM	NEWSPAPER	SHOE SALESMAN	RAILROAD
FURNITURE DEALERS	OIL FIELD	SOCIAL WORK	MISCELLANEOUS

ADVERTISING

POUSLAND, EDWARD.
The kind of slang to use in advertising. (Printers' ink. New York, June 10, 1926. 8°. v. 135, p. 153–154.)   TWA
Deals largely with terms "put it over" and "come across." "Whether one incline toward or away from the use of slang in advertising copy, the question remains one of infinite delicacy — for the most eminent philologists themselves cannot predict the expressions which are destined to gain acceptance in the standard language."

AQUARIUM

MELLEN, IDA M.
Aquarium English. (American speech. Baltimore, 1928. 4°. v. 3, p. 460–463.)   RNA
A highly specialized jargon, with few expressions of the slang variety, noted by one connected with the Aquarium in New York City.

BOOK TRADE

HOLDEN, JOHN ALLAN.
The bookman's glossary; a compendium of information relating to the production and distribution of books. New York: R. R. Bowker Co. [etc.], 1925. 127 p. 8°.   * I
Appeared originally in *The Publishers' weekly*, New

York, 1924, v. 106, p. 118–120, 188–190, 290–293, 442–444, 498–499, 543–545, 601–602, 714–717, †* GAA.

—— 2d ed., rev. and enl. New York: R. R. Bowker Co. [etc.], 1931. 153 p. 8°. M.R.R. Desk
This compilation includes a few slang terms known to the book trade and librarians.

BUSINESS

MARTIN, DOUGLAS S.
Business jargon and the American language. (Living age. New York, Aug. 8, 1914. 8°. v. 282, p. 373–375.)   * DA
Reprinted from the *Academy*, London, * DA.
"In ten years' time I think that there will be very little English left in America. There will be nothing but slang — the commercial jargon of the office and the store." Gives a few samples of American commercial lingo.

SIMMONDS, PETER LUND.
Commercial dictionary of trade products, manufacturing and technical terms... A new edition, revised and enlarged. London: George Routledge and Sons, 1872. 463 p. 12°.   TLD
Good for older business terms, coin names, provincialisms, etc.

Occupational Jargon — Business, continued

WINGATE, JOHN WILLIAMS.
Manual of retail terms... New York: Prentice-Hall, 1931. 562 p. 8°.   TLD
This is a technical dictionary, but some of the terms such as "teaser advertising," "strim," "spiff," "floater," and "hopper" belong to the realm of jargon, if not to slang proper.

COOKERY

See also QUICK LUNCH

ROGERS, SUSAN F.
Colonial cookery terms. (Dialect notes. New Haven, 1915. 8°. v. 4, p. 239–240.)   RNZ
Short list taken from old recipes in Chimney Corner Inn, Cambridge, Mass., built in 1657.

COWBOY

ADAMS, RAMON F.
Cowboy lingo. Boston: Houghton Mifflin Co., 1936. 257 p. 12°.   RNM
Contents: The cowboy and his lingo; the ranch; the cowboy and his duties; his costume and furnishings; his riding equipment; ropes and roping; cattle; horses; riding; the round-up; brands and ear-marks; the trail; the commissary; rustlers and outlaws; guns; nicknames; the cowboy dance; miscellaneous expressions; figures of speech; more figures of speech; index.
Includes more cowboy lingo than any other work on the subject.
Each chapter contains the lingo peculiar to it.
Reviewed by Florence Finch Kelly in *New York Times*, April 5, 1936, p. 6, * *A*.

Cowboy speech. (American speech. Baltimore, Dec., 1927. 4°. v. 3, p. 168–169.)   RNA
Reprinted from the *Baltimore Sun*, Aug. 13, 1927. Appeared originally in the *Dallas News*.

ALLEN, JULES VERNE.
Cowboy lore... San Antonio, Texas: Naylor Printing Co., 1933. 165 p. 8°. * MP (U. S.)
"Cowboy dictionary," p. 57–62.
Compiled by the "Singing cowboy."
Reviewed in the *New York Times*, June 4, 1933, p. 10.

BRADDY, HALDEEN.
Some southwestern cowboy lingo. (American speech. New York, April, 1937. 4°. v. 12, p. 153.)   RNA

BRANCH, EDWARD DOUGLAS.
The cowboy and his interpreters. New York: D. Appleton Company, 1926. 277 p. 8°.   IW
There is no glossary of cowboy terms in the book, but many cowboy words are mentioned in the text. It has a bibliography of the books and magazine articles treating of cowboy life, which would serve as a starting point for the compiler of a dictionary of cowboy terms.

C., S. C.
Cowboy camp expressions. (The Editor. Highland Falls, N. Y., Sept. 5, 1917. 8°. v. 46, p. 309.)   NARA
A short list of the more common cowboy terms.

C. G. LELAND collection. Vol. x. The cattle range idiom. (British Museum catalogue of additions to manuscripts, 1916–1920. London, 1933. 8°. p. 45, no. 39561.)   * GXB (British)
The Leland manuscript should prove of interest. Leland was co-author with Albert Barrière of *A Dictionary of slang, jargon & cant* (q.v.).

COWAN, JOHN L.
Lingo of the cow country. (Outing magazine. New York, Aug., 1909. 8°. v. 54, p. 620–623.)   MVA
"It is not the intention in this article to try to explain the obvious, but rather to trace the origin of a few words that cast interesting sidelights upon the history of the cow country."

FISHER, GAIL WISDOM.
Some strictly Wyoming colloquialisms. (The Editor. Highland Falls, N. Y., May 20, 1916. 8°. v. 43, p. 533–534.)   NARA
Cowboy lingo of Wyoming, by an "ex-rider."

FURLONG, CHARLES WELLINGTON.
Let 'er buck. A story of the passing of the old West... New York: G. P. Putnam's Sons, 1921. xxxviii, 242 p. 8°.   IW
A glossary of cowboy terms, entitled "Tips to the tenderfoot," p. 235–242.

HALLIDAY, DICK.
The makin's of a rodeo. (Billboard. Cincinnati, Dec. 10, 1927. f°. v. 39, p. 90.)   † MZA

HOLMES, ABERCROMBIE.
Cowboy colloquialisms. (Texas ranger. v. 51, no. 7, March, 1936, p. 32.)

LARKIN, MARGARET.
Singing cowboy. A book of western songs ... New York: Alfred A. Knopf, 1931. 196 p. 8°.   * MO (U. S.)
"Glossary," p. 179–193. The definitions are quite full.
Reviewed in *The Nation*, New York, Dec. 16, 1931, v. 133, p. 674, * *DA;* Herald Tribune *Books*, New York, Nov. 29, 1931, p. 5.
Cowboy songs are published from time to time in the *Journal of American folk lore*, HBA.

LINDERMAN, FRANK BIRD.
Idioma. (The Frontier. Missoula, Mont., Nov., 1928. 8°. v. 9, p. 55–56.)   * DA
A handful of words peculiar to the Northwest, taken from fur trader and cowboy lingo.

McTIMMONDS, JIM.
Cowboy slang. (Writer's digest. Cincinnati, Oct., 1932. 8°. v. 12, p. 47–49.)   * IH
"We're comin' through with a whole herd of cowboy words, and terms, all rounded-up an' close herded for your special convenience. Take down that old reata, spread a loop and rope out the ones you may want to use."

MEREDITH, MAMIE.
"Waddies" and "Hoboes of the old West." (American speech. Baltimore, April, 1932. 4°. v. 7, p. 257–260.)   RNA
Based largely on *Lyrics of the lariat,* by N. K. Griggs, published in 1893 by Fleming H. Revell, Chicago.

POUND, ROBERT T.
Western terminology. (Writer's monthly. Springfield, Mass., May, 1923. 8°. v. 21, p. 418–422.)   * IH
Deplores ignorance of short-story writers who attempt cowboy themes. Gives correct terms under general headings of ranch, cattle, wagon outfit, men, expressions.

Occupational Jargon — Cowboy, continued

REEVES, FRANK.
Tips on the rangeland. (Writer's monthly. Springfield, Mass., Nov., 1931. 8°. v. 38, p. 195–201.)   * IH
"An authoritative glossary of terms used in the cow country and among western horsemen." Reeves is a well-known writer of "westerns."

What the cowboys say. (Writer's monthly. Springfield, Mass., Oct., 1927. 8°. v. 30, p. 314–317.)   * IH
"An informal glossary of terms and customs on cow-land arranged as a guide to writers who at times may be in doubt."

RIGGS, LYNN.
Green grow the lilacs. A play. New York: Samuel French, 1931. 166 p. 12°.   NBM
This is a cowboy play.
Glossary, p. 165–166.
There are a number of cowboy books which do not contain glossaries but which are liberally sprinkled with cowboy lingo. All the books by Will James fall into this class, as do Frank J. Dobie's *The Vaquero of the brush country* (1929) and J. E. Haley's *The XIT ranch of Texas* (1929) and the collections of cowboy songs by John A. Lomax. Lomax is now with the Library of Congress and is building up a large collection of cowboy and prison songs and ballads, preserved on phonograph records and available for public use.

ROLLINS, PHILIP ASHTON.
Definitions and cowboy ways. (In his: The cowboy... New York: Charles Scribner's Sons, 1922. 8°. p. 39–64.)   IW
The whole book contains authentic cowboy expressions, but the above chapter contains the most.

SIMMONS, O. D.
Expressions of the Southwest. (Writer's monthly. Springfield, Mass., Oct., 1926. 8°. v. 28, p. 295–297.)   * IH
Short essay on cowboy speech.

STANDISH, JOHN K.
Up the Texas trail. (The Producer, the national livestock monthly. Denver, August, 1932. f°. v. 14, p. 3–5.)   † VPOA
Excerpts of cowboy slang taken from Granville Stuart's *Forty years on the frontier.*

THORP, N. HOWARD.
Songs of the cowboy... Boston: Houghton Mifflin Company [1921]. 184 p. 16°.   NBH
Glossary, p. 177–178. Includes only such words as appear in the poems.

Tales of the chuck wagon. [No place or date of publication, but probably privately printed at Santa Fe.] 123 p. 8°.
                              NBF p.v.88, no.10
These tales, written in the lingo of the cow country by N. H. (Jack) Thorp, preserve the real flavor of cowboy speech.

VAN DEN BARK, MELVIN.
Nebraska cow talk. (American speech. Baltimore, Oct., 1929. 4°. v. 5, p. 52–76.)   RNA
An intelligent and sympathetic study of the speech and ways of the cowboy. This preservation of the homely expressions peculiar to the cow country is of the utmost philological and historical value.

FARMING

PRESCOTT, RUSSELL T.
Middlewestern farm English. (American speech. New York, April, 1937. 4°. v. 12, p. 102–107.)   RNA

FIRE INSURANCE

BERNSTEIN, HERBERT B.
Fire insurance lingo. (American speech. Baltimore, July, 1926. 4°. v. 1, p. 523–528.)
                              RNA
Not a slang list. A good example of how technical terms baffle the lexicographer.

FISHING

MAURER, DAVID W.
Schoonerisms. (American speech. Baltimore, June, 1930. 4°. v. 5, p. 387–395.)   RNA
Some speech peculiarities of the North Atlantic fishermen. Good glossary appended.

WHITE, FREDERICK.
British and American fishing terms. (Outlook. New York, Aug., 1934. 4°. v. 74, p. 33–34.)   MYA
About fifty technical terms of the British and American fishermen, arranged in parallel columns.

FRUIT FARM

MORTON, IVY GRANT.
Fruit-drying phraseology. (Writer's monthly. Springfield, Mass., Aug., 1928. 8°. v. 32, p. 104–105.)   * IH
California fruit farm lingo.

FURNITURE DEALERS

MILLER, CHARLES.
Furniture lingo. (American speech. Baltimore, Dec., 1930. 4°. v. 6, p. 125–128.)   RNA
Words used by the retail dealers in Chicago. A number of German and Yiddish words have crept into the furniture jargon.

GLASSBLOWING

GLASSBLOWERS' lingo. Bridgeton, N. J., Evening News, Aug. 24, 1889.
Not in The New York Public Library.

HOP FIELD

SHULTERS, JOHN RAYMOND.
Hop-field terms from western New York. (Dialect notes. New Haven, 1922. 8°. v. 5, p. 182–183.)   RNZ
A short list from the Bristol valley fields in New York.

HOSPITAL

BARKLEY, DOROTHY.
Hospital talk. (American speech. Baltimore, April, 1927. 4°. v. 2, p. 312–314.)   RNA
Hospital talk expands as new discoveries are made, and when personalities like Nightingale and Lister enter the field.

Occupational Jargon, continued

LAW

CORPUS JURIS; being a complete and systematic statement of the whole body of the law... New York: The American Law Book Company, 1914–35. 4°.   * R–XAB
Arranged in dictionary form. Many slang words are defined, and cases cited in which they appear. *Corpus juris secundum*, 1936–date, is a new and revised edition. See also *Judicial and statutory definitions of words and phrases*, St. Paul: West Publishing Company, 1904–33, series 1–4, * R–XAB.

MABEY, RICHARD A.
The English of the courtroom as heard by the shorthand reporter. (American speech. Baltimore, Feb., 1926. 4°. v. 1, p. 264–268.)   RNA
The slang of court witnesses often involves a rigid cross-examination in order to arrive at true meanings. The lawyer's request: "Tell the story in your own words" brings forth odd narratives.

THE SLANG of the specialist. (The Nation. New York, April 23, 1908. 4°. v. 86, p. 369–370.)   * DA
Comment on reform of French legal terminology, and on scientific vocabularies in general. These latter have been called "slang of the specialist." The old legal terms change but little, and have kept alive the original meanings.

LIBRARY

BURKE, WILLIAM JEREMIAH.
Library cant. (The New York Sun. March 29, 1935. p. 26, col. 8.)   * A
A letter to the editor commenting on the use of *accessioned*, and giving a number of library slang terms such as "green pig," "dummy," etc.

COMPTON, NELLIE JANE.
Library language. (American speech. Baltimore, Nov., 1926. 4°. v. 2, p. 93–95.)   RNA
A few library terms. Library work has produced little slang. A dictionary of library terminology is being compiled by the American Library Association.

LUMBER INDUSTRY

ALLEN, CHANDLER BRIGGS.
The last frontier of American romance. (The Writer's monthly. Springfield, Mass., Jan., 1926. 8°. v. 27, p. 3–7.)   * IH
Speech of the Maine lumberjack of the old days as told by "old timers" who remember tales of the "Windigo."

BECK, E. C.
Lumberjack ballads and songs. (English journal. College edition. Chicago, 1932. 8°. v. 21, p. 52–57.)
This article appears only in the College edition, which the Library does not have.

BERRY, EDWARD.
Sawmill talk (East Texas). (American speech. Baltimore, Oct., 1927. 4°. v. 3, p. 24–25.)   RNA
Small list of words, many of them being general, rather than peculiar to sawmill workers.

THE BRITISH COLUMBIA logger in his shirt. (British Columbia magazine. Vancouver, Jan., 1911. 8°. v. 7, p. 13–18.)   HWA
Contains much of the logger jargon of the Canadian West.

CLARK, J. W.
Lumberjack lingo. (American speech. Baltimore, Oct., 1931. 4°. v. 7, p. 47–53.)   RNA
The author of this article knows the lumber camp from first hand experience, and he presents an imposing list of words familiar to the American lumberjack.

EMERY, C. A.
Ways and words of the woodsmen. (Writer's monthly. Springfield, Mass., Feb., 1927. 8°. v. 29, p. 126–129.)   * IH
The old-time lumberjack of the Pacific Northwest is becoming legendary. The machine age has played havoc with old words and customs. Some of the changes in lingo are here recorded.

ERICKSON, ORRIN.
A woodsman's vocabulary. (Writer's monthly. Springfield, Mass., Feb., 1925. 8°. v. 25, p. 128–129.)   * IH
Glossary of lumberjack terms common in the Allegheny mountains in Pennsylvania, where the author worked for four years.

HIGGINS, JOHN C.
The lumberjack in American literature: his life and customs, his slang, his ballads and shanties, and his folk-epic of Paul Bunyan. 1935. 147 p.
Master's thesis submitted at the University of Southern California. Slang of the lumberjacks of northern United States and eastern Canada. The study was based on personal experience. The bibliography contains ninety-nine titles, some of them helpful in the study of slang.

JENKINS, CHARLES.
Colloquialisms of the north woods. (The Editor. Highland Falls, N. Y., June 17, 1916. 8°. v. 43, p. 631–632.)   NARA
"There is no fiction so persistently 'murdered' as the North Woods story. Only by years of occasional contact could one hope to absorb the peculiar color of the lumber camp and the winding Indian trails of that vast stretch of untamed country that lies between the north shore of Lake Superior and Hudson's Bay." A glossary follows.

MONROE, BENTON SULLIVAN, AND CLARK S. NORTHUP. Some lumber and other words. (Dialect notes. New Haven, 1904. 8°. v. 2, p. 394–403.)   RNZ
Lumberman's lingo. Many of the words taken from *A History of the lumber industry in the state of New York* (U. S. Forestry Division. Bulletin 34. 1902). Glossary form.

MORRISON, J. W.
Lumberjack rhetoric. (American forests and forest life. Washington, Dec., 1924. 4°. v. 30, p. 722–724, 754.)   VQN
An intelligent study of the customs of modern lumberjacks in America and Canada, with emphasis on their picturesque speech.

PENDLETON, PAUL E.
How the "Wood hicks" speak. (Dialect notes. New Haven, 1930. 8°. v. 6, p. 86–89.)   RNZ
Lingo of the lumber camp in Upshur Co., West Virginia.

Occupational Jargon—Lumber Industry, cont'd

STARLUND, GEORGE C.
Talk in the tall timber. (Writer's monthly. Springfield, Mass., May, 1930. 8°. v. 35, p. 298–300.) * IH
Woodsman's vernacular. Not a glossary, but a story written in the argot of the logger.

STEVENS, JAMES.
Logger talk. (American speech. Baltimore, Dec., 1925. 4°. v. 1, p. 135–140.) RNA
Workers in the woods of the Pacific Northwest like the word *logger* instead of *lumberjack*. The machine age had modified their speech, but many of the old words remain. Several hundred logger words are given.

STUART, ROBERT YOUNG, AND OTHERS.
Glossary of terms used in fire control. Prepared by Forest Service. Washington: U. S. Gov. Printing Office, 1930. 22 p. 8°. (United States. Department of Agriculture. Miscellaneous publication no. 70.) VPZ
Foreword by R. Y. Stuart.
Includes a large number of slang terms. The glossary was issued originally in 1924 in mimeographed form.
Other forest terms of a technical nature may be found in *Journal of forestry*, Jan., 1917, v. 15, p. 68–101, *VQN*.

WILLIAMS, GUY.
Logger-talk. Some notes on the jargon of the Pacific Northwest woods. Seattle: University of Washington Book Store, 1930. 30 p. 12°. (University of Washington chapbooks. no. 41.) STG (Washington)
Words used in Washington, Oregon, and California, written by one who "was born and raised in the logging camps of Puget Sound."

WOODFORD, JOSEPH L.
"Logger" language. (Writer's digest. Cincinnati, April 1, 1930. 8°. v. 10, p. 34–35.) * IH
Slang of the Northwest woods. Differentiates among kinds of loggers. "A 'logger' is any man who is engaged in the activities of bringing timber from the woods and making it into lumber ready for use."

MEN'S WEAR

BAKER, WILLIAM HENRY.
A dictionary of men's wear. Embracing all the terms (so far as could be gathered) used in the men's wear trades expressiv of raw and finisht products and of various stages and items of production; selling terms; trade and popular slang and cant terms... Cleveland: William Henry Baker, 1908. 326 p. 8°. 3–VLV
Has a bibliography. "It has been the aim of the author to make simply a handy reference book, 'popular' rather than learned." — *Preface.*

MINING

All of the dictionaries of mining terms contain some jargon. See, for instance, Albert H. Fay, *A Glossary of the mining and mineral industry*, Washington, 1920, 754 p. (United States. — Bureau of Mines, Bulletin 95), *VH*, which contains terms in many languages; William Stukeley Gresley, *Glossary of terms used in coal mining*, London: E. & F. N. Spon, 1883, 296 p., *VHW*; and R. W. Raymond, "A Glossary of mining and metallurgical terms," in *Transactions* of the American Institute of Mining Engineers, v. 9, 94 p., *VH*.

BRUFF, HAROLD JOHN LEXOW.
A glossary of mining terms in common use among the miners of Greentrow Hill in Yorkshire. (Yorkshire Dialect Society. Transactions. York, April, 1923. 8°. v. 4, p. 23–54.) RNY
Extensive glossary of about 300 terms, defined at great length.

DAVIDSON, LEVETTE J.
Mining expressions in Colorado. (American speech. Baltimore, Dec., 1929. 8°. v. 5, p. 144–147.) RNA
Gold and silver mining terms, not so much the lingo of the miner as of the mine, for the expressions have to do with the actual work.

DERBYSHIRE lead-mining terms. (English Dialect Society. Series B. Reprinted glossaries. VIII–X. Edited by the Rev. Walter W. Skeat. London: Published for the English Dialect Society, by Trübner & Co., 1874. 8°.) RNXA
Contains *The Liberties and customes of the lead-mines within the wapentake of Wirksworth...,* by Edward Manlove, printed in London in 1653. This ancient mining poem contains mining jargon. A special glossary of the terms used in the poem is appended. There is also a reprint of the glossary of mining terms in Thomas Houghton's *Rara Avis in Terris; or, The Compleat Miner,* London, 1681. The terms relate to the lead mines within the wapentake of Wirksworth, Derbyshire. There is also a reprint of the glossary from John Mawe's *Mineralogy of Derbyshire,* London, 1802.

HAMILTON, MARIAN.
California gold-rush English. (American speech. New York, Aug., 1932. 4°. v. 7, p. 423–433.) RAN
Useful article in that it gives the source, by means of bibliographical footnotes, for every term used in the text. 180 expressions are identified.
See also Henry Degroot's "Glossary of terms in common use among the miners of California" in California. — Natural Resources Department: Mines and Mining Division, *Second annual report,* 1880/82, p. 280–288, *VHCA.*

LOPUSHANSKY, JOSEPH, AND MICHAEL LOPUSHANSKY.
Mining town terms. (American speech. Baltimore, June, 1929. 4°. v. 4, p. 368–374.) RNA
Words from a coal mining town near Pittsburgh, Pa. A good list for this particular locality.

MOORE, HELEN L.
The lingo of the mining camp. (American speech. Baltimore, Nov., 1926. 4°. v. 2, p. 86–88.) RNA
A few words from the vocabulary of the American gold miner.

PRYCE, W.
Mineralogia Cornubiensis... To which is added an explanation of the terms and idioms of miners. London, 1778. 331 p. f°. † VHB
The terms are those used by tinners. See p. 315–331. Most of the terms are Cornish.

MOTOR BOAT

SCHNURMACHER, DOC.
Outboard glossary. (Motor boat. New York, June 25, 1929. 4°. v. 26, p. 40.) † VXA
The popularity of outboard motor racing in America gave rise to such slang as "elephant breath," "donkey fuzz," "coffee grinder," etc.

Occupational Jargon, continued

NEWSPAPER

BASTIAN, GEORGE C., AND LELAND D. CASE.
Editing the day's news... Rev. ed. New York: The Macmillan Company, 1932. xiv, 309 p. illus. 8°. NARP
Appendix A, p. 265–276, gives a number of newspaper terms, arranged alphabetically. Includes a good deal of slang.

BEIRNE, FRANCIS F.
Newspaper English. (American speech. Baltimore, Oct., 1926. 4°. v. 2, p. 8–12.) RNA
Defends the grade of English used by newspapermen, and shows how carefully each article is edited. The snappy slang is relished by most newspaper readers, and the editors bow willingly to this demand.
Cf. Adams Sherman Hill, *Our English*, New York: Harper & Brothers, 1889, *RNC*. This book contains a chapter on "English in newspapers and novels."

COLBURN, DOROTHY.
Newspaper nomenclature. (American speech. Baltimore, Feb., 1927. 4°. v. 2, p. 238–243.) RNA
Standard American newspaper terms known to the "fourth estate," and the followers of the "art preservative."

DANE, CLEMENCE, PSEUD.
American tomorrows. (World today. London, March, 1925. 8°. v. 45, p. 290–294.) *DA
"Journalese is the material out of which the American 'little nations' are fashioning the most original language since Babel."
Thinks good English is being put to rout by facile journalese, and that this jargon may become the *lingua franca* of the new world.

HALL, WILLIAM EARL.
Reporting news... Boston, New York [etc.]: D. C. Heath and Company [1936]. vi, 441 p. illus. 8°. NARP
Slang is discussed on p. 131–139. Quotes from an article in the *Christian Science Monitor* entitled "The Virtues of slang." The free use of slang is condemned as bad newspaper practice, but a judicious use of the better slang locutions is approved. Vulgarity and crudity, so often associated with slang words, should be shunned by a good newspaper man.

HICKLIN, MAURICE.
Scribes seek snappy synonyms. (American speech. Baltimore, Dec., 1930. 4°. v. 6, p. 110–122.) RNA
Newspaper editors clamor for brevity and "punch" in their headlines. If a snappy synonym is not in the dictionary one is coined to meet the emergency. An alphabetical list of these synonyms is given.

HOOVER, DONALD D., AND WILLIAM L. MAPEL.
"Copy!" A handbook for reporters and students of journalism. New York: Thomas Y. Crowell Co. [c. 1931.] xi, 327 p. 8°. NARP
"Why do we talk like that?" p. 296–316.
"The jargon of the gentlemen of the press contains terms, contractions, and, if we may be permitted to say so, slang, which have become the language of the craft through usage."

LANDON, HERMAN.
Newspaper "trade talk." (The Editor. Highland Falls, N. Y., June 3, 1916. 8°. v. 43, p. 582.) NARA
American newspaper slang. Some twenty-five expressions explained. Additions are made by A. L. Weeks in the Sept. 23, 1916, issue, v. 44, p. 291–292.

MATTHEW, FRANKLIN.
Newspaper English. (Chautauquan. Meadville, Pa., June, 1895. 8°. v. 21, p. 302–305.) *DA
Newspaper English is far better than the English used in business, in the pulpit, and in ordinary conversation, but it becomes careless at times, pandering to popular taste. The reasons for the use of poor English, including slang, in newspapers, are briefly outlined.

NEWSPAPER slang. (American notes and queries. Philadelphia, June 25, 1892. 8°. v. 9, p. 86–87.) *DA
Ten slang words familiar in the newspaper office.

NORRIS, ARTHUR C.
Newspaper lingo. (Writer's digest. Cincinnati, Jan., 1932. 8°. v. 12, p. 28–41.) *IH
"In his everyday speech the newspaper man uses the slang of the printer, the policeman, the theatre, the underworld, and the gutter, but he rarely goes to extremes." A number of slang words are mentioned.

PERRY, GEORGE B.
Composing room slang. (The Writer. Boston, 1888. 8°. v. 2, p. 9–11.) *DA
Informal essay on the language of the newspaper composing room. The lingo of the "art preservative" changes less through the years than most technical jargon.

POST, LOUIS F.
English of the melting pot. (The Freeman. New York, 1923. f°. July 25, v. 7, p. 464–466; Aug. 1, p. 490–493; Aug. 8, p. 512–514; Aug. 15, p. 537–539; Aug. 22, p. 560–562.) *DA
This series of articles is confined to newspaper English and newspaper policies, particularly the New York newspapers. Contains very little slang.

ROCKWELL, HAROLD E.
"Going to press." (American speech. Baltimore, Dec., 1928. 4°. v. 4, p. 134–136.) RNA
Modern newspaper slang.

SOME xxth century English notes on journalistic <and other> jargon of the day. By a west-country wiseacre. Torquay: A. Iredale & Son, 1909. 24 p.
Kennedy 12396.
Chiefly newspaper jargon.
Not in The New York Public Library.

TUNISON, JOSEPH SALATHIEL.
Newspaper jargon. (Dialect notes. Norwood, Mass., 1892. 8°. v. 1, p. 204–209.) RNZ
Haste, and not a desire to be picturesque, leads to the creation of newspaper slang. A few terms carefully defined.

WALKER, STANLEY.
City editor... New York: Frederick A. Stokes Co., 1934. 336 p. 8°. NARF
Filled with newspaper jargon. The style is in the racy idiom of the gentlemen of the press. The chapter on sports is particularly rich in slang. Says Charley Dryden was the father of American sports writing as we know it today. He worked in San Francisco beginning in 1890 and came to New York in 1898. See articles on Charles Dryden in *New York Times*, Feb. 13, 1932, * *A.*

WILLIAMS, TALCOTT.
Newspaper English. (The North American review. Boston, Nov., 1920. 8°. v. 212, p. 631–640.) *DA
"Keats added over one hundred and fifty words to the vocabulary of verse...'Lewis Carroll' <Charles L.

Occupational Jargon — Newspaper, continued

WILLIAMS, TALCOTT, *continued*

Dodgson> added at least two-score. These are of imagination all compact. New thought; new words. The closer to daily life and speech is the writer's pen or the click of the typewriter keys, the more active, the more efficient, the more effective is the utterance of the writer and the life of the people." Journalism offers an opportunity for word coinage. The great literary periods of the world are traced and it is shown how and where and when the language became fixed and artificial. The spoken language lived, with all its slang, and variety, and red-bloodedness. Benjamin Franklin saved us from the heavy literary tongue of Samuel Johnson. "The literary world in England and here accepted the style of Johnson; the world of men and of events the style of Franklin."

OIL FIELD

ADAMS, E. RUSSELL.
Oil-field lingo. (The Writer's monthly. Springfield, Mass., May, 1919. 8°. v. 13, p. 269.)
*IH
Short list of oil field terms for the use of writers.

Oil field talk. (The Editor. Highland Falls, N. Y., Sept. 9, 1916. 8°. v. 44, p. 250–251.)
Fourteen slang phrases defined.   NARA

McTEE, A. R.
Oil field diction. (Texas Folk-lore Society. Publications. Austin, May, 1925. 8°. v. 4, p. 64–67.)   ZBA (Texas)
Slang from the Texas oil fields.

NORTHUP, CLARK SUTHERLAND.
The language of the oil wells. (Dialect notes. New Haven, 1903–04. 8°. v. 2, p. 338–346, 373–393.)   RNZ
"As the American oil industry has been wholly developed since 1859, it will be seen that this specialized vocabulary is mainly of recent growth." Northup, who was connected with Cornell University, was one of the first to make a plea for the preservation of American speech, and his bibliographies have been drawn upon freely by other writers in the field.

POND, FREDERICK R.
Language of the California oil fields. (American speech. Baltimore, April, 1932. 4°. v. 7, p. 261–272.)   RNA
Lengthy glossary. "Although investigation has been confined to California publications and California oil fields, the terms collected, with few exceptions, are current in fields throughout the country where both cable-tool and rotary drilling are employed. Migratory oil workers tend to keep usage general."

SANFORD, WINIFRED, AND CLYDE JACKSON.
Derrick jargon. (Southwest review. Dallas, 1934. 8°. v. 19, p. 335–345.)   *DA
Many of the southwestern oil field terms have found their way into common speech. The origins of some of the more striking ones are traced. At the end of the article is a glossary, p. 341–345, compiled by Lee Brooks.

STEVENS, HELEN K.
Oil field expressions. (American speech. New York, April, 1937. 4°. v. 12, p. 153–154.)   RNA

TEMPLE, HELEN CHAFFEE.
Local color in the oil fields. (Writer's monthly. Springfield, Mass., July, 1926. 8°. v. 28, p. 40–43.)   *IH
Oil field life is described and a selection of oil field terms is given, with adequate definitions.

OYSTER FISHERY

INGERSOLL, ERNEST.
The oyster industry. Washington: Gov. Prtg. Off., 1881. 251 p. f°. (United States Department of the Interior. Tenth census of the United States. The history and present condition of the fishing industries.)   †VRY
Glossary of terms. An oysterman's dictionary, p. 241–250.
The specialized lingo of the oysterman, chiefly technical, but containing a few picturesque expressions peculiar to America.

POLITICS

BUCHER, LOTHAR.
On political terms. (Philological Society. Transactions. London, 1858. 8°. 1858, p. 42–62.)
RAA
Not slang words; but useful to the student of political phrases and their backgrounds.

FIRESTONE, CLARK BARNABY.
Sycamore shores. New York: Robert M. McBride & Company [1936]. xi, 247 p. 8°.   IV
American political phrases, p. 126–127.
This is an account of the author's voyages on several American rivers, and in the account of Salt River he explains the origin of "up Salt River" as a political expression and lists many others besides.

GIRARD.
Campaigns as word-makers. (Journal of education. Boston, Oct. 19, 1916. f°. v. 84, p. 383.)
SSA
Reprinted from an article in the Philadelphia *Ledger*, by Girard. Political Americanisms. Not limited to one era.

MONTGOMERY, HUGH, AND PHILIP G. CAMBRAY.
A dictionary of political phrases and allusions. With a short bibliography. London: Swan Sonnenschein & Co., 1906. 406 p. 12°.
*R–*AY
Long historical definitions, carefully documented, and composed almost exclusively of political terms peculiar to the British Empire. Bibliography, p. 373–400, is classified by subject. Has an index.

NORTON, CHARLES LEDYARD.
Political Americanisms. A glossary of terms and phrases current at different periods in American politics. London: Longmans, Green, and Co., 1890. 135 p. 16°.   ID
The earliest compilation of its kind and one of the standard references. Most of these phrases appeared originally in *The Magazine of American history*, New York, Dec., 1884, v. 12, p. 564–566; Jan., 1885, v. 13, p. 98–99; Feb., 1885, v. 13, p. 199–202; March, 1885, v. 13, p. 295–298; April, 1885, v. 13, p. 394–396; May, 1885, v. 13, p. 495–497, *IAA.* See v. 13, p. 599–600, for an extra note.
Reviewed in *The Nation*, New York, March 19, 1891, v. 52, p. 240, *DA; Popular science monthly*, New York, v. 39, p. 134–135, *DA; Saturday review*, London, Nov. 28, 1885, v. 60, p. 709–710, *DA.

OLIVER, ROBERT T.
Electionisms. (American speech. Baltimore, Feb., 1933. 4°. v. 8, p. 20–22.)   RNA
Slogans and campaign expressions of the 1932 election.

POLITICAL slang. (Cornhill magazine. London, June, 1887. 8°. v. 55, p. 624–629.)   *DA
American political slang. This is a review of a *Dictionary of American slang.* A few British terms are included.

Occupational Jargon — Politics, continued

SCHERF, CARL. Slang, slogan and song in American politics. (The Social studies. Philadelphia, Dec., 1934. 4°. v. 25, p. 424–430.)
† BAA

One of the more up-to-date collections of American political slang phrases. The compiler claims to have listed during the past few years some twelve hundred "cases of slang, slogans, songs, and cartoons used more or less effectively in our politics, foreign relations, wars, teaching, business relations, and social life." Many examples are cited. Some of the derivations are open to question.

SMITH, EDWARD CONRAD. A dictionary of American politics. Comprising accounts of political parties, measures, and men... New York: A. L. Burt Company, 1924. 496 p. 12°.
ID

Contains many slang political phrases, slogans, nicknames, catchwords, etc., of American politics from the earliest times to the present, the whole arranged in one alphabet. Many dates are given.

This makes a good companion volume to Montgomery and Cambray (q.v.), and supplements the earlier work of Norton.

TOWNSEND, MALCOLM. Handbook of United States political history ... Boston: Lothrop, Lee & Shepard Co. [cop. 1905.] 441 p. 8°.
ID

"Political vocabulary," p. 195–266, 415–423.
"Political parties," p. 149–194, 414–415.
Both groups contain many slang terms, Americanisms, etc.

URBAN, SYLVANUS, PSEUD. [Political slang.] (Gentleman's magazine. London, May, 1878. 8°. v. 244, p. 630–631.)
A few current political locutions. * DA

WIMBERLY, LOWRY CHARLES. American political cant. (American speech. Baltimore, Dec., 1926. 4°. v. 2, p. 135–139.)
RNA

"Our political jargon is thoroughly indigenous to America." Gives many of the old words found in Norton, and adds a few of the very latest coinage. Additions to this are made by Charles Lindsay, *American speech*, July, 1927, v. 2, p. 443.

For the "Americanisms" of orators see Frank Moore Colby, *Imaginary obligations*, New York: Dodd, Mead & Company, 1905, p. 49–53, *NBQ*.

POST OFFICE

BISGAIER, PAUL. Speech in the post office. (American speech. Baltimore, April, 1932. 4° v. 7, p. 278–279.)
RNA

Short but useful list of terms used in New York City. "Interwoven as the Post Office is with the lives of the people it has evolved a vocabulary which is virtually unknown to any but its employes."

QUICK LUNCH

BOY, page American Speech. (The Kalends of the Waverly Press and the Williams and Wilkins Co. Baltimore, Nov., 1926. 12°. v. 5, p. 17.)
TLNA

Slang of the "short order" restaurant, excerpted from the *William Feather magazine*.

COFFEE and —— (World's work. New York, Feb., 1932. 4°. v. 61, p. 26–29, 71.) * DA
Some of the most amusing slang terms in America

are those which are created by the cooks and waiters in wagon restaurants, quick lunch stands, and "coffee pots." Many such terms are local, but some gain popularity and are known from coast to coast.

QUICK-LUNCH lingo. (The Literary digest. New York, March 18, 1916. f°. v. 56, p. 766–767.) * DA

A writer in the *Boston Post* lists a few expressions overheard in a Boston restaurant. Two eggs on toast are called "Biddies on a raft," and an order for rump steak rare is phrased, "Slab of moo — let him chew it!" etc. *See also* Word study, v. 10, Nov., 1934, p. 6, *RNA*.

SEA

ANSTED, A. A dictionary of sea terms...with appendix of additional words, fully illustrated, and in almost every case from the object described. Glasgow: Brown, Son & Ferguson, Ltd. [1933.] iv, 327 p. 12°.
VXB

A reprint, with appendix added, of the 1917 edition. Published originally in 1898.
A few sea words which might well be classified as sea slang appear in this work.

BASSETT, FLETCHER STEWART. Some curious sea-words. (The American magazine. New York, Sept., 1887. 8°. v. 6, p. 621–627.) * DA

Several hundred sea words, mostly descriptive of parts of a ship. The author was a lieutenant in the U. S. Navy. The etymology of most of the words is traced, and a great many foreign equivalents are given.

BECKETT, WALTER NAPIER THOMASON. A few naval customs, expressions, traditions and superstitions. 2nd ed... Portsmouth: Gieves, Ltd. [1931?] 87 p. 12°.
VYB

Commander Beckett, of the Royal Navy, has collected an interesting assortment of sea terms which he has attempted, with some pains, to trace historically.

BENSTEAD, CHARLES RICHARD. The landsman's guide to sea lore. London: Methuen & Co., Ltd. [1935.] vii, 184 p. 12°.
VXF

Index and glossary, p. 177–184.
Contains sea slang.

BISH. Naval language. (The Spectator. London, Jan. 24, 1920. f°. v. 124, p. 104–105.) * DA

A few modern sea terms treated informally by a plain observer of sea lingo. The sailor creates slang "for the purpose of expressing in the smallest number of words a big quantity of fact."

BOWEN, FRANK C. Sea slang... London: Sampson Low, Marston & Co., Ltd. [1929?] vi, 154 p. 16°.
M.R.R. Desk

Handbook of English sea slang. "When I enlisted as a seaman in the early days of the war the old hands...used a slang that was practically the same as that of the late Victorian navy... When I went down to the Mediterranean fleet in 1927, I found that this language had practically disappeared."

Reviewed in the London *Times literary supplement*, June 13, 1929, p. 468, *NAA*.

BRIDGE, SIR CYPRIAN ARTHUR GEORGE. Old sea terms and duties. (The United service magazine. London, 1920. 8°. new series, v. 60, p. 179–182.) * DA

Sea terms of the British navy of the middle Victorian period, as recalled by an admiral.

Occupational Jargon — Sea, continued

CHERRY, ANDREW.
Spanish dollars! or, The priest of the parish. An operatic sketch... London: Barker and Son, 1806. 32 p. 8°.   NCO p.v.67
Abounds with slang, mostly nautical. Contains some rollicking songs.

COLCORD, JOANNA CARVER.
Sea terms ashore. (Yachting. New York, Dec., 1935. f°. v. 58, p. 32–33, 82–83.) † MVRA
Our modern American speech is filled with salty expressions which have nautical origins. Some of these expressions fall into the category of sea slang. There is a short glossary appended.

COWAN, FRANK.
A dictionary of the proverbs and proverbial phrases of the English language relating to the sea... Greenesburgh, Pennsylvania: The Oliver Publishing House, 1894. 144 p. 8°.
                                          * R–NAX
A rather odd volume which contains many of the old sea terms. Quotations are plentiful.

CROUCHER, E. J.
Sailor words. (Word-lore. London, April, 1928. 12°. v. 3, p. 61–63.)   ZBA
"Steam and electricity have transformed ships, and with the passing of sails, new sailors, trained to the new ways, have coined new words." Certain of these neologisms are mentioned, along with some of the ancient survivals.

DAVIS, JOHN.
The Post-captain; or, The wooden walls well manned...by the author of 'Edwards', 'A view of society in France', &c. [John Davis.] The third edition, corrected... London: Thomas Tegg, 1808. 232 p. 12°.   NCW
Contains much sea slang.
This edition was reprinted, with an introduction by R. H. Case, in 1928, London: The Scholartis Press, 8°, 247 p., *NCW*. In addition to the slang explained in the footnotes there is a glossary, p. 242–247. This book has been attributed to Dr. John Moore, and others. It seems that Tegg, the publisher, perpetrated a fraud as to the earlier editions. Supposed to have been printed as early as 1802, nothing earlier than 1805 has been found. In the *Naval chronicle*, 1806, v. 15, a reviewer says: "Every page abounds in sea terms, sometimes delivered like a seaman; but there is a vast deal, which betrays the slang of a land-lubber." Davis wrote *Travels in America* (q.v.), and *The American mariners*, Salisbury: Brodie and Dowding [1822], 12°, 384 p., *NBHD*, which also contains much sea lingo. *The Post captain* has been called the parent of all English nautical novels.

FAIRBANKS, R. JONATHAN.
Nautical terms. (Writer's monthly. Springfield, Mass., Oct., 1928. 8°. v. 32, p. 314–315.)
                                          * IH
A few technical terms familiar to seamen and useful for the writer of sea tales.

FITZGERALD, EDWARD.
Sea words and sea phrases. (In his: A Fitzgerald medley. Edited by Charles Ganz... London: Methuen, 1933. 8°. p. 59–144.) NDH
The words are only those in common use along the Suffolk coast in England, particularly at Lowestoft. Also includes Fitzgerald's annotations of sea phrases in Charles Richardson's *The New dictionary of the English language*, 1858.
This is a sample of inspired lexicography, compiled by a learned poet who loved the sea and who wrote in his manuscript book these words: "Burke to Kep-

pel: 'I am perfectly convinced that "Englishmen" and "seamen" are names that must live and die together',"
"Sea words and sea phrases along the Suffolk coast" appeared originally in the *East Anglian notes and queries*, Lowestoft, 1868, v. 3, p. 347–363, 1869, v. 4, p. 261–264, *CA*, and were signed: E. F. G. The entries sometimes vary from the list edited by Ganz. Fitzgerald seems to have added to his definitions from time to time.

GLASCOCK, WILLIAM NUGENT.
Land sharks and sea gulls. By Captain Glascock, R. N. [William Nugent Glascock]... Philadelphia: Lea & Blanchard, 1838. 2 v. 12°.
                                          NCW
Filled with sea slang, with a number of English flash terms thrown in. Some of the words are explained in footnotes. Glascock also wrote *Tales of a tar*, London: Henry Colburn and Richard Bentley, 1830, 12°, 333 p., *NCW*, which likewise abounds in sea slang. He was one of the authors of *The Naval sketch book*.

GODDARD, L. F.
Slang. (London Daily Herald, Aug. 4, 1936.)
Article on English sailor slang.

GRANDPIERRE, CHARLES.
A systematic dictionary of sea terms. Abstracts from "The book of the sea, ships, seafarers" (systematic marine encyclopedia) by C. Grand Pierre. Valley Cottage, N. Y.: Printed at sea, aboard American Legion, Munson Line [1928]. 95 p. 16°.   * C p.v.3023
An odd little volume with some authentic sea terms, technical and slang, compiled by the editor of Greenwich Village bohemian newspapers, etc.

HARVEY, BARTLE T.
Navy slang. (Dialect notes. New Haven, 1914. 8°. v. 5, p. 150–151.)   RNZ
"The following 'slang of the sea,' current among United States bluejackets, constitutes extracts from a collection made by Mr. Bartle T. Harvey. — Ed."

"JACKSTAFF," PSEUD.
Sailor talk. (London Daily Mail, May 5, 1917, p. 2.)

JONES, CLAUDE E.
A note on sailor slang. (American speech. New York, Feb., 1935. 4°. v. 10, p. 78–79.)
                                          RNA
A short glossary of slang words used by the American sailor.

LARK, C.
Paddy Hew; a poem, from the brain of Timothy Tarpaulin, whistled by a sea lark [C. Lark] ... London: Printed for Whittingham and Arliss, 1815. 195 p. 12°.   NDF
Col'd front. by C. Lark. Contains much sea slang, and some of the colloquialisms in common use at the time there was marked anti-Napoleon sentiment in England.

LAUGHTON, L. G. CARR.
A bibliography of nautical dictionaries. (Mariner's mirror. London, Feb., 1911. 8°. v. 1, p. 84–89.)   VXA
Feeling the need of a bibliography of the sea, the compiler submitted a plan for such a work. His scheme included: 1. Encyclopedias and dictionaries, (a) in English, (b) in a single foreign language, (c) in two or more languages; 2. Glossaries or word books, (a) of two languages, (b) polyglot. The books were located for the most part in the Admiralty Library, the British Museum, the Patent Office Library,

Occupational Jargon — Sea, continued

the Library of the Royal Institution, and the Public Record Office. Sotheby's catalogue of the library of John Scott (1905) was also used. A tentative list of the books examined appears in this issue of the *Mariner's mirror.* All the volumes of this interesting and valuable periodical should be scanned by the collector of sea terms. Each volume has a special notes and queries section. For further details about the nautical dictionary see the July, 1924, issue, v. 10, p. 227–242, and the July, 1926, issue, v. 12, p. 335–338.

LEIGH, MAGDA.
Expressions used in the merchant marine. (The Editor. Highland Falls, N. Y., Dec. 2, 1916. 8°. v. 44, p. 518–520.)   NARA
"I shall not try to include the Navy usages, but only such expressions as I have picked up in the merchant marine."

LOWRY, ROBERT GRAHAM.
The origins of some naval terms and customs. London: Sampson Low, Marston & Co. [1930?] ix, 102 p. 16°.   VXB
The section devoted to "Terms and customs," p. 10–56, will be of interest to the slang collector. Some effort is made to trace origins.

MERCIER, HENRY JAMES, AND WILLIAM GALLOP.
Life in a man-of-war; or, Scenes in "Old Ironsides" during her cruise in the Pacific. By a fore-top-man... [Henry James Mercier and W. Gallop.] Philadelphia: Lydia R. Bailey, printer, 1841. 267 p. 8°.   VYE
This is filled with the naval slang of the period so well portrayed by Dana in his *Two years before the mast.* It has many words not mentioned in Dana and a great many of the words are earlier than the examples cited in the N. E. D.
The work was reprinted in 1927 by Houghton Mifflin Co., Boston, with a preface by Rear Admiral Snow, 288 p., 4°, *VYE.*

NAUTICAL slang. (The Bookfellow. Sydney, April 15, 1915. f°. new series, v. 4, p. 79.) * DA
A short study of "boozed" and "tight" with a hint of their nautical origin. Also a word about the Australian slang words "pommies" (tramcar conductors) and "jimmygrants." Thinks "dagoes" came from "Diegos," from a line from William Davenant's *The Triumph of Sir Francis Drake* (1659).

PARTRIDGE, ERIC HONEYWOOD.
Sailors' language. (Everyman. London, Feb. 5, 1931. f°. v. 5, p. 44.)   * DA
A short review of books on sea slang.

READER.
Navy slang twenty years ago. (Writer's monthly. Springfield, Mass., Sept., 1928. 8°. v. 32, p. 235–236.)   * IH
Reprint of an article in the *Boston Post,* addressed to the editor. Contrasts hardships of old days with the comforts of the modern navy, and the slang of the old and new.

RICHARDSON, C. B. W.
Elegy for a dying tongue. (Scribner's. New York, Aug., 1935. 4°. v. 98, p. 120–122.) * DA
Some notes on the language of the sea and the passing of the picturesque sea slang of an older generation.

ROBERTS, EDWIN F.
Tom Coxe's "Traverse." A "tough" yarn. (United service magazine. London, July, 1854. 8°. v. 75, p. 344–355.)   * DA
Couched in the lingo of the British sailor.

RUGGLES, LOGAN E.
The navy explained... New York: Edwin N. Appleton [1918]. 161 p. 12°.   VXB
An encyclopedia of the American navy — including many expressions which may properly be classified as slang.

RUSSELL, WILLIAM CLARK.
Sailors' language. A collection of sea-terms and their definitions... London: Sampson Low, Marston, Searle, & Rivington, 1883. 164 p. 12°.   VXB
Includes a few slang terms. William Clark Russell is best known for his novels of the sea, particularly for his *The Wreck of the 'Grosvenor.'*
One may read along with this a similar dictionary compiled by Richard Henry Dana in any of the numerous editions of his *The Seaman's friend.*

Sea phrases. (Living age. New York, Jan. 8, 1887. 8°. v. 172, p. 67–73.)   * DA
Reprinted from *Contemporary review.*
Etymological study of over a hundred British sea phrases by one conversant with the history of the subject. Sailors love short words. "Everything must be done quickly at sea; there is no time for sesquipedalianism."

SAM SPRIT, PSEUD.
[Sea sketches.] (United service magazine. London, 1830–32. 8°.)   * DA
A number of letters addressed to the editor appeared in the years 1830–1832, and were signed Sam Sprit. They were written entirely in the vernacular of the sailor. This magazine, which ran for almost a hundred years, contains many other sea stories which would yield the word-hunter a rich harvest.

SLANG in the British navy. (T. P.'s weekly. London, July 9, 1909. f°. v. 14, p. 45.)   * DA
A review of the British navy slang occasioned by the naval manoeuvers of 1909. About 100 expressions are defined.

STRIDE, W. K.
Sea lingo. (The Argosy. London, July, 1901. 8°. v. 75, p. 58–61.)   * DA
Mentions a few English sea words which have been applied to persons and things on shore, such as "above board," "A1," "knows the ropes," etc.

TOMLINSON, HENRY MAJOR.
Sailor language. (In his: Waiting for daylight. London: Cassell and Co., Ltd., 1922. 8°. p. 125–130.)   NCZ
An essay based on W. H. Smyth's *Sailors' word book, VXB.*
Another edition, New York: A. A. Knopf, 1922, *BTZG.*

VAUX, PATRICK.
As heard in 'Andrew.' (In his: Gadgets. London: Hodder and Stoughton, 1917. 12°. p. 49–59.)   VXCB
British navy slang, ancient and modern, but chiefly the slang as used at the time of the World War. About 100 expressions are defined.

WASSON, GEORGE SAVARY.
Our heritage of old sea terms. (American speech. Baltimore, June, 1929. 4°. v. 4, p. 377–384.)   RNA
"Let us try to trace the pedigree of a few old sea terms in most common use on shore today." The author writes from Bangor, Maine.

Occupational Jargon — Sea, continued

WELLS, GERARD.
Naval customs and traditions... [London:] Philip Allan, 1930. 195 p. 8°.   VYB
An alphabetical arrangement of miscellaneous sea lore, customs, and slang. The definitions tend to fullness.

WESTCOTT, ALLAN FERGUSON.
Sea words on shore duty. (United States Naval Institute. Proceedings. Annapolis, July, 1926. 8°. v. 52, p. 1330–1338.)   VXA
Most of the American nautical words were taken over from the Dutch, the Spanish, the Scandinavian, and the English of Queen Elizabeth's reign. A few were coined in America, at the time of our great maritime activity following the War of 1812. Caboose, all aboard, close quarters, berth, round robin, bluff, grog, etc., are samples of sea words which have been taken over into land speech.

YEXLEY, LIONEL.
Grog time yarns. Spun by the merry clan of 17 mess, and showing how Shiner Green joined the clan, and eventually parted Brass-rags with Pincher Martin... London: The Westminster Press, 1904. 153 p. 8°.   VYC
These yarns of the British sailor are written in slang and make a useful adjunct to sea slang dictionaries. Other works by the same writer contain naval jargon.

United States Naval Academy

AGETON, ARTHUR AINSLEY.
Annapolis, cradle of the navy. (National geographic magazine. Washington, D. C., June, 1936. 8°. v. 69, p. 789–801.)   KAA
Gives a few slang words heard at the Naval Academy.

BRACKBILL, HERVEY.
Midshipman jargon. (American speech. Baltimore, Aug., 1928. 4°. v. 3, p. 451–455.)   RNA
United States Naval Academy slang of the present day. About 100 words are defined.

RILEY, ELIHU SAMUEL.
A new naval tongue. (Army and navy life. New York, Nov., 1906. 4°. v. 9, p. 497–500.)   VWA
A study of the slang of the United States Naval Academy students, from 1845 to 1906.

W., J. V.
Beach combings. Slanguage of Bancroft Hall. n.p. [cop. 1928.] 38 p.
A little dictionary of midshipman slang at the United States Naval Academy.

Sealing

GREENE, WILLIAM HOWE.
The wooden walls among the ice floes... London: Hutchinson & Co., Limited, 1933. xix, 298 p. illus. 4°.   VRX
A sealing glossary, p. xv–xvi. Terms from the Newfoundland sealing industry.

Whaling

DENHAM, EDWARD.
Expressions, chiefly of whalers, noted at New Bedford, Mass. (Dialect notes. New Haven, 1915. 8°. v. 4, p. 240–242.)   RNZ
Thirteen expressions known to whalers. Full definitions given.

EDWARDS, EVERETT JOSHUA, AND JEANNETTE EDWARDS RATTRAY.
"Whale off!" The story of American whaling... New York: Frederick A. Stokes Company, 1932. xv, 286 p. 12°.   VRW
Nautical and local terms used, p. 279–283. Bibliography, p. 283–285.

REYNOLDS, JOHN N.
Mocha Dick; or, The white whale of the Pacific. (Knickerbocker magazine. New York, May, 1839. 8°. v. 13, p. 377–392.)   *DA
This was probably the inspiration for Melville's *Moby Dick*. It is filled with the special slang of Nantucket whalers.

SHEEP HERDING

LINDSAY, CHARLES.
The idiom of the sheep range. (American speech. Baltimore, June, 1931. 4°. v. 6, p. 355–359.)   RNA
The special language of the western sheep herders — words from the range and the shearing pen.

SHOE SALESMAN

GELLER, DAVID.
Lingo of the shoe salesman. (American speech. New York, Dec., 1934. 4°. v. 9, p. 283–286.)   RNA
Due partly to chain shoe stores a special lingo has been created by shoe salesmen which is used all over the United States. There is a short addendum by J. S. Fox.

SOCIAL WORK

BOWMAN, LEROY EDWARD.
The terminology of social workers. Vogues in social work terms. (American speech. Baltimore, June, 1926. 4°. v. 1, p. 478–480.)   RNA
Not slang, but a few of the special phrases peculiar to social work.

SODA FOUNTAIN

BENTLEY, HAROLD WOODMANSEE.
Linguistic concoctions of the soda jerker. (American speech. New York, Feb., 1936. 4°. v. 11, p. 37–45.)   RNA
"To foreigners in search of local American color, the soda fountains are as good as made to order." The soda fountain business was firmly established in America by 1876. It has its special cant from coast to coast. A glossary of about 300 words is given.
See *New York American,* May 12, 1931, p. 17 (O. O. McIntyre). Also *New York American,* Aug. 7, 1936 (Alice Hughes).

STEEL INDUSTRY

SLANG of steel. (Fortune. New York, Dec., 1935. f°. v. 12, p. 44.)   †TMA
Thirty-eight slang terms used in the American steel industry, "chosen, to be frank, more for picturesqueness than for importance."

STOCK YARDS

PRESCOTT, RUSSELL T.
Language of the livestock mart. (American speech. New York, Dec., 1935. 4°. v. 10, p. 269–272.)   RNA
Glossary of the trade jargon of the stock yards of the American Middle West.

Occupational Jargon, continued

SUGAR INDUSTRY

DAVIDSON, LEVETTE JAY.
Sugar beet language. (American speech. Baltimore, Oct., 1930. 4°. v. 6, p. 10–18.) RNA
Terms used in the sugar beet industry in Colorado and neighboring states.

PADDOCK, W. EARL.
Local color from the maple sugar camps. (Writer's monthly. Springfield, Mass., May, 1929. 8°. v. 33, p. 405–407.) *IH
Familiar words from the New England sugar camps, probably bordering more on the technical than the slang side.

TELEGRAPHY

ALLAN, E. A.
Slang of the telegraph operators. (The Editor. Highland Falls, N. Y., Aug. 26, 1916. 8°. v. 44, p. 200.) NARA
Twenty-three slang expressions.

BRACKBILL, HERVEY.
Some telegraphers' terms. (American speech. Baltimore, April, 1929. 4°. v. 4, p. 287–290.) RNA
"Telegraph no longer has but a single meaning for Americans, even when land-wire telegraphy alone is alluded to. Throughout the country the Morse system has been supplanted to a considerable extent by the automatic printing telegraph. Some of the words relating to the vanishing Morse system are herein preserved."

LOOMIS, CHARLES P.
Lineman's English. (American speech. Baltimore, Sept., 1926. 4°. v. 1, p. 659–660.) RNA
The lingo of the Texas linemen.

MITCHELL, MINNIE SWAN.
Lingo of telegraph operators. (American speech. New York, April, 1937. 4°. v. 12, p. 154–155.) RNA

TELEPHONY

WALDO, EDNA L.
Telephone shop talk. (The Writer's monthly. Springfield, Mass., May, 1927. 8°. v. 29, p. 406–409.) *IH
Slang words for the writer of stories that have to do with the American telephone industry, from the "hello" girls to the linemen.

TRANSPORTATION

Airplane

BEATH, PAUL ROBERT.
Aviation lingo. (American speech. Baltimore, April, 1930. 4°. v. 5, p. 289–290.) RNA
A short list of the most-used terms in flying.

COULSON, EDWIN R.
Aeroplane factory English. (American speech. New York, April, 1938. 4°. v. 13, p. 155–157.) RNA

GIMPERS, goophers, and other new aviation wrinkles from France. (The Literary digest. New York, Aug. 24, 1918. f°. v. 58, p. 36.) *DA
Excerpted from the *New York Evening Sun;* an

article by the American flying ace, Eddie Rickenbacker. He says: "A gimper is a bird who would stick by you through anything...it means more than good scout, or pal, or comrade."

GLOSSARY of aviation terms. (The Playbill. New York, May, 1935. 8°. p. 19–21.)
Theatre Collection
The playbill for "Ceiling zero," by Frank Wead, contained a glossary of the aviation terms taken from the play.

MAYS, BROCK.
Aviation in slang. (Popular science monthly. New York, May, 1928. 8°. v. 112, p. 72, 141.) *DA
An interesting article which confines itself to the more colorful of the slang words. "That kiwi was up on a payhop; he put her on hot down-wind and washed out the only peppy crate in the outfit." "He's a Chinese ace" is perfectly intelligible to a flyer.

SNYPP, WALTER WYATT.
The airplane story. (Writer's monthly. Springfield, Mass., Nov., 1926. 8°. v. 28, p. 394–396.) *IH
The commercial development of aviation had created a reading public for air stories. A glossary of terms is arranged for the use of writers.

STUBBLEFIELD, BLAINE.
Aviation terms. (Writer's monthly. Springfield, Mass., Feb., 1928. 8°. v. 31, p. 122–124.) *IH
An article on "kiwi" writers. "A kiwi is anyone connected with a flying organization who is himself not a flyer." These writers used so many incorrect words that the author felt he would serve the writing profession a good turn by giving a number of genuine flying terms.

WATTS, RAYMOND.
Parlance of the flying fields. (The Editor. Highland Falls, N. Y., April 21, 1917. 8°. v. 45, p. 358–359.) NARA
Technical terms of aviation, just coming into popularity as a result of the Great War.

Automobile

BOTKIN, BENJAMIN ALBERT.
The lore of the Lizzie label. (American speech. Baltimore, Dec., 1930. 4°. v. 6, p. 81–93.) RNA
The labels painted on dilapidated Ford cars reveal a certain type of American humor. "The language of the Lizzie label is vigorous and vulgar with colloquialisms and slang."

An anthology of Lizzie labels. (American speech. Baltimore, Oct., 1931. 4°. v. 7, p. 32–39.) RNA
Additions to the first list.

CURTISS, ELLIOTT, JR.
Slang on wheels. (Automobile trade journal. Philadelphia, 1937. 4°. Jan., 1937, p. 30–31, 50.) 3-TOL

DAVIDSON, LEVETTE JAY.
Auto-tourist talk. (American speech. New York, April, 1934. 4°. v. 9, p. 110–114.) RNA
The automobile has given rise to new travel terms. Along the routes patronized by tourists has developed a strange language of signs, advertisements, etc.

Occupational Jargon — Transportation, cont'd

GILLILAN, STRICKLAND W.
Gasoline cocktails for old Noah Webster.
(Motor life. New York, May, 1920. f°. v. 15,
p. 40, 88.)   3–† TOL
Words connected with the automobile have passed
over into daily speech. "Step on the gas" is an example. "Flat tire" is another. Reprinted in condensed
form in *Literary digest*, New York, May 22, 1920,
v. 65, p. 120–125, * *DA*.

GOULD, PAUL.
A glossary of taxicab words and phrases.
(The New Yorker. New York, Nov. 3, 1928.
4°. v. 4, p. 94.)   * DA
Eighteen slang expressions peculiar to the New
York taxi driver are defined.

HORNBERGER, THEODORE.
The automobile and American English.
(American speech. Baltimore, April, 1930. 4°.
v. 5, p. 271–278.)   RNA
"The automobile dialect has been determined...by
the people most concerned, rather than by the scholars."
A good historical study of the subject.
See also M. R. Eiselen, "The Horseless carriage,"
Yale review, Autumn, 1936, v. 26, p. 134–147, * *DA*,
in which the various early names of the auto are
traced.

MILBURN, GEORGE.
The taxi talk. (Folk-say. A regional miscellany. Edited by B. A. Botkin. Norman:
The Oklahoma Folk-lore Society, 1929. 8°.
p. 108–112.)   ZBA
The slang of the Chicago taxi drivers. Compare
this with the slang of the New York taxicab drivers,
as given by Frank J. Wilstach in the *New York Times*,
Nov. 11, 1928, * *A*.

MOVING words. (New York Evening Journal,
Sept. 29, 1936.)
The men who operate the moving vans in New York
have a language of their own. *Fiddle, mousetrap,
chowder, rough stuff, bottom, top, firehouse, swing,*
and *dutch up*, are defined.

STEELE, A. N.
Slang. (London Daily Herald, Aug. 5, 1936.)
A brief vocabulary of the London busmen.

STREET, JAMES H.
Knights of the line. (New York World Telegram, April 8, 9, 10, 1937.)   * A
Three lengthy articles on long-distance truck drivers,
written in their lingo. In the April 8th article is a
short glossary of "Truckman talk."

WILSTACH, FRANK JENNERS.
The slang of taxi cab drivers. Four type-
written sheets of ms. given to The New York
Public Library by the author.
Printed in the *New York Times*, Nov. 11, 1928,
section 5, p. 21, col. 2, * *A*.

Railroad

BATIE, RUSSELL V.
Railroad lingo. (American speech. New
York, Feb., 1934. 4°. v. 9, p. 73–74.)   RNA
Terms in common use in the West, particularly on
the Union Pacific system and the Denver and Rio
Grande Western.

FOREMAN, EARL H.
Railroad vernacular. (Writer's monthly.
Springfield, Mass., Oct., 1929. 8°. v. 34, p. 228–
233.)   * IH
List of words for the use of the fiction writer. "Most

slang words and phrases used on the railroads are
coined and circulated by 'boomers,' who are usually
adept and capable workmen but of independent and
migratory dispositions."

GLOSSARY of pullman service terms. (The Pullman news. Chicago, Sept., 1922. 4°. v. 1, p. 137.)
      TLNA
This is a colorful and highly-specialized jargon. The
observation car, for instance, is called the "bird cage"
and a railroad official is called a "brass hat."

HARPER, ROBERT S.
Lingo of locale. (Writer's digest. Cincinnati,
May, 1931. 8°. v. 11, p. 40, 42, 64.)   * IH
Slang for the short-story writer. Gives a few aviation
terms and a long list of railroad terms.

JONES, GROVER.
Railroad lingo. A story in dialect — with an
essay on the rails. (Bookman. New York, July,
1929. 8°. v. 69, p. 524–527.)   * DA
Railroad workers have always had a rich argot, but
few of their expressions have found their way into
common speech. Many of these words have been re-
placed as electricity and oil supplanted coal as a moti-
vating power. This glossary pertains to the coal burners.

PANGLE, MARY ELLEN.
Railroad parlance. (The Editor. Highland
Falls, N. Y., Aug. 30, 1932. 4°. v. 98, p. 130–
134.)   NARA
Authentic railroad lingo for the use of writers who
wish to portray genuine railroad activities.

POWER, J. P.
Railroad slang. (The Editor. Highland Falls,
N. Y., Oct. 21, 1916. 8°. v. 44, p. 376–377.)
      NARA
A few slang phrases for the fiction writer.

SCHREIBER, R. L.
Electric railway parlance. (Writer's digest.
Cincinnati, Dec., 1929. 8°. v. 10, p. 35–37.)
      * IH
Glossary of terms arranged alphabetically. This
speech of the rails, as overheard around the car barns,
was compiled for the use of writers seeking local color.

SCHULTZ, J. R.
Railroad terms. (American speech. New
York, April, 1937. 4°. v. 12, p. 154.)   RNA

SIDNEY, F. H.
Railroad terms. (Dialect notes. New Haven,
1916. 8°. v. 4, p. 355–357.)   RNZ
From notes made in 1916, by F. H. Sidney, secretary of the Boston Manuscript Club, and for many
years a railroad man in many parts of the country.

SMITH, STEPHE R.
Romance and humor of the rail... New
York: G. W. Carleton & Co., 1873. 343 p. 12°.
      TP
Contains a few railroading terms, and numerous
songs as sung by American railroad men.

YOUNG, EDGAR.
Some railroad slang. (The Editor. Highland
Falls, N. Y., March 25, 1916. 8°. v. 43, p. 343.)
      NARA
A short list of American railroad terms.

MISCELLANEOUS

B., H. W.
Occupations. (American speech. New York,
Feb., 1937. 4°. v. 12, p. 83–84.)   RNA
Slang names of various occupations.

SLANG AND JARGON OF SPORTS, THE THEATRE, THE GAMBLING WORLD, AND ASSOCIATED GROUPS

SOME of the professions in the above classification are highly respectable and speak a technical jargon rather than slang. This is notably the case in the theatre and the broadcasting studio. Others are on the confines of low life and speak the argot of the underworld. Broadly speaking all of them fall under the general heading of professional entertainment. A candid study of such groups reveals that money-making is a paramount factor, and that this is more often than not an exploitation of gullibility or of the gambling instinct. When this is the express or hidden motive a language of deception is invented to conceal the modus operandi.

The sports pages of the daily newspapers are almost unintelligible without a slight knowledge of the various jargons spoken by each sport's devotees; and even a cursory glance at the contents of *Variety* and the *Billboard* reveals that the amusement world has a language of its own, to the utter despair of grammarians and dictionary-makers, but to the endless delight of the initiated.

ORDER OF ARRANGEMENT

GENERAL	SPORTS, *continued*	THE STAGE
SPORTS	FOOTBALL	VAUDEVILLE
SPORTS IN GENERAL	GOLF	MOTION PICTURES
THE RACE TRACK		RADIO
THE PRIZE RING	GAMBLING	JAZZ ORCHESTRAS
BASEBALL	STOCK MARKET	CHAUTAUQUA
CRICKET	MONEY	CIRCUS AND CARNIVAL
		PITCHMEN

GENERAL

BUCHANAN, BARRY.
[Encyclopedia of the amusement world.]
This work is still in manuscript. It covers the whole field of American amusement slang, including theatre, circus, vaudeville, movies, radio, amusement parks, burlesque, and many other entertainment groups. Buchanan spent two years with the circus, a year in a broadcasting studio, and several years in the theatre business along Broadway in order to collect his material from first hand sources. It is to be classified and carefully cross-indexed.
See "Oddities fill encyclopedia of show world," *New York Herald Tribune*, Feb. 17, 1937, * A.

SPORTS

Sports in General

BADCOCK, JOHN.
A dictionary of the turf, the ring, the chase, the pit, the bon-ton... London: T. Hughes, 1823. 8–RNM
For full description see entry in *Part One: Nineteenth Century*.

BINSTEAD, ARTHUR M.
...The works of Arthur M. Binstead ("The Pitcher")... With a foreword by J. B. Booth ("Costs"). London: T. Werner Laurie, Ltd., 1927. 2 v. 12°. NCG
Contents: A Pink 'un and a pelican; Pitcher in Paradise; Houndsditch day by day; Gal's gossip; More gal's gossip; Mop fair.
Binstead was a writer on the *Sporting times*, the "Pink 'un," and was a master of slang. For reminiscences of "Pitcher" see the half dozen or so books written by his colleague, J. B. Booth.
Lord Rosebery once said to John Corlett, the editor of the "Pink 'un": "I have just finished reading 'Mop fair.' Some of Pitcher's slang puzzled me as much as did the language of Thucydides when I was a boy at Eton, but, once mastered, Pitcher is as entertaining as the old Greek."
When an undergraduate at Oxford once mentioned Pitcher to Sir Walter Raleigh, that eminent scholar replied: "That, my boy, is literature."

BOOTH, JOHN BENNION.
London Town... London: T. Werner Laurie, Ltd. [1929.] 324 p. 8°. COB (London)
Contains sports slang, stage slang, journalese, etc. See particularly the chapters on the "Gaiety girls" and the old music halls.

"Master" and men. Pink 'un yesterdays... London: T. Werner Laurie, Ltd., 1926. 380 p. facsims., front., plates, ports. 8°. AN (Booth)
This work has much slang in its pages, including considerable music hall slang. The "Great Vance," of music hall fame, was just about to sing a line containing the word "bloody," but seeing two policemen enter the hall, suddenly changed the word to "blolly," which became slang immediately. From it we have "bally" and "ruddy" and other synonyms.

Old Pink 'un days. New York: Dodd, Mead & Co., 1925. 413 p. front., plates, ports. 8°. NARL
The English publication *The Sporting times*, was known as the "Pink 'un." It was started Feb. 11, 1865. Its columns were filled with slang. This history of the personalities associated with the "Pink 'un" is couched in the slang so familiar to its readers. The cricket term "the ashes" was originated in *The Sporting times*, in 1882. Likewise "masher," "bounders," "oof bird," "spoof," etc. The slang specialist of the "Pink 'un" was Arthur M. Binstead "Pitcher" (q.v.). There are two chapters on music halls.

Pink parade... London: Thornton Butterworth, Ltd. [1933.] 317 p. front., illus., plates, ports. 8°. AN (Booth)
In a foreword to this book, Charles B. Cochran said that he wrote some slang articles for *The Man about town*, which was printed on blue paper and followed the style of the "Pink 'un." "I wrote some articles for it, one or two of which were on the new topic of the growth of American slang. (This was in the epoch of 'The Belle of New York') which I still cherish."
There is much sporting and theatrical slang in this work. As in all of Booth's works there is a detailed account of the music halls of the day and snatches of many song hits.

Slang and Jargon of Sports, etc., continued

EGAN, PIERCE.
Pierce Egan's book of sports, and mirror of life: embracing the turf, the chase, the ring, and the stage. Interspersed with original memoirs of sporting men, etc. ...Dedicated to George Osbaldeston, Esq. London: Printed for T. T. and J. Tegg, 73, Cheapside, and R. Griffin and Co., Glasgow, 1832. 414 p. illus. 8°.   MY
A repository of slang in true Egan vein. Excerpts from sporting chronicles, ballads, anecdotes, and scenes of high and low life, make this collection a "bonanza" for the prospector of slang.
Most of the articles are on the subject of the turf, but all other English sports are represented. The book was issued in twenty-five parts, price three pence each.

Sporting anecdotes, original and selected; including numerous characteristic portraits of persons in every walk of life... v. I. New-York: Johnstone & Van Norden, 1823. 280 p. illus. 16°.   MV
v. 1 only.
The article "A sporting biographical sketch of William Habberfield, slangily denominated 'Slender Billy,' " p. 267–274, is filled with flash slang, and many of the other anecdotes contain slang.
The original edition appeared in London, 1820, and was published by Sherwood and Co. It was reviewed in the *London magazine,* London, Aug. – Sept., 1820, v. 2, p. 155–161, 268–276, * DA. The review contains some slang.

GRISWOLD, FRANK GRAY.
The horse and buggy days. [Norwood, Mass.,] Privately printed [1937]. 12°.
Sporting metaphors, p. 102–110.

HALLOCK, CHARLES.
Hallock's American club list and sportsman's glossary... New York: Forest and Stream Publishing Co., 1878. 77, xiii p. 12°.   MYA
Glossary, p. i–xiii. Over 600 words used by sportsmen in America are listed. All the major sports are included.

KIERAN, JOHN.
The sportsman's lexicon. (The Saturday review of literature. New York, July 22, 1933. f°. v. 10, p. 1–3.)   † NAA
Starting with the phrase "It's in the bag" which was incorrectly defined in the *Literary digest,* the sports columnist of the *New York Times* takes up the whole field of sports jargon and traces some of the more popular phrases — some of them back to the time of Pierce Egan. Kieran's essay was reprinted in the *1934 essay annual,* edited by Erich A. Walter, and published by Scott, Foresman and Co., Chicago, p. 254–262, *NBP.*

ORR, JOHN.
Les anglicismes du vocabulaire sportif. (Le Français moderne. Paris, Oct., 1935. 8°. année 3, p. 293–311.)   * DM
Rich contributions to all sports has been made by the English-speaking peoples.

O'TOOLE, RICHARD F.
Sports slang in Latin America. (American mercury. New York, Nov., 1930. 4°. v. 21, p. 336–338.)   * DA
Gives examples of American sporting slang which have crept into the Latin American newspapers.

PHILLIMORE, WALTER G. F.
"Sporting terms in common speech." (The Monthly review. London, Nov., 1906. 8°. v. 25, p. 81–90.)   * DA
Terms from various sports, including a few words which may be classified roughly as slang, are traced.

RIDINGS, JOSEPH WILLARD.
Use of slang in newspaper sports writing. (Journalism quarterly. Iowa City, Dec., 1934. 8°. v. 11, p. 348–360.)   NARA
A study based on eleven representative American newspapers. All of the American sports are included and a colorful glossary results from the study. A special list of dated slang comparisons and similes is given.

ROCKWELL, HAROLD E.
Color stuff. (American speech. Baltimore, Oct., 1927. 4°. v. 3, p. 28–30.)   RNA
Slang of the sports writer. Newspaper readers want stories of their favorite sports written with color. Prize ring slang is emphasized in this article.

ROSE, HOWARD N.
A thesaurus of slang... New York: The Macmillan Company, 1934. 120 p. 8°. RNM
"Sports slang," p. 70–81. Includes baseball, p. 70–71; boxing, p. 72–75; football, p. 75–77; golf, p. 77–79; polo, p. 79–80; turf, p. 80–81.

WEEKLEY, ERNEST.
National sports and national metaphor. (Cornhill magazine. London, March, 1921. 8°. v. 50, p. 311–325.)   * DA
Many old sporting terms are traced, and their relation to the English character is pointed out. A few French terms are included.

WESEEN, MAURICE HARLEY.
A dictionary of American slang... New York: Thomas Y. Crowell Company [1934]. 543 p. 8°.   M.R.R. Desk
"Baseball slang," p. 203–225. A good list.
"Football slang," p. 226–228.
"Boxing and prizefighting slang," p. 229–245. Good for modern prizefighting slang as well as the old.
"Sports slang — miscellaneous," p. 246–271.

The Race Track

BOOKMAKING. (All the year round. London, June 13, 1868. 8°. v. 20, p. 13–16.)   * DA
A few slang phrases used by the English bookmaker at horse races, particularly the unscrupulous type of bookmaker known as the "welcher."

CRICKMORE, HENRY G.
Dictionary or glossary of racing terms and slang... Reprinted from "Krik's guide to the turf." Compiled and published by H. G. Crickmore, with "The World," 35 Park Row, New York [1880]. 30 p. 16°.   MXS
Autographed copy. "H. C. from Krik."
American racing slang. Some of the definitions include English racing slang for purposes of comparison.

FAIRFAX-BLAKEBOROUGH, JOHN.
Racing stable terms. (Notes and queries. London, April 15, 1922. 8°. series 12, v. 10, p. 286–287.)   * R–* DA
"Some years ago when living at the famous Hambleton Yorks training stables (and later at Middleham) I compiled a list of technical terms." A note is added by Herbert W. Greene, in the May 6, 1922, issue, v. 11, p. 177, and a companion list of paddock jargon is added by Fairfax-Blakeborough in the Sept. 9, 1922 issue, v. 11, p. 206–207.

Slang and Jargon of Sports, etc., continued

FANE, MICHAEL.
Racecourse swindlers. London: Hutchinson
& Co., Ltd. [1936.] 288 p. front., plates. 8°.
SGS
Contains modern English race track slang and
swindler's cant. The English Derby has been called
by Samuel Cushing Lucas, "that carnival of slang."

MORRIS, JOHN, AND ERIC H. PARTRIDGE.
Epsom's attic salt. (Cornhill magazine. London, June, 1933. 8°. new series, v. 74, p. 696–
703.) *DA
A dramatic scene at the Epsom race-course at the
annual derby. A number of race-course habitues discourse on the race, entirely in the slang of the race
track. The words are defined in footnotes.

SARL, ARTHUR J.
Horses, jockeys & crooks. Reminiscences of
thirty years' racing... London: Hutchinson &
Co. [1935.] 288 p. illus. 8°. MXS
Contains no glossary, but sufficient race track
slang fills the pages to warrant the book's inclusion
in a list of sources for this type of jargon.

VANCE, L. J.
Race-track slang. (American notes and queries. Philadelphia, Aug. 23, 1890. 8°. v. 5,
p. 196–197.) *DA
Mentions a few of the terms most commonly heard
around the American race-track at that time.

The Prize Ring

ANSTEY, CHRISTOPHER.
The patriot. A Pindaric address to Lord
Buckhorse. [By Christopher Anstey.] [Quot.
from Virgil.] Cambridge: Printed by Fletcher
and Hodson: and sold by J. Dodsley, in Pall-
Mall; S. Crowder, in Pater-Noster Row; J.
Almon, in Piccadilly; and M. Hingeston, near
Temple-Bar, London. 1747. 44 p. 4°.
NCI p.v.66, no.1
Lord Buckhorse was in reality Buckhorse, the prize-
fighter. The poem is filled with the slang of the day,
including many terms known to the "Fancy"; i.e., the
followers of pugilism.
Anstey's most celebrated work was his poetical
satire, entitled *The Bath guide*, which ran through
several editions.

CREIGHTON, ROBERT E.
Jargon of fistiana. (American speech. New
York, Oct., 1933. 4°. v. 8, p. 34–39.) RNA
American prize-fight slang as gleaned from the
pages of the San Francisco *Chronicle*, from 1919 to
1931.
It might be added that at this time appeared H. C.
Witwer's articles called "Slanguage in a book shop"
in the Sunday issues of the *New York American*.
They were letters by "One Punch McTague" and
abounded in prize-ring slang. Ring Lardner and
George Ade were writing their slang articles in the
same section of the Hearst newspapers at this time,
and the files of these papers are a rich field for the
collector of American slang. The New York tabloid
newspapers are perhaps the most prolific source of
all for racy sports jargon and neologisms of all kinds.

EGAN, PIERCE.
Boxiana; or, Sketches of ancient and modern
pugilism, from the days of the renowned
Broughton and Slack to the championship of
Crib. London, 1818–29. 5 v. 4°.
Set in Princeton University Library.

There has been a great deal of bibliographical confusion concerning this well-known set, filled with the
argot of the boxing world. Henry Downes Miles, in the
preface to the first volume of his *Pugilistica*, Edinburgh, 1906, p. xi, comes the closest to settling the
matter. He says: "This very scarce volume [referring
to Boxiana: sketches of antient and modern pugilism.
vol. 1. London: G. Smeeton, 139, St. Martin's Lane,
Charing Cross, July, 1812. 8°.], which was the production of George Smeeton, a well known sporting
printer and engraver, was the basis of the larger work
Boxiana, subsequently written and edited by Pierce
Egan, and of which *five* volumes appeared between
1818 and 1828. The well-written 'Introduction', much
disfigured by the illiterate editor, were incorporated,
and the handsome copperplate title page will be found
bound into the later work published by Sherwoods,
Jones & Co. Pierce Egan was, at one time, a com-
positor in Smeeton's office, and continued the work
for Sherwoods.
"*Boxiana. Sketches of Ancient and Modern Pugilism,
from the days of the renowned Broughton and Slack
to the Championship of Crib.* By Pierce Egan. In
two volumes. London: Sherwood, Neely, and Jones,
Paternoster Row, 1818.
"This was the first complete book. A third volume
followed in 1825. There are *two* fourth volumes owing
to a circumstance which requires explanation. That
published by George Virtue, and bearing the name of
Pierce Egan, has for its title *New Series of Boxiana:
the only Original and Complete Lives of the Boxers.*
By Pierce Egan. London: George Virtue, Ivy Lane,
Paternoster Row. Vol. I, 1828. Vol. II., 1829. These
are generally bound as Vols. IV., and V., in sets of
Boxiana. The other volume, IV., is identical in title,
but not in contents, with Pierce Egan's first volume
of the 'new series', omitting those words. It was
written by John Bee, for Messrs. Sherwoods, who
moved an injunction against Pierce Egan for selling
his fourth volume to another publisher. Lord Chan-
cellor Eldon merely compelled Pierce Egan to prefix
the words 'new series' to his book, and the matter
ended."
Grantley Berkeley in his *My life and recollections*,
v. 1, p. 107–108, says: "His [Egan's] 'Boxiana' was
considered as a text-book on fight and fighting men;
and his description of a 'mill', as prize-fights were
designated, were stuffed full of slang, the delight
of a large circle of male readers."
Henry Downes Miles, in his *Pugilistica*, v. 1,
p. 239, corrects some of Berkeley's misstatements concerning Pierce Egan.
A good account of Egan and his period may be
found in the *Cambridge history of English literature*,
v. 14, p. 212–239, under the chapter "Caricature and
the literature of sport."
A long review of *Boxiana* made up largely of extracts from the work, appeared in *Blackwood's magazine*, London, July, 1819, v. 5, p. 439–443; Aug., 1819,
v. 5, p. 593–597; Sept., 1819, v. 5, p. 663–669; Oct.,
1819, v. 6, p. 66–69; Dec., 1819, v. 6, p. 279–284;
March, 1820, v. 6, p. 609–615; June, 1820, v. 7, p. 294–
306 (a review of Peter Corcoran's *The fancy*); Oct.,
1820, v. 8, p. 60–67; March, 1821, v. 8, p. 671–677
(a letter addressed to Pierce Egan by Christopher
North, in which we learn that the articles on *Boxiana*
in *Blackwood's* were written by "Odoherty" or William
Maginn).
"The sketch of Professor Wilson (by Maclise),
which appeared in *Fraser's magazine* for April, 1831.
is accompanied by a semi-biographical, one-page notice,
by Maginn, in which he speaks of 'Boxiana' being
Wilson's. Elsewhere, in later volumes of *Fraser*
they are attributed to Maginn himself." — Dr. Shelton
Mackenzie, in his memoir of Maginn in v. 5, p. xxxii,
of *The Miscellaneous writings of the late William
Maginn*, New York: Redfield, 1857, *NCG*.
For a background study of the *Fancy* see Eric R.
Watson, *Trial of Thurtell and Hunt...*, Edinburgh:
William Hodge [1920], *SLN*, particularly the intro-
duction, p. 1–50.

An impartial enquiry into the existing doubts
and various reports relative to the late pugilistic
contest between the renowned Dutch Sam and
Nosworthy, at Moulsey Hurst, Dec. 8, 1814...
Dedicated to the sporting world, with great
respect and deference by the editor of Boxiana... London: Printed by and for G. Smee-

Slang and Jargon of Sports, etc., continued

EGAN, PIERCE, *continued*

ton, 17, St. Martin's Lane. Price one shilling [1815]. 29 p. 12°.   * C p.v.640, no.1

Filled with the boxing slang of the period, the flash language of "the Fancy." On the last page is an advertisement of a new series of *Boxiana*, no. 1, to appear Feb. 1, 1815. Price 6d. Egan's name does not appear on the title-page, but it is presumed he wrote the book, although Smeeton himself may have had a hand in it. If, as Henry Downes Miles says, Egan did not bring out the first volume of his *Boxiana* until 1818, it would appear that the above work was Smeeton's, since it is known he edited an 1812 edition of *Boxiana*, which became the basis of Egan's work.

THE FANCY; or, True sportsman's guide: being authentic memoirs of the lives, actions, prowess, and battles of the leading pugilists, from the days of Figg and Broughton, to the championship of Ward. By an operator. London: Published by J. M'Gowan and Son, Great Windmill street, 1826. 2 v. 8°.

Vol. 1 has an extra title-page in color and twenty-six plates, mostly portraits of pugilists. Issued in parts numbered 1–28. No. 1 is dated April 21, 1821; no. 2, May 5, 1821; no. 3–6, 16–19, 21–28 are not dated; no. 7–15, 20, are dated A. D. 1821. 680 p.
Vol. 2 has an extra title-page in color and twenty-five plates, mostly portraits of pugilists. Issued in parts numbered v. 2, no. 1–3, 22–55. The first three are dated A. D. 1822. 743 p.
The above set is owned by the Racquet and Tennis Club, New York.
Each volume is filled with the picturesque slang of pugilists and those who follow that sport. Cf. Jon Bee, Pierce Egan, Thomas Moore, and John Hamilton Reynolds.

GILBERT, JOHN.
Language with a punch. The spread of boxing slang. (T. P.'s and Cassell's weekly. London, Oct. 24, 1925. f°. v. 5, p. 12.)   * DA

Some of the boxing slang derives from the time of Pierce Egan, but most of it is modern, and of American origin. Some of the terms have spread to France and Italy and other countries.

LEXICON fisty-cuff-glutton. (Spirit of the public journals. London, 1813. 12°. v. 16, p. 37–38.)   * DA
A few pugilistic terms known to the "fancy."

LITTELL, ROBERT.
Is zat so? (New republic. New York, April 1, 1925. f°. v. 42, p. 160.)   * DA
Review of play by that name, written by James Gleason and Robert Tater. Mentions the prize fight lingo which runs through the dialogue.

LYNCH, JOHN GILBERT BOHUN.
The prize ring, by Bohun Lynch. Illustrated by reproductions of old prints, several oil paintings, and of the famous Byron screen. London: Country Life, Ltd., 1925. 137 p. col'd front., plates, ports. f°.   † MWI
An historical survey, well illustrated, of the English boxing world of the early nineteenth century. The flash language of the Regency flavors the book. This is the era of Pierce Egan and Jon Bee [Badcock]. There is a flash song "The true bottom'd boxer; or, The champion of fame" included in the book.

McCLINTOCK, THEODORE.
English and American sport terms in German. (American speech. New York, Dec., 1933. 4°. v. 8, p. 42–47.)   RNA
The Germans took over many of our sport terms

intact, particularly those connected with boxing. A list is given.

MILES, HENRY DOWNES.
Pugilistica; the history of British boxing...
v. I [to 1820]. London, 1866. 8°.   MWI
No more published.

Pugilistica; the history of British boxing, containing lives of the most celebrated pugilists; full reports of their battles from contemporary newspapers, with authentic portraits, personal anecdotes, and sketches of the principal patrons of the prize ring, forming a complete history of the ring from Fig and Broughton 1719–40, to the last championship battle between King and Heenan, in December, 1863. Edinburgh: John Grant, 1906. 3 v. illus. pl., ports. 8°.   MWI
Filled with boxing slang.
Miles was editor of *The sportsman's magazine*, etc. He gives a bibliography of boxing in the preface to v. 1, p. x–xiii.
He was the author of the curious novel, *Dick Turpin*, London, 1841, *NCW* (q.v.) said to be a plagiarism of Ainsworth's *Rookwood*. This novel is filled with criminal argot.
There is a good chapter on boxing in William B. Boulton, *The amusements of old London*, London: John C. Nimmo, 1901, p. 71–121, *COB (London)*.

MOORE, THOMAS.
Jack Randall's diary of proceedings at the house of call for genius. Edited by Mr. Breakwindow. To which are added, several of Mr. B's minor pieces. London: Printed for W. Simpkin and R. Marshall, Stationers' Court, Ludgate Hill, 1820. 75 p. 12°.   NDF
The authorship of this poem is not definitely established, but it is in exactly the same style and feeling of Thomas Moore's "Tom Crib's memorial to congress" (q.v.). Jack Randall was a celebrated English pugilist, and this work is filled with pugilistic slang.
Hotten mentions another Randall item entitled *A few selections from his scrapbook, to which are added poems on the late fight for the championship*, 1822, but we have not located a copy.

Tom Crib's memorial to Congress with a preface, notes and appendix. By one of the fancy [Thomas Moore], author of Fudge family, &c., &c... London: Printed, 1819. New York: Reprinted for Kirk and Mercein, C. Wiley and Co., W. E. Gilley, and A. T. Goodrich and Co. William A. Mercein, Printer, 1819. 120 p. 16°.   * KF 1819
Attributed to Thomas Moore, the poet. Thomas Cribb was a noted English pugilist. This poem is filled with pugilistic slang, some of the terms being defined in footnotes. The appendix contains flash songs.
Another copy in *RNM*.
A prototype of Moore's poem, lacking the slang, was Paul Whitehead's *The gymnasiad; or, Boxing match. A very short, but very curious epic poem...*, London, 1744. It gave an account of the fight between Broughton and Stephenson. This edition is in the Huntington Library. The New York Public Library has later editions.

PARKER, DAN.
Lexicon of a fight manager. (New York Daily Mirror. Jan. 7, Jan. 21, 1933.)
Glossary of modern pugilistic slang in America.

Slang and Jargon of Sports, etc., continued

REYNOLDS, JOHN HAMILTON.

The fancy: a selection from the poetical remains of the late Peter Corcoran, of Gray's Inn, student at law [John Hamilton Reynolds]. With a brief memoir of his life... London: Printed for Taylor and Hessey, Fleet street, 1820. xxx, 107 p. 12°. *KL

Lowndes, Hotten, Nodal, Kennedy and others have listed this under the name of Peter Corcoran without further elucidation. Reynolds was Thomas Hood's brother-in-law, and a close friend of Keats. He was a frequent contributor to London magazines. There is a bibliography of Reynolds by George L. Marsh in *University of North Carolina studies in philology*, Chapel Hill, Oct., 1928, v. 25, p. 491–510, *RNA*. See also George L. Marsh, "New data on Keats's friend Reynolds," in *Modern philology*, Chicago, Feb., 1928, v. 25, p. 319–329, *NAA*, and W. B. Gates, "A sporting poet of the Regency," *Sewanee review*, Sewanee, Tenn., Oct., 1927, v. 35, p. 433–447, *DA*.

The fancy is filled with flash slang and the language of the prize ring and may be compared with Thomas Moore's *Tom Crib's memorial to congress*, 1819. The contents: Preface, p. v–xxx, King Tims the First: an American tragedy, p. 1–48, The fields of Tothill: a fragment, p. 49–79, poems, p. 84–107, glossary, p. 109–110.

The fancy was reprinted in 1905 by Elkin Mathews, London, with a prefatory memoir and notes by John Masefield and thirteen illustrations by Jack B. Yeats.

Part of *The fancy* was reprinted in *John Hamilton Reynolds. Poetry and prose. With an introduction and notes by George L. Marsh*, London: Humphrey Milford, 1928. 195 p. 12°, *NCM*.

The 1820 edition was reviewed in *Blackwood's magazine*, June, 1820, v. 7, p. 294–306, *DA; London magazine*, London, July, 1820, v. 2, p. 71; *New monthly magazine*, London, Aug., 1820, v. 14, p. 174–177, *DA;* and E. W. Gosse has a chapter on Reynolds in his *Gossip in a library*, London, 1891, p. 271–281, *NCZ*.

SMEETON, GEORGE.

Boxiana; or, Sketches of ancient and modern pugilism, from the days of the renowned Broughton and Slack to the heroes of the present milling era... London: Printed by and for G. Smeeton, 139, St. Martin's Lane, and sold by Sherwood, Neely, and Jones [etc.], 1812. 484 p. 8°.

Illustrated by George Cruikshank. He did not illustrate the later volumes of *Boxiana*, which were the work of Pierce Egan [q.v.].

THE SPORTING repository... London: Kegan Paul, Trench, Trübner & Co., 1904. 478 p. 4°. MVF

Reprint of the original *Sporting repository* which "ran its course as a magazine in the year 1822, and has long commanded a high price in its complete form on account of the excellence of many of the plates by H. Alken." It contains much sports slang, particularly that of boxing, termed "the fancy." There is also a good account, accompanied by a colored portrait by Dighton, of Richard Vaughan, alias Hell-Fire Dick, the Cambridge coachman, in the Feb. 15, 1822, issue. See note under *Lexicon balatronicum*, by Captain Grose.

In this edition some of the original plates have been omitted and others substituted.

WESEEN, MAURICE HARLEY.

A dictionary of American slang. New York: Thomas Y. Crowell Company [1934]. 543 p. 8°. M.R.R. Desk

"Boxing and prizefighting slang," p. 229–245. Good for modern prizefighting slang as well as the old.

WITWER, HARRY CHARLES.

The leather pushers... New York: Grosset & Dunlap [1921]. 341 p. 12°. 8–NBO

A story of the American prize ring, written in boxing lingo. It was made into a movie. Witwer, Damon Runyon, sports writer, and James Gleason, author of "Is zat so?," the popular play featuring a prize fighter and his manager, were deft at handling the jargon of the prize ring. Boxing slang was introduced by Pierce Egan and his school, and the words he used are still current, but American sports writers have added many picturesque phrases of their own.

Baseball

Baseball slang is an American contribution to sports lingo. The daily newspapers abound with the expressions of the diamond. The historian of baseball will find a rich collection of material in The New York Public Library, thanks to the generous gifts from the private collections of Albert Goodwill Spalding and Bradshaw Swales. The game of baseball is popularly believed to have been founded by Abner Doubleday, at Cooperstown, New York, in 1839. A baseball museum has been formed at Cooperstown in commemoration of this first game of baseball. The student of baseball terminology has a hundred years of baseball history to examine. For the Spalding collection see *Bulletin*, The New York Public Library, Feb., 1922, v. 26, p. 86–127, *HND*, and for the Swales collection, v. 33, p. 653–654. See Robert W. Henderson's article in *The Bulletin*, New York Public Library, April, 1937, v. 41, p. 287–291, tracing the game to England.

CONNERS, R. J.

Baseball makes slang of its own. (The New York Times. June 2, 1929, section 9, p. 2, col. 7.) *A

Over a hundred slang terms common to the sports reporter who describes the big league baseball games.

ENGLISH and baseball. (The Nation. New York, Aug. 21, 1913. 4°. v. 97, p. 161.) *DA

Comments on the attempt of the Chicago *Record Herald* to eliminate slang from the accounts of baseball games. The fans wrote in and clamored to have "baseballese" back again.

HARVARD ties the can to slang. (The New York Times. May 5, 1915, section 5, p. 15.) *A

The school authorities at Harvard objected to the baseball slang used by undergraduates in student publications.

LEE, GRETCHEN.

In sporting parlance. (American speech. Baltimore, April 1, 1926. 4°. v. 1, p. 369–370.)

Baseball lingo. RNA

PARROTT, HAROLD.

Bewildering are slang terms used in talk of baseball players. (Brooklyn Daily Eagle. Aug. 9, 1936.)

A few slang terms are explained.

PERIL of the baseball lingo. (The Literary digest. New York, Sept. 6, 1913. f°. v. 47, p. 379–380.) *DA

The Charleston *News and Courier* supports a movement started in Chicago to improve baseball slang. Grave injury to the language might result from the free use of uncontrolled baseball slang. The Washington *Post* took the opposite view. The Atlanta *Constitution* is for slang reform in this species of colorful reporting.

Slang and Jargon of Sports, etc., continued

POWERS, JIMMY.
Dugout slang. (Daily News. New York, Jan. 12, 1937, p. 42; Jan. 17, 1937, p. 80; Jan. 21, 1937, p. 54; Jan. 31, 1937, p. 80.)
Baseball slang as spoken by the players in the dugout. Powers, in his daily sports column, has contributed a great deal to the files of baseball slang, of which the above are merely samples, rather than a complete rcord.

TAMING the sports slangsters. (Literary digest. New York, April 18, 1931. f°. v. 109, p. 40–41.)   *DA
The sports writers, according to an article in the *New York Evening Post*, by Westbrook Pegler, go out of their way to invent new words. Under no circumstances would they call a hit a hit, or a baseball a baseball. That would be a sure sign of imaginative sterility. Some of the baseball terms are downright silly, and Pegler thinks the sports writer's language could be improved.

WESEEN, MAURICE HARLEY.
A dictionary of American slang. New York: Thomas Y. Crowell Company [1934]. 543 p. 8°.   M.R.R. Desk
"Baseball slang," p. 203–225. A good list.

WITWER, HARRY CHARLES.
There's no base like home... New York: Grosset & Dunlap, 1920. 284 p. 12°.   NBO
Written in the Ring Lardner style. This is the story of a big league baseball player, and is filled with the slang of the diamond.

Cricket

LEWIS, W. J.
The language of cricket with illustrative extracts from the literature of the game. London: Oxford University Press, Humphrey Milford, 1934. 316 p. 12°.   MVFC
A dictionary on historical principles. Includes all the expressions used in cricket. Bibliography, p. 305–310. Reviewed in London *Times literary supplement*, Dec. 13, 1934, p. 894, † *NAA*.

Football

VALK, MELVIN.
Die Entwicklung der deutschen Fussballsprache. (Journal of English and Germanic philology. Urbana, Ill., 1935. 8°. v. 34, p. 567–571.)   RKA
Gives English football terms with German equivalents, p. 569–570.
See also entries under Rose, Howard N., and under Weseen, Maurice Harley, in the sub-section Sports — General.

Golf

ANGEL, ANNE, PSEUD.
Golf gab. (American speech. Baltimore, Sept., 1926. 4°. v. 1, p. 627–633.)   RNA
Traces the etymology of terms used in golf. Golf has a technical jargon of great antiquity.

CAHILL, MARGARET ERSKINE.
A caddy's compendium. (American speech. New York, April, 1937. 4°. v. 12, p. 155–156.)   RNA

HERNDON, CHARLES.
Golf made easier. Los Angeles, Cal.: Parker, Stone & Baird Co. [cop. 1930.] 220 p. 8°. MVFE
"Golf terms defined," p. 185–220.
All of the technical terms of golf are explained, and some of the slang expressions, chiefly American, are included.
See also entries under Rose, Howard N., and under Weseen, Maurice Harley, in the sub-section Sports — General.

GAMBLING

A'BECKETT, GILBERT ABBOTT, AND MARK LEMON.
St. George and the dragon... London: Published at the National Acting Drama Office, 19 Suffolk street, Pall Mall East [etc., n. d.]. 24 p. 12°.   NCO p.v.662, no.7
Contains gambling cant. All of A'Beckett's farces abound in slang.
See Ralph Samuel's "The well-known name of a little known man" in Quarto Club, New York, *Papers*, New York, 1930, 1928/29, p. 42–54, * *KP (Quarto)*.

BARRYMORE, WILLIAM.
The two swindlers; or, There he goes! A farce in one act as represented at Astley's Theatre, Oct. 9, 1820. London: John Dicks, n. d. 13 p. illus. 12°.   NCO p.v.636
Contains flash and gambling slang.

THE COMPLEAT gamester; or, Instructions how to play at billiards, trucks, bowls, and chess. Together with all manner of usual and most gentile games either on cards, or dice. To which is added, The arts and mysteries of riding, racing, archery, and cock-fighting. The second edition. London: Printed for Henry Brome at the gun at the West-end of St. Pauls, 1680. 175 p. 16°.   8–MZ
Thomas Westwood's copy, with his bookplate. Westwood, in a note on the flyleaf, says: "Ascribed to Charles Cotton, in the edition of 1754. It is possible that the 'Epistle to the Reader,' and the chapter entitled, 'Of gambling in general, or an ordinary described,' may have been from Cotton's pen. The rest is a mere compilation."
The chapter "Of gaming in general, or an ordinary described," is certainly in the Cottonian vein, and is filled with canting terms. The cheats of *rooks* are exposed in some detail.
Reprinted in *Games and gamesters of the Restoration* ...*With an introduction by Cyril Hughes Hartmann* ..., London: George Routledge and Sons [1930], p. 1–114, *YFP*. In this same volume is reprinted *Memoirs of the lives, intrigues, and comical adventures of the most famous gamesters and celebrated sharpsters... By Theophilus Lucas, Esq.*, London, printed for Jonas Brown without Temple-bar, and Ferdinando Burleigh in Amen-Corner, 1714. This work contains a few gambling terms.

DUNNE, CHARLES.
Rouge et noir. The Academicians of 1823; or the Greek of the Palais Royal and the clubs of St. James's... By Charles Persius, Esq., Garde Nationale de Paris [Charles Dunne]. London: Lawler and Quick and Stephen Couchman, 1823. 456 p. 12°.
This edition was called in on account of libellous matter and reissued without the offending chapter. Contains much gambling information.

Slang and Jargon of Sports, etc., continued

FAR-WESTERN gamblers. (All the year round. London, Oct. 31, 1868. 8°. v. 20, p. 489–493.)
*DA
Specimens of gambling in the American West. The same author contributed other articles on the Far Westerner in the same volume of *All the year round*.

THE GAMBLERS, a new melodrama in two acts, of peculiar interest, as performed for the 1st and 2d times November 17 & 18, 1823, suppressed by order of the court of King's Bench. Re-performed for the 3d time, Monday, January 12, 1824, at the New Surrey Theatre... Printed by and for John Lowndes, 36, Bow Street, Covent Garden. 22 p. 8°. NCO p.v.224, no.7
Contains a few words of gambling slang.

HARTMANN, CYRIL HUGHES.
...Games and gamesters of the Restoration. The compleat gamester by Charles Cotton, 1674 and Lives of the gamesters by Theophilus Lucas, 1714... London: George Routledge and Sons, Ltd. [1930.] xxx, 281 p. 8°. (The English library, edited by F. Isaacs.) YFP
Cotton's works have been described in the section of this bibliography devoted to cant. In the appendix to Lucas is an explanation of some of the terms of basset, a French game. Very little gambling slang occurs in Lucas.

HECKETHORN, CHARLES WILLIAM.
The gambling world. Anecdotic memories and stories of personal experience in the temples of hazard and speculation. By 'Rouge et Noir' [Charles William Heckethorn]... New York: Dodd, Mead & Co., 1898. viii, 373 p. 8°. YFP
Many gambling terms occur in the pages of this book, and a special glossary of stock exchange terms is given, p. 163–172.

JESSEL, FREDERIC.
A bibliography of works in English on playing cards and gaming. London: Longmans, Green, and Co., 1905. vi, 312 p. 8°. MZMB
1733 separate entries arranged in dictionary form. Entries are full. Includes magazine articles as well as books. Many of the items contain gambling slang.
An earlier bibliography is Norton Townshend Horr's *A bibliography of card-games and of the history of playing-cards*, Cleveland, O.: Ch. Orr, 1892. 79 p. sq. f°, *MZMB*. The Library has three copies, one autographed. Horr has 1348 entries in dictionary form, including items in foreign languages. Especially good for bibliography of whist.

KEATE, JAMES HENRY.
The destruction of Mephisto's greatest web; or, All grafts laid bare... By H. K. James [James Henry Keate]. Salt Lake City, Utah: Published by the Raleigh Publishing Company, 1914. 313 p. 8°. SLE
Has no glossary, but much gambling slang is revealed.

LEXICON balatronicum. A dictionary of buckish slang, university wit, and pickpocket eloquence ... London: C. Chappel, 1811. RNM
Contains much gambling lingo. For full description see Underworld Cant: Eighteenth Century, under entry for Francis Grose.

MATSELL, GEORGE WASHINGTON.
Vocabulum: or, The rogue's lexicon... New York: Published by George W. Matsell & Co.

Proprietors of the National Police Gazette No 3 Tryon Row [1859]. 130 p. 12°. RNM
"Appendix. The gambler's flash," p. 107–118.
The compiler has a copy of Matsell, with identical text and pagination, but it is 16° in format, and has the date 1859 in the imprint. It also lacks the frontispiece (port.).

MATTHEWS, BRANDER.
Poker-talk. (In his: Pen and ink papers on subjects of more or less importance. New York and London: Longmans, Green & Co., 1888. 12°. p. 187–226.) NBQ
Some of the language of poker is traced in this informal essay, and British poker terms are contrasted with American terms.

THE MINOR jockey club; or, A sketch of the manners of the Greeks... Printed for R. Farnham, and sold by the booksellers at Bath, Newmarket, York, and London [179–?]. 98 p. 8°. YFP p.v.2
This rare little work is filled with the cant and flash used by London gamblers. A thinly veiled account of the lives of the better-known gamblers of London is given. Cant expressions are explained.

POLLOCK, ALBIN JAY.
The underworld speaks... San Francisco: Prevent Crime Bureau [1935]. 8°. RNM
Contains much gambling lingo. Pages are unnumbered.

PROSKAUER, JULIEN J.
Suckers all. New York: The Macaulay Company [1934]. 318 p. 12?. AN (Kelly)
Biography of "Honest John" Kelly, written from his diaries and notes. Contains much gambling terminology.

QUINN, JOHN PHILIP.
Fools of fortune, or gambling and gamblers... Chicago: The Anti-gambling Association, 1895. 640 p. illus. port. 4°. YFP
Contains gambling slang. Quinn hoped that his book would "extenuate his twenty-five years of gaming and systematic deception of his fellow-men."

STOCKDALE, JOHN JOSEPH.
The pigeons. Dedicated to all the flats, and showing the artifices, success, and crimes of gaming, gamesters, and gambling houses... Second edition. London, 1817. 8°.
Copy in Huntington Library.

Stock Market

DICE, CHARLES AMOS.
The stock market... New York: McGraw-Hill Book Company, Inc. [1929.] xiv, 667 p. 8°. TG
Appendix. Stock market terminology, p. 635–656.
Includes the slang of Wall Street.
A narrative account of Wall Street written in financial lingo is William Worthington Fowler's *Twenty years of inside life in Wall Street*, New York: Orange Judd Company, 1880. 576 p. 8°, *TG*.

FOWLER, JOHN FRANCIS.
Introduction to Wall Street... New York and London: Harper & Brothers, 1930. 265 p. 8°. TG
"Glossary of terms used in this book," p. 241–257. Chiefly technical, but some financial slang is included.

Slang and Jargon of Sports, etc., continued

FOWLER, WILLIAM WORTHINGTON.
Ten years in Wall Street; or, Revelations of inside life and experiences on 'change... Hartford, Conn.: Worthington, Dustin & Co. [etc.], 1870. 536 p. illus. 8°.   TG
Many terms from the lingo of Wall Street speculators may be found here.

JARGON: talk in Wall Street where bulls feast on melons. (News week. New York, July 4, 1935. 4°. v. 8, p. 33–34.)   *DA
Glossary of stock market lingo.

PRATT, SERENO STANSBURY.
The work of Wall Street... New York: D. Appleton and Co., 1921. 447 p. 12°.   TG
"The language of Wall Street," p. 231–238.
"Definitions of terms," in index, p. 435–437.
The jargon of the financial district of New York. Earlier terms may be found in Hartley Withers, *Stocks and shares*, 1910, p. 357–362, TG.

SMITH, MATTHEW HALE.
Twenty years among the bulls and bears of Wall Street... Hartford: J. B. Burr & Company, 1870. xxii, (1)24–577 p. illus. 8°. TG
"Language of Wall Street," p. 61–74. A few terms defined at length.

STODDARD, WILLIAM LEAVITT.
Financial racketeering and how to stop it. New York and London: Harper & Brothers, 1931. 217 p. 8°.   TG
Glossary, p. 4–5. This is a short list, but one of the best for the argot of the financial racketeer.

WILSON, ALEXANDER JOHNSTONE.
A glossary of colloquial, slang and technical terms in use on the stock exchange and in the money market. Edited by A. J. Wilson. London: Wilsons & Milne, 1895. 210 p. 16°.   TG
British terms, plus a few borrowed from the United States. The definitions are of unusual length. Consequently relatively few terms are listed. There are very few dictionaries of financial jargon. Even Wall Street lacks its lexicographer, although a few attempts have been made to explain the more common expressions.

Money

For lack of a better place in which to classify it, money slang is included here. Most of the slang terms for money were invented by gamblers and criminals, being cant terms originally created for the purpose of concealment and to facilitate the "plucking" of "suckers." Most of the canting dictionaries listed in Part One contain money slang, but there is no need to duplicate the entries. Many stray references to money slang will occur throughout the bibliography. It is impossible to group them all here.

ABRACADABRA, AND OTHERS.
Slang nomenclature of coins. (Notes and queries. London, 1860. 8°. series 2, v. 10, p. 171, 237–238, 295.)   *R–*DA
Origin of old English coin names.

FREY, ALBERT ROMER.
A dictionary of numismatic names. Their official and popular designations. 311 p. (American journal of numismatics. New York, 1916. 4°. v. 50.)   MHA
Includes foreign as well as English terms for money. Popular or slang terms for paper money and coins are given. An excellent historical compendium.

HOTTEN, JOHN CAMDEN.
A dictionary of modern slang, cant, and vulgar words... By a London antiquary [John Camden Hotten]... Second edition... London: John Camden Hotten, 1860. 290 p. 12°.   RNM
Money slang, p. 79–82. See other editions of Hotten.

JOHN O' LONDON, PSEUD. *See* WHITTEN, WILFRED, AND OTHERS.

MENMUIR, CHARLES, AND OTHERS.
Bank note slang. (Notes and queries. London, Dec., 1919, Feb., April, 1920. 8°. series 12, v. 5, p. 309–310; v. 6, p. 51–52, 159.) *R–*DA
English money slang. Some old terms are traced.

[MONEY slang.] (Town talk. London, Aug. 8, 1859. 4°. p. 207.)
Copy in Library of Congress.
A Hiawathian jingle containing the following money terms: mopus, pewter, shiner, brad, dough, spoons, ready, rowdy, stumpy, cash, rhino, tin, dibs, browns, chip, dust, chinkers, dimes, horse-nails, brass, needful, spoondolix, buttons, rocks, mint-drops, lumps, lucre, gelt, heavy, sweet pecuniary, hard, root of every evil, circulating mediums, mammon.

OWEN, DOUGLAS, AND OTHERS.
[American coin names.] (Notes and queries. London, 1906–07. 8°. series 10, v. 6, p. 381; v. 7, p. 36, 136–137, 154–155.)   *R–*DA
American money terms, especially those familiar to Californians.

POLLOCK, ALBIN JAY.
The underworld speaks... San Francisco: Prevent Crime Bureau [1935]. 8°.   RNM
"Banking, money, checks, securities," 5 unnumbered pages.
"Counterfeiting," 2 unnumbered pages.

PRENNER, MANUEL.
Slang terms for money. (American speech. Baltimore, June, 1929. 4°. v. 4, p. 357–358.)   RNA
American expressions for coins and bank notes.

TOWNSEND, MALCOLM.
Money slang. (In his: U. S. An index to the United States of America. Boston: D. Lothrop, 1890. 8°. p. 426–427.)   IAG
One hundred and sixty-six slang expressions for United States currency. No definitions.

WALLIS, H. W.
Slang names for coins. (Notes and queries. London, Sept. 23, 1893. 8°. series 8, v. 4, p. 248–249.)   *R–*DA
Commentary on Hotten's vulgar names of coins. W. C. Richardson and S. J. Adair Fitz-Gerald reply in the Jan. 27, 1894, issue, series 8, v. 5, p. 76.

WESEEN, MAURICE HARLEY.
A dictionary of American slang... New York: Thomas Y. Crowell Company [1934]. 543 p. 8°.   M.R.R. Desk
"Money slang," p. 294–300.

WHITTEN, WILFRED, AND OTHERS.
The riff-raff of speech. By John o' London [pseud.] and others. (T. P.'s weekly. London, 1905. f°. v. 5, Feb. 3, p. 136; Feb. 10, p. 188; Feb. 17, p. 220; March 3, p. 284; March 24, p. 380.)   *DA
Modern London money slang, with a few older terms recalled by correspondents.

Slang and Jargon of Sports, etc., continued

THE STAGE

A., G. L.
Theatrical slang. (The Graphic. London, April 10, 1886. f°. v. 33, p. 399.) *DA
    English theatrical slang, old and new, chiefly Elizabethan and Victorian.

AMEND, OTTILIE.
Theatrical lingo. (American speech. Baltimore, Oct., 1927. 4°. v. 3, p. 21–23.) RNA
    Stage slang, with a paragraph on the origin of the word "up stage."

ARNOLD, JOSEPH.
Show talk and stage slang. (Theatre magazine. New York, June, 1929. f°. v. 49, p. 33, 64.) † NBLA
    Current words "in colloquial use on Broadway." Contains about one hundred words and phrases.

BENCHLEY, ROBERT CHARLES.
The king's English: not murder but suicide. (The Bookman. New York, 1929. 8°. v. 70, p. 387–390.) *DA
    British criticism of American pronunciation as heard in the talking pictures is met with a counter attack purporting to demonstrate the even worse effects produced by visiting English actors.

BETTS, EDWARD W.
A dictionary of stage terms. (In: Harold Downs, editor, Theatre and stage, a modern guide to the performance of all classes of amateur dramatic, operatic, and theatrical work. London: Sir I. Pitman & Sons, Ltd., 1934. 8°. v. 1, p. 91–104.) MZB
    This list, compiled by the assistant editor of *The Era*, contains besides technical expressions, many slang words familiar to the London stage folk.

CARTMELL, VAN H.
A handbook for the amateur actor... New York: Doubleday, Doran & Co., Inc., 1936. xiv, 203 p. illus. 8°. MZB
    "A glossary of stage terms and parlance," p. 85–98.

DE WITT, MARGUERITE E.
Stage versus screen. (American speech. Baltimore, Jan., 1927. 4°. v. 2, p. 165–181.) RNA
    Traces the oral influence of the stage. The stage became the guide to good speech, and actors were instructed in the art of proper speech. The printed word on the screen was not always so meticulous. Perhaps the "talkies" will revive the earlier stage tradition in this matter.

EDWARDS, JAMES CARTER.
Good old "Stock." (Era almanack. London, 1894. 8°. p. 87–91.) NCOA
    Contains theatre slang. Another article in the same magazine, 1878, p. 55–56, by Edward Spencer, entitled "Squaring the press," also contains a few slang terms. All the issues of the *Era almanack* contain theatrical lingo. Such slang experts as Henry J. Byron, George R. Sims, E. L. Blanchard, and G. Edwards, were frequent contributors. The Edward Spencer mentioned above may be the Edward Spencer Mott who wrote *Cakes and ale* and *The flowing bowl*, under the pseudonym of Edward Spencer, *Nathaniel Gubbins*.

EGAN, PIERCE.
The show folks! ...Embellished with nine designs on wood, by the late Mr. Theodore Lane, and engraved by Mr. John Thompson. To which is added, a biographical sketch of the life of Mr. Theodore Lane. Dedicated to the president of the Royal Academy, Sir Martin Archer Shee, Knt. London: Printed for M.

Arnold, Tavistock street, Covent Garden; and Simpkin and Marshall, Stationers' court, 1831. 59 p. illus. 24°. NCM
    Filled with Regency slang, flash, and theatrical lingo. The life of Theodore Lane is written in slangy vein. Egan also wrote *The life of an actor*, London: C. S. Arnold, 1825, which has some theatre slang in it. The Library has two reprints of this: the Methuen edition, London, 1904, 12°, *NCW*, and the John Dicks edition, London, n. d., 8°, *NCE p.v.13, no.4.*

ENGLISH show slang. (The Billboard. Cincinnati, Dec. 18, 1915. f°. v. 27, p. 193.) † MZA
    This selection was compiled by one Massey, known as the tattooed man. Includes the definition of "Johnny Audley," which means "a signal for the abbreviation or conclusion of a performance. 'John Audley' was originated by Shuter, a comedian, who performed at the famous Richardson Show, at the old Bartholomew Fair, London."

GABLE, J. HARRIS.
American stage-hand language. (American speech. Baltimore, Oct., 1928. 4°. v. 4, p. 67–70.) RNA
    Gives common stage terms. "Perhaps they deserve to be called slang, as they are abbreviations or catchwords; yet they constitute a well-known and much-used vocabulary that does not vary the country over."

GREEN, HELEN.
At the actors' boarding house, and other stories... New York: The Nevada Publishing Co., 1906. 380 p. 8°. NBO
    These stories of stage folk in New York appeared originally in the New York *Morning Telegraph*, in 1905. They abound in stage slang as well as the Newyorkese of the period.

The Maison de Shine. More stories of the actors' boarding house... New York: B. W. Dodge & Co., 1908. 298 p. 12°. NBO
    The slang of Broadway fills the pages of this book.

HERTZMAN, CHARLES L.
Idioms of the stage. (The Green book album. Chicago, Dec., 1909. 8°. v. 2, p. 1223–1227.) NAFA
    "There is an accepted term for every article on the stage. Each piece of scenery is designated by some peculiar name, and every member of the stage crew is known by some queer sounding title. The same applies to every implement used on a stage and to every conceivable condition peculiar to theatrical life." Many of these are defined, along with some circus slang and some vaudeville slang.

JENNINGS, HERBERT.
The actor's craft... London: Simpkin Marshall, Ltd. [1930.] 258 p. 8°. MWEQ
    Glossary, p. 243–258. Not a slang glossary, but technical terms of great antiquity.

KINGSLEY, WALTER J., AND LONEY HASKELL.
A stageland dictionary. (New York Times. Oct. 14, 1923, section 8, p. 4, col. 1.) *A
    The backstage lingo of the actors and stage hands.

MATTHEWS, BRANDER.
The vocabulary of the show-business. (In his: The principles of playmaking... New York: Charles Scribner's Sons, 1919. 12°. p. 251–264.) NAFD
    Stage talk is a special technical vocabulary and is not to be considered as slang, except in a few instances. Few of the stage expressions find their way into the dictionaries. This fairly large list of stage words has been added to considerably in recent years by other writers, but for a long time it was one of the few readily available reference tools on the subject of theatrical jargon.
    Printed originally in *The Billboard*, Cincinnati, Dec. 22, 1917, v. 29, p. 8–9, † *MZA.*

Slang and Jargon of Sports, etc., continued

MOSS, ARNOLD.
Jewels from a box office. The language of show business. (American speech. New York, Oct., 1936. 4°. v. 11, p. 219–222.)   RNA
New York theatre slang, chiefly that used by producers of plays.

MOTHERWELL, HIRAM.
The language of lobster alley. (The Bookman. New York, Dec., 1930. 4°. v. 72, p. 396–399.)   *DA
Lobster Alley is the theatrical section of New York. Its language is due in part to the theatrical newspaper *Variety* and its slangy editor, Sime Silverman. Excerpts from *Variety* reveal the crisp and exact language Silverman always demanded of his staff. "Silverman, I think, will go down in newspaper history, like Dana of the *Sun*, for his permanent influence on our language and the use of it."

ROSE, HOWARD N.
A thesaurus of slang... New York: The Macmillan Company, 1934. 120 p. 8°.   RNM
"Theatre slang," p. 82–88; "Cinema slang," p. 88–93; "Circus and carnival slang," p. 94–103; "Chautauqua slang," p. 103–105.
All of the above are listed under the general heading of "Theatre slang," instead of "Slang of the amusement world" which would have been a happier generalization.

SOBEL, BERNARD.
The language of the theatre. (The Bookman. New York, April, 1929. 8°. v. 69, p. 148–151.)   *DA
"...Modern American stage slang is not nearly so extensive as might be expected." Mentions a few stock slang phrases still in vogue. Credits Jack Conway, George Ade, and Walter Winchell with popularizing slang in America.
Excerpts from this article appeared in *Writer's monthly*, Springfield, Mass., Jan., 1930, v. 35, p. 37–39, which in turn had copied them from the *Literary digest*.

THEATRICAL slang. (The Family herald. London, July 3, 1886. 4°. v. 57, p. 159.)   *DA
Excerpts from an article in the *St. James Gazette*, giving London stage slang.

TRAUBE, SHEPARD.
So you want to go into the theatre? A "manual"... Foreword by Barrett H. Clark. Boston: Little, Brown, and Company, 1936. 258 p. 12°.   MWED
"Broadway glossary," p. 243–247. The modern jargon of the New York stage folk.

WESEEN, MAURICE HARLEY.
A dictionary of American slang... New York: Thomas Y. Crowell Company [1934]. 543 p. 8°.   M.R.R. Desk
"Theatre slang," p. 135–156.

WILSTACH, FRANK JENNERS.
A stage dictionary. (New York Times. Sept. 9, 1923, section 8, p. 2, col. 1.)   *A
Useful glossary of modern Broadway argot. Definitions are brief. Wilstach collected his slang from the actors and stagehands themselves. He had a wide acquaintance among the accredited slangsters of the moving picture, theatre, and newspaper circles.

WINCHELL, WALTER.
A primer of Broadway slang. (Vanity fair. New York, Nov., 1927. f°. v. 29, p. 67, 132, 134.)   *DA
"Broadway is the slang capital of the world... Perhaps, *Variety*, known as the Bible of the theatrical profession, is responsible for most of the show business slang... Jack Conway (until his death the most prolific slangster of *Variety*)...is conceded to be the ace 'slanguage' hurler in the world." Winchell claims that Walter Kingsley popularized the word "jazz."
See John F. DeVine's article on Walter Winchell in the *Writer's digest*, Cincinnati, April, 1930, v. 10, p. 19–21, 56, 66, *IH.
Reprinted in part in New York *Daily Mirror*, May 23, 1936, p. 10.

Vaudeville

THE ARGOT of vaudeville. (New York Times. Dec. 16, 1917, section 4, p. 7, col. 5; Dec. 23, section 4, p. 6, col. 1.)   *A
Excellent articles containing vaudeville slang of the World War period. (Incidentally, not listed in *New York Times Index!*)

CONWAY, JACK.
Why I write slang. (Variety. New York, Dec. 29, 1926. f°. v. 85, p. 5, 7.)   NAFA
Conway was considered to be the most versatile creator of slang on Broadway. He wrote for *Variety*. He died in Bermuda, Oct. 2, 1928. An obituary may be found on p. 11 of the Oct. 10, 1928, issue of *Variety*. See the editorial on Conway in the *New York Times*, Oct. 5, 1928, p. 24, col. 5. Also Walter Winchell's article, "A primer of Broadway slang," in *Vanity fair*, New York, Nov., 1927, v. 29, p. 67, *DA. Reprinted in v. 92, p. 10.

LEE, GRETCHEN.
Trouper talk. (American speech. Baltimore, Oct., 1925. 4°. v. 1, p. 36–37.)   RNA
The talk of the vaudeville travellers is little known outside the profession.

SILVERMAN, SIME, 1873–1933, editor of *Variety*.
Sime Silverman started the magazine *Variety* in 1905. He soon began to write of Broadway in the slang of the day, and invented many slang expressions himself. His assistant, Jack Conway, became the most gifted coiner of slang terms in New York. As Walter Prichard Eaton said, "*Variety* became, and remained, a place where philologists could study the popular language in evolution." See Eaton's biography of Silverman in *The Dictionary of American biography*, v. 17, p. 169–170.
There is a long obituary of Silverman in *Variety*, Sept. 26, 1933, p. 1, 50–51, *NAFA*. In the same issue appear memorial articles by Epes W. Sargent and Jack Lait. See also the articles in the *New York Herald Tribune*, Sept. 25, 1933, editorial page, and the *New York Times*, Sept. 23, 1933, p. 15. See also Hiram Motherwell, "The language of lobster alley," in *Bookman*, New York, Dec., 1930, v. 72, p. 396–399, *DA*; and also Allene Talmey, "Broadway's Bible — *Variety*," in *The Stage*, New York, March, 1935, p. 35–36, *NAFA*.

[VAUDEVILLE slang.] (New York Times. Oct. 7, 1923, section 9, p. 2, col. 1.)   *A
Review of *Vaudeville dictionary*, by W. J. Kingsley, a Broadway press agent. Kingsley also contributed to *Broadway anthology*, New York: Duffield & Company, 1917. 60 p. 12°, *NBH*.

WHITE, PERCY W.
Stage terms. (American speech. Baltimore, May, 1926. 4°. v. 1, p. 436–437.)   RNA
Vaudeville glossary. The word "hokum" is treated at length.

Slang and Jargon of Sports, etc., continued

MOTION PICTURES

ACADEMY OF MOTION PICTURE ARTS AND SCIENCES. Recording sound for motion pictures. Edited by Lester Cowan... New York: McGraw-Hill Book Company, 1931. xv, 404 p. 8°.   MFLC

"A glossary of motion-picture terms," p. 355–392. Includes jargon and slang.

ALLVINE, GLENDON.
Studio lingo. (In: Roger Whately and others, The silver streak...by Roger Whately, Jack O'Donnell and H. W. Hanemann... Los Angeles: Haskell-Travers, 1935. 8°. p. 241–268.) MFLK

A glossary of movie slang, "science and wisecracks unite in unholy wedlock to produce a strange language heard only in darkest Hollywood." A list of censorable words which producers have learned by experience will not be tolerated on the screen, may be found on p. 244–245.

BARNUM, MERRITT H.
Cinema slang. (Writer's digest. Cincinnati, Dec., 1931. 8°. v. 12, p. 32–33.)   * IH

Studio slang of Hollywood, "picturesque because it is born of a business that is a strange combination of art, science, and ballyhoo."

THE BEST moving pictures of 1922–23... Edited by Robert E. Sherwood... Boston: Small, Maynard & Company [1923]. 346 p. 12°. MFLA

"The movie vocabulary," p. 340–346.

BRUNEL, ADRIAN.
Filmcraft. The art of picture production. London: George Newnes, Ltd. [1933.] x, 238 p. 12°. (The filmcraft series.)   MFL

"Abbreviated glossary," p. 153–168. These are terms in use in the British film industry, and although technical include some slang.

EARLY, DUDLEY.
Hollywood has a word for it. (The Family circle. New York, May 28, 1937. 4°. v. 10, p. 14–15.)

Sixty-one movie terms defined.

FLOHERTY, JOHN J.
Moviemakers. New York: Doubleday, Doran & Company, Inc., 1935. 100 p. 4°.   MFL
Movie slang, p. 90–95.

GREGORY, CARL LOUIS.
Motion picture photography. Second edition. Edited by Herbert C. McKay...Director, New York Institute of Photography. New York: Falk Publishing Co., Inc. [1927.] 435 p. 8°.   * R–MFL

"Glossary," p. 404–422.

How the "movies" corrupt the English language. (The Literary digest. New York, July 19, 1913. f°. v. 47, p. 97–98.)   * DA

Comments on W. G. Faulkner's article in the London *Daily Mail* which held the movies responsible for the insidious growth of Americanisms in England. It creates mental indiscipline and corrupts advertising.

JESCO, JOHN, JR.
The movie dictionary. 1925?   MFL

Seventeen typewritten sheets, given to the Library in the Frank J. Wilstach collection. Bound with this is *A movie dictionary*, by Harry Carr, which appeared in *The Classic*, March, 1925.

KERST, WALTER D.
Glossary of movie terms. (A dictionary for beginning amateurs.) (Movie makers. New York, Oct., 1928, p. 660; Nov., 1928, v. 3, p. 726.)   † MFLA

About 100 technical terms are defined. They are familiar to the studio technicians, but not to the general public.

KNOX, EDMUND GEORGE VALPY.
Cinema English. (The Living age. New York, April, 1930. 8°. v. 338, p. 187–189.) * DA

Reprinted from the London *Sunday Times*. Gives some startling examples of cinemese, or "lingua calefornica" as exhibited in the sub-titles of American movies.

LANE, TAMAR.
The new technique of screen writing... New York: Whittlesey House [cop. 1936]. 8°.   MFLF

"Dictionary of studio terms," p. 111–125. Contains Hollywood studio jargon.

PARRY, ALBERT.
Movie talk. (American speech. Baltimore, June, 1928. 4°. v. 3, p. 364–368.)   RNA

"Movie talk is the youngest of all the American lingoes... Besides its youth, another outstanding feature of the movie talk is its genuine American character." Gives the more common expressions used by directors, photographers, stars, extras, and other movie folk.

PATTERSON, FRANCES TAYLOR.
Scenario and screen... New York: Harcourt, Brace and Company [1928]. 232 p. 12°.

"Diction on the lot," p. 211–224.   MFLF
Includes a few slang expressions used by American movie technicians on "location."

PHILLIPS, HENRY ALBERT.
Photodrama... Larchmont, N. Y.: The Stanhope-Dodge Publishing Company [cop. 1914]. xxv, (1)28–221 p. 16°.

Copy in the Library of Congress. Has a vocabulary of early movie terms.

RAMSAYE, TERRY.
Movie jargon. (American speech. Baltimore, April, 1926. 4°. v. 1, p. 357–362.)   RNA

Dates the use of the words *movie, cinema, film, photoplay*, etc. Gives a brief history of the movies.

ROSE, HOWARD N.
A thesaurus of slang... New York: The Macmillan Company, 1934. 120 p. 8°.   RNM
"Cinema," p. 88–93.

[SLANG.] (Film daily. New York, August 22, 1929. f°. v. 49, p. 15.)   † MFLA

Forty-seven words from prison slang for the use of movie producers in making crime pictures.

SOUND picture slang. (Bell laboratories record. New York, April, 1930. 4°. v. 8, p. 363.) TTA

A few of the more graphic expressions heard round the sound studio.

Slang and Jargon of Sports, etc., continued

TALKIE language. (The Writer's monthly. Springfield, Mass., March, 1931. 8°. v. 37, p. 159.)   * IH

"The Academy of Motion Picture Arts and Sciences ...has through its technical bureau issued a glossary for the motion picture technician."
Glossary is reprinted from the *Springfield Union.*

U's slang glossary for British parts in talkers. (Variety. New York, Nov. 20, 1929. f°. v. 97, p. 4.)   † NAFA

Universal Pictures prepared a glossary of English and British slang for use in their London office. A few excerpts are given.

WEINBERG, MAXWELL.
Crix nix hix pix. (Cue. New York, Aug. 1, 1936. 8°. v. 4, p. 6–7, 30–31.)   NBLA

Movie jargon, drawn chiefly from the current files of *Variety.*

WILSTACH, FRANK JENNERS.
A glossary of motion picture terms. (Congressional digest. Washington, Nov., 1928. f°. v. 7, p. 316–317, 321.)   † SEA

Defines about 200 slang terms of the movie studio and its adjuncts.

Scrapbook of movie slang. f°. † MFL n.c.157

This scrapbook was presented to The New York Public Library as a part of the Wilstach collection. It contains numerous clippings from newspapers and magazines, mostly glossaries of slang. The scrapbook also contains many of Wilstach's articles on slang, either magazine clippings, or typewritten sheets. The period covered is 1927–1930.

The slang of the audible picture. 12 typewritten pages of ms. given to the Library by the author. About three hundred technical terms associated with the production of "talkies."

Printed in *The New York Times* under title: "Sound studio slang," Oct. 13, 1929, section 9, p. 8, col. 5, and Oct. 20, 1929, section 9, p. 8, col. 5, * A.

Slang of film men. (New York Times. March 11, 1928, section 8, p. 6, col. 1.)   * A

Short dictionary by a movie press agent; some of it technical.

Speaking the motion picture's language. (The Motion picture. New York, 1928–29. 8°. v. 4, no. 12, p. 6; v. 5, no. 1, p. 2; v. 5, no. 2, p. 6; v. 5, no. 3, p. 6.)   MFLA

Based on the original list which appeared in the *New York Times.*

RADIO

BENTLEY, JULIAN T.
The fifth estate vocabulary. (American speech. New York, April, 1937. 4°. v. 12, p. 100–101.)   RNA

Radio expressions, compiled by one connected with station WLS, in Chicago.

COLE, HILDA.
Radio slang. (Radioland. New York, March, 1935. v. 4, p. 70.)

Copy in Library of National Broadcasting Company. There is also a short article on radio slang in *Sound waves,* Hollywood, California, Jan. 1, 1930, which the compiler has not seen.

FRY, MACON.
Ham lingo. (American speech. Baltimore, Oct., 1929. 4°. v. 5, p. 45–49.)   RNA

"The language of the radio amateur is the quintessence of all that is craft slang." Glossary is appended.

HOGAN, JOHN VINCENT LAWLESS.
The outline of radio... Boston: Little, Brown, and Company, 1924. xviii, 256 p. illus. 12°. (The useful knowledge books, ed. by G. S. Bryan.)   TTF

Contains a glossary, p. 221–237.

IRWIN, JOHN R., AND ARTHUR NILSON.
Radio up to the minute... New York: E. J. Clode, Inc. [cop. 1926.] x p., 1 l., 402 p. 12°. TTF

Definitions, p. 305–336.

LEWIS, LEONARD.
Radio dictionary. (Printer's ink. New York, 1937. 4°. v. 34, April, p. 49, 54; May, p. 39–40, 42, 45.)   TWA

A good list of studio jargon, with short definitions. Includes a few "swing" terms.

LOWELL, MAURICE.
Listen in. An American manual of radio... New York: Dodge Publishing Company [1937]. 114 p. 12°.   TTT

"Glossary of radio terms," p. 1–14. Contains such examples of studio jargon as "fluff," "in the mud," "drooling," "on the nose," and "delight box."

REID, LOUISE.
Radio bandmen speak a strange language at their labors. (New York American. June 22, 1935.)   * A

Studio jargon.

UNITED STATES. — Office of Education. Educational radio project. Radio glossary: a wordbook of terms used in the production of radio programs; prepared by Maurice Lowell. Washington, D. C., 1936. 10 p.

WESEEN, MAURICE HARLEY.
A dictionary of American slang... New York: Thomas Y. Crowell Company [1934]. 543 p. 8°.   M.R.R. Desk

"Radio slang," p. 165–172.

WEST, ROBERT.
So-o-o-o you're going on the air!... New York: Rodin Publishing Company, Inc., 1934. 215 p. 8°.   TTF

"The radio speech primer," p. 171–201.
Does not contain slang, but shows how the speech requirements of the studios all but bans the use of underworld argot.
Very little has been written on the slang of the broadcasting studio. Most of the glossaries are purely technical, such as *Drake's Radio cyclopedia...*, Chicago: Frederick J. Drake & Co. [1927], TTF.

WILLETS, GILSON V.
Radio nomenclature. (Writer's monthly. Springfield, Mass., Sept., 1928. 8°. v. 32, p. 224–227.)   * 1H

"An authoritative and up-to-the-minute explanatory lexicon of technical and slang terms used in radio," according to the sub-title.

Slang and Jargon of Sports, etc., continued

JAZZ ORCHESTRAS

The jazz orchestra has developed a vocabulary of its own, and the colorful technical jargon is as well known in Paris and London as in New York. What is slang itself but the jazz of language? Jazz music started in New Orleans at the turn of the century, but in a few years it swept the world. It has an interesting history, and the word *jazz* itself has caused no end of controversy. It is claimed that Lafcadio Hearn used the word circa 1880, but the compiler has not been able to document this. Without going into the various arguments it will suffice merely to mention some of the references which deal with the word's disputed origin. See: Henry O. Osgood's *So this is jazz*, Boston: Little, Brown, 1926, * *MF*; also the same author's article "Jazz," *American speech*, Baltimore, 1926, v. 1, p. 513–518, *RNA; Vanity fair*, New York, Nov., 1927, p. 132, † *VSM*; "Where the word jazz started," *Music trade review*, New York, May 3, 1919, v. 68, p. 50, * *MA*; "Jazz origin again discovered," *Music trade review*, June 14, 1919, p. 32–33, * *MA*; J. A. Rogers, "Jazz at home," in *The new negro... edited by Alain Locke...* New York: Albert and Charles Boni, 1925, p. 216–224, *IEC*; "A negro explains jazz," *Literary digest*, New York, April 26, 1919, v. 61, p. 28–29, * *DA; The Etude*, Philadelphia, August, 1924, v. 42, p. 515–528; Sept., 1924, p. 593–596, * *MA* (this is a symposium dedicated to the subject of jazz).

See also the notes under the following entries.

ARMSTRONG, LOUIS.

Swing that music... London: Longmans, Green and Co., 1936. 136 p. illus. front. (port.) 8°.   * MF

"Glossary of swing terms," p. 135–136.

This is a biography of Louis Armstrong, the Negro swing artist. He gives the history of the "Dixieland Five," the original jazz orchestra, of New Orleans. It was led by Nick LaRocca, who organized it in 1909. He took the orchestra to New York in 1916 and jazz music swept the world. Jazz went from New Orleans to Saint Paul, via the Mississippi showboats. From there it went to Chicago, San Francisco, and New York.

Jazz started in New Orleans, but the "Blues" started in Memphis. W. C. Handy popularized the singing of "blues" with his song, "Mr. Crump," which was later changed to "Memphis Blues." For this story see George W. Lee, *Beale street. Where the blues began*, New York: Robert O. Ballou [1934], 296 p., *IEC*.

CHAPMAN, JOHN.

[Jazz orchestra slang.] (New York Daily News. Oct. 21, 1935.)

Glossary compiled by Lou Frankel and printed in Chapman's daily column "Mainly about Manhattan." Jazz orchestra leaders are called "hot men" and their bands "jam band." The slang names for the instruments and the players are given.

CONS, CARL.

Jargon of jazz. (American mercury. New York, May, 1936. 8°. v. 38, supplement, p. x.)   * DA

The "slanguage" of swing-terms the "cats" use. (Down beat. Chicago, Nov., 1935. f°. v. 2, p. 1, 8.)

The slang of the jazz orchestra which goes in for "hot" jazz. 103 terms are defined. This magazine confines its columns exclusively to "hot" jazz and swing artists. Swing is defined in the *New York World-Telegram*, Dec. 28, 1935, p. 1, and the history of "hot" jazz is outlined. It has been the subject of serious study in France since 1920, and two or three books have been written about it. Periodicals on the subject are also mentioned in the *World-Telegram* article.

EGG, BERNHARD.

Jazz-Fremdwörterbuch. Leipzig: W. Ehrler & Co., Music-Verlag, 1927. 47 p. 24°.   * MG p.v.12, no.1

A dictionary of jazz terms, chiefly American, with their German equivalents.

GOLDBERG, ISAAC.

Tin Pan Alley. A chronicle of the American popular music racket. New York: John Day Company, 1930. 341 p. 8°.   * MF

Contains some of the slang of Tin Pan Alley. The origin of the word jazz is gone into, p. 268–271.

HART, JAMES D.

Jazz jargon. (American speech. New York, April, 1932. 4°. v. 7, p. 241–254.)   RNA

Popular song writers do not hesitate to take liberties with the English language. Several Tin-Pan Alley coinages are listed, and much attention is given to the songs known as "blues." Jazz music is analyzed in detail. Radio crooners propagate jazz jargon.

HARVEY, HOLMAN.

It's swing! With glossary of swing terms. (Delineator. New York, Nov., 1936. f°. v. 129, p. 10–11, 48–49.)   †VSA

Reprinted in *Readers digest*, Pleasantville, N. Y., Jan., 1937, v. 30, p. 99–102, * *DA*.

MARKS, EDWARD BENNET.

They all sang, from Tony Pastor to Rudy Vallee, as told to Abbot J. Liebling by Edward B. Marks. New York: Viking Press, 1934. 321 p. 8°.   * MF

The student of slang who wishes to cull words from popular songs will find in the list of songs, p. 223–269, a rich field for investigation. Old variety and vaudeville stars are listed, along with famous minstrels, the restaurants, saloons, dives, dance halls, hotels, and other centers of high and low life in New York.

MILA, MASSIMO.

Jazz hot. (Pan. Milano, 1935. 8°. v. 4, p. 84–96.)   * DO

Excellent article on jazz from the viewpoint of an Italian writer. All the current tendencies of jazz are reviewed, including swing music. A number of English slang terms occur in the article. Includes portraits.

NICHOLS, E. J., AND W. L. WERNER.

Hot jazz jargon. (Vanity fair. New York, Nov., 1935. f°. v. 45, p. 38, 71.)   †VSM

Differentiates between straight jazz and hot jazz. The terms used by members of the hot jazz orchestras are given. The noted French work on the subject *Le jazz hot*, by Hugues Pannassié, Paris: Éditions R. A. Corréa, 1934, 432 p., 8°, * *MF*, is mentioned. This book was translated by Lyle and Eleanor Dowling, under the title, *Hot jazz. The guide to swing music* ... New York: M. Witmark & Sons [1936], 363 p. 8°, * *MF*. Cf. Robert Goffin's *Aux frontières du jazz*, Paris: Kra, 1932, 256 p. 12°, * *MF*. The French have made a more serious study of jazz than the Americans.

NYE, RUSSEL.

A musician's word list. (American speech. New York, Feb., 1937. 4°. v. 12, p. 45–48.)   RNA

Special vocabulary of the American dance orchestra.

OSGOOD, HENRY OSBORNE.

So this is jazz. Boston: Little, Brown, and Company, 1926. 258 p. illus. 8°.   * MF

A good survey of American jazz music and its origins. The origin of the word jazz itself is discussed, p. 9–19, and the first jazz orchestras are traced, p. 28–41.

See Osgood's article entitled "Jazz" in *American speech*, Baltimore, 1926, v. 1, p. 513–518, *RNA*.

Slang and Jargon of Sports, etc., continued

SPAETH, SIGMUND GOTTFRIED.
Onward and upward with the arts. (The New Yorker. New York, Nov. 3, 1934. 4°. v. 10, p. 89–94.) * DA
The language of the popular song hits is dissected. We meet such expressions as *boop-boop-a-doop, scat-singing, hot-cha* and *corny.*

STEIG, HENRY ANTON.
Alligators' idol. (The New Yorker. New York, April 17, 1937. 4°. p. 31–34, 36, 38.) * DA
Biographical sketch of the swing orchestra leader, Benny Goodman. Defines many swing terms.

WEBB, H. BROOK.
The slang of jazz. (American speech. New York, Oct., 1937. 4°. v. 12, p. 179–184.) RNA
Short history of jazz, with glossary.

CHAUTAUQUA

ROSE, HOWARD N.
A thesaurus of slang... New York: The Macmillan Company, 1934. 120 p. 8°. RNM
"Chautauqua," p. 103–105.

SCHULTZ, JOHN RICHIE.
Chautauqua talk. (American speech. Baltimore, August, 1932. 4°. v. 7, p. 405–411.) RNA

CIRCUS AND CARNIVAL

For authorities on the circus and collectors of circus books see *Holden's Private book collectors in the United States and Canada, 8th rev. ed.,* New York: R. R. Bowker Co., 1936, p. 140.

BIRSS, JOHN H.
Additional circus expressions. (American speech. New York, April, 1932. 4°. v. 7, p. 316–317.) RNA
A list reprinted from the article "The land of sawdust and spangles" in the *National geographic magazine,* New York, Oct., 1931, p. 463, *KAA.*

BRAATHEN, SVERRE O.
Circus slang. [Photostat copy of a letter dated March 11, 1937, addressed to the compiler. 7 p.] Theatre Collection
Glossary contains one hundred circus expressions. Sverre O. Braathen claims to have the world's foremost circus room at Lake Waubesa, Madison, Wisconsin. His collection includes all the programs issued by the Ringling show, most of that show's route books, etc. He also has books, prints, posters, scrapbooks, curios, miniature circus models, autographs, and other historical matter, American and foreign.

C. G. LELAND collection. vol. 10. Circus slang from one of Hengler's men. (British Museum. Catalogue of additions to the manuscripts, 1916–1920. London, 1933. 4°. p. 45, no. 39561.) * GXB (British)
This manuscript is still unpublished. Charles, John Milton, and Edward Henry Hengler were noted circus men of the 1860's and 1870's in England, and held their shows chiefly in Argyle Street, London.

CHIPMAN, BERT JESSE.
The language of the lots. (In his: "Hey Rube." [Hollywood, Calif.: Hollywood Print Shop,] 1933. 8°. p. 193–197.) MWF
Written by one who has spent a lifetime in the circus.

CIRCUS folk use picturesque lingo. (New York Evening Post. April 10, 1931, p. 22, col. 4.) * A
Over 50 words and phrases are defined. "Well, there I was, under the rag, sitting in the blues, getting some junk from the butcher, and glomming the kinkers" is good circus lingo. Dexter Fellows, the circus publicity man, was considered an authority on circus argot. See Dexter William Fellows, *This way to the big show,* New York: The Viking Press, 1936. 362 p. 8°, *MWES.*

CIRCUS glossary. Lot lingo. (The White tops. Evansville, Ind., 1928. 4°. v. 2, no. 3, July, 1928, p. 7–8; v. 2, no. 4, August, 1928, p. 4.) MWA
A good glossary contributed by circus people, chief among them being I. C. Speers, of Santa Monica, Cal., and Joe Cook, the comedian.

CONKLE, ELLSWORTH PROUTY.
Carnival slang. (American speech. Baltimore, Feb., 1928. 4°. v. 3, p. 253–254.) RNA
Glossary of carnival slang from the popular stage success *The Barker.*

FOREMAN, EARL H.
Vernacular of the "white tops." (Writer's monthly. Springfield, Mass., Feb., 1932. 8°. v. 39, p. 76–80.) * IH
Circus jargon written by one who knows the "big top."

FROST, THOMAS.
Circus slang. (In his: Circus life and circus celebrities... London: Tinsley Brothers, 1875. 12°. p. 276–284.) MWF
Lists a number of circus words used in England. It is interesting to note that the gymnasts call their performance a "slang." Eric Partridge cites this work in the *Times literary supplement,* London, June 15, 1933, v. 32, p. 412, † *NAA.*

HIGGINS, RAY.
Big top ballyhoo. (Writers digest. Cincinnati, April, 1932. 8°. v. 12, p. 41–45, 50.) * IH
The lively circus jargon, known only to those who "belong," is presented here for the benefit of those wishing to write about circus folk.

KELLEY, FRANCIS BEVERLY.
The land of sawdust and spangles. (National geographic magazine. Washington, D. C., Oct., 1931. 8°. v. 60, p. 463–516.) KAA
Excellent article on circus life. Contains some circus slang, p. 512, 514. Whether the technical language used on the lots is really slang or not is disputed. John S. Clarke, in his *Circus parade,* New York: Scribner, 1937, says it is not. "Circus folk very seldom talk the slang of the showground. The circus has a vocabulary like every other profession or art, but it is not a slang vocabulary... If a circus artiste speaks slang at all it is the current slang of the day." The compiler has gone into this question in his review of Clarke's book in the *Book buyer,* May, 1937.

MAURER, DAVID W.
Carnival cant: a glossary of circus and carnival slang. (American speech. Baltimore, June, 1931. 4°. v. 6, p. 327–337.) RNA
The old carnival jargon is passing. The motor caravan and mechanical aids have done away with the picturesque circus hands. Carnival slang is cosmopolitan, racy, colorful. This has an excellent glossary.

MILBURN, GEORGE.
Circus words. (American mercury. New York, Nov., 1931. 4°. v. 24, p. 351–354.) * DA
The vocabulary was "selected from the conversation of H. L. Johnson, a veteran circus man. He has worked in American circuses for many years in every capacity from privilege car attendant to paymaster."

Slang and Jargon of Sports, etc., continued

MORRIS, RUTH.
A carnival grifter in winter. (Variety. New York, Jan. 8, 1930. f°. v. 97, p. 123.) † NAFA
Carnival slang. Includes regular carnival words, also slang of the racketeer, spieler, etc.

ODDITIES fill encyclopedia of show world. (New York Herald Tribune. Feb. 17, 1937.) * A
This article, almost a column in length, gives an account of a talk on circus slang delivered at the Town Hall Club by Barry Buchanan. Mentions *The encyclopedia of the amusement world*, in process of compilation by Buchanan.

PANCOAST, CHALMERS LOWELL.
Circus slang. (Writer's monthly. Springfield, Mass., July, 1928. 8°. v. 32, p. 48–49.) * IH
A list of American circus slang reprinted from the Boston *Evening Transcript*. Pancoast was one of the moving spirits in the organization of the Circus Fans Association, and knows circus life from first-hand observation. See *White tops*, Evansville, Ind., July, 1929, v. 3, p. 3, *MWA*.

PEANUTS and pink lemonade. (Scholastic. The American high school weekly. Pittsburgh, April 24, 1937. 4°. v. 30, p. 8.) * DA
"Glossary of circus terms." Reprinted from an article in *Fortune*. It also appeared in *Correct English*, Evanston, Ill., May, 1937, v. 37, p. 143, *RND*.

PEGASUS, PSEUD.
Circus slang. (World's fair. Oldham, England, April 3, 1937.)

ROSE, HOWARD N.
A thesaurus of slang... New York: The Macmillan Company, 1934. 120 p. 8°. RNM
"Circus and carnival," p. 94–103.

SCULLY, FRANK.
Slanguaged language. (Variety. New York, Jan. 8, 1930. f°. v. 97, p. 77.) † NAFA
Mostly about carnival lingo. Tribute is paid to Jack Conway for his contribution to American slang. To the purists who profess to be shocked by these changes don't matter, since they never in their life knew the holy joy of creating a new word."

SEAGO, EDWARD.
Circus company. Life on the road with the travelling show... With an introduction by John Masefield. London: Putnam [1933]. xv, 295 p. col'd front., illus. plates. 8°. MWF
Glossary, p. 294–295.
In this modern English circus slang the word "slang" itself means "the show" and the "slanger" means a "showman." A few gipsy words have found their way into circus slang.

Sons of sawdust, with Paddy O'Flynn's circus in western Ireland... London: Putnam [1934]. viii, 219 p. col'd front., plates, ports. 8°. MWF
Glossary, p. 217–219.

SMITH, LLOYD EDWIN.
The glamour of circus words. (The Circus scrapbook. Jersey City, N. J., Jan., 1931. 16°. no. 9, p. 27–32.) MWA
A few words associated with the circus are traced with some care.

TOWN and country circus life. (All the year round. London, Nov. 16, 1861. 8°. v. 6, p. 181–186.) * DA
Contains a great deal of English circus slang in the days of the Chirper brothers.

WESEEN, MAURICE HARLEY.
A dictionary of American slang... New York: Thomas Y. Crowell Company [1934]. 543 p. 8°. M.R.R. Desk
"Circus and carnival slang," p. 157–164.

WHITE, PERCY W.
A circus list. (American speech. Baltimore, Feb., 1926. 4°. v. 1, p. 282–283.) RNA
A selective list of circus slang. Circus fiction is always popular, and the best writers are those who have actually been with a circus.

More about the language of the lot. (American speech. Baltimore, June, 1928. 4°. v. 3, p. 413–415.) RNA
A continuation of the above.

WOLVERTON, CHARLES.
Mysteries of the carnival language. (American mercury. New York, June, 1935. 8°. v. 35, p. 227–231.) * DA
"The carnival workers' language is...a deliberately disguised speech." Lists over a hundred words from American carnival cant. One notes in this list the absence of the gipsy element, which had such an influence at one time, and the ascendancy of native American slang.

PITCHMEN

BALTIMORE, IRVING.
About carnival and pitchmen. (The Editor. Highland Falls, N. Y., Dec. 2, 1916. 8°. v. 44, p. 518.) NARA
Nineteen expressions of a pitchman "one who sells merchandise and novelties, from a little case resting on tripods which he pitches on a street corner or empty lot, whence the origin of the term."

FLYNN, JOHN THOMAS.
Something for nothing. (Collier's. New York, Oct. 8, 1932. 4°. v. 90, p. 15, 47–48.) * DA
The slang of the street salesman. His crooked game is called a "jam auction." Excerpts are made from *Pipes for pitchmen*, edited by Gasoline Bill Baker.

JOHNSTON, ALVA.
The Billboard. (The New Yorker. New York, Sept. 12, 1936. 4°. p. 32, 34, 36–42.) * DA
The latter part of this article is devoted to pitchmen and their language. "Billboard's not only the pitchman's Bible but his business barometer, legal guide, book of etiquette, and letter from home."

STOUT, WESLEY WINANS.
Alagazam. The story of pitchmen, high and low. (Saturday evening post. Philadelphia, Oct. 19, 1929. f°. v. 202, p. 26.) * DA
Pitchmen are salesmen of bogus articles who usually tour the country looking for suckers. This story was told to Mr. Stout by Dr. N. T. Oliver (Nevada Ned). It contains a glossary of terms.

WAR SLANG

NAVAL slang appears in the section on occupational jargon. This arrangement is arbitrary. More logically it belongs with war slang, but sea slang, of which naval slang was a part, contained much jargon which has no connection with the fighting forces.

ABBATT, WILLIAM.
The colloquial who's who... Tarrytown, N. Y., 1924. 2 v. 8°.   Ref. Cat.
World war phrases are given in v. 1, p. 97–99, and v. 2, p. 125–127. Those in v. 1 are chiefly French phrases; those in v. 2, English and American.

ACTIVE-SERVICE slang. (The Literary digest. New York, April 17, 1915. f°. v. 50, p. 907–908.)   * DA
Copied from the *Toledo Blade.* A few words of English slang as overheard in a cafe in France during the World war.

BAKER, ERNEST A.
English in war-time. (Athenæum. London, May 23, 1919. f°. v. 150, p. 359–360.)   * DA
The purists thought that the war was killing the English language. These conservatives tend to emasculate the language. Science and invention led to a great revival in word-coining in the nineteenth century. The many vernaculars of the British Empire brought fresh words to the English language, and the Great war brought many more. Some of these words are listed.
Reprinted in *Living age,* New York, July 5, 1919, v. 302, p. 23–26, * DA.

BAKER, ERNEST A., AND OTHERS.
Slang in war-time. (Athenæum. London, 1919. f°. v. 151, July 11, p. 582–583; July 18, p. 632; July 25, p. 663–664; Aug. 1, p. 694–695; Aug. 8, p. 727–729; Aug. 15, p. 759; Aug. 22, p. 791; Aug. 29, p. 822–823; Sept. 26, p. 957; Oct. 10, p. 1012; Nov. 7, p. 1163.)   * DA
The slang commonly used in the World war is reviewed by a host of contributors in the correspondence section of the *Athenæum.* The war had just ended and the words were fresh on the lips of soldiers. Eric Verney, who brought the discussion to a close, made a recapitulation of the correspondence and showed that 288 words had been discussed, 100 of them being definitely war slang; 65 were pre-war slang, 62 old army slang, 11 American and colonial, and 50 of doubtful origin.

BALDRY, W. Y.
Regimental nicknames. (Society for Army Historical Research. Journal. London, 1921. 8°. v. 1, p. 29–30, 74–75.)   VWZH
An alphabetical list of several hundred British regimental nicknames. See also Johns, W.

BENKEMA, HERMAN.
West Point and the gray-clad corps. (National geographic magazine. Washington, D. C., June, 1936. 8°. v. 69, p. 777–789.)   KAA
A few terms heard at the United States Military Academy.

BROPHY, JOHN.
The five years... London: Arthur Barker, Ltd. [1936.] 320 p. 8°.   BTZE
"A glossary of common technical terms of the Great war," p. 181–205. Includes slang expressions.

The soldier's war. A prose anthology... London: J. M. Dent & Sons, Ltd. [1929.] xv, 272 p. 12°.   8–BTZK
"Glossary of military and foreign words and war-time slang," p. 263–272.
The glossary was compiled by Brophy.

BROPHY, JOHN, AND E. H. PARTRIDGE.
Songs and slang of the British soldier. 1914–1918. London: Eric Partridge, Ltd. at the Scholartis Press, 1930. 200 p. 8°.   BTZE
The slang of the British soldier is presented in an informal manner not common to the works of lexicographers as a whole, and this entertaining method of defining words adds delight as well as instruction. The definitions are full. The compilers have written much on the subject of slang and the World war.
Reviewed in *John o' London's weekly,* London, July 26, 1930, v. 23, p. 561–562, * DA (J. B. Priestley).

—— 3. ed. London: Scholartis Press, 1931. 383 p. 8°.   BTZE
The songs occupy p. 23–89; the glossary, p. 93–181; additional songs, words, notes, etc., p. 185–383.
See in connection with war songs Edith Aulhorn's "Vom englischen Soldatenlied" in *Germanisch-Romanische Monatsschrift,* Heidelberg, 1920, Jahrg. 8, p. 29–44, RAA.

CASSELL'S New English dictionary. With an appendix. Edited by Ernest A. Baker... 2d ed. London: Cassell & Co. [1919.] 8°.   RNI
Supplement, p. 1281–1300 contains "words coined, introduced, or brought into popular use during the Great war." A good list, with pronunciation indicated. Contains much slang.

COLBY, ELBRIDGE.
Notes on soldier speech. (The Military engineer. Washington, D. C., July – August, 1932. 4°. v. 24, p. 327–330.)   † VWA
This is not an article on the speech of the World war. It deals with general terms known in English and American army circles. Some very old expressions are traced, and reasons given for the creation of some modern ones.

Soldier slang. (Our army. Brooklyn, N. Y., 1929–30. 4°. v. 2, Oct., 1929, p. 20–21, 40–41; Nov., p. 26–27; Dec., p. 24–25, 48; Jan., 1930, p. 20–21, 46–47; Feb., p. 20–21, 43–46; March, p. 28–29; April, p. 30–31, 45–48; May, p. 30–31; June, p. 26–27.)   † VWA
A dictionary of army slang by a recognized authority. The definitions are fully documented in the accepted historical manner.

Soldier speech. (American speech. New York, Feb., 1936. 4°. v. 11, p. 50–63.)   RNA
An historical study of military word origins, English and American, with a few examples of army slang.

COOK, SIR EDWARD TYAS.
Words and the war. (In his: Literary recreations... London: Macmillan and Co., Limited, 1919. 8°. p. 142–175.)   NCZ
"The new horrors of the war are told in such words as *gassed, tear-shells, shell-shock, barbed-wire disease;* its heroisms in the story of those who went *over the top.*"
Other war words are carefully traced, and certain French and German influences are noted.

COWDEN, ROY WILLIAM.
Current glossary... Ann Arbor, Mich.: Educators Association, 1917. 29 p. 16°.
Cover-title: War dictionary, atlas and gazetteer. Pocket edition.
Copy in Library of Congress.

War Slang, continued

DEKOBRA, MAURICE.
Tommy Atkins's vocabulary. (Current history: a monthly magazine of the New York Times. New York, Nov., 1916. 8°. v. 5, p. 259–260.)   BAA
A handful of war words picked up by a correspondent of the *Paris Journal* at the British front during the World war.

DOWNING, W. H.
Digger dialects. A collection of slang phrases used by the Australian soldiers on active service. Melbourne and Sydney: Lothian Publishing Co., 1919. 60 p.
Kennedy 11354.
Not in The New York Public Library.

EICHLER, WILHELM.
Wortschatz und Wirtschaft im Grossbritannischen Kriegsenglisch. Greifswald: H. Adler, 1923. 36 p. 8°.
Reviewed in *Anglia, Beiblatt*, Sept., 1923, Jahrg. 34, p. 266–267, *RNA* (Hermann M. Flasdieck); *Archiv für das Studium der neueren Sprachen*, 1925, Bd. 148, p. 121–122, *RAA* (F. Liebermann).

EMPEY, ARTHUR GUY.
"Over the top," by an American soldier who went...together with Tommy's dictionary of the trenches... New York: G. P. Putnam's Sons, 1917. x, 315 p. 12°.   BTZE
The slang dictionary, p. 281–315, was one of the first compilations of trench argot to reach American readers. The words were coined by the British soldier.
In the same author's *First call*, New York: G. P. Putnam's Sons, 1918, p. 348–365, *BTZE*, there is also a slang glossary.

ESCOTT, THOMAS HAY SWEET.
Post-war English as she is spoke. (London quarterly review. London, July, 1922. 8°. v. 138, p. 63–75.)   * DA
Emphasis on slang is very light, but the point that John Bull as fighter in foreign wars is a slang-carrier extraordinary, is well taken.

FALLS, DE WITT CLINTON.
Army and navy information... New York: E. P. Dutton & Company [1917]. xxii p., 1 l., 192 p. 12°.   VWG
"Army slang": p. 84. Slang of the World war.

FARROW, EDWARD SAMUEL.
A dictionary of military terms... New York: Thomas Y. Crowell Co. [cop. 1918.] xii, 682 p. 16°.   M.R.R. Desk
Not a slang dictionary, but a few outstanding slang words, particularly those relating to the World war, are included. Farrow was a former instructor at West Point.
Reviewed in *English studies*, Amsterdam, June, 1922, v. 4, p. 125–127, *RNA* (F. P. H. Prick van Wely). There is also a London edition, Library Press, 1919.

FRANK, GLENN.
Slang and jargon. (The Century magazine. New York, Nov., 1920. 8°. v. 101, p. 137–139.)   * DA
Essay on war slang with some definitions of slang and jargon. "Jargon is the fog of language; slang the lightning of language."

FRASER, EDWARD, AND JOHN GIBBONS.
Soldier and sailor words and phrases. Including slang of the trenches and Air Force; British and American war-words and service terms and expressions of everyday use; nicknames, sobriquets, and titles of regiments, with their origins... London: George Routledge and Sons, 1925. vii, 372 p. 8°.   * R–RNM
This is one of the better dictionaries of the World war from the standpoint of the number of words defined. Popular rather than historical treatment.
Reviewed, with additions, by Elbridge Colby, *American speech*, Jan., 1926, v. 1, p. 243–244, *RNA; Saturday review of literature*, New York, Sept. 5, 1925, v. 2, p. 111, *NAA; Notes and queries*, London, July 25, 1925, v. 149, p. 71–72, * R–* DA. Other reviews in *Moderna Sprak*, Dec., 1925, v. 19, p. 235–238 (Einar Ekblom); and *Anglia, Beiblatt*, July, 1926, Bd. 37, p. 201–214, *RNA* (G. Kirchner).

FRENCH soldier-slang. (The Literary digest. New York, March 11, 1916. f°. v. 32, p. 643.)   * DA
From the London *Evening Standard*. The argot of the trenches is chiefly the creation of the French, with a few words contributed by the Tommy. Over a hundred examples.

GLOSSARY of terms commonly used in aviation. By a flight commander. (Sea, land and air. The Australian monthly journal. Sydney, Jan., 1919. 8°. v. 1, p. 638–643.)   * DA
Technical glossary, with several slang terms born of the experience of the World war.

HAL.
Soldier slang. (The Globe. New York, Feb. 16, 1916.)   * A
Three columns of war words, mostly British.

HERRMANN, ALBERT.
Kriegsenglisch. (Zeitschrift für französischen und englischen Unterricht. Berlin, 1919. 8°. Bd. 19, p. 14–26.)   NAA
A close study of English war words and their origins, based largely on excerpts from the *Saturday review*.

HOLMES, ROBERT DERBY.
A Yankee in the trenches... Boston: Little, Brown & Co., 1918. 214 p. 12°.   BTZE
"Glossary of army slang," p. 209–214.
World War slang as recorded by an American soldier.

How war enriches language. (The Literary digest. New York, May 8, 1915. f°. v. 50, p. 1081–1082.)   * DA
Quotations from the London *Times*, showing the influence of wars on the English language, particularly the wars with the Dutch, the Crimean war, and the World war. The French contributed much to the latter group.

JAEGER, P. L.
On English war-slang. (Englische Studien. Leipzig, 1926. 8°. Bd. 60, p. 272–299.)   RNA
A review of Fraser and Gibbons's *Soldier and sailor words and phrases* (q.v.). "We learn very little, in fact in most cases nothing at all about etymology... If the authors had but taken the trouble to consult the 7 vols. of Farmer and Henley's slang dictionary, and 'Hobson-Jobson' not to speak of the Oxford Dictionary, we all should be the wiser." Although the authors spoke of the forcible language of the war, "bloody" was the only example in the whole volume. Jaeger supplies a few of these forcible words. He gives two alphabetical lists of words, one containing

War Slang, continued

JAEGER, P. L., *continued*
comments on words given in Fraser and Gibbons, and
the other containing words "which may be of use
to the compilers for a second edition."

JOHNS, W.
...Regimental nicknames... London: Spottiswoode & Co., 1881. 16 p. 8°.
                                            VWZH p.v.22, no.6
In July, 1881 a new territorial scheme for the
British army came into effect, and with it a change
of regimental titles. The old nicknames were in most
cases discarded. This brochure is an attempt to preserve some of them.
The New York Public Library copy bears the autograph inscription: "With the author's compliments.
Thomas Preston." Newspaper clippings containing
regimental nicknames are pasted in the pamphlet.
In connection with regimental nicknames there is much
to be gleaned from the index volume of *The Journal
of the Society of Army Historical Research*, 1921–
1933, *VWZH*. Notes and queries also contains information.

KEELEY, MARY PAXTON.
A. E. F. English. (American speech. Baltimore, June, 1930. 8°. v. 5, p. 372–386.)   RNA
Writer spent ten months in France as canteen worker.
Traces origins of many war words, lists those borrowed from the British and French, and gives a glossary.

LEMBERGER, J.
War notes. [By J. Lemberger.] (Bodleian
quarterly record. Oxford, 1918. 4°. v. 2, p. 123–
126, 152–154.)   * HPD (Oxford)
"There is no reason why documents admitted to these
columns should be old... Accordingly we print our
very latest manuscript acquisition, a glossary of war
terms..."
Includes corruptions of Hindustani, corruptions of
French and German, rhymed slang, and ordinary slang.

LÜDECKE, WINFRIED.
Wie spricht Tommy Atkins? (Grenzboten.
Berlin, Nov., 1916. 8°. Jahrg. 75, Vierteljahr 4,
p. 185–189.)   * DF
Slang words coined by the British soldiers during
the World war. Over fifty words are defined.

McCARTNEY, EUGENE STOCK.
Additions to a volume on the slang and the
idioms of the World war. (Michigan Academy
of Science, Arts and Letters. Papers. Ann
Arbor, 1929. 8°. v. 10, p. 273–337.)   * EA
Words added to the volume by Fraser and Gibbons
entitled *Soldier and sailor words and phrases* (q.v.).
This list is fully documented in a scientific manner.
"Literature on war slang," p. 335–337.
There is a separate reprint of this paper, *M.R.R.Desk*.

Linguistic processes as illustrated by war
slang. (Michigan Academy of Science, Arts
and Letters. Papers. New York, 1924. 8°. v. 3,
p. 289–299.)   * EA
A study of vocabulary in the making. World War
slang is analyzed with etymological skill by a recognized authority. Portions of the article appeared originally in *The Texas review*, v. 4, p. 73–87, * *DA* (q.v.).
There is a bibliography of war slang, p. 299–300.

Trench talk. (Texas review. Austin, 1918.
8°. v. 4, p. 73–87.)   * DA
"A soldier in a dugout regards linguistic conven-
tions as little as did his troglodytic ancestor." The

French were especially prolific in the creation of war
slang. The American soldiers brought a great wave
of new slang to the trenches. Most of the words in
this study are French, and a few German words are
included.

MASON, WILLIAM LESLEY.
Principal new words brought into use since,
or as the result of, the great World war. (In
his: Troublesome words and how to use them.
New York: George Sully & Co., 1924. 8°.
p. 282–289.)   RND
Not all of the words in this glossary are war words.

MOSS, JAMES ALFRED.
Officers' manual... 6. ed. Menasha, Wis.:
George Banta Pub. Co. [1917.] 353(1) p., 5 l.
12°.   VWC
See paragraph 484 for a glossary of United States
army slang.

MOTHES, RUDOLPH.
Das Flugwesen und der neuenglische Wortschatz. (Anglia. Halle, 1918. 8°. Bd. 42, p. 337–
344.)   RNA
A comparative study of British and German aviation
terms as they were known to those in active service
on both sides of the line. This article was submitted
"Im Felde."

MÜGGE, MAXIMILIAN A.
The war diary of a square peg... London:
George Routledge and Sons, 1920. 224 p. 8°.
                                            BTZE
Appendix II. A dictionary of war words, p. 217–224.
Most of the words are those of the British soldier
at the front during the World war.

MUIR, WARD.
Slang in a war hospital. (In his: Observations of an orderly. London: Simpkin, Marshall, Hamilton, Kent & Co. [1917.] 12°. p. 219–
232.)   BTZW
World war slang as heard from the hospital cot.

NETTLEINGHAME, FREDERICK THOMAS.
Tommy's tunes... London: E. MacDonald,
Ltd., 1917. 12°.   * MP
There is also a second volume entitled: *More Tommy
tunes*. These songs contain a great deal of British
soldier slang of the World War period.

OUR army slang charms the British. (Literary
digest. New York, Nov. 23, 1918. f°. v. 59,
p. 38, 41.)   * DA
Excerpts from an article in the London *Daily Mail*.
The charm of the American soldier slang was refresh-
ing to the war-weary people of England and France.
He regarded the war as a lark and never lost his
humor. His cocksureness in putting an end to the
war before Christmas acted as a tonic to the allies.

PARTRIDGE, ERIC HONEYWOOD.
Byways of soldiers' slang. (In: A Martial
medley... London: Scholartis Press, 1931.
8°. p. 127–133.)   BTZE (Medley)
"This is new" the author says, and is not to be
confused with articles he wrote on the same subject
for various magazines. This is the intimate slang
of the trenches, connected with the daily life of the
soldier; terms for food, for lice, for the places of
detention, etc.

Soldiers' slang. (Everyman. London, Jan.
29, 1931. f°. v. 5, p. 12.)   * DA
World War slang.

War Slang, continued

POWLETT, N., AND OTHERS.
[War slang.] (Notes and queries. London, 1916–19. 8°. March 4, 1916, series 12, v. 1, p. 194; April 8, 1916, series 12, v. 1, p. 292; Oct., 1918, series 12, v. 4, p. 270–271; Nov., 1918, series 12, v. 1, p. 306–308; Dec., 1918, series 12, v. 4, p. 333; Jan., 1919, series 12, v. 5, p. 18–19; March, 1919, series 12, v. 5, p. 79; April, 1919, series 12, v. 5, p. 108; May, 1919, series 12, v. 5, p. 136; June, 1919, series 12, v. 5, p. 159; July, 1919, series 12, v. 5, p. 182, 195.) * R–* DA
Starting with a discussion on the word "blighty," a host of correspondents contribute a great many other war words. See Sieveking for a more extensive list of war words.

PRESTON, EDGAR.
War words. (The National review. London, 1917–22. 8°. v. 70, Dec., 1917, p. 466–474; v. 78, Jan., 1922, p. 633–640.)   * DA
Slang coined by the soldiers in the World war, including the German soldier as well as the allied soldiers. A few words coined immediately prior to the war are also discussed. No American slang is included, and no naval slang is listed. In the second article the dictionary of army slang, compiled by the Imperial War Museum, under the direction of the librarian, A. Forbes Sieveking, is mentioned. This dictionary was approved by Dr. Henry Bradley, of Oxford, "perhaps our greatest living authority on slang."
See W. W., "What the soldier said," in *John o' London's weekly,* Jan. 14, 1922, v. 6, p. 480, for favorable comment on Preston's articles in the *National review.*

PRICE, WARWICK JAMES.
War's gift of words. (Overland monthly. San Francisco, Aug., 1919. 8°. v. 74, p. 115–118.)   * DA
A few of the early slang creations of the World war, such as boche, poilu, rookie, slacker, etc.

PRICK VAN WELY, F. P. H.
War words and peace pipings. (English studies. Amsterdam, 1922. 8°. v. 4, Feb., p. 10–19; April, p. 60–64.)   RNA
"Materials for a study of slang and neologism." An attempt to give an historical account of the origins of war words, each word being definitely dated.

PROTHERO, SIR GEORGE WALTER.
A select analytical list of books concerning the Great war. London: Printed and published by His Majesty's Stationery Office, 1923. 8°.   * RB–BTZF
"Linguistic works," p. 376–382, includes dictionaries of war slang.

RANDERSON, JEFFRY HOWARD.
"On His Majesty's service." By Prince Reichstadt-Napoleon [Jeffry Howard Randerson]... Albany, New York: J. Howard Randerson, 1925. 54 p. 8°.   BTZE
Privately printed.
"There is presented in the following pages an account of the extraordinary experiences of Prince Reichstadt-Napoleon v. in the World war, with special reference to the circumstances surrounding his origination of war terms which were destined to become part of our popular vocabulary."
First printed under the title: *The Origin of the war term "no man's land" as applied to the World war,* [Albany, cop. 1922] 14 p. 4°. *BTZE p.v.683, no.9.*

RECRUITS' primer of trench idiom. (The Literary digest. New York, 1917. f°. v. 55, Oct. 27, 1917, p. 64–65.)   * DA
Glossary of war slang copied from the *Philadelphia Enquirer.* The list was prepared originally by the British recruiting mission for the benefit of the American troops going into the trenches. It was the work of Colonel St. George Steele.

SCOBEE, BARRY.
Parlance of the army. (The Editor. Highland Falls, N. Y., March 11, 1916. 8°. v. 43, p. 296–297.)   NARA
A few slang words of the United States Army.

SIEVEKING, A. FORBES, AND OTHERS.
English army slang as used in the Great war. (Notes and queries. London, 1921–22. 8°. Oct. 29, 1921, series 12, v. 9, p. 341–348; Nov. 5, 1921, series 12, v. 9, p. 378–379; Nov. 12, 1921, series 12, v. 9, p. 383–385; Nov. 19, 1921, series 12, v. 9, p. 415–419; Nov. 26, 1921, series 12, v. 9, p. 423–425; Dec. 3, 1921, series 12, v. 9, p. 455–459; Dec. 10, 1921, series 12, v. 9, p. 465–467; Dec. 17, 1921, series 12, v. 9, p. 499; Dec. 24, 1921, series 12, v. 9, p. 502–504; Dec. 31, 1921, series 12, v. 9, p. 538–539; Jan. 7, 1922, series 12, v. 10, p. 7; March 18, 1922, series 12, v. 10, p. 201–202; April 8, 1922, series 12, v. 10, p. 279; May 20, 1922, series 12, v. 10, p. 295; May 27, 1922, series 12, v. 10, p. 415.) * R–* DA
The first contribution goes into the history of slang in general before listing specific words and phrases of the Great war. The glossary which follows was compiled by members of the staff of the London *Times.* The glossary in the Dec. 24, 1921, issue is made up entirely of airmen's slang.
See also Powlett, N., and others.

SLANG. (The New statesman. London, Aug. 25, 1917. f°. v. 9, p. 488–489.)   * DA
The revolutionizing effect of the World war on speech leads this essayist to an investigation of the whole subject of slang. War slang is briefly reviewed, some American slang is mentioned, as is drinking slang, etc. Ward Muir's *Observations of an orderly,* which contains a chapter on soldier slang, is quoted.
Reprinted in *Living age,* New York, Nov. 3, 1917, v. 295, p. 377–380, * *DA.*

SLANG of the airmen. (The Literary digest. New York, June 23, 1917. f°. v. 54, p. 1957–1958.)   * DA
Digest of an article in London *Answers.* Most of the words are taken from Flight Lieutenant Harold Rosher's book, *In the Royal Air-Service.*
"The Great war has developed a tendency to slang among the British allies who have always heretofore handed the palm to America for verbal inventiveness."

SMITH, CHARLES ALPHONSO.
New words self-defined... Garden City, N. Y.: Doubleday, Page & Co., 1920. 215 p. 12°.   RNM
A dictionary of words which, for the most part, grew out of the World war. The definitions are taken verbatim from newspapers and magazines. The definitions are lengthy, only two or three words being defined on a page.

STOREY, HEDLEY V.
New words in war. (Chambers's journal. London, Oct., 1915. f°. v. 96, p. 660–665.) * DA
Traces origins of war words from the Indian mutiny (1857–58), which gave England the word "khaki," to the World war. A number of words derived from aerial combat are noted, along with some words contributed to English slang by the Germans.

STRANGE slang used by Tommy Atkins. (New York Times. April 14, 1915. Section 5, p. 2.)   * A
A handful of words used by the British soldier during the early days of the World war.

War Slang, continued

SULLIVAN, MARK.
Our times. The United States, 1900–1925.
v. 5. New York: Charles Scribner's Sons, 1933.
8°.   IL
On p. 326–330 an alphabetical list of war slang,
used by the United States troops in the World war,
is given, with full definitions.

WARNER, ARTHUR H.
Slang and slogans of war in France. (The
New York Times. Oct. 7, 1917. Section 3,
p. 10.)   * A
A review of the general war slang of 1914–1917.

WORD-SMITH, PSEUD.
War slang. (The Saturday review. London,
Sept. 2, 1916. f°. v. 122, p. 220–221.)   * DA
The profession of war brings a new argot into being.
The World war had not produced many new words

up to the time this article was written. The writer
pointed out that slang of the Boer war had already
been forgotten. A number of terms were listed and
most of them are still in use. A note on the word
"Rosalie" is added in the Sept. 9 issue, p. 250, by
A. Beresford-Horsley.

WORDS born out of conflict. (Literary digest.
New York, Oct. 14, 1916. f°. v. 53, p. 990, 992–
993.)   * DA
Short résumé of war slang from London *Answers.*
"Contraband" and "embargo" grew out of the wars
between England and Spain in the sixteenth century.
"Khaki" originated in the Boer war. "Free lance"
goes back to the crusades. A list of American political
slang is given.

WYETH, JOHN ALLAN BENEDICT.
This man's army. A war in fifty-odd sonnets. London: Longmans, Green and Co., 1929.
60 p. 8°.   NBI
Glossary, p. 59–60. World War slang.

SCHOOL AND COLLEGE SLANG

SCHOOL SLANG

General Works

AUSTIN, HELEN H.
"Almost everyman," a "better English" play
... Minneapolis: Northwestern College of
Speech Arts, 1929. 14 p. 12°.   NBL p.v.220
A school play to show the evils of slang. O. U.
Slang is being tried for the murder of Miss English
Language, and other linguistic culprits are personified.

CLARK, A. BESS.
Slang: a lesson in ninth-grade composition.
(The English journal. Chicago, Sept., 1925.
8°. v. 14, p. 541–546.)   RNA
Dialogue between teacher and pupils on the subject
of slang. In this Socratic method the minds of the
pupils are clarified regarding the nature and function
of slang. The conclusion reached was that a slang
word survives if it is not too offensive.

CONRADI, EDWARD.
Children's interests in words, slang, stories,
etc. (The Pedagogical seminary. Worcester,
Mass., Sept., 1903. 8°. v. 10, p. 359–404.)   SSA
Compiled by a Fellow of Clark University with the
aid of normal school students. It is a detailed study
of student speech habits. Question 6 of the syllabus
read: "At what age are the young most prone to slang?
Give a brief vocabulary of slang phrases that have been
favorites (a) with girls and (b) with boys. What can
be said in its favor, and what against it?" The tabulated results of this question are given on p. 369–380.

EASTMAN, MAX.
Poetic education and slang. (The New republic. New York, 1916. f°. Dec. 9, v. 9, p. 151–
152; Dec. 16, p. 182–184.)   * DA
An indictment of the smug schoolroom atmosphere
of boredom and fettering dignity, and of the teachers
who forbid the use of slang. Slang is poetic, virile,
joyous. A digest of this article appeared in the
Literary digest, New York, Jan. 13, 1917, v. 54, p. 71,
* DA. It was also digested in *Current opinion,* New
York, Feb., 1917, v. 62, p. 119–120, * DA.

EDDINS, A. W.
The state industrial school boys' slang.
(Folk-Lore Society of Texas. Publications.
Austin, 1916. 8°. v. 1, p. 44–46.)   ZBA
"The boys who come to the state juvenile training

school have full knowledge of the underworld life,
and are adepts in the use of common criminal slang."

FARMER, JOHN STEPHEN.
The public school word-book. A contribution to a historical glossary of words, phrases,
and turns of expression obsolete and in present
use peculiar to our great public schools. Together with some that have been or are modish
at the universities... London: Privately issued for subscribers only. By Hirschfeld Brothers, 13 Furnival Street, E. C., 1900. 243 p. sq. 8°.
                                                    SSYH
This comprehensive work by the author of *Slang
and its analogues* is arranged according to strict historical principles. Some of the words have great
antiquity, as the quotations prove. Few dictionaries
designed for popular use have been so elaborately
printed.
Reviewed by Nowell Smith in *Cornhill magazine,*
London, 1902, v. 85, p. 686–694, * DA.

FRY, ROBERT J.
The salvation of Jemmy Slang. [Spokane,
Wash., cop. 1920.] 16 p. 8°.   NBL p.v.77, no.4
A comedy in two acts, written for the sophomore
English class of the Lewis and Clark High School,
Spokane, Washington. An attempt to create a love of
good English by personifying slang, good English,
ignorance, culture, etc. The speech of Jemmy Slang
is filled with modern American slang.

FURBER, DOUGLAS.
The influence of Thesaurus. (In his: The
"All star" cast... London: Samuel French
[1931]. 8°. p. 47–51.)   NCO p.v.635, no.4
A burlesque playlet on the use of a thesaurus. Some
of the characters speak entirely in modern slang synonyms.

GORE, WILLARD CLARK.
Notes on slang. (Modern language notes.
Baltimore, Nov., 1896. 4°. v. 11, p. 193–198.)
                                                    RAA
Professor Gore had his University of Michigan
students collect slang specimens. The purpose was to
determine definitely what kind of images were aroused
in the minds of slang users, and what feelings slang
engenders. The students were questioned on the psychological aspects of slang and their answers classified
and interpreted. This article is a digest of those
answers.

School and College Slang, continued

HOWLAND, MRS. FRANCES LOUISE (MORSE).
Children and good English. By Kenyon West
[pseud.]. (Outlook. New York, Aug. 14, 1897.
8°. v. 56, p. 943–946.) *DA
General statements about the slipshod speech of
children, with a brief closing note on the pernicious
effects of slang.

A LITTLE study of school slang. (T. P.'s
weekly. London, Aug. 31, 1906. f°. v. 8, p. 270.)
*DA
Boy's slang at a nonconformist school in England.
Expressions current in 1906. About two columns of
material.

MELVILLE, A. H.
An investigation of the function and use of
slang. (The Pedagogical seminary. Worcester,
Mass., March, 1912. 8°. v. 19, p. 94–100.) SSA
An investigation of the slang used by boys and
girls of the Madison, Wisconsin, High School. Each
person was asked to: 1. Write as many slang expressions as you know; 2. Tell why you use slang.
There were 909 different slang expressions turned in
by the pupils. Of this total the boys used 691 or 76%
and the girls 516 or 57%. The slang words are tabulated.

MORGAN, FAY HOUSE.
"Who killed old slang?" (Normal instructor
and primary plans. Dansville, N. Y., Feb., 1924.
f°. v. 33, p. 46, 92.) †SSA
Account of Good English week, with posters made
by pupils at Mt. Morris, N. Y. Slang is put before
the school children as a "bad egg" and a "bum" — not
to be admitted into polite society.

PASCOE, CHARLES EYRE, EDITOR.
Everyday life in our public schools. Sketched
by head-scholars... Edited by C. E. P...
London: Griffith & Farran, 1881. 314 p. 8°.
Listed in British Museum catalogue. Contains some
school slang.

RUSSELL, ELSA.
Slang — face to face. (The English journal.
Chicago, Nov., 1934. 4°. v. 23, p. 740–744.) RNA
A compendium of up-to-the-minute American slang.
A ninth-year English class was requested to make out
a list of slang words and in another column to express
the same ideas in good English, to determine if the
slang expression was more forceful. After the lists
were collected the slang was classified as forceful,
vulgar, meaningless, specialized, etc.

SCHOOL and college slang of England; or,
Glossaries of the words and phrases peculiar
to the six great educational establishments of
the country. London: J. C. Hotten, 1872.
Kennedy 12048.

SCHMIDT, FREDRIK.
A study of English school-life and schoolboy slang, as represented by Kipling's *Stalky
& Co.* (Englische Studien. Leipzig, 1908. 8°.
Bd. 39, p. 240–274.) RNA
The samples are taken from the Macmillan edition
of 1899. A thorough examination of Kipling's famous
book, couched in the philological nomenclature so dear
to scholars. There is an index to the slang words,
p. 272–274.

SIEPMANN.
[Slang.] (Paedagogium. Leipzig. v. 9, p. 384–
393, 808–811.)
The compiler has not seen this article, but it has
been pointed out as a significant contribution.

SCHWESINGER, GLADYS CLOTILDE.
Slang as an indication of character. (Journal
of applied psychology. Worcester, Mass., June,
1926. 8°. v. 10, p. 245–263.) YEA
"The research here reported is an exploratory attempt in the field of character detection and measure-
ment. The aim was to find an instrument which would
differentiate delinquent children from non-delinquents."
A list of slang words was given with a number of
synonyms. The child taking the test was asked to
underline the word which he thought was the best
synonym. This list is given in the appendix.

SELLING, LOWELL SINN, AND SEYMOUR P.
STEIN.
Vocabulary and argot of delinquent boys.
(The American journal of sociology. Chicago, March, 1934. 8°. v. 39, p. 674–677.) SA
Abstract of a study "made on a group of delinquent
boys comprising 100 cases at the St. Charles Corrective
School and was controlled by a group of Austin <Chi-
cago> High-School boys from one of the areas of
lowest delinquency in the city. A scale was made
of 24 words used largely by delinquents, and 26 without such connotation. These were mixed together by
chance, with four choices by definition."

SEWELL, JAMES WITT.
Colloquialism at the bar. (The English journal. Chicago, 1929–30. 8°. Dec., 1929, v. 18,
p. 818–822; Feb., 1930, v. 19, p. 127–132.) RNA
Slang and colloquialisms of a boy in high school.
"He sees only two extremes: on the one hand familiar
vulgarisms which make up the language of some of his
less fortunate associates, and on the other a stilted
and artificial speech that would make him unduly
conspicuous, if not ridiculous. You know which style
of expression a youth of good red blood is likely to
choose." Samples are given, and the impression is
created that the writer believes that purist teachers
should not tamper too much with the vivid language
of boys.

SHAW, CLIFFORD ROBE.
The jack-roller. A delinquent boy's own
story... Chicago: The University of Chicago
Press [cop. 1930]. 205 p. 8°. SLL
A sociological study of a juvenile delinquent's narrative. It contains many tramp and underworld expressions.

SMITH, NOWELL CHARLES.
The language of schoolboys. (Cornhill magazine. London, 1902. 8°. v. 85, p. 686–694.) *DA
Based on John S. Farmer's *The public school word
book*, but the author draws from a similar work by
R. G. K. Wrench and from personal experience. The
slang of the Wykehamists comes in for analysis.
Schoolboy slang is the offspring of "two prolific brethren, the one of *Usus*, the other of *Lusus*. *Usus* we
know from Horace as the great begetter of language."
Many slang words are defined.

VIVID slang urged by Barnes of N. Y. U. (New
York Times. Nov. 27, 1936. f°. p. 5, col. 1.) *A
Professor Walter Barnes, of New York University,
addressing the National Council of Teachers of English, in New York, advocated the free use of slang
in schools. "We must define and teach a more
natural, idiomatic and comfortable mode of communication."

WEST, KENYON, PSEUD. *See* HOWLAND, MRS.
FRANCES LOUISE (MORSE).

WORDS often mispronounced, or Jack Downing-
isms. (The Common school journal. Boston,
1839. 8°. July 1, 1839, v. 1, p. 203–204; July
15, v. 1, p. 218–219; Aug. 1, v. 1, p. 236–237;

School and College Slang, continued

WORDS often mispronounced, *continued*

Nov. 15, v. 1, p. 347–348; Dec. 2, v. 1, p. 361–363.)   SSA
The English reviews regarded the letters of Jack Downing as typical specimens of American speech. The *Common school journal,* edited by Horace Mann, points out that these errors of speech should be eradicated, and submits this list for the use of teachers.

Chefoo

CROFTS, ALFRED.
Vernacular of an English school in the Orient. (American speech. New York, Feb., 1935. 4°. v. 10, p. 24–29.)   RNA
Words from the primary and secondary school at the Chinese treaty port of Chefoo. Many hybrid expressions are listed, but English slang predominates. Numerous samples are given.

Christ's Hospital

LA TOUCHE, WILLIAM MARTIN DIGUES.
Christ's Hospital from a boy's point of view. 1864–1870... Cambridge: W. Heffer and Sons, Ltd., 1928. xii, 82 p., 2 ports. 12°.
"School slang," p. 76–78.   STK (Christ's)
This list was compiled by T. H. D. La Touche. He says: "A vocabulary of Christ's Hospital words is given by Mr. Blunden in an appendix to his book mentioned in the preface, partly drawn from a list compiled by Mr. W. H. Blanch, *The Blue Coat boys, or School life in Christ's Hospital,* W. Allen, 1877. A concise list is also given by Mr. Francis in *Christ's Hospital sixty years ago.* The following list comprises those used by my brother in this book, some of which are not included in either of the above lists, or have a somewhat different meaning attached to them."

Eton

AINGER, ARTHUR CAMPBELL.
Memories of Eton sixty years ago... London: John Murray, 1917. 353 p. 8°.   STK
"Language," p. 287–293. Eton slang of the 1850's.

BRINSLEY-RICHARDS, JAMES.
Seven years at Eton, 1857–1864. 2d ed. London: Richard Bentley and Son, 1883. 447 p. 12°.   STK
This book contains no formal glossary of school slang, but it is filled with Eton slang from beginning to end.

GRILDRIG, SOLOMON, PSEUD.
The miniature, a periodical paper, by Solomon Grildrig [pseud.] of the College of Eton ... Windsor: C. Knight, 1805. viii p., 1 l., 368 p. 8°.   NCE
No. 21, p. 235–246, deals with the importation of French phrases into English speech, and a few Etonian cant words are discussed on p. 244–246.

GUIDE to Eton. Eton alphabet. Eton block. Eton glossary. London: Whittaker, 1861. 71 p. 12°.
Not in The New York Public Library.
Mentioned in Harcourt's *An Eton bibliography,* London, 1898, p. 25, *STK.*

LUBBOCK, ALFRED.
Memories of Eton and Etonians... London: John Murray, 1899. 320 p. 8°.   STK
Contains a great deal of Eton slang for the period 1854–1863. Henry S. Salt's *Memories of bygone Eton,* London: Hutchinson, 1928, *STK,* also contains some slang. For other works on Eton see L. V. Harcourt, *An Eton bibliography,* London: Swan Sonnenschein, 1898, 45 p., *STK.*

NUGENT-BANKES, GEORGE.
A day of my life; or, Every-day experiences at Eton. By a present Eton boy [George Nugent-Bankes]. New York: George R. Lockwood, 1877. 184 p. 16°.   STK
"Explanatory chapter," p. 179–184, gives a glossary of Eton slang.

PARKER, ERIC.
Floreat; an Eton anthology. London: Nisbet & Co. [1933.] 333 p. 8°.   STK
"Glossary," p. 332–333.
Slang phrases of Eton, which occur in the book, are explained.

STONE, CHRISTOPHER REYNOLDS.
The Eton glossary. Eton: Spottiswoode & Co., Ltd., 1902. 4 p.l., 55 p. 12°.
Copy in Library of Congress.

—— 4th edition. Eton: Spottiswoode & Co., Ltd., 1909. 4 p.l., 79 p. 12°.
Copy in Library of Congress.

Haileybury

DANVERS, FREDERICK CHARLES, AND OTHERS.
Memorials of old Haileybury College. Westminster: Archibald Constable and Co., 1894. xxv, 668 p. 8°.   STK
On p. 258 of this history of the old East India College, at Haileybury, are a number of slang words, with a reference to some early source material.

Rossall

N., T.
School slang at Rossall. (Notes and queries. London, Feb. 16, 1907. 8°. series 10, v. 7, p. 125–126.)   * R–* DA
Slang current at Rossall School, England, in July, 1906.

Rugby

KARES, OTTO.
Hermeneutische und phraseologische Anmerkungen zu Tom Brown's schooldays. (Englische Studien. Heilbronn, 1883–84. 8°. Bd. 6, p. 327–351, 387–415.)   RNA
A detailed background study of the words and phrases, including slang, in the popular English classic of schoolboy life.

Winchester

ADAMS, HENRY CADWALLADER.
Wykehamica. A history of Winchester College and commoners, from the foundation to the present day... With nineteen illustrations ... Oxford and London: James Parker and Co.; Winchester: J. Wells, 1878. 496 p. 12°.
Glossary, p. 414–439.   STK (Winchester)
The text contains additional school slang.
Adams seems to have based his glossary on an earlier work by Robert Blackford Mansfield (q.v.) but he has added a few words and gone more into the etymologies.

MANSFIELD, ROBERT BLACKFORD.
School life at Winchester College; or, The reminiscences of a Winchester junior. With a glossary of words, phrases, and customs, peculiar to Winchester College. By the author of "The log of the Water Lily," "The Water-Lily on the Danube," &c. &c. [R. B. M., i.e.

School and College Slang, continued

Robert Blackford Mansfield.] London: John Camden Hotten, Piccadilly, 1866. 243 p. illus. 12°. STK (Winchester)

Glossary, p. 197–243.
Kennedy, no. 12056, mentions a third edition, London: D. Nutt, 1893. The second edition was published in 1869.
Wright's dialect dictionary, v. 6, p. 41 of the bibliographical section, mentions a manuscript entitled "Commoner word-book, or dictionary of words and phrases current in Winchester School," 1864. This may have been the basis of Mansfield's work.

R., W. J.
Winchester school slang. (American notes and queries. Philadelphia, May 30, 1891. 8°. v. 7, p. 51.) *DA

Comment on a book by R. G. K. Wrench, entitled *Notions,* excerpted from the London *Daily News.* Further comment is added by Ramon in the June 20, 1891, issue of the *American N. & Q.,* v. 7, p. 95.
See also Thomas De Quincey, "The nation of London," in his *Collected works, NCG,* which contains an account of the Ziph language as used at Winchester. Eric Partridge has a note on Ziph in his *Slang to-day and yesterday,* London: Routledge, 1935, p. 278–279, *M.R.R. Desk.*

WINCHESTER College notions. By three Beetleites. Winchester: P. & G. Wells, 1901. 161 p.
Kennedy 12061.

WRENCH, ROBERT GEORGE KENSINGTON.
Winchester word-book. A collection of past and present notions. Winchester: J. Wells; London: D. Nutt, 1891. 53 p.

2d ed. 1901. Copy in Boston Public Library.
Reviewed in *Athenæum,* London, Sept. 12, 1891, v. 98, p. 350–351; *Academy,* London, v. 39, p. 562–563; *American notes and queries,* 1891, v. 7, p. 51, *DA.*

COLLEGE SLANG

General Works

BABBITT, EUGENE HOWARD.
College words and phrases. (Dialect notes. New Haven, 1900. 8°. v. 2, p. 3–70.) RNZ

Nineteen pages of introductory matter give the best account of college slang to be found. Compares American and foreign universities. A word list drawn from 87 American colleges and universities gives an excellent idea of the geographical distribution of certain expressions, for each definition is followed by the name of the college or colleges using the word or phrase.
A brief description of this work, with a few words as samples, was written by Babbitt for *The Chautauquan,* Cleveland, April, 1900, v. 31, p. 22–24, *DA.*

BASS, ALTHA LEAH (BIERBOWER).
The university tongue. (Harper's magazine. New York, March, 1922. 8°. v. 144, p. 529–530.)
A short essay couched in college lingo. *DA

BOLWELL, ROBERT GEORGE WHITNEY.
College slang words and phrases. (Dialect notes. Boston, 1915. 8°. v. 4, p. 231–238.) RNH
A general list of college words current at the time of the World war.

COLLEGE slang. (Bookman. New York, August, 1897. 8°. v. 5, p. 448.) *DA
Contrasts a few college slang phrases of 1897 with the college slang twenty years earlier.

DOUGHRITY, KENNETH L.
Handed-down campus expressions. (American speech. Baltimore, Dec., 1930. 4°. v. 6, p. 129–130.) RNA
Gives a few campus expressions not listed in previous articles in *American speech.* Suggests a comparative study of the language of our schools and colleges.

HALE, SWINBURNE.
College criticism and "literary slang." (Harvard monthly. Cambridge, Feb., 1904. 8°. v. 38, p. 186–192.) STG
Undergraduate literary criticism is studded with the "obvious." Literary slang in this instance may more properly be called jargon, the result of a tendency towards triteness.

HALL, BENJAMIN HOMER.
A collection of college words and customs ... Cambridge: John Bartlett, 1851. 319 p. 12°. SSYH
One of the first college glossaries, and one of the best. The slang terms are taken for the most part from American colleges, but words from foreign universities are included. The definitions are full, and the quotations adequate.
Reviewed in *Harvard magazine,* Cambridge, Oct., 1855, v. 1, p. 416–422, * DA.

—— Rev. and enl. Cambridge, 1856, vi, 508 p. 12°. SSYH

—— New York: M. Doolady, 1859. vi, 508 p. 12°. SSYH

McPHEE, M. C.
College slang. (American speech. Baltimore, Dec., 1927. 4°. v. 3, p. 131–133.) RNA
Present-day terms in use in the Middle Western colleges.

MONROE, BENTON SULLIVAN, AND G. S. NORTHUP.
Contributions of the Cornell University Dialect Society. (Dialect notes. New Haven, 1901. 8°. v. 2, p. 135–150.) RNZ
"The following word-list represents the accumulation of the above society of students and instructors between 1896 and 1900." Mostly college slang, but of no one locality.

STEADMAN, JOHN MARCELLUS.
Language taboos of American college students. (English studies. Amsterdam, June, 1935. 8°. v. 17, p. 81–91.) RNA
A list of taboo words submitted by 361 students, men and women, of Emory University, Georgia. There are three long lists of provincial words, common "tacky" words, and illiterate and ungrammatical words and constructions. Does not contain much slang.

STUDIES in current colloquial usage by a group of graduate students in a practicum course in the School of Education, New York University, under the direction of Professor Walter Barnes. No. 1. 1933.
Mimeographed.
Part III. "Report of the committee on slang." 25 p. An historical introduction to the subject of slang is followed by lists of slang words, collected from two hundred college, high school and elementary school teachers in New York, New Jersey, and Pennsylvania. 432 slang expressions were submitted and the reactions noted and tabulated. The expressions were classified as acceptable, trite and forceless, offensive, doubtful, and omitted. The reactions of the men towards the list of slang words were compared with the reactions of the women, and many other statistical charts were drawn up from a study of the results.

School and College Slang, continued

WESEEN, MAURICE HARLEY.
Crowell's dictionary of English grammar and handbook of American usage. New York: Thomas Y. Crowell Company [cop. 1928]. ix, 703 p. 8°.   RND
Contains a special vocabulary of American college slang, p. 123–128.

Brown

COLLEGE slang a language all its own. (The Literary digest. New York, March 14, 1925. f°. v. 84, p. 64–65.)   *DA
From *The Providence Journal*, and *The Brooklyn Eagle*, based on an article by Fredson Bowers, editor of the Brown University daily newspaper. Current campus lingo of Brown.

Bryn Mawr

SAVAGE, HOWARD JAMES.
College slang words and phrases from Bryn Mawr College. (Dialect notes. New Haven, 1922. 8°. v. 5, p. 139–148.)   RNZ
Words collected at Bryn Mawr from 1915 to 1922.

Cambridge

AN ENEMY to all ambiguity [Cambridge slang]. (Gentleman's magazine. London, Dec., 1794. 8°. v. 76, p. 1084–1085.)   *DA
• Introduces a number of slang terms in common use at Cambridge University, and asks readers to enlighten the author as to some of the meanings. This is done in the Jan., 1795 issue, v. 77, p. 18–22, in an article signed "Cantab."

BRISTED, CHARLES ASTOR.
The Cantab language. (In his: Five years in an English university... New York: G. P. Putnam & Co., 1852. 12°. v. 1, p. 30–35.)
STK (Cambridge)
Written for Americans by an American, and he inserts a glossary of slang terms for the benefit of his readers.

THE CANTAB. (The Satirist. London, 1808. 8°. June, 1808, v. 2, p. 364–369; Dec., 1808, v. 3, p. 476–483.)   *DA
A number of articles appeared in *The Satirist* under the heading "The Cantab," but these two contain a great deal of student slang.

GRADUS ad Cantabrigiam: or, A dictionary of terms, academical and colloquial, or cant, which are used at the University of Cambridge... London: W. J. and J. Richardson, 1803. 139 p. 12°.   RNM
Contemporary expressions, with scholarly etymological "notes and quotes" which ramble on delightfully.

TEICHMAN, OSKAR.
Colloquial or cant terms peculiar to the University of Cambridge in 1824. (In his: The Cambridge undergraduate of 100 years ago... Cambridge: W. Heffer & Sons, 1926. 8°. p. 96–103.)   STK (Cambridge)
Many of these terms are still in use at Cambridge. They were taken from the *Gradus ad Cantabrigiam* (q.v.).
A good deal of Cambridge slang may be garnered from *Alma Mater; or, Seven years at the University of Cambridge. By a Trinity-man [John Wright]...* London: Black, Young, and Young, 1927. 2 v. 12°. *STK (Cambridge)*.

Colgate

RUSSELL, JASON ALMUS.
Colgate University slang. (American speech. Baltimore, Feb., 1930. 4°. v. 5, p. 238–239.)
RNA
A short list. An illustrative sentence follows each expression in order that its meaning may be made more clear to the reader.

Columbia

BANKS, J. R. MCREYNOLDS.
An unabridged collegiate dictionary. (Columbia jester. New York, 1927–28. 4°. Dec., 1927, v. 27, p. 10; Jan., 1928, v. 27, p. 19; Feb., 1928, v. 27, p. 14; March, 1928, v. 27, p. 12.)
STG
Campus slang of Columbia University, New York.

Dartmouth

SELLMER, R. A.
They called them babes. The story of Dartmouth slang. (Jack-o-Lantern. Hanover, N. H., March 28, 1933. 4°. v. 25, p. 16.)
STG (Dartmouth)
Reviews campus slang of Dartmouth College — some old, some modern.

Denver

PATTON, MARY.
[College slang.] (The Clarionette. March 18, 1937.)
Slang of the University of Denver.

Hampden Sidney

WOODWORTH, R. B.
College slang, Hampden Sidney. (American notes and queries. Philadelphia, Nov. 30, 1889. 8°. v. 4, p. 60.)   *DA
Nineteen words and phrases common to Hampden Sidney, in Virginia.

Harvard

B., R. G.
College slang, Harvard. (American notes and queries. Philadelphia, Nov. 9, 1889. 8°. v. 4, p. 22.)   *DA
Sixteen words and phrases commonly heard on the Harvard campus.

COLLEGE dialect. (The Harvard magazine. Cambridge, May, 1858. 8°. v. 4, p. 174–177.)
*DA
A defence of college slang. "How many a thought would be left unuttered, if this ever-ready means of expression did not exist!" The slang words "toot," "scrub," and "squirt," were then in vogue.

Johns Hopkins

KUETHE, J. LOUIS.
Johns Hopkins jargon. (American speech. Baltimore, June, 1932. 4°. v. 7, p. 327–338.)
RNA
One of the longer lists of college slang of the twentieth century.

Kansas

PINGRY, CARL, AND VANCE RANDOLPH.
Kansas University slang. (American speech. Baltimore, Feb., 1928. 4°. v. 3, p. 217–221.)
Glossary collected in 1926–1927.   RNA

[SLANG.] (The Nation. New York, March 28, 1912. 4°. v. 94, p. 303.)   *DA
Short notice on the proposal of the University of Kansas to campaign against slang. Further comment appears in the April 25 issue, p. 410.

School and College Slang, continued

Lincoln

SEBASTIAN, HUGH.
Negro slang in Lincoln University. (American speech. New York, Dec., 1934. 4°. v. 9, p. 287–290.)   RNA
Lincoln University is located at New Oxford, Pennsylvania. A special slang has been developed by Lincoln students.

Michigan

GORE, WILLARD CLARK.
Student slang. [Ann Arbor, 1896.] 29 p. 8°. (Contributions to rhetorical theory. Edited by Fred Newton Scott. [no.]2.)   RNM
"Reprinted, with some changes and additions, from *The Inlander* [a student publication of the University of Michigan] for November and December, 1895."
Aided by collections turned in by some two hundred students, Professor Gore arranged the words into a descriptive glossary. Etymologies were given, when known. The slang is local to the extent that only those words used by students at the University of Michigan were included.
Bibliography, p. 25–29, contains all the important books and articles on slang then known, including a number of French and German titles.

Missouri

CARTER, VIRGINIA.
University of Missouri slang. (American speech. Baltimore, Feb., 1931. 4°. v. 6, p. 203–206.)   RNA
Terms in daily use at the University of Missouri. Some borrowed from other schools.

Oxford

BRADLEY, EDWARD.
The adventures of Mr. Verdant Green. By Cuthbert Bede [Edward Bradley]. With illustrations...by the author... London: James Blackwood, 1858. 118, 108, 112 p. 12°.   NCW
This popular work which ran through many editions is a mine of Oxford slang, and Victorian slang in general. The first part of this work appeared in 1853.

—— London: James Blackwood [187–?]. 271 p. 12°.   NCW

—— New York: Carleton, 1875. 3 parts in 1 v. 12°.   NCW

—— New York: Carleton, 1878. 3 parts in 1 v. 12°.   NCW

GODDARD, E. H.
Brasenose ale. Oxford: Privately printed, 1878.
Contains some slang.

MORGAN, JOHN AINSWORTH.
Oxford observations. New York: F. H. Hitchcock, 1925. xii, 84 p. illus. 8°.   STK (Oxford)
Glossary, p. 73–84. Current Oxford expressions, mostly slang.
Slang did not become popular at Oxford until after 1825. "When I went up to Oxford, 1823–4, there were two things unknown in Christ Church, and I believe very generally in Oxford — smoking and slang. I never saw a man smoking until Michaelmas Term, 1826. I never heard a word of slang until about the same time." — Archdeacon Denison, *Our memories, shadows of old Oxford, edited and printed by H. Daniel*, Oxford, 1893.

OXFORD slang. (Macmillan's magazine. London, Nov., 1869. 8°. v. 21, p. 68–72.)   *DA
"Oxford slang may be divided into two classes: there is the slang of the place, and there is the slang of the people." Current expressions explained.

Smith

FARRAND, MARGARET L.
The slang at Smith. (The Delineator. New York, Oct., 1920. f°. v. 97, p. 119.)   †VSA
A few expressions from Smith College, Northampton, Mass.

South Dakota State College

SEBASTIAN, HUGH.
Agricultural College slang in South Dakota. (American speech. New York, Oct., 1936. 4°. v. 11, p. 279–280.)   RNA
South Dakota State College of Agriculture and Engineering has its own brand of slang.

Stanford

MORSE, WILLIAM R.
Stanford expressions. (American speech. Baltimore, March, 1927. 4°. v. 2, p. 275–279.)   RNA
Lists expressions used at Stanford University, and a few general on the Pacific coast.
See also John Ashton Shidler, "More Stanford expressions," *American speech*, 1932, v. 7, p. 434–437.

Southern California

COLLEGIANS have a language all their own. (Word study. Springfield, Mass., Sept., 1927. 4°. v. 3, no. 1, p. 3–4.)   RNA
Reprinted from a United Press dispatch. College slang in California. Mentions a pamphlet entitled *Campus cant*, compiled at the University of Southern California.

Virginia

SHORT dictionary of slang, jargon, cant and popular customs. (University of Virginia alumni news. Charlottesville, Jan., 1936. 4°. v. 24, p. 80–81.)   STG
Twenty-four terms of campus slang, old and new, known to the students at the University of Virginia. The most interesting one is *calathump*, "an organized student riot," dating back to 1844 and lasting until the '60's.

Yale

BAGG, LYMAN HOTCHKISS.
Four years at Yale. By a graduate of '69 [Lyman Hotchkiss Bagg]. New Haven, Conn.: Charles C. Chatfield, 1871. xiv, 713 p. 12°.   STG (Yale)
List of college slang at Yale, p. 42–49. The entire text is studded with college slang of the period.

DIALECT

In studying American speech one cannot afford to overlook the regional dialects. The connection between slang and dialect may seem remote, but the speech habits involved are very much the same, and it seemed wise to add the following references to the general study of slang in the hope that the speech of America will be viewed from all angles and thus lead eventually to a better understanding of speech psychology. The practice of splitting the study of speech into many pedantic categories has driven students from this most attractive and significant field of research. Over-refinement and hair-splitting have given philology a very stuffy atmosphere. It needs the fresh air of informality. The compiler of this bibliography is not a philologist, but he would like to feel that this work, already extended beyond the original plan, has been of some help to those more capable of pursuing the odds and ends of speech. Since the field of English dialect is so vast no attempt has been made to include it in this work. The publications of the English Dialect Society will repay any student who wades through them.

GENERAL WORKS

BLOCH, BERNARD.
Reviewing for the linguistic atlas. (American speech. New York, Feb., 1935. 4°. v. 10, p. 3–9.) RNA
Chiefly a description of the field work being done by the students who are assisting in bringing together the material for the atlas of American dialect and other regional speech variations. Cf. the articles by Handley and Kurath.

BOOKS containing American local dialects. A series of lists compiled by the St. Louis Public Library. St. Louis, 1914. 16 p. 8°.
* GAH p.v.3, no.16
"The following lists have appeared at various times in the *Monthly bulletin* of the St. Louis Public Library, beginning in February, 1913, and ending in June, 1914... The word 'dialect' is used throughout in the popular rather than in the strict philological sense." — *Preface.*
Contents: New England, by Arthur E. Bostwick, p. 5–6; The Pennsylvania German, by C. C. Ziegler, p. 7–8; The Middle West, by Clara Chew, p. 8; Missouri, by William Clark Breckenridge, p. 9–10; The Southern states, by Mary Denson Pretlow, p. 11–12; The Creoles of Louisiana, by Helen Tutt, p. 13–14; The cowboy country, by Genevieve Pierson, p. 14; The negro, by Helen Tutt, p. 15–16.
Chiefly a list of American dialect novels. The entries are annotated.

BURT, N. C.
The dialects of our country. (Appleton's journal. New York, Nov., 1878. 8°. v. 20, p. 411–417.)
* DA
Examples of dialectal differences in the United States, by region and by race, with emphasis on the speech of New England and the South.

BURTON, WILLIAM EVANS.
The cyclopedia of wit and humor... New York: D. Appleton & Co., 1867. 2 v. 8°. NAP
Most of the first volume is devoted to American humorous literature, arranged chronologically from 1625 to 1856. Contains many dialect stories from every part of the country. Still one of the best anthologies to be had.

CHANNING, GRACE ELLERY, AND J. W. CALD-WELL.
The abuse of dialect in fiction. (Belford's monthly and democratic review. Chicago, Nov., 1891. 8°. v. 7, p. 304–315.)
* DA
This article is in two parts. The first, by Grace Ellery Channing, is entitled "Foreign languages in

English fiction," and the second, by Joshua W. Caldwell, is entitled, "The manufacture of dialect." The introduction of foreign words into our fiction is decried. Simplicity and good taste are against word borrowing. The second article describes the work of the southern dialect writers, with particular attention to Miss Murfree. Her writings set the fad for dialect and "has been a positive injury to the cause of American literature."

GILMAN, ARTHUR.
The Dialect Society and some English "Americanisms." (The Literary world. Boston, Aug. 16, 1879. 4°. v. 10, p. 267–268.) * DA
Finds that the words contained in the *Glossary of words and phrases peculiar to the dialect of Cumberland,* published by the Dialect Society, are strikingly like the words spoken in certain sections of America. Selects about 300 words to prove this.

HANFORD, G. L.
Metaphor and simile in American folk-speech. (Dialect notes. New Haven, 1922. 8°. v. 5, p.·149–180.) RNZ
Dialect expressions, colloquialisms, Americanisms, exclamations, and other colorful examples of American speech are listed alphabetically, defined, and their geographical locale designated.
Addenda by B. Q. Morgan appeared in v. 5, p. 289–291.

HANLEY, MILES L.
Progress of the linguistic atlas. (Dialect notes. New Haven, 1931–37. 8°. 1931, v. 6, part 3, p. 91–98; 1932, v. 6, part 4, p. 235–236; 1932, v. 6, part 5, p. 281–282; 1933, v. 6, part 6, p. 335; 1933, v. 6, part 7, p. 365–367; 1934, v. 6, part 8, p. 391–392; 1934, v. 6, part 9, p. 417–419; 1935, v. 6, part 10, p. 449–452; 1935, v. 6, part 11, p. 481–485; 1936, v. 6, part 12/13, p. 513–516; 1937, v. 6, part 15, p. 622–624.) RNZ
The later reports are mostly by Hans Kurath.

HEIL, JOHANN ALBERT.
Die Volkssprache im Nordosten der Vereinigten Staaten von Amerika, dargestellt auf Grund der Biglow papers von James Russel [!] Lowell. (Giessener Beiträge zur Erforschung der Sprache und Kultur Englands und Nordamerikas. Breslau, 1927. 8°. Bd. 3, p. 205–311.)
Copy in Harvard University Library.

Dialect, continued

HEMPL, GEORGE.
The study of American English. (The Chautauquan. Chautauqua, N. Y., Jan., 1896. 8°. v. 22, p. 436–441.) *DA
A plea is made by the secretary of the phonetic section of the Modern Language Association of America, for assistance in collecting regional speech. A great many words are analyzed to show the method desired. A circular on the subject of regional speech is reprinted in the article. See also *The Nation*, New York, Nov. 29, 1894, v. 59, p. 406, * *DA*.

KURATH, HANS. *See* HANLEY, MILES L.

LONG, PERCY WALDRON.
The American dialect dictionary. (American speech. Baltimore, May, 1926. 4°. v. 1, p. 439–442.) RNA
Brief notes on the American Dialect Society, and the proposed new dictionary undertaken by Professor W. A. Craigie.

MENNER, ROBERT JAMES.
Linguistic geography and the American atlas. (American speech. Baltimore, October, 1933. 4°. v. 8, p. 3–7.) RNA
The linguistic atlas is based on the one edited by Jules Gilliéron in France. "The aims of most linguistic atlases so far undertaken have been the same: to record dialectal differences in phonology, morphology, and vocabulary." Hopes a similar atlas will be undertaken in England. The American project is under the direction of Prof. Hans Kurath, of Yale.

VAN PATTEN, NATHAN.
Source material for study of dialects. (American speech. Baltimore, Aug., 1929. 4°. v. 4, p. 425–429.) RNA
Outlines a plan of procedure for those who wish to contribute to American dialect studies. The suggestions are concrete and should prove of value to the student.

WARNER, L. R. R.
American dialect literature. (Methodist review. New York, Sept., 1915. 8°. v. 97, p. 763–771.) *DA
A brief survey of American regional fiction containing dialects.

WELLARD, JAMES HOWARD.
Some observations on American speech. (Nineteenth century and after. London, March, 1935. 8°. v. 117, p. 374–384.) *DA
Comments on the scientific survey of American dialects by the Council of Learned Societies, begun in 1931. The great size of the American continent makes this task complicated. Regional accents are commented upon, and the differences between American and English speech are noted. Mentions slang. Bibliographical footnotes.

REGIONAL DIALECTS

Alabama

PAYNE, L. W.
A word list from east Alabama. (Dialect notes. New Haven, 1908–09. 8°. v. 3, p. 279–328, 343–391.) RNZ
Several hundred southernisms, negro and white.

Arkansas

CARR, JOSEPH WILLIAM.
A list of words from northwest Arkansas. (Dialect notes. New Haven, 1904. 8°. v. 2, p. 416–422.) RNZ
Glossary of words used in Fayetteville, Arkansas, and vicinity. Many of the quotations are from *Three years in America*, by Marion Hughes.

Words from northwest Arkansas. (Dialect notes. New Haven, 1905–09. 8°. v. 3, p. 68–103, 124–165, 205–238, 392–406.) RNZ
Contributions made by the English Club of the University of Arkansas. Several hundred words are given. In the last compilation words common to different parts of the country are enumerated.

Arizona

MAN, A. P., Jr.
Arizona. (Dialect notes. New Haven, 1914. 8°. v. 4, p. 164–165.) RNZ
Desert terms collected from Stuart Edward White's *Arizona nights*.

California

LEHMAN, BENJAMIN HARRISON.
A word-list from California. (Dialect notes. New Haven, 1921. 8°. v. 5, p. 109–114.) RNZ
General words, local words, occupational words, student slang, imported words, flower terms, animal terms, words for the automobile.

OWEN, DOUGLAS, AND OTHERS.
California English. (Notes and queries. London, 1906–07. 8°. Nov. 17, 1906, series 10, v. 6, p. 381–382; Jan. 12, 1907, series 10, v. 7, p. 36–37; Feb. 16, 1907, series 10, v. 7, p. 136–137; Feb. 23, 1907, series 10, v. 7, p. 154–155; March 9, 1907, series 10, v. 7, p. 197.) *R–*DA
A number of West Coast words, strange to English ears, are brought out in the course of this correspondence. The imaginary coin, called a "bit," is rather fully discussed.

Colorado

SWINBURNE, LOUIS.
The bucolic dialect of the plains. (Scribner's magazine. New York, Oct., 1887. 8°. v. 2, p. 505–512.) *DA
Indian, Spanish, and cowboy words of the country immediately south of Denver, Colorado, with particular emphasis on the cowboy lingo.

Connecticut

BABBITT, EUGENE HOWARD.
The dialect of western Connecticut. (Dialect notes. Boston, 1894. 8°. v. 1, p. 338–343.) RNZ
"A group of towns near the New York line, halfway up the state of Connecticut, forms a 'speech island' of more than usual interest."

FULLER, M. CORDELIA.
Word list from Danbury, Connecticut. (Dialect notes. New Haven, Dec., 1932. 8°. v. 6, p. 283–284.) RNZ
"These words and phrases have been used by members of Miss Fuller's family, especially by her mother, Mrs. Virginia Fuller, who is now ninety-three years old." — *Editor*.

Dialect, continued

MEAD, WILLIAM EDWARD, AND G. D. CHASE.
A central Connecticut word list. (Dialect notes. New Haven, 1905. 8°. v. 3, p. 1–24.) RNZ
Compiled by three students of Wesleyan University. Most of the expressions are common to Middletown. Includes slang.

Far West

MIGHELS, HENRY RUST.
Our good talkers of the Far West. (In his: Sage brush leaves. San Francisco: Edward Bosgui & Co., 1879. 12°. p. 189–195.) NBQ
Commends the use of lingo in Bret Harte's and Mark Twain's writings. "We are a race of people — we Pacific Coasters of the early immigration — peculiar in ourselves."

Georgia

COMBS, JOSIAH HENRY.
A word-list from Georgia. (Dialect notes. New Haven, 1922. 8°. v. 5, p. 183–184.) RNZ
Words taken from *Uncle Remus*.

Hawaii

REINECKS, JOHN E., AND AIKO TOKIMASA.
The English dialect of Hawaii. (American speech. New York, 1934. 4°. Feb., 1934, v. 9, p. 48–58; April, 1934, v. 9, p. 122–131.) RNA
A good many Americanisms crop up in Hawaiian speech. The development of pidgin English is traced, and the influence of American movies, newspapers, and schools is taken into account. The factors involved in hybrid speech creation are all present in Hawaii.

SMITH, WILLIAM C.
Pidgin English in Hawaii. (American speech. New York, Feb., 1933. 4°. v. 8, p. 15–19.) RNA
"Necessity demanded a medium of communication between the polyglot people of Hawaii. Pidgin, a mixture of several languages into one curious but serviceable jargon, grew out of this situation." Gives samples.

Illinois

RICE, WILLIAM O.
The pioneer dialect of southern Illinois. (Dialect notes. New Haven, 1902. 8°. v. 2, p. 225–249.) RNZ
The inhabitants of this section were influenced by the speech of the South. About 600 words and phrases are explained.

Indiana

BROWN, ROLLO WALTER.
A word-list from western Indiana. (Dialect notes. New Haven, 1912. 8°. v. 3, p. 570–593.) RNZ
See also the works of James Whitcomb Riley, Edward Eggleston's *The Hoosier school-master* and other works, and some of the writings of George Ade, for Indiana colloquialisms.

HANLEY, O. W.
Dialect words from southern Indiana. (Dialect notes. New Haven, 1906. 8°. v. 3, p. 113–123.) RNZ
Expressions known to the compiler in Vigo county, Indiana, in the Wabash valley. Most of the inhabitants are Scotch-Irish.

Kansas

RUPPENTHAL, J. C.
A word-list from Kansas. (Dialect notes. New Haven, 1914–16. 8°. v. 4, p. 101–114, 319–331.) RNZ
"I have tried to note words and phrases in common or even occasional use, printed or spoken, colloquial, vulgar, low, even coarse slang... Many words have been picked up in the courtroom."

Kentucky

BRADLEY, WILLIAM ASPENWALL.
In Shakespeare's America. (Harper's magazine. New York, Aug., 1915. 8°. v. 131, p. 436–445.) *DA
Study of the dialect, manners, and customs of the Kentucky highlands, with an attempt to show the survival of words which belong to the days of Shakespeare.

EARLY English slang survivals in the mountains of Kentucky. (Dialect notes. New Haven, 1921. 8°. v. 5, p. 115–117.) RNZ
Many of the slang words came from England in the seventeenth century.

FRUIT, JOHN PHELPS.
Kentucky words and phrases. (Dialect notes. Boston, 1890–92. 8°. v. 1, p. 63–69, 229–234.) RNZ
Negro words as well as the slang and dialect of the whites. Has observations on pronunciation and grammar.

SHEARIN, HUBERT GIBSON.
An eastern Kentucky dialect word-list. (Dialect notes. New Haven, 1911. 8°. v. 3, p. 537–540.) RNZ
About one hundred words and phrases.

WEEKS, ABIGAIL E.
A word-list from Barbourville, Ky. (Dialect notes. New Haven, 1910. 8°. v. 3, p. 456–457.) RNZ

Louisiana

PEARCE, J. W.
Notes from Louisiana. (Dialect notes. Boston, 1890. 8°. v. 1, p. 69–72.) RNZ
The compiler writes from Tulane University, New Orleans.

RIEDEL, E.
New Orleans word-list. (Dialect notes. New Haven, 1916. 8°. v. 4, p. 268–270.) RNZ
Words used by the non-French white population.

ROUTH, JAMES EDWARD.
Terms from Louisiana. (Dialect notes. New Haven, 1916–17. 8°. v. 4, p. 346–347, 420–431.) RNZ
Expressions from New Orleans, De Soto parish, and on the Texas border; bird names, and animal names.

Maine

CARR, JOSEPH WILLIAM, AND G. D. CHASE.
A word-list from Aroostook. (Dialect notes. New Haven, 1909. 8°. v. 3, p. 407–418.) RNZ
Aroostook county, Maine. Words collected by Prof. Horace Melvyn Estabrook. Period covers years 1849–1872.

A word-list from eastern Maine. (Dialect notes. New Haven, 1907. 8°. v. 3, p. 239–251.) RNZ
Words from Orono, Maine, seat of the State University.

Dialect, continued

CHASE, GEORGE DAVIS.
Lists from Maine. (Dialect notes. New Haven, 1913–14. 8°. v. 4, p. 1–6, 149, 151–153, 239.)
                                                        RNZ
Lists from Lewiston and Bingham, compiled by Arthur N. Leonard. Some logging terms by Bartle T. Harvey, and a miscellaneous list.

MAXFIELD, EZRA KEMPTON.
Maine list. (Dialect notes. New Haven, 1926. 8°. v. 5, p. 385–390.)   RNZ
Terms from all parts of the state. Obsolete words are designated.

PERKINS, ANNE E.
Vanishing expressions of the New England coast. (In: William Abbatt, Colloquial who's who. Tarrytown, 1924. 8°. v. 1, p. 101–107.)
In *Boston Transcript*, Dec. 2, 1922. Ref. Cat. 187 "Originally published in the *Boston Transcript* and rewritten by Dr. Perkins for our use." — *Abbatt.*
Rewritten with a few changes in *American speech*, Baltimore, Dec., 1927, v. 3, p. 134–141, *RNA.*

More notes on Maine dialect. (American speech. Baltimore, Dec., 1929. 4°. v. 5, p. 118–131.)   RNA
Additions to the above list.

SMITH, SEBA.
The life and writings of Major Jack Downing, of Downingville. Away down east in the state of Maine. Written by himself... [Seba Smith.] Second edition. Boston: Lilly, Wait, Colman, & Holden, 1834. 260 p. 12°.   NBX
The first edition was printed a year earlier by the same publishers. Seba Smith created a humorous character in Jack Downing, and his first letters appeared in newspapers, beginning with the *Portland Courier*, Jan. 18, 1830. Jack Downing was a mixture of Maine philosopher and politician and was a good friend of the President, Andrew Jackson, going with him on his travels. The Yankee dialect used in the letters set a fad, and Haliburton's *Sam Slick* owes its model to Smith. The same may be said of Lowell's *The Biglow papers*, and the writings of Artemus Ward, and later humorists. Smith and his wife, Elizabeth Oakes Smith, contributed heavily to the newspapers and magazines of their period, and a bibliography of their works may be found in Mary Alice Wyman, *Two American pioneers. Seba Smith and Elizabeth Oakes Smith*, New York: Columbia University Press, 1927, *NBC*. Seba Smith had many imitators who brought out Jack Downing books in spurious editions. The chief pirates were Charles Augustus Davis and James Brooks. For real and spurious editions see Wyman, op. cit., p. 233–240. The *Cambridge history of American literature*, v. 2, p. 148–159, * *R–NBB*, gives an account of early American humorists, and the bibliography of the same, p. 503–511, gives a number of titles by Smith and his contemporaries.

—— Third edition. Boston: Lilly, Wait, Colman, & Holden, 1834. 288 p. 16°.   NBX

Jack Downing's letters. By Major Jack Downing... Philadelphia: T. B. Peterson and Brothers, n.d. 119 p. 12°.   NBX p.v.4, no.6
A reprint of the edition by Burgess, Stringer & Co., New York, who copyrighted the work in 1845.

My thirty years out of the Senate. By Major Jack Downing. Illustrated with sixty-four original and characteristic engravings on wood. New York: Oaksmith & Company, 1859. 458 p. 12°.   NBX
This is the first edition.

'Way down east; or, Portraitures of Yankee life. By Major Jack Downing. New York: J. C. Derby, 1854. 384 p. 12°.   NBO
For a review of the Jack Downing books see *Quarterly review*, London, April, 1835, v. 53, p. 396–406, * *DA.*

Massachusetts

CHASE, GEORGE DAVIS.
Cape Cod dialect. (Dialect notes. New Haven, 1903–09. 8°. 1903, v. 2, p. 289–303; 1904, v. 2, p. 423–429; 1909, v. 3, p. 419–422.) RNZ
Cape Cod dialect as it was in 1850 or thereabouts. Includes the "Herring song." H. W. Smith added to this list in *Dialect notes*, 1913–14, v. 4, p. 55–58, 155–156.

NANTUCKET. (Dialect notes. New Haven, 1916. 8°. v. 4, p. 332–337.)   RNZ
Dialect words taken from *The Nantucket scrap basket*, by William F. Macy and Roland B. Hussey.

READ, ALLEN WALKER.
Nantucketisms of 1848. (American speech. New York, Feb., 1935. 4°. v. 10, p. 38–42.) RNA
Glossary of James Mitchell's compilation, who sent it to John W. Bartlett in 1848 after receiving a copy of Bartlett's *Dictionary of Americanisms*.

REES, BYRON JOHNSON.
Word-list — Chilmark, Martha's Vineyard, Mass., 1917. (Dialect notes. New Haven, 1918. 8°. v. 5, p. 15–17.)   RNZ
Words from the fishing village of Menemsha, in the town of Chilmark. A few of the terms may be traced to the Gay Head Indians.

Minnesota

KLAEBER, FREDERICK.
A word-list from Minnesota. (Dialect notes. New Haven, 1913. 8°. v. 4, p. 9–12.)   RNZ
About a hundred words from various sections of Minnesota.

Missouri

CRUMB, D. S.
The dialect of southeastern Missouri. (Dialect notes. New Haven, 1903. 8°. v. 2, p. 304–337.)   RNZ
A glossary of about a thousand words and phrases containing many genuine Americanisms, as well as Elizabethan survivals.

RANDOLPH, VANCE.
A word-list from the Ozarks. (Dialect notes. New Haven, 1926. 8°. v. 5, p. 397–405.) RNZ
Words from McDonald, Barry, Stone and Taney counties in Missouri, and Benton, Washington, Carroll, and Boone counties in Arkansas.

More words from the Ozarks. (Dialect notes. New Haven, 1927. 8°. v. 5, p. 472–480.) RNZ
Continuation of the above.

A third Ozark word-list. (American speech. Baltimore, 1929. 4°. v. 5, p. 15–21.)   RNA

A fourth Ozark word-list. (American speech. New York, Feb., 1933. 4°. v. 8, p. 47–53.) RNA
Cites other works on the same subject and continues his glossary.

A fifth Ozark word list. (American speech. New York, December, 1936. 4°. v. 11, p. 314–318.)   RNA
Randolph was assisted in this study by Nancy Clemens.

Dialect, continued

READ, ALLEN WALKER.
Attitudes towards Missouri speech. (The Missouri historical review. Columbia, July, 1935. 8°. v. 29, p. 259–271.)   IAA
Shows the formative influences exerted on Missouri speech by the Southern, French, New England, Spanish, and other speech elements. Reviews the speech studies of the Ozark region, gives various etymologies of the word "Missouri" and its pronunciation, and supplies helpful bibliographical footnotes.
In connection with Missouri speech one may read with profit the stories of Alphonso Wetmore, in the appendix to his *Gazetteer of the state of Missouri*, St. Louis: C. Keemle, 1837, p. 281–350, *ZZME*.

TAYLOR, JAY LAIRD BURGESS.
Snake county talk. (Dialect notes. New Haven, 1923. 8°. v. 5, p. 197–225.)   RNZ
Speech of the Ozark folk in McDonald county, Missouri. Several hundred words and phrases are defined.

WEEKS, R. L.
Notes from Missouri. (Dialect notes. Boston, 1892. 8°. v. 1, p. 235–242.)   RNZ
Chiefly from Jackson county, Mo. Includes Kansas City district. Those which are common to Michigan are so noted.

WILSON, CHARLES MORROW.
Backwoods language. (In his: Backwoods America. Chapel Hill: The University of North Carolina Press [1934]. 8°. p. 61–71.)   IVP
The homely language of the Missouri and Arkansas hill folk of the Ozark region.

Montana

GLOSSARY of common speech in Montana. (Frontier and Midland. Missoula, Mont., 1938. 8°. v. 18, p. 246–248.)   *DA

HAYDEN, MARIE GLADYS.
A word-list from Montana. (Dialect notes. New Haven, 1915. 8°. v. 4, p. 213–245.)   RNZ
Words collected at Judith Basin, Montana.

Nebraska

CONKLE, ELLSWORTH PROUTY.
Crick bottom plays. Five mid-western sketches... New York: Samuel French [1928]. 99 p. 12°.   NBM
Dialogues of the Nebraska farm folk, written in the homely colloquialisms of the soil.

POUND, LOUISE.
Dialect speech in Nebraska. (Dialect notes. New Haven, 1905–16. 8°. v. 3, p. 55–67, 541–549; v. 4, p. 271–282.)   RNZ
Glossary of dialect terms, chiefly from eastern Nebraska.

VAN DEN BARK, MELVIN.
Nebraska pioneer English. (American speech. Baltimore, 1931–32; New York, 1933. 4°. April, 1931, v. 6, p. 237–252; Oct., 1931, v. 7, p. 1–17; Feb., 1932, v. 7, p. 161–171; Dec., 1933, v. 8, p. 48–52.)   RNA
"Pioneer 'talk' began its currency about seventy-five years ago." Words crept in from early explorations, fur trade, military occupation, trails, trains, stage coaches, Indians, the buffalo, homesteaders, and the pony express.

Nebraska sandhill talk. (American speech. Baltimore, Dec., 1928. 4°. v. 4, p. 125–133.)
    RNA
The Kincaid Act, in 1904, gave the homesteader 640 acres of land in the sandhills. "There was a steady flow of settlers who became 'Kincaiders' into the hills." The nature of the country gave rise to many homely expressions. Includes many cowboy terms.

New England

BRIGGS, LE BARON RUSSELL.
A few New England words. (Dialect notes. Boston, 1892. 8°. v. 1, p. 209–211.)   RNZ
New England in general, and Plymouth, Mass., in particular.

DANIELL, MOSES GRANT.
New England notes. (Dialect notes. Boston, 1892. 8°. v. 1, p. 211–213.)   RNZ
About twenty-five dialect words.

ELWELL, EDWARD HENRY.
Fraternity papers... Portland: Elwell, Pickard & Co., 1886. 310 p. 12°.   NBQ
Humors of dialect, p. 72–99.
A rambling essay on dialect in general with a few examples from New England, based chiefly on the writings of James Russell Lowell.

ENGLAND, GEORGE ALLAN.
Rural locutions of Maine and northern New Hampshire. (Dialect notes. New Haven, 1914. 8°. v. 4, p. 67–83.)   RNZ
An attempt to save from oblivion the vanishing expressions of the simple country-folk of New England.

HALIBURTON, THOMAS CHANDLER.
The Attaché; or, Sam Slick in England. By the author of "The clockmaker; or, Sayings and doings of Sam Slick," etc., etc., etc. [Thomas Chandler Haliburton]... Paris: Published by A. and W. Galignani and Co., 1843. 314 p. 12°.   NDF
One of the best known books written in the so-called Yankee dialect. It is a continuation of the adventures of "Sam Slick." See Haliburton's *The Clockmaker.*

—— New revised edition. New York: Stringer and Townsend, 1856. x, 359 p. 12°.
    NCW

—— New revised edition. New York: Dick and Fitzgerald [1880?]. x, 358 p. 12°.   NCW

The clockmaker; or, The sayings and doings of Samuel Slick, of Slickville [by Thomas Chandler Haliburton]... Second edition. Philadelphia: Carey, Lea, and Blanchard, 1837. 218 p. 12°.   NDF
The first edition appeared in 1836, and was published by Joseph Howe, Halifax. vi, 221 p. 12°. Howe published another issue from the same type in 1837. The second edition was published in London by Richard Bentley, 1837. xii, 367 p. 8°. The first American edition was published by Carey, Lea & Blanchard, 1837. 218 p. 12°.
For complete bibliographies of Haliburton's works see John Daniel Logan, *Thomas Chandler Haliburton*, Toronto: The Ryerson Press [1924], p. 155–173, *NDF;* V. L. O. Chittick, *Thomas Chandler Haliburton,* New York: The Columbia University Press, 1924, p. 654–686, *AN;* and Arthur Henry O'Brien, "Haliburton <Sam Slick>. A sketch and a bibliography," in Royal Society of Canada, *Proceedings and transactions,* series 3, v. 3, section 2, p. 43–66, Ottawa, 1910, *EC.* Various reviews of Haliburton's books may be found

Dialect, continued

in Chittick, p. 665–667, and in Logan, p. 169–170, and for that reason space will not be taken here to enumerate them.

Haliburton was born in Nova Scotia, in 1796, and died in Isleworth, England, in 1865. He was appointed a judge of the Supreme Court of Nova Scotia in 1840. In 1835 he began to publish in the *Novascotian* some satiric sketches with Sam Slick, the Yankee clockmaker, as hero. When it appeared in book form it became one of the most popular humorous books in England and America, and its Yankee speech was considered to be a genuine reproduction, but linguists of later years have proved that such was not the case. Neither was he the "father of American humor" as has often been said, for the Yankee prototype existed in numerous plays and tales such as Royal Tyler's *The Contrast* (1787), J. N. Barker's *Tears and smiles* (1808), Morris Barnett's *The Yankee peddler* (acted in England by "Yankee Hill" in 1836), and particularly in the works of Jack Downing, the pseudonym of Seba Smith. For a discussion of the precursors of Haliburton's "Sam Slick" see Chittick, p. 358–384.

—— Third edition. Concord: Published by Israel S. Boyd; Boston: Benjamin B. Mussey, 1838. vi, 262 p. 16°. NDF

—— London: Richard Bentley, New Burlington Street, 1838. xii, 329 p. 12°. NDF

—— Second series. Philadelphia: Carey, Lea and Blanchard, 1838. 220 p. 12°. NDF
First American edition of the second series.

The clockmaker; or, The sayings and doings of Sam Slick, of Slickville. To which is added, The bubbles of Canada, by the same author... Paris: Baudry's European Library...1839. 421 p. 8°. NDF

The clockmaker; or, The sayings and doings of Samuel Slick, of Slickville... Third series. Philadelphia: Lea and Blanchard, 1840. iv, 13–215 p. 12°. NDF

—— First series. New York: William H. Colyer, 1840. 240 p. 12°. NDF

...The clockmaker. Sayings and doings of Samuel Slick of Slickville by Thomas Chandler Haliburton. Illustrated by F. O. C. Darley. Boston: Houghton Mifflin & Co. [1871.] xi, 271 p. 12°. NDF

—— New York: Published by Hurd and Houghton, 1874. xi, 271 p. 16°. NDF

...Sam Slick, the clockmaker. By Judge T. C. Haliburton... New York: John B. Alden, 1887. 84 p. 12°. NDF

Sam Slick, by Thomas Chandler Haliburton. Edited with a critical estimate and a bibliography by Ray Palmer Baker... New York: George H. Doran Company [cop. 1923]. 420 p. front. (port.) 8°. NDF
Contains the three series of *The Clockmaker*; the two series of *The Attaché*; *Sam Slick's wise saws*; *Nature and human nature*; *The Old judge*; *The Season ticket*; *The Letter-bag*"; and a bibliography, p. 413–420.

The clockmaker; or, The sayings and doings of Samuel Slick of Slickville. By Thomas Chandler Haliburton. Introduction by Ray Palmer Baker. New York: The Leviathan Press, 1927. xviii, 338 p. illus. 12°. NDF
Bibliography, p. 331–338.

Judge Haliburton's Yankee stories...with illustrations. Philadelphia: Lindsay & Blakiston, 1847. x, 192 p. illus. 12°. NDF
Lithographs by Sinclair.

The letter-bag of the Great Western; or, Life in a steamer... By the author of "The Sayings and doings of Samuel Slick," &c. &c. Philadelphia: Lea & Blanchard, 1840. xvi, 189 p. 12°. NDF
First American edition.

—— New York: William H. Colyer, 1840. viii, 25–112 p. 12°. NDF

Nature and human nature. By the author of "Sam Slick, the clockmaker," "Wise saws," "Old judge," etc... New York: Stringer and Townsend, 1855. xi, 336 p. 12°. NDF
The first edition was published by Hurst & Blackett, London, 1855.

The old judge; or, Life in a colony. By Judge Haliburton... Complete in one volume. New York: Stringer & Townsend, 1849. 239 p. 8°. NCT p.v.53, no.4
Blue paper cover, with illustration on front. Two v. in 1.

Sam Slick's new work. The old judge; or, Life in a colony. By Judge Haliburton... New York: Stringer & Townsend, 1849. 114 p. 8°. NDF
Incomplete.

The sayings and doings of Samuel Slick, Esq., together with his opinion on matrimony. By Judge Haliburton... New York: Dick & Fitzgerald, publishers, n.d. 263 p. 12°. NDF

Sam Slick's wise saws and modern instances; or, What he said, did, or invented... Philadelphia: Blanchard and Lea, 1853. xii, 291 p. 12°. NDF

Wise saws; or, Sam Slick in search of a wife. By the author of "Sam Slick, the clockmaker," "Old judge," etc. New York: Stringer & Townsend, 1855. xii, 291 p. 12°. NDF

Sam Slick's wise saws and modern instances; or, What he said, did, or invented... London: Hurst and Blackett, 1859. v, 329 p. front. 12°.
Engraved frontispiece by John Leech. NDF
Many of the terms used by Sam Slick may be found in "Newfoundland dialect terms" by George Allan England in *Dialect notes*, New Haven, 1925, v. 5, p. 322–346, *RNZ*. Over a thousand expressions are included in this article.

HARRIS, RACHEL S.
New England words for the earthworm. (American speech. New York, Dec., 1933. 4°. v. 8, p. 12–17.) RNA
Results of the field work of the linguistic atlas. Includes a map.

KURATH, HANS.
New England words for the see saw. (American speech. New York, April, 1933. 4°. v. 8, p. 14–18.) RNA
This study is an outgrowth of the field work of the Linguistic atlas of New England. A map is given to show the geographical distribution of the word "see saw" and its synonyms.

Dialect, continued

LOWELL, JAMES RUSSELL.
...The Biglow papers, edited with an introduction, notes, glossary, and copious index by Homer Wilbur [James Russell Lowell]... Cambridge: Published by G. Nichols; New York: G. P. Putnam, 1848. 12, xxxii, 163 p. 12°.   *KL
   First edition.
   At head of title: Meliboeus-Hipponax.
   Some copies of this edition have the imprint: Cambridge: Published by G. Nichols, 1848.
   This is the first series of *The Biglow papers.*
   The Biglow papers, written in Yankee dialect by a scholarly poet and philologist, offers with its introductory remarks on dialect, its voluminous notes, and its glossary, the most outstanding study of New England speech yet written. The characters are drawn true to life and their speech reflects the native wit and homespun philosophy of the true New Englander.
   Lowell began writing *The Biglow papers* in 1846. The first five numbers appeared in *The Boston Courier* and the remaining four in *The Standard,* a New York anti-slavery journal edited by one of Lowell's friends. The series began in June, 1846, and ended in September, 1848.

...The Biglow papers. Second series... Boston: Ticknor & Fields, 1867. lxxv, 258 p. 12°.
                                              *KL
   First American edition. The second series appeared originally in the *Atlantic monthly* between January, 1862, and May, 1866.
   No attempt is made to list the various editions in the Library's collections. *The Biglow papers* also appear in the various editions of Lowell's collected works, and in the many editions of his *Complete poetical works,* most of which are in The New York Public Library. Space will not permit a list.
   See Marie Killheffer, "A comparison of the dialect of 'The Biglow papers' with the dialect of four Yankee plays," in *American speech,* Baltimore, Feb., 1928, v. 3, p. 222–236, *RNA;* Johann Alfred Heil, "Die Volkssprache im Nordosten der Vereinigten Staaten von Amerika dargestellt auf Grund der Biglow Papers von James Russell Lowell," *Giessener Beiträge zur Erforschung der Sprache und Kultur Englands und Nordamerikas,* Breslau, 1927, v. 3, no. 2, p. 205–311; Edward M. Chapman, "The Biglow papers fifty years after," *Yale review,* New Haven, Oct., 1916, v. 6, p. 120–134, *DA;* William Lenhart McPherson, *The Biglow papers...an essay,* 1883, 16 p., *NBH p.v.25, no.5.*

PENZL, HERBERT.
   New England terms for 'poached eggs'. (American speech. New York, April, 1934. 4°. v. 9, p. 90–95.)   RNA
   This study was made by field workers of the Linguistic atlas of the United States and Canada. It is accompanied by a map.

STEPHENS, ANN SOPHIA (WINTERBOTHAM).
   ...High life in New York. By Jonathan Slick, Esq., of Weathersfield, Connecticut [Ann Sophia Winterbotham Stephens]. Second edition. New York: Edward Stephens. Brother Jonathan office, 162 Nassau-street: Wadleigh's, 459 Broadway. 1843... 136 p. 8°.   NBO
   Title from brown paper covers.
   In three parts. Part 1 as above; parts 2 and 3 have the imprint: New York: Burgess, Stringer & Co., 222 Broadway, corner of Ann street. Redding and Co., Boston. — G. B. Zieber and Co., Philadelphia. — Wm. Taylor, Baltimore. — Bravo and Morgan, New Orleans. 1844...
   Jonathan Slick's letters appeared originally in the *New York Express* and later letters by him appeared in the 1843 issues of *Brother Jonathan,* New York, *DA.* They were attributed in part to Thomas Chandler Haliburton, the author of "Sam Slick," and a long book review in the *Irish quarterly review,*

Dublin, June, 1856, v. 6, p. 217–267, *DA,* was based entirely on the assumption that Haliburton was the author.
   The creator of Jonathan Slick was Mrs. Ann Sophia Winterbotham Stephens. She was born at Derby, Conn., 1813, and died at Newport, R. I., in 1886. She came to New York in 1837. In 1842 she succeeded Edgar Allan Poe as editor of *Graham's magazine,* and was editor of *Peterson's magazine* for over twenty-five years. She helped establish *Brother Jonathan* and many other magazines, mostly ladies' magazines. She wrote about fifty novels, many of them appearing in Beadle's dime novel series, which she helped to popularize. Her Jonathan Slick letters were written in genuine New England dialect and were more faithful specimens of the Yankee dialect than the more celebrated works of Judge Haliburton.

—— New York: Edward Stephens. Brother Jonathan office, 162 Nassau-street: Wadleigh's, 459 Broadway, 1843... 48 p. 8°.
   Part one only. Letters 1–11.   NBN p.v.25, no.7
   Title from cover.

—— London: Printed for Jeremiah How, 132 Fleet Street, 1844. 2 v. 12°.   NBX
   "Glossary of such Yankee words and phrases as are not likely to be generally understood by English readers," v. 1, p. ix–xii.

—— New York: Bunce & Brother, publishers, 134 Nassau Street, 1854. xii, 299 p. illus. 12°.   NBX

—— Embellished with illustrative engravings. Philadelphia: T. B. Peterson and Brothers, 306 Chestnut Street [1873]. xii, 299 p. illus. 8°.   NBX

WOLFE, JULIA W.
   Some New England neologisms. (American speech. Baltimore, Dec., 1929. 4°. v. 5, p. 134–136.)   RNA
   The free use, without acknowledgment, of a longer article written by C. W. Ernst, which appeared in the *New England magazine,* 1896, v. 21, p. 337–344, *DA,* under the title, "Words coined in Boston."

New Hampshire

ALLEN, FREDERIC.
   Contributions to the New England vocabulary. (Dialect notes. Boston, 1890. 8°. v. 1, p. 18–20.)   RNZ
   Words and phrases in use in Portsmouth, N. H.

CARR, JOSEPH WILLIAM.
   A word-list from Hampstead, S. E. New Hampshire. (Dialect notes. New Haven, 1907. 8°. v. 3, p. 179–204.)   RNZ
   The compiler admits that all of the expressions are not localisms, but may apply to the whole state.

WIENER, LEO.
   New Hampshire. (Dialect notes. New Haven, 1914. 8°. v. 4, p. 153–155.)   RNZ
   Collected from an old farmer at East Jaffrey, who had lived in New Hampshire since 1858.

New Jersey

LEE, FRANCIS BAZLEY.
   Jerseyisms. (Dialect notes. Boston, 1894–95. 8°. v. 1, p. 327–337, 382–383.)   RNZ
   Mostly dialect and slang terms from Cape May and the lower counties. Includes terms used in the glass industry, p. 335–336, and the shingle industry, p. 336–337.

Dialect, continued

New York

BOWEN, B. L.
A word-list from western New York. (Dialect notes. New Haven, 1910. 8°. v. 3, p. 435–451.) RNZ
Chili, Monroe county, N. Y.

WHITE, HENRY ADELBERT.
A word-list from central New York. (Dialect notes. New Haven, 1912. 8°. v. 3, p. 565–569.)
Mostly the Syracuse region. RNZ

North Carolina

KEPHART, HORACE.
A word-list from the mountains of western North Carolina. (Dialect notes. New Haven, 1917. 8°. v. 4, p. 407–419.) RNZ
A list of words noted down on the spot. Many of them appear in his *Our southern Highlanders.*

STEADMAN, JOHN MARCELLUS, JR.
A North Carolina word-list. (Dialect notes. New Haven, 1918. 8°. v. 5, p. 18–21.) RNZ
Includes slang.

Pacific Northwest

GARRETT, ROBERT MAX.
A word-list from the Northwest. (Dialect notes. New Haven, 1919–20. 8°. v. 5, p. 54–59, 80–84.) RNZ
Collected in 1917, in and near Seattle.

HARVEY, BARTLE T.
A word-list from the Northwest. (Dialect notes. New Haven, 1913–14. 8°. v. 4, p. 26–28, 162–164.) RNZ
Washington, Oregon, Idaho, Montana, and Wyoming. Includes a few cowboy words.

LEHMAN, BENJAMIN HARRISON.
Word list from northwestern United States. (Dialect notes. New Haven, 1918. 8°. v. 5, p. 22–29.) RNZ
"They represent the jargon of college students and teachers, of miners and lumbermen and farmers and 'sodysquirts,' as well as the idiom of Mrs. Grundy."

Ohio

HART, JAMES MORGAN.
Notes from Cincinnati. (Dialect notes. Boston, 1890. 8°. v. 1, p. 60–63.) RNZ
Includes slang and dialect. Collected by members of the Philadelphia Society of the University of Cincinnati.

KENYON, JOHN SAMUEL.
Western Reserve. (Dialect notes. New Haven, 1917–21. 8°. v. 4, p. 386–404; v. 5, p. 122–123.) RNZ
Dialect of the Connecticut Western Reserve of northeastern Ohio. The settlers were almost exclusively New England people. Several hundred words and phrases are listed.

Pennsylvania

For a list of books containing Pennsylvania German dialects see William L. Werner's article "Pennsylvania German. 1927–1937" in *American speech,* New York, April, 1938, v. 13, p. 122–127, *RNA.*

Philippine Islands

BARRY, JEROME B.
A little Brown language. (American speech. Baltimore, Oct., 1927. 4°. v. 3, p. 14–20.) RNA

CLINCH, BRYAN J.
The new language despotism in the Philippines. (American Catholic quarterly review. Philadelphia, 1902. 8°. v. 27, p. 369–388.) * DA
The compiler has not read this article.

DUNLAP, MAURICE P.
What Americans talk in the Philippines. (American review of reviews. New York, Aug., 1913. 8°. v. 48, p. 198–204.) * DA
The new language growing up in the Philippines is a strange admixture of English, Spanish, Chinese, and native tongues. The author traces a few of the interesting word origins.

FOSTER, HERBERT HAMILTON.
Über den amerikanischen Versuch, die englische Sprache auf den Philippinen-Inseln durch die Schule einzuführen... Jena: Bernhard Vopelius, 1908. 84 p. 8°. STE p.v.11
Bibliography, p. 7–11.
American speech in the Philippines.

YULE, EMMA SAREPTA.
English language in the Philippines. (American speech. Baltimore, Nov., 1925. 4°. v. 1, p. 111–120.) RNA
The Philippines had to choose between Spanish and English languages, and English, through the efforts of pioneer teachers, has triumphed. The story of this great struggle is recorded by a teacher in the College of Agriculture, Los Baños, Philippines.

The South

ANDREWS, ELIZA FRANCES.
Cracker English. (Chautauquan. Meadville, Pa., April, 1896. 8°. v. 23, p. 85–88.) * DA
The dialect of the Atlantic seaboard cotton states, particularly of the poor whites or "sandhillers." It is more often defined as "Georgia English."

COMBS, JOSIAH HENRY.
Dialect of the folk-song. (Dialect notes. New Haven, 1916. 8°. v. 4, p. 311–318.) RNZ
Taken from the folk-songs of the southern highlands, from Georgia to West Virginia. A word-list, with the name of the song from which the word or phrase was taken. Includes slang.

Old, early and Elizabethan English in the southern mountains. (Dialect notes. New Haven, 1916. 8°. v. 4, p. 283–297.) RNZ
The highlands from West Virginia to northern Alabama.
"Much of the slang of the Elizabethan period is still used."
Not a word-list.
Addenda and corrigenda, by J. M. Steadman, Jr., p. 350–352.

A word-list from the South. (Dialect notes. New Haven, 1919. 8°. v. 5, p. 31–40.) RNZ
Includes words from Kentucky, Arkansas, North Carolina, Oklahoma, Tennessee, and Virginia.

DINGUS, L. R.
Appalachian mountain words. (Dialect notes. New Haven, 1926–27. 8°. v. 5, p. 468–471, 472–479.) RNZ
Words taken largely from James Watt Raine's *The Land of the saddle bags.*

Dialect, continued

HUDSON, ARTHUR PALMER.
Humor of the old deep South. New York: Macmillan and Company, 1936. 584 p. 8°. NBW
A rich anthology of southern humor, taken from old newspapers, magazines, and early books. Many of the stories are in the dialects of the Mississippi River valley. This river has been called the "highway of humor" and the home of the *tall* story. The contents treat of the Indians of Misslouala; hunters and fishermen; doctors; lawyers, judges and catchpolls; politicians; preachers; players and showmen; barkeepers and bonifaces; broadhorn boys and steamboat bullies; captains, colonels and privates; pirates and picaroons; schoolmasters and collegians; duelists; ha'nts; greenhorns; the ladies; darkies; the fourth estate.

P.
Provincialisms. (Southern literary messenger. Richmond, Aug., 1849. 8°. v. 15, p. 482–484.) *DA
Holds that the inhabitants of the southern states use a purer English than the people of New England. Cites a few speech differences. This article may have been written by Edgar Allan Poe, although it is not exactly in the typical Poe manner.

PORTER, WILLIAM TROTTER.
A quarter race in Kentucky, and other sketches...with illustrations by Darley. Philadelphia: T. B. Peterson and Bro. [cop. 1858.] 203 p. 12°. NBX
A collection of humorous stories from the South and West, abounding in dialect and picturesque Americanisms. Bound with this is *The Drama in Pokerville ...by* "Everpoint," *J. M. Field, Esq. of the St. Louis Reveille with eight illustrations...by F. O. C. Darley,* Philadelphia: T. B. Peterson [cop. 1850], *NBX,* which is another collection of tales, rich in pioneer slang. It includes the "Death of Mike Fink." The title-page for the two combined volumes is *Colonel Thorpe's scenes in Arkansas.* This is part of a series known as *Peterson's illustrated uniform edition of humorous American works.*
Porter was the founder of the New York *Spirit of the times.* His life was written by Francis Brinley, his brother-in-law, and published by Appleton in 1860.
A list of southern dialect stories may be found in *Library of southern literature,* New Orleans, 1913, v. 16, p. 39–41, of the analytical index, * *R–NBF.*

POWERS, STEPHEN.
Afoot and alone; a walk from sea to sea, by the southern route... Hartford, Conn.: Columbian Book Co., 1872. 2 p.l., (i)xii–xvi, (1)18–327 p. 12°. ILD
Passing through the "piney woods" country and the land of the "sandhillers" in the reconstruction days following the Civil war, the author picked up a wide collection of southernisms, which dot the pages of his narrative. The lingo of the Southwest is also included.

RAINE, JAMES WATT.
The speech of the land of saddle-bags. (Quarterly journal of speech education. Chicago, June, 1924. 8°. v. 10, p. 230–237.) NANA
Study of the dialect of the southern Appalachians.

REYNOLDS, J. J.
The Allen gang. Outlaws of the Blue Ridge Mountains... Baltimore: I. & M. Ottenheimer, cop. 1912. 182 p. 12°. SLG
Copyright 1912, by Kerner & Getts.
Contains dialect of the moonshiners.

SMITH, CHARLES FORSTER.
Southern dialect in life and literature. (The Southern bivouac. Louisville, Nov., 1885. 8°. new series, v. 1, p. 343–351.) IKLD
A study of southern speech and southern writers,

chiefly those who write in dialect. Mentions the more important dialect writers and the stories which most faithfully record the actual speech of the poor whites and negroes. Cable, Harris, and Craddock are considered the best.

Southernisms. (American Philological Association. Transactions. Boston, 1883–86. 8°. v. 14, p. 42–56; v. 17, p. 34–46.) RAA
Gives an excellent list of dialect words used in the southern states, with notes on their origin. Even then the compiler called attention to the rapidity with which southern dialect words were passing out of speech, and out of memory. The breaking down of regional isolation since his day has accelerated this disintegration.

THOMPSON, WILLIAM TAPPAN.
Major Jones' chronicle of Pineville...by the author of "Major Jones' courtship" [William Tappan Thompson]...with twelve illustrations from original designs by Darley. Philadelphia: T. B. Peterson and Brothers [cop. 1843]. 186 p. 12°. NBX
Copyrighted by Carey & Hart.
Specimens of "cracker" dialect.
Bound with this is: *Polly Peablossom's wedding... Edited by T. A. Burke,* Philadelphia: T. B. Peterson [cop. 1851].
This is a collection of stories in the dialect and slang of the South from Georgia to Mississippi. This collection of tales is a lexicographer's paradise.
Thompson wrote several other books in the same humorous manner and was one of the precursors of Mark Twain.
The preliminary title-page has the collective title: *Major Jones' scenes in Georgia.*
Thompson (1812–1882) created the Major Jones character for *The Miscellany,* a weekly published in Madison, Georgia. In 1845 he joined with Park Benjamin in the publication of *The Western continent,* a weekly in Baltimore. See *Library of southern literature,* New Orleans, 1910, v. 12, p. 5283–5307, * *R–NBF,* and *The American,* Philadelphia, Oct. 21, 1882, v. 5, p. 23–24, * *DA.*

South Carolina

PARLER, MARY CELESTIA.
Word-list from Wedgefield, South Carolina. (Dialect notes. New Haven, 1930. 8°. v. 6, p. 79–85.) RNZ
"South Carolina may be divided socially, geographically and linguistically into two sections by a line drawn through Columbia parallel with the coast. The speech of the coastal half of the state is close to that of Georgia, while the speech of the other section is nearer that of North Carolina."

The Southwest

HYACINTH, SOCRATES.
Southwestern slang. (Overland monthly. San Francisco, Aug., 1869. 8°. v. 3, p. 125–131.) *DA
One of the early attempts to collect the peculiar expressions used by Texans, and still one of the useful sources for the study of the southwestern speech. Contains many cowboy terms.
Reprinted in M. M. Mathews, *The Beginnings of American English,* 1931, p. 151–163, RNZ.

Tennessee

BROWN, CALVIN SMITH.
Dialectal survivals in Tennessee. (Modern language notes. Baltimore, Nov., 1889. 4°. v. 4, p. 205–209.) RAA
A few Elizabethan survivals in the speech of Tennessee folk.

Dialect, continued

EDSON, H. A., AND OTHERS.
Tennessee mountains. (Dialect notes. Norwood, Mass., 1895. 8°. v. 1, p. 370–377.) RNZ
Words and usages from the mountains of Tennessee and the adjoining regions of Kentucky and North Carolina.

POLLARD, MARY O.
Terms from the Tennessee mountains. (Dialect notes. New Haven, 1915. 8°. v. 4, p. 242–243.) RNZ
Terms picked up at Gathinburg, Tennessee.

Texas

BUCKNER, MARY DALE.
Ranch diction of the Texas Panhandle. (American speech. New York, Feb., 1933. 4°. v. 8, p. 25–32.) RNA
The old ranchers are now but a small part of the Texas population. Their picturesque language is dying out. This is a glossary of the scraps of speech still alive.

HAMMETT, SAMUEL ADAMS.
Piney woods tavern; or, Sam Slick in Texas. By the author of "A Stray Yankee in Texas," "Adventures of Captain Priest," etc., etc. [Samuel A. Hammett.] Philadelphia: T. B. Peterson and Bros. [cop. 1858.] 309 p. illus. 12°. NBX
Every page of this book is filled with the slang and dialect of the Southwest. It is also filled with "tall talk." See also William Tappan Thompson and William T. Porter for other Peterson books.
Hammett (1816–1865) was a native of Connecticut. He spent about a dozen years in the Southwest, but moved to New York in 1848, where he contributed to the *Spirit of the times* and other journals.

ROLLINS, HYDER EDWARD.
A west Texas word-list. (Dialect notes. New Haven, 1915–16. 8°. v. 4, p. 224–230, 347–348.) RNZ
A list verified by students attending the University of Texas.

TALLICHET, H.
A contribution towards a vocabulary of Spanish and Mexican words used in Texas. (Dialect notes. Boston, 1892–94. 8°. v. 1, p. 185–195, 243–253, 324–326.) RNZ
Many of the words have now become common in the Southwest and may be called Americanisms.

VAN EMDEN, FRIEDA W.
Sure enough, How come? San Antonio, Texas: The Naylor Company, 1933. 70 p. 12°. RAE p.v.165
Verses to illustrate the curiosities of Texas popular speech.

Utah

JENSEN, PAUL.
Desert rats' word-list from Idaho. (American speech. New York, Dec., 1931. 4°. v. 7, p. 119–123.) RNA
Speech of the Mormon farmers in eastern Idaho.

LINDSAY, DOROTHY N.
The language of the "Saints." (American speech. New York, April 1, 1933. 4°. v. 8, p. 30–33.) RNA
Expressions peculiar to the Mormons of Utah, mostly those used in church matters.

Vermont

WORDS from West Brattleboro, Vt. (Dialect notes. New Haven, 1910. 8°. v. 3, p. 452–455.) Over one hundred Vermont idioms. RNZ

Virginia

BARNETT, MORRIS.
Yankee peddler; or, Old times in Virginia. New York: Samuel French, n. d. 16 p. 12°. NCO p.v.490, no.1
This play was popular in the middle western states in the 1840's.

DINGUS, L. R.
A word-list from Virginia. (Dialect notes. New Haven, 1915. 8°. v. 4, p. 177–193, 349–350.) RNZ
Words taken from Clinch Valley, Scott county, Va.

GREEN, BENNETT WOOD.
Word-book of Virginia folk-speech. Richmond: Wm. Ellis Jones' Sons, Inc., printers, 1912. 530 p. 8°. RNZ
An excellent glossary. The appendix gives a list of Indian place names, p. 499–530.
An earlier edition was published in 1899, 435 p., *RNZ.*

MAN, A. P., JR.
Virginia. (Dialect notes. New Haven, 1914. 8°. v. 4, p. 158–160.) RNZ
Words from Mineral, Louisa county, collected during 1901–07.

The West

DAVIDSON, LEVETTE JAY.
Old trapper talk. (American speech. New York, April, 1938. 4°. v. 13, p. 83–92.) RNA
Speech of the trapper and trader in the fur trade era.

FRANCIS, FRANCIS.
Saddle and moccasin... London: Chapman and Hall, 1887. 322 p. 8°. ILD
Contains many western Americanisms and colloquialisms of the Yellowstone region, the Sierras, and northern Mexico. Some of the terms are defined in footnotes.

McCOY, COL. TIM.
A dictionary for dudes. (Harper's bazaar. New York, June, 1936. f°. p. 79, 141–144.) *DA
Contains forty Westernisms.

MACLEAN, JOHN.
Western Americanisms. (In his: The Indians. Their manners and customs. Toronto: William Briggs, 1889. 12°. p. 197–201.) HBC
Includes a few cowboy terms, frontier words, and westernisms in general, such as "sky-pilot," "painting the town red," etc.

MULLEN, KATE.
Westernisms. (American speech. Baltimore, Dec., 1925. 4°. v. 1, p. 149–153.) RNA
An assortment of expressions peculiar to the lands west of the Mississippi. From these words we catch the character and the spirit of the people.

Dialect, continued

PARDOE, T. EARL.
Some studies of Rocky Mountain dialects.
(Quarterly journal of speech. Chicago, June,
1935. 8°. v. 21, p. 348–355.)   NANA
Dialect notes from the Rocky Mountain basin. Con-
tains many place-names as well.

WESTERN slang. (All the year round. London,
Sept. 23, 1871. 4°. v. 26, p. 402–405.)   * DA
Speech of the American West, chiefly that of the
gold miners of California. An interesting proclamation
by the governor of British Columbia, in the gold miners'
jargon, is a linguistic gem.

Wisconsin

SAVAGE, HOWARD JAMES.
Word-list from southwestern Wisconsin.
(Dialect notes. New Haven, 1923. 8°. v. 5,
p. 233–240.)   RNZ
Divided into miscellaneous expressions, similes and

metaphors, jocular expressions and exclamations, euphemisms.

Wyoming

DUNN, ALTA BOOTH.
Western (Wyoming and Montana) collo-
quialisms. (The Editor. Highland Falls, New
York, March 11, 1916. 8°. v. 43, p. 297.) NARA
A few westernisms, mostly the well-known ones,
briefly defined.

PETERSEN, SARAH CHRISTINE.
Yellowstone Park language. (American
speech. Baltimore, Oct., 1931. 4°. v. 7, p. 21–
23.)   RNA
A number of college boys and girls get vacation jobs
in Yellowstone Park. Around their various jobs has
sprung a language.
Additions to this list were made by Dorothy Cook
in *American speech*, New York, Feb., 1935, v. 10,
p. 75–76, *RNA*.

MISCELLANEOUS

African Slang

BESSELAER, GERRIT.
Der Ursprung Burensprache oder des "Afrikaans." (Germanisch-romanische Monatsschrift. Heidelberg, 1931. 8°. Bd. 19, p. 268–
273.)   RAA

BRUCHHAUSEN, P.
The commonwealth's youngest language.
(New statesman and nation. London, April 7,
1934. f°. new series, v. 7, p. 507–508.)   * DA
Essay on Afrikaans, a language spoken by one-
half the white population of South Africa; with a
few observations on South African corruptions of
English.

"BUSH-NIGGER" English. (Manchester Guardian weekly. Manchester, England, Oct. 2, 1931.
v. 25, p. 275.)

DRENNAN, C. M.
Kitchen Dutch and cockney English. An
eirenicon. (The South African quarterly. Johannesburg, March, 1920. 8°. v. 2, p. 4–9.) * DA
An account of the English language in South Africa
with a note or two on slang. The author is a professor
in University College, Johannesburg.

PETTMAN, CHARLES.
Africanderisms. A glossary of South African
colloquial words and phrases and of place and
other names... London: Longmans, Green and
Co., 1913. xviii, 579 p. 8°.   * R-RNYL
Bibliography: p. vii–xvii.
Historical sketch: p. 1–17.
"The glossary was begun on the day of the author's
landing in Cape Town in October, 1876, when he
jotted down a few of the strange words that then
fell upon his ears."

Australian Slang

The compiler is indebted for much of the following
to Mr. John Metcalfe, Deputy Principal Librarian of
the Public Library of New South Wales, Sydney, and
to Mr. Alan Mulgan, of Wellington, New Zealand.

AKHURST, WILLIAM M.
Gulliver on his travels! or, Harlequin, Old
Father Christmas and the Fairy Queen of the
silver acacias!... [Melbourne:] Abbott and
Co., machine printers [1866]. 23 p. 12°.
                                   NCO p.v.665
First performed at the Theatre Royal, Melbourne,
Dec. 26, 1866. Written in slang.

Harlequin Robinson Crusoe; or, The nimble
naiad, the lonely squatter, and the lively abo-
riginal. Melbourne: R. Bell, steam printer
[1868?]. 33 p. 12°.   * KL

King Arthur or Launcelot the Loose, Gin-
Ever the square, and the knight of the round
table, and other furniture. A burlesque extravaganza... Melbourne: R. Bell, steam printer,
97 Little Collins Street East [1868?]. 31 p. 16°.
                                   NCO p.v.683

Paris the Prince, and Helen the Fair; or, The
Giant horse, and the siege of Troy. A classical
burlesque extravaganza... Third edition. Mel-
bourne: R. Bell, steam printer, Little Collins
Street East, 1869. 34 p. 12°.   NCO p.v.665
First performed at the Theatre Royal, Melbourne,
April 11, 1868. Written in slang.

Tom Tom, the piper's son, and Mary Mary,
quite contrary; or, Harlequin Piggy Wiggy,
and the good child's history of England... Melbourne: R. Bell, steam printer, Little Collins
Street, n.d. 31 p. 16°.
First acted at Theatre Royal, Melbourne, Dec. 26,
1867.
These burlesques contain much Australian slang.

AUSTRALIA needs slang. (Daily Telegraph,
Sydney, N.S.W., July 14, 1936.)
A long article on slang inspired by H. L. Mencken's
The American language.

AUSTRALIAN colloquialisms. (All the year
round. London, July 30, 1887. 8°. v. 61, p. 65–
68.)   * DA
Larrikin is the best-known Australian slang word.
Swag, jackaroo, brumby, grog-shanty, lime-juice, and
others are mentioned.

Miscellaneous, continued

AUSTRALIAN slang. (Encyclopedia Britannica. 14th edition. London: Encyclopedia Britannica, 1929. 4°. v. 20, p. 770.)   * R–*AL
Glossary taken largely from Jice Doone's *Timely tips for new Australians*, London, n. d.

AUSTRALIAN slang dictionary. n. p., n.d. 11 p. 8°.

CROWE, C.
Australian slang dictionary. [Melbourne:] Fitzroy [1895]. 105 p. 12°.

CUNNINGHAM, PETER MILLER.
Two years in New South Wales; a series of letters, comprising sketches of the actual state of society in that colony; of its peculiar advantages to emigrants; of its topography, natural history, &c., &c. By P. Cunningham, Surgeon, R.N. London: Henry Colburn, New Burlington street, 1827. 2 v. 12°.   BHM
Cunningham made four trips to New South Wales as surgeon-superintendent of convict ships. His narrative is filled with the slang of the period, including some indigenous Australian slang. "A number of slang phrases current in St. Giles *Greek* bid fair to become legitimatized in the dictionary of this colony: *plant, swag, pulling up,* and other epithets of the Tom and Jerry school, are established — the dross passing here as genuine, even among all ranks, while the native word *jirrand* (afraid) has become in some measure an adopted child, and may probably puzzle our future Johnsons with its *unde derivatur.* In our police-offices, the slang words are taken regularly then in examinations." He goes on to mention a few so-called Americanisms heard during a trip to America.

DENNIS, CLARENCE JAMES.
The moods of Ginger Mick... New York: John Lane [1916]. 150 p. 16°.   BTZI
Glossary: p. 125–150.
This glossary contains many of the words employed in the author's *The Sentimental bloke*, a little classic of Australian slang. The poems in this volume deal with the Australian soldier in the Great War.

The songs of a sentimental bloke... Sydney: Angus & Robertson, Ltd., 1916. viii p., 2 l., 13–126 p. 12°.   NCM
Glossary: p. 117–126.
Australian poems in slang. They appeared originally in the Sydney *Bulletin*, except numbers 12 and 14. Foreword by Henry Lawson.

Doreen and the sentimental bloke. New York: John Lane Company; Toronto: S. B. Gundy, 1916. 90 p. 12°.   NCM
Glossary: p. 81–90.
The same as the Angus & Robertson edition. One poem "The Stoush o' day" is omitted from the American edition.
Reviewed by E. V. Lucas in his *Cloud and silver,* New York, 1916, p. 101–109, *NCZ.*

EHRENSPERGER, C.
Australianisms. (Taalstudie. 1889. v. 9, p. 367–368.)
Kennedy 11336.
Not in The New York Public Library.

FINGER, CHARLES JOSEPH.
A dog at his heels... Philadelphia: The John C. Winston Company, 1936. 304 p. illus. 8°.   NAS
"Words from far places": p. 303–304.
Includes a few Australianisms and South Americanisms. A story of an Australian sheep dog.

FURPHY, JOSEPH.
Such is life, being certain extracts from the diary of Tom Collins (Joseph Furphy). Melbourne: The Specialty Press [1917]. 297 p. [2. ed.] 8°.   NCW
This book was first published by the Sydney *Bulletin,* 1903. Contains the slang of the Australian frontier. Furphy was a bullock driver, a farmer, a gold-hunter, and a wanderer.

GARTH, JOHN.
Some Australian slang. (Australian magazine. 1908. p. 1249–1252.)

HANCOCK, WILLIAM KEITH.
Australia. London: Ernest Benn, Ltd., 1930. 326 p. 8°.   * R–BHD
A list of Australian slang words appears on p. 292–293, with a few remarks concerning the differences between the English and Australian vocabularies.

—— New York: C. Scribner's Sons, 1931. 326 p. 8°.   BHD

LAKE, JOSHUA.
A dictionary of Australasian words, compiled and edited under the supervision of G. L. Kittredge. (In: Webster's international dictionary. Australasian edition. Springfield, Mass.: G. & C. Merriam Co., 1898. p. 2015–2034.)
Kennedy 11346.
Not in The New York Public Library.

LAWSON, HENRY HERTZBERG.
In the days when the world was wide, and other verses... Sydney: Angus and Robertson, 1898. 234 p. 12°.   NCM
A number of the poems contain Australian slang.
See also the same author's *Verses popular and humorous,* London: Angus and Robertson, Ltd., 1913, *NCM.* Lawson wrote several novels of Australian life, all of which contain a good deal of Australian slang and dialect. Among them are *While the billy boils, On the track and over the sliprails, Children of the bush, Joe Wilson and his mates, The Country I come from,* etc.

LENTZNER, KARL AUGUST.
Dictionary of the slang-English of Australia and of some mixed languages. With an appendix. Halle-Leipzig: Ehrhardt Karras, publisher, 1892. 237 p. 8°.   RNM
Contents: Australian and Bush slang, p. 1–50; Anglo-Indian slang, p. 51–77; Chinese pidgin, p. 79–92; West Indian slang, p. 93–98; South African slang, p. 99–102; Addenda, p. 103–128; Appendix, p. 129–237.
A scholarly study of Australian slang by a linguist who resided for several years in New South Wales and Victoria. Quotations from Australian authors add to the usefulness of the dictionary.

MCCARTHY, JUSTIN, AND MRS. CAMPBELL PRAED.
The Ladies' gallery... New York: D. Appleton and Company, 1889. 352 p. 12°.   NCW
The first two chapters of this novel are filled with the slang of the Australian bush.

MARSHALL, VANCE.
Timely tips for new Australians. London: Empire Publishing Co. [1928?] 21 p. 8°.

Miscellaneous, continued

MORRIS, EDWARD ELLIS.
Austral English. A dictionary of Australasian words, phrases and usages. With those aboriginal-Australian and Maori words which have become incorporated in the language, and the commoner scientific words that have had their origin in Australasia... London: Macmillan and Co., 1898. 526 p. 8°.   RNYL
This dictionary grew out of the labors of Professor Morris, of the University of Melbourne, in behalf of the *O. E. D.* It is done on historical principles and fulfils the requirements of a good etymological dictionary. New Zealand expressions are included.
The copious quotations are of great value to the literary historian.
Reviewed in *Literature,* London, March 19, 1898, v. 2, p. 314–315, * DA.

O'BRIEN, STEPHEN EDWARD, AND A. G. STEPHENS.
Materials for a dictionary of Australian slang. 1900–1910.
Typescript manuscript purchased by The New York Public Library from the Mitchell Library.

PALMER, NETTIE.
Austral English. (In her: Talking it over. Sydney, Australia: Angus & Robertson, 1932. 12°. p. 38–43.)   NCZ
Comment on *Austral English,* a dictionary compiled by Professor Edward E. Morris in 1898, with a few new Australian slang words not included in that work.

Cobbers. (In her: Talking it over. Sydney, Australia: Angus & Robertson, 1932. 12°. p. 85–89.)   NCZ
Cobbers is an Australian slang word for pal or chum. In this study it is made the basis of an essay encouraging a wider use of slang.

PARTRIDGE, ERIC HONEYWOOD.
Slang today and yesterday... London: George Routledge & Sons, 1933. 476 p. 8°.
M.R.R. Desk
See description under main entry in the section devoted to general dictionaries.

PATERSON, ANDREW BARTON, EDITOR.
The old bush songs. Composed and sung in the bushranging, digging, and overlanding days... Sydney: Angus and Robertson, 1905. 135 p. 12°.   NCI
Contains many Australian slang words, some of which are explained in footnotes. These songs compare favorably with the American cowboy ballads. Paterson was a ballad writer and slangster in his own right.

R., L. G.
Australian slang. (Notes and queries. London, May, 1917. 8°. series 12, v. 3, p. 296.)
* R–* DA
Lists a few words from a current popular success called *Songs by a sentimental bloke.* Wants to know the source of these words. C. W. Firebrace responds with a few definitions in the Aug., 1917, issue, p. 401. H. Maxwell Prideaux questions the definition of the word *bloke* in the Dec., 1917, issue, p. 521.

SADLEIR, JOHN.
Recollections of a Victorian police officer... Melbourne [etc.]: George Robertson & Company, Propy. Ltd. [1913.] 312 p. 12°.   SLG
Contains many Australian slang words and some criminal cant. Claims that "larrikins" was coined by

Sergeant James Dalton, and that it first appeared in print in a police court report furnished by "Barney" O'Hea, a reporter on the Melbourne *Argus,* in the 1860's.

STRONG, H. A.
Austral English and slang. (University extension journal. 1897–98. v. 3, p. 70.)
Kennedy 11345.
Not in The New York Public Library.
Although not containing slang, "The spoken English of Australasia," by Thomas C. Trueblood, in *Quarterly journal of speech education.* Chicago, April, 1920, v. 6, p. 1–10, *NANA,* is of interest to the student of Australian speech.

YOUTH and its elders. (Sydney Morning Chronicle, Sydney, July 25, 1936.)
A two-column article on slang.

ZIRKLER, F.
A few words from Australia. (Writer's monthly. Springfield, Mass., April, 1929. 8°. v. 33, p. 322–325.)   * IH
A native of Australia sends in a group of Australian slang words for the instruction of American writers.

Canadian Slang

See also some of the entries under the special heading The Lumber Industry in the section devoted to Occupational Jargon.

CAMERON, AGNES DEANS.
New words with crops of yellow wheat. (Canadian magazine. Toronto, June, 1908. 8°. v. 31, p. 141–143.)   * DA
"With the one exception of Johannesburg, the city of Winnipeg last year had a greater diversity of languages spoken within her gates than any other city in the world." As the great horde of newcomers trek to the land of the golden wheat they soon take on the speech and habits of the natives. It is a homely speech which has a great deal in common with the cowboy speech of western United States. The literature of the country consists largely of "the Bible, Burns, and the Breeder's gazette."

CHAMBERLAIN, ALEXANDER FRANCIS.
Dialect research in Canada. (Dialect notes. Boston, 1890. 8°. v. 1, p. 43–56.)   RNZ
Notes with additions from articles on Canadian English written by A. C. Geikie and W. D. Lighthall (q.v.). Contains a good bibliography, p. 53–56.

CLAPIN, SYLVA.
Dictionnaire canadien-français... Montréal: C. O. Beauchemin & fils [1894]. xlvi, 388 p. 8°.   RFW
Americanisms and Briticisms are listed on p. xxvii. Anglicisms are listed on p. xxviii–xxx.
Bibliography: p. xliii–xlvi.
There are 123 words of Canadian origin in Clapin's *Dictionary of Americanisms* (q.v.).

DIONNE, NARCISSE EUTROPE.
Le parler populaire des Canadiens français ou lexique des canadianismes, acadianismes, anglicismes, américanismes [etc.]. Québec: Laflamme & Proulx, 1909. xxiv, 671 p. 8°.   RFW
Bibliography: p. xxiii–xxiv.
The Americanisms and Anglicisms are scattered profusely through the dictionary. No dates are given.

Miscellaneous, continued

GEIKIE, A. CONSTABLE.
Canadian English. (The Canadian journal of industry, science, and art. Toronto, Sept., 1857. 8°. new series, v. 2, p. 344–355.) *EC
Paper read before the Canadian Institute, March 28, 1857.
This is among the earliest and best of the few lengthy articles on the subject of Canadianisms. Some of them are imported Americanisms. A great many words are compared with synonyms of a purer strain current in England. The verbal modesty of Canadians is roundly criticized.

LIGHTHALL, WILLIAM DOUW.
Canadian English. (The Week. Toronto, Aug. 16, 1889. f°. v. 6, no. 37.)
Not in The New York Public Library.
Mentioned in *Dialect notes*, 1890, v. 1, p. 45, *RNZ*.

MONTIGNY, LOUVIGNY TESTARD DE.
La langue française au Canada... Ottawa: Chez l'auteur, 1916. 187 p. 12°. RFW
The bibliographical notes in the "appendice," p. 137–187, contain many references to Canadian slang, including what the author calls "yanko-franco-canadien." Includes an excerpt from a letter on slang, which appeared in the Ottawa *Evening journal*, Oct. 31, 1916. Anglicisms are fully treated in the text. There is a lively note on jargon.

SANDILANDS, JOHN.
...Western Canadian dictionary and phrase-book. Explaining in plain English, for the special benefit of newcomers, the meaning of the most common Canadianisms, colloquialisms, and slang... Winnipeg: Telegram Job Printers, Limited [1912]. [30] p. 16°. RNB p.v.38
Contains much slang, a great many Americanisms, and a few Canadian colloquialisms of the western provinces.

WIGHTMAN, F. A.
Maritime provincialisms and contrasts. Words, phrases and expressions. (The Canadian magazine. Toronto, May, 1912. 8°. v. 39, p. 3–7.) *DA
Homely provincialisms that touch upon the daily life of the seaboard provinces of Canada. A few traditional words may be culled from the author's articles in succeeding issues of the same magazine.

YOUNG, R. H.
"Deacon" McGraw. (British Columbia magazine. Vancouver, April, 1914. 4°. v. 10, p. 192–194.) HWA
A humorous story of British Columbia characters, written in the slang and colloquialisms of the period. See also his story "Black Jack Macdonald" in the July, 1914, issue, v. 10, p. 370–371.

Gipsy Slang

BORROW, GEORGE.
Romano lavo-lil: word-book of the Romany; or, English gipsy language... London: John Murray, Albemarle Street, 1874. 331 p. 12°.
8–*OKXE
In the word-book, p. 17–101, are several gipsy words which have come into use in the English language as slang, such as "bango," "bloen," "blowing," "bob," "fake," "pal," "mash," "mort," etc.
In any edition of Borrow's *The Zincali; or, An account of the gypsies of Spain*, one may find an account of "The robber language," which goes into the history of cant, including English cant. Borrow denies that Romany is a cant language or that the gipsies invented English cant.
See also Kluyver's "Romani words in Dutch slang," in Gypsy Lore Society, *Journal*, 1934, v. 13, p. 1–8, *QOX*, a review of J. G. M. Moormann's *De Geheimtalen*.

CUTTRISS, FRANK, PSEUD. OF FRANK R. HINKINS AND R. CUTTRISS HINKINS.
Romany life... London: Mills & Boon, Limited [1915]. xii, 283 p. 12°. QOX
"Glossary": p. 277–283. Includes "Romany or slang."

H., J. C. M.
Slang terms, and the gipsy tongue. (Bailey's magazine of sports and pastimes. London, Nov., 1871. 8°. v. 21, p. 20–26.) MVA
Describes the life of English gipsies, and goes into the etymology of some of their words — mostly of Hindustanee origin, and shows how they have crept into the English language as slang terms.

LELAND, CHARLES GODFREY.
The English gipsies and their language. 4th ed. London: Kegan Paul, Trench, Trübner & Co., 1893. 259 p. 12°. QOX
Author says his information was gathered directly from gipsies themselves.
The gipsy words appearing in this volume furnish many clues to English slang words.
Leland was the author of the popular *Hans Breitmann's ballads,* which first appeared in 1856, and co-compiler with Albert Barrère of *A Dictionary of slang...*, [Edinburgh,] 1889, 2 v., *M.R.R.Desk*.

McCORMICK, ANDREW.
The tinkler gypsies. Dumfries: J. Maxwell & Son, 1907. xxiv, 538, xxx p. 2. ed. 12°. QOX
"Tinkler-gypsy cant vocabulary": p. ix–xxiv of the appendix.
Cant: p. 433–447; glossary: p. 438, 444–447. Gives list of authorities. There is a fusion of speech between the tinklers and the gipsies. The result is cant or cainnt speech. Galloway tinklers have a different language than that commonly known as Shelta. Sir Walter Scott's *Guy Mannering* was influenced by manuscript notes on gipsies sent him by Joseph Train.

MACRITCHIE, DAVID.
The speech of the roads. (The Nineteenth century. London, Sept., 1911. 8°. v. 70, p. 545–554.) *DA
"In addition to genuine Romani language, there are many species of jargon, or 'cant', in use among the wanderers along European highways." Gipsy argot is discussed, particularly Shelta. "Professor Meyer (Kuno Meyer) has proved beyond any reasonable doubt that the secret language used by many of our modern British vagrants was artificially created about a thousand years ago, from Gaelic, and by a cultivated caste."

PETULENGRO, GIPSY.
A romany life. London: Methuen & Co., Ltd. [1935.] 276 p. 8°. AN
Glossary: p. 273–277.
This glossary of gipsy terms includes some slang and cant. Cant is spelled "Kant," which is Hindustani for "diddikai language," diddikai being Romany for a half-breed gipsy. This lends support to the theory that "cant" is of gipsy origin.

Miscellaneous, continued

SIMSON, WALTER.

A history of the gipsies: with specimens of the gipsy language by Walter Simson. Edited with preface, introduction, and notes, and a disquisition on the past, present and future of gypsydom... London: Sampson Low, Son, and Marston...1865. 575 p. 8°.

Language: p. 281–340.

Much English slang has come from gipsy speech, and many of the words are given in this book. Some of the later editions of Bampfylde-Moore Carew (q.v.) borrowed their gipsy words from Simson's book.

See also Frederick J. Arnold, "Our old poets and the tinkers," in *Journal of American folk-lore*, Boston, 1898, v. 11, p. 210–220, *HBA*, which contains a cant glossary; A. T. Sinclair, "The secret language of masons and tinkers," in *Journal of American folklore*, 1909, v. 22, p. 353–364; and R. A. S. Macalister, *The secret languages of Ireland*, New York: The Macmillan Company, 1937, 284 p., *RP*.

SMART, BATH CHARLES, AND H. T. CROFTON.

The dialect of the English Gypsies. London: Asher & Co., 1875. xxiii, 302 p. 2. ed. 8°.
                                                *OKXE

STARKIE, WALTER FITZWILLIAM.

Don Gypsy... London: John Murray [1936]. xvi, 525 p. 8°.   BXY

"Index and glossary": p. 499–505.

Spanish gipsy terms in use to-day in Andalusia and La Mancha and Barbary.

Pidgin English and Chinook Jargon

AIREY, FREDERICK WILKIN IAGO.

Pidgin Inglis tails and others... Shanghai: Kelly & Walsh, Ltd., 1906. 94 p. 12°.   NCM

Glossary, p. 11–14.

CANNON, PHILIP SPENCER.

The "Pidgin English" of the China coast. (Journal of the army educational corps. London, Oct., 1936. 8°. v. 13, p. 137–140.)

Pidgin occurs "whenever races, unable or unwilling to learn one another's languages, come into contact." Urdu or Hindustani was the result of the Mussulman's invasion of India. Gives many examples of pidgin in Cantonese districts of China. Mentions a rare book written by a native scholar entitled *Words used by the red-faced barbarians.*

FENN, HENRY C.

A pidgin English vocabulary. (Editor. Highland Falls, N. Y., July 25, 1917. 8°. v. 46, p. 121.)   NARA

About forty expressions, briefly defined.

GREEN, O. M.

Pidgin-English. (Fortnightly review. London, Sept., 1934. 8°. new series, v. 136, p. 331–340.)   *DA

"Classical pidgin-English is very rarely heard now. Even the modified pidgin, which is hardly more than a sort of slang adapted to the Chinese idiom and very easily acquired, is going out."

Gives some samples of pidgin English, and hopes it will never die. "In some indefinable way one associates pidgin-English with all that is most endearing in the Chinese nature."

JACOBS, MELVILLE.

Notes on the structure of Chinook jargon. (Language. Baltimore, 1932. 4°. v. 8, p. 27–50.)
                                                †RAA

"The best earlier treatment of the jargon is Horatio Hale's *'Manual of Chinook jargon* (1890).'" Gives short history of the jargon and a long study of the grammatical structure.

THE "JARGON," or trade language of Oregon. (The Literary world. New York, Feb. 3, 1849. 8°. v. 4, p. 104–105.)   *DA

"Mr. [Albert] Gallatin, in his philological papers contained in the forthcoming <second> volume of the Transactions of the Ethnological Society, takes notice of a very singular phenomenon in philology, the trade-language; or, as it is called, the *Jargon*, in use on the North-West coast and in Oregon." Gives examples.

POWERS, ALFRED.

Chinook jargon as a literary language. (In his: History of Oregon literature. Portland, Oregon: Metropolitan Press, 1935. 8°. p. 74–88.)   NBB

Gives a number of excerpts in Chinook with English translations.

Yiddish

ATROFSKY, RALPH.

"Tromenicks" or Jewish hoboes. (The Jewish social service quarterly. New York, March, 1928. 8°. v. 4, p. 226–234.)   *PYS

Lists many tramp terms known to the Jewish hoboes in America.

BRODY, ALTER.

Yiddish in American fiction. (American mercury. New York, Feb., 1926. 4°. v. 7, p. 206–207.)   *DA

"There arises in the popular American fiction of the day, a new dialect, which, by analogy with pidgin English, may be called yidgin English. Its basis is theoretically Yiddish, in form it is ostensibly a translation of Yiddish into English. Accordingly, it is a purely imaginary language, logically related to neither of its parents." Gives some samples, and has a word to say about ghetto psychology.

JUDAISM in the "comics" corrupting our native tongue. (The American standard. New York, April 15, 1924. f°. v. 1, p. 7.)   *DA

"The 'comic strip' and the 'Sunday comics'...are peculiar to America. Before 1890 they were unknown. They made their appearance since the Jews came here in large masses." Samples of the slang English as spoken by the Jews in the comic strips are given.

RUMYANECK, J.

The Jew in English slang. (The Jewish chronicle. Supplement. London, May, 1933. f°. p. v–vi.)   †*PBE

Jewish contributions to London slang from 1750 onwards. "Smouch," "ganof," "Jew bail," "mandozy," "sheeny," "kosher," "shemozzle," "smear gelt" and other expressions are traced. "From 1600 onwards Jew is a derogatory word and a derogatory prefix in the English language, meaning cheat, hard bargainer and sharking usurer." This is one of the better articles on the Jewish influence on English slang. An additional note on "smoutchy," an earlier synonym for "sheeny" was contributed to the June 30, 1933, issue, by J. D. Applebaum.

Miscellaneous, continued

MENCKEN, HENRY LOUIS.

Yiddish. (In his: The American language. 4. ed. New York: A. A. Knopf, 1936. 8°. p. 633–636.) *RR–RNZ

Although many Jews look upon Yiddish as a barbarous jargon, it has attained great circulation in the United States. There were thirty-seven Yiddish periodicals, including twelve daily newspapers, in 1936. The impact of the American vulgate on Yiddish is briefly outlined.

WELLS, H. B.

Notes on Yiddish. (American speech. Baltimore, Oct., 1928. 4°. v. 4, p. 58–66.) RNA

Drinking Slang

ADAMS, F., AND OTHERS.

"Max," slang for gin. (Notes and queries. London, 1900. 8°. Sept. 1, 1900, series 9, v. 6, p. 161–163; Oct. 13, 1900, v. 6, p. 286; Dec. 15, 1900, v. 6, p. 475–476.) *R–*DA

In the course of this correspondence a great many slang names for gin are mentioned, bolstered by apt quotations.

CRAUFORD, J. R.

Queer drinks. (Era almanack. London, 1884. 8°. 1884, p. 56.) NCOA

Slang names for drinks, heard by an English actor in Tom Gould's place just off of Broadway, in New York.

FIJN VAN DRAAT, P.

Drunkard's English. (Englische Studien. Leipzig, 1904. 8°. Bd. 34, p. 363–372.) RNA

Shows the transformation of words by a drunken person. "Assimilation, svarbhakti, and the reverse process of dropping vowels in consequence of which certain consonants become syllabic; rhotacism, the weakening and dropping of vowels...must all be set down to a tendency on the speaker's part to utter his sounds with least trouble to himself." Gives examples.

[DRINKING slang.] (Town talk. London, March 19, 1859. 4°. v. 1, p. 547.)

Copy in Library of Congress.
Australian drinking terms, heard around Sydney.

EARLE, ALICE (MORSE).

Customs and fashions in old New England... New York: Charles Scribner's Sons, 1902. 387 p. 12°. IQ

Old colonial drinks and drinkers: p. 163–183.
Slang names for beverages have always been plentiful, and this historical essay lists many of the very earliest, such as "stonewall," "black strap," "calibogus," "bellows-top," etc. More New England colloquialisms may be found in other chapters.

HARDIN, ACHSAH.

Volstead English. (American speech. Baltimore, Dec., 1931. 4°. v. 7, p. 81–88.) RNA

The slang which grew out of the Volstead Act soon reached amazing proportions. Some of these are tabulated, and supplemented by some of the older drinking terms.

JUNIPER, WILLIAM.

...The true drunkard's delight... London: The Unicorn Press [1933]. 375 p. 12°. VTZF

Drinking slang: p. 224–254.
This is the best book written in recent years on the subject of drinking. It is a happy blend of erudition and humor.

LARSON, CEDRIC.

The drinkers dictionary. (American speech. New York, April, 1937. 4°. v. 12, p. 87–92.) RNA

Reprint, with notes, of a glossary of drinking terms which appeared originally in the *Pennsylvania Gazette*, Jan. 6, 1737, and the *South-Carolina Gazette*, April 30, 1737. Contains over 225 phrases. This is one of the earliest lists of American slang expressions.

THE LEXICON of prohibition. (New republic. New York, March 9, 1927. f°. v. 50, p. 71–72.) *DA

Over a hundred slang expressions in common use in the United States to denote the varying degrees of drunkenness.

M., C. P.

Language of the speakeasy. (American speech. Baltimore, Dec., 1930. 4°. v. 6, p. 158–159.) RNA

Twenty-one expressions common to the New York speakeasy. Appeared originally in the *New York Sunday News*, Nov. 3, 1929.

MOTT, EDWARD SPENCER.

The flowing bowl... By Edward Spencer ...[Edward Spencer Mott.] Sixth edition. London: Stanley Paul & Co., Ltd. [1925.] 242 p. 12°. VTW

Contains a good many popular or slang names for drinks. Includes a chapter on the drinks mentioned by Dickens.

NORWORTH, T.

Observations on drunkenness. (The Gentleman's magazine. London, Dec., 1770. 8°. v. 40, p. 559–560.) *DA

A list of seventy-nine slang words and phrases "to express the condition of an Honest Fellow, and no Flincher, under the Effects of good Fellowship." Many of these eighteenth-century words for *drunkenness* are still current.

PRENNER, MANUEL.

Slang synonyms for "drunk." (American speech. Baltimore, 1928–29. 4°. Dec., 1928, v. 4, p. 102–103; Aug., 1929, v. 4, p. 441.) RNA

Lists forty-nine common American expressions for "drunk." Lowry Axley adds to this list in v. 4, p. 440–441.

RANDOLPH, VANCE.

Wet words in Kansas. (American speech. Baltimore, June, 1929. 4°. v. 4, p. 385–389.) RNA

Kansas has been officially dry since 1881, but there is no dearth of liquor terms in circulation.
Reprinted in *Kansas magazine*, Manhattan, Kan., 1934, p. 91–93, *DA.

REEVES, IRA LOUIS.

Ol' rum river. Revelations of a prohibition administrator. Chicago: Thomas S. Rockwell, 1931. 383 p. 8°. VTZR

Filled with the slang of the bootleg era in the United States, including many terms familiar to the underworld.

Miscellaneous, continued

SVARTENGREN, T. HILDING.

Intensifying similes in English. Lund: Printed by Aktiebolaget Skånska Central-tryckeriet, 1918. 512 p. 8°.   RNL

Includes much slang. Has extensive bibliography, including a few slang dictionaries. The section devoted to drinking terms, p. 191–213, is of particular interest, and the quotations are of historical value in tracing terms.

Index verborum prohibitorum
Verbal Taboos

BRYAN, GEORGE S.

Cant in language. (Quarterly journal of speech education. Chicago, June, 1920. 8°. v. 6, p. 79–82.)   NANA

"The form of cant that we mean, is an assumed and pretentious super-nicety in the choice and use of certain words to the disparagement, or even exclusion, of certain others." Deplores the taboo on such words as "bloody," "hell," "skunk," "belly," and "sweat."

CHESTERTON, GILBERT KEITH.

On the prudery of slang. (In his: All is grist; a book of essays. London: Methuen & Co., Ltd. [1931.] 16°. p. 1–5.)   NCZ

"There is a queer sort of prudery about slang, and modernity shows it most in what it calls 'facing the facts of nature'... It is obvious to me that calling the old gentleman 'father' is facing the facts of nature. It is also obvious that calling him 'bean' is not facing the facts of nature."

JESPERSEN, OTTO.

Veiled language. (Society for Pure English. Tract no. 33. Oxford, 1929. 8°. p. 420–430.)   RND

"In the popular speech of many nations are found instances of a peculiar class of round-about expressions, in which the speaker avoids the regular word, but hints at it in a covert way by using some other word." Much slang originates from this common practice. Jespersen takes a good many expressions from the works of Captain Grose.

MEREDITH, MAMIE.

Inexpressibles, unmentionables, unwhisperables, and other verbal delicacies of the mid-nineteenth century Americans. (American speech. Baltimore, April, 1930. 4°. v. 5, p. 285–287.)   RNA

The various appellations for "nether garments" reveal the American's verbal modesty.

RANDOLPH, VANCE.

Verbal modesty in the Ozarks. (Dialect notes. New Haven, 1928. 8°. v. 6, p. 37–64.)   RNZ

"One of the most interesting peculiarities of the Ozark hillman's speech is the extraordinary character of his conversational taboos — the singular nature of his verbal reactions to sexual and skatological matters." Gives a list of expressions.

READ, ALLEN WALKER.

Lexical evidence from folk epigraphy in western North America, a glossarial study of the low element in the English vocabulary. Paris: Privately printed, 1935. 83 p. 8°.   8–RNM

Based on those anonymous gems found scrawled in jails, railway stations, public wash rooms, etc.
Reviewed in *Revue anglo-américaine*, Dec., 1935, p. 146–147 (F. Mossé). * *DM.*

Noah Webster as a euphemist. (Dialect notes. New Haven, July, 1934. 8°. v. 6, part 8, p. 385–391.)   RNZ

"Changing fashions in language can be illustrated at their best in the matter of euphemisms. What is innocuous in one period may become indecent in the next in a manner quite unpredictable." Verbal taboos are mentioned, and Webster's omission of certain words is commented upon, and the words themselves are given.

An obscenity symbol. (American speech. New York, Dec., 1934. 4°. v. 9, p. 264–278.)   RNA

An historical study of the verbal taboo in English literature. English is rich in "four-letter words" of obscene meanings. The public attitude towards words of this nature has changed generation by generation, now narrow, now broad. A few words are traced through several dictionaries, and there are many bibliographical footnotes.
One should read along with this D. H. Lawrence's *Pornography and obscenity*, London: Faber & Faber, Ltd. [1929.] 32 p. 12°. * *C p.v.2056.*

SHOEMAKER, ERVIN C.

Noah Webster, pioneer of learning. New York: Columbia University Press, 1936. x, 347 p. 8°.   AN

"Webster was in sympathy with nineteenth-century tendency to euphemize," p. 291–296.
The Puritan priggishness in the use of words relating to sex had its influence on Webster's lexicography.

STEADMAN, JOHN MARCELLUS.

A study of verbal taboos. (American speech. New York, April, 1935. 4°. v. 10, p. 93–103.)   RNA

The characteristics of verbal taboos: 1. coarse, obscene words; 2. words of an unpleasant suggestion; 3. innocent words that have become contaminated.
Based on a study of such words made by 361 students at Emory University. The bibliographical footnotes which accompany the glossaries are of value. The basis of a study of the taboo idea in folk custom and speech is naturally Sir J. G. Frazer's *Taboo and the perils of the soul*, London: Macmillan & Co., 1911. 446 p. 8°. (Golden bough, v. 3.) * *R–ZAC.* See also the article on verbal taboos in *English journal* (college edition), Sept., 1936, v. 25, p. 573–588.
Other references to verbal taboos may be found in *Blackwood's magazine*, April, 1861, v. 89, p. 421–439, * *DA;* in *Our English*, by A. S. Hill; in Richard Burton, *Why do you talk like that?* p. 89–100, *RND;* in Frederick Marryat, *Diary in America;* and in W. C. Benet, *Americanisms*, 1880.

Swearing

GRAVES, ROBERT.

The future of swearing and improper language. London: Kegan Paul, Trench, Trubner & Co., Ltd., 1936. 100 p. 12°.   RNM

Study of the art of swearing, with examples drawn chiefly from British annals. Verbal taboos and the psychological implications of intensifying similes are outlined. The decline of lusty and picturesque asseveration is deplored. Wars revive our swearing proclivities.
This is a revision of his *Lars Porsena or the future of swearing and improper language*, London, 1927, 94 p. 16°, *RNM.*

HAYDEN, MARIE GLADYS.

Terms of disparagement in American dialect speech. (Dialect notes. New Haven, 1915. 8°. v. 4, p. 194–223.)   RNZ

An extensive and valuable list of terms such as "boob," "jade," "crumb," "numbskull," "silly," etc. Also adjectives such as "daffy," "runty," "cracked." cf. E. L. Wornock's "Terms of approbation and eulogy," *Dialect notes*, 1913, v. 4, p. 13–35, *RNZ.*

Miscellaneous, continued

HILLS, ELIJAH CLARENCE.
Exclamations in American English. (Dialect notes. New Haven, 1924. 8°. v. 5, p. 253–284.) RNZ
Present-day exclamations, classified under headings: Inarticulate exclamations, articulate interjections, onomatopoetic words, substitutes for God, for "Jesus," for "Christ," for "Jesus Christ," for "Lord," for "Saints," for "Devil," for "Hell," for "Damn," general list of exclamations.

JOESTEN, JOACHIM.
Calling names in any language. (American mercury. New York, Dec., 1935. 4°. v. 36, p. 483–487.) *DA
Each nation has disparaging phrases for foreigners. Some of them are traditional, some are of current coinage. A few English locutions are given, but German, French, Spanish, Italian, and Dutch words are also included.

JOHNSON, BURGES.
The every-day profanity of our best people. (The Century magazine. New York, June, 1916. 8°. v. 92, p. 311–314.) *DA
A few old-time oaths, exclamations of surprise and wrath, and a few modern variants are discussed. A few social and psychological implications are woven into the background of the article.

Modern maledictions, execrations and cusswords. (North American review. Boston, Nov., 1934. 8°. v. 238, p. 467–471.) *DA
Short essay on the transfer of epithets from the "God" category to modern maledictions, chiefly those social strata labels such as bolshevik, rotarian, plutocrat, etc.

JOYCE, PATRICK WESTON.
Swearing. (In his: English as we speak it in Ireland... London: Longmans, Green, & Co., 1910. 12°. p. 66–74.) RNY
Irish swearing terms compiled by the "late president of the Royal Society of Antiquaries, Ireland."

REINIUS, JOSEF.
On transferred appellations of human beings. Chiefly in English and German studies in historical sematology... Göteborg: Wald. Zachrissons boktryckeri A. B., 1903. 291, 10 p. 4°. RNF
Dissertation for the degree of Doctor of Philosophy at the University of Upsala, Sweden. It is filled with English and German slang. A number of slang dictionaries are listed in the bibliography. When one is called a Shylock, a Judas, a Moll, a hoodlum, a yahoo, a cadger, a sissy, a dandy, etc., certain definite meanings are applied. Thousands of these appellations are historically studied. There is a word index, arranged according to language.

SWAEN, ADRIAAN ERNST HUGO.
Figures of imprecation. (Englische Studien. Leipzig, 1898. 8°. Bd. 24, p. 16–71, 195–239.) RNA
A study of the old Dutch and English dramatists with particular attention to the oaths, phrases involving the irreverent use of the word God, etc. Hundreds of dated quotations are given.

SWEARING and low language. (The Family herald. London, Feb. 24, 1849. 4°. v. 6, p. 683–684.) *DA
Includes a few mild epithets. Slang is discussed.

TALLENT-BATEMAN, CHARLES T.
The etymology of some common exclamations. (Manchester Literary Club. Papers. Manchester, 1886. 8°. v. 12, p. 345–356.) NAA
Histories of some of the familiar exclamations, such as "Fudge," "By Gad," "Go to Jerico," etc., are carefully traced. The *Papers of the Manchester Literary Club* are the same as the *Manchester quarterly*, *DA.

VALDES, EDGAR.
The art of swearing. (Belgravia. London, Dec., 1895. 8°. v. 88, p. 366–379). *DA
An historical study of swearing. A great many common "swear words" are traced through the world's literature.

Classic Slang

BENNETT, KATHRYN S.
Slang, Latin vs. American. (Classical journal. Chicago, Oct., 1935. 8°. v. 31, p. 35–41.) BTGR
Application of the principles set forth by F. K. Sechrist's *The psychology of unconventional language* to Latin slang, principally that found in Petronius, Plautus, and Terence.

CONANT, R. W.
Classic slang. (The Dial. Chicago, Feb. 1, 1896. 4°. v. 20, p. 63.) *DA
Traces the origins of two or three slang terms to the Greek and Roman classics.

Marbles

COMBS, JOSIAH HENRY, AND OTHERS.
Marbles. (Dialect notes. New Haven, 1922. 8°. v. 5, p. 186–188.) RNZ
"Several contributors, chiefly Professor J. H. Combs and the Reverend Mr. F. L. Palmer, sent in the terms from the game of marbles." — *Editor.*

FRUIT, JOHN PHELPS, AND OTHERS.
Marbles. (Dialect notes. Boston, 1890–92. 8°. v. 1, p. 24, 76, 219–220.) RNZ
The first article gives marble terms from Kentucky, and was compiled by J. P. Fruit. The second is a list from New York and New Jersey, compiled by E. F. Griffing. The third is from Georgetown, District of Columbia, and was sent in by Angelo Hall. A. A. Berle adds a few words from the game of marbles as it is played in Missouri.

JONES, JOSEPH.
More on marble names and games. (American speech. New York, April, 1935. 4°. v. 10, p. 158–159.) RNA
A short glossary from southeastern Nebraska.

T., J. S. M., AND OTHERS.
Marbles. (Notes and queries. London, Jan. 28, 1899. 8°. series 9, v. 3, p. 65–66.) *R–*DA
A number of slang words connected with the game of marbles as played at Belfast, Ireland, circa 1850. Occasioned by remarks on the game which appeared in N. & Q., series 9, v. 2, p. 76, 314–315, by George Marshall, F. J. Candy, John P. Stilwell, Nemo, and C. C. B. The contributions were continued in series 9, v. 3, p. 97–98, 272, by John T. Page, Thos. Ratcliffe, and John Pickford. The whole series of notes was occasioned by the publication of Percy Fitzgerald's *Pickwickian manners and customs*, London, 1898.

ZUGER, JOHN A.
Technical terms in the game of marbles. (American speech. New York, Feb., 1934. 4°. v. 9, p. 74–75.) RNA
Glossary of phrases used at Bismarck, North Dakota.

Miscellaneous, continued

Reduplicated Words

MÜLLER, MAX.
Die Reim- und Ablautkomposita des Englischen... Strassburg: Buchdruckerei M. Du Mont Schauberg, 1909. vi, 106 p. 8°. RNB p.v.4
Double words, such as huff-puff, tirra-lirra, etc., which abound in the English language, are examined in a scholarly manner in this inaugural dissertation.

WHEATLEY, HENRY BENJAMIN.
A dictionary of reduplicated words. London: Published for the Philological Society by Asher and Co., 1866. 104 p. 8°. (Philological Society, London. Transactions, 1865, Appendix.)
RAA (Philological)
Dates the expressions and gives many quotations.

WOOD, FRANCIS ASBURY.
Iteratives, blends, and "Streckformen." (Modern philology. Chicago, Oct., 1911. 8°. v. 9, no. 2, p. 1–38.)   NAA
A long list of such familiar combinations as chit-chat, dilly-dally, knick-knack, jim-jam, hurly-burly, and blends such as needcessity, animule, frockaway coat, chortle, swellelegant, skittenish, etc., and the words with the prefix ker, ca, etc., such as kerchunk, kersmash, cahoots, caboodle, etc.

Tall Talk

McHUGH, VINCENT.
Caleb Catlum's America... New York: Stackpole Sons [cop. 1936]. 340 p. 8°.   NBX
A Gargantuan tale of the heroic deeds of Caleb Catlum, a glorified composite character based on Paul Bunyan and other imaginary "tall talkers." This narrative is filled with homely Americanisms and regional dialect.

THOMPSON, WILLIAM F.
Frontier tall talk. (American speech. Baltimore, Oct., 1934. 4°. v. 9, p. 187–199.)   RNA
"Perhaps the most familiar variety of tall talk is that which consists in a copious flow of derisive or abusive epithets." Another form is exaggerated boasting. Sometimes it takes the form of fight talk, a tale of physical prowess, although the frontier tall talk makes little use of the Paul Bunyan story. Davy Crockett and Mike Fink are examples. Frontier oratory and fanatic loyalty to a native state are other examples.

Olla Podrida

ALEXANDER, LOUIS CHARLES.
On the artistic dialect. (In his: Echoes of Whistler. London: John Long, 1910. 12°. p. 51–61.)   NCZ
"Slang is the stronghold of specialization. It is, too, the wit of the feeble, the mark of the bold, the bliss of the vulgar, and the tongue of the dissolute and dishonest." The jargon of the art world as given in an imaginary conversation between three artists.

ANCIENT modernisms. To-day's slang in yesterday's authors. (John o' London's weekly. London, Oct. 2, 1926. f°. v. 15, p. 807.)   *DA
Mentions a few Jacobean Americanisms, and a number of old slang words from English authors.

THE ANGLO-SAXON tongue. The Anglo-Indian tongue. (Blackwood's magazine. Edinburgh, May, 1877. 8°. v. 121, p. 541–551.)   *DA
"The mixture of English and native words, which we call Anglo-Indianisms, constitutes an idiom in the speech of the governing class, and really forms a bond of union between them and the governed."

BERGEN, FANNY DICKERSON.
Popular American plant names. (Journal of American folk-lore. Boston, 1892–98. 8°. v. 5, p. 89–106; v. 6, p. 135–142; v. 7, p. 89–104; v. 9, p. 179–193; v. 10, p. 49–54, 143–148; v. 11, p. 221–230, 273–283.)   HBA
An attempt to preserve many of the old American folk names, which have become in a sense legitimate Americanisms. "As a rule, I have here entered only such popular names of wild plants as are not recorded in the new edition of Gray's Manual."
See also Willard N. Clute, *The common names of plants and their meanings,* Indianapolis, 1931. 160 p. 8°, QEC.

BOMBAUGH, CHARLES CARROLL.
Gleanings for the curious... Hartford, Conn.: A. D. Worthington, 1875. 864 p. 8°.
NAZ
A repository of eccentric and out-of-the-way information, including verbal novelties and word origins.

BYRON, HENRY JAMES.
Ali Baba; or, The Thirty-nine thieves, in accordance with the author's habit of taking one off! London: Thomas Hailes Lacy, n.d. 38 p. 12°.   NCO p.v.642
Filled with the slang and puns of the mid-Victorian burlesque extravaganza.

CAMP, ELWOOD W., AND H. C. HARTMAN.
C. C. C. speech. (American speech. New York, Feb., 1937. 8°. v. 12, p. 74–75.)   RNA
Some of the slang words of the Civilian Conservation Corps in the states of the Middle West.

CARY, HENRY NATHANIEL.
The slang of venery and its analogues. Compiled from the works of Ash, Bailey, Barrere, Bartlett, B. E., Bee, Cleland, Cotgrave, Dunton, D'Urfey, Dyche, Egan, Farmer, Florio, Grose, Halliwell, Harman, Johnson, Mayhew, Matsell, the Lexicon Balatronicum, and other sources. Chicago: Privately printed, 1916. 2 v. f°.
Typewritten sheets, bound. Compiled on historical principles. Very few copies of this interesting compilation are available.
This set is accompanied by a printed bibliography, 22 p., f°, which gives considerable biographical and bibliographical information. There is also a bibliographical index, listing the authors and titles, but with no bibliographical details. 47 p. f°.

Synonyms of the slang of venery. Collated from the Slang of venery and its analogues. Chicago: Privately printed, 1916. 208 p. f°.
Typewritten pages, bound. The order of arrangement for each word or phrase is the definition, followed by English synonyms, analogues, French synonyms, and Italian synonyms or other languages, when synonyms are known.

CHAMBERLAIN, ALEXANDER FRANCIS.
Algonkian words in American English. (Journal of American folk-lore. Boston, 1902–08. 8°. v. 15, p. 240–267; v. 16, p. 128–129; v. 21, p. 82.)   HBA
An extensive alphabetical list of Indian names which have been absorbed into the daily speech of Americans. The definitions are long, and the etymological notes are extensive. Chipmunk, moose, woodchuck, persimmon, 'possum, mugwump, Tammany, tomahawk, totem, skunk, and squash, are but a few of the words traced to the Algonkian language.

Miscellaneous, continued

COUES, R. W.
Odd terms in a writer of letters. (Dialect notes. New Haven, 1928. 8°. v. 6, p. 1–6.) RNZ
Words taken from the works of Susan Hale (1833–1910), sister of Edward Everett Hale. Some are creative words made by mingling colloquial and dialectal forms.

CULBERTSON, ELY.
Terms in contract bridge. (American speech. New York, Feb., 1934. 4°. v. 9, p. 10–12.) RNA
A few slang terms are presented by the well-known American bridge expert.

CULIN, STEWART.
Street games of boys in Brooklyn, New York. (Journal of American folk-lore. Boston and New York, July/Sept., 1891. 8°. v. 4, p. 221–237.) HBA
Contains a great deal of street slang. Thirty-six games and their nomenclature are given. Added to the list are forty-one games known to the boys of Philadelphia, submitted by Leland Harrison, but they are not described. There is also a note on street "gangs."

CUNARD, NANCY.
Some negro slang. (In her: Negro anthology. London: Wishart & Co., 1934. 4°. p. 75–78.) QPF
The highly imaginative slang of the Harlem negro. The negro has coined a secret language of his own called "sanguadny."

FLAPPERS' words and others. (Literary digest. New York, Nov. 1, 1924. f°. v. 83, p. 30.) *DA
Extracts from an article in *The New York Sun.* The flapper era brought in many new words, such as "dumbell" and "dumbdora," etc. The result of an interview with Dr. Frank Vizetelly, published in the Brooklyn *Daily Eagle* anent the inclusion of new slang words in the Standard Dictionary, Funk and Wagnalls, is also commented upon. See also *Manchester quarterly,* 1919, v. 38, p. 205–210, *DA; New York Times,* April 23, 1922, sec. 6, p. 8, col. 4.

HOWARD, LEON.
Walt Whitman and the American language. (American speech. Baltimore, Aug., 1930. 4°. v. 5, p. 441–451.) RNA
Whitman was vitally interested in the American language and wanted to free it of "delicate ladywords" and "gloved gentleman-words." His attempts at philology are outlined, and his influence weighed.

KUETHE, J. LOUIS.
Q. K. Philander Doesticks, P. B., neologist. (American speech. New York, April, 1937. 4°. v. 12, p. 111–116.) RNA
A brief sketch of the life and works of Mortimer Neal Thomson (Doesticks), and a list of words he coined.
Note: It is not safe to assume that Thomson coined the words listed simply because they are earlier examples than those listed in the O. E. D., Thornton, etc. Cases in which a word can be traced indisputably to one person are rare indeed.

MATTHEWS, BRANDER.
The outskirts of the English language. (Munsey's magazine. New York, Nov., 1913. 8°. v. 50, p. 260–265.) *DA
A review of Thornton's *An American glossary* and Pettman's *Africanderisms* (q.v.). Thinks the Americanisms are more apt and energetic than the Africanderisms. "There is a pitiful modesty in the way

in which Americans refer to a dictionary as if it were inspired. While this obeisance to a book is peculiarly American, it is only another aspect of an attitude observable half a century ago in Great Britain, in the deference paid to the prescriptions of the grammar promulgated by Lindley Murray." Thinks this opinion would have been less noticeable had the British known that Lindley Murray was an American.

Parts of speech. Essays on English... New York: C. Scribner's Sons, 1901. 350 p. 12°. RNB
Contents: 1. The stock that speaks the language. 2. The future of the language. 3. The English language in the United States. 4. The language in Great Britain. 5. Americanisms once more. 6. New words and old. 7. The naturalization of foreign words. 8. The function of slang. 9. Questions of usage. 10. An inquiry as to rime. 11. On the poetry of place-names. 12. As to "American spelling." 13. The simplification of English spelling. 14. Americanisms — an attempt at a definition.

MEREDITH, MAMIE.
Charivaria. (American speech. New York, April, 1933. 4°. v. 8, p. 22–24.) RNA
Continued in same issue by Miles L. Hanley, under the title of "Serenade in New England," p. 24–28. A great many dialect words for this popular wedding celebration are listed.

The human head in slang. (American speech. Baltimore, June, 1928. 4°. v. 3, p. 408–409.) RNA
"Appellations or circumlocutions for the human head are very numerous. Some now belong to accepted English, others are colloquial, and others are branded as slang."

MERRYWEATHER, L. W.
The argot of the orphan's home. (American speech. Baltimore, Dec., 1932. 4°. v. 7, p. 398–407.) RNA
Has sociological value as a character index to orphans. "The slang of the institution was originated or collected almost entirely by the children themselves." Has a glossary.

AN OLD UNIVERSITY MAN.
Slang. (Cope's tobacco plant. Liverpool, Aug., 1874. f°. v. 1, p. 636–637.) †VTY
"Hotten speaks as if slang were one of the necessary utterances of human nature, and could be traced even in the writings of the ancients. In truth, however, slang is entirely a modern phenomenon, and is radically opposed alike to the antique and to the classical spirit." Says modern times are the offspring of "medieval chaos, monstrosity, and madness." Slang began to make inroads with the breakdown of scholarly Latin, and the secret orders of the middle ages, the crusaders, the guildsmen, the explorers, the gipsies, the Free Masons, the mendicant orders — all were fashioners of new argots. Changing fashions also brought new slang. "The apotheosis of slang has been accomplished in the United States of America.
"It is fatal to that true reverence in which so many of the diviner virtues are rooted; it is a horrible, a detestable desecration; it would suffice of itself to ruin the wisest, most valiant people," he says of slang.
This is an introductory essay, and an admirable one, to two articles on the slang connected with the use of tobacco. See the following:

Nicotian slang. (Cope's tobacco plant. Liverpool, 1874. f°. v. 1, p. 646–648, 662–664.) †VTY
This is the first and most noteworthy essay on tobacco slang, and is of great value to the "tobaccophile." A glossary of French nicotian slang, selected from Lucien Rigaud's *Dictionnaire du jargon parisien,* appears in the July, 1880, issue, p. 498–500.
The introductory essay was reprinted in part in *Public opinion,* London, Aug. 15, 1874, v. 26, p. 204, *DA.*

Miscellaneous, continued

ORR, LYNDON.
The nicknames of famous Americans. (Munsey's magazine. New York, Sept., 1908. 8°. v. 39, p. 738–743.) *DA
Most nicknames are meant to convey either affection or opprobrium. Nicknames of the presidents, notable politicians, and famous soldiers are given.

PAUL, HARRY GILBERT.
Slang — the language jester. (In his: Better everyday English. Chicago: Lyons and Carnahan [cop. 1924]. 12°. p. 121–134.) RND
An essay for teachers and students — its aim being speech improvement. There are sections on Americanisms vs. Briticisms, p. 81–84, 143–151.

PEACOCK, W. F.
Charles Dickens's nomenclature. (Belgravia. London, April – May, 1873. 8°. v. 20, p. 267–276, 393–402.) *DA
A study of 971 created personages in Dickens, and a few dialectal and slang inventions and adaptations. "Concerning slang, Dickens knew it well."

PIPER, EDWIN FORD.
Quadrille calls. (American speech. Baltimore, April, 1926. 4°. v. 1, p. 391–395.) RNA
The old square dance terminology contains many Americanisms. The French influence is also evident. The Middle Western states still cling to these dances and the old terms.

POLLOCK, F. WALTER.
Courtship slang. (American speech. Baltimore, Jan., 1927. 4°. v. 2, p. 202–203.) RNA
A few remarks anent the words "petting," "flapper," "gold-digger," "stepping out," "heavy date," etc.

POUND, LOUISE.
American euphemisms for dying, death, and burial. (American speech. New York, Oct., 1936. 4°. v. 11, p. 195–202.) RNA
"Flippant and slang expressions," p. 198–199.

American indefinite names. (American speech. Baltimore, April, 1931. 4°. v. 6, p. 257–259.) RNA
"The grotesqueries of language usually deserve to be recorded, for they have a certain sociological significance alongside their interest for linguists." Includes such words as "doodinkus," "widget," "thingabob," "gimcrack," etc.

Notes on the vernacular. (The American mercury. New York, Oct., 1924. 4°. v. 3, p. 233–237.) *DA
Shows how the innate love of humor among Americans leads them to coin strange words, and odd linguistic devices. The humorous "R"; novel comparison of adjectives; American indefinite names; and abridged writing, are the four divisions of the article.

"Stunts" in language. (The English journal. Chicago, Feb., 1920. 8°. v. 9, p. 88–95.) RNA
"A few generations ago dignity was an asset in speech, literary or oral, and novelty or informality was not... The phrase-makers of our popular reading vie with one another in their zest for picturesque idiom." Adding and dropping suffixes, portmanteau words, popular inversions, agglutinations, etc., give modern language its "punch."

Vogue affixes in present-day word coinage. (Dialect notes. New Haven, 1918. 8°. v. 5, p. 1–14.) RNZ
"Contemporary coinages which exemplify the particular set of prefixes and endings now having special popularity." Examples: hoboette, filmdom, crookdom, golfitis, Hooverization, printery, etc.

RANDOLPH, VANCE, AND ISABEL SPRADLEY.
Quilt names in the Ozarks. (American speech. New York, Feb., 1933. 4°. v. 8, p. 33–36.) RNA

STEUERWALD, K.
Die Londoner Vulgärsprache in Thackeray's Yellowplush Papers... Leipzig: Verlag von Bernhard Tauchnitz, 1930. 62 p. 8°. (Beiträge zur englischen Philologie. Heft 14.) RNA
Dissertation, University of Munich.
Includes some slang, but the emphasis is on orthography.

THIELKE, KARL.
Slang und Umgangssprache in der englischen Prosa der Gegenwart (1919–1937). Mit Berücksichtigung des Cant... Emsdetten i. Westf.: Verlagsanstalt Heinr. & J. Lechte, 1938. 234 p. 8°. (Münsterer anglistische Studien. Heft 4.) RNA (Münsterer)
This scholarly study of contemporary English slang, with its wealth of quotations, and its useful bibliography (p. 212–222) and word index (p. 223–234) is recommended to all students of slang and dialect.
See also the same author's "Slang und Umgangssprache in der englischen Lyrik der Gegenwart" in *Zeitschrift für neusprachlichen Unterricht*, Berlin, 1938, Bd. 37, p. 238–249.

WARNOCK, ELSIE L.
Terms of approbation and eulogy. (Dialect notes. New Haven, 1913. 8°. v. 4, p. 13–25.) RNZ
Good list of nouns such as "crackerjack," "peach," "humdinger," "bully," "dandy," etc. Cf. Marie Gladys Hayden's "Terms of disparagement in American dialect speech," in *Dialect notes*, 1915, v. 4, p. 194–223, RNZ.

WESTENDORPF, KARL.
Das Prinzip der Verwendung des Slang bei Dickens. Greifswald: Adler, 1923. 31 p. 8°.
A short study of the technique employed by Dickens in his utilization of popular speech.
Dissertation, University of Greifswald.

WITHINGTON, ROBERT.
More "portmanteau" coinages. (American speech. New York, Feb., 1932. 4°. v. 7, p. 200–203.) RNA
Lewis Carroll set the style for "portmanteau" words. The magazine *Time* is foremost among modern periodicals in the matter of word coinage. Other cases cited.
See also Howard Wentworth, "Twenty-nine synonyms for 'portmanteau words,'" *American speech*, Dec., 1933, v. 8, p. 78–79.

Rehabilitated words. Notes for a chapter on "Regeneration of meaning." (American speech. Baltimore, Feb., 1930. 4°. v. 5, p. 212–218.) RNA
Speaks of a chapter in Greenough and Kittredge on the "Degeneration of meaning." Sometimes derisive nicknames have been accepted by those to whom it

Miscellaneous, continued

applied, and thus risen to a normal word; *Yankee, Hoosier, Whig*, etc.

Gilbert M. Tucker has a chapter in his *Our common speech*, New York, 1895, entitled "Degraded words." See also "Down-hill words" in *Sewanee review*, April, 1913, v. 21, p. 148–154, * *DA*, by Reed Smith.

WITTMANN, ELISABETH.
Clipped words. (Dialect notes. New Haven, 1914. 8°. v. 4, p. 115–145.)   RNZ
Different explanations are given for the use of clipped words. Student slang is made up largely of clipped words. Newspapers shorten words in headlines. Some are whimsical or humorous. Bike from bicycle, bus from omnibus, are examples of clipped words. A long list is given in this article.

WOOD, FRANCIS ASBURY.
Language and nonce-words. (Dialect notes. New Haven, 1913. 8°. v. 4, p. 42–44.)   RNZ
Such words as swellelegant from swell and elegant, gawkward from gawky and awkward, etc.

WYLD, HENRY CECIL KENNEDY.
A history of modern colloquial English... London: T. Fisher Unwin, Ltd. [1920.] xvi, 398 p. 12°.   RNX
"Colloquial idiom": p. 359–398.
Filled with slang and idiomatic expressions, taken from well-known English authors, with a good deal of attention paid to oaths and expletives.

IN the course of compiling this bibliography many stray newspaper references were noted, and many were put aside for annotation when the opportunity arose. Unfortunately this opportunity never came, owing to conflicting duties imposed upon the compiler. As this work was going to press it became manifest that a great number of newspaper references would have to be left out altogether or put in without annotations. Realizing that some of these articles might contain material of some value to future historians of slang it seems justifiable to list them, even in this unscholarly and inadequate manner. Readers are forewarned that some of the following articles are of little importance, but the compiler, who took note of them over a period of years, cannot at this late date recall the length or the subject matter of a large part of them, and can only hope that in the main they have some useful information in them. Newspapers are a rich source of slang, and almost every American newspaper has had special articles on slang at one time or another.

Baltimore Evening Sun, Oct. 20, 1910; Oct. 25, 1910; Sept. 15, 1910; Sept. 7, 1916; Nov. 18, 1920; Jan. 31, 1935 (H. L. Mencken contributed a great many articles to the *Baltimore Evening Sun* over a period of years, and the files of this newspaper are well worth consulting).

Boston Herald, Nov. 20, 1892.

Boston Transcript, March 1, 1893; Sept. 7, 1921, part II, p. 2.

Bridgeton, N. J., Evening News, Aug. 24, 1889.

Chicago Daily Tribune, Nov. 18, 1917.

Kansas City Star, May 16, 1915.

Manchester Guardian, June 19, 1926.

Manchester Guardian weekly, Aug. 20, 1926, section XV, p. 153; Sept. 20, 1929, 21:228; Aug. 19, 1932; Aug. 11, 1933, 29:116.

New York Evening Mail, Oct. 25, 1917; Oct. 29, 1917; Nov. 22, 1917; April 11, 1918.

New York Evening Post, May 7, 1899, p. 2; May 31, 1919, Books, p. 3; June 11, 1921.

New York Herald Tribune, Dec. 22, 1938 (obituary notice of Dr. Frank H. Vizetelly).

New York Sun, Oct. 17, 1894; Dec. 9, 1894, p. 6; Oct. 14, 1895, p. 6; Oct. 27, 1895; Nov. 3,

1895, p. 6; Feb. 25, 1916 (Cleo Mayfield); March 10, 1918.

New York Times, Aug. 7, 1897 (bicycle slang); March 30, 1918, p. 8, col. 3 (war slang); June 12, 1919, p. 17, col. 4 (Owen Wister comments on American slang in England); April 23, 1922, sec. VI, p. 8, col. 4 (flapper); July 6, 1924, p. 8, Book review section; Dec. 15, 1926, p. 26, col. 4 (college slang); Feb. 5, 1928, section V, p. 21, col. 1 (London slang); June 9, 1929, section IX, p. 2, col. 7 (college slang); July 14, 1929, section X, p. 8, col. 1; Sept. 14, 1930, section VIII, p. 11, col. 7 (forest rangers); April 19, 1931, section V, p. 14, col. 1; June 5, 1931, p. 22, col. 5 (editorial on G. K. Chesterton's criticism of American slang); July 8, 1931, p. 19, col. 2; July 19, 1931, section IX, p. 2, col. 3; April 19, 1931, section V, p. 14, col. 1; Jan. 3, 1934, p. 17, col. 5; Jan. 4, 1934, p. 18, col. 4; Jan. 10, 1934, p. 20, col. 7; Dec. 22, 1938 (obituary notice of Dr. Frank H. Vizetelly).

New York Tribune, Jan. 19, 1913.

New York World, Dec. 29, 1929 (article by McGrath on new slang).

Philadelphia Public Ledger, April 16, 1915.

St. Louis Post Dispatch, Sept. 20, 1925 (article by Elsie McCormick).

INDEX OF AUTHORS

[Numbers refer to pages]

Authors mentioned in the notes are not indexed

B

D

D., H.:
The life of Jonathan Wild, 78.
Dane, Clemence, pseud.:
American tomorrows, 103.
Daniel, George:
"Sworn at Highgate," 80.
Daniell, M. G.:
New England notes, 140.
Danvers, F. C., and others:
Memorials of old Haileybury College, 132.
Darling, C. H.:
The jargon book, 3, 91.
Dauncey, Enid C.:
The American language, 37.
The snobbery of synonyms, 41.
Davidson, L. J.:
Auto-tourist talk, 109.
Mining expressions in Colorado, 102.
Old trapper talk, 145.
Sugar beet language, 109.
Davies, Maurice:
Slang, 21.
Davies, T. L. O.:
A supplementary English glossary, 4.
Davies, W. H.:
Beggars' slang, 91.
Davis, E. B.:
John Mason Peck and the American language, 18.
Davis, John:
The Post-captain, 106.
Davitt, Michael:
Leaves from a prison diary, 80.
Dawson, A. H.:
A dictionary of English slang and colloquialisms, 4.
De Bekker, Leander, joint author. *See* Vizetelly, F. H.,
and Leander De Bekker.
De Blaquier, Dora:
American slang, 32.
Defoe, Daniel:
Street robberies considered, 71.
Dekker, Thomas:
The Belman of London, 64.
The Guls Horne-booke, 64, 65.
Lanthorne and Candle-light, 65.
O per se O, 65.
See also Middleton, Thomas, and Thomas Dekker.
Dekobra, Maurice:
Tommy Atkins's vocabulary, 127.
De Lenoir, Cecil:
The hundredth man, 97.
Denham, Edward:
Expressions, chiefly of whalers, noted at New Bedford, Mass., 108.
Denike, C. W.:
"Pull down your vest," 25.
Dennis, C. J.:
Doreen and the sentimental bloke, 147.
The moods of Ginger Mick, 147.
The songs of a sentimental bloke, 147.
The Dens of London exposed, 80.
Desmond, Shaw:
London nights in the gay nineties, 32.
De Vere, M. S.:
Americanisms, 4.
DeVere, William:
Tramp poems of the West, 91.
De Witt, Marguerite E.:
Stage versus screen, 119.
Dibdin, C. I. M.:
Life in London, 81.
Dice, C. A.:
The stock market, 117.
A Dictionary of American English on historical principles, 4.
Dilnot, Frank:
The written and spoken word, 41.

Dingus, L. R.:
Appalachian mountain words, 143.
A word-list from Virginia, 145.
Dionne, N. E.:
Le parler populaire des Canadiens français, 148.
Dixon, J. M.:
English idioms, 5.
Dodge, N. S.:
Guesses and queries, 23.
Dodsley, Robert:
A select collection of old English plays, 71.
Dollard, John:
Dictionary of English in America, 4.
Doolittle, Maud M.:
Rhymes in prose on my verbal throes, 41.
Doughrity, K. L.:
Handed-down campus expressions, 133.
Downey's Peter Napoleon campana old sport songster, 80.
Downing, W. H.:
Digger dialects, 127.
Drennan, C. M.:
Kitchen Dutch and cockney English, 146.
Ducange, Anglicus, pseud.:
The vulgar tongue, 80.
Duncombe, John?:
Duncombe's dictionary of the cant words...now in use in flash cribb society, 80.
Dunlap, M. P.:
What Americans talk in the Philippines, 143.
Dunn, Alta B.:
Western (Wyoming and Montana) colloquialisms, 146.
Dunne, Charles:
Rouge et noir, 116.
D'Urfey, Thomas:
The bath, 71.
Wit and mirth, 72.
The Dutch Whore, 65.
Dutcher, E. W.:
Slang, 32.

E

E., B., Gent.:
A new dictionary of the terms ancient and modern of the canting crew, 65.
Earle, Alice (M.):
Customs and fashions in old New England, 151.
Early, Dudley:
Hollywood has a word for it, 121.
Eastman, Max:
Poetic education and slang, 130.
Eddins, A. W.:
The state industrial school boys' slang, 130.
Edson, H. A., and others:
Tennessee mountains, 145.
Edwards, E. J., and Jeannette E. Rattray:
"Whale off!" 108.
Edwards, Eliezer:
Words, facts, and phrases, 5.
Edwards, J. C.:
Good old "Stock," 119.
Egan, Pierce:
Boxiana, 113.
An impartial enquiry into the existing doubts and various reports relative to the late pugilistic contest between Dutch Sam and Nosworthy, 113.
Life and extraordinary adventures of S. D. Hayward, 82.
Life in London, 80–81.
Pierce Egan's book of sports, 112.
Pierce Egan's finish to the adventures of Tom, Jerry and Logic, 81.
Real life in Ireland, 82.
Real life in London, 82.
The show folks!, 119.
Sporting anecdotes, 112.
Tom and Jerry, 81.

H

S

WITHDRAWAL